TELEVISION
AND THE CHILD

TELEVISION
AND THE CHILD

*An empirical study of the effect
of television on the young*

BY

HILDE T. HIMMELWEIT

A. N. OPPENHEIM   PAMELA VINCE

In collaboration with

D. BLUMENTHAL   M. NEWELL
E. W. CROFT-WHITE N. A. STANDEN
A. G. MACLAINE   J. WHELDON

Published for
THE NUFFIELD FOUNDATION
by the OXFORD UNIVERSITY PRESS
LONDON   NEW YORK   TORONTO

Oxford University Press, Amen House, London E.C.4

GLASGOW NEW YORK TORONTO MELBOURNE WELLINGTON
BOMBAY CALCUTTA MADRAS KARACHI KUALA LUMPUR
CAPE TOWN IBADAN NAIROBI ACCRA

FIRST PUBLISHED 1958
REPRINTED 1960

PRINTED IN GREAT BRITAIN

Foreword

IN 1954 the Audience Research Department of the BBC suggested to the Nuffield Foundation that it should sponsor an inquiry into the impact of television on children and young people. At that time there were nearly three million television sets installed in the fifteen million homes in this country and their number was increasing rapidly. A good deal of concern was felt about the effect of this new medium on children and especially on very young children. Some maintained that television was on balance bad, that young children were intent on the screen when they should be out at play, that older children spent on it time that should have gone to their homework, and that adolescents were diverted from their youth clubs and their games. Some stressed the dangers arising from the passive character of television viewing, fearing that it would make young people mentally lazy. Some, on the other hand, thought that viewing could help young children, make their homes more attractive, expand their horizons, stimulate new interests, and provide a new basis of contact between the generations. These were the questions which the BBC had in mind. It felt that the proposed inquiry should be authoritative and independent and that it should be made while a large proportion of homes were still without television so that effective comparisons could be drawn between the habits of viewers and of non-viewers.

The Foundation agreed that such an investigation would be useful, if it could be done with sufficient scientific precision. An approach was made to Dr. H. T. Himmelweit, Reader in Social Psychology at the London School of Economics and Political Science, who had had wide experience of research in social and clinical psychology. Dr. Himmelweit accepted appointment as consultant director. A further member of the staff of the London School of Economics, Dr. A. N. Oppenheim, Lecturer in Psychology, collaborated in the study. Both he and Dr. Himmelweit worked on a part-time basis with Miss Pamela Vince, also a psychologist, as full-time senior research officer. The statistical adviser was Mr. Alan Stuart of the London School of Economics.

Including the writing of the report the inquiry has taken four years to complete. In the early stages particularly, while the design of the inquiry was under consideration, the team has had the guidance and support of a strong advisory committee. As chairman of that committee, I wish to express to its members the warm thanks of the Foundation for their help, especially to those who have been in touch with the actual execution of the inquiry, and who have given the draft report close critical attention. I wish also to express the gratitude, felt by the Foundation, to Dr. Himmelweit and her colleagues for their skill in handling so complex a problem and for their fortitude in coping with so formidable a mass of material. The whole credit and the final responsibility for the report is theirs and theirs alone, and not the Foundation's. I associate the Foundation in the acknowledgements to many helpers which Dr. Himmelweit makes elsewhere.

The Foundation has thus supported one of the most comprehensive studies ever done of the effect of any mass medium on children. The report, the Foundation believes, succeeds in showing that techniques of scientific investigation can be applied to such a set of problems as those originally presented by the BBC. By these methods, fact can be separated from opinion so that constructive, and possibly practicable, recommendations can be made. The social scientist is often criticised for merely charting the obvious. Even this, of course, has its uses. But, as will be seen in this report, the investigation disclosed that numerous supposed facts were not facts at all. And this, too, may be added: no research of this kind is ever final. The situation itself changes, and the methods of inquiry become more refined. So there is nothing here that can be said to have been done once and for all. Within our present experience, the results have a high degree of reliability. But the most certain result is that continuing study of this and of related problems is both necessary and possible. The Foundation hopes that one outcome of this long and, in Britain, pioneering enterprise will be that, in the appropriate places, other similar investigations will, in due course, be undertaken.

HECTOR HETHERINGTON
Chairman of the Advisory Committee

MEMBERS OF THE
ADVISORY COMMITTEE

———————

Table of Contents

PART IX

Future Research

Appendixes

Introduction

EVERY new medium of communication has in its time aroused anxiety—the cinema, radio, and at one time (a chastening thought) even reading. Now it is the turn of television. This present study was started at a time when public concern about the effects of television on children was at its height. There were few facts available about children's behaviour and reactions to viewing; there were also few documented facts about the way children spent their time before television came on the scene.

Television itself is continuously changing. For example, our main survey work was carried out in 1955 when only BBC television was on the air. When the second channel was introduced, we were able to make a small-scale study of its effects. Since then there have been further changes in programme content and transmission time. In minor ways, therefore, our data were out of date even before they were tabulated, but the major findings and conclusions have not been affected. The role of television in children's lives, the manner of children's reactions and the underlying principles that determine them remain constant in the face of the superficial changes in television itself.

The presentation of this report has not been easy; it covers a wide range of subject-matter; and it is intended for a varied audience (including teachers, parents, programme planners, experts in communication research, and other social scientists). For the sake of the critical reader, we decided not to publish findings without giving the methods by which they were obtained, so as to facilitate the evaluation of one in terms of the other.

Many people may wish to read this book rather like a reference book, consulting mainly those chapters that deal with subjects of special interest to them. Acting on this assumption, we have divided the book into a number of parts, within which the various chapters are relatively self-contained. To the same end, we have, wherever possible, put tables in the Appendix and explained in a glossary such specialist terms as have been used.

The usual order of presentation has been reversed by putting into Part I what goes customarily at the end of the book—namely, the summary of the main findings and the implications and suggestions that arise from them.

The summary of the main findings is given in question and answer form; this seemed the simplest way to give a clear account of the many different effects, the relative importance of which will vary with the interests of the reader. Since it is a digest of the book's main contents, appropriate chapter references to the fuller account are given after each finding.

Part I ends with *implications* and *suggestions*. These recommendations (based on our findings and also on impressions gained as psychologists in the course of three years' study of the effects of television) inevitably suggest criticism of the way television is used. They should, however, be read in the context of the whole report, which makes it clear that there is much about television that is useful and valuable.

Television is used by different children in different ways. In describing television's effects we had, therefore, time and again to consider the way these effects differed according to the ability, maturity, background, and personality of the children concerned. This has not contributed to lightness of presentation, but to gloss over the differential effects of television would have vitiated the whole purpose of the survey.

As an integral part of the study, we have collected a great deal of information about the lives, outlook, background, intelligence, and personality of two age groups of children. This material, based on a large sample drawn from five cities, yields systematic information about children's attitudes, interests, and behaviour. Since a proportion of the children were re-examined a year later, it provides data about the development of the children's attitudes and interests. The material has been analysed only in so far as it bears on the effects of television; it is to be hoped that one day it will be looked at in a broader context, to see how far the various factors of social background, sex, and intelligence determine children's behaviour.

It has often been said, and rightly, that socio-psychological field studies lack the scientific precision of laboratory experiments. In this inquiry we had in some ways the best of both worlds: an experimental set-up within a real-life situation. In 1955 less than half the population had been regularly exposed to television, so that we were able to base our research design on the comparison of an experimental (television) group with a control (non-viewing) group. In Norwich, moreover, the opening of a new television transmitter in an area where up to then little television could be seen, coincided with an early stage in our investigation and provided us with a ready-made experimental situation. We tested nearly all the Norwich children in two age groups, and then waited for the arrival of television sets into children's homes. Almost a year later, those children who had since acquired a set were re-examined and compared with a group of children who did not have television.

An understanding of the true character of mass communication is vital in the present world. This study has shown how urgently research is needed into the content of television entertainment; too many programmes appear to be built on conjecture about what people want or can take, too few on fact-finding and experimentation. So far as television in this country is concerned, we have been able to map some aspects of the present situation, but far more detailed charting remains to be done. We would venture, for instance, to suggest that research is needed to examine the effects of television on the country child, the very young child, and the disturbed child; and in addition much needs to be done in the way of testing reactions to particular programmes and particular programme types.

Like research in the natural sciences, social research depends for its value on continuity and on systematic progress towards a deeper understanding of each problem. This applies particularly to a field such as communication research which, in this country, is still in its infancy.

H. T. H.
A. N. O.
P. V.

Acknowledgements

WE should like to record our indebtedness to the trustees of the Nuffield Foundation for giving us the opportunity to carry out this inquiry and to the Director, Mr. L. Farrer-Brown, for his continued interest and support. We owe a great deal to Sir Hector Hetherington, chairman of the advisory committee, who gave much time and guidance to the team, and also to the members of this committee, particularly to Professors M. G. Kendall, A. R. Knight, and P. E. Vernon, and to the secretary Mr. J. C. Beavan and his predecessor, Mr. J. E. Morpurgo.

We are grateful to Sir Alexander Carr Saunders, the then Director of the London School of Economics, and to Professor D. V. Glass for allowing us to take on the inquiry and for providing accommodation for the research staff during the first year.

Most inquiries in the social sciences depend for their success on the co-operation of outside organisations. In this inquiry we sought more help than is customary, and gained much more assistance than we had ever hoped to receive. The Head of the Audience Research Department of the BBC, Mr. Robert Silvey, tendered every possible assistance; as did other members of the Corporation, especially Mrs. Mary Adams and Miss Freda Lingstrom. We must likewise thank Captain T. M. Brownrigg of Associated Rediffusion for making tele-recordings and films available to us, and Miss J. Elman for arranging their showing. Through the courtesy of Mr. Norman Collins we were given similar facilities by Associated Television.

We are greatly indebted to the Directors of Education and the Education Committees of Bristol, London, Norwich, Portsmouth, and Sunderland for allowing the inquiry to be carried out in their schools. We have received a great deal of co-operation from heads of the schools and their teaching staff.

In Norwich we were allowed to approach every single school in the city, to administer diaries and tests, and then to retest a year later. For these unusually good facilities we should like to thank the Director of Education, Mr. J. W. Beeson, the Education Committee, the heads of the city schools and their teachers.

We are also grateful to the Chief Education Officers of Derbyshire, Devonshire, East Sussex, Middlesex, and the West Riding of Yorkshire for organising the distribution of questionnaires to teachers in their areas, as well as to Mr. R. C. Steele of the Schools Broadcasting Council who made the initial contacts for us.

We have had a great deal of assistance from teachers and from parents. We should like to thank them most warmly as well as the children from over 123 schools for co-operating so well and for making our task so rewarding.

Originally the fieldwork and coding were to have been carried out by an outside organization; for a variety of reasons this proved impossible. At short notice, our small staff undertook these tasks, supervised the work of over a hundred fieldworkers, and assumed responsibility for the coding. These were heavy demands on their versatility and patience. We were exceptionally fortunate in having a group of collaborators who not only met these demands most ably, but who also contributed substantially in terms of research ideas. Each of the collaborators was in charge of the fieldwork in one of the cities; in addition, each undertook special responsibilities with regard to some particular aspect of the research: Nellie Standen with the time analysis of programme content and the analysis of drama; Doris Blumenthal and Jacqueline Wheldon with the content analysis of Westerns and crime serials and a study of children's reactions to them; Dr. A. G. Maclaine with an investigation into teachers' opinions and with the construction of the general knowledge tests; Mrs. E. W. Croft-White with the organisation of the two-stage testing in Norwich; and Mary Newell with the supervision of much complex tabulation. It was a pleasure to work with this group; we owe them much more than can be expressed here.

We are also very grateful to Mrs. Judith Evered and other temporary research staff and to the secretaries who carried the administrative burden and typed the drafts.

Many others have made contributions to the study: we should like to mention in this connexion Dr. W. H. King of the Institute of Education, University of London, through whose research seminar we obtained facilities for conducting pilot tests; to Mr. M. Abrams of Research Services Ltd. for inserting comparable questions in one of his surveys; to Mr. H. D. Wilcock of the Social Survey for his advice on the design of questions; and to the Curator of the Ashmolean Museum, Oxford, for allowing us to interview young visitors.

During the analysis of the data we had much expert assistance. For statistical advice we are indebted to Mr. Alan Stuart. We should also like to thank Mr. J. A. Everingham of the South-Western Regional Hospital Board, the Director of the National Physical Laboratory, and Dr. F. Garwood of the Road Research Laboratory, for permitting much of the statistical work to be done by their staff, and Miss L. D. M. Gabriel, Miss F. A. Rigg, Mr. K. A. Morris,

Mr. J. Woolgar, and Miss P. Keating (of the London School of Economics) for their valuable help.

The topic we have been investigating has been little studied in this country and discussions in the United States proved most helpful, in particular those with Dr. Eleanor Maccoby, Miss Marjorie Fiske, Dr. J. Klapper, Mr. R. Meyersohn, and Dr. and Mrs. Riley. In the course of their visits to London we were fortunate in having the advice of Professors J. K. Bruner and R. K. Merton.

To comment on a draft manuscript is a thankless task; we are, therefore, much in the debt of Mr. R. Silvey, Mr. B. Emmett, Miss Marghanita Laski, and our colleagues Dr. Marie Jahoda, Mr. N. Hotopf, Mr. D. R. Price-Williams, and Dr. W. E. Belson. In the final editing of this report we have had the expert help of Mr. John Gray and Mrs. S. McRobic, to whose skill we owe a great deal. The responsibility for the views expressed remains, of course, our own. We are grateful to Mr. P. Perrin for the skilful preparation of the index.

We must thank the British Radio Equipment Manufacturers' Association for the loan of a television set and the Controller of Her Majesty's Stationery Office and the Secretary of the Association of Optical Practitioners for permission to quote from their reports.

We are very grateful to the staff of the Foundation for the co-operation we have enjoyed throughout our stay at its headquarters.

Finally, research workers on projects of this kind find themselves working long and irregular hours. Our families have accepted this with admirable grace and we should like to thank them very much for their forbearance.

H. T. H.
A. N. O.
P. V.

PART I

Summary and Suggestions

I

The Problem

OUR terms of reference in this inquiry were to study the impact of television on children and young people. In 1954, when the study was officially planned, as many as 3,000,000 homes had television sets. It was known that, compared with radio listening, children viewed more and began viewing at an earlier age. The possible effects of this situation, while the subject of much public speculation, had not been systematically investigated. There was urgency about this research, not only because of public concern about the potentially harmful effects of television, but also because the rate of buying television sets was increasing so rapidly. If such a study, based on a comparison of an experimental (television-viewing) group of children with a control (non-viewing) group, had been left to much later, it would not have been possible to do it at all. One of the difficulties in attempting this type of research in the United States had been just this; namely, that research workers had often to rely on retrospective accounts of pre-television behaviour, rather than on current comparisons of the behaviour of viewers and non-viewers.

Our assignment proved a difficult one because there was no baseline on which to build. Some individual studies apart, there was little knowledge about how much children viewed, or the significance that television had assumed in their lives. Even more important, there was no systematic knowledge about the manner in which children spent their leisure, or about their outlook and attitudes, before television had had a chance to change them.[1]

This was one problem. In addition, we were faced with the difficulty that the 'effects' of television could manifest themselves in almost every aspect of children's lives. To find out what to measure, and where to draw the line, we therefore turned to the many opinions that had been expressed about the effects of the medium. Not surprisingly, such opinions tended to be heavily influenced by personal attitudes, and were often contradictory. For instance:

> Television, it was said, ruined children's sleep and eyesight, made them passive, made them aggressive (through seeing so many adventure and murder plays); led to a falling off in schoolwork as a result both of tiredness and declining interest. Others, more favourably disposed to television, claimed that it widened children's interests, that it made them more active by encouraging hobbies, that it made them less aggressive (again as a result of watching adventure and murder plays which this time were seen as offering a harmless outlet for pent-up aggression); it was also suggested that school work improved because television stimulated children's interest in some of the subjects taught.

The variety of opinions advanced by well-informed people suggested that we could take nothing for granted. It meant that we had to test hypotheses and establish results which many people would regard as 'obvious'. It also meant that our inquiry had to include a large number of children, since one reason for the divergent opinions about the effects of television was that these were generalisations based on observations of different groups of children. But television, like any other influence, is likely to have differing effects on children of different ages, intelligence levels, personality, home background, and so on. Moreover, not only do children vary in what they choose to watch on television, they also perceive and react to the same programmes differently, according to their idiosyncratic needs.

By establishing the variations, we hoped to discover some of the principles underlying television's influence. The survey was consequently designed to find out how television affects different types of children in different aspects of their lives, at different points of time, and according to different sets of viewing circumstances. This procedure also enabled us to locate 'problem areas' where action might be needed.

Assessment of the good or harmful effects of television must depend, in part at least, on the nature and quality of the activities it displaces. This again will vary from child to child; in some cases, for instance,

---

[1] Some figures were available about how often children went to the cinema and what they read, but there was no coherent picture of the total leisure life of the child into which television had to be fitted.

television will push out comic reading, in other instances homework will suffer.[1]

Broadly speaking, two main types of effects can be distinguished: those (which we have called displacement effects) which stem essentially from the time taken up by viewing; and those which relate, more specifically, to the content of television programmes.

Displacement effects

Consciously or unconsciously, children exercise choice in how much they view, and in the way they make time for viewing. They may drop a few activities completely, reduce them all proportionately, or reduce some more than others. We have tried to isolate the principles on which these choices tend to be made; in this way it should be possible to predict what will happen, for instance, if television is newly introduced into a community. To do this effectively, we had to chart, as fully as possible, the leisure pattern of the children's lives; the casual as well as the organised activities, the useless as well as the useful ones.

The effects of programme content

The second type of effect depends more on the content of television programmes, and for the most part consists of the stimulation of interests and activities. We wanted in particular to examine the effects of content on children's knowledge and school performance, and on their outlook and values. In the latter case we studied the subtle, almost imperceptible ways in which children's outlook is affected by the view of the world and society which television tends to offer. This is a realm of intangibles, difficult to chart and measure.

We were concerned here with the content of programmes as children perceive them. This does not necessarily coincide with the perceptions of experienced adults, including producers. Similarly, the standards which adults use to assess violence, aggression, or realism in a programme may well differ from those of children. It is important to bear this in mind, particularly in the case of evening programmes intended primarily for adults.

[1] One paper even came to the conclusion that 'television is helping to turn our youth back from the paths of insobriety which it has been increasingly following in recent years' (30).* If this finding were true, then in this particular area at least, there would be little doubt about the beneficial effects of television!

* See Bibliography, p. 504.

These two types of effects—those due to the time spent watching television, and those due to the content of the programmes watched —often have a conflicting impact on the same activity. For instance, it will be shown later that many children cut down their book-reading as a result of the time they gave to television, but that at the same time they were stimulated to read some of the books which had been dramatised on television.

Other types of effects

There are other types of effects not dealt with under the two main categories already outlined. These include the effects of television on family life (the extent to which it increases the amount or quality of family contacts, or stimulates conflict between parent and child); and the effect television has on the pattern of children's emotional reactions (on their relationships with their friends, on their general capacity for adjustment, on passivity, aggressive behaviour, sleep, and level of anxiety).

This inquiry, then, was not a simple study of 'the effect' of television on 'the child', but a more complex investigation of many different types of effects on many different types of children. But there were other differentiating factors which complicated the picture further. It was thought, for example, that the effect of television might vary with the context in which viewing takes place, whether alone or with adults, whether in the dark or with familiar objects clearly visible; and also according to the attitude to television of the adults in the child's environment, in particular his parents and teachers.[1] Finally, we had to design the study remembering that some of the effects may be short term, others more lasting. We therefore needed to compare the veteran viewers with relatively new viewers.

Essentially the effects of television can best be seen as an interplay between the characteristics of the viewer and the characteristics and content of the medium.

AN OUTLINE OF THE DESIGN

Our task lay in building up a picture of the changes brought about by television. To do this, we adopted the conventional experimental method: we compared two groups, only one of which had been exposed to the variable (these were the *viewers*, who had television at

---

[1] A parent who views a great deal himself sets a different example from one who views sparingly, and his example may affect the child's viewing. Equally, the teacher who works the content of suitable television programmes into his teaching creates a different situation from the one who does not link the children's viewing experience with the teaching at school.

home); the other group were the *controls* (who had no television at home and were also not regular guest viewers).

For such comparison to be valuable, the two groups—viewers and controls—must in all other respects *start off* as alike as possible. To this end, we matched each viewer individually with a 'twin' control child; the members of each pair were, therefore, of the same sex, age, intelligence, and social background; in addition, as far as possible, they were selected from the same class-room in order that they might share the same neighbourhood and school atmosphere. This system of *individual matching* (which is described in detail in Chapter 6) was more rigorous and precise than is customary in research of this kind.

In carrying out this type of comparison, the choice of criteria for matching the viewers and controls is, of course, of paramount importance. We chose four (sex, age, intelligence, and social class) which previous research had shown to account for many of the important differences in children's outlook and leisure-time activities. Inevitably, however, they leave other factors out of account; as a result, the two groups could only be very approximate replicas of each other.

This inquiry, which is in effect a comparative study of matched viewers and controls, will be referred to as the *main survey*. It was carried out in four English cities, London, Portsmouth, Sunderland, and Bristol. A total of 4,500 children was tested, leaving us (after the guest viewers and unmatchable cases had been discarded) with 1,854 matched viewers and controls.

The main survey provides a picture of the way in which the viewers differed from their controls. Such differences cannot, however, be automatically ascribed to viewing; our matching criteria were, of course, not exhaustive and there remains the possibility that the differences might already have existed before the viewers acquired their television sets. We knew already that the two groups must have been to some extent different, in that in one case their families decided to buy a television set, whilst the others despite similar incomes—preferred to use their money in other ways. Such differences in home background might well find expression in the children's attitudes and behaviour.[1] If this were so, some of the differences found in the main survey would not be due to the effects of viewing but would be due to pre-existing differences between children from homes which bought television early and those which did not.

Ideally, therefore, we would require a different type of inquiry— a *before-and-after* study in which children, examined before they had

---

[1] That is to say, the purchase of a television set may be an expression of a particular home atmosphere, and of particular interests on the part of both parents and children.

access to television, can be examined again after they have come under its influence. In such a study a control group (which continues to lack access to the medium) is necessary in order to ensure that any change between the first and second testing was not in fact due to such extraneous factors as, for example, the passage of time. With this type of research design, changes found between the first and second testing of those children who had acquired television, between test and retest, could be more confidently ascribed to the effects of viewing.

The opening of a new television transmitter in Norwich provided us with the opportunity for a natural *before-and-after* study. Taking advantage of this circumstance, we gave our main survey questionnaires to all the 10–11 and 13–14 year olds in nearly every Norwich school, at a time when hardly any family had a television set. After a year we compared a group of children who had since acquired sets with a group who had not, by matching them, individually in pairs, as in the main survey. By relating the results to those obtained in the main survey, one could see whether the differences emerging in the main survey represented after-effects of viewing, or had existed prior to the arrival of the set; i.e. the extent to which the *future viewers* (those who acquired television in the course of the year) differed from children whose families proved less eager to acquire a television set.[1] Out of the original 2,200 children tested on our first visit to Norwich, we subsequently obtained 370 cases, consisting of all children who had television and of their controls.

One example may serve to illustrate the need for distinguishing between pre-existing differences and after-effects brought about by television. In the main survey we found that viewers went less regularly to Sunday school compared with controls. It would be tempting to argue that this was due to the counter-attraction of television, or to the materialistic attitude fostered by it. The before-and-after study, however, showed that this difference already existed between future viewers and their controls before television came on the scene. The less regular attendance at Sunday schools was not the result of acquiring a television set, but due to a relatively low level of religious interest and observance among those families who responded most promptly to the appeal of television.

Since the before-and-after study—referred to in this report as the *Norwich study*—appeared to be so much more precise than the main

[1] Even then we could not be absolutely sure that we were dealing with after-effects, since one cannot ever be sure of having controlled for all the relevant factors. All we can say is that the Norwich before-and-after study greatly increased the likelihood of getting at differences due to viewing, rather than those caused by extraneous factors.

survey, it might be asked why we did not confine the inquiry to this study alone. This would have been unwise, not only because our final sample could only be small, but also because in Norwich only the immediate effects of television could be examined. We were anxious also to assess the effects which occur once television has become an established feature in the home.[1]

Further, what the Norwich study could not do was to answer our second question, namely, how far the effects of television varied according to the sex, age, intelligence, and social background of the viewers. For this we needed large numbers; we also needed a special type of sample design—a *factorial design* (described in detail in Chapter 6) which makes it possible to study the influence of one background characteristic (for example, age), while holding the others constant. To achieve this, we used not a representative sample, but one in which we had equal numbers of middle- and working-class children,[2] of bright and dull children, and of boys and girls.[3]

The number of viewers included in the main survey was sufficiently large to permit two comparisons to be made within the viewing group. The first examines the effects of television over time, by comparing *recent viewers* (those who have had a television set for between three months to one year) with *experienced* and *veteran* viewers (the last being viewers who have had television for at least three years). The second comparison examines the degree to which the effects vary with the weekly amount of time which children devoted to viewing, and so compares *occasional*, *moderate*, and *heavy* viewers with one another.

The age groups studied

Since the design called for a great deal of information about each child, we decided to concentrate in the survey on two age groups.[4]

---

[1] In the main survey, we excluded for this reason all viewers who had had television for less than three months.

[2] Throughout this report the term *working class* has been used to describe children whose fathers do manual work, and the term *middle class* to describe those whose fathers are white-collar workers. Since the inquiry was restricted to state schools, the sample includes few children from upper middle-class homes.

[3] In using a factorial design we gained great advantages. We had, however, to forfeit any type of representative sample, since to fit our sample into the design it was necessary, of course, to have more middle class and bright children than any type of random sample would provide. We felt that the advantage of the factorial design outweighed the disadvantage of having an unrepresentative sample; but in considering the results outlined in this report it must throughout be remembered that they are (from the point of view of representativeness) in certain respects over-weighted.

[4] Some additional studies, described later, were used to gain information about the reactions of younger children.

These were 10–11 and 13–14 year olds, the former being the youngest group able to deal with written instructions and to give answers in written form, the latter the oldest group still fully represented at school. All the children were drawn from state schools, the 10–11 year olds from the top form of the primary school, the 13–14 year olds from the two main types of secondary schools within the state system: the grammar and the secondary modern schools. Although only 2–3 years apart, preliminary exploration made it clear that the two age groups were sufficiently dissimilar in their interests and behaviour as well as in their emotional and social development to bring out age variations in the effects of television.

The research instruments used

In both surveys the children wrote their own answers to our questionnaires under conditions of anonymity. In Chapter 6 we discuss the advantages and disadvantages of interviews and questionnaires in studies with children. For a variety of reasons, interviews were not feasible in our case. What we did do, however, was to use a number of devices to make the questionnaires as much like an interview as possible, so that the children could answer in their own characteristic ways. The various testing instruments went through many revisions before being used in the survey.

Two main techniques were employed. First, the children were asked to keep a diary, filled in privately at school each day for one week, in which they recorded everything they did between leaving school and going to bed. At this point there had been no mention of our interest in television; the inquiry was presented to the children as a study of their leisure activities. The diaries gave a consecutive account of children's leisure activities which has proved very valuable. The children also indicated each day which were their three most enjoyed activities, so that we could tell how important a role television really played, and what relationship there was between the time and interest devoted to it. Secondly, questionnaires were given to the children some six weeks later, containing detailed questions about their leisure activities and interests, and parallel questions for each of the mass media—the cinema, radio, and reading. (The questionnaire on reading contained questions about comics and magazines, as well as books.)

In addition, measures of children's personality were obtained, as well as ratings by the teachers of the children's behaviour and personality characteristics. The assessment of personality in particular was used to account for differences in emotional impact; to show, for example, whether being frightened by a particular programme reflected a general tendency to anxiety, or whether it was really a function of the programme, so that fear was experienced also by children not particularly predisposed to anxiety.

By including these techniques, we tried to obtain the type of material normally collected in a case study, but within the framework of an extensive survey dealing with large numbers.

Additional studies

Special studies were also carried out to examine groups not covered by the survey, and to investigate problems for which other techniques were needed. Some of these studies again used pencil and paper tests and questionnaires, but others, this time, relied more on the qualitative data that could be obtained through observational methods or through long, informal interviews with individuals or groups.

Altogether, there were eleven such studies: one enrolled the help of mothers to keep seven-day diaries of the viewing habits and reactions of their young children. Two were opinion studies carried out among teachers and parents. Three studies dealt with the assessment of the impact of specific programmes (one by observing children while watching a programme, one by measuring children's understanding and recall of certain programmes, and the third by investigating the extent to which child attendance at a museum had increased after some of its exhibits had been shown on television). One study dealt with the effect of television on school performance. Two aimed at understanding the role that television plays in children's lives, the one by interviewing 9-10 year olds, the other by group discussions with a similar age group, this time with special reference to their reactions to Westerns, crime and detective series. One very different study systematically examined the content of television programmes, in terms both of the amount of programme time given to different types of programmes, and of the values, attitudes, characterisation, and themes contained in television plays.[1] Finally, a study was included to measure the effect of an alternative television channel on the amount of children's viewing, and on their programme choice.

One final point needs to be made here. Our first task lay in charting the manner in which children who see television differ from those who do not: in their way of life, interests, knowledge, and values. Such a study is essentially a comparative one which is concerned

---

[1] Although the main survey and the Norwich study were conducted with children who had access to BBC only, the content analysis was carried out for both BBC and ITV, so as to be more representative of television entertainment today.

with the children's total viewing experience. In the course of this work we have also tried to answer certain other questions—which are not all specific to this medium alone. Here is a sample of such questions:

1. What factors determine consumption of a mass medium?
2. Do children reach satiation point in their desire for spectator entertainment?
3. To what extent can tastes be developed?
4. What frightens children, and how do the fears induced by television vary according to the sex and age of the child? Are there any discoverable principles about the sort of programmes or incidents that are most likely to arouse fear?
5. What is the effect on children of programmes featuring aggression and violence?
6. To what extent do children turn for their entertainment to programmes designed primarily for adults?
7. How far does television entertainment put over a constant set of values? How far are such values taken over by the children?
8. To what extent do children become so preoccupied by television that it dominates their lives and interests?
9. How does television affect family life?

Lastly, we should point out that in many ways a 13–14 year old does not differ much from an adult in his tastes and reactions. For this reason, and also because the research develops general principles about consumption of, and reactions to, television, many of the findings may have relevance to adults as well as to children.

2

Summary of Main Findings

T HIS chapter is designed to give a general picture of the main findings. It divides into two main sections. Section I gives the effects for each area in turn, while Section II provides the broader picture of the way different factors determine children's reactions. To keep the presentation brief, we may on occasions sound more categorical than the evidence warrants. This summary should, therefore, be read in conjunction with the main report, where the evidence is presented with its necessary qualifications and where the implications of the findings are more fully discussed. The relevant chapters are indicated in brackets throughout this summary. Unless specifically stated otherwise, the findings refer to children with access to BBC television only and are based on the results obtained from 10–11 and 13–14 year old children.

Who are the early viewers? (Ch. 7)

Apart from various social and economic determinants, we found that the first people to buy television were those with the strongest need for ready-made entertainment. In the United States research among adults has shown that the early set buyers were originally more avid cinema-goers and radio listeners. Our work with children also indicates that those from homes which bought television early were more dependent on outside stimulation—they had an unusually high interest in comics, radio, and clubs, and their taste in book reading tended to be narrower. All this suggests a home atmosphere which would seek the stimulation of outside entertainment rather than rely on its own resources.

SECTION I

THE AMOUNT CHILDREN VIEW

How many hours per week do children view television? (Ch. 8)

At the time of our survey, viewers in both age groups watched television for an average of 11–13 hours a week, or just under two hours a day; they spent more time on television than on any other single leisure activity. While older and younger children devoted about the same amount of time to television, the time was in each case differently distributed; the 10–11 year olds watched more children's television and less evening television than the adolescents. On average, children's television was watched by grammar, secondary modern, and primary school children respectively for four, five, and six hours a week. Viewing was fairly regular throughout the week, Saturday being the favourite viewing night.

[The popular image of the child glued to the television set, watching whatever is on, did not fit the facts. Most children viewed reasonably selectively, turning to other things when something was on which they did not like. Many also consulted the *Radio Times* or the newspapers before they settled down to viewing, despite the fact that in many of the homes—two-thirds, according to the children—the set was left on for most of the evening. This happened as often in middle- as in working-class homes.]

What factors reduce interest in and time spent on viewing?   (Ch. 8)

The single, most important background factor was undoubtedly intelligence; the higher the child's intelligence, the less his viewing. This difference was already clear cut among the 10–11 year olds and became more pronounced in early adolescence—where the grammar school pupils, of all the children tested, proved the least interested and the least prepared to spend a lot of time on television.

In both age groups boys and girls spent roughly the same amount of time in front of the set.

Viewing seemed to become a habit on which the child fell back when nothing more interesting was available. Consequently, the child with many interests, the active child, and the outdoor type tended to view less than the other children. But for all children, outdoor play and (in adolescence in particular) social activities proved television's strongest rivals. For the average child, viewing took second place to these.

The social level of the home (whether it was a middle- or a working-class home) proved of little importance in affecting how much children viewed. Only among the younger children was there any difference. Middle-class children tended to view a little less than working-class children, largely because of their earlier bedtimes. What proved much more important was parental example, and to a lesser extent, parental control. In homes where the parents themselves were selective and moderate viewers, the children also tended to view relatively little. While this was the general pattern, we also found much individual variation between members of the same family.

It would appear that the amount a child views depends in the first instance on his intelligence, secondly on his personality and on how full and active a life he had led before television came on the scene, and thirdly on parental example.

How does the amount of viewing change (a) *over time and* (b) *with the introduction of a second channel?*   (Ch. 8)

Viewing rapidly becomes a habit—within the first three months the children settled to a routine in keeping with their age, intelligence, and personality, and one which seemed relatively independent of how long they had had television. The veteran viewers (those with television for over three years), compared with recent viewers, reduced their viewing by only two hours a week although they were more critical and less attached to television.

Even the attractions of an alternative channel, offering many more of the children's favourites, did not change this pattern. A study carried out with children who had access to both channels showed that the average number of hours they viewed was about the same as for children with access to BBC alone.

Do the children watch many programmes designed for adults?   (Ch. 8)

From the age of 10 onwards, at least half the children watched adult programmes in the first part of the evening (until 9 p.m.). Even after 10 p.m. one-third of the 13–14 year olds was still watching. On evenings not followed by school days, the children viewed until a later hour.

An assessment of the effects of television on children which did not take evening programmes into account would, therefore, be seriously misleading.

CHILDREN'S TASTE IN TELEVISION

What kinds of programme do children like best?   (Ch. 9)

Three-quarters of the votes for the most favoured programme went to adult programmes, particularly to crime thrillers and, to a lesser extent, to comedies, variety programmes, and family serials. Westerns were much favoured by the younger children. Other types of programme—such as puppets, nature and animal programmes, and how-to-make programmes—were not especially popular. Only among the 8–10 year olds did children's television programmes or *Watch with Mother* appear among the top five favourites.

As with time, so with taste. We found that age and intelligence affected preferences, while the social level of the home made little difference. A child's liking for a given programme is a function of his sex, emotional and intellectual maturity, and of his own idiosyncratic needs.

The preferences of adolescent girls and boys differed more than did the tastes of the younger boys and girls. Rather unexpectedly, girls seemed as much interested as boys in crime and detective series.

Adult political programmes, documentary and discussion programmes such as *Panorama* or the *Brains Trust* held little appeal, even for the more intelligent grammar school children.

One finding was of special interest; even the most popular programme or programme type was mentioned by no more than one-third of the children. Within any given age and intelligence group there is thus a great deal of variation in taste, a fact which seems to be considerably underestimated in popular discussion.

Do children's tastes in television reflect their tastes in other mass media?
(Ch. 11)

On the whole we found they did. Children liked similar types of programmes whether they occurred on television, or radio, or in the cinema, or whether they formed the content of a book. Tastes in television were further linked with interest in other activities. Children have a general underlying pattern of preferences, and it is therefore possible to predict (within limits) a child's television likes and dislikes from a knowledge of his age, intelligence, and taste in other mass media.

Can children's tastes be developed by seeing programmes which are not on the whole popular with children?
(Ch. 10)

When programmes such as *Science Review*; *Animal, Vegetable, or Mineral?*; *Meet the Commonwealth*; *From Tropical Forests*; *Have You a Camera?* come on the screen, children with access to one channel only must either stop watching or view programmes which they do not expect to be very interesting. Under these circumstances, quite a number of children chose to see such programmes and in fact enjoyed them. Children with access to one channel only get the chance to discover such programmes, but those with two channels hardly ever.

The more the child can follow his favourite choices by switching from channel to channel, the less likely is he to come in contact with programmes which, from an educational viewpoint, would prove more worth-while and which would enable him to experience new things and so broaden his taste.

How is taste affected by access to a second channel?   (Ch. 10)

While the amount of viewing did not increase, children now tended to concentrate more on their favourites, switching from channel to channel. They therefore saw other kinds of programmes less often. Thus, child audiences for adult crime and detective series, panel games, Westerns, drama and variety programmes remained high, while information and documentary programmes suffered a disproportionate loss (from 48 per cent down to 13 per cent). Once there is a choice of channels, with programmes as at present distributed, those with educational value or those which have been especially produced for children are most likely to suffer.

Family conflict over the choice of channel was rare; only about 10 per cent of the children on any one day could not watch a programme they wanted to see because (they said) the rest of the family preferred to view something else on the other channel.

On the whole, children in homes where a second channel had recently become available much preferred ITV. It offered more of their favourites, and many liked the advertisements. This was particularly true of the 10–11 year olds; the older and the more intelligent children tended to be more critical both of the advertisements and of the interruptions they cause.

What constitutes television's appeal for children?   (Ch. 12)

[The interviews with the children suggest that part of television's appeal lies in its easy availability and its consequent value as a time filler.]

Television offers the satisfaction of being in the know, of going behind the scenes and of learning about the world and about people. On the emotional side, television appeals in different ways to different children. [It offers security and reassurance through the familiar format and themes of many of its programmes, notably the family serials and the Westerns. It offers constant change, excitement, and suspense. It provides escape from everyday demands with lightheartedness, glamour, and romance, and permits the child to identify himself with different romantic heroes.]

Television also offers the appeal of personalities, presented more intimately and in more everyday terms than the stars of the cinema. The personalities of television seemed to be liked by the children in particular for their warmth and friendliness.

THE CONTENT OF ITV AND BBC TELEVISION PROGRAMMES

As a preliminary step in the study of the effects of television on the child's values and outlook, a content analysis was made of the programmes on both channels, first when ITV had only just come on the air and again about nine months later.[1] The allocation of time to different types of programme was charted and a detailed analysis made of the themes, motives, values, and characterisation of adult plays (excluding comedies) and of children's Westerns.

What does television offer to the child in terms of programme content? (Ch. 13)

Taking both children's and evening television together, the staple fare consisted of plays—chiefly Westerns, crime, and adventure. Without overstaying his bedtime the child with access to both channels could watch well over twenty-five plays a week. In one rather typical week, between 5 and 9 p.m., eighteen plays were shown which dealt with one or other aspect of lawbreaking and retribution,[2] fourteen of them on ITV (nine of these were designed for adults). In the same week, the BBC during these hours offered four programmes of this kind (two designed for children).

In the evening, ITV offered twice as many plays or playlets as the BBC, half of them episodes from crime, adventure, and adult Western series; the BBC devoted about one-fifth of its plays to such episodes, the remainder being comedies or problem plays.

In children's television the BBC allotted about one-third of its time to information programmes and one-third to plays. On ITV, plays occupied first 50 then 73 per cent of the time. While both channels offered mainly adventure plays, in the case of ITV these amounted to 96 per cent. They consisted of Westerns, swashbuckling adventure and animal adventure series, most of them produced in America. 73 per cent of BBC children's plays were adventure plays; they covered a wider range of topics than those shown on ITV, with more of them being live productions.

That such programme uniformity is not an inevitable by-product of commercial television is seen in comparison with New York television; where programme output for children proved more varied, even though New York has seven stations competing for audiences.

[1] The analysis was based on programmes put on the air by the BBC and by the two programme companies serving the London region (Associated Rediffusion and Associated Television); for brevity's sake these will be referred to as ITV. The analysis was carried out in 1956.

[2] These figures were obtained in May 1958 and are similar to those of 1956.

In consequence, children's information programmes on ITV compared with BBC were fewer, shorter, and covered a smaller number of topics. There were no programmes to correspond to the BBC programmes on foreign countries, fewer 'making and doing' programmes, and fewer programmes about the ways of life of people in different occupations. Apart from current affairs programmes like *This Week* and the news, children missed nearly all ITV evening information programmes, as these were on too late. In the case of the BBC, information programmes were more uniformly spread over the evening, so that children could see more of them; but even so they would miss most of the BBC science programmes (which might well appeal to children) and all the programmes on art.

In the course of the last year, ITV programmes for children have become more varied.

EFFECT OF TELEVISION ON VALUES AND OUTLOOK

What view of life and what values do adult television plays offer the child?
(Ch. 17)

Analysis of the content of randomly selected adult plays from both channels (excluding comedies, crime and detective series), showed the values put over to be remarkably consistent from play to play. Since children see and enjoy a great number of plays, we set out to discover how far there was a cumulative effect on their outlook and values.

[The world of television drama tends to be that of upper middle-class urban society. The occupations of people of this social level are depicted as worth-while, while manual work is presented as uninteresting. Television plays teach that self-confidence and toughness are needed to achieve success—goodness of character is not enough; that life is difficult, especially for women; that marriages are frequently unhappy, and parent-child relationships often strained. Events rarely turn out satisfactorily and virtue seldom brings happiness in its train. Violence is an inevitable part of life, and good people often resort to it.] For the adult observer a hackneyed view of life emerges, similar in many ways to that offered in films or in the theatre; [for the child television may afford a glimpse of adult life which he would otherwise gain less often and only at a later age.]

To what extent is the child's outlook coloured by what he sees on television?
(Chs. 18–21)

We have found a number of instances where viewers and controls differed in their outlook, differences which did not exist before television came on the scene. There was a small but consistent influence of television on the way children thought generally about jobs, job values, success, and social surroundings. In their wishes about jobs the viewers proved more ambitious than children not exposed to television; in their job values they were more 'middle class', and in their assessment of the factors making for personal success they more often stressed the need for self-confidence. Some of their descriptions of the homes of rich people reflected the hall-marks of wealth depicted on television.

Adolescent girl viewers proved more concerned than their controls about growing up and marrying—possibly a reaction to the difficulties of adult life of which television made them aware at an age when they are much in need of reassurance.

Probably as a result of BBC programmes about foreign (and especially European) countries, viewers made fewer value judgements about foreigners; where stereotypes were given, they tended to reflect those offered by television.

Television tended to make no impact where the child could turn for information to his immediate environment, parents, and friends; it had little effect on the jobs children expected to do, as distinct from their wish dreams about them.

The most affected were the less intelligent 13–14 year olds. The lesson of television was not absorbed by a child bright enough to be well informed, or critical of what he viewed, or by one too young to perceive or to take an interest in the implied values.

All in all, the values of television can make an impact if they are consistently presented in dramatic form, and if they touch on ideas or values for which the child is emotionally ready. Extrapolating from these findings, one would expect that in the crime and detective series the constant display of aggression by both the criminal and the upholder of the law would also make an impact on those children sensitised to such cues.

REACTIONS OF FEAR AND ANXIETY

What frightens children on television?   (Chs. 14, 15)

Westerns tended to frighten only the very young or the insecure; it is likely that the majority of children can enjoy them without fear by the time they are about 7. On the other hand, detective, murder and crime thrillers were often mentioned as frightening by adolescents as well as by the 10–11 year olds. Violence in these plays, unlike Westerns, is realistic, not stylised, and forms less often part of a stereotyped plot sequence.

Many children were frightened by incidents in horror programmes, space fiction, and even such dramatisations as *Jane Eyre*. On the other hand, real events of a violent nature seen on newsreels were rarely mentioned as frightening. Fiction made a deeper impact than reality.

Where children mentioned incidents that had frightened them, they often spoke of nightmares and of difficulty in falling asleep. It is in such effects as these that the disturbance caused by frightening programmes can best be seen.

Children tended to be more readily frightened when viewing in the dark, and when watching programmes in the evening without an adult present. Television in so far as it is more of a family activity than radio listening is likely to arouse less fear, but television's visual impact in darkened rooms could well make up for this. In general, television emerged from our survey as very similar to the cinema and radio, both in the amount of fear it engendered and in the types of programmes which children found frightening.

What types of aggression prove most disturbing to children?   (Ch. 15)

Guns and anything to do with guns, proved least and daggers and sharp instruments most disturbing, with swords somewhere in between. Fist-fights and fighting on the ground were disturbing only when they occurred in sports programmes, i.e. in real life, rather than in fictional programmes.

We found young children unmoved by a scene in which polecats devoured a rat; but they were very disturbed by danger to animals like the dogs in *Lassie* and *Rin-Tin-Tin*, for which they had a particular attachment or which had been cast in a special role.

Verbal acts of aggression, reprimand, and ridicule sometimes occasioned more unease than physical aggression, particularly when they occurred in real-life situations, in panel games, or sports programmes. Children were disturbed by situations with which they could identify themselves; this is a more important factor than the sheer amount of force of the physical violence shown.

Children enjoy being a little frightened; they like suspense for the sake of the relief that follows. There is a narrow margin between pleasurable suspense and intolerable fear. The children themselves made a clear distinction between exciting and frightening programmes, enjoying the former and not the latter.

THE EFFECT OF WESTERNS, AND OF CRIME AND
DETECTIVE SERIES

Do these programmes make children aggressive?   (Ch. 16)

We did not find that the viewers were any more aggressive or maladjusted than the controls; television is unlikely to cause aggressive behaviour, although it could precipitate it in those few children who are emotionally disturbed. On the other hand, there was little support for the view that programmes of violence are beneficial; we found that they aroused aggression as often as they discharged it. We also found that they taught the one-sided lesson that to offend against the law is bad, without teaching its positive counterpart.

By taking up such a disproportionate amount of viewing time, these programmes prevent the showing of more varied types of programmes that could offer children a broader view of life.

Do these programmes fill an urgent demand?   (Ch. 16)

While *Fabian of Scotland Yard* was the first favourite, as many as two-thirds of the children mentioned quite different programmes as their favourites. Also, when asked to plan an ideal evening's entertainment, only 10 per cent of the adolescents and 26 per cent of the younger children mentioned these programmes in their bill of fare. It would seem, therefore, that the number of these programmes could safely be reduced without fear of losing the child audience.

TELEVISION'S EFFECT ON GENERAL KNOWLEDGE AND
SCHOOL PERFORMANCE

Does television improve children's general knowledge?[1]   (Chs. 22–26)

On the whole the gain was very slight, but varied with the type of child. Children can undoubtedly learn from television; but viewing takes time, some of which might be spent with books or other sources of information. It incurs, therefore, both gain and loss. We found a net profit only for the younger, duller children.

There were several reasons for the absence of gain. Documentaries and the discussion programmes offered a good deal of information; but the type of information contained in programmes designed especially for children is also readily available to the controls from other media, so that there is little advantage to be gained from viewing. Adult information programmes were not very popular and did

---

[1] We were examining the increase of knowledge obtained not from school's television, but from general television entertainment.

not always get their points across even to adolescents. In any case, younger children do not remember the content for any length of time, so that there is little storing of information. Paradoxically, our results suggest that gains in general knowledge come mostly from adult non-information programmes; these contain useful details of plot and circumstance which are more readily remembered because of their dramatic content.

For most children in our survey, television proved neither a help nor a hindrance as far as general knowledge was concerned, except for the younger or duller children (as yet able to read very little), for whom it proved a real advantage. Their gain in knowledge proved the equivalent to what a child would normally gain in the course of four to five months of intellectual development. For these children, television provided information in the form and the pace best suited to them—in dramatic and above all in visual form. Grammar school viewers, on the other hand, did not gain; in fact they proved a little less knowledgeable than their controls. Viewing offered them little that was new and took time away from other sources of knowledge, such as reading or radio.

Although children remembered nature programmes well, they carried over little of such programmes into their general knowledge of this subject or into their performance in related subjects taught at school. Gain in knowledge of current affairs was negligible because children had little interest in these programmes. There was equally little gain in cultural interests. Few children, for example, went to a museum after seeing exhibits from it in a children's programme.

How does television affect children's school work?   (Ch. 25)

On the whole, viewers more or less held their own with class mates of similar age, sex, social class, and intelligence; but the brighter children in both age groups tended to fall a little behind.

Television created no particular interest in any school subject, nor were viewers markedly better or worse at any of them.

Viewers and controls also spent much the same amount of time on homework. But the closing of the transmission gap between 6 and 7.30 may well make a difference here, and a repeat inquiry is needed under these new conditions.

Does television make children listless and lead to poor concentration at school, and reduce interest in school?   (Chs. 33, 20)

Our findings suggest that it does not. There was no difference between viewers and controls in children's subjective assessments of tiredness in the morning, nor in ratings by class teachers of each child's concentration.

On the other hand, half the teachers, when asked for their opinion, said that one of the three most important effects of television was the children's tiredness in the morning and consequent lack of concentration. Their views reflected their general attitude to television and their class-room experience with viewers; our findings were likely to be more valid since they were derived from a comparison of viewers and controls, taking into account the number of children without television who nevertheless lacked concentration and felt tired.

Children's interest in school or school societies did not seem to be affected. Viewers and controls differed neither in the age at which they would like to leave school, in the frequency with which they took part in extra-curricular activities, nor in their attitude to school as judged by their class teachers.

THE EFFECT OF TELEVISION ON LEISURE

Are children's lives dominated by television? (Ch. 27)

This proved true in only a minority of cases—just as only a minority of children are obsessed with the cinema or radio. Children gave much of their time to television, but far less of their interest. There was an age difference here: the 10–11 year old in the survey proved more attached to television than the adolescent and, within each age group, the child of below average intelligence more than the bright child.

How much television is wanted depends on the relative emptiness of the child's life before he had television and also on his emotional needs. For a minority of cases the vicarious companionship and excitement offered through television is very important, and in such cases television occupies a central place in their lives. But about half the children said they would not very much miss television if they had to do without it, and most children on most ordinary days of the week had other activities which they enjoyed more than viewing.

What makes room for viewing? (Ch. 27)

Viewing takes up a good deal of children's time—on average just under two hours a day. Something, then, must make room for viewing. We consider first the two mass media which are most closely akin to television: cinema and radio; then reading; and finally other leisure activities.

How has television changed children's interest in the cinema?   (Ch. 29)

Cinema and television are seen by many children as interchangeable. Both provide entertainment, one with the added advantage of convenience and of not having to pay. Younger viewers therefore reduced their cinema visits and continued to go less often even after viewing for some years. More among them only went once a fortnight rather than once or twice a week. The cinema, however, is also a social occasion, a way of meeting friends away from home. This proved more important for the adolescents than for the younger children; recent adolescent viewers went to the cinema only a little less often than before, but those who had already been viewing for a year had returned to the number of cinema visits characteristic of the adolescent control group.

Individual films made less impact on viewers than controls, accustomed as the former were to the rapid panorama of television programmes with their juxtaposition of emotion and content. But admiration for film stars continued undiminished—television here helps with the many personal appearances of film stars that it features.

How has television affected listening to the radio?   (Ch. 29)

Children with access to television listen very little to the radio. While future viewers were keener listeners than their controls, once they had television they stopped listening almost completely. Half the older and a third of the younger viewers still spent a little time with the radio—on average, about one hour a week. One exception here were the frequent viewers who were also relatively heavy consumers of whatever other ready-made entertainment was available; when television was off the air, they would turn to radio. However, for the majority of children, there is a limit to the amount of ready-made entertainment they require—given enough of one mass medium, they cut down severely on the others.

Children who had been viewing for several years showed a very slight revival of interest in the radio. Where listening to the radio continued, viewers assigned it a specialist role. They listened to sports commentaries, discussions, panel games, and musical programmes, rather than to plays; these they enjoyed more on television.

What is the effect of television on reading and skill in reading?   (Ch. 28)

Children, once they started viewing, certainly read less than before; by how much depended on the type of child and on how long he had been viewing; it also differed for book- and comic-reading.

The future viewer read more comics than his control, but once he had been viewing for a time his comic-reading came down to the level of that of the control children. Ultimately, then, viewers read no fewer comics than their controls, although before they had television they read more. Books, on the other hand, were read equally often by future viewers and their controls (even though the quality of books read by the former tended to be lower); but with the arrival of television, the viewers reduced their book-reading more severely than their comic-reading. This reduction was most marked among older children and those of medium intelligence; the bright children were little affected and the dull children read very little in any case.

At first, television decreased the proportion of books to comics read. But as children got used to viewing they gradually reverted to books; so that after a few years the viewers were once again reading as many books as the controls, and the duller children had even increased their share. Ultimately, therefore, television favours book—rather than comic-reading.

[Book-reading comes into its own, not despite television but rather because of it. Television stimulated interest in reading, through its serial dramatisation of books; it also aroused the child's interest and curiosity so that he became interested in a wider range of books than before, including non-fiction.]

Television may reduce children's reading skill at first, but not in the long run. The present generation of children, who first meet with television at a crucial stage of development, come off worst in this respect, especially since those who reduce their book-reading most tend to be most in need of reading practice. But it must be remembered that book-reading (and therefore reading practice) revives after several years of viewing, and that duller children come to read more than their controls. Ultimately, when television sets have become as commonplace as radio and children grow up accustomed to viewing, there is likely to be no loss in reading skill.

Does television reduce social contacts outside the family?   (Ch. 30)

Entertaining at home tended to increase with the acquisition of a television set, but visiting other children was not affected. What did suffer somewhat was the time spent in casual companionship with other children; this is in line with other effects we have noted, the more clearly defined activities being the least affected.

As a result of television, children's lives become more structured; less time is spent on doing 'nothing in particular' either alone or with other children. There is less time 'to stand and stare'.

Whether this is desirable or not will depend on the use to which such time is put and how much of it a child has. A distinction needs to be made here between aimless, bored loafing, on the one hand, and 'healthy' idleness on the other, which enables the child to draw on his own resources rather than on ready-made entertainment.

EFFECT ON FAMILY LIFE

Does television keep the family together? (Ch. 34)

Television does keep members of the family at home more. But it is doubtful whether it binds the family together in more than this physical sense, except while the children are young. As they grow older, their viewing becomes more silent and personal. Also, as children grow into adolescence, the increased time spent with the family may set up strains, since it runs counter to their need to make contacts outside; they may therefore do less in the way of other joint activities with their parents than formerly .

Does television cause conflict in the family? (Ch. 34)

Conflict about television does occur, especially over bedtimes, mealtimes, and the banning of certain programmes. But in many cases this conflict is only indirectly due to television; it may arise from existing poor parent–child relations, from unwise handling by the parents of problems thrown up by television (failure, for instance, to understand the child's absorption in what he views), or from emotional disturbance within the child. In all this television does not create conflicts, although it may precipitate them; it provides a whole new range of situations about which conflict can occur—but the root cause of the conflict normally goes much deeper than television.

Do parents control their children's viewing? (Ch. 34)

Many parents are greatly in favour of television, even to the point of being defensive about it. To some extent television helps them to keep an eye on the children. Also, if they themselves enjoy television and view a lot, they have a vested interest in defending it. Perhaps for these reasons many parents do not admit to a need to control the amount and content of children's viewing. Also, of course, when parents view unselectively themselves, such control becomes difficult to enforce. Two-thirds of the children we questioned said that the television set was left on all the evening in their homes.

There were also signs—though many children and parents tended to deny it—that television is used as an instrument of discipline, for punishment and reward.

Does television make children passive?   (Ch. 31)

In the opinion survey, as many as a quarter of the teachers (and an even higher number among those who disliked television) believed that television made children more passive.

This vague term 'passivity' seems to be used in five different senses; taking each sense in turn and comparing the viewers' behaviour with that of the controls, we found no evidence whatsoever of increased passivity.

1. Children, it is said, absorb television like a sponge; this view (in which physical and mental inactivity are confused) proved untenable, judging from the observations of mothers and the subjective reports by children of their reactions to programmes. Inherent in this view is a confusion between what to the adult may appear poor entertainment, and the way such programmes may appear to the less sophisticated child.

2. Viewing, it is argued, leads children to prefer an edited version of life to the 'real thing', since they can have the screened version without effort. We found no evidence of this.

3. It is also said that viewing leads to loss of initiative. But both viewers and controls enjoyed the same types of activity; and in fact children mainly tended to make room for viewing by cutting down on other ready-made entertainments, notably the cinema and radio, rather than on hobbies and play. Similarly, teachers' ratings of the children's initiative were identical for the two groups.

4. A fourth assertion is that television leads to a jaded palate; we found if anything that the opposite was true, especially among dull adolescents and bright 10–11 year olds; as a result of viewing, they had become interested in a wider range of subjects than their controls.

5. Finally, it is thought that viewing dulls the imagination. Yet when the teachers in our survey were asked to rate each child as 'unusually' or 'moderately' imaginative or as 'unimaginative', no difference emerged between viewers and controls.

The consistently negative results obtained for each one of these five aspects give confidence in our findings. Children's love of activity and exploration is very strong. When there was a choice between sports or hobbies and viewing, television was often the loser.

Can television broaden and stimulate children's interests? (Chs. 28, 31)

The power of television in this respect is most evident in relation to reading. We found that future viewers, before they got their sets, showed less interest than controls in specialised and non-fiction subjects, but that after they had been viewing for a time their interests expanded. This change seemed to occur most often among children of a mental age of about 12; the duller 13–14 year olds and the brighter 10–11 year olds proved most receptive to television's benefit.

Does television make children more enterprising, or stimulate them to make things, enter competitions, visit places of interest, or develop new hobbies? (Ch. 31)

On the whole it does not. We found few children had made anything after seeing it modelled on television, and those who did tended to be the hobby-minded, generally alert children—the ones least in need of stimulation. Only 2 per cent of the older and 3 per cent of the younger children had made and sent things to the BBC Television Centre for a competition.

The under-nines, according to their mothers' accounts, became interested in things shown on television and tried to copy them more often than did the older children. Apart from an increased interest in sport, children of nine years and older proved little responsive.

Visits to museums and art galleries increased little after the viewing of specific programmes.

Viewing, it seems, stimulates interest rather than activity. This may be due to the methods of presentation and choice of topics; but it is probably in large measure due to the nature of television entertainment—a rapid succession of programmes allowing little time for reflection and so only stimulating children with initially strong interest in a given topic. Serialised dramatisations of books are effective possibly because each episode ends on a note of suspense, so retaining the children's interest after the programme has finished.

EFFECT OF TELEVISION ON NIGHT REST AND EYESIGHT

Do child viewers get less sleep than their controls, and have more trouble in falling asleep? (Ch. 33)

Within the two age groups studied, viewing caused a slight postponement of bedtime on weekdays; on average not more than twenty minutes a night. Moreover, the controls spent more time than viewers playing or reading in bed, before they turned out the lights; there was, therefore, very little difference between viewers and non-viewers in effective sleeping time.

Bedtimes were postponed especially among those who would otherwise go to bed early, that is girls and younger children from middle-class homes. Contrary to popular belief, really late bedtimes occurred as often among controls as among viewers; they reflect not so much the lure of television as the general home atmosphere, of which excessive viewing may be just another facet. In fact, the Norwich findings suggested that more relaxed parental control of bedtime was characteristic of parents who were among the first to buy television sets.

We had many reports of difficulties in falling asleep, and of nightmares after some specially frightening programme. But, in general, viewing did not seem to over-excite children; viewers had no more difficulty in falling asleep and reported no more frightening dreams than their controls. Younger children may, however, be more seriously affected than the two age groups we studied.

Is there more defective eyesight among viewers than controls?   (Ch. 33)

Defective eyesight was no more frequent among viewers than controls, at least when assessed in terms of the number wearing glasses or complaining of eyestrain. In fact, adolescent girls without television—those who read most—complained of eyestrain more often than the viewers. Of course, some children with poor eyesight may find that their eyes hurt after viewing. Our findings suggest, however, that if these children had used their eyes in other ways (as in reading) the effect would have been much the same.

Do children view under optically suitable conditions?   (Ch. 33)

A fair proportion viewed under poor conditions. Children often sat on the floor with the screen above eye level; and as many as one in four viewed in the dark, thus maximising the glare. Viewing in the dark, we found, had a further disadvantage: it enhanced the emotional impact of potentially frightening programmes. There is need for more education of parents and children on the correct conditions for viewing, so as to lessen the possibility of eyestrain for those predisposed to it.

THE CHARACTERISTICS OF THE TELEVISION ADDICT—THE EFFECTS OF HEAVY VIEWING

What type of child becomes a television addict?   (Ch. 35)

It is difficult to characterise the television addict or heavy viewer, since addiction is, of course, not simply a matter of heavy viewing.

For classification purposes, however, we have been forced to treat it in these terms and have defined as addicts or heavy viewers the 30 per cent in each age group who viewed the most. We have already shown on p. 12 the different factors that correlate with amount of viewing. The most important was intelligence, the duller children viewing more than those of high intelligence; in addition, in the younger age groups, heavy viewing occurred rather more frequently among working-class children.

But personality make-up tends to be at least equally important, and here an addict type emerged who is not exclusive to television; his emotional insecurity and maladjustment seem to impel him towards excessive consumption of any available mass medium. If television is available to such a child, he will view excessively; if not, he will go very often to the cinema, listen a great deal to the radio, or become a heavy reader of comics (but not of books). Such children were characterised by lack of security, by being ill at ease with other children. Their teachers often described them as shy and retiring.

The television addicts in our sample showed less initiative than occasional viewers. They preferred plays of two escapist types— adventure or mystery, and family serials. The first type of play offers them the vicarious pleasure of an active, dangerous life, while the family serial facilitates identification with a happy and united family, offering them reassurance.

While the occasional viewers cut heavily into radio listening and cinema-attendance, the addict managed to fit in something of them all. He listened to the radio when there was no television to watch, and went to the cinema as often as two or three times a week in spite of spending over half his free time in front of the television set.

A comparison of television addicts with control children who were frequent cinema-goers showed that both groups need a great deal of ready-made entertainment; both were insecure and afraid of striking out for themselves. These characteristics are more likely to be the cause than the result of heavy viewing, but the intensive viewing which addiction entails can only make matters worse. With escape through television so readily available, the heavy viewer's outside contacts become more restricted still. Such contacts demand much effort and offer little promise of success; they therefore compare unfavourably with the certain, undemanding companionship of television.

Within a given intelligence level, social class, and age group, the amount a child views gives an indication of the degree to which his life is satisfactory; heavy viewing is a symptom of unsatisfactory adjustment or of inadequate environmental facilities.

SECTION II

THE WAY IN WHICH DIFFERENT CHILDREN REACT
TO TELEVISION

Throughout the summary we have discussed each effect in turn and indicated how it varied for different types of children. Here we shall look at the picture from the other point of view and attempt to show how the various factors of intelligence, age, sex, social class, personality and home background determine television's role in the child's life.

Effects on children of different intelligence

The relationship between intelligence and the effects of television is complex, depending on the one hand on the ability to comprehend what is offered, and on the other hand on the level of programme content, compared with that of other sources of information with which children are likely to come into contact.

In this survey intelligence emerged as the single most important determinant. This is shown both in the amount children view and in their interest in viewing; the more intelligent the child, the less inclined he will be to watch television and the less interest in it will he show.

In the case of the 13–14 year olds the picture is clear-cut, irrespective of the effects examined; grammar school children, compared with the less intelligent children of the same age group, proved the less interested, devoted less time to viewing, and also were the less affected by what television offered in the form of values or knowledge. This was partly because for these children television offered little that was new; also because in the case of knowledge, television even hampered intelligent adolescents by reducing the time they might otherwise spend on different sources of information, such as books or the radio, for instance.

In general, we found that the 13–14 year olds of average and below average intelligence and the bright 10–11 year olds were the most responsive both in terms of gaining wider interests (though not activities) and also in terms of their absorption of the values television offered. It would, of course, also follow that they would be similarly affected by inadequate or harmful values, if these were consistently presented. These two groups of children have approximately the same mental age of about 12 years, an age at which television still offers sufficient that is new to the children and where at the same time other sources of stimulation are unlikely to be more adequate than television.

The 10–11 year old of average or below average intelligence can absorb only the simplest of values from television entertainment. However, it is this group—whose reading and access to other sources of knowledge is the most limited—who has gained most from television as far as general knowledge is concerned.

In the matter of gaining knowledge, television has narrowed the gap between the more and the less intelligent 10–11 year olds; in the case of values and outlook it has brought about the same equalising process between the more and the less intelligent older children.[1]

When a child of relatively low intelligence views a great deal, this has quite a different significance than with a child of about average intelligence. With the former, television provides his main source of stimulation; such a child tends to have few hobbies, and often comes from a home with equally few interests; television for him takes the place of the newspaper and the book; it becomes his main source of information, offered in a manner and at a pace which suits him.

In the case of the intelligent child, the same amount of viewing would more often be a sign of an environment poorly equipped in resources, or else of personal problems within the child himself. Such a child can read and engage in hobbies; under these circumstances, with the majority of children television occupies a less central role.

Effects on children of different ages

At adolescence, television becomes less important; this is not so much because its content no longer interests the children, but rather because viewing occurs among the family at home and so fails to meet the adolescent's social needs. For this reason, the cinema, for instance, by providing opportunities for meeting friends as well as entertainment, gains in popularity as children grow older.

Tastes also change; some of this change comes from increased intellectual maturity, some from changing emotional needs and circumstances. The adolescent ceases to be interested in Westerns (so popular with the 10–11 year olds) with their stereotyped plots and straightforward action; he prefers the more varied action and more complex motivation of detective and other adult plays.

[1] In the study of teachers' opinions, some teachers from schools for educationally subnormal children mentioned that television had helped their pupils not only in providing them with a common talking point with the rest of the family, but also by offering them a source of information which they could easily comprehend.

At all ages, children respond to the programmes in terms of their own needs and of their personal capacity for understanding; in adolescence this involves greater responsiveness to information about personal relationships, and about adult life. About to leave school, the adolescent responds to cues about the type of jobs and about the social values contained in much television drama, which as yet make no impact on the younger child. Similarly, only the older children reacted, and some of them with anxiety, to the problem-laden view of adult life that inevitably forms part of so many evening television plays.

The younger child likes action; his capacity for perceiving motives, unless they are explicitly stated, is as yet limited. Consequently, he responds to episodes or incidents rather than to the overall theme (unless through repetition the theme has been learnt, as in Westerns). This factor must be borne in mind in evaluating the manner in which a child will respond to a given programme; the younger the child the greater the tendency to respond to particular incidents rather than to the story as a whole. He prefers clear-cut characterisation, provided there is also excitement and suspense; as a result he enjoys both the stereotyped Western and the less stereotyped detective series. At the same time he likes family serials and shares with the older child enjoyment of programmes which invite laughter.

In their enjoyment of funny programmes and in their susceptibility to the fear potential in various programmes, no age difference was found. The older child, because he is more concerned with problems of interpersonal relationships and able to understand a wider range of situations, can be as readily disturbed as younger children, albeit by different types of situations. This is important; particularly since older children compared with younger ones are less ready to admit to fear or disturbance.

Effects on boys and girls

Girls, especially among the adolescents, proved more responsive than boys to television's impact even though they gave no more time to viewing. Girls were more often influenced in their outlook, and also more often than boys admitted to fears and disturbances after seeing certain television programmes.

Television's impact on girls may be stronger than on boys because they tend to be the more interested in plays dealing with problems of human relationships; also because television tends to reinforce girls' feelings of insecurity (characteristic of adolescence) by failing to provide them with reassuring models. The sympathetic female characters in television plays tend to be unhappy and troubled, and to be dominated by events of which they are unable to take command.

Considering that half the child audience consists of girls, it is indeed surprising to see how few children's plays seem to take account of this factor; their themes tend to relate to boys' rather than to girls' interests, providing adequate heroes for the former, but inadequate heroines for the latter.

Yet, this survey evidence provides little support for the popular view that girls compared with boys are more squeamish about violence. Westerns appealed to girls a little less than to boys, but they were just as, indeed more, interested in the detective series *Fabian of Scotland Yard.*

Effects on children from middle- and working-class homes

Contrary to popular opinion, social background exercised an almost negligible influence on children's reactions to television.[1]

It must be remembered that when we looked at social-class differences, we held intelligence constant, that is, we ensured that there were as many bright, medium, and dull children in the working- as in the middle-class sample.

Under these circumstances, social-class differences were still found; many examples of them, in terms of the children's behaviour and outlook, have been cited in this report, but not usually in relation to amount of viewing or to children's taste in programmes. In the case of cinema visits, for instance, social-class differences were found; paradoxically, social background was less influential in respect of the home-bound media (radio and television); the children's use of these readily accessible media depends less on social conventions and more on personal choice.[2]

The same would seem to be true for adults; we found that as many children in middle- as in working-class families claimed that their television sets were left on all the evening; nor was there any class difference in the amount of parental viewing reported. Social conventions would seem to enter more into those activities which take place outside the home, and into such traditional patterns of upbringing as are expressed in the selection of appropriate bedtimes rather than into the use to which children put this new and readily available medium.

[1] Social background is defined here in terms of differences in parental occupation. The group of 'working-class' children consisted of children whose fathers engaged in manual work. The middle-class sample, since it was restricted to state schools, included only a few children whose fathers did professional work or held higher executive posts.

[2] There was similarly no difference among the controls between middle- and working-class children listening to the wireless.

Effects on children of different personalities

One important factor determining the amount of time a child watches television and the importance viewing assumes for him, lies in the personality of the child, in the quality of his relationships with his friends and family, and in the general home atmosphere.

The active child, socially at ease and with a happy home background, is the least likely to become preoccupied by television. On the other hand, children who view a great deal do so (particularly the intelligent ones) because they have difficulties in making friends or problems in their family relationships. They retreat into viewing or into ready-made entertainment of other types. A vicious circle is then set up whereby the ready access to television aggravates those problems of the children which led them to view heavily in the first instance.

The child's personality also affects his reactions to the content of television programmes; the extent to which these frighten and disturb him and the extent to which he identifies himself with the characters on the screen.

Equally important in this context is family atmosphere and parental example. Where parental viewing is high the children will tend to adopt a similar pattern.

3

Principles and Generalisations

FOR some of television's effects we have been able to arrive at a set of principles which would help to predict, for instance, what would happen if television, or some other medium, were newly introduced into a community comparable to our own; or if at some time in the future a medium capable of satisfying three, instead of two, senses were to make its appearance.

These principles can be grouped into four main categories:

1. The principles of leisure displacement.
2. The principles underlying television's effects on children's outlook and values.
3. Generalisations about taste.
4. The principles which determine what types of incident arouse fear and emotional disturbance.

THE PRINCIPLES OF LEISURE DISPLACEMENT

With television available, the child finds himself in a conflict situation: consciously or unconsciously, he has to decide how much to view, and how to make room for viewing. The resulting compromise seems to be made on the basis of three principles: first, he will sacrifice most readily those activities which satisfy the same needs as television but less effectively—those activities which are *functionally similar*. Secondly, some activities will be so thoroughly cast in the shade by television that in order to continue with them at all children will come to use them in a specialised way so that they do not overlap with viewing: these are the *transformed* activities which must either change in character or cease to exist. And thirdly, the child will tend to make room for television at the expense of activities on which he places little value, or of those which are of an unspecific, indefinite character (the *fringe* or *marginal* activities).

Functional similarity: the first of these principles concerns functional rather than objective, similarity, or equivalence. For instance, cinema visits are considerably reduced by the younger viewers, for whom cinema and television are relatively interchangeable; but amongst adolescent viewers cinema visiting is little affected—and then only temporarily—because for the adolescent the cinema represents an opportunity to meet friends and to develop a social life away from home, a need which television cannot gratify.

Other activities are little affected by viewing, because they are of great importance to children and yet functionally different from viewing, as, for example, outdoor play, and activities which permit self-expression. When there is competition between viewing and activities of this kind, viewing often turns out to be the weaker rival.

Transformed activities: there were two examples of transformed activities. Radio, in particular, comes to take on a specialised role for those viewers who turn to it at all. To a lesser extent, something of the same kind happens with reading: the circulation figures for adult magazines in general have dropped but not for the specialised and non-fiction ones.[1] Among children, interest in non-fiction subjects increases under the impact of television, turning reading slightly away from the well-trodden paths of television.

Marginal or fringe activities: we found that in so far as outdoor activities or social pastimes are affected at all, the more casual, unstructured activities are the ones that suffer, rather than the organised or more clearly purposive ones. There is a consequent reduction of *leisure itself* as children's lives inevitably become more crowded.

These two basic principles are illustrated particularly well in the case of reading. Book-reading is most severely reduced among those children who start off with only a marginal interest; and comic-reading, it will be remembered, was permanently reduced by television. But whereas television can provide an effective substitute for a good deal of comic-reading, in the case of books the position is very different. Book-reading is temporarily reduced because the satisfactions offered by books and viewing at first seem similar. In the long run, viewing cannot offer the same freedom of choice or diversity of subject matter; as a result, after a few years, both viewers and controls are once again reading a similar number of books.

---

[1] Bogart shows that in the United States this trend has gone much further, with specialised magazines flourishing, and magazine articles increasingly dealing with informational topics. Fiction is more and more left to television. Between 1946 and 1955 there was a much increased demand for non-fiction books (19).

THE PRINCIPLES UNDERLYING TELEVISION'S
EFFECTS ON CHILDREN'S OUTLOOK AND VALUES

Gradually, almost imperceptibly, television entertainment brings about changes in children's outlook and values, even though the programmes that achieve this do not deliberately set out to influence. It is rather that the similarity of views and values conveyed in television programmes, particularly in plays, make their cumulative impact.

The following principles indicate the conditions under which maximal effect is likely to occur (i.e. from the cumulative impact of a number of programmes rather than from the impact of a particular programme):

1. If the values or views recur from programme to programme;
2. if the values are presented in dramatic form so that they evoke primarily emotional reactions;
3. if they link with the child's immediate needs and interests;
4. if the viewer tends to be uncritical of and attached to the medium;
5. if through his friends, parents, or immediate environment the viewer is not already supplied with a set of values which would provide a standard against which to assess the views offered on television.

Provided these conditions are fulfilled, values may be taken over from the main themes of plays or programmes, and also from the subsidiary touches used in presenting them. Children have an inconvenient way of responding to isolated incidents rather than to overall themes.

These same principles apply equally whether the views and values are worth-while or worthless. The process is likely to be a slow and gradual one, reflecting not so much the impact of individual programmes as the cumulative effect of them all. Over and above this slow effect (composed of the accumulation of minute influences from many programmes) individual programmes also make their impact, either because of their dramatic excellence or because they touch on something of specific importance to the child. For most children both types of effects are likely to operate.

GENERALISATIONS ABOUT TASTE

Five generalisations can be made on the basis of our findings:
1. Taste in one medium is linked, not only to taste in other media, but to the child's interests generally. Already by the age of 10, children have a fairly integrated set of taste patterns.

2. Children tend to prefer adult to children's programmes and watch more of them; it may therefore be adult rather than children's programmes which have the larger share in forming tastes.

3. Children appear to be quite capable of enjoying programmes without understanding them fully.

4. When children are brought inadvertently into contact with programmes which do not, 'in anticipation', interest them, they often like them and may later even seek them out again. To develop children's tastes, it is therefore important to provide in programme planning for such experiences. It is possible to achieve this in a one-channel situation where the choice lies between watching such a programme and switching off, but it is more difficult where there is access to two channels—under these circumstances the child can more easily limit himself to his favourite types of programme. This will ultimately lead to a narrowing of taste.

5. The diversity of taste among children of the same sex, age, and intelligence is so great that in our survey even the most popular programme was the first favourite of no more than 30 per cent of children in any one age or intelligence group. It follows that firm predictions about what children will like or reject cannot be easily made; this is even more so when considering favourite television personalities.

THE PRINCIPLES WHICH DETERMINE WHAT TYPES OF INCIDENT AROUSE FEAR AND EMOTIONAL DISTURBANCE

In the last resort, children's fears are idiosyncratic, determined by the nature of the stimulus (or programme), by the child's own needs, and also by the extent to which particular incidents touch on personal preoccupations. Nevertheless, certain general principles can be laid down about the type of incidents which tend to arouse fear. Emotional disturbance of this kind is not only aroused by episodes of killing, wounding, and lethal weapons; fist-fights are also disturbing (whether in plays or in the boxing-ring), and incidents of verbal aggression such as quarrelling and one person telling another off. Children can also be upset by portrayal of adult relationships where unhappiness is stressed more than violence. Finally, the uncanny may frighten, as, for instance, the sleep-walking of the mad wife of Mr. Rochester in *Jane Eyre* or the invasion from outer space in *Quatermass*.

In general, we found that violent or aggressive episodes tend to cause far *less* disturbance where the following conditions are fulfilled:

1. If the presentation of violence is stylised, as in Westerns.

2. If the programme forms part of a series, so that the child can become familiar with the conventions; if the ending falls into an accepted pattern; and if there is a hero figure who appears in each of the episodes.

3. If the setting in which the violence occurs is unfamiliar, so that children are the less likely to imagine that similar events might occur in their own home or street. But at the same time the setting and violence should not be so unfamiliar as to be uncanny (as in the case of *Quatermass*).

4. If the characters are black and white rather than grey. Detective plays, with their emphasis on the psychological exposition of character, often arouse sympathy with the criminal; this is absent in Westerns, whose villains usually remain shadowy, unsympathetic figures.

5. If the child can feel sure that the events are make-believe rather than real; although it must be remembered that with smaller children this distinction tends not to be clear-cut.

6. In general, children tend to be less concerned about the magnitude of the disaster or the seriousness of its consequences, than about the prospect of hurt to *someone with whom they can identify*. For this reason, disasters in newsreels may be less disturbing than a heated discussion on television in which one person may be made to look foolish, or the threat of injury to the dogs in *Lassie* and *Rin-Tin-Tin* (the same children, however, remained quite undisturbed by the sight of animals in nature programmes being attacked and eaten by other animals). Differences were also found with regard to the type of physical aggression. Fighting on the ground proved no more disturbing than other kinds of fighting. Any gun fight, whether 'real' or fictional, was enjoyed, probably because children play at shooting, and see so much of it in Westerns, that they treat gun fights as spectacles, whatever the context in which they are shown. On the other hand, knives, used at close quarters, quite often proved disturbing.

Finally, there are the differential effects of violent and disturbing programmes. While familiarity with the series tends to reduce emotional impact, familiarity with viewing does not; we found that children who had been viewing for many years were as readily affected as those who had as yet little experience of television entertainment. Moreover, programme impact was no greater for heavy viewers than for those who saw less television.

Nor does susceptibility to fear decrease with age, although the types of situation capable of arousing fear do undergo change. Equally, susceptibility to fear does not appear to be related to intelligence: even though the intelligent children viewed less and were more critical of programmes than the other children, they were as readily disturbed by them.

Perhaps most important of all, television does not seem to induce fear any more readily than sound radio. There is, however, evidence to suggest that the emotional impact of reading may be slighter than those of radio and the two visual media—television and films.

THE BROAD PICTURE

The final picture of the influence of television on children's leisure, interests, knowledge, outlook, and values proves to be far less colourful and dramatic than popular opinion is inclined to suppose. Effects occur in each one of the various fields, but not to such a degree that the children would have been fundamentally changed.

Television, then, is not as black as it is painted, but neither is it the great harbinger of culture and enlightenment which its enthusiasts tend to claim for it. If television is a window on the world, it gives a view not very different from that provided in books, comics, films, and radio programmes. Similarly, its capacity for broadening a child's horizons is not spectacularly different from that of any of the other mass media.

Part of the reason why popular opinion produced a picture considerably at variance with the facts lay in each observer's tendency to generalise from the children he knew. Part, however, stems from the distrust with which people tend to view new technical inventions (particularly in the field of culture): the radio, the cinema, and now television. Each tends to be seen as bringing about a change for the worse, a lowering of standards and behaviour. In such an atmosphere of distrust three things combine to distort the picture of television's true effects; the intrinsic power of the medium is exaggerated, the resilience of the children tends to be seriously underestimated, while at the same time the past is idealised. The same factors operate in reverse with those people who welcome the medium and are among the first to use it.

With each new medium the experience gained from the introduction of the previous one counts for little. Each time the attractions of the new technique loom so large that once again its potential effects are exaggerated.

It is important to gain a proper perspective, not only for correct understanding and recording of contemporary events, but also for finding the best ways of effecting change. Unless the effects are known to be undramatic, there is the danger that untoward reactions (such as very heavy viewing, very late bedtimes, loss of concentration or interest at school)—aspects which have to do with the child and his environment rather than with the lure of television—may be mistakenly passed off as the inevitable by-product of having television in the home.

In the course of this inquiry we have often been asked to sum up briefly what we have found, particularly to evaluate whether television is good or bad for children. It will be clear from the findings reported in the preceding chapter that any answer to such a question would require innumerable qualifications in order to be even approximately accurate.

In fact, this question makes no more sense than asking a doctor 'Are injections good or bad for children?' He will answer that it depends on the type of injection, the dosage, the particular condition and age of the child, the appropriateness of the injection to the illness, and the context in which it will be administered. Similarly, whether television is good or bad for children depends on the programmes, the amount the child views, the type of child, the type of effects to be examined, and the context in which viewing takes place. In the last resort, it is an individual matter with the effects varying from child to child. Nevertheless, just as in immunology it is possible to lay down certain rules or broad guiding principles as to when injections should or should not be used, so here we have been able to make certain generalisations.

At *best*, television can implant information, stimulate interests, improve tastes, and widen the range of the child's experience so that he gains some understanding of people in other walks of life; this can make him less prejudiced and more tolerant. It can make him less susceptible to over-simplified value judgements; it can raise the level of his aspirations. At *best*, viewing can reduce the child's less worth-while activities (such as comic-reading), whilst leaving the more worth-while ones intact.

At *worst*, on the other hand, viewing can lead to a reduction in knowledge (in that it takes up time which could be spent more profitably), keep children from relatively worth-while activities (like outdoor play and book-reading), and implant or accentuate one-sided, stereotyped value judgements—if the content of television is such as to convey this kind of attitude. Depending on content, television can frighten and disturb, particularly those who are emotionally insecure or those who are preoccupied with a particular problem.

While the majority of children are not drastically affected, it must nevertheless be remembered that each minority group represents a large section of the child population, whose needs must be considered.

Lastly, two further generalisations can be made. First, the extent to which the introduction of a new medium forces a greater differentiation into the existing ones—radio and to some extent reading show signs of taking on specialised roles. We have signs of this in our survey, and also a good deal of confirmatory data from surveys in the United States (19).

Secondly, the introduction of any new element into an existing structure requires assimilation and integration. We have shown that this takes place smoothly in the majority of cases; but with children who have problems, families which have conflicts, or (for example) clubs which have a decreasing membership, television may just tip the scale.

4

Implications and Suggestions

AT the beginning we showed how, in the absence of data, the public's views about television and children tended to be heavily influenced by their own attitude to the medium and often to consist of generalisations based on observing a very small number of children. They were neat, global views. After some years of research, during which many so-called 'facts' about viewing and children were found not to be facts at all, the inaccuracy of these neat images became apparent; children differ too widely and the impact of the medium is not such as to stamp out these differences. Nevertheless, as has been shown in the last chapter, for each effect in turn or for each type of child, a fairly tidy picture can be built up and some generalisation made.

It is not just the research worker's desire to stay in business which prompts him to end his inquiries with a plea for further research; it is the inevitable consequence of seeking a pattern to explain the facts which have been uncovered. For example, when we began the inquiry we asked ourselves why is television so attractive to children? We end by asking why is television not more attractive? What is the pull of the everyday activities which children are unwilling to give up even to view a favourite programme? This leads to a re-examination of existing concepts about children's needs and requirements. Many similar examples could be cited. How many such questions are raised depends not only on the scope of the inquiry, but also on the existing state of knowledge in the field. In this instance, the questions are many because few facts were known about the way children spend their leisure or react to television, and also because there is hardly any systematic body of knowledge or theory about the development of children's needs and tastes or about their acquisition of knowledge. Chapter 3 indicates some of the principles that derive from the inquiry; other general issues and questions are dealt with in Chapter 36. Here we shall discuss only issues relevant to the suggestions which follow.

First, any division into children's and evening entertainment has little meaning; children view both and derive impressions from both. The assessment of the effect of television on attitudes and knowledge must therefore be based on both sets of programmes.

Second, any division into programmes designed to instruct and those designed to entertain is unjustified. Children often acquire a good deal of knowledge from entertainment programmes and may learn little from instructional programmes if the level is pitched too low. We have shown that the child's outlook and store of information are derived from all kinds of programmes; in fact, those which make an immediate emotional appeal seem to have the greater effect. The division between instruction and entertainment should disappear altogether; the distinction should rather be in terms of the topic to be covered. All programmes, if successful, entertain; and all programmes provide the child with some information.

Once the problem is considered in this light, it becomes clear that devices successful in entertainment programmes should be tried when dealing with instructional topics. More will be said of this later.

Third, it is also incorrect to suppose that supervision of viewing is a matter of the social level of the home; it is no greater in middle-class than in working-class homes. Certainly, we found evidence of a positive relationship between children's viewing and parental example, but one which cuts across social-class divisions. Excessive viewing and crude, narrow tastes are to be found as often in both sets of homes.

We also found that the focus of public concern had been misplaced. The public had been concerned chiefly with the effects of children spending so much *time* in viewing. Our research suggests that the amount of time spent is a less important cause of concern than the nature of the programmes the children see. There has been public anxiety about such supposed consequences of long hours spent in viewing, as strain on the eyes, insufficient sleep and fresh air, neglect of school work, reduced club attendance, and the development of a generally passive attitude to recreation. These anxieties we have found to be largely unfounded—they were based on an insufficient appreciation of children's resilience and flexibility. More important questions are: what determines the kinds of interests or activities the child will give up in favour of viewing and what are the programmes giving him in compensation?

The impact of television gains its strength from the large number of programmes of similar content that the child sees. There is need therefore to think in terms of *programme balance*. It is important not to concentrate too exclusively on the effects of programmes containing violence, but instead to focus on the whole range of pro grammes that present a view of life to the child, and, in particular, examine the *implicit* values contained in plays, serials, and panel games.

Looking at the problem in this way immediately suggests the need for diversification, for seeing that the views and values presented are not too one-sided and for producers of children's programmes, in particular, to add to their diversity.

Finally, we have seen that an assessment of how much is learnt from television must be done in terms of a profit-and-loss account—in terms of gain in knowledge from television and in reduced opportunity of acquiring knowledge from other sources such as books. This at once shows why intelligent children with ready access to books profit little from television while duller children, who rarely turn to books, often profit more.

The research has destroyed a number of bogies; we hope that it will also indicate areas where concern and interest could more usefully be placed so as to minimize the harmful effects and increase the beneficial ones.

In the remainder of this chapter we outline various suggestions to the general public, in particular to parents, teachers, and youth leaders. In the next chapter we shall try to make suggestions which relate to the planning of television entertainment.

Many of our suggestions will not be new; too many thoughtful people have written about what might be done; and some of our suggestions have already been tried. They are still worth stating here, however, as they derive closely from our findings and thus we have some confidence in their appropriateness. Moreover, an uninvolved observer may draw attention to certain reforms which have not been carried out for organisational reasons—because old ideas are too deeply ingrained, or because they cost too much.

However much one tries, it is difficult in formulating suggestions not to sound obvious.

This is a risk the research worker takes, once he steps out of his role of fact finder and assumes that of interpreter. We feel, however, that in being asked to undertake this inquiry it was partly in the hope that positive suggestions would result from our findings.

SUGGESTIONS TO THE GENERAL PUBLIC

How much should a child be allowed to view? A fixed number of hours cannot be laid down; too much depends on the child's age, intelligence, on his family, and also on the resources in his environment. If we were judging from an educational standpoint alone, we should say that viewing is comparatively unprofitable for the grammar school child, but may teach a good deal to younger children, to adolescents of average and below average intelligence, to children who read little, and to those who live in isolated rural areas. The assessment of the value of television to the child must therefore take into account what else he would do with his time.

Nevertheless, one can say more generally that it is useful to reduce children's viewing by providing more attractive alternatives—viewing, we have seen, takes more time than any other leisure activity and there is no evidence that it is correspondingly more profitable, be it from an emotional or an intellectual point of view. Much viewing is relatively casual, for want of something better to do. Children have a lively curiosity, an enjoyment in exploring and doing things for themselves, so that it is not really difficult to wean them away; the more active the alternative provided, the more likely is it to compete effectively with viewing. A child with many hobbies who leads an active social life has generally a limited interest in viewing; a child who views a great deal, may have few resources or may experience difficulties in making relationships. Thus his viewing is a refuge. Such a child needs to be helped to make better relationships and to be given better environmental opportunities. As far as the majority of children are concerned, there is no need for great concern about the effects of the amount of time they spend viewing. They will view less if their attention is directed towards other activities.

We have been surprised, however, by the small amount of concern that has been expressed about the effect of the *content* of programmes. Violence is the only feature that seems to cause anxiety among parents and educators. There is little evidence of effective parental control or supervision of children's choice of programme, though in some families children are forbidden to see programmes thought to frighten.

Our research suggests that the positive and negative effects of the content of television may be quite powerful. The following need to be borne in mind:

1. Children's interests can be extended by what they see, and their receptiveness to new ideas and their understanding of situations and people outside their immediate experience broadened. But by the same token, if the values portrayed on television are slick and materialistic and give a stereotyped and one-sided view of societies and groups, these values too will be absorbed.

2. Such effects on outlook and values are cumulative; each play and each programme makes only a small effect, but the sum total is considerable.

3. Children are not so much frightened by the amount of violence shown and the physical seriousness of its consequences, as by the context in which it occurs and the way in which it is presented; some programmes disturb not so much through the violence or aggression they contain, as through the picture they give of adult relationships which (in the case of an adolescent, for instance) may heighten the child's concern about the difficulties of adult life. We have evidence that girls particularly suffer from this adverse effect.

It follows that parents and teachers should inform themselves about the programmes which are being shown, not only to prevent the child from seeing what is harmful, but—more important—to encourage him to view some of the worth-while programmes. The public should urge producers to experiment more than they do, by lending support to the worth-while; too much of the criticism of television has been negative and destructive.

In addition, there is need for discussion of programmes, with the child, both at home and at school, to show up the unreality and one-sidedness of the views television frequently offers. Equally, discussion may help to reinforce the impact of good programmes.

Such discussions need not be on a high plane—casual comments are often sufficient. With adolescents, shy in talking about their feelings, a particular play may even serve to get them to talk about emotional problems of concern to them.

With the younger child in particular, the emotional impact can be reduced by making him aware of the production tricks. Reduction of emotional impact, correction of faulty views, and reinforcement of valuable experience are all ways in which parents and teachers can help to make viewing less harmful and more valuable.

Finally, television stimulates interests, but only fleetingly. It is up to the adults around the child to maintain these interests and turn them into action: by rendering accessible the books that have been dramatised, by helping the child to find materials needed to make things suggested on television, by encouraging him to visit places (such as art galleries or exhibitions) that have been featured. Advertisers have long known the importance of making immediate use of the demand which an advertisement has aroused, by having the advertised goods in the local shops the same day, not merely in a few large stores two weeks later. Similarly, at present too much of the child's interest aroused by television programmes is allowed to become dissipated, to be swamped by the impact of the succeeding programme. Adults could do much more to ensure that interest is kept alive.

Specific suggestions to parents

Many homes have worked out useful rules to discourage indiscriminate viewing and to prevent television from becoming an interminable source of conflict. It may, for instance, be decided that the children be allowed to watch the early evening programmes, but nothing (except under exceptional circumstances) after a certain hour; that there will be no viewing until homework is done; or that each child has the right to watch certain programmes regularly. This latter alternative also helps to avoid family conflict over choice of channel.

Children become readily absorbed in what they view and to interrupt their viewing unexpectedly, even with the best intentions (be it for bed, homework, or running errands), is likely to provoke unnecessary conflict; children in this respect should be given the same consideration as adults expect to receive.

Control of children's viewing does not mean using television as a means of discipline—as punishment or reward; extensive use of it in this way would only add to the value which children set on viewing.

More attention needs to be paid to the optical conditions of viewing. Viewing in the dark increases the emotional impact of a programme; it also maximises glare.[1]

Television can be used too readily as a means of keeping the children quiet, a temptation which often faces the busy mother, especially with several young children. It is also a temptation to use television unquestioningly as a means of 'keeping the family together', of encouraging the children to stay under their parents' eye instead of following their own interests farther afield. Television is, of course, unlikely by itself to bring the members of the family closer together.

Each member of the family will to some degree absorb what he views into his private world of experience; a sense of shared experience can, however, be built up through talking about programmes afterwards or even by doing together some of the things suggested. Discussion is particularly necessary with the older children who see so many adult plays. The young child has a small store of experience, as yet little detachment or ability to differentiate between reality and fiction; his response is to incidents, he cannot yet comprehend the broader theme. This is why it is so useful if parents can find the time to watch with the younger children or,

---

[1] Other conditions of correct viewing as laid down by the Association of Optical Practitioners are given in Appendix H.

failing that, encourage them to talk to them about the programme afterwards. In this way one can see if there is anything that disturbs the child, and use the opportunity for building on the new impressions he has gained.

Undoubtedly care should be taken not to expose children to programmes which might frighten and disturb, taking into consideration here each child's personality and predisposition. In general, murder and crime thrillers should not be seen just before going to bed.

Altogether, children should not watch too many murder plays or programmes which feature violence and aggression, not so much because they may frighten, as because they offer a one-sided view of life, implying that all conflict has to be resolved by force. The danger lies less in imitation than in acceptance of violence as manly and inevitable.

Similarly care should be taken to see that children do not watch too many adult plays for which they are not emotionally ready, plays which cumulatively convey too much of an anxiety-laden view of adult life.

Since television can do much to broaden or narrow children's tastes, some guidance as to what children should view might be unobtrusively given. This is particularly important in the two-channel home, where children switch from favourite programme to favourite programme, and so limit themselves to a very narrow range. Here control may have to be more direct to ensure that children select a more balanced diet.

We cannot stress too much the importance of parental example; if parents view continuously and indiscriminately themselves, hushing their children's questions because they might interrupt the next programme, then their children are likely to view equally unselectively. Our survey has shown that as many as 60 per cent of the children claimed that in their homes television was left on all the evening.

Finally, there is a strong temptation to see in television the cause of symptoms that in fact derive from other sources. We suggest that it may be more profitable for the purposes of diagnosis to assume that television itself is unlikely to be the primary cause and that at most it acts as a catalyst.

Recommendations to youth club leaders

We have seen that television has little effect on club attendance or membership. Some clubs have even brought television into the club on an experimental basis and with good results; it is put on for special programmes thought to offer opportunities for informal education.

The National Advisory Committee for Television Group Viewing has been established to experiment with this approach to television.[1] This committee co-ordinates group-viewing activity, advises youth clubs, promotes training courses, and issues a bulletin with advance notices of programmes of likely interest to clubs. Here are some examples of the use to which television has been put in some clubs:

One club used a programme on delinquency to bring together different groups from the same district; in this instance the local magistrate and probation officer were introduced into the club—an experiment from which the magistrate learnt as much as the club members. Similarly, the club's sports instructor watches sports programmes with his team.

In another club, a programme on textiles was accompanied by a visit from instructors from a sewing-machine company; they demonstrated their technical skill, with the result that some of the girls began to take up sewing lessons. In the same club, a local drawing master watched a series of programmes on art with the club members, got them sufficiently interested to look up books on painting, and induced a number of them (this time, not only the converted) to join him on sketching excursions.

Television can be used as a means of starting discussion of a subject which is not easily broached. One club, for instance—joining with marriage guidance counsellors to view a BBC documentary on *Patterns of Marriage*—finished with a lively discussion of the problem; this also offered an easy way of informing young people about the services of the Marriage Guidance Council.

Such examples show how the appeal of television can be exploited as a means of informal education. They also show how much of the success of the venture depends on detailed planning, and on the enthusiasm and devotion of the experts who are brought in. In every district there is usually sufficient local talent to call on, so that television could in fact help to develop closer ties between members of youth clubs and the community.[2]

France was the pioneer in setting up the first tele-clubs (28). Holland, Austria, Japan, and Italy are now also forming national advisory committees on group viewing. In all these countries special attention is being paid to group viewing for young people.

---

[1] This committee was established under the sponsorship of the National Federation of Community Associations within the National Council of Social Service.

[2] The examples are taken from T. Monks's report on *Television and the Youth Services* (1953). The report also offers an account of the formation of a television appreciation group in Wembley, Middlesex.

Suggestions to the teaching profession

Finally we come to teachers, discussing the role that they might play, not in relation to schools' television, but to television entertainment viewed by children at home. Many of the suggestions have been followed for many years by the Society of Film Teachers. They are, nevertheless, set down here because they have not been widely applied in schools in relation to television, and because the problem is one which, in our view, concerns every teacher, not only those specially interested in film appreciation.

While our study of teachers' opinions showed that about half judged the effects of television on their pupils to be beneficial rather than harmful,[1] only 6 per cent regularly suggested to their pupils programmes to view, and even fewer referred to programmes in their teaching.

We should like to suggest that the child's viewing experiences be linked with teaching or discussion wherever feasible so as to bridge the gap between the teacher's and the child's world and interests, to counterbalance some of the values conveyed by television, and to utilise television as a means of getting children interested in certain topics. This is particularly important with the younger children and the adolescent of average and below average intelligence.

Some programmes prove useful starting points for discussion. Teachers from schools in isolated areas commented particularly on the way television had widened children's horizons and had helped to bring home certain lessons, with greater force, than would have been possible through discussion and books alone.

We have seen that television at first reduces reading, and does so particularly with the marginal reader (the boys and the less intelligent children). Some remedial action might be necessary here, a special watch being kept on the amount such children read out of school.

Programmes of any kind, the good and the less good ones, can, of course, be used as exercises for composition, comprehension, and accurate perception. We should welcome, for instance, discussions and analysis of the build-up of detective plays, or comparative analyses by the children themselves of the different Westerns they know so well. All this would help towards more detached, critical viewing.

[1] Only 11 per cent thought that, taken all in all, television's effect on their pupils was harmful rather than beneficial, and a further 39 per cent were undecided. Among those who had television and observed the effects on their own children, three out of four thought the good effects outweighed the harmful ones. The rate of purchase of television sets among teachers was the same as among other groups of comparable income and education.

We see the teacher's role also as one of suggesting future programmes to be viewed, of interesting children in the better plays or in some non-fiction programmes which, through the switching from channel to channel, they are likely to miss. Children who have no television at home could guest-view on these occasions.

The extent to which teachers will make systematic use of television (apart from schools' television) will, of course, depend on the demands of the time-table, the pressure of examinations, and the intelligence and age of the child. Every teacher can do a little, even if only in the form of a casual comment and guidance about viewing. Television is too important a source of values and of knowledge (correct and incorrect) for the teacher to take no positive action. Expression of dislike of the medium as such is of little value here.

Finally, teachers could do a great deal in drawing the attention of producers of children's television to suitable books for dramatisation and to topics of likely interest. The link between children's television and teachers should, in our opinion, be as close as that between the teaching profession and schools' television. Television seen at home touches a far larger audience, without the correcting influence of the teacher's presence.

How best to utilise television could with profit be taught at the training colleges; it is something that teachers can, of course, do effectively only if head-teachers and educational administrators, too, accept that this task should be done by them. If it is not done, the development of taste, the ability to view critically, will be left too much to chance.

5

Suggestions to Television Producers[1]

PERHAPS the most difficult problem that faces television is its large child audience up to nine o'clock in the evening. Three out of four 10–11 year olds view regularly until that hour. Three out of four 13–14 year olds go on until nearly ten o'clock.

In the course of this inquiry a good deal of evidence has been collected about the impact of adult programmes. We know that they make more of an impact on children than those programmes specifically designed for them; that plays in particular convey implicit and explicit values which influence children (at least from the age of 11 onwards) and that this occurs because of the large number of adult plays they see with fairly uniform underlying themes and characterisation (Chapters 13, 14, 17).

Problem plays, particularly those of high calibre, may disturb children as much as murder plays. After all the essence of drama is the portrayal of tension which in some of the more sophisticated plays is purposely left unresolved. Young, insecure adolescents, through seeing so many of these plays may, as we have seen, become anxious about their own competence to enter the adult world. While women's magazines are often criticised for protecting the adult reader from the tragedy of life, we have to criticise television for introducing it to the child before he has the emotional and intellectual resources to cope with it.

The responsibility that falls on adults concerned with children's viewing is then a serious one, and the producers cannot maintain that all responsibility lies with the parents and none with them. Viewing is after all a family affair; it often takes place in the only room available in a home containing children of very different ages. Whether we like it or not, we have to accept the fact that young children stay up until 8.30 or 9 o'clock; effectively they cannot be sent out of the room. Also—and this is the decisive argument—the parents often do not know, until the programme is well under way,

---

[1] The term 'producer' is used as a generic term and includes also those responsible for programme planning.

whether or not it is suitable for children. The present method of warning parents at the beginning of a programme presupposes that the majority hear the opening announcements; this, investigation has shown, is rarely the case. Also, if children heard it without an adult present, it would be the exceptional child who would not be eager to view!

What is to be done? The example of an older mass medium that faced similar problems might serve as a guide here. The cinema either takes responsibility completely out of the hands of the parents (the 'X' certificate) or offers a choice under certain conditions (the 'A' certificate, where the child has to be accompanied by an adult). Prohibition and restriction cannot, of course, be enforced in home viewing, but at least action along the following lines could be taken. Programmes intended for the marginal period of 6–9 p.m. could be vetted, bearing the children in mind in the following ways:

1. Plays which contain incidents of violence or horror essential to the dramatic story should be shown after 10 p.m.
2. Plays which contain such incidents merely as frills for the sake of sensationalism (we quote two such examples in Chapter 14) might be able to replace them by other dramatic devices. (The impression gained is that this might quite often be the case in murder plays and thrillers.)
3. Some programmes may be too sophisticated for the young viewer in the problems they raise or the themes they present. We suggest, not that these programmes be taken out of evening television, but that the parents be informed through the medium of the *Radio Times* or *TV Times* that these programmes are not suitable for children below the age of 10 or below the age of 15, whichever the case might be. It can then be left to the parents to decide how to use this information. The comment has been made that such procedure will only make children keener to view unsuitable programmes. This will depend on the home and the amount of supervision exercised by the parents. In any case it is one of those generalisations which are easy to make but which have yet to be put to the test.

What are suitable programmes? Just as with films, the dividing line is difficult to draw. Roughly speaking, unsuitable programmes, from the child's point of view, are problem plays[1] and programmes where violence is depicted realistically with much camera play on the preparation of attack, the attack itself, and the injury that follows. The less a detective play is a battle of wits and the more it

[1] Especially those which deal with alcoholics, drug addicts, prostitutes, and tense parent–child relationships.

becomes an exposition of psychopathic or sadistic behaviour, the less suitable it is for the entertainment of children. Trial and error would gradually produce some working classifications. It would have the advantage of teaching parents to consider what programmes their children view.

It is in no way our intention to suggest that adult entertainment should be reduced to the level of the 10–11 year old. Intellectually, unfortunately, too much of it is already well within his competence; it is rather that undue concentration on particular themes be avoided, or parents alerted to them.

Programme balance. In this connexion, programme planners should consider more carefully the *balance of their programmes* than they do at present; reducing in particular the number of murder or detective series shown between 6–9. Insistence on a more varied picture of life could only improve the quality of television entertainment, not devitalise it. The Children's Advisory Committee of ITA, which, as at present constituted by the charter, is concerned with children's programmes only, should recognise that the main effects on children are produced by evening television and not by television designed for children. If it is good in quality, in diversity, contains laughter as well as conflict, is devoid of sadistic, sensational episodes, it will help to broaden the child's outlook; if it remains as at present (i.e. if ITV remains as at present) this is not likely to be the case.

Taking the question of programme balance one step further, we find that producers of children's programmes have a greater responsibility and also a greater opportunity than has perhaps been fully realised. It is not enough to have the children's programmes merely balanced among themselves. The number of adventure programmes shown on children's television must be added to those presented in the early evening, but outside the children's hour. With the help of content analysis of those adult programmes which children will view anyhow, children's television could consciously try to counteract, in its plays and programmes, any stereotyped one-sided views presented in adult programmes. This is not a Utopian view; it simply means that children's adventure plays should search for other types of heroes than cowboys and detectives. Our suggestion throws a greater burden of inventiveness on the producers of children's programmes, but one which their past performances show them more than capable of bearing, provided they are given adequate facilities.

Action and suspense must remain an integral part of children's plays, but we ask for their appearance in the varied settings in which they occur in real life. This, like our suggestions for a better programme balance of adult plays, requires above all good scripts.

There is a third type of balance that should be struck and one perhaps most difficult to achieve. It is the *balance of juxtaposition of programmes* on the two channels. An example may help to illustrate the point: if, for instance, ITV produced a perfect programme balance, but each time it showed an instructional programme the BBC at the very moment offered an adventure play, then the programme balance of the one channel would count for little; it would simply lose its audience to the other channel. We should like to put forward the 'revolutionary' suggestion that the television companies concerned, i.e. ITV and BBC, for their children's hour, agree to show educational programmes at the same time. It is not an easy thing to arrange, but with a fair measure of give and take quite possible, and in our view, very important. This would deprive children of absolute choice; for adults, such restrictions on choice would be inappropriate. We have produced a great deal of evidence to show that *l'appétit vient en mangeant*, that, for example, programmes showing the way of life of children in other countries can be enjoyed by children who, given a free choice, would opt for something more exciting and of more immediate appeal.

Balance of adult programmes, balance of children's programmes in relation to the adult ones, and finally the balance of children's programmes for both channels, and later for the third channel, are suggestions that we put forward with confidence and with some urgency.

Presentation of violence. There is a great deal of talk about the need for research into the effects of showing so much violence. We feel that the need for research is used too readily as an excuse. There is no need to prove that such programmes do harm; it is the responsibility of the companies which show a large number of them to prove that they are worth the time given to them, particularly in children's hour: i.e. that they are not merely entertaining but that they are also broadly educative, intellectually and emotionally. For this, the evidence would seem to go the other way. On these grounds, therefore, and for the reasons outlined more fully in Chapter 16, we recommend a reduction in the number of murder-thrillers and detective series shown at times when children view (in particular those which have more complex characterisation (the psychological angle) and those which show the detective to be as aggressive as the criminal, a common feature in many of the plays). Of course, these programmes will not make normal children delinquent, though they may have an effect on latent delinquents. However, the strongest reason for criticising them is their reiteration that life is cheap and that conflict is to be solved by violence—because they are all so similar, they do not offer a sufficient diversity of models for identification.

There has, however, been too much talk about the number of gun shots fired in children's Westerns and the possible harm that may result from them. These we have seen make little impact, if any; instead, more consideration ought to be given to the range of incidents which disturb children.

It is not whether a man is only shaken by an aggressor or seriously injured that makes the difference to the child; it is rather the way the incident is presented, how much of the man's fear is depicted, how the close-ups are used. The sight of a man falling off a building does not lead to much anxiety, but a man caught after a long chase whose laboured breathing conveys fear, may frighten and disturb. We are mentioning this because in several of the BBC episodes of classics (*David Copperfield, Jane Eyre*) much play was made of fear and anxiety. Had their disturbing effect on children been appreciated, they might have been toned down without losing too much of the atmosphere. A first-rate presentation of a classic can disturb as readily as a second-rate murder play.

From the foregoing it should be clear that if the Independent Television Authority is to fulfil its responsibilities—which include making judgements about the suitability of programmes which children view, it must concern itself with the situation as it really is and do periodic content analyses of the kind described. The charter lays down the need for ensuring balanced programmes, but does not stipulate the unit of time within which this balance is to be assessed. There ought to be two units within which balance is evaluated; the unit between 6 and 9 o'clock, and then the overall balance. The balance within the first unit has not always been achieved; on certain days, adventure succeeds crime and is followed in turn by adult Westerns.

Our trend analysis showed that in the course of the first year the programme balance of ITV became increasingly more narrow, more packaged. One wonders if the Authority could not have taken more notice of this trend and stopped it earlier. Also, through direct supervision, or through request, ITA should ensure that no national or social groups appear too exclusively in the role of either villain or fool; stereotypes of television we have seen are taken over by children.

We are, of course, aware that we have studied Independent Television during its experimental period when it had to cope very quickly with a mass of problems of which BBC had many years' experience. It also had to ensure its own survival by getting audiences big enough to attract advertisers. Independent Television has got over its early difficulties and is now in a strong enough position to bear its social responsibilities; there are many signs that it is aware of them and a wider range of programmes, including non-fiction programmes, is now being shown. Nevertheless, the programme balance could do with much improvement.

PROGRAMME PRODUCTION AND RESEARCH

The suggestions, so far, have been concerned with overall planning and control; those which follow relate more to individual programmes. We are conscious that we are invading the territory of experts without having any expert knowledge of production. Our suggestions derive from information concerning the consumer's and the observer's point of view. Producers have not been able to get any systematic information about children's tastes, the number who view different programmes, or about the effects of their programmes.

We are presenting here ideas as they suggest themselves from a study of children's reactions and an analysis of television content. Once again the suggestions we make are ones that producers have carried out many times, or would have liked to carry out, had they had the right facilities. Nevertheless, the suggestions are worth making, because they are based on actual data and not on hunches, and because television entertainment as it is today presents too little evidence that these ideas have in fact been widely applied.

We know that experiment is often not possible because of limitations of time, production facilities, and money; but it is not for us in making suggestions to be bound by these limitations. Indeed, we hope that our suggestions for more experiment and more fact finding about the impact of programmes will lead to the provision of better facilities, particularly for children's television and informational programmes, the two Cinderellas of television.

Our suggestions are aimed at two things: to encourage more experiment and less reliance on the safe formula and the packaged series, and to show that research, carried out in close collaboration with the producer, is an essential aid to production when dealing with so heterogeneous an audience.

Apart from money and time, two things stand in the way of greater adventurousness in programming: the producer's tendency to underestimate the viewer's taste, and inadequate information of audience reactions.

The producer's scapegoat is the public and its poor level of taste, just as the public's scapegoat for the ills of society is television. The public, it is said, can take little of the worth-while, hungers for the mediocre, and so accepts the better programmes only if the pill is heavily sugared.

We can quote many findings which contradict this view. For

example, as many as 24 per cent of our grammar and 12 per cent of our secondary modern school children mentioned a non-fiction programme as one of their favourites, impressive figures when seen against the figure of 30 per cent for the most popular programme (*Fabian of Scotland Yard*). Among adults, we find that some informational programmes interest sizeable audiences. Programmes on social and political problems (*Panorama*), archaeological discoveries, painting, under-water fauna, anthropology, and medical science have all found a good measure of popularity.

If three or four information programmes covering very different topics interest a large number of viewers, then we can no longer say that people in general will accept only the frivolous and mediocre; rather we have to ask ourselves: what makes these programmes acceptable where others fail? We must look for the ingredients that make for their success so as to produce more programmes of a different kind on the same level.

The difference between producer and audience is not so much one of difference in interest in such topics as in having different habits of communication. Without detailed study of viewers' reactions, barriers of language might inadvertently be set up between the audience and the topic simply because the expert (or the producer advising the expert) is not sufficiently familiar with the phraseology and way of thinking of his target audience.

This brings us to another impediment to effective experiment; lack of information about viewers' reactions. Information about the adult audience's reactions are to a limited extent provided by measures of audience size and popularity ratings. For children's programmes even that is missing—there is no systematic information available about the age-composition and number of children who view programmes, nor about their reactions. In fact, planning of children's programmes has gone on for years without regular 'feed-back'. Fan-mail is notoriously unrepresentative.

This we suggest is due to two kinds of stereotypes, namely, that children do not know their own mind and that there is no way of questioning them. Children, as we have seen, know what they like. They can also express their views; it is simply that the techniques for questioning differ from those suitable for adults.

Paradoxically, such information becomes the more important to obtain the more a programme company aims at diversity and at putting on good programmes (i.e. at achieving a high level); we suggest that in this respect the need for research and feed-back is particularly great for BBC children's television, where there is a great deal of diversity, and where one would learn from its successes as well as from programmes which are less popular. The less frequently the safe formula is used, the more comprehensive must be the information service.

Nor can one argue that such feed-back is not required because children's tastes are uniform and well known. We have shown in Chapter 10 how inaccurate are the assessments of experts and how little uniformity there is in children's tastes.

Research as aid to effective programme production

We should like to illustrate the need for research by one specific example. Our study showed that the BBC programmes asking children to make models, produced a response rate of only 2 per cent. Surely there is an important area here for fact finding—how to stimulate children through television. Was the topic the right one, the vocabulary appropriate, the pace suitable, were the instructions clear? What impression did the instructor make on the children? Did they fail to respond because it seemed too babyish or too boring, or because they had not the materials at hand or because they were given too lonely and long a task? Once the reasons for lack of response have been ascertained, a producer is in a better position to experiment. For example, he may decide to cater for a narrower age range, so that the level of exposition can be more effectively geared to that group, or he may ask for group rather than individual products.

Of course television entertainment is an art, but an art within certain rules; research can help here. It can also show that certain 'rules' which have been built up about the type of things which disturb children have little justification. One such example is the rule laid down to producers of children's television against showing fights on the ground. Children find little to disturb them in such scenes, unless they occur in a boxing match; more disturbing are attacks with sharp instruments, about which there are no rules.

Research, as we see it, depends on very close collaboration between research worker and producer. This we envisage ideally as four or preferably five stages:

Stage 1. The producer indicates what he is trying to convey, in terms of ideas and values, or whatever emotional responses he wishes to evoke.

Stage 2. When the programme is on the air, the research worker and preferably a colleague who is not familiar with the producer's intentions, carry out a content analysis of what is in fact conveyed—listing ideas, themes, moods (those intended as well as those not intended).

Stage 3. Using the ideas derived from the content analysis and the producer's ideas, an effects study is done with children of different ages and intelligence levels. Information is sought about their interests, emotional responses, and about their comprehension of the programme, possibly at two points of time to see if there have been subsequent effects.[1] The children would be matched with children who did not see the programme.

Stage 4. A post-mortem on the points of agreement and of discrepancy between producers' intentions, the content of what was put over, and the viewers' reactions.

In this way a great deal could be learnt which may help the producer on other occasions.

In many instances a *fifth stage* is needed, as was done in several BBC Audience Research studies (8, 17), where information is collected, before the programme is planned in detail, about the existing knowledge and attitudes about the topic. This is very important in the case of children's documentaries, for example, where, as we have shown, many are pitched too low and provide information which children of 10–11 already possess.

These stages sound rather formidable; they need not necessarily be so, and can to some extent be made simpler, depending on the purpose for which they are needed.

Information programmes

We should like to make more specific suggestions about informational or educational programmes. Evidence from our study shows that when children see such programmes they often enjoy them, but given a choice, will not seek them out.

The analysis of viewing in two-channel homes showed that instructional programmes are losing audiences to fiction programmes. It is for this reason that we have earlier suggested a kind of 'educational truce' between the two channels, so that the child, whichever programme he turns to, comes across a programme of this type. To make these programmes more interesting, more of the devices which ensure for the entertainment programmes their large audiences could be adopted: among them the creation of suspense, greater use of the action sequence, the conscious building up of star qualities of the principal exponents. Some programmes do this very successfully, they have the pace and tempo of a play without in any way— and this is important—forgoing careful exposition. Science is inherently dramatic; there is no reason why, from the age of 10 onwards, children could not enjoy the presentation of scientific topics. Adult informational programmes can, on occasions, be used for children, but they may have to be made shorter and given a different, simpler dialogue drawing attention to rather different features from the ones believed to interest adults.

Much could be done by conveying to the children that scientists

---

[1] Hovland found quite often that attitude change was greater with a longer time interval between first contact and re-examination.

and explorers, as people, can be as interesting and have as exciting a life as detectives. Here, more than in any other type of programme, follow-up is needed. Gradually a set of principles could be built up about the children's capacity for comprehension. Such research should also be used to see whether increase in knowledge produces a change in attitude and, if so, whether the change in attitude is in the desired direction.[1]

Research and experiment are two sides of the same coin. In one respect, there is more need for experiment here than in the United States, where some of these functions are taken over by the twenty or more educational television stations. (These are unlikely to be opened here; they would require too much subsidising.)

Quite a number of successful programmes from education stations were bought by American commercial television companies. In their absence from the British scene, we should like to suggest that each television company, for one half-hour a week during children's television and a somewhat longer period during evening television, has an *experimental period*, announced as such to the audience, giving new writers and new expositors a chance to try things out. It should be a period, too, during which certain educational films could be shown with a view to obtaining the reactions of the audience.

Such an idea is not too Utopian—one thing is certain: that, apart from the need for experiments and research to fulfil television's social responsibilities, they are necessary as an investment against the future. The American example has shown that soap opera, more recently quiz programmes, are declining in popularity and there is need to look ahead for new ideas. No more shots can be put into a Western, no more psychological twists into a detective series; after a time their sameness will inevitably begin to bore.

We should like to end our recommendations with some specific suggestions for the content of children's television, which has set itself the impossible task of attempting to cater for an age range of 5–14. The impossibility of catering for all their needs and levels of maturity should be recognised, and specific days might be devoted to programmes for given age groups, with the week-end offering something for them all. In this way the programmes could be far more specifically geared to the target audience, and each age group would feel that there was one day on which *its* interests were considered. In particular, the programmes inviting children to partici-

---

[1] The BBC showed in one study (8) how increased knowledge about travel to France and knowledge of French words went hand in hand with greater anxiety about travel. The programme had made people aware of problems by describing the process of travelling, which, for the first time, brought home to people how different France is from England.

pate could be related to the level of skill and staying power of the age group. A system such as this would make time for programmes for adolescents, a group insufficiently catered for. Of course, other age groups will 'guest view', but this would not matter; it might be all to the good.

It would, however, make the parents more aware that their children might be watching programmes not designed for them, since they would know in advance that on a given day the entertainment was intended for a different age group.

If one could envisage a truce between BBC and ITV, sufficiently firmly founded, then much would be gained if each company were to select a different day from that of the other company for a given age group.

Programmes for adolescents are badly needed, whatever time they might be put on the air. Adolescents, as yet, are offered too few personalities of sufficient stature to act as models. This is an age when young people talk about social and economic problems, about jobs, about ways of behaving, about moral issues—our data show that they would be interested in discussion programmes for young people, specifically aimed at matters which are of concern to them. Television could give a great stimulus in encouraging community and group activities.[1] Group competitions are likely to meet with more success than those asking for individual contributions. Great care, however, must be taken to pitch the level right, and there is need for the most careful follow-up.

Children's plays could be built on the ingredients of the existing adventure plays, but contain a far wider range of models, settings, and problems. They should interest children in the excitement that comes, not from exploits against the law or in its defence, but from the conquest of difficulties. The range of models that television could offer the children is very wide. At present the heroes are usually cowboys or detectives or escaped prisoners of war; heroes who fight against disease, are generally figures from the past, dressed in historical costumes (Pasteur and Florence Nightingale). Through this, they lose much of their model value for children. Such models should be living ones, or fictional shown in today's setting.

There is a particular need for models for girls—women whom they would admire and whom they would feel like imitating. The fact that girls form half the child audience seems sometimes to be forgotten.

To move away from the stereotyped plot to more diversity requires greater skill in writing. Many of the BBC children's programmes

---

[1] More could be done, for instance, about interesting adolescents in such activities as competing for the Duke of Edinburgh awards.

have shown what can be done in this direction; we should like to see it more widely applied.

Finally, more could be done to make use of the child's spirit of adventure in order to encourage activity—instead of showing exhibits in a museum, producers could encourage them to compete with one another in finding the largest number of such exhibits in their local museums, or in obtaining detailed information through reference books, or exploration of towns. We should like to see a wide range of such programmes attempted.

We have felt it our task in these recommendations to point in the main to weaknesses and to the type of changes that might be made. These in no way detract from the many excellent programmes that are shown, or from the ingenuity and enterprise that has made BBC children's television a model of its kind. It is because we are so much aware of what children can take and of the potentialities of the medium that we have sounded this critical note.

Our findings are based on careful examination of data; our recommendations on predictions that derive from these facts and from the close study of television and children. We are offering them as hypotheses, which, if tried out, need in turn to be checked for their correctness. What we have tried to do is to indicate that experiment is not as difficult as it sounds, nor is the forgoing of the safe formula as risky an enterprise as has often been thought.

Schools' television

The inquiry was confined to an investigation of the effects of television viewed in the home after school; nevertheless, many of the findings, concerned with the acquisition of knowledge, have a bearing on schools' television; for this reason they are brought together here. They relate to the teacher's decision on whether or not to use television for his class, to the age and intelligence level of children likely to profit most, and to the type of research needed for effective programme planning, for which schools' television offers a unique opportunity.

How is a teacher to decide whether it is useful for his class to watch schools' television? We suggest that such an evaluation be made in terms of profit and loss; by deciding whether television can provide a greater gain in knowledge, interest, and liveliness of discussion than could have been obtained through a period of free reading, open discussion, or class-room teaching. Once put in this way, the decision will vary, not only with the age and intelligence level of the pupils, but also with the particular programme, the topic and the manner of its presentation.

Our findings suggest that the age group most likely to profit might well be rather younger children than those at present served by schools' television; an age group for whom alternate sources of information are less readily available through lack of reading skill and lack of vocabulary and who are also at the age where visual presentation adds greatly to their comprehension. We are thinking here of the 10–11 year old in the last year of his primary school career. For schools' television to be of value to the grammar school child, it has to face much keener competition; it must show that it can offer the pupil more in the half-hour than he might derive from books to which he has easy access, and for which he has acquired the appropriate vocabulary. The usefulness of schools' television in the case of grammar school children may then depend almost exclusively on whether the level of presentation is pitched sufficiently high. This may require straight exposition and demonstration rather than more indirect methods of putting information across.

In the case of schools' television, much can be gained if the research worker works closely with the producer right from the inception of the programme; in fact carries out quite systematically the five stages of inquiry outlined on p. 60.

In this way, over time, much can be learnt about the ways in which information can best be put over: the relation of word to image, the appropriateness of the vocabulary, the visual as well as the auditory presentation of specialist terms, the relation of dramatic illustration to central narrative and of interview versus straight exposition.

Research should and must form an integral part of schools' television. It is not something that can be done casually in an unsystematic way. It requires the closest collaboration between producers, teachers, and research workers. As we have said earlier, we know so little about how information is to be put across, that here we have an unusual opportunity for building up a systematic body of knowledge. We would go so far as to say that without research of a thorough kind, schools' television cannot live up to the high standards that it has set itself.

Of course, the value of schools' television is not to be assessed in terms of gains in factual knowledge alone; it may help to develop a critical or thoughtful approach to a problem, stimulate discussion, or get children interested in topics which they previously thought were outside their province or of whose existence they were unaware. Nevertheless, such gains are as amenable to straight research as gains in factual knowledge. Too little is known about the relation between interest and gain in knowledge or attitudes to infer from children's apparent interest in a programme that it has achieved its necessary goal.

Research carried out by the teachers themselves would be very useful here; for example, three comparable classes could agree to an experiment in which one used the half-hour period to watch schools' television, the second to have a lesson on the same topic, while the third did reading on the subject. The relative effectiveness of the different methods could then be shown.

A great deal of research can be done by outside bodies, by university and other departments. However, this in no way lessens the need for integral research on the spot, financed and used by those who put schools' television programmes on the air.

*   *   *   *   *

In conclusion, we should like to make two points: first, since these suggestions are aimed at more balanced and diversified programming and affect adult as well as children's television, they may well improve the quality of television content. Secondly, experiment in programming with adequate follow-up is as necessary in television as is research into the development of new products in industry; without it, television cannot flourish. Our suggestions for more research into the effects of television should be seen, not as an interference with the artistic process of production, but as a valuable information service for it; nor as a luxury, but as an integral part of effective planning.

PART II

The Design of the Study

6

IN Chapter 1 we have outlined the problem and the way in which the research design took shape. Here we shall consider the stages in the design, indicate how the review of the literature led to certain ways of thinking about the problem, describe the research instruments used, the selection of the sample, the conduct of the field work, the process of matching, and the analysis of the data. We have tried to present here a more general account, leaving details and technical considerations to an appendix on methods.

EXAMINATION OF THE LITERATURE

The size of the problem and the shortage of time made it particularly important to survey the existing literature on the effects of television and also on the effects of the older, more fully documented media such as films, radio, newspapers, and comics.[1] In addition we looked at communication research, as carried out, for instance, by Hovland (47), which is primarily concerned with the process of communication itself, and with the way in which attitudes or behaviour respond to given messages contained in the programmes. Were we to present a list of what we have read, without discussion, it would

---

[1] The survey was far from complete since it was difficult to gain access to many interesting studies, notably those carried out on the Continent as, for example, by Keilhacker and others in Germany (54), and by Zazzo in France (106).

add nothing to our report except respectability; it has therefore not been given. Instead we refer the reader to the various summary accounts by Lazarsfeld (56), Hovland (46), Merton (65), Schramm (82), and Berelson (12); and also to the pre-war Payne Fund studies into the effects of the cinema on the child summarised by Charters (22).

Studies on the effect of television have been summarised well by Coffin (24), Meyerson (67), and more recently by Bogart (19). In the main, these studies examine the effects of television on leisure pursuits and on buying habits. Special mention should be made here of the rather more imaginative inquiries of Maccoby (58, 59) and Riley (78, 79), both relating children's television behaviour to factors in their environment and social relations.

In forming our plans we profited most from the accounts of Maccoby and Riley, and from two reports published by the Bureau of Applied Social Research, Columbia University—one by McPhee (64), the other by Klapper (55). Klapper's report has been especially useful. It describes the various short- and long-term effects that television was thought to have, as hypotheses for examination. Wherever possible, we have tried to investigate these (cf. Chapter 31 on passivity and stimulation). Herzog's (40) analysis of children's radio listening proved similarly fruitful in suggestions and hypotheses.

In this country, studies fall into various distinct types: those which deal with comprehension, of which the work of P. E. Vernon (97), M. D. Vernon (96), and Kay (52) are examples, as well as the many studies carried out by the BBC Audience Research Department (6, 8, 17), especially by Belson (7, 11), and by Trenaman (94). Then there are the studies concerned with children's tastes and with the effect of the cinema on children, notably the interesting work of Mary Field (32), and the studies by Wall (98), by Mayer (61), as well as the report of the departmental committee on children and the cinema published by the Home Office in 1950 (44). Finally, there are the BBC Audience Research Department's studies of the effect of programmes on attitudes (8, 10) and their occasional studies of children's preferences for given types of programmes (15, 16). One or two of these studies include children's reactions to television programmes; they tend to sample preferences for given programmes rather than obtain an overall view of children's tastes.

From the survey of the literature the following points emerged which proved relevant to the way we built up our research design:

1. That the effects of any medium, when examined objectively, tend to be far smaller than popularly supposed; consequently to

detect its effects the number of cases to be studied would have to be fairly large.

2. That the use to which the medium is put, and the child's reactions to it, depend on his needs, which in turn relate to his age, sex, intellectual ability, and home life (40, 59, 78). A design should therefore make it possible to relate variations in effect to certain known characteristics of the viewer, including some information about his home life.

3. That there is differential displacement—the time taken up by any medium is gained not by reducing all other activities by equal amounts, but by reducing some more than others (19). While isolated studies pointed to this, there was need for establishing principles which would permit prediction of the types of activity most likely to be affected.

4. That communication research, as described by Hovland (46) and Merton (65), had built up a set of theories, backed by substantial empirical evidence, concerning the effectiveness of communications. Our task lay in extending such inquiries to a problem little touched upon, i.e. the extent to which an influence is exerted by the values and ideas contained in programmes designed to entertain. Any such influence, we postulated, would be cumulative. To explore this issue we first had to establish how far television entertainment was in fact putting over certain values consistently, and second, how far these affected the outlook of the young viewers. Through studying children of differing age, intelligence, sex, and social background we hoped to obtain differences in effects which might be built up into a coherent set of principles, similar to the ones obtained for communications which put over a specific point of view.

We also examined the literature to see what pitfalls must be avoided in the design and in the research techniques. The main pitfalls seemed to be these:

1. Mothers' reports tended to be unreliable; compared with the children's own accounts, mothers tended to underestimate the amount their children viewed and were rarely familiar with their children's programme preferences. Moreover, Maccoby (58) has shown that mothers tended to belittle the effects of television, since any changes might reflect adversely on their maternal skill.

2. Teachers' reports also lacked objectivity. Too often they assessed changes brought about by television in the light of their own overall attitude towards the medium.

3. Certain studies have little chance of success—as, for example, the testing of a causal relationship between seeing violence on the screen and its resultant effect on behaviour and emotion; this type of problem requires more indirect techniques of assessment.

4. The whole body of communication research, as exemplified by the work of Hovland (47), Peterson and Thurstone (73), and Franck (34), shows that one

cannot infer from the content analysis of television programmes what may actually be perceived and absorbed by the child. Communication research has shown that such inferences are faulty even for adults, and are likely to be more so for children, where programmes designed by adults are viewed by children of different ages. Consequently any analysis of the impact of television programmes must consist both of a content analysis and of effects studies.

5. Researches which sought information about subjects other than television in the child's life seemed to come closest to showing the effect of television. This statement may seem paradoxical, but an example, namely the work of Maccoby (58), will make the point clear. Maccoby, interested in studying patterns of upbringing, carried out a set of detailed interviews with mothers of young children in the Boston area. In the course of this study, but not as a central part of it, she asked certain questions about television ownership and about the children's viewing pattern. Re-analysing her results, this time around television, she showed how much the television experience forms part of a broader pattern of the child's home life and reflects the parent–child relationships. Her research is valuable to the extent to which she has information on other aspects of the child's life, to which his television experience could be related.

6. Many of the findings pertaining to children were so similar to those obtained for adults that some of the results of our inquiry would quite likely be applicable to adults.

THE MAIN SURVEY AND THE NORWICH STUDY

For reasons outlined in Chapter 1 we decided to devote most of our research effort to the two surveys; the main survey, in which matched *viewers* and *controls* (non-viewing children) were compared with one another, and which was conducted in London, Bristol, Portsmouth, and Sunderland; and the Norwich *before-and-after* study in which we tested children both at the time of the main survey (May–July 1955) and again a year later (using the same instruments). In 1956, we tested only those children who had in the meantime acquired a television set, together with their controls. We shall discuss these surveys under four headings: design of the research instruments, selection of the sample, field work, and analysis of data.

DESIGN OF THE RESEARCH INSTRUMENTS

Decision to use written questionnaires

In social psychology, stereotyped views have grown up about the sensitivity, quality, and validity of given research instruments. Like other stereotypes they exist to some extent independently of the conditions which gave rise to them. One view is that honest answers cannot be obtained from questionnaires—that personal interviews are always more informative and flexible. This is true where highly trained interviewers are available, together with ample time to establish *rapport* with respondents and to clarify their answers by means of supplementary questions. The interview is certainly superior to written techniques when these conditions are fulfilled. But for the reasons listed below, personal interviews in this survey would have fallen far short of these optimal conditions:

1. *Likelihood of interviewer bias*: all interviews had to be conducted within the same period of time. To do this would have required a very large body of interviewers. We would have run the risk of not having sufficient numbers of the right calibre, fully conversant with the objectives of the inquiry. Lacking these, interviewers would have had to abide by a rigid schedule, so losing one major advantage of personal interviewing, especially where children are concerned.
2. *The rumour bias*: where it is necessary to interview a considerable number of children from the same class-room, one after the other, this could mean that a child might come to the interview primed by his predecessors. This would introduce bias and make all but the first child's interview valueless.
3. *Accommodation bias*: in a crowded school often the only room which can be freed is that of the headmaster, hardly suitable for the conducting of relaxed interviews. Further, under these conditions, the continued presence of the interviewer for several days at a school would prove an intolerable burden.
4. *Parental bias*: alternatively, to interview each child at home would have proved not only a formidable task, but would have introduced the additional bias intrinsic in the parents' presence.

Effectively, there was no choice. We had to aim at devising class-room administered questionnaires which would allow for maximum flexibility and spontaneity. This meant, too, that the youngest age group we could study was 10–11 years of age. Below that age, written instructions and spontaneous answers would have proved too difficult for all but the brightest.

Research instruments used

The following questionnaires and devices were used:

1. A diary, in which every day for one week, children recorded their previous day's activities, and in which they also indicated the three things each day which they had most enjoyed.

2. Programme recall lists: children were asked every day for one week to indicate which of a list of wireless and television programmes they had seen or heard; and for each of these, how much they had liked it.

3. Questionnaires asking for factual information about length of television ownership, viewing habits and also attitudes to television, preferred and disliked programmes and personalities. As far as possible parallel questionnaires were designed about cinema-

going, listening to the wireless, and reading, although in the latter case especially, many additional questions were included, separately covering book-reading, comic-reading, and reading of magazines and newspapers.

4. Questionnaires containing background questions about the home and general leisure interests as well as about attitudes to school and vocational aspirations.

5. Open-ended questions, essays, and sentence-completion devices, to reflect children's attitudes and outlook, as described in Chapters 19, 20.

6. Questions designed to assess the importance of television in children's lives and interests.

7. Interest inventories covering children's participation and interest in different activities, as well as their liking for given types of subject-matter presented on television and radio, in films and books.

8. Tests of information, designed to assess children's general knowledge, and also knowledge specifically derived from television (cf. Chapters 22, 23).

9. In addition to the background factors already discussed, some measure of the child's adjustment and personality was needed, to which differences in the effect of television could be related. To obtain this—which is really an attempt at fitting a case study into a survey—we devised three personality inventories, dealing with children's wishes, worries, and fears, respectively. We also obtained the class teacher's assessment of each child's behaviour and personality characteristics; whenever the teacher felt that some out-of-school condition had a bearing on the child's school performance or general adjustment, he was invited to make a note of this. In addition, he recorded attendance at child-guidance clinics, as well as any physical disabilities.

All the research instruments are described more fully in Appendix A. Here we have singled out for description the diary and the programme recall lists, both central to our main survey.

The diary

We decided on a diary as the best device to measure the current after-school behaviour of the children, to obtain spontaneous information about their viewing, and especially to chart unorganized leisure activities. In addition, we hoped to gain a measure of the relative amounts of social contact that the child had with his family and friends of his own age. The design of the diary raised many problems. First, we experimented with the time unit within which children were asked to record the day's happenings; we presented them with a sheet of ruled paper and asked them simply to write down everything they had done after school on the previous day. This produced scanty results, but the introduction of hour-by-hour divisions yielded much fuller accounts. We also found we obtained more accurate accounts about bedtimes when we ended the diary with *What did you do between 10 and 11 o'clock*, so making it look acceptable that the child might only have gone to bed at this late hour.

In addition, we had to decide on the right layout for discovering which of the day's events the child had experienced alone, and which with someone else. The layout we came to use, complete with the answers of a bright working-class girl of 11, is presented on p. 74. The detail given is characteristic even of 10–11 year olds of average intelligence. Below that level reports were scantier, yet still informative.

The diary was given to all the children in the same week, beginning 9 May 1955. Administratively this proved difficult, and became possible only through the excellent collaboration we received from the teachers concerned.

To ensure frank rather than prestige-oriented replies, three devices were used. First, we began the study with a letter to each child, explaining the objective of the inquiry, stressing that we were interested in leisure activities generally, and the need to record all details, however unimportant. The letter is reproduced in Appendix A. Second, the children were given code numbers which they were asked to use instead of their names. The teacher alone had a list aligning the code numbers with the children's names, so that anyone else picking up a diary would not be able to identify the writer. This technique proved a success; children enjoyed the secrecy and importance that it conveyed and saw that our assurance of anonymity was genuine.[1] The third device lay in demonstrating to the children that the teachers would have no chance to read the diaries. In the letter read to the children they were told that the diaries would be collected by the teachers, placed in an envelope, and sealed.[2] We had previously asked the teachers to do this rather ostentatiously in the children's presence.

This material, in its hour-by-hour record of one week of children's leisure, drawn from five cities and from several thousand children

---

[1] It also proved of clerical convenience since the children did the numbering of the questionnaires for us. They retained the same code number and used it for all subsequent questionnaires.

[2] The pilot survey had further shown that the accounts became briefer as the week went on. To guard against this, different letters of thanks and reminders were read out by the teacher on several occasions.

DIARY RECORD OF A 10–11 YEAR OLD GIRL WITH NO TELEVISION AT HOME

| To be filled in, on Tuesday, May the 10th | Diary sheet for MONDAY afternoon and evening | Code Number 6929 |

WRITE DOWN ALL THE THINGS WHICH YOU DID	For each thing you did, say whether you did it by yourself or with someone else. If you did it with someone else, say who this was.
Between 4 and 5 o'clock in the afternoon: Came out of school and got on the school bus. Got off bus and went home and had my tea.	Alone. Sister.
Between 5 and 6 o'clock in the afternoon: After my tea I got my bike out and rode down to my sister's house to baby sit.	With friends.
Between 6 and 7 o'clock in the evening: Got baby to sleep then read *The Lone Ranger* and *Billy the Kid*. Then I washed up the dishes.	Alone.
Between 7 and 8 o'clock in the evening: Wrote a letter to my pen pal. Then listened to the wireless called *Double Your Money*. Ate sweets while listening to it.	Alone Girl friend.
Between 8 and 9 o'clock in the evening: Listened to *Double Your Money*. Then made some supper. Then ate it, and then made the baby's bottle.	Girl friend. Girl friend. Alone.
Between 9 and 10 o'clock in the evening: Gave baby his bottle. Then sat in the chair to read *The Wizard*. Sister came in, then went home.	Alone. Girl friend.
Between 10 and 11 o'clock in the evening: Arrived home, then got washed, had a cup of tea then went to bed.	Alone.

Please think back again over **everything** *you did yesterday afternoon and evening. Write down the three things you* **really** *enjoyed:*

(a) *I enjoyed most of all* listening to *Double Your Money*.

(b) *I enjoyed next most* reading *The Lone Ranger* and *Billy the Kid*.

(c) *I enjoyed third most* getting baby to sleep.

whose background and intelligence level are known, is unique in this country and provides a wealth of material well worth further analysis. The problems of coding this vivid individual material proved difficult; the technique developed is described in Appendix A. Since seven diary sheets had to be coded for each child, we were able to code fully only a small number of randomly selected cases for each sub-group, 336 in all.

Programme-recall lists[1]

Our main objective was the spontaneous charting of children's leisure, but a secondary objective was to obtain precise information about their daily viewing and radio-listening. The hour-by-hour account from the diaries proved adequate for determining the week's viewing in broad units. To obtain more precision, for the week following the diary period, a daily programme-recall list was designed which covered the previous day's radio and television programmes. On this list, children were asked to indicate whether they had seen or heard the programme and, if so, whether they had liked it or had not cared for it; they were also asked to record any film they had seen.[2]

SELECTION OF THE SAMPLE FOR THE MAIN SURVEY

It will be remembered that the main survey had two chief aims: first, to find out what differences, if any, existed between viewers and controls—differences which were associated with (and might be due to) viewing; and second, to study the variations in these differences due to age, sex, social class, and intelligence, so as to find the sub-groups within which particular effects were most marked. The first objective depended for its success largely on the efficacy of our matching, the second on finding and testing the necessary children to fill the cells of the factorial design.

The factorial design

Matching of viewers and controls ensured similarity between the two groups to be compared. At least equally important was the overall design, controlling the internal composition of these two samples. Here we were above all concerned to find out how the

[1] We should like to thank the BBC very much for making available advance information of programmes for the preparation of these lists.

[2] In the pilot study we affixed programme-recall lists to each day's diary, but found that this influenced the spontaneous description of the other leisure activities; consequently, apart from overlap during the week-end, we administered diaries only in the first week and recall lists only in the second.

effects varied with age, sex, intelligence, and social class, and to do this in a way which would permit the study of the effect of one of these factors while holding the others constant. As explained in Chapter 1, this was done by means of a *factorial design*, which requires equal numbers of children in each of the cells and sub-groups.

It is a well-recognised fact among statisticians that the analysis of any body of experimental material is greatly simplified if the experiment has been carried out in a factorial design. The principal reason for this, while fundamentally mathematical, is readily appreciated from a common-sense point of view: if one is analysing simultaneously the effects of a number of factors upon a particular variable, and each possible combination of these factors occurs with equal frequency among the observations, we can be sure that, when we combine these factors for a particular comparison, no undue weight will be given to one combination at the expense of another.[1]

An example will make the advantage of such a design clear. We found that middle-class children were keener book-readers than children from working-class homes, and that the bright children read more books than the dull. In a study which did not employ a factorial design, it might well be that when one was comparing the effect of television on dull with that on bright children, the picture would be misleading if in the duller group there were more working-class and in the brighter group more middle-class children. The factorial design ensures that the dull and the bright groups both contain equal numbers of children from working- and middle-class families.

Although a factorial design permits considerable gain in efficiency, the number of cells required—and therefore the size of the sample—mounts rapidly as soon as more than one or two variables are included. Because of this, not more than four main variables could be used, each divided into two or three categories, as follows:

1. Two age groups (10–11 and 13–14 years).
2. Boys and girls.
3. Three levels of intelligence within each age group. (Children with I.Q.'s of 115 and above; 100–114; and below 100. In the case of the older group, children from grammar schools constituted the group of children with I.Q.'s above 115.)
4. A twofold social class division (middle class and working class).

[1] Similarly, if we are interested in the extent to which two of these factors interact upon the variable being studied, the fact that observations are equally frequent in all cells of the design permits us to look separately at the effect of the interaction of the two factors, and at the effects of the two factors acting separately. This property, usually described by its mathematical name, 'orthogonality', gives the factorial design its importance in research experimentation of all kinds.

In addition, there would be equal numbers of viewers and controls, so that the design would consist of 48 cells. Since the minimum acceptable number of cases per cell was thought to be 40, a total of 1,920 cases was required. Even though the number of cases per cell was kept as low as possible we did not expect to be able to fill each cell, since our previous studies had shown, for instance, that there were few middle-class children in secondary modern schools (42). Later, we shall indicate how we dealt with this problem.

The procedure adopted to find suitable cases

Our pilot work in greater London showed that about two-thirds of the children had television at home, while a large number of the remaining children from non-television homes were frequent guest viewers. This meant that our potential controls (i.e. children who were not subjected to the influence of television, whether as guest viewers or as set owners) might consist merely of the small minority of children who viewed very rarely; apart from the fact that such children would be atypical, this would restrict the number of viewer/control pairs to the small number of controls available. It was therefore necessary to go outside London, concentrating on areas (and within areas on schools and even classes) which promised the best return of viewers and controls. To find the most suitable areas, we looked at the Postmaster General's regional returns for television licences[1] (making allowances for elapsed time), and then carried out a viewing census in eighteen of the more profitable of these. We aimed at those urban areas in which approximately one-third of the children would have television at home, with a further one-third potential controls, and the remainder guest viewers.[2] Any other ratio of viewers to non-viewers would have restricted the proportion of usable cases, either by offering too few set owners or too few controls. This was especially important since we intended to carry out the matching within class-rooms.

To each Director of Education in the eighteen selected areas we sent a personal letter explaining the purpose of the proposed census, asking for his co-operation, and for the return of a form indicating the number of schools of different types in his area. Next, each local education office was supplied with count forms, which they distributed to the schools under their authority. After examination of

[1] *G.P.O. Quarterly Statistics of Wireless Licences Current, by Head Post Office Districts.* The Auditor General's Department, Ledger Branch 3.

[2] It proved impossible to include the urban/rural division as one of the variable factors in our basic design. We had to concentrate on urban areas, for the sake of speedy field-work organisation.

647 returns, we selected Bristol, Portsmouth, and Sunderland. (The count form is shown in Appendix A.)

A similar count was carried out in London County Council schools. The census proved useful in selecting not only cities, but also schools, and within schools those classes which had the most favourable ratio of viewers to controls. Each head also described the type of occupations which his pupils' parents followed; this information helped us to select classes with the appropriate social background to fill the forty-eight cells of the factorial design. The final selection of classes within schools worked out towards a fairly even distribution over the five cities (Table 1).

TABLE 1. Selected schools and classes for the main survey

City and type of school:	No. of schools	No. of classes	No. of children
Bristol:			
Primary	9	14	603
Secondary modern . . .	4	9	288
Secondary technical[1] . . .	1	2	55
Grammar.	4	10	333
Total	18	35	1,279
Portsmouth:			
Primary	12	19	719
Secondary modern . . .	6	11	323
Secondary technical[1] . . .	—	—	—
Grammar.	2	8	234
Total	20	38	1,276
Sunderland:			
Primary	8	9	314
Secondary modern . . .	10	13	407
Secondary technical[1] . . .	—	—	—
Grammar.	3	10	302
Total	21	32	1,023
London:			
Primary . . .	14	19	666
Secondary modern[2] . . .	7	11	417
Secondary technical[2] . . .	1	2	34
Grammar[2]	3	5	143
Total	25	37	1,260
Grand total	84	142	4,838

[1] Since there were too few secondary technical schools to permit a special subdivision they were combined with the secondary modern school pupils.

[2] The secondary schools in London cannot readily be classified in general terms. The labels which we have attached to them can therefore only be regarded as approximations, and have merely been used as a matter of convenience.

(a) The main survey

The schools which were selected from the census returns were asked whether they would agree to take part in the inquiry. Permission was almost invariably given.

The work with the children fell into two main parts, separated by about six weeks. The first stage began on 10 May 1955; it involved the filling in of diaries for one week, followed in the subsequent week by completion of the daily programme-recall list. Both diaries and programme-recall lists were given out to the children by their class teachers, who proved extremely helpful to the whole conduct of the research. The inquiry had first been discussed with each teacher by a member of the research team. The instructions on how to administer the diaries and programme-recall lists were given to the teachers both orally and in writing. This method assured considerable uniformity in administration.

The second stage, some six weeks later, consisted in the filling out of questionnaires and test papers. Each class was visited for two or sometimes three half-day sessions. This part of the inquiry was carried out by members of the research team, assisted by over a hundred trained and supervised helpers, who had been recruited locally. The teachers took no part at this stage. The helpers were organised into two groups; those who were capable of taking charge of classes, and their assistants. The former had the task of explaining the nature of the inquiry to the children, and of demonstrating (with the help of black-board examples) the various procedures for answering different types of questions.

In the case of the grammar schools, we had two assistants to each class, in the other classes three or even four. In some cases it was even necessary for a child to dictate his answers to one of the assistants, who spent most of their time in going from child to child, and giving help where needed. The questions had been divided into a number of booklets, and we found it necessary to have sufficient staff in each class-room to check each booklet when handed in, returning it to the child where necessary, pointing out questions he had omitted. A friendly, rather grown-up atmosphere of mutual collaboration was preserved. On the whole the children enjoyed the tests; they were mostly at an age when they liked giving their opinions, and had not yet become self-conscious. Judging by the children's replies, our emphasis on the need to write what they felt, rather than to worry about how to spell the words seems to have been effective.

(b) Norwich

Norwich was visited twice, once in 1955 and then again in 1956; in 1955 the field work was carried out at the same time as that of the main survey. Here, however, *all* schools with children in the age groups of 10–11 and 13–14 took part. Table 2 shows the number of schools in which the testing was carried out.[1]

TABLE 2. Number of children tested in the first part of the Norwich study (May–June 1955)

Type of school:	No. of schools	No. of classes	No. of children
Primary	16	34	1,346
Secondary modern	13	26	682
Grammar	3	7	213
Total	32	67	2,241

In April 1956 we obtained the necessary information to tell us which children in Norwich had acquired television since our first visit. After collecting this information we returned to Norwich in June 1956, and retested all the children who had television at home, as well as children of the same age, sex, intelligence, and social background to act as controls.[2] To be on the safe side, we tested very many more potential controls, so that altogether during this second visit, 109 grammar school and 550 secondary modern school pupils were tested—ultimately providing 185 pairs of matched viewers and controls. Table 3 gives the distribution of these pairs by social class, sex, intelligence, and age.

It will be seen that in Norwich we could not aim at equal numbers for each sub-group, but had to take all available cases.

The distribution of cases is uneven. In particular, the ratio of older to younger children was 1:3. This was due, not to differential purchase of television sets in the children's families, but to early school-leaving. More than half of the older children who had tele-

[1] At the beginning of the survey, questions which we had asked were taken up and in some cases misquoted by the local press, and subsequently in the national press, with the result that the inquiry received adverse publicity. In consequence two Norwich schools withdrew from the survey and, at the request of one of these, the questionnaires already filled out by the children were destroyed. We immediately informed every headmaster and headmistress, not only in Norwich but also in the other cities, of the publicity, showed them the full range of questionnaires, and asked if they would like to withdraw from the inquiry. Apart from the two schools in Norwich, only one school in London did so. We have much appreciated the teachers' continued support of this inquiry.

[2] The very few children who already had television at the time of our initial visit were not included.

vision at home could not be retested, because they had left school just before the retest. We were in a difficulty here to which no adequate solution could be found. On the one hand, it was essential to carry out the first test with children of the same age as those tested in the main survey, as their answers were to serve as a base-line to indicate pre-existing differences. On the other hand, we could not return to the schools in less than a year, as otherwise the season would have been different, and also there would not have been sufficient time for the effects of viewing to make themselves felt.

TABLE 3. Distribution of the Norwich sample of matched pairs of viewers and controls by age, sex, social class, and intelligence

		BOYS		GIRLS		
		Middle class	Working class	Middle class	Working class	Totals
10–11 year olds:						
Primary I.Q. above 115.	.	2	3	1	4	10
Primary I.Q. 100–115 .	.	4	17	10	24	55
Primary I.Q. below 100.	.	8	18	6	32	64
Total number of pairs .	.	14	38	17	60	129
13–14 year olds:						
Grammar . . .	.	16	11	—	—	27
Sec./mod. I.Q. above 100	.	1	3	—	5	9
Sec./mod. I.Q. below 100	.	1	10	4	5	20
Total number of pairs .	.	18	24	4	10	56

The process of individual matching

The need for careful individual matching in exploring differences between viewers and non-viewers was of great importance. In order to keep the study within manageable bounds, the factorial design had of necessity to be rather crude: two age groups (10–11 and 13–14 years), two social class groups, and just three levels of intelligence do not give very fine discrimination. If we had simply filled the design with viewers and non-viewers without matching, it might easily have happened that we would have found differences between viewers and controls which were due not to viewing but to a bias in the selection of cases, within the two cells or sets of cells being compared. For instance, we might have found that viewers scored higher than non-viewers on measures of school performance; this might be due to viewing, or it might have happened that within each of our three levels of intelligence we had selected viewers who were a little brighter (and consequently a little better at schoolwork) than non-viewers within the same I.Q. range.

Every viewer was individually matched against a control subject of very nearly the same age, sex, intelligence, and social background, so that in all comparisons between viewers and controls these main variable factors were, in effect, much better controlled than the outline of the factorial design would lead one to expect. As far as possible, the matching was also done within the same class-rooms, so that geographical factors, and the influence of the teachers, the school, and of the other children were also, as far as possible, held constant. The better the matching, the greater the likelihood that any differences between viewers and controls would in fact be attributable to television and not to extraneous factors.

The choice of the matching characteristics presented problems; strictly speaking, one might need different matching criteria for each new factor under investigation. Thus, in order to assess television's effect on school performance, we would ideally need to match viewers and controls for all those factors which influence school performance, such as age, intelligence, social background, persistence, quality of the teachers, size of class, &c. But in studying the effects of viewing on frequency of cinema visiting, some other factors might be involved: social maturity, emotional characteristics, &c. For each issue under investigation one would need to match on the factors most relevant to it. But for many forms of behaviour such determinants are not known or are only partially understood, and in any case the need constantly to rematch the samples for different factors would have created prohibitive problems, even if the necessary cases could have been found. In choosing to match only on age, sex, social class, and intelligence (and often on school class as well) we tried to employ the four factors most often and most closely associated with the problems we wished to study.

The necessary information for matching was obtained from a brief questionnaire, given to the children on the first day on which they filled out the diaries. In this questionnaire we asked for sex and age, how often the child listened to the wireless, how often (if at all) he viewed television, and how long his family had had a television set. In addition we asked what kind of work he would like to do when he left school, as well as two questions about his father's occupation: *What is the name of your father's job?* followed by *Describe carefully the sort of work he does.* We used the father's occupation as an approximate indicator of the social level of the home; it is a rough measure but has been shown to be the most effective single indicator of social class (38).

The question arises as to how far children know, and can correctly describe, their father's job. In a previous investigation we had found a correlation of 0·88 between the occupations of the fathers as described by 13–14 year olds and as given by the fathers themselves.

In the present inquiry we found that even the dull 10–11 year olds were able to describe their father's job with sufficient detail. When we classified the occupations on the basis of the Hall–Jones scale of occupational prestige (38), over 90 per cent could be placed into one or other of the eight groups.

Here are some examples of the children's responses. First, some exceptionally careful descriptions:

> An inspector of refrigerators. My father finds the dents and scratches in the doors and cabinets of refrigerators. If he finds a scratch he marks it with a crooked line, and a dent he marks with a circle and he marks it 'ding'.

> Mosaic terrazzo. It is an Italian name. He puts in fireplaces, floors, &c., with mosaic. This is a sort of coloured marble chips. He cements the floor, then adds the marble chips. After that he has to polish it up. It is a very hard job.

The following are more typical of the general level of the replies:

> A constable in the Z borough police. My father sees that shop doors are closed at night and gives advice to passing motorists.

> Plumber's mate. He does all of the dirty work for the plumber. He works in a shipyard and he has no skilled job as he was in the Army.

> Sorter in the Post Office. He sorts letters into one of 68 holes in a wooden frame. There are different frames for every town.

Here are some examples of shining admiration:

> At —'s. He serves people with clothes. He is second to Head and could have been head of the shop. It is not his own shop.

> Barber. He cuts men's hair and small boys' too and big boys'.

> Grocer and sub-Postmaster. He serves on the post office and does all post office and grocery accounts. This means he does a lot of brain work.

Finally, some very flat descriptions:

> Clerk in War Department. He writes.

> Electrician. He cuts the lights off of people who do not pay the bill.

> Sanitary attendant. He works down the lavatory. He sells towels so people can have a wash.

> Bus driver. He goes to work at the Depot and gets a bus and he goes.

The inquiry was restricted to state schools. In consequence, the sample of middle-class children consisted mainly of those whose fathers' occupations were of lower middle- and middle middle-class status.

Table 4 gives the composition of the main survey sample, in terms of the Hall–Jones classification of occupational prestige.

TABLE 4. Detailed distribution of children in the main survey, in terms of the prestige rating of their fathers' occupations

	13–14 YEAR OLDS		10–11 YEAR OLDS	
Hall–Jones grading of occupational prestige:	v %	c %	v %	c %
1. Professional and high administrative	4	2	5	3
2. Managerial and executive . .	3	5	5	6
3. Inspectional, supervisory, and other non-manual (higher grade) .	10	9	13	13
4. Inspectional, supervisory, and other non-manual (lower grade) . .	14	14	13	13
5. Routine grades of non-manual .	9	10	11	12
6. Skilled manual	38	38	37	36
7. Semi-skilled manual . . .	19	17	13	13
8. Routine manual	3	5	3	4
Total cases	473	473	454	454

NOTE. In this and all subsequent tables, V denotes viewers, C controls.

This table also shows the close similarity of the social-class composition of the viewers and the controls.

Measures of intelligence were obtained from the schools, or where these were not available, a special intelligence test was given, devised by Professor P. E. Vernon.

It will be remembered that for administrative reasons all the children in each form had to be tested, and that the selection of matched cases was only subsequently made. The actual matching procedure is described in Appendix A. The matching standards were especially rigorous: the two members of each pair were of the same sex, within six months in age, within six points of I.Q., and within one grade either way in the eight-point Hall–Jones scale of occupational prestige. Towards the end it was not always possible to confine the matching to children from the same classrooms, and at that point we had somewhat to relax our rigorous requirements; they remained, however, more stringent than is customary in survey inquiries. As a rule, a viewer was individually matched with a child who not only had no television set at home but who also viewed no more than once a fortnight. This procedure, while increasing the precision of the design, meant discarding no more than a handful of suitable cases for whom no 'twin' could be found. Individual matching was used both in the main survey and in Norwich. The distribution of the Norwich pairs has already been given in Table 3. Table 5 presents the distribution of pairs of viewers and controls for the main survey.

TABLE 5. Distribution of the matched pairs in the main survey by age, sex, social class, and intelligence

NOTE. The planned distribution of the factorial design aimed at 40 pairs per sub-group.

| | BOYS | | GIRLS | | |
	Middle class	Working class	Middle class	Working class	Total pairs
10–11 year olds:					
I.Q. above 115 . . .	49	36	51	32	168
I.Q. 100–115 . . .	46	48	37	43	174
I.Q. below 100 . . .	19	42	15	36	112
					Total 454
13–14 year olds:					
Grammar . . .	38	40	69	47	194
Sec./mod. I.Q. above 100 .	20	47	29	56	152
Sec./mod. I.Q. below 100 .	14	55	10	48	127
					Total 473
Total number of pairs . .	186	268	211	262	927

Weighting procedure adopted

Table 5 shows that in a number of cells we fell short of the desired forty cases. If we had proceeded with the analysis without equalising the numbers we would have been faced with serious problems of inspection of the tabulated results; even more important, we would have created the very situation we had wanted to avoid: one sub-group, by being numerically stronger than others, would create spurious differences between combined groupings. On statistical advice, a process of *weighting* was therefore used.

This is a system whereby, using a random procedure, the cells can be made up to the required numbers. Where the cells contained too many cases, the requisite number was discarded at random; where there were too few cases, some (drawn from the cells at random) were mechanically duplicated. The system of weighting and its implications for statistical analysis are discussed more fully in Appendix A.

The results of the questionnaires were coded and machine tabulated. Inevitably, the coding process was slow, since so many of the questions were open-ended and in addition often needed coding frames which were interpretative as well as analytical. The coding of the week's diaries for each child proved particularly cumbersome, so that in this case only 168 viewers and 168 controls were fully analysed.

Machine tabulation of the results was complex, due partly to the number of Hollerith cards needed for each child (by the time summary and area-score cards had been punched the total came to over forty 80-column cards per child) and partly as a result of having to deal with matched pairs.

The following comparisons were made:

1. In Norwich, a comparison of future set owners and their controls, to see how far there were pre-existing differences.

2. A comparison of the differences between the 1955 and 1956 replies of Norwich children who had acquired a television set with similar differences obtained from a matched group of controls.

3. A comparison of the viewers and controls in the main survey: here we looked first for overall differences, but also for differential effects, such as between different social classes, different intelligence levels, &c. In every case all the comparisons made possible by the factorial design have been carried out, but only the significant ones have been reported. However, in some instances consistent minor tendencies have been mentioned, which helped to throw light on children's reactions to the medium.

4. The extent to which effects change over time. Here we compared viewers who had had television for less than one year (*recent viewers*) with those who had had television for between one and two years (*experienced viewers*), and finally with those who had had television for three years or more (*veteran viewers*). All these comparisons, unless otherwise stated, were carried out on matched groups, that is to say the recent, experienced, and veteran viewers were equated for age, sex, intelligence, and social class.

5. Finally, how much do effects depend on the amount children view? We divided the viewers into *occasional*, *moderate*, and *heavy* viewers, and, again using matched groups, compared their reactions with one another.

The tests of statistical significance used were χ^2 and analysis of variance, together with certain special correlational techniques such as the tau coefficient.

To indicate the significance of the differences at every turn would have made for cumbersome reading; similarly the tables would have become difficult to inspect, if we had always shown levels of significance on them. Instead, we have as far as possible restricted ourselves to a discussion of only those differences which were statistically significant at the 5 per cent level of confidence, or higher. Otherwise, such descriptions as 'a slight trend', 'a small tendency', 'a minor difference', &c., indicate that the findings were not statistically significant. Where appropriate, a one-tail test has been used.

Generally, in table headings and elsewhere, we have indicated the text of the actual questions as used in the questionnaires by putting them in italics.

ADDITIONAL STUDIES

To examine problems for which the main survey and the Norwich study could not be used, we undertook a number of supplementary inquiries. Ideally, we should have waited with these until the results of the main survey were at hand; lack of time prevented this, and many of the studies had to be started at a time when the coding of the main survey was still in progress. Most of the studies were carried out in the course of 1956.

In all, eleven supplementary studies were undertaken. Some of these studies are referred to throughout the report, others are presented in more detail in particular chapters.

1. *Interviews with parents.* Two groups of thirty children from television homes, representing occasional and heavy viewers respectively, were matched in pairs, for sex, social class, age, and intelligence. The children had been selected from the main survey sample and were drawn from a number of primary schools in the London area. The homes of each of these sixty children were visited and the mothers interviewed. The interview started with a discussion of the mother's general attitude to television and her views about its effects on her children; this was followed by questions dealing with television in relation to the children's learning and education, their interests and hobbies, and their relationships with other members of the family. Questions were also asked about listlessness and the stimulation of new interests, about the child's social relationships outside the home and the extent to which television entered into his play activities, and about control by the parents of the children's viewing. In the analysis a special point was made of comparing and contrasting the occasional and heavy viewers. These data are only partially analysed and will mostly be written up separately.

2. *The teachers' opinion study.* Over 500 teachers answered questionnaires which sought their observations and opinions about the effects of television on children in their class-rooms, and (for television-set owners only) on their own children. The teachers were drawn from different areas of the country and from all types of school in the state system, from infant and E.S.N. schools to grammar schools. A substantial number of rural teachers was included. Teachers were asked for their opinions on many different alleged effects of television on children—lack of concentration and tiredness, improvement in children's general knowledge, the potential value of educational television in the schools, and so on. This study has been written up separately as a Ph.D. thesis. Reference will be made to it throughout this report.

3. *A study of television's effect on school performance.* The class teachers of children who had taken part in the main survey assessed the performance of selected children in a number of different school subjects. Each teacher was given the code numbers of pairs of children, each pair constituting a viewer and his control 'twin'. Only by reference to his class list was the teacher able to identify the children. He was then asked to indicate which member of the pair was better at a given subject or whether their level of performance was the same. This was done for a number of school subjects in turn, and finally for an overall assessment of their respective school performance. Whether television improved or led to a deterioration in school performance could then be assessed by seeing whether more viewers than controls received higher ratings, or vice versa. By adopting this method of comparisons within pairs we were able to use results obtained from many different schools, in spite of differences in syllabus and different systems of marking. Altogether 172 pairs were assessed in this way (cf. Chapter 25).

4. *A study of the viewing habits and reactions of young children* (*Mothers' diaries*). So far, the studies had, in the main, been confined to two age groups—the last year of the primary and the third year of the grammar and secondary modern schools. To obtain information about younger children, a study was carried out in which a group of twenty-two mothers was asked to keep a week's record of their own and their children's viewing. They also recorded what they observed of their children's reactions and gave their own views about the manner in which television entered into their children's lives. Only mothers with children under 7 were approached, although in fact they recorded the viewing of the whole family. The sample was selected with the help of the BBC Audience Research Department and the results provided a check on *family* viewing as well as offering information about the viewing of young children in the home. The sample contained families with different social backgrounds.

5. *Content analysis of programmes.* It is only possible to understand the influence of television on children if one knows what kinds of programmes are offered to them. At the most superficial level this involved a simple classification of BBC and ITV programmes over selected periods, by subject-matter, time of day, and day of the week. Subsequently, we developed a system of content analysis, aimed at analysing programmes in terms not merely of their structural characteristics, but also of the values, attitudes, stereotypes, and themes portrayed (Chapters 13, 14, and 17).

6. *Observation of children's reactions during viewing.* On four occasions, groups of children aged 9–11 were observed while watching Westerns, an episode from a children's dramatic serial (*The Prince and the*

Pauper), and an information programme about polecats. These observations threw light on such problems as the extent to which children became involved in the happenings on the screen, how much they identified themselves with them, how much they listened to dialogue, and how much they attended to action.

7. *Group sessions.* One small group of five 10–11 year old children met two research workers on nine occasions to talk about television programmes and their reactions to television. The children's homes were also visited. This study was carried out in order to find out more about children's reactions, especially to programmes containing violence and aggression, and to get to know from the children themselves what kind of incidents they found disturbing. The sessions ended with the children re-enacting scenes from different television programmes for the benefit of the research workers. These sessions, which were tape-recorded, are discussed in the main in Chapter 12.

8. *Intensive individual interviews.* Ten interviews were carried out with 9–10 year old boys and girls about several different aspects of their viewing reactions. In the course of these interviews (each lasting over an hour and recorded on tape) the children were encouraged to talk about television as freely as possible. In particular they were asked to give an account of certain selected programmes which had appeared on television during the previous seven days, and of which a content analysis had been carried out. These interviews explored the children's perception of these programmes, together with the nature of the appeal of television generally, all within the context of the child's own personality as it emerged in the course of the interview. Additional information about these children in terms of intelligence, social adjustment, and personality was obtained from the headmaster through whose co-operation the children were contacted; the interviewer also visited the children's homes.

9. *Comprehension studies.* A number of studies were carried out immediately after certain selected programmes had been on the air, to test understanding and recall not only of facts, but also of plot, characterisation, and motives.

Members of the research team viewed and analysed each programme, then constructed questionnaires about it. These were given the following day to children who had seen the relevant programme. In addition to dealing with the comprehension of plot and situation, we also tried, within the limits of the written questionnaire, to analyse perception of character and motives, different 'levels' of comprehension and understanding of the values and attitudes presented by the programme (Chapters 15 and 23).

10. *Stimulation of museum visiting.* We studied children's attendance

at the Ashmolean Museum, Oxford, before and after some of its exhibits had been shown in a BBC *Children's Television* programme (Chapter 24).

11. *The change brought about by ITV.* Towards the end of our period of study the first ITV programmes came on the air. We therefore carried out a small follow-on survey of viewing habits in the first week of July 1956, nine months after the start of ITV. Programme-recall lists were prepared, listing all the programmes on both channels for one week. These were given every day to 219 children by their teachers; the children were asked to record which programmes they had seen and how much they had liked them; they were also asked questions designed to find out how often they switched from one channel to the other. At the end of the week, a final questionnaire was administered covering general preferences, attitudes to programmes, and viewing frequencies.

PART III

The Child Audience

7

The First Viewers

TELEVISION in this country restarted after the war in 1946. Between then and 1955, in no more than nine years, the number of families who owned television sets increased from less than 20,000 to approximately five million.[1]

Owning a television set will soon be as commonplace as owning a radio. But there is still time to learn about the needs that television satisfies by looking at those families who, in an area where television is newly introduced, are among the first to acquire a set. The Norwich study provided such an opportunity. We shall start by considering the manner in which such homes and their children differ from families less eager to purchase a television set.

Previous studies, so far as we have been able to ascertain, have been concerned with this problem in its relation to family size, income, and education. On the whole, within any one social class the less well educated proved more eager to provide themselves with sets than the better educated, and the families with more than one child more so than families without children or with only one child (Emmett, Bogart, 19, 31). With regard to income, the position has shifted over the years; at first, a greater proportion of the higher-income groups bought sets, but by now comparison of households

[1] These figures are based on information obtained from the Audience Research Department of the BBC.

with and without television sets shows their income distribution to be much the same.

What is more interesting, however, is to get at the character and way of life of these two types of families. Our study was well adapted to this end; by matching our future viewers with their controls, we could compare two groups of families of similar social class and with at least one child in each family of similar age and intelligence. Consequently, we could ask what factors other than income determine the alacrity with which a family will buy a television set. The two groups (future viewers and controls) proved also to be similar in family size; as a result we have in the end eliminated all those variables, one by one, which in previous studies have differentiated the two groups. What other factors remain?

It will be remembered that in the Norwich study we did not interview the parents. We have therefore to infer something about the type of home from which these children come, and about the type of people their parents might be, from differences found in the behaviour, attitudes and values of future viewers and their controls.

It will also be remembered that the comparison of future viewers with their controls determined whether differences found in the main survey were pre-existing differences or the after-effects of viewing. As a result, these comparisons will be referred to throughout this report as they become relevant. Here we are bringing all the differences together. They are not a haphazard collection of chance differences, but instead present a meaningful picture.

The children of the early set-owners

Four main qualities tended to characterise children of Norwich families which bought television sets in 1955/6—during the first year after the opening of the local transmitter:

1. They proved more eager for ready-made entertainment; their tastes were narrower, less mature, and less developed.
2. They tended to have lower and more limited aspirations for their future.
3. Home supervision was more relaxed.
4. They tended to be more gregarious, and more extraverted.

Appetite for popular entertainment

Not unexpectedly, the future viewers were already in 1955 more involved than the controls with the whole idea of viewing; they knew more about television programmes, and were more eager to have a chance to view.

What was more interesting was their unusually strong interest in the cinema and radio.[1] Seven per cent of the future viewers mentioned cinema or radio as their favourite spare-time activity, compared with only 2 per cent of the controls. Future viewers more often said they would like to be a film star and seemed to immerse themselves more in the films they saw: for example, in answer to one question they indicated significantly more often than the control group that they sometimes wanted to see a film a second time, or that they would think or talk about it afterwards. They also showed a rather less critical attitude to the cinema than other children: more of them said they would go on looking at a film they disliked rather than walk out.

Mass entertainment of any kind would appear to be more important to future viewers than to other children. In addition, their tastes in entertainment tended to be less highly developed and narrower: in reading, for instance, future viewers read more comics than other children, although they read the same number of books. Table 6 shows the number of comics and magazines the two groups claimed to read in one week:

TABLE 6. *How many comics, children's newspapers, or magazines do you read in one week?*

(Distribution of answers of 10–11 year old Norwich children (1955))

Number read:					Future viewers %	Controls %
2 or less	.	.	.	.	17	34
3 or 4	.	.	.	.	30	29
5 or more	.	.	.	.	53	37
Total cases	.	.	.	.	114	115

When, however, the better children's newspapers and magazines[2] were considered by themselves, no difference was found. In other words, only for popular mass entertainment did future viewers show a stronger appetite.

Both groups spent an equal amount of time on books, but the future viewers spent more time reading comics. As a result, when children were asked: *On which do you spend most time—reading books, comics, newspapers, or magazines?*, two-thirds of the future viewers said they spent most of their time on comics, compared with only half of the other children (Table 7).

[1] Nevertheless (possibly through force of circumstances) they spent no more time than other children on these types of entertainment.
[2] Magazines such as the junior national papers (now defunct), the *Children's Newspaper, Young Elizabethans,* and the technical papers such as *Meccano Magazine.*

TABLE 7. *On which do you spend most time—reading books, comics, newspapers, or magazines?*

(Distribution of answers of 10–11 year old Norwich children (1955))

Spend most time on:	Future viewers %	Controls %
Books	32	44
Comics	63	49
Newspapers . . .	4	4
Magazines . . .	1	3
Total cases	96	106

A similar trend towards the more popular, less demanding forms of reading was seen in children's tastes in newspapers and magazines: the future viewers mentioned *Reveille* as their favourite adult magazine more often than other children, and the pictorial newspapers such as the *Daily Mirror, Graphic, Sketch,* and *Sunday Pictorial.*[1]

Tastes in films, radio, and books also tended to be less mature than those of other children. More often than the controls, the future viewers mentioned the family serials and thrillers among their favourite radio programmes, and the Enid Blyton series as their favourite books. Perhaps most conclusive of all, when the children were presented (in separate questionnaires) with lists of different types of reading matter, films, and radio programmes, and asked to indicate for each item whether or not they would like to read about it (watch it, or listen to it), the future viewers were interested in considerably fewer non-fiction and specialist subjects.

Generally, then, the future viewers tended to be unusually interested in mass entertainment of the more popular type, and their tastes were more immature and restricted. This is all the more interesting since we were comparing children of the same age, sex, social background and ability, attending the same type of school.

Lower and more limited aspirations

Just as the future viewers' tastes tended to be less 'ambitious' than those of other children, so were their personal aspirations. Significantly more of the future viewers than of the controls thought in terms of an early school-leaving age, and were little interested in going to a university. The jobs they expected to do, and also those they day-dreamed about, tended to be of a slightly less ambitious and enterprising type than those mentioned by the other children; they

---

[1] This taste reflects very considerably that of the parents, since, of course, the children read what papers are available in the home.

were also less aware of prestige symbols than the controls, and were less often able to recognise the significance of dress and speech as indicators of social status. Their outlook showed them to be generally less alert to social distinctions and considerations of prestige.

More relaxed supervision at home

Side by side with a more easy-going approach to life, and with acceptance of the more readily absorbed forms of mass entertainment offered them, we found evidence of a less strictly controlled and possibly less moralistic home atmosphere. Our research provided two symptoms of this trend. The bedtimes of future viewers tended to be a little later than those of their controls—Gorer has pointed out the moral undertones attached to the importance we accord in this country to early bedtimes (37). Equally, regular church and Sunday school attendance was less frequent among future viewers than amongst other children; this is more likely to be due to parental attitude than to the children's own inclinations.[1]

More gregarious and extraverted behaviour

Compared with the controls, the future viewers proved more gregarious, more often wanting to be with a crowd; their need for external stimulation was greater and they tended less often to rely on their own resources. We have a series of findings in support of this conclusion. The future viewers attended clubs more often than other children. Asked whether they preferred to play 'with a whole crowd', 'by themselves', or 'with just one or two others' they more often chose to play with a number of children. The pattern of their favourite spare-time activities showed no greater stress on playing outdoors, but in their outdoor play they placed more emphasis on competitive and organised games than on those of a more individual sort. Indoors, in addition, they were less interested in creative activities—in writing, painting, acting, handicrafts, &c.—of the type which also tend to be solitary in nature, and are intellectually more demanding.[2]

---

[1] Taking both age groups together, 45 per cent of the future viewers said they attended church and 37 per cent Sunday school, either weekly or every other week. The percentages for the controls were 54 per cent and 49 per cent, respectively.

[2] This agrees well with their preference for comics rather than books, and with their reduced interest in non-fiction reading matter.

CONCLUSIONS

In this chapter we have brought together the differences that were found in the outlook and behaviour of children whose families acquired television early compared with other children. These differences were assessed at a time when neither group had as yet had regular access to television; they were therefore pre-existing differences, not after-effects of viewing.

The particular design of our inquiry enabled us to look beyond such factors as age, sex, social background, intelligence, and education to such more psychologically determined factors as leisure interests, social outlook, and values.

The differences form a consistent pattern. The children in families which were first to get television, compared with their controls, tended to be more extraverted and gregarious, more in need of external stimulation, and less demanding in their tastes.[1] This was not due to differences in intelligence or social background, since the two groups were equated for these factors, but to personality and outlook. The future viewers were also less ambitious. Their attitudes and behaviour generally were more easy-going, just as their home background tended to be less moralistic and controlled.

This was the pattern among the early viewers, a pattern by now obscured by the fact that ownership of a television set has become commonplace for the majority of families.

---

[1] This type of individual and the type of child we have described as characteristic of the early set owner resembles in some respects the *other-directed* individual so vividly drawn by Riesman (77).

8

Amount of Viewing

How much do children view?

IN most discussions on this subject, a vivid picture is painted of the mesmeric power of television. Children are often seen as voracious, unselective viewers who spend all their free time in front of the television set, and who can be coaxed only with great difficulty into going outside to play, having their meals, or going to bed. How much truth is there in this image? How much time do children, in fact, spend in viewing and in what ways does this vary from child to child?

This kind of information is, of course, basic to our inquiry. We must be able to compare the time television takes up with the amount of time the child spends on other leisure activities in order to see what proportion of his total available leisure time is taken by television, and this will differ for children of different ages. Then we must go further. What happens to the number of viewing hours after the novelty has worn off, when the set has been in the home for several years? Does the introduction of a second channel increase the amount of viewing? And, on the other hand, what are some of the circumstances that limit viewing? Must the parents step in and restrict the child's viewing hours, or can children in any case limit themselves, by finding more interesting things to do, such as sports, or going to the cinema? Do children have pronounced likes and dislikes in television programmes, and do they perhaps stop viewing whenever something is being shown that does not interest them? These are some of the questions to which we shall try to find answers.

To find out how much children view, previous investigators have used different methods, such as interviews with mothers, questionnaires given out by teachers, diaries kept by the children, recall lists of programmes, &c. Each of these methods has its weaknesses, and there is probably no single technique which is entirely adequate. In Appendix B we discuss the various ways in which this problem has been studied by other research workers, and describe the three techniques which we have adopted (questionnaire, diary, and programme-recall lists).

A special analysis of children who viewed a great deal—the tele-vision addicts—is presented in Chapter 35.

Viewing hours per week

The average child in our main sample viewed for just under two hours a day, or 11–13 hours a week. The actual amount varied to some extent according to the inquiry technique adopted, and there were considerable variations between sub-groups and between dif-ferent children within the same sub-group (see Fig. 1).

To give more meaning to these results, we may compare them to adult viewing hours, to the total amount of television on the air, and to American data. We find that the average for adults is about the same ($12\frac{1}{2}$ hours a week for evening viewing in the first quarter of 1958, according to BBC audience research figures (18)). Our figure represents just under half the number of potential viewing hours available to children at the time of our survey.[1] It falls far below the figures quoted for American children (see Appendix B), even after making due allowance for differences in sampling, techniques of in-quiry, television hours on the air, and age ranges studied.

These findings certainly represent a picture which differs markedly from that of the voracious viewer described earlier. As we shall see, children tended after a little while to take television in their stride, giving it an important but not usually exclusive place in their leisure activities, and retaining or acquiring a selective and critical attitude towards it.

On the other hand, television generally took up more time than any single other leisure activity, far more time, for instance, than non-viewers gave to cinema or the radio. This was particularly true of the younger children. On an ordinary week-day, assuming that children got home from school by 4 p.m., the younger ones (aged 10–11 years) had on average five hours of spare time before going to bed at 9 p.m., while the older ones (aged 13–14 years) had about fifty minutes longer. Thus, even though both groups viewed for almost the same average number of hours, viewing took up a larger share of the younger than of the older child's spare time. Expressed as a proportion of the children's leisure time on week-days, viewing took up about one-third—depending, as we have seen, on the amount of viewing, and on age and bedtimes.

[1] At the time of the main survey, television (BBC only) was on the air for brief periods every afternoon, and children's television ran for one hour—5–6 p.m. There was a break from 6–7.30 p.m.; then the adult evening programmes began, con-tinuing usually until about 10.30 p.m. During any week in term time, a child viewer could have 7 hours of children's television and 21 hours of evening television, plus a few hours of early afternoon television over the week-end.

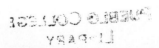

It is clear also that even the younger age group regularly watched a great many adult programmes in the first half of the evening (until 9 p.m.), while the adolescents, because of their later bedtimes, could view most of the programmes designed for adults. On evenings not followed by school-days even more children regularly saw evening programmes.

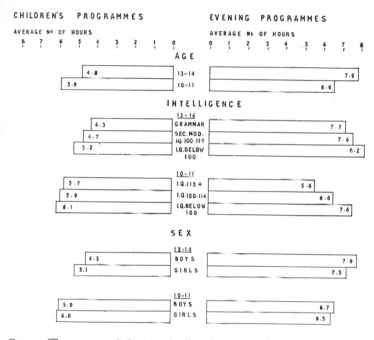

CHILDREN'S PROGRAMMES

AVERAGE Nº OF HOURS

8 7 6 5 4 3 2 1 0

EVENING PROGRAMMES

AVERAGE Nº OF HOURS

0 1 2 3 4 5 6 7 8

AGE

13–14   4.8   7.9
10–11   5.9   6.6

INTELLIGENCE

13–14
GRAMMAR   4.3   7.2
SEC.MOD. I.Q.100-114   4.7   7.6
I.Q.BELOW 100   5.2   8.2

10–11
I.Q.115+   5.7   5.6
I.Q.100-114   5.9   6.6
I.Q.BELOW 100   6.1   7.6

SEX

13–14
BOYS   4.5   7.9
GIRLS   5.1   7.3

10–11
BOYS   5.9   6.7
GIRLS   6.0   6.5

FIG. 1. The amount of viewing of children's and evening programmes, by age and intelligence, in terms of hours per week.

Only a very small number of children felt frustrated in their desires to view. Asked *Would you like to see more television than you do now, or do you see it as often as you want?*, only 15 per cent of the older and 30 per cent of the younger age group expressed the wish to see more television. Not unexpectedly, the reasons most often given for not viewing more were parental control and bedtimes.

The amount of viewing is influenced by a number of factors, each telling us something about the function of television for different kinds of children. As we have seen in Fig. 1, the total amount of viewing differs very little between the two age groups, in spite of the fact that the older children had more leisure time available. This is because they distributed their viewing time differently. On the whole, the 13–14 year olds had outgrown children's television and looked at it only spasmodically, generally preferring the evening programmes, whereas the 10–11 year olds were still very regular viewers of the children's programmes but were limited in their access to evening television. With approaching adolescence, children become less interested in viewing, less willing to give up other activities for it, and more ready to turn to other things when something is shown in which they are not interested.

The amount of viewing is greatly influenced by intelligence (see Fig. 1). On the whole, the duller the child, the more he viewed. Throughout this inquiry we have generally found a relationship between children's intelligence and their reactions to viewing. The more intelligent the child, the more critical and detached he is of television, and the less time he devotes to it. This is typical of the grammar school children, but it is also true of the brighter pupils in the primary schools.

On an average, boys tended to view a little more than girls, but the difference was not important. Rather surprisingly, class differences in total amount of viewing were also slight and inconsistent. However, working-class children were more inclined to outgrow children's television at a relatively early age. This finding is of interest, since we have not found any marked class differences with regard to overall amount of viewing or programme tastes.

Table 8 gives the distribution of those children who were strongly attached to children's television, viewing it almost daily. We note the much greater and relatively homogeneous interest of the younger age group, while among the older children there are sharp differences due to social class, sex, and intelligence. The grammar school boys were least interested in children's television, but the duller middle-class children, especially girls from white-collar homes, still viewed these programmes very regularly. On an average, children from grammar, secondary modern, and primary schools saw respectively four, five, and six hours of children's television a week.

These variables of age, sex, intelligence, and social class by no means fully account for all the many differences in the amounts that children view. Even where we find considerable differences between the averages of two sub-groups, there is generally a good deal of overlap, and Standard Deviations usually amount to about seven hours a week. In the paragraphs that follow we shall turn our attention to several factors which may cause children to view more, or less, such as the example set by their parents, the availability of a second channel, length of set ownership, the power of alternative attractions, and the child's own needs and tastes.

TABLE 8. Percentage of children from television homes who viewed children's television six or seven times per week

(Distribution by age, sex, intelligence, and social class)

13–14 YEAR OLDS

	Total %	Boys		Girls	
		Middle class %	Working class %	Middle class %	Working class %
Grammar . . .	31	19	19	42	44
Sec. mod. (I.Q. above 100)	42	38	38	52	38
Sec. mod. (I.Q. below 100)	58	50	29	95	62
Total cases (weighted) .	504	126	126	126	126

10–11 YEAR OLDS

	Total %	Boys		Girls	
		Middle class %	Working class %	Middle class %	Working class %
I.Q. above 115 . .	68	71	60	69	73
I.Q. 100–115 . . .	70	76	71	56	76
I.Q. below 100 . .	76	52	83	86	81
Total cases (weighted) .	504	126	126	126	126

Week-ends v. weekdays

The children did not view with equal frequency on every day of the week. Table 9 shows that the percentage who 'nearly always' watched evening television was the highest on Fridays and Saturdays, i.e. on evenings not followed by school-days. The younger children viewed evening television about as often as the older ones, but for shorter periods.

TABLE 9. Percentage of viewers who 'nearly always' watched children's television and evening programmes on each day of the week

	13–14 YEAR OLDS		10–11 YEAR OLDS	
	Children's television %	Evening programmes %	Children's television %	Evening programmes %
Monday .	45	66	71	61
Tuesday .	59	67	81	64
Wednesday .	46	66	71	68
Thursday .	52	61	77	62
Friday .	68	67	87	78
Saturday .	50	77	78	79
Sunday . .	55	63	76	63
Total cases (weighted)	507		507	

The large proportion of children who said they viewed 'nearly always' for each day of the week in turn highlights the extent to which viewing becomes a regular habit.

Parental example

The overall amount of time children spent in front of the television set did not, we have seen, depend on social background; it was, however, in part related to the example set by parents.

We had no first-hand data on how much parents viewed. To get some impression we asked the children to indicate whether their mothers and fathers viewed 'most evenings', 'some evenings', or 'hardly ever'. The question was put separately for each parent.[1]

TABLE 10. Comparison of frequency with which children and parents (according to their children) viewed

	13–14 YEAR OLDS			10–11 YEAR OLDS		
	Light %	Medium %	Heavy %	Light %	Medium %	Heavy %
Both parents viewed little .	18	6	7	10	4	1
Both parents viewed some evenings. . . .	29	30	24	52	28	15
One parent viewed most evenings	26	24	30	13	17	21
Both parents viewed most evenings. . . .	27	40	39	25	51	63
Total cases . . .	51	81	170	103	138	95

There was a marked relationship between the amount children viewed and the amount they suggested their parents viewed. This was particularly the case with the 10–11 year olds. When the younger children were divided into three groups on the basis of their weekly viewing we found, for instance, that 1 per cent of the heavy viewers had parents who viewed little and 63 per cent had parents who viewed a great deal. The figures for the older children were almost as striking. While not too much reliance need be placed on the children's assessment of their parents' viewing, and while there may also be a strong tendency to perceive the parents as doing the same things as the child, the results were nevertheless too clear-cut to be discounted altogether on these grounds. Furthermore, the relationship is not unexpected, but its particular interest lies in the fact that it cuts right across social class differences.

[1] The results were analysed for each parent separately, and for both parents together, in relation to the child's own viewing habits, for the different sub-groups in the sample.

In answer to another question, two-thirds of the children (60 per cent of the older, and 71 per cent of the younger ones)[1] said that after 7.30 p.m. television was left on for most of the evening irrespective of the programmes. We found that children from such unselective homes differed to some extent from children in selective homes (see p. 110).

Changes in viewing over time

With continued access to television, one of two things may happen: either the child will become more and more interested in viewing, adjusting his leisure time to the demands of the new medium; or else the amount he views will decrease when the novelty wears off. We found, however, comparatively little change over time. After three to five years of ownership, children viewed on an average only about two hours a week less than recent viewers of similar background. It would seem, therefore, that children get over the first impact of television within three months, and that subsequently they settle down to the habitual pattern of viewing which is common for most children of their age and intelligence. Veteran viewers do not diverge markedly from this norm. Fig. 2 shows the results in outline.

We have seen that, while the amount of viewing does fall with increasing length of ownership, the fall is less dramatic than has been suggested. Could this be due to the fact that the different length-of-ownership groups were not strictly comparable in terms of age, sex, social class, or city of origin? We had in mind here, for instance, the fact that over half the London children in our sample had had television for three or more years, while in Portsmouth only 5 per cent were of this category and over 62 per cent had had their set for less than a year.

Because of the importance which we have attached throughout this report to amount of viewing and length of set ownership, it became important to examine the correlation between them more closely. To do this, we again made use of our matching procedure. Now, for each veteran viewer we tried to find an experienced and a recent viewer of the same age, sex, social class, type of school, and level of intelligence. This appreciably reduced the number of cases available for comparison, but yielded greater precision than the results in Fig. 2. We found that, when these various other influences were thus removed, the moderate negative correlation between length of set ownership and amount of viewing became more marked, especially with regard to the regular viewing of children's television.

[1] The difference between these figures must be treated with caution because the younger children went to bed earlier.

For instance, in the younger age group this was seen daily or almost every day by only 55 per cent of the veteran viewers, compared to as many as 81 per cent of the recent viewers.

We carried out separate analyses for each type of school, and for the various intelligence levels within each age group, and found the relationship confirmed each time, the trend being sharper among the duller than the brighter children. We conclude, therefore, that the

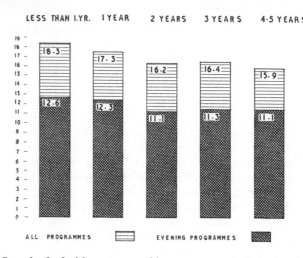

FIG. 2. Length of television set ownership *versus* amount of viewing, in terms of average number of hours per week. (Both age groups are included here.)

relationship between length of set ownership and amount of viewing is genuine and not merely due to the differences in background between veteran and recent owners.

In the rest of the report, we often return to the length of the viewing experience and to the amount of viewing the child does. The relationship between these two is not, as we have seen, sufficiently close to regard them as interchangeable.

The effect of a second channel

The added attraction of a second television channel did not markedly alter the amount of viewing, or the pattern of differences due to intelligence.

It will be remembered that the main survey was carried out with children who had access to BBC only. When the second channel came on the air, we carried out a small supplementary study in which we gave programme-recall lists for one week to 13–14 and 10–

11 year old children in a number of London schools and selected for analysis those who had access to both channels.

Table 11 gives the results of the comparison. Allowing for differences between the samples, we found no evidence of any marked increase in viewing.[1] (The effects of the introduction of a second channel on the children's taste are discussed in Chapter 10.)

TABLE 11. Average amount of viewing in one-channel and two-channel homes

(Distribution by age and type of school)

	13–14 YEAR OLDS				10–11 YEAR OLDS	
	Grammar		Sec. mod.		All	
	BBC	ITV & BBC	BBC	ITV & BBC	BBC	ITV & BBC
Hours per week .	11·5	12·7	12·8	13·6	12·5	12·7
Total cases .	122	62	284	52	402	105

NOTE. *BBC & ITV* refers to a group of London children only, in 1956, whereas *BBC* refers to the main 1955 survey sample from London, Bristol, Portsmouth, and Sunderland.

Fig 3 shows the results in more detail. In two-channel homes much more time was spent in viewing ITV than BBC, especially on Sundays. Again, age differences were slight, the younger children viewed the children's programmes more frequently than the older ones, and Saturday was the most popular viewing night. Grammar school children, more often than others, retained their interest in BBC programmes.

Viewing is very much a family affair, and in the evening, at least, the parents' taste may largely determine what is viewed. How often, then, are children disappointed in their viewing, and unable to see their favourite choices?

In the 1956 programme-recall lists we asked two questions every day for a week:

Did you and your family all want to see the same programmes during the evening?

Did you yourself want to see something you couldn't see because the others wanted to watch something different on the other channel?

Only a few of the children reported disagreement with their family on any day, the averages being 8 per cent for the grammar school children and 5 per cent and 6 per cent for secondary modern and primary school children, respectively. Also, children rarely missed a programme because the rest of the family wanted to see a programme on the other channel. For each day of the week an average of 12 per

[1] The BBC has reported the same finding for adults.

cent of the grammar school, 15 per cent of the secondary modern, and 8 per cent of the primary school children reported such a disappointment.

In the 1956 programme-recall lists we also asked a set of questions concerning the frequency of switching from one channel to the other, and back. Briefly, the results indicated that grammar school children were the most selective, secondary modern school pupils less so, while

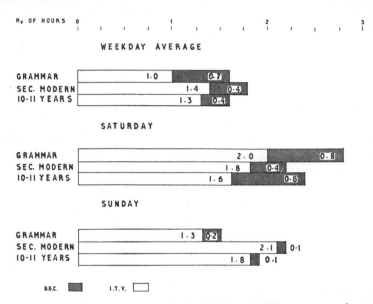

Fig. 3. Proportion of time spent viewing BBC and ITV programmes in two-channel homes, on week-days and at week-ends, for grammar, secondary modern, and primary school children.

those from primary schools switched comparatively little, least of all during the children's programmes. Again, when we asked the children whether they made a point of always seeing certain favourite pro-grammes, this most often occurred among the grammar school children, and least often among the primary school children. As we shall see, the older and brighter children generally tended to be more critical and more discerning in their tastes.

In line with this is the finding that younger children liked adver-tisements better than the older ones. They found them amusing, helpful, good, and reasonable, and were less prone to say harsh things about them. We further asked the children: *How do you feel when advertisements come in the middle of a programme?* Though the numbers were small, the results showed the same trend: advertisements were better liked/by the younger children, even when shown in the middle of a programme. Among the older, more critical and selective children, boys tended to dislike advertisements more often than girls did, possibly because the advertisements are more often aimed at girls and women.

TABLE 12. *Advertisements can come at the beginning, at the end, or in the middle of programmes. How do you feel when advertisements come in the middle of a programme?*

(Distribution of the answers by age and type of school)

	13–14 YEAR OLDS		10–11 YEAR OLDS
	Grammar %	Sec. mod. %	All %
I never notice them	2	3	6
I hate having the programme interrupted . .	29	20	17
I wouldn't mind, if they didn't come at such bad moments	21	30	17
I don't mind them, it makes a break . . .	33	30	26
I look forward to them	15	17	34
Total cases	58	40	89

Selectivity in viewing

At the beginning of this chapter we found that the stereotyped image of children mesmerised by television, spending all their waking hours in front of the set, was not borne out by our research. Children viewed selectively. In one-channel homes they viewed, on an average, for only half the number of television hours available to them, and the introduction of a second channel had not caused them to step up their viewing. Children, it would seem, will spare only so many hours for viewing and no more, even when offered a wider choice of programmes.

What reasons do children give for not viewing? We asked: *If there are some days on which you hardly ever see children's TV (Evening TV), why is that?* Table 13 shows how the answers were coded. Programme preferences, as a reason for regular abstention from viewing, had considerable prominence. Children's television evoked such phrases as 'too babyish', 'grown out of it', while disinterest for evening programmes was shown in responses such as 'don't like the programmes', 'not interesting', 'don't want to watch'. The question dealt not with occasional but with regular abstentions, and that explains why it was answered by no more than one-third of the children in the sample. Moreover, it was answered in the affirmative by twice as many of the older children as of the younger ones; this is because secondary school children were out more often in the evenings, either at youth clubs or school activities, or at other organised evening pursuits, or out with friends or visiting, playing, doing jobs, &c. (non-organised activities). The older children were also more often at the cinema on certain regular days, and they were generally more critical of television programmes.

TABLE 13. *If there are some days on which you hardly ever see children's TV (Evening TV), why is that?*

	Children's television		Evening programmes	
	13–14 YEAR OLDS %	10–11 YEAR OLDS %	13–14 YEAR OLDS %	10–11 YEAR OLDS %
Out, out with friends, not at home, visiting, playing, busy, jobs, paper round, helping in home, other activities (non-organised) . . .	41	49	26	18
Youth clubs, clubs, church choir, school activities, evening classes (organised)	18	13	44	18
Cinema	4	2	11	—
Too babyish, grown out of it, don't like programmes, not interesting, don't want to watch	35	36	14	26
Parental prohibition	—	—	—	13
Bedtime	—	—	3	25
Homework	2	—	2	—
Total cases	196	99	132	68

Later the children were asked: *Did you see any TV last night? If you did not watch TV last night, why was that?* Dislike or criticism of programmes came fourth in importance in both age groups. Obviously, the positive demands of counter-attractions and interests were the main factors for reduced viewing. However, even when it was perfectly possible for the child to view, there was an appreciable number of children who simply did not want to see what was on. It is of interest that when we asked similar questions with regard to cinema visiting, selectivity or dislike for what was being shown was rarely mentioned as a reason for not going. On the other hand, children were at least as critical of radio programmes as they were of those on television.

We have further evidence of selectivity in the responses to the following question: *When you watch children's television, for how long do you usually watch it?* (As a rule children's television lasted one hour, and usually consisted of two or three separate programme units.) The reply 'part of it' was given by 35 per cent of the older children and by only 15 per cent of the younger ones. We found the older children more selective in respect of children's television, and in both groups the boys were more selective than the girls.

Selectivity showed itself in other ways. For instance, about two-thirds of the viewers and about half of the controls often consulted the *Radio Times*, which gives both radio and television programmes for the BBC. Television and radio programmes are usually also available in the newspapers. To what extent did children use this information when deciding what to view? We asked them: *Do you yourself usually know what is on TV before it is switched on?* Eighty-five per cent of the older children and 74 per cent of the younger children said they knew what was on before turning to watch.[1] As before, we found the older children more selective and we also found somewhat higher scores for the brighter children. Part of this trend may be accounted for by a greater readiness on the part of the older and brighter children to consult any printed reference matter.

What happens when a programme comes on which the children dislike? Table 14 shows the results for the one-channel home. Again,

TABLE 14. (a) *While you are watching a children's TV (Evening TV) programme, something may come on that you dislike. Which of these do you do?*

	Children's television		Evening television	
	13–14 YEAR OLDS %	10–11 YEAR OLDS %	13–14 YEAR OLDS %	10–11 YEAR OLDS %
I just go on looking	24	34	20	30
I stop looking for a time . . .	26	26	31	31
I stop looking and do something else .	50	40	49	39
(b) *And what usually happens to the set?*				
It is kept on	44	49	47	54
It is switched right off . . .	38	30	35	28
The sound is turned down, but not the picture	16	18	15	15
The picture is turned down, but not the sound	2	3	3	3
Total cases (weighted) . . .	512	536	538	514

the older children were more selective, especially those from grammar schools. Selectivity usually took the form of doing something else, rather than just not looking. But when a disliked programme or incident came on, in at least half the homes the television set was nevertheless not switched off, and so children made their own choice to continue to view or turn away. About one family in seven turned down the sound, when a disliked programme came on, but very few turned down the picture but not the sound.

We must of course remember that children are not always free to

[1] These figures are very high and may, of course, be inflated. Also they are not unequivocal evidence for selectivity, since even the unselective viewer may wish to gain an impression beforehand of what he is going to view.

switch the television sets in their homes on or off, even for the children's programmes. Nevertheless, these results show quite clearly that children can exercise a selectivity of their own accord, whether or not the television set is switched off. If they dislike a programme they quite often either just stop viewing or go away and do something else.

These findings should be seen against the children's home background, which is often one of apparently undiscriminating parental viewing, i.e. switching the set on early in the evening and allowing it to run right through the evening's programmes. When we asked the children: *If you have a TV set at home, is it left on most of the evening, or switched on for some programmes only?* as many as 60 per cent of the older and 71 per cent of the younger age group claimed that their set was left on for most of the evening. (Among the new viewers in Norwich, the percentages were slightly higher: 70 per cent and 78 per cent, respectively.)[1] Obviously, such estimates cannot altogether be taken at their face value, but they suggest that the majority of children have an *impression* of continuous television in their homes. Against this background, the children's selectivity is all the more remarkable.

None the less, as we have seen, the children are not impervious to their parents' example. Children who are heavy viewers often report that their parents view a great deal, and vice versa. Similarly, it is more difficult for a child to become a 'selective' viewer when in his home the television set is left on all evening. To examine this, we compared the 13–14 year old viewers from homes which were selective with viewers from 'unselective' homes. The results were not unexpected: in the unselective homes, the children were more attached to television and viewed more, and so did their parents; they were more inclined to go on viewing when a programme came on which they disliked, instead of leaving the set; and they expressed less criticism of the programmes. Often, in such homes, the television set provided a continuous background to other activities. Consequently, we found that selective viewing resulted in somewhat greater emotional impact.[2] Less frequent viewing, but under conditions of

---

[1] The younger children, because of their earlier bedtimes, could only report on the first half of the evening.

[2] Emotional impact was assessed by means of three questions:

1. After seeing a TV programme, people sometimes pretend to themselves, or daydream, that they are one of the people they have seen. Have you ever done this?

2. Sometimes after watching a TV programme, people try to act or make up games about it. Have you ever done this?

3. Have you ever seen anything on TV you couldn't get out of your mind—that you have been thinking about a lot?

The selective viewers gave positive answers to all three questions significantly more often. It may, of course, be that the more reflective, imaginative children more often view selectively.

greater interest, concentration, and motivation, is likely to be more conducive to lasting impressions than being subjected rather uncritically to a continuous stream of television programmes.

CONCLUSIONS

Children in our sample viewed television for an average of just under two hours a day, or from 11–13 hours a week. This represented about one-third of their available leisure time on week-days; the children spent more time on viewing than on any other leisure activity. A large proportion of even the younger age group regularly watched evening television programmes until 9 p.m. or later, and adolescents could often view most of the programmes designed for adults.

Compared to children in the USA the children in this country view far less, and this difference can only partly be accounted for by differences in sampling, methods of inquiry, school hours, television broadcasting hours, &c. The children in our sample viewed for only about half the number of potential viewing hours available to them at the time of our survey; when more television hours became available to them with the introduction of the second channel, this did not cause a marked increase in viewing

Altogether it is clear that while children view a great deal, television has not by any means come to occupy an exclusive place in their leisure activities, and there is little truth in the stereotyped image of the mesmerised, voracious child-viewer.

The amount of viewing is influenced by many factors. In terms of the child's background, intelligence is probably the most important variable: the duller the child, the more he views. Age differences were slight (but older children divided their viewing time differently, spending more time on evening programmes and less time with children's television), boys viewed a little more than girls, and, rather surprisingly, social-class differences amounted to very little.

Apart from age, sex, and intelligence, other factors influence the amount a child views. Parental control of bedtimes, relaxed on days not followed by school-days, was an important limiting variable, and parental example had considerable influence. Viewing was also limited by the many counter-attractions available to the child.[1]

---

[1] Television viewing, because it necessarily takes time, is in direct competition with many other leisure activities and interests. In Part VII we show in detail what has been television's impact on the child's leisure. Looked at in another way, however, all the other leisure interests compete with viewing, and tend to limit it. Television's most powerful rivals, we found, were outdoor play and unorganised social activities.

Contrary to expectation we did not find that the introduction of a second channel made the children view more; after the first few months of hectic viewing, television was absorbed into a habit pattern which fitted in with the child's needs and interests, a habit which was neither increased when extra viewing time became available, nor markedly reduced after the first year or so. Generally, most children viewed as much as they wanted to, and only a small minority on any one night were frustrated in their desires to see a particular programme because of conflict with the rest of the family.

Most important of all, children viewed selectively. Generally, they knew in advance which programmes were on the air, and even if the set was left on for most of the evening they were quite able to leave it and do something else when a programme came on which they did not like. Children develop their own tastes and preferences, as we shall see in the following chapters, and the older and the more intelligent the child, the more critical is he of television programmes. It is important to note, however, that the emotional impact of television was sometimes greater on the selective child than on the unselective one.

Though the popularity of children's television began to decline after the age of 8 or 9, nevertheless a substantial number of the older children still saw these programmes regularly, in particular dull middle-class girls. Children from grammar, secondary modern, and primary schools viewed children's programmes for an average of four, five, and six hours a week, respectively.

9

Favourite Programmes

IN the chapters that follow we shall examine the children's taste in television and in the other mass media, showing the extent to which there is a common taste pattern underlying children's preferences in television, radio, films, and books. We shall further show the extent to which such taste patterns may be related to children's other interests and general outlook.

The present chapter will deal primarily with children's tastes in television programmes. How uniform or diverse are their likes and dislikes? How far does intelligence rather than age determine what children like best? What is the influence on taste of the social milieu of the home? What proportion of children choose their favourites from adult programmes rather than from programmes specially designed for children? These are some of the questions which we shall explore.

In one of their early studies of programme preferences the BBC Audience Research Department wrote:

> No apology is necessary for showing the voting of children so young as 7–11. Naturally the factors which affect their choice are often quite different from those which affect the choice of adults. Nevertheless nothing is clearer than that quite young children do frequently watch a wide range of TV programmes and hold opinions about them, opinions which, whatever the adult may think of them, should not be ignored in an analysis of this kind (VR/50/1).

In our own work we have found much confirmation for this point of view. School children regularly view large numbers of adult programmes, and most of them view selectively. Yet too little is known about the factors that determine their preferences.

To find out how much adults know about children's tastes in television programmes, we carried out a little experiment, using groups to whom we lectured about our inquiry, such as parents, teachers, and even producers of children's programmes. We offered them a list of programmes and asked them to select the children's top three favourites for the two age groups we had studied; to indicate how many would select any given type, i.e. how uniform

children's tastes were; and also to indicate how far the list would
vary with children of different intelligence and coming from different
social backgrounds. Not a single group gave an answer which was
even approximately correct, nor did any two groups offer the same
list. All groups overestimated the uniformity of children's tastes and
the extent to which social background played a part. This little
experiment suggests that all generalisations about children's tastes,
even those made by experts, need to be verified by asking the children
themselves.

To examine what children like on television is, of course, essential
for programme planning. Both ITV and BBC obtain daily viewing
figures and audience reactions from adults, and adjust their programme policies in the light of this information. Such data about
audience response are even more necessary for the planning of
children's programmes not only because so little is known about
children's tastes generally, but also because children form a rather
less homogeneous audience than adults, so that there are very real
difficulties in adjusting the level and content of a programme to
their needs.

The comparative scarcity of knowledge about the popularity and
appeal of different programmes among children has in part been
due to the need for more specialised methods of questioning. The
BBC has included children in several of its television preference
studies, and their Minors' research (16) included audience figures
for a number of programmes, but felt that this problem could perhaps best be taken further by an outside organisation—hence the
approach to the Nuffield Foundation which led to the present
research project. The data which we present are, however, merely a
beginning. There are no technical reasons now why regular audience
research should not be carried out with children as with adults.
Indeed, there is much scope for regular and close collaboration
between producers and audience researchers in both the planning
and the evaluation of many different kinds of programmes.

In the course of the inquiry the children were asked about their
programme preferences. These questions were 'funnelled', starting
with broad ones such as *Of all the TV programmes you have watched,
which three have you liked best?*, followed by more specific questions
about children's and evening programmes, favourite plays, favourite
personalities, and their attitudes to certain selected programmes.
Among other things we also asked the children for their own programme suggestions. Details about individual programmes were
collected even though these quickly became outdated, because this
made it possible to outline more general patterns of children's taste
and to indicate the *type* of programme that children like or dislike.

CHILDREN'S FAVOURITES ON TELEVISION

To obtain the general pattern of preferences, the children were asked: *Of all the TV programmes you have watched, which three have you liked best?* The distribution of choices for the twelve most popular programmes is shown in Table 15.

This Table shows a number of interesting findings. First, children overwhelmingly chose their favourites from evening television. This was the case even for the younger ones, who were still regular viewers of children's television. Second, one programme was the universal favourite, irrespective of age, sex, or intelligence, namely the detective series *Fabian of Scotland Yard*. Most other choices reflected differences in the children's age, sex, or intelligence. Third, social-class differences were almost entirely absent; this suggests that the child's taste depends much more on his age, intelligence, and sex, and on individual interests and needs, than on the social level of the home.

Essentially, the children's main preference was for drama; especially for crime drama and Westerns, but also for family serials. The wish-fulfilling *Ask Pickles* programme also obtained a high rating, and comedy shows were popular, more so among the older children. The interest in children's programmes, Westerns apart, was already declining even among the 10–11 year olds.

A more detailed analysis was carried out of all the programmes mentioned by the children. Generalising from this, and from Table 15, we may say first of all that the tastes of the 10–11 year olds were more uniform than those of the older children, where differences due to sex and intelligence manifested themselves more often. In general, the older children were more often interested in sport and in war documentaries, and of course less interested in Westerns and in children's programmes generally. A liking for Westerns, with their stereotyped plot and presentation, was more marked among the duller children, especially in the younger age group. The intelligent child, even at the age of 10–11, loses interest and turns to comedy and variety shows instead, with their constant change of acts and opportunities for laughter.

After *Fabian of Scotland Yard*, the universal favourite, the duller adolescents showed a greater preference for the *Ask Pickles* requests programme, and for the family serials; to some extent they also retained an interest in Westerns. The more intelligent 13–14 year olds, on the other hand, more often mentioned documentary programmes. It would seem that, at adolescence, the more intelligent children turn to television for suspense, laughter, and information,

TABLE 15. The twelve favourite programmes arranged by programme type
(Distribution of first three choices by age and sex, and by intelligence)

| | 13–14 YEAR OLDS | | | 10–11 YEAR OLDS | | | 13–14 YEAR OLDS | | | 10–11 YEAR OLDS | | |
	All %	Boys %	Girls %	All %	Boys %	Girls %	Grammar %	I.Q. 100–114 %	I.Q. below 100 %	I.Q. 115+ %	I.Q. 100–114 %	I.Q. below 100 %
EVENING PROGRAMMES:												
Detective series *Fabian of Scotland Yard*	29	26	33	29	29	30	28	30	31	29	33	26
Requests programme *Ask Pickles*	16	16	16	20	16	24	7	17	22	18	21	21
Comedy shows *The Benny Hill Show*	11	11	11	7	8	7	12	7	14	10	7	5
Before Your Very Eyes	5	6	4	6	7	5	6	4	4	13	3	2
Family serial *The Grove Family*	11	12	10	16	12	20	7	10	16	15	16	17
Panel game *What's My Line?*	9	7	11	6	6	7	12	4	12	8	7	4
Documentary *War in the Air*	8	14	1	3	6	—	11	6	7	3	4	3
Filming in Africa	6	7	5	5	2	7	10	4	4	7	6	2
Adult play cycle *Terminus*	1	1	2	3	2	5	1	2	1	5	3	2
CHILDREN'S PROGRAMMES:												
Westerns *Cisco Kid, Range Rider*	6	8	3	19	23	14	3	6	9	9	18	29
Hobbies programme *All Your Own*	2	1	2	6	4	9	3	1	1	7	6	6
Family serial *The Appleyards*	4	2	6	7	2	3	1	7	4	8	6	7
Total cases (weighted)	540	270	270	540	270	270	180	180	180	180	180	180

NOTE. The totals may exceed 100 per cent because they include three choices; this does not mean that all choices went to the twelve programmes mentioned.

while the less intelligent ones more often seek the 'human interest' element.

In general, differences in taste between boys and girls became more marked as the children grew older. The choices of the younger boys and girls were rather similar (except for the boys' more marked liking for Westerns), but in the older group the girls preferred plays, family serials, and panel games more often, while the boys more often enjoyed Westerns and documentaries—in particular the *War in the Air* series, dealing with the air battles of the Second World War. Boys of that age generally take a keen interest in what happened during the war; they may also identify themselves with the skill and daring of the pilots.

These expressions of taste differ considerably from some popular preconceptions. It is not generally realised, for instance, how overwhelmingly the children—even at the age of 10—prefer evening programmes to those specially designed for them. The popularity of Westerns was well known, but not the great interest in crime programmes, by girls as well as by boys. Many would have expected *What's My Line*, or puppet shows, or animal programmes, or sports programmes, or science fiction, children's variety, or school stories to be more popular than they were. Again, there is the popular belief that taste is largely a function of the social level of the home; we have shown that intelligence, rather than social background, is influential here. In this way some light is thrown on the functions which children assign to television.

How representative are these findings?

Appendix Table 3 gives the results of a similar question which was put to 620 children from homes with television by Research Services Ltd. in April 1955 (1), roughly the same time as our main survey. About two-thirds of the votes went to adult programmes. The results were broadly similar to ours, despite differences between the samples, categories, and ways of collecting data. The top five favourites of each age group were the same in both surveys, though the order was different. In particular, *Fabian of Scotland Yard* did not rank as high in this sample as in ours. In both investigations the older children showed less interest in Westerns and in *The Grove Family*, while boys showed more interest than girls in programmes like *Fabian* and Westerns, and girls more often voted for *Ask Pickles* and *The Grove Family*. The Research Services survey showed that only in the youngest age group (8–10) did *Children's Television* or *Watch with Mother* appear among the top five favourites.

Children's and evening programmes

More can be learned by asking children for their favourite programme on children's television and evening television, respectively (Appendix Tables 1 and 2). Understandably, their favourite evening programmes coincided with the general favourites, though plays and serials appeared a little higher on the list, especially among the older children.

As for children's television (which many of the older children had outgrown), when specifically asked to name a programme they liked, there was a marked interest in plays and serials (especially among girls), in family programmes like *The Appleyards*, and in variety shows. Westerns were always very popular, but children's panel games and quiz programmes were less popular than those designed for adults. Very few children gave sport, news and newsreels, nature programmes, or music as their favourite, whether presented for children or adults. *All Your Own* was third in popularity among the older children, especially the brighter girls. This is interesting because the programme was undramatic and unspectacular; a 'live' programme, shown on Sunday afternoons, it presented children from all over Britain who had unusual or interesting hobbies or talents. One girl of 12 wrote:

> My favourite programme is *All Your Own* because it is for children and only children appear on the programme. The children do all different things.

What makes programmes popular?

It is not always easy to decide why children like certain types of programme or what it is they like. We asked new viewers in Norwich a number of questions about variety programmes, panel games, and serials to help throw some light on this question.

The variety shows were very well liked largely because of the comedians and the comedy turns. When children were asked *Supposing Variety shows had to be made shorter, what part would you leave out?*, both age groups almost unanimously suggested that singing and dancing (including excerpts from opera or ballet) should be left out.

Quiz programmes, panel games, or guessing games (BBC only) were liked about as much for the questions as for the opportunity they gave the child to take part ('trying to guess the answer', 'playing the game afterwards'). Children also claimed to find these games instructive ('learn from them', 'increases your intelligence'), and enjoyed the competitive aspect ('the excitement of seeing who wins'). They rarely mentioned that they were funny or amusing.

What's My Line? was easily the favourite panel game and contained most of the favourite panel members, even though it was rarely mentioned as the children's best-liked programme.

To study the appeal of serials more closely we put the following question: *If you could choose for a month, which would you rather have on TV—a serial play that is on once a week, or a new play every week?* The children were almost evenly divided, but a small majority favoured serials. They found them more thrilling and exciting and liked the element of suspense. Those who preferred single plays often said they could not bear the suspense of waiting for the next instalment. Others preferred a change of theme and subject-matter, and a few were worried that they might miss an episode in a serial and so be unable to follow the plot.

Since there are more plays on television than any other kind of programme, we asked the children: *What sort of thing do you like TV plays to be about?* The results (Appendix Table 4) are in many ways similar to the general preferences: suspense, excitement, and adventure were the favourite diet. Most frequently mentioned were crime thrillers (27 per cent), Westerns (18 per cent), and comedies (10 per cent). Romantic plays and war stories were better liked by the adolescents, and mentioned more often by the older girls and the older boys, respectively. At adolescence, it would seem that the boys look for real-life heroes which they find in the detective series and in the war plays, while girls look for models in romantic dramas, and in plays about children or families. The younger girls' preferences were interesting. They liked thrillers, detective, murder, and mystery plays better than any other group, and plays with child characters.

PROGRAMMES CHILDREN DISLIKE

The pilot inquiry showed that few children would commit themselves to saying that they did not like a television programme. We therefore used two successive questions to invite criticism: *Is there any TV programme which you have really disliked?* and *If there has been none that you really disliked, which programmes are you not so keen on?* This second, more restrained question was the more productive. The answers to both questions have been combined in Appendix Tables 5 and 6. In spite of the extra care taken with the wording of these questions, about one-third of the sample could think of no programme which they had disliked or were not keen on; the younger and less intelligent children were the least critical.

Unpopular children's programmes

We first asked children which programmes on children's television they disliked or were not keen on. Appendix Table 5, which summarises the results, unexpectedly contains some of the favourites—variety programmes like *Jigsaw* and *Sugar and Spice*, and *All Your Own*. The former, it seems, are popular with the younger and duller children and so are disliked by the older and brighter ones, as are puppet programmes and *Watch with Mother*. In the case of *All Your Own* its very undramatic, 'ordinary' quality may appeal to some but may make it uninteresting to others, particularly to boys.

Westerns were not popular with some of the younger girls. It would be tempting to conclude that this was because they disliked violence; but, as we have already seen, girls of this age were keen viewers of crime thrillers. In fact their dislike for Westerns was sometimes based on quite other grounds:

> Each time there is a cowboy film on it is always the same thing. Some men rob a bank and then they put the blame on a good cowboy and he gets put in jail and then somebody comes and helps him and in the end they find out the real person.

> I also dislike some cowboy films on children's television because everything happens at once and before you know where you are they have caught the criminals and they are in prison.

Among the informative programmes, *Sketch Club* was disliked by a number of children. Once again it is easy to attribute this to a lack of interest in painting or in worth-while programmes generally, but the following answer by a girl of 10 shows that her dislike was not based on the subject-matter, but on the method of presentation. In fact, she would prefer to have had more time to enjoy the drawing:

> One night at 5 o'clock we saw sketch club and I hate it because he chatters too much and every picture he draws, he does not finish it but takes it off the stand and starts another one.

Unpopular adult programmes

We found the older children to be more critical of evening programmes than the younger ones. They particularly expressed dislike for discussions, serious programmes, and political talks. The 1955 General Election was about to be held when we were putting the questions, and television and radio programmes included an unusually high number of party political broadcasts and talks on politics, which may have affected replies. Otherwise, the results were, broadly speaking, in line with our analysis of favourite programmes; those less often mentioned as favourites, e.g. sport or musical programmes, tended to be more frequently disliked. (Appendix Table 6.)

Here are comments by an 11 year old boy on the Sunday afternoon programme, *The Brains Trust*:

> I don't like *The Brains Trust* because we think it is too clever and there's nothing exciting about it, and another reason is because it is too slow and I think it is mainly for grown-ups. They are always talking about things which I haven't heard about and the people always seem to use big words and I never understand them and they never seem to agree with one another and they are always smoking, making noises with their chairs and they are always interrupting so that you cannot understand a word they say. It's always the same scenery, all dark colours, bits of old pictures hanging on the wall and it's all dull, the whole thing is dull.
>
> I think it all ought to be done away with. They are always talking of uninteresting things and always leaning back in their armchairs smoking away as though they were millionaires, they ought to be sacked and never heard of again.

A 10 year old girl commented in similar vein on a number of serious programmes:

> I don't like discussions especially when they get angry and all talk at the same time. I think *Panorama* is boring when they talk about things that we don't know anything about. I don't like *Concert Hour* either, I don't know why I don't like it, I expect it's because I don't like opera and things like that.

Plays disliked

Appendix Table 7 shows the kinds of plays which were not popular; only a few children mentioned any at all. Among those who did, twice as many older as younger children were critical of some plays. Girls more often disliked detective plays, war plays, and historical plays; boys more often disliked Shakespeare and romantic love themes. This pattern was found among both grammar and secondary modern school children. Age and sex seemed to determine dislike, rather than intelligence. The small number of younger children who mentioned any plays they were 'not keen on' confined their answers chiefly to thrillers and detective plays.

These data, though scanty, confirm the lack of uniformity in taste even among relatively homogeneous sub-groups. While age, sex, and intelligence do affect children's preferences, taste is also determined by the child's needs and personality make-up.

Suggestions on programmes by the children themselves

Another way to study children's taste is to ask them to plan their own programmes, though this is influenced by the viewing diet to which they are accustomed. In the Norwich study we asked the new viewers what sort of programmes they would put on if they could arrange children's television for an hour and adult programmes for a whole evening. The replies on the whole were not very imaginative; they mostly followed existing types of programme, but with a change in emphasis.

Almost half the children wanted the whole hour of children's television devoted to one programme, and most others recommended two parts. Few mentioned three or more short programmes, which was the usual arrangement of BBC children's television at the time. Otherwise, they mostly wanted drama, variety, and Westerns, in that order. They also included sports programmes, but not hobbies programmes.

The suggestions for adult programmes again tended to reflect existing tastes. The younger age group suggested more plays, family serials, detective stories, and variety. Few mentioned comedy shows, Westerns, adventure and mystery plays, either because their needs for these were already well satisfied, or else because they regarded at least the latter two types of programme as more suitable for children's television. The older children, who suggested mainly drama and variety, also wanted more comedy shows; fewer of them mentioned crime plays or family serials. News, music, dancing and ballet, or documentary programmes were rarely mentioned.

Here are some of the children's ideas (afternoon and evening programmes suggested have been placed together):

A girl of 14 (I.Q. 95):

> *Children's Television*: 'From 5 p.m. to 5.30 p.m. I would put on a show like *Playbox*, then I would put on a show where boys and girls can do what they like, sing, etc.'
>
> *Evening programmes*: 'At 7 to 7.15 *News*, then *Highlight* to 7.30 then *The Grove Family*. At 8 *Puzzle Corner*, 8.45 *Camera One*, 9.30 Victor Sylvester ballroom dancing. At 10.30 *News*.'

A girl of 11 (I.Q. 108):

> *Children's Television*: 'I would put on *The Appleyards* for an hour.'
>
> *Evening programmes*: 'I would begin with *Life with the Lyons*, then arrange for some kind of sport.'

A boy of 11 (I.Q. 110):

> *Children's Television*: 'A good play and *Sooty* and a cowboy film.'
>
> *Evening programmes*: 'A play and a variety show.'

A boy of 12 (I.Q. 102):

> *Children's Television*: 'A puppet show, a quiz game and then a Western film.'
>
> *Evening programmes*: 'A space play, the news, a comedian, some singing, a talk on birds, another good play for grown-ups and then the weather forecasts.'

At the time of our survey, programmes for adolescents were few and far between. We wanted to see what kinds of topics for discussion would interest them, and what role they would assign to television— for example, would viewers and controls suggest different subjects? We therefore asked the children in the main survey the following question: *There are sometimes discussion groups on TV where young people talk over different problems. What would you like them to talk about?*

TABLE 16. (*Young people's discussion groups on television.*) *What would you like them to talk about?*

(Distribution of first and second choice)

	13–14 YEAR OLDS		10–11 YEAR OLDS	
	v	c	v	c
	%	%	%	%
SUBJECT:				
Politics	14	17	18	15
Information	13	10	16	19
Television	13	5	13	6
School	13	21	13	8
Social problems of young people . .	11	10	5	5
Personal problems	8	5	5	3
Sports	8	7	8	10
Job information	5	4	2	3
Social problems (general) . . .	3	4	4	5
Relations with parents	3	5	3	4
Films	1	1	2	3
Miscellaneous	8	11	11	19
Total number of answers	870	826	747	729

NOTE:

v = Viewers.

c = Controls, i.e. children without television at home who viewed not more than once a fortnight.

These abbreviations have been used throughout this report.

There was plenty of variety in the answers, which suggest that, while discussions between adults were far from popular, and their topics of little interest, discussions between young people would be well liked if they were better geared to the children's needs. There was a lively interest in social, political, personal, and other problems (Table 16). A more detailed analysis is given in Appendix Table 8. The age differences reflect the different needs of the 10–11 year olds and the young adolescents. The older children tended to show more interest in discussions about jobs, about personal difficulties and the social problems of young people. The younger children were somewhat more interested in discussions on nature topics, such as bird-watching. Not surprisingly, boys tended to be more interested than girls in discussions about sport, how things work, the H-bomb, and space travel. Girls showed somewhat greater interest in art and music, and in discussions about personal problems like dress, bed-time, the school-leaving age, and the right age to start using make-up.

Viewers and controls listed the same types of topic. This suggests that these must be subjects of genuine interest to the children, and not just replicas of discussions featured on television. The con-siderable interest shown in politics, social problems, and information of all kinds may, of course, have been exaggerated, but it should be seen against the children's general dislike of discussion programmes of any kind. It may well be that children's interest in programmes of this type could be better maintained by means of discussions between young people rather than between experts.

EFFECT OF AMOUNT OF VIEWING AND LENGTH OF SET OWNERSHIP

It might be thought that heavy viewers, because they see so many programmes, would develop tastes that differ from the average. This was not the case. The choices of heavy, frequent, and occasional viewers were, on the whole, similar. Minor differences within this general pattern will be discussed in Chapter 35: *The Television Addict.*

Similarly, several years of regular viewing had surprisingly little effect on children's taste for programmes and personalities. Dif-ferences between veteran and recent viewers were small.

EFFECT OF ALTERNATIVE PROGRAMMES

While our inquiry was in progress, commercial television was introduced. This provided us with a unique opportunity for examin-ing differences in preferences between children with access to one channel and those with a choice of two. The effect this had on the amount children viewed has been discussed in Chapter 8. Here we shall consider the effect on taste.

Not all the differences can be attributed to the second channel: many other factors may well have played a part. The composition of the two samples differed, the 1956 one being drawn from London only; the supplementary inquiry was carried out in summer, not late spring (this affected programme planning as well as the time children gave to television); also the BBC, faced with competition, had somewhat changed its programmes; finally, families who were among the first to convert sets for the reception of both channels may well have differed in their tastes from the general run of viewers who formed part of the main survey.

In Table 17 the children's three favourite television programmes are classified, irrespective of time and channel. The most popular programmes spontaneously mentioned are given in Appendix Table 9.

TABLE 17. The three favourite television programmes of children with access to both channels

(Distribution by age and sex)

| | BBC or ITV | | | |
| | 13–14 YEAR OLDS | | 10–11 YEAR OLDS | |
	Boys %	Girls %	Boys %	Girls %
ADULT PROGRAMMES:				
Crime: (*Fabian of Scotland Yard, Dixon of Dock Green, My Friend Charles, Judge for Yourself, Dragnet, Inner Sanctum, Highway Patrol, Gun Law*)	72	39	81	60
Comedy and variety shows: (*Jack Jackson Show, Tony Hancock, Patti Page, Sunday Night at the London Palladium, Val Parnell's Startime, Arthur Askey, Billy Cotton, Charlie Chester*)	43	45	35	27
Family comedy: (*I Love Lucy, I Married Joan, Life of Riley, Life with the Lyons*)	24	53	14	23
Plays	21	26	4	7
Sport	23	13	16	12
Documentary and information: (*Look in on London, Science Review, Look, Brains Trust, Panorama, Buried Treasure*)	21	8	4	3
Panel games: (*What's My Line, Yackity Yak, Spot the Tune*)	5	2	2	15
Give away shows (ITV only): (*64,000 Question, Take Your Pick*)	2	2	7	8
CHILDREN'S PROGRAMMES:				
Westerns: (*Gun Law, Roy Rogers, Cisco Kid, Range Rider, Hopalong Cassidy, Rin Tin Tin*)	25	36	29	33
Adventure: (*Robin Hood*)	17	18	37	43
Other children's television: (*Gordon Honour, Peter in the Air*)	4	6	12	15
Miscellaneous, no answer, don't know	6	8	2	2
Total cases	66	48	45	60

NOTE. Representative programmes mentioned by the children are given in brackets. The figures add up to over 100 per cent because most children gave two or three answers.

The following points stand out clearly:

As before, adult programmes were mentioned far more often as favourites than children's programmes.

Crime series, comedy and variety shows, plays, and Westerns were still the most favoured types of programmes, but the American type of humorous family serial was also highly popular, especially among the girls, who probably identified with the female leads in such programmes as *I Love Lucy* and *I Married Joan*.

In general, the children's preferences were more narrowly distributed than in the one-channel homes. This is reflected by the considerable magnitude of the figures in Table 17; children tended to mention as their first, second, and third favourites programmes which were of the same type. As we shall see in Chapter 10, in the two-channel home children tend to switch from channel to channel in pursuit of their first or second favourites, and more rarely view anything else. This in turn brings about a narrowing of their taste pattern.

On the whole, the children in these homes (whose television sets had but recently been converted to receive the second channel) preferred ITV programmes. The only category in which BBC programmes were mentioned more often than those of ITV was documentary and information programmes.

CONCLUSIONS

The following main findings emerge:

Even the younger children watch very many adult programmes. By the age of 8 or 9 they take a keen interest in adult programmes like *Ask Pickles*, *The Grove Family*, and adult comedies, and also to a lesser extent in crime serials and panel games. After this age their interest in children's programmes, then at its height, steadily declines. By adolescence, the only children's programmes which still attract substantial numbers are Westerns. This trend depends on age, sex, and intelligence, but not on social background.

By and large the popular programmes—drama, crime, adult comedies, family serials, variety, and panel games—are also the programmes that adults like; of course the very fact that these programmes are not intended for children may make them more attractive. The child, through sharing the viewing with his parents, may be developing adult tastes rather earlier. Alternatively, the results may show that the tastes of most adults are like those of the young teen-ager. Or, more simply, the popularity of adult programmes with children may be due to the fact that they are shown at a time of day when the child is often at home and wants to be entertained; if children's television were shown later, it might be much more popular than at present. We cannot yet say which of these explanations is the most likely.

When a child gains access to a second channel he narrows his interests in programmes, viewing the serious ones less often and developing an almost exclusive predilection for the popular favourites, on whatever channel these may appear. From the educational standpoint, this narrowing and sharpening of preferences is to be regretted. By watching the sort of programme he likes best on either channel the child avoids documentary and information programmes more easily than when he has only one channel. By concentrating almost exclusively on a particular type of programme he reduces the chance of seeing a new type of programme that might interest him. His tastes are in a rut.

Perhaps the most consistently popular type of programme is the adult serial crime thriller, even among the younger girls. Apart from this, variety and comedy shows, panel games, family serials and plays of all kinds are highly popular. Children's programmes are not widely favoured, except for Westerns, which primarily appeal to the younger, duller child. Documentary, informational, and discussion programmes have little appeal for children.

A programme such as *All Your Own*—realistic, 'live', and featuring children—was well liked by some but disliked by others. However, a programme like *Ask Pickles*, where a wish may be granted, was universally popular. Grammar school children are less keen on drama, on human interest programmes, and on crime programmes, and more often mention information and sports programmes.

Our findings suggest that a young people's discussion programme dealing with politics, social and personal problems, and information of different kinds geared to the children's needs (e.g. about jobs) would probably be well received.

The preferences of children who viewed a great deal did not seem to follow a markedly different pattern; they merely viewed more of the programmes that were popular with other children of their age, sex, and intelligence.

Ultimately, further research will have to show the reason or cause for such preference patterns as have been found. It is frequently suggested that watching television satisfies certain needs, but very little is actually known about the changing needs of boys and girls at different ages. It is believed, for instance, that Westerns are popular with young boys because they offer a vicarious outlet for aggression, or that romantic themes are favourite with adolescent girls because of their maturing sex needs. Similarly, it could be suggested that family serials are popular with children who are unhappy at home. Such 'explanations' sound plausible, and may well be true, but they have often been arrived at by means of circular argument. Preferences are explained in terms of underlying needs whose existence is then 'proved' by listing the type of programmes or books children enjoy. Our findings underline the need for further research into the needs of children of different age, sex, and intelligence.

I O

Actual Choice of Programmes

Factors which determine the child's choice of programmes

MANY factors apart from tastes and preferences determine the child's actual choice of programme—how much and how often he views (which in turn is determined by his age and intelligence), what programmes the two channels have to offer him, parental influence on selection of both channel and programme, counter-attractions inside and outside the home, season and weather, time of day and week, the circumstances of a particular day or week (holidays, Wimbledon tennis, General Election), a general bias towards one of the two channels, the length of the programme, whether it is a serial, whether it appears on children's television or in the evening, and what comes before and after it.

Audience statistics reflect the interaction of factors like these; their strength lies in showing how many children, or what proportion of the total, viewed a given programme; but further knowledge is required to *predict* what programmes children will look at, except for occasions when all the relevant conditions are the same. An example may help to clarify this point:

> Plays are very popular with children, so that one would have expected a big child audience for a play like *Under the Red Robe* shown on ITV on Sunday, 1 July 1956, between 8–9 p.m., particularly since it was preceded by a popular panel game. In fact, however, it had a relatively small audience, no more than 39 per cent of the older and 33 per cent of the younger children. Here are some of the factors that may account for the smallness of the audience: (1) competition from the other channel, which showed a crime series, followed by a popular panel game; (2) the length of the programme (one-hour plays are rather long for young children); (3) the time at which it was shown, which was close to the bedtimes of some of the children; (4) the weather; on a fine evening many children preferred to play out of doors rather than watch television.

The size of the audience for any one programme depends on an interplay of these various factors; it is therefore not a very sure guide to children's taste.

There are, however, two ways by which children's taste can be inferred from the programmes they choose. The first applies to children with access to one channel only, the second to children with access to two channels. In the one-channel situation, one examines the viewing figures for a sufficient number of programmes of a given type so that the various extraneous factors tend to cancel out. When this is done in turn for various programme types, a picture of the children's actual programme choice is obtained.

In the two-channel situation, one can deduce the child's regular choice pattern by finding out which, of two programmes shown concurrently, is viewed. This method has the advantage of enabling us to hold constant all extraneous variables except parental influence, length of programme, serialisation, preceding or following programmes, and bias towards one channel. We examine first a single programme type in rivalry with various other types of programme, and then repeat this process for each programme type in turn.

Programme directors, too, recognise some of the variables affecting the size of their adult audience, and arrange their programmes accordingly. The evening's main attraction is shown at peak viewing time (about 8–9 p.m.). Newsreels are shown early or late, but not at peak time; similarly, scientific or documentary programmes tend to appear late, serials or panel games early. With the arrival of a second channel, producers started to compete directly with their rivals by putting similar programmes on at the same time, or else they tried to gain a more substantial share of the audience by putting on programmes they thought would draw large audiences at times when their competitors were thought to be showing less attractive programmes. Thus certain types of programme are put on consistently at favourable (or unfavourable) times, so making direct comparisons between different programme types difficult.

It follows that the timing of programmes is partly due to popularity, and that popularity is partly due to timing; there is a circular process here, and it is difficult to disentangle its components.

Average audiences for BBC programmes

In the main survey (May 1955) we obtained from the programme-recall lists a record of what the child had seen on television in the course of one week. Table 18 shows the viewing frequencies for various types of programmes.

Where comparisons are possible, we find that the audience figures reflect the children's tastes fairly well. They confirm the great popularity of crime and other plays, and variety and comedy shows; the more modest popularity of children's television programmes (apart from Westerns); and the lack of interest in information, documentary, and news programmes. But it must, of course, be remembered that the timing of programmes favours the existing taste pattern—known favourites are put on at times when children have a ready chance to view.

TABLE 18. Average percentage of viewers who saw BBC programmes of various types during the week beginning 13 May 1955, in order of audience size

	Number of programmes shown	13–14 YEAR OLDS %	10–11 YEAR OLDS %
Westerns (children's television) . . .	3	73	83
Crime drama	1	73	73
Comedy shows	1	71	51
Other drama	3	69	53
Variety	4	65	53
The Appleyards (children's television) . .	1	64	74
Have you a Camera?	1	64	53
Panel games	3	54	45
The Grove Family	1	53	68
Sport	2	52	28
Information or documentary	4	50	47
Other children's programmes	14	49	64
Programmes about the cinema . . .	2	47	49
Party political broadcasts	3	34	41
Weather, news, and newsreel . . .	7	28	44
Music recital	1	23	13
Total cases (weighted)		369	366

NOTE. The data were obtained from the programme-recall lists.

Two comments on Table 18 are necessary. First, adult comedy shows, which are very popular with children, were scarcely represented in the week chosen for study. Only one (*Secombe Here*) occurred in that week and was shown late at night, so that its audience figures were certainly not representative of the taste of the younger children for this type of programme.

Secondly, *Have you a Camera?*, which formed part of a series of practical programmes on photography, had a large child audience, partly because it was shown early on Wednesday evening after *Fabian of Scotland Yard*, a top favourite, and before a variety programme. This illustrates how a programme which is not intrinsically popular can hold a considerable audience because it comes between two more popular ones. Another example of this kind was a documentary programme about Devon and Cornwall shown on children's television, which was both preceded and followed by Westerns. The viewing percentages were as follow:

	13–14 YEAR OLDS %	10–11 YEAR OLDS %
Cisco Kid (Western)—25 minutes . .	76	85
Devon and Cornwall (documentary)—10 minutes	60	72
Range Rider (Western)—25 minutes . .	75	83

Normally documentary programmes do not attract such a large audience. For instance, in the same week an information programme *Out of Doors* was seen by only 36 per cent and 49 per cent of viewers, respectively.

When a programme is sandwiched like this between two programmes, it is the *preceding* rather than the following programme which affects the size of the audience.[1] For example, the fact that three General Election broadcasts were followed by programmes popular with children hardly increased their audience:

Percentage of viewers who saw election broadcasts and contrasting programmes on three selected days

	13–14 YEAR OLDS %	10–11 YEAR OLDS %
Monday:		
Weather, news, and newsreel	29	47
Election broadcast—Labour Party	34	47
Showcase	63	72
Tuesday:		
Weather, news, and newsreel	30	47
Election broadcast—Conservative Party	41	47
Away from the Nest	58	55
Thursday:		
Weather, news, and newsreel	28	35
Election broadcast—Liberal Party	27	34
Film extracts—Greta Garbo	49	53
Total cases (weighted)	369	366

Children's viewing habits, taken as a whole, were very regular, almost irrespective of the type of programmes shown. On any one day, about half of them—more of the younger ones, fewer of the older ones—looked at children's television. The younger children viewed as much as they could of the early evening programmes, the figures rising sharply after the news, and falling again after 9 p.m. Fig. 4 represents a typical hour-by-hour sequence of viewing figures for one day.

On occasions, a reversal of the normal pattern occurred. On the Thursday night a telerecording of Billy Graham, the evangelist, was shown fairly late in the evening. During earlier programmes the child audience had gradually dwindled to 13 per cent of the older ones and 9 per cent of the younger ones. When Billy Graham came on it rose to 38 per cent and 16 per cent respectively. Some children may have been persuaded by their parents to watch this special

[1] This applies primarily to the situation in the one-channel home.

programme, but on other occasions when the trend was reversed
they probably followed their own taste. For example, the percentage
of older children viewing rose from 33 to 51 for a boxing match
shown late at night, and from 54 to 71 for a late comedy programme.

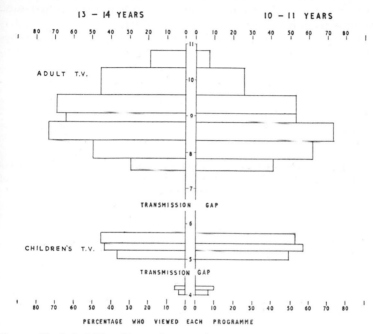

FIG. 4. Typical child audiences for successive programmes on an ordinary week-
day, for the two age groups. The three sets of programmes are those for the very
young, children's, and evening programmes. (The width of each bar indicates the
length of the programme.)

Table 18 also shows that of the two family serials *The Appleyards*
was seen by more viewers than *The Grove Family*, although *The
Grove Family* was mentioned more than twice as often by both age
groups as their favourite programme. This discrepancy was largely
due to the timing. *The Appleyards* was shown during children's television on Saturday afternoon—generally a favourable day and
time for viewing; while *The Grove Family* was the first feature programme after the news on Friday night. Moreover, the rest of that
evening's programmes—a documentary, a film programme, a horse
show, part of the Bath Festival, and a science programme—were
not very tempting to a child—an interesting reflection once again
of how selective children are in their viewing.

In Table 19 we list the *children's* programmes shown during the week of the programme-recall lists. The table indicates the percentage of children who viewed, and the percentage of those who liked the given programme very much. The *types* of programmes which were popular and those which were little liked are the same as those which are being shown today, even though the individual programmes may, of course, be partly out of date.

The most popular programmes were Westerns, followed by the first instalment of a new serial (*The Explorer*), a family serial (*The Appleyards*), and a play (*Alibi Children*). Lower down the list came children's variety programmes, animal programmes (for the older children), sports programmes, a newsreel, and the third in a series of how-to-make-it programmes (*Our Port*). Least popular were programmes about music and books.

TABLE 19. Percentage who viewed certain children's programmes during the week beginning 13 May 1955 and the percentage among them who liked each of these programmes very much

	Percentage who viewed		Percentage who liked the programme very much	
	13–14 YEAR OLDS %	10–11 YEAR OLDS %	13–14 YEAR OLDS %	10–11 YEAR OLDS %
Friday:				
Cisco Kid	75	81	76	91
Filming in Africa .	58	76	76	90
Saturday:				
Sugar and Spice (variety)	51	71	41	69
The Appleyards	64	74	88	95
Sunday:				
Our Port (3)—serial	54	68	16	44
Newsreel	63	70	65	85
Play—Alibi Children	63	74	83	93
Monday:				
Cisco Kid	76	85	77	91
Devon and Cornwall	60	72	57	63
The Range Rider .	75	83	84	93
Tuesday:				
The Explorer (1)—serial.	68	82	80	85
Wednesday:				
Out of Doors	36	49	21	51
Comic Turn (Peter Glazer)	43	57	42	70
Sport .	45	53	41	42
Thursday:				
Billy Bean .	41	59	29	61
Ten Minutes Music	35	54	24	31
Chessington Zoo .	40	57	70	84
People in Books	35	49	52	53
Total cases (weighted)	369	366		

Table 19 also gives a 'reaction index'—the number who ticked 'I like it very much' as a percentage of those who saw the programme. The younger children viewed children's television more often than the older ones and enjoyed it more. On the other hand, they were also less critical of programmes in general—adults' as well as children's. Grammar school children, once they decided to view children's programmes, were not much more critical than those from secondary modern schools.

The reaction index gives in some ways a clearer reflection of taste than does size of audience; but it refers only to those children who saw a programme and depended more on the virtues of one particular programme, as distinct from the category of programme. Thus *The Appleyards* episode came fifth or sixth in size of audience but first in the reaction index; evidently this particular episode was highly successful.

With most other programmes the two measures (audience size and reaction index) seemed to correspond, but there were some interesting exceptions. Several programmes were not liked by the older children who saw them; but one—the Chessington Zoo programme—though seen by only two-fifths of this age group, was very well liked. (Appendix Table 10 gives details.) Westerns once again were most often liked by the duller, younger children, and the *People in Books* programme was very well liked by the brighter girls[1] but not by the brighter boys; the reaction among duller children was moderately favourable. Several comparatively unpopular programmes were well liked by a fair number of those who saw them.

The reaction indices of a selected number of *evening programmes* are presented in Table 20, selected as typical of their kind or else as throwing light on a particular issue. Appendix Table 10 gives the audience size as well as the reaction indices and further details of the two groups of children.

These figures are interesting not so much because they confirm children's liking of variety and comedy shows, plays, panel games, and crime series, but because of the unexpectedly favourable reactions to informational and documentary programmes. Only the election broadcasts and *Panorama*, which tend to rely on verbal rather than pictorial presentation, obtained really low reaction indices; otherwise, at least half the children who saw these programmes liked them very much. These figures are still well below those of the top favourites, and the audiences are rather more self-selected, but they show that such programmes, if seen, are not by any means universally disliked.

[1] Girls, we found, read more books and enjoyed them more than boys did (Chap. 28).

TABLE 20. Percentage of children who very much liked certain evening programmes shown during the week beginning 13 May 1955, as a proportion of those who saw them

	REACTION INDEX	
	13–14 YEAR OLDS	10–11 YEAR OLDS
	%	%
What Every Woman Knows (play) . . .	56	70
Showcase (variety)	97	94
Fabian of Scotland Yard (crime series) . .	96	96
Secombe Here (comedy show). . . .	92	92
Have you a Camera?	54	52
In Town Tonight (reportage)	57	68
Filming in Africa	68	78
Panorama	30	31
Election broadcasts	17	18
Meet the Commonwealth.	60	63
From Tropical Forests	57	65
Science Review	52	78
Cities of Europe—Rome (documentary) . .	43	53
Animal, Vegetable, or Mineral	61	68
Find the Link (panel game)	75	82

It is quite striking, for instance, to see how well the archaeological panel-game *Animal, Vegetable, or Mineral* has been received; it was almost as well liked by those who saw it as *Find the Link*, a different type of panel game. Quite possibly knowledge conveyed in the form of a game (aided in this case by the personality of Sir Mortimer Wheeler) is more attractive to children than knowledge conveyed verbally. An essay, written by a boy of 11, shows the ingredients of *Animal, Vegetable, or Mineral* that appeal to him:

> I prefer this programme (*Animal, Vegetable, or Mineral*) because I like to see people, like Sir Mortimer Wheeler, who I think has a great personality, revive relics of thousands of years ago, and who devotes his life to his work. Sometimes the programme is devoted to art; this I like very much and sometimes the pictures are really beautiful, I admire art very much. I also like to try and guess what an object or fragment of a painting is.

The Appendix Table 10 gives the reaction indices for boys and girls and for children of different intelligence levels. Again we shall make reference to the non-fictional programmes. Contrary to expectation, the less intelligent children were as interested in the archaeological panel game and in *Science Review* as those of grammar school calibre. The reaction index was the same for the bright and the less bright children. On the whole, girls proved a little less interested in these programmes than boys.

The appeal of television personalities is discussed in Chapter 12.

Developing new tastes

One other important point needs to be made which has a bearing on the results just discussed: so long as children can only view one channel, they will occasionally see programmes in which they are not primarily interested, and which they would not choose to watch if an alternative channel were available. Yet, as we have seen, reaction indices for such programmes were often unexpectedly favourable. Some of these programmes were seen by children who continued watching after seeing highly popular preceding programmes. The audience, therefore, contained many children who were not in the habit of viewing this type of fare. Nevertheless, reactions ranged from favourable to highly favourable.

In the one-channel home, children often get the chance to discover such programmes; in the two-channel home, hardly ever. Our results suggest that there is a good deal of room for more imaginative and varied programme planning. Children's tastes are flexible; they respond well to the new and the unfamiliar.

EFFECTS OF A SECOND CHANNEL

We have seen in Chapter 8 that children with access to two channels spent about as many hours viewing television before as after the advent of ITV. They divided this time between the two channels. If taste played no part in such a division, and the viewers were assigned at random to one channel or the other, the effect would be that of halving the audience sizes characteristic of the one-channel situation.

TABLE 21. Proportion of the audience retained in the two-channel situation, for various types of programme

(See Appendix Table 11)

	Proportion of audience kept	
	13–14 YEAR OLDS	10–11 YEAR OLDS
	%	%
Crime	73	63
Film programmes	55	31
Westerns	51	52
Panel games	48	78
Variety	43	44
Drama	42	51
Children's television (excluding Westerns)	34	36
Information and documentary	24	29

Taste, of course, does play a part. In Table 21 it can be seen that crime programmes, Westerns, and panel games held their audiences much better, irrespective of channel, than other programmes on children's television or information programmes. The latter almost invariably lost two-thirds or three-quarters of their former viewers to programmes on the other channel. Children kept to the programmes they preferred, following them from one channel to the other and back again. Unfortunately, the programmes most likely to suffer were those which had educational value or were specially produced for children.

Two factors modify this trend slightly. One is a general bias towards ITV; this can make the diet a little more varied provided ITV is willing to make it so. The second and more important factor is variation in the degree of competition between the two channels; for instance, information programmes and plays seem to meet strong competition on the alternative channel more often than other programmes, and this helps to explain why drama has not held its audiences as well as, say, panel games. However, these qualifications do not greatly affect the general trend—the switching from channel to channel in pursuit of favourite programmes.

ANALYSIS OF COMPETING PROGRAMMES

We now come to the second approach outlined at the beginning of this chapter—a comparison of choices between programmes on at the same time. This method, as we have said, is restricted to the two-channel situation, and is handicapped by a general bias towards one channel; nevertheless it offers an opportunity to hold constant many influences other than taste preferences.

We took from the 1956 programme-recall lists pairs of programmes which appeared concurrently or overlapped. The programmes of a single week did not give us all the pairs we needed for an accurate order of preference; nor were sufficient programmes available to permit confident generalisations. However, we were able to deduce the following tentative preference order:

1. Crime programmes draw more viewers than variety.
2. Comedy draws more viewers than serious drama.[1]
3. Serious drama attracts more viewers than panel games.
4. Light drama attracts more viewers than
   (a) comedy shows;
   (b) serious drama;
   (c) information programmes.

From this emerged the following rough-and-ready order of preference for evening programmes:

1. Light drama.
2. Comedy shows.

· [1] In this particular analysis drama was subdivided into light and serious drama.

3. Serious drama.
4. Crime and detection.
5. Variety.
6. Panel games.
7. Information and documentary programmes.
8. Film programmes.

For children's television, an insufficient number of programmes was available for detailed ranking. But one fact stood out clearly: Westerns easily attracted audiences away from all other types of programme.

We put these comparisons forward with some diffidence, because three factors impair their accuracy. First, each is based on only a few programmes. Second, the general bias in favour of ITV gives ITV programmes an advantage. Third, not all items within each programme category are equally attractive. Also, some of the influences which we could not hold constant—such as length of programme, serialisation, preceding and following programmes, parental influence, and the effect of personalities no doubt reduce the accuracy of such comparisons. Quite possibly in a different week a somewhat modified order of preference might emerge, due to particularly popular or unpopular programmes. On the other hand, this method of paired comparisons allows us to eliminate the influence of many extraneous factors such as time of day, or the attractiveness of other activities.

CONCLUSIONS

The most important finding presented here concerns the effect of a second channel. As we have seen earlier, the introduction of a second channel has not increased the number of viewing hours, so that the same amount of viewing time is divided between two channels. In this choice of channel, children's taste plays a dominant role: they switch from channel to channel following their favourite programme types. In this way, irrespective of the programme balance on either channel, the children create for themselves a narrow viewing diet, consisting mainly of their first or second favourites. Under these circumstances, documentary and informational programmes, and programmes specially designed for children (apart from Westerns), suffer a disproportionate reduction in audience size. Compared with the one-channel situation, these programmes are reduced to about one-third of their former audience.

Many factors influence the size of the child audience for any particular programme. Among these are the available counter-attractions, the time of day and the day of the week, parental influence, the appeal of the programme which precedes and of the one which follows it. Yet by careful analysis of audience statistics it is possible to show that notwithstanding these various situational factors, by and large the child's taste still influences his viewing. A tentative order of preference for given programmes has been suggested from a consideration of programmes shown concurrently.

Taste is reflected even more clearly in the children's liking or disliking of programmes they have actually seen (i.e. in the size of the reaction index). In particular, even in our quite limited set of data, there were a number of documentary or informational programmes, not obviously of a kind to interest children, which when seen were well liked. It is therefore important for children to have contact with such programmes, in order that their tastes may have a chance to develop. Such findings should be a stimulus to the producer, but in the two-channel home, children will discover such programmes less often for themselves, and so are even more in need of parental guidance and encouragement.

II

Patterns of Taste

IN this chapter several basic questions are raised concerning children's tastes in television, in other mass media, and in other leisure activities. Do programme preferences develop in relation to a particular type of programme or performer, or on broader patterns? And if on broader patterns, do these in turn form part of general patterns found in the other mass media? How far are these patterns related to the child's other values and interests.[1]

Methods. At varying times in the main survey and in Norwich the children were given four lists—one each for television, cinema, radio, and reading—and asked to tick one of three columns for each of more than forty subjects:

1. 'I would like to read this' (see this, hear this);
2. 'I would not mind whether I read this or not' (hear it, watch it);
3. 'I would not like to read this' (hear it, watch it).

The items were selected either according to subject-matter— 'cowboys and the Wild West', 'crime, detectives and mystery', 'science and inventions'—or to the nature of the contents, for example, 'things that make you sad'. In each inventory we listed all or most of the usual subjects for that medium and included items common to all four media so that we could compare these directly. To give one illustration, the inventory on reading contained items common to all four media—like 'space travel and space men', 'things that happened in the Bible', and 'your hobbies'—along with items which had no parallel in the other media, like 'the sea', 'fairy tales', 'poems', 'comics and comic strips', and 'dictionaries'.[2]

---

[1] In trying to answer these questions we shall largely ignore differences of sex, class, and intelligence within the sample; these have been considered in Chapter 9. Also, we shall be concerned less with individual programmes than with types or groups of programmes.

[2] Because this technique of questioning imposes a closed framework on the responses, it was preceded at an earlier testing session by an open-ended question about children's tastes in programmes and reading matter.

We have tried to measure associations between programme types by means of a special correlation coefficient known as Kendall's Tau.

In Appendix C further details are given about this coefficient and its computation. In Appendix Table 12 we present evidence to show that the data obtained by means of these inventories bear a close relationship to those obtained in the open-ended question about tastes.

PATTERNS OF TELEVISION TASTE

Does the child's liking for a particular television programme, or type of programme, form part of a pattern of taste shared by a number of programmes?[1] Three popular programme types were selected, differing as widely as possible from one another: Westerns, ordinary families, and variety. Each of these was correlated (separately for each age group) with twenty other types of television programmes. The results offer substantial evidence of an underlying pattern of taste and have enabled us to isolate tentatively five fairly distinct clusters of related types of programme.

1. *The excitement cluster*

Westerns showed significant coefficients with only three other types of programme; all other coefficients were close to zero, some above, others below.[2]

Type of programme:	13–14 YEAR OLDS	10–11 YEAR OLDS
Adventure	0·48	0·48
Crime, detectives and mystery . . .	0·29	0·17
Space travel and space men	0·34	0·27

Provisionally, we may call this small but most popular set of programmes the 'excitement cluster'.

2. *The social empathy cluster*

Preference for programmes about ordinary families correlated with a variety of programmes:

[1] The only proper way of answering this question is by means of a factor analysis, which is inappropriate for Tau coefficients and would have involved us in the computation of 903 coefficients for each age group. However, by confining our study to selected clusters of relationships we can answer the question in part and suggest findings which a factor analysis might show with greater confidence.

[2] Perhaps the most useful way of examining these coefficients is to ignore those below 0·20, which are likely to be determined mainly by chance fluctuations.

Type of programme:	13–14 YEAR OLDS	10–11 YEAR OLDS
About famous people	0·33	0·34
Things that make you laugh	0·32	0·23
Things that happened in the Bible . . .	0·30	0·25
People in other countries	0·28	0·24
Cowboys and the Wild West	0·24	0·22
Adventure	0·24	0·31
Painting	0·24	0·20
Things that make you sad	0·22	0·13
Crime, detectives and mystery . . .	0·21	0·28
Your hobbies	0·21	0·19
Horror plays or stories	0·21	0·26
Love and romance	0·20	0·28
School life	0·20	0·25
Things that happened in history . . .	0·19	0·24

It would seem that children who like programmes about ordinary families also tend to be those with an interest in programmes about people generally (famous people, people in other countries, happenings in history), a desire for vicarious emotional experiences (laughter and sadness, love and romance, with some crime, adventure, and horror), and enjoyment of creative activities (painting and hobbies).

This large group, which may be loosely labelled the 'social empathy' cluster, is of special interest because in family serials ordinary families are brought to the screen in a way which is comparatively rare in the cinema or magazines (though radio has some examples). These serials have had a very great appeal, and it is interesting to see some of the factors related to it. This cluster to some extent overlaps with the previous one, but both differ from the intellectual and artistic clusters which we describe later on.

3. *Mixed social empathy and excitement cluster*

Variety correlated with about a dozen programme types:

Type of programme:	13–14 YEAR OLDS	10–11 YEAR OLDS
Things that make you laugh	0·60	0·50
Crime, detectives and mystery . . .	0·55	0·48
Things that happened in the war . . .	0·34	0·27
Things that happened in the Bible . . .	0·30	0·25
Adventure	0·30	0·45
Horror plays or stories	0·26	0·24
Famous people	0·23	0·34
People in other countries	0·22	0·24
Things that happened in history . . .	0·21	0·27
Ordinary people	0·20	0·26
Cowboys and the Wild West	0·20	0·28

The very word 'variety' suggests a long series of short performances with quick changes from jokes to juggling, singing to satire, and from tailcoats to tights; laughter is its primary ingredient for children. This cluster overlaps with the 'excitement cluster' (crime, adventure, Westerns, horror, and war) and with the 'social empathy cluster'.

4. The artistic cluster

It was possible to identify a small 'artistic' cluster from the correlations with ballet:

						13–14 YEAR OLDS	10–11 YEAR OLDS
Type of programme:							
Ballroom dancing	.	.	.	.	.	0·54	0·69
Painting	.	.	.	.	.	0·29	0·24
Love and romance	.	.	.	.	.	0·29	0·32

5. The intellectual cluster

We also found an intellectual cluster, including liking for architecture, news and current affairs, books and politics.

These taste systems are put forward mainly as hypotheses for further research. They should be seen as types of interest, and discussed in terms of the types of children who have these interests and how they differ from other children. They may also be regarded as underlying types of appeal, which are shared by apparently dissimilar programmes and which 'explain' the popularity of these programmes with different groups of children.

Contrary to expectation, we did not find that the older children had a more differentiated taste. The taste structure of both age groups was very similar.

TASTE PATTERNS IN TELEVISION AND OTHER MEDIA

Are these patterns specific to television or common to several of the mass media? How far is a child's taste for a particular topic confined to one medium and how far does it extend to others? For example, how far does a child who enjoys Westerns on television choose to read books about the Wild West and watch films and listen to radio programmes on the same topic?

Ten items which appeared on all four inventories were selected, and the equivalent items for radio, cinema, and reading correlated with those for television to see how far subject-matter liked in one medium was liked in all four. The results (in Appendix Table 13) indicate that the taste for excitement clearly extended into all other media. So did the social empathy and artistic clusters, though less clearly. Television news extended slightly into radio and cinema news, but not into newspaper-reading. Chapter 28 shows that reading diverged in several ways from the pattern followed by the other three mass media: children who enjoyed reading about a certain subject did not necessarily enjoy it when it was broadcast or shown on a screen.

We next correlated the *reading of comics and comic strips* with liking for twenty types of television programme. The following coefficients were significant:

Type of television programme:				13–14 YEAR OLDS	10–11 YEAR OLDS
Crime, detective and mystery	.	.	.	0·34	0·39
Adventure .	.	.	. . .	0·30	0·41
Westerns .	.	.	. . .	0·25	0·36
Love and romance	.	.	. .	0·26	0·14
About famous people	.	.	.	0·21	0·31
About other countries .	.	.	.	0·30	0·32
About things that happened long ago	.	.	0·28	0·26
About farming and country life	.	.		0·29	0·29
Things that happened in the Bible .	.	.		0·24	0·31
Things that happened in history	.	.	.	0·24	0·25

Thus, the main link between comics and television was through the excitement and social empathy clusters. Reading comics seems to go with an interest in unusual people (famous people, historical or Biblical personages, romantic or foreign people) but hardly at all with an interest in ordinary families. As might be expected, there was no link here with the artistic and the intellectual clusters.

A slightly more elaborate analysis was carried out for the three chief favourites in the *excitement cluster*—programmes on crime, adventure, and space travel. Each was correlated in turn with the main items in the excitement clusters of the other three media. The following points emerge from inspection of Appendix Table 14:

Each item correlated best with its nearest equivalent in the other three media; with the others it had a smaller, though still positive relationship. For instance, a taste for crime on television correlated reasonably well with a liking for adventure in the other media.

An exception was space travel on television, which showed very little relationship with the excitement items in other inventories. A similarly isolated taste, rather surprisingly, was the reading of cowboy and Wild West stories; it had hardly any relationship with crime or adventure programmes on television.

The data show that most patterns of taste do extend through all four mass media. To some degree a child's television tastes can be predicted from his radio, reading, and cinema preferences.

TASTE PATTERNS AND OTHER INTERESTS

How far are the child's taste patterns linked with his other interests, and with his values and outlook? To what extent are they an expression of his personality?

Appendix Table 15 links favourite pastimes found in our study of leisure activities[1] with the television programmes list. The three pastimes most often mentioned were: games (competitive, athletic, and mainly team games); outdoor play (non-competitive informal sports and outdoor activities); and reading (including looking at comics or books, and going to a library). Those whose favourite pastimes fell in each of these groups were examined for their preferences in television programmes.

There were significant differences between the three groups, especially between reading and the other two. Among the older children the reading group tended to be rather more interested than others in Westerns, adventure, school-life stories, love and romance, ordinary families, painting and sculpture, ballet, ballroom dancing, serious music, popular music, children's television, puppet shows, fashion parades, and, of course, programmes about books. They were less interested in programmes about things that happened in the war. These differences were by no means due merely to the fact that the reading group contained more girls than the games group.

Thus, on this prima facie evidence, there do seem to be links between the child's favourite leisure activities and the type of television programmes in which he is interested. As the analysis proceeds, the pictures become more recognisable and distinct; the television tastes of each kind of child reflect to some extent his other interests, as well as his age, intelligence, sex, and social background.

Having first compared an open-ended question about favourite pastimes with a 'closed' inventory about television programmes, we next adopted the opposite approach and compared some of the children's spontaneously mentioned television preferences with a 'closed' inventory of children's interests (described in Chapter 6).

[1] Open-ended questions were asked about the child's home and family, and about the things which he liked to do in his spare time. For example, the following question was included: *There never seems to be enough time to do all the things one likes doing. Write down the three things you like doing best, that is, in the time after school.* See Part VII.

Fig. 5 shows the results for the older children. We selected three groups, according to their favourite programme: those who chose *Fabian of Scotland Yard*, those who chose *Ask Pickles*, and the much smaller group who preferred documentary types of programme. The three groups' mean scores for the sixteen areas in the interests inventory were compared with the corresponding mean scores for their age group as a whole. The straight horizontal line in Fig. 5 represents this series of sixteen means—one for each area—while the other lines show how each of the three groups deviated from the mean of their age group, as well as from the other two.

The scores of children who gave *Fabian of Scotland Yard* were mostly very near the average. The only deviation of any size was a below-average interest in more cultural and intellectual pursuits, such as going to the theatre, writing a story, discussing politics, or playing chess.

Those who gave documentary types of programme as their favourites stood farther from the mean. They had an above-average interest in indoor games such as cards, crossword puzzles, or ludo, in hobbies such as woodwork or metal work, making models, finding out how engines work, and in cultural and intellectual interests. But they were below average in their interest in domestic pursuits (cooking, shopping, looking after small children), and in the mass media (passive light entertainment). This pattern was characteristic of the intelligent, more intellectually inclined older child.

The group who preferred *Ask Pickles* (a programme with a homely, sentimental atmosphere and containing a large element of wish-fulfilment) comprised mainly duller children from secondary modern schools. They tended to be below average in most of the interest areas, including watching sport; on the whole their pattern of interest was the reverse of that described above for the more intellectual child. They cared less for sedentary games and all forms of cultural and intellectual interests; on the other hand, they enjoyed domestic tasks and also dressing up and acting. This is a rather typical picture of an unintellectual, rather inactive, dreamy adolescent.

A similar analysis was carried out for those who gave *variety* programmes as their favourites, but their scores generally approximated to the average and so did not yield a particular 'type'. Variety would seem to have a very general appeal.

We now relate these associations between programme preferences and leisure-time interests to the various measures of attitude, opinion, and personality described in Chapters 6 and 20. For this, we have taken four groups of children very similar to the previous three: those whose favourites were adult plays (mostly *Fabian of Scotland Yard*, but also *The Grove Family* series), those who liked

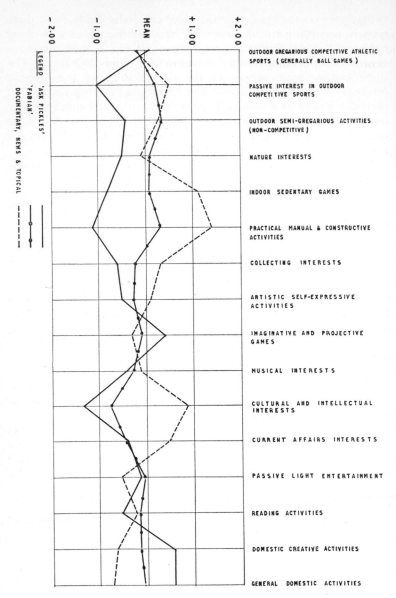

FIG. 5. Deviations from the mean for each area of the Interests Inventory by children whose favourite programme was *Ask Pickles*, *Fabian of Scotland Yard*, or documentary and topical programmes, respectively

variety and comedy shows best, those who preferred documentary types of programme, and those who liked *Ask Pickles*. As there were not enough cases the groups were not matched for sex or intelligence. Appendix Table 16 gives the results for the older children.

We thought that preference for each of these four favourites might be linked with distinct differences in outlook, and we selected questions accordingly. Turning to values and attitudes, we thought that preference for any one of the four favourite types of programmes might be associated with superstitious and irrational beliefs, with attitudes towards foreigners, and with general attitudes towards life and people. Questions were therefore selected to bring out these associations. Plays, especially family serials, might give children ideas about roles, so we included projective questions about the good father. Children worried about growing up might readily seek escape in certain types of programmes, therefore questions were included to measure these attitudes.

We found that children who liked *documentary* types of programme diverged from the others in describing the good father a little less often as a provider and more often in terms of his emotional relationship with his family. They also tended to be less gullible and more resistant to clichés than the others, less prone to dislike political or news-discussion programmes, and more prone to dislike panel games. But when they did watch panel games they tried a little more often to guess the answers rather than look at them.

Children who favoured *Ask Pickles* most often saw the father in the role of provider; being duller they were also the most gullible and the most cliché-ridden. They admitted to a little more anxiety about growing up, and about their parents' attitude towards them, than other children; possibly they saw the 'fantasy come true' character of this programme and the fatherly figure of Wilfred Pickles as a temporary escape from reality. Their dislike of news and discussion programmes was more pronounced than in any other group.

Finally, as part of a further analysis we found that children who chose sports as their favourite programme admitted to fewer worries of any kind.

These differences should be regarded as pointers only, their statistical significance being slight. However, taken together with the other differences analysed in this chapter, they do suggest some links between the child's viewing tastes and his leisure interests, attitudes, and personal needs.

CONCLUSIONS

In this chapter we have presented evidence to show that, while many factors help to determine the popularity of individual programmes, there is a broad pattern of taste which underlies different groups and types of programmes. It is not true, therefore, to suggest that children's preferences are haphazard and idiosyncratic; in the background there is always a regular taste pattern clearly discernible already at the age of 10.

Furthermore, we have tentatively identified five types or clusters of programmes. These have been provisionally labelled as the excitement, social empathy, variety, artistic, and intellectual clusters. Further research is needed to confirm and define these clusters more precisely. These clusters are not specific to television but form part of a wider taste pattern, shared to a greater or lesser extent by the other mass media. It should be possible therefore to predict a child's taste in television with a fair amount of accuracy from his tastes in radio, reading, and the cinema.

These taste patterns are in their turn linked with the child's personality and outlook. At any one moment, the child's preferences in mass media reflect not only his age, sex, and intelligence, but also his general outlook, spare-time interests, anxieties, and needs.

1 2

Attractions of Viewing

In this chapter we provide some conjectures about the attractions which children find in viewing. Our material comes partly from answers given to questions in the survey, and partly from qualitative and more detailed material collected in greater depth from much smaller numbers of children, from mother's observations and reports, and from lengthy interviews with 9–10 year old children.[1] The more conjectural parts of this chapter (particularly those concerned with the emotional appeals of viewing) are included despite their uncertain validity, in the hope that they may lead to further research.

The various attractions of viewing are discussed under different headings: the negative, or nondescript attractions, visual appeals and emotional appeals, and the appeal of television personalities.

THE NONDESCRIPT OR NEGATIVE ATTRACTIONS OF VIEWING

To speak of nondescript or negative attractions is in some ways a contradiction in terms; yet a great deal of television's appeal for many children is of this kind. Viewing is used as a time-filler, requiring neither money nor effort.

Evidence of this attitude emerged when children were asked what they thought was the best thing about television. The easy, and obvious, answer was to refer (however vaguely) to the programmes—saying, for instance, that they were 'interesting', 'nice', or 'good'. Two-thirds of the older viewers and nearly as many of the 10–11 year olds did reply in these terms. Yet as many as one child in five

---

[1] Particularly from ten intensive interviews, which were intended to provide a type of case-history evidence, throwing light on the manner in which children react differently to television according to the needs of their own personalities. Each child was interviewed at length, and in addition the interviewer visited his home, and talked to his headmaster.

avoided the obvious way out and mentioned the relatively negative advantages of television—as something to do when bored or lonely, something to turn to when it is raining outside, something which involves none of the trouble or expense of going to the cinema.

Moreover, as Table 22 shows, the proportion expressing this attitude was even higher (two-fifths) when the question was slightly rephrased to emphasise home viewing: *What would you say is the best thing about having a TV set at home?*

TABLE 22. *What would you say is the best thing about having a TV set at home?*

(Viewers only)

	13–14 YEAR OLDS %	10–11 YEAR OLDS %
Answers in terms of content:		
TV is entertaining, exciting, there are good, interesting, nice programmes	25	31
TV is educational—you learn about things and people . .	17	10
Nondescript answers:		
Viewing is a way of filling time, something to do when bored, always available	27	21
Is not necessary to go out, to the cinema or otherwise, keeps children off the streets	18	17
Other answers:		
Able to have friends in, keeps family together, makes everyone happy	8	4
Miscellaneous answers	6	5
Don't know, no answer	8	16
Total cases (weighted)	538	539

NOTE. These percentages add to slightly over 100 per cent because some children gave more than one type of answer.

This vague attitude to viewing appeared more often among the less intelligent children, who may be more aimless than the others, and among the 13–14 year olds, who were becoming less interested in television.

Some of the reasons for this type of nondescript appeal emerged when children were asked to compare viewing with going to the cinema.

Television versus the cinema

Although television has an advantage over the cinema (because it can be seen at home) children did not greatly prefer it. For many of them television cannot provide superior content of programmes, or the attractions of colour and size, or (for older children in particular) the pleasure of being away from home.

These results emerged from three questions, asked in three separate questionnaires: children were asked—

(a) Whether they agreed or disagreed with the statement: '*I find it more fun to watch TV than to go to the pictures.*'
(b) *Would you say that going to the pictures is better than watching television, or not so good?* and *What makes you feel that way?*
(c) *Imagine that the same story could be seen on television, at the pictures, or listened to on the wireless—which would you choose?*

The first question was deliberately framed as an extreme statement to measure maximal feeling for television. Yet even among viewers only 40 per cent of the older children and 58 per cent of the 10–11 year olds expressed agreement with it. In both age groups it was the girls more than the boys who favoured television.

The second question was less biased. It also gave children the chance to say they had no preference for either medium, and between a quarter and a third availed themselves of this opportunity. The remainder distributed themselves in the same proportions as with the first question, the balance being tipped slightly in favour of the cinema among older children and towards television among younger ones (Table 17 in the Appendix).

The reasons given for preferring the cinema showed that the cinema has many social attractions for adolescents at least. In the words of one secondary modern school girl, the cinema was better because 'I can neck with my fellow', and a bright grammar school girl put the same point less bluntly: 'you can sit by friends you can't have home because they are of the opposite sex'.

A third question was asked to find out how much of the cinema's superior appeal lies in the interest of its stories. When in this way the programme content of both media was thought of as identical '*Imagine that the same story could be seen on television or at the pictures, or listened to on the wireless: which would you choose?*'), television emerged as much more popular than the cinema: well over half of the older children and nearly three-quarters of the younger ones chose it[1] (Appendix Table 17a).

The relatively nondescript appeal that television made to a sizeable minority of children was thus underlined by comparison with the cinema—the latter being much more widely liked for the sake of its programmes and presentation.

---

[1] The remainder chose the cinema, with only about 2 per cent preferring to listen to the wireless.

THE VISUAL APPEAL OF TELEVISION

BBC figures have shown that at times when adult viewers can either watch television or listen to the radio, only one listens for every 10 or 11 who view (14). Chapter 29 shows that children are affected in much the same way. A study of children's preference for viewing over various forms of reading makes it possible to understand more about the visual appeal of television. The children were presented with a problem of choice:

> Imagine a boy or girl who has been ill in bed. When he—or she—was getting better, he was allowed to choose from anything he liked to amuse himself with in the evening. Which one of these things do you think he would most likely choose: comics, books, TV, wireless, or toys or games?

For practical purposes, radio can be ignored; only very few viewers chose it. Toys and games were equally unimportant for older children, and only moderately interesting to 10–11 year olds. The main effective choice lay between reading books or comics and watching television. Television won, but only just (Table 23).

TABLE 23. *Which one of these things do you think a boy who has been ill in bed would most likely choose—comics, books, TV, wireless, or toys or games?*

(Viewers only)

Would choose:	13–14 YEAR OLDS %	10–11 YEAR OLDS %
Television	52	44
Books	28 ⎫ 38	24 ⎫ 39
Comics	10 ⎭	15 ⎭
Radio	5	2
Toys, games	5	15
Total cases (*weighted*)	475	475

In general the advantages of reading and viewing were the same Both are home media, always available. But when they competed against each other, television (with the extra enticemen of sound and vision) had more appeal than reading.

Nevertheless there remained an interesting minority, especially among girls, and among the more intelligent younger children, who said they would rather read than view; for them the advantage o selecting their own reading matter proved stronger than that of the pictorial content of television.

THE EMOTIONAL APPEAL OF TELEVISION

Emotionally, television made some of its main appeals through romantic heroes, through satisfying curiosity, and through providing unreality, security, action, and constant change. It also attracts through the infringement of conventions.

The appeal of romantic heroes

Important to both younger and older children were the romantic heroes, invariably right, clever, and strong, and moving in a generally unfamiliar setting. The younger children liked the heroes of Westerns, and also Robin Hood (romantic in his historical setting) and *Superman* (romantic in fantasy). The heroes of modern crime—*Dixon of Dock Green, Fabian of Scotland Yard*, and Joe Friday (*Dragnet*)—were even more popular and appealed strongly to older children as well.

Their appeal varies with the child's age, sex, ability, and personal needs. Wolfe and Fiske (105), in their study of children's comic-reading, concluded that the heroes of comics gratify special needs for each type of child. The comic 'fan', who often shows signs of emotional disturbance, tends to see the hero as a god-like figure on whom he can rely emotionally, but the more stable child more often identifies himself with the hero, using him as a means of experiencing heroism and adventure.

One such example of the 'fan' was a 10 year old girl, Joan—intelligent, socially active, and very down to earth. But she was also an only child, and her companionship was over-important to her mother. She reacted to this by retreating from the claustrophobic atmosphere of her home to the bigger world of television.

A romantic fictional hero can seem very real, as this further extract from Joan's interview shows:

> Roy Rogers is the best! . . . I like his horse and dog. I think he never dies . . . I think he's a religious man because Mummy says he goes to Church every Sunday now. I think he's a very *nice* man, you know.

Much the same need to believe in the reality of the hero was shown by Henry, a 9 year old only child of working-class parents. Of average intelligence— but nervous, diffident, and backward at school —he was described by his headmaster as suffering from a strong sense of inferiority. He, too, found comfort in romantic larger-than-life heroes, emphasising their all-powerful role setting wrong to right. He relished the fact that the *Dragnet* stories were true, insisted that there really was a *Dixon of Dock Green*, and at least half believed in the fantasy of *Superman*.

The appeal of unreality

We found much incidental evidence of the appeal of unreality in television—even in programmes apparently dealing with everyday life, such as *The Grove Family*. One of the many appeals of this serial lies in the cosy sense of security it can provide, enhanced rather than destroyed by the larger-than-life figure of the great-grandmother, 'Gran Grove'. The family's *reality* and the *unreality* of Gran's exaggerated behaviour complement and highlight each other.

Most children in the survey, when asked which member of the Grove family they preferred, chose the great-grandmother. One child, for instance, bored with the everyday life of the rest of the Grove family, welcomed the crossness and picturesqueness of 'Gran': asked how the Groves got on with each other, she said:

> Oh, very well, not a row between them (laughs). . . . But Gran doesn't get on with everybody, she just rocks and grumbles (laughs). Especially about a lady called—oh, another lady that calls her 'cherub', that she absolutely *hates* . . . and she hates being called cherub and she says 'don't call me cherub'. And she *bangs* her stick on the floor. And she says '*I want my elevenses, oh come on, I want my elevenses*'—(laughs).

A 10 year old boy, Kenneth, who showed symptoms of obsessive fears and fantasies, had much the same need for escape from the problems of everyday living. When a programme threatened to come too close to his personal problems, he showed signs of amending it so that it would cease to apply to himself. For example, he watched a *Dixon of Dock Green* episode in which a girl of his own age had run away from home when she thought she had failed her 11-plus examination; Kenneth, who was about to sit for his own examination, stressed that his examination was quite different from the one mentioned in the programme—so forcing the programme into unreality.

Much television entertainment offers a light-hearted treatment of almost any theme. This, naturally, is especially true of the variety programmes and comedies, which appealed strongly to children in the survey. But variety, of course, has other attractions besides light-hearted unreality; there is violence disguised as slapstick, the glamour of the singing and dancing acts and the skill of acrobats and conjurors. The results of a question asked in the Norwich study suggested that it was the funny parts of variety that were best liked by boys, although girls tended to be divided fairly equally between the comedy acts and the musical interludes (as well as showing some interest in conjurors). Much the same result emerged when children were asked which part they would leave out if variety shows had to be made shorter: both girls and boys would dispense with the singing and dancing in the main, but would leave the comic turns.

The appeal of security and familiarity

Television helps to satisfy the need for security in that it is always here, providing companionship and comfort. A 10 year old girl, for instance, remarked:

> Well, it never stops. Till I go to bed. If you go out to play, somebody goes in, and another person goes in, and you're only left with people you don't like.

Reassurance is also gained by seeing and reseeing familiar programmes or types of programme, familiar themes, faces, and personalities.

The importance of this familiarity is stressed elsewhere in this report. The television Western—to a casual observer prolific with shock and surprise—is shown in Chapter 14 to be thoroughly cushioned with certainties. Only very young or very insecure children fail to see that it is rather like a fairy tale and so are unpleasantly frightened by Westerns.

Variety programmes, even in 'slapstick' episodes, provide the reassurance of play-acting, and also of familiar personalities; 'our Jimmy' was the label given affectionately by one 10 year old to the *Jimmy Wheeler* series. Panel games offer the security of familiar personalities and structure, together with a light-hearted presentation which is equally familiar. Their main source of insecurity lies in the prospect of a competitor suffering loss and humiliation. Less certain and secure are discussion programmes, which always contain the possibility of conflict and genuine anger.

But above all, security is found in the family serials, like *The Grove Family*, discussed on p. 156. Among girls and the 10–11 year olds the appeal of this programme was especially strong. Children's written answers to a question asking what they liked about the programme stressed the united character of the family (in spite of frequent squabbling), the family's ordinariness in the face of unusual adventures, and the predictability of each character's reactions. There was also a good deal of self-identification with younger members of the Grove family.[1]

A sense of security was also created by a quite different type of

---

[1] Children were asked which member of the family they liked best. The younger children in the serial were more often preferred by the younger children in the sample, and the older children more by the 13–14 year olds. Lenny (the younger boy) was more often a favourite of the boys, whilst Daphne (the younger girl) found her only following amongst the girls.

programme—the series *Dixon of Dock Green*, dealing with episodes in the life of a London policeman. All the main characters were ordinary and nice people, and there was stress on the triviality of much of their routine. The series was described by Celia, a 10 year old, socially rather isolated girl:

> It's a sort of little serial, if you know what I mean. Well, I can't give you much more to it, well, it was a nice programme, you know—a time to enjoy yourself, you know, to sit down and make yourself comfortable and watch it.

Lastly, television ownership can itself offer a sense of security. In one sense, television has created a gigantic club, of which all viewers are automatically members. A 13 year old boy wrote:

> I think it's a good thing to have a television in the house, because when you go to work or school, the people are always talking about the programmes, and it is not nice when you are the odd one out, and you don't know what the programmes are like.

The other members of the club are the television personalities themselves. The perpetually amiable personnel of television are everyone's uncles and aunts. They can offer children a refuge from the relationships of their everyday life—if this is what they desire—and also provide a reassuring sense of being surrounded by friendly people who are part of their own environment.

The appeal of satisfied curiosity

Television helps to satisfy children's desire to be in the know, to find out what really happens. They can watch Scotland Yard in action, see dress rehearsals in Drury Lane, wander round family mansions, mix with petty criminals in Soho and head-hunters in Sarawak.

Watching programmes of this type, children can feel part of the lives and events going on around them. They can also actively explore other social and geographical worlds, relationships and behaviour in culture patterns quite different from their own, as well as those just sufficiently different to be interesting. In this last sense the suburban household of *The Grove Family* may satisfy as much curiosity as the lives of cowboys or Eskimoes. One child, for instance, liked the programme: 'because you are inside the house and can see what goes on'

But the romanticism of the exciting subject adds greatly to the interest of purely intellectual exploration. A 9 year old girl, for instance, enthusiastic about *Fabian of Scotland Yard*, preferred it to *Dixon of Dock Green* because it was not only intimately interesting but also romantic:

> Oh, it's nice. It's more like—more *police* thing. It's more—what would you call it?—more *crimey*. It's more *dangerous*. And it's nice because you don't have

lot of people and there isn't all this talking and friendly business. They get down to work, and you see them down in Scotland Yard . . . Fabian is more exciting (than *Dixon of Dock Green*). And (the police are) much differenter, because it's in the police station. (*Dixon of Dock Green*) isn't a great big Scotland Yard thing. This, this Fabian, it's down in all the big rooms where they go 'Calling', 'calling', 'over'. It's done in all the big rooms, and you can see them moving the flags where the areas are and where the accidents have been taken, and all the *working out* and stuff, and all the *finger prints*. And I think it's (pause) more *nicer*.

The mothers' diaries provided examples of television satisfying and inspiring curiosity in children of very different ages. A 9 year old boy, for instance, watching the *Royal Tournament*:

He talked excitedly through most of the programme. Thought it was the best show of the year—lots of variety in it. He discussed last year's tournament with Richard, his friend. Decided he liked seeing the scaling of the cliffs and putting the jeep together best. He was very interested in the bands' leopard skins. Got up and started marching like a band. Asked how long the arena was. Said he would like to ride on one of the gun carriages. Asked what a chasm was—and lots more . . .

The main survey results gave evidence of the ultimate confidence that children place in television, *vis-à-vis* the other mass media. They were asked to rank the media according to a number of criteria, including *Which tells you what things are really like?* Among the viewers, television emerged as an easy winner over the other mass media—books, newspapers, comics, cinema and radio.

The appeal of action and constant change

For younger children especially, one of television's biggest pleasures lies in the excitement of action and constant change. Only as children grow older do they become equally interested in what is said, in the implications of the action as much as in the action itself.

Television offers action both in the ordinary sense and in a way that is individual to broadcasting: an evening's television represents a succession of different programmes each constituting a change from the previous one. For children this constant change is as important a means of maintaining interest as the lure of dramatic adventure and physical movement.

Children's interest in action (rather than in the development of character or ideas) emerged clearly in personal interviews in which they were asked to describe certain programmes they had seen. These 9–10 year olds tended to give episodic accounts, with little concern for the causal links and with little interest in why things were said or done. The characters tended to be used as pegs on which to hang the action.

A similar picture emerged in children's attitude to comedy and jokes; slapstick and comedy of action appealed to pre-adolescent children, but the jokes themselves were often seen as boring. 'Sometimes they're hard', said an intelligent 10 year old, 'you can't really understand them very well.' And another girl of the same age liked variety programmes, but qualified:

> . . . *some* programmes, you get so *bored*. Some of these funny men! They try to make jokes, and they *don't* make you laugh.

Many intelligent adults would agree with this verdict. Moreover, to perceive the humorous implications of a verbal joke may demand a capacity for abstraction which children cannot manage; in addition, of course, many jokes depend on a knowledge of topical events with which children would be unfamiliar. When ninety London school children aged between 9 and 13 were presented with three jokes taken from current variety programmes and asked to say why they were funny, we found only a minority of 9–11 year olds who were able to give reasonably correct explanations (Table 24).

TABLE 24. Percentage of viewers who gave reasonably correct answers to these jokes taken from current variety programmes

	9–11 YEAR OLDS %	12–13 YEAR OLDS %
(a) A flying machine landed in America. A door opened and a Martian came out. He went up to a petrol pump and said: 'Take me to your leader.'	17	58
(b) This machine saves a lot of time. It does the work of one man, and takes ten men to run it	29	67
(c) The cost of living is terrible. We've bought a new suite of furniture and have just finished paying off the instalments on the deposit	13	33
Total cases	38	52

At the age of 10, children prefer action to talk. Observation of young children watching Westerns showed a drastic drop in interest during the talking parts, but interest revived as soon as action sequences appeared.[1]

Linked to the appeal of action is the interest born of tension and excitement. This, of course, is important to all ages, although the ability to stand tension increases with age, and is likely to be weaker for the more insecure child. There is no point in offering examples of this appeal—it is an obvious feature of very many programmes, including not only plays but also panel games and quizzes, discussions and even variety. The fear that arises when tension oversteps the bounds of what the child can tolerate is discussed in Chapter 15.

[1] One experiment in a cinema club produced the startling conclusion that the children themselves made too much noise even to hear the dialogue.

The appeal of infringed conventions

Finally, television offers the appeal of defiance. Many programmes (through self-identification) offer children enjoyment of momentary infringement of the conventions by which they are normally bound. This is safely enjoyable because it is vicarious, because the whole audience shares in the responsibility and also because the infringement is disguised—either as innuendo or else as play-acting and make-believe. The audience is offered the best of both worlds: non-conformity secure within the safe trappings of conformity.

One social and moral convention frequently infringed by television, is the principle of non-aggression. *Physical aggression* is enjoyed in variety, Westerns, and detective programmes. The point at which its portrayal arouses unease rather than enjoyment is discussed in Chapters 15 and 16.

Verbal aggression is part of the stock-in-trade of discussions and panel games. For example, the panelist Gilbert Harding's appeal has been built on the fascination of rudeness. His verbal aggression is rendered legitimate by the absence of reprisal; it arouses ambivalence, however, because it is unexpected and cuts across conventions. To some children, his aggressive comments cause uneasiness rather than pleasure. Here, for example, is the comment of Joan, herself a rather aggressive child:

> Well, I don't like him. Some people like him, I think he's horrible. He's such a—well, people seem to think he's got humour, and *I* don't think he has. *I* don't think he's in the least bit funny. Well, he *is* funny, but he never *laughs*, to show people that he can laugh—he's always *serious*. And he's always *rude* to some people. I think he's very rude. And he's just horrible. I don't *like* him. Everybody claps when he comes on, but I think he's absolutely disgusting. He's absolutely born to disgust me. I hate him.

Joan rather overstates her case; it seems unlikely that her fury of resentment against Gilbert Harding does not conceal some element of fascination, alongside the uneasiness he causes her. He offers the satisfaction of vicarious aggression, but at the same time angers her by virtue of her own response to it.

As we shall show in Chapter 15, verbal aggression in plays and discussions often proved more disturbing to the child than physical acts of aggression. Only when verbal aggression is light-heartedly offered, as in variety back-chat, can it be enjoyed wholeheartedly.

There is also infringement of the convention that adults (and particularly parents) must be respected, obeyed, and regarded as generally in the right. Many television programmes show children scoring off adults: proving them on minor issues to be wrong, bringing them (in the case of the child-sleuths and criminals) to justice, being cheeky to them, and generally reversing the usual pattern of adult and child relations.

Such programmes are mostly confined to children's television, especially to plays in which children take the part of detectives and track criminals to justice. In such cases the child characters get the best of adults in both morals and cunning. For the child audience the satisfaction is likely to be great and the effects harmless: the presentation is recognisably play-acting, and the adult victims are firmly stamped as social outcasts.

In *The Grove Family* also the adults are occasionally shown in an unfavourable light. In particular, 'Gran' (by siding with the children against the parents) can help to put the parents to a disadvantage. 'Gran's' role is that of a grown-up child; the parents have two generations in league against them.

There is also the type of programme where adults appear without children, but in a foolish and ineffectual light. This only proves satisfactory for children if it need not be taken seriously—as in comedy and variety programmes. There adults are seen making fools of themselves, losing face and suffering comic humiliation, and the child is offered the chance to laugh at them. The light-hearted treatment allows him to do so without conflict.

Finally, children find satisfaction in hinted infringement of the social taboos, in hints at the outrageous—implying what is conventionally left unsaid. There is, of course, a great deal of this on television, mostly in variety programmes and the more light-hearted panel games. The satisfaction for all age groups is immense, the more so as it is masked by innuendo and sanctioned as a joke.

THE APPEAL OF TELEVISION PERSONALITIES

Much of the appeal of television lies in its personalities. Plays apart, television characteristically introduces and gives prominence to personalities as themselves and not as actors playing a fictional part. The panelist Gilbert Harding appears in the role of Gilbert Harding, the comedian Benny Hill as Benny Hill. On the stage or cinema screen, in contrast, the actor, by assuming the personality of a different character, creates a barrier between his audience and himself.

Also conducive to personality interest is the manner of presentation adopted on television, with its emphasis on intimacy and casualness. One symptom of this is the frequent use of Christian names, intended to produce a sense of easy equality between viewers and performers.

Television personalities appear on the screen at no more than life-size, at conversational distance, and within the family context. As a result they are likely to seem more human and ordinary than film stars.

Something of these differences emerged from the children's completion of the following two sentences:[1]

A good TV actor or actress is one who . ..
A good film star is one who . . .

In both cases the single most frequent response stressed acting ability—the obvious answer that the question invited. But this obvious answer was given far less often in relation to the television actor than in relation to the film star. Altogether, children's perceptions of these two types of actors differed in that film actors were seen principally in terms of their acting ability and looks, while in the case of television actors stress was also laid on keenness and hard work, the need to remember their lines, and to take their part seriously. In addition, the younger children stressed the personality qualities demanded of a television actor ('makes people listen', 'holds interest', 'has personality'), while the older children (especially the grammar school girls) stressed the need for realistic and natural acting.

TABLE 25. *A good TV actor or actress is one who . . .*
A good film star is one who. . . .

	Television actor or actress		A good film star	
	13–14 YEAR OLDS %	10–11 YEAR OLDS %	13–14 YEAR OLDS %	10–11 YEAR OLDS %
Good acting, versatile. Good acting generally. Speaks well, good acting technique	37	37	66	57
Realistic, lifelike, natural, makes you feel you are there, emphasis on naturalness of acting	22	6	8	7
Works hard, keen, interested in the job, remembers lines, takes it seriously .	15	15	7	9
Has personality, makes people listen, holds interest, puts it over, confidence	12	15	14	5
Good looks, good expression, good figure, pretty, attractive . .	8	5	22	12
Stress on character qualities, e.g is nice, pleasing, does not show off, is kind, amusing	7	6	9	7
Miscellaneous	12	17	4	7
No answer, don't know . . .	11	14	6	10
Total cases (weighted) . . .	540	540	480	480

NOTE. The figures add up to more than 100 per cent since some of the children gave more than one type of answer.

[1] The sentences were given in two separate questionnaires.

In other words, there is a tendency to think of the television actor in terms of the ordinariness of the parts he plays; and to think of him also with his feet firmly on the ground in that he does not simply act well, but must work hard at acting. He is more like other people than the film star. The cinema is essentially a purveyor of fantasy, its stars regarded as superlative beings.

In contrast, comparable questions on radio and film personalities showed that the children liked *radio* personalities most of all because they are funny or amusing.

Types of television personalities

It is possible to classify television personalities into three categories: first, personalities appearing as themselves (a category exclusive to the broadcasting medium)—the announcers, commentators, panelists, and visiting experts. Secondly, there are those with a role to play which heavily colours their personality—the variety artists, comedians, singers, and musicians. Thirdly, there are the actors, whose personalities are usually entirely submerged in the character or part they play.

Something of the relative popularity of these three types of television personalities can be judged by children's answers to the question: *Of all the people on television that you have heard about or seen, whom do you like best?*

The form of this question, by asking about 'people', tended to make mention of fictional characters less likely. The most interesting aspect of these results, therefore, lies in the relative frequency with which persons appearing on television in their own right were mentioned, compared with the comedians, singers, and musicians, whose personality (as shown on television) would be much coloured by their role. The older children more often chose announcers and panelists, whilst the younger children put slightly more stress on comedians and characters from plays. This preference ties up well with the interest in action that is characteristic of children of that age.

Intelligence and social class made little difference to children's susceptibility to the appeal of different types of personalities. There were, however, differences between the tastes of boys and girls: boys were the more interested in comedians, girls in panelists and singers; but both tended to give as their favourite a member of their own sex, one possible indication of the self-identification factor running through preferences. In all this, it is difficult to disentangle the appeal of personalities from that of the programmes in which they feature; the two sets of preferences coincide closely, each helping to determine the other:

TABLE 26. *Of all the people on television that you have heard about or seen, whom do you like best?*

	13–14 YEAR OLDS			10–11 YEAR OLDS		
	All %	Boys %	Girls %	All %	Boys %	Girls %
Personalities appearing as themselves:						
Panelists	15	11	18	6	3	8
Announcers, commentators, interviewers, sporting personalities . . .	14	12	15	5	6	4
Experts	1	1	—	2	3	2
Wilfred Pickles* . . .	13	16	11	13	9	16
Total	43	40	44	26	21	30
Personalities playing a role:						
Comedians . . .	18	23	14	23	28	17
Singers and musicians .	8	3	10	8	3	12
Total	26	26	24	31	31	29
Actors, actresses, characters in plays:						
Characters . . .	4	3	6	10	11	8
Actors, actresses . . .	5	1	8	2	—	5
Puppets	—	—	—	3	3	2
Total	9	4	14	15	14	15
Other answers . . .	2	5	—	—	1	—
No answer, don't know .	20	25	18	28	33	26
Total cases (weighted) .	540	540	270	270	270	270

* Wilfred Pickles appeared a good deal on both sound radio and television, specialising in human interest programmes in which he would chat humorously with ordinary people. Difficult to classify, he was half comedian, half compère.

The interviews we conducted showed clearly how much television personalities meant to children. However, there were so few clear-cut favourites that their appeal would seem to be largely a composite one, residing not so much in certain individuals as in the whole range of personalities. Even the most popular personality, Wilfred Pickles, was mentioned by no more than 13 per cent of either age group. Here are the seven most popular television personalities:[1]

	13–14 YEAR OLDS %	10–11 YEAR OLDS %
Wilfred Pickles (human interest requests) .	13	13
Benny Hill (comedian) . . .	6	6
Arthur Askey (comedian) . . .	3	3
Bruce Seton (*Fabian of Scotland Yard*) .	2	5
Ruby Murray (singer)	2	3
Macdonald Hobley (announcer and compère) .	4	1
Gilbert Harding (panel member) . .	3	1

[1] Since the popularity of performers depended partly on the type of programmes shown at the time of the survey, the importance of the results should not be over-emphasised. However, they do broadly reflect the children's taste pattern.

Why should Wilfred Pickles be chosen more frequently than other personalities? We suggest that it is in part due to the role that his programme requires of him—that of granter of favours; and in part to an admixture of role and *persona*, being kind, warm-hearted, and jocular. He seems to be Father Xmas and the Yorkshire uncle rolled into one.

In children's reasons for liking Pickles, two themes tended to reoccur: that he is kind and helps people, and that he is happy:

> He would do anything in his power to help people, and to make them happy.
> He is so happy and he never grumbles.
> He is so nice and kind-hearted.

It is clearly impossible to predict what type of person will become a favourite with children, since even Wilfred Pickles appealed strongly to only a small minority of children. Moreover, it is worth noting that none of the favourite personalities most frequently mentioned were drawn exclusively from programmes designed for children. As a result, there would seem to be an opportunity for experimenting with a range of personalities, especially in the children's programmes.

We used the opportunity of the re-test in Norwich to investigate further the problem of the perception of television personalities. This time we presented the children with a number of personality profiles, asking them to think of persons on television who fitted each description:

> Here are some descriptions of different types of people whom you often see on television. We would like to know which people on television you think of when you read each of these descriptions—which persons fit them best.[1]
>
> This is a person on television who always means what he says, someone you can really believe.
> This is a very well-educated television person, to whom you can look up.
> This is a television person who is very like someone in your family, or someone living in your street.
> This is a person on television whom you would like to have as a friend.
> This is a television person with very good manners.
> This is a very good-hearted television person.
> This is a television person whom you feel you know really well.

The single, most popular individual, on these ratings, was Eamonn Andrews—the easy-mannered compère who appeared a good deal at that time, not only in the adult panel game *What's My Line* but also in children's programmes. One child in six chose him as the person they felt they knew really well. He was *not*, however, chosen as 'like someone in the family'—two children in five could think of no one to

---

[1] Only the answers of the 11–12 year olds are considered here, as only a small proportion of the older Norwich children were asked the questions.

fit this category, and those who succeeded in finding someone for it thought mainly of members of the Grove family or of comedians. Wilfred Pickles, together again with the comedians, scored as 'good-hearted' (rather than as someone they knew well; his role had placed him on a different plane). And the panelists, especially Isobel Barnett (the titled panel member on *What's My Line*), tended to feature as 'an educated person to whom you can look up'.

The Grove Family aims at depicting the life of an average family—how well it has succeeded can be seen from the fact that members of the Grove family were most often mentioned as 'like someone in the family', or potential personal friends. Here the fictional role of the television personality had become very real to children.

As a group, the comedians emerged as most popular of all (this was among younger children); they were chosen particularly as friendly equals ('a person you would like to have as a friend'), as good-hearted, as someone whom the child felt he knew really well, and as ordinary ('like someone in your family, or living in your street'). The announcers and commentators, in contrast, were less often chosen, and emerged with a very different profile. Their role tended to invest them with rather colder and remoter qualities: they were seen as well-mannered, as people to be trusted and believed, and as educated; even though they are constantly seen on the screen, few children thought of them as people they knew really well.

Here are the seven profiles, arranged in the order in which comedians and announcers were each associated with them. (Panelists showed a very similar pattern to announcers.) The interest of the lists lies in their contrasting orders:

Comedians

A very good-hearted person.
A person you would like to have as a friend.
The person you feel you know really well.
Like someone in your family, or living in your street.
A person who always means what he says, that you can believe.
A person with very good manners.
An educated person to whom you can look up.

Announcers, news-readers, commentators

A person with very good manners.
A person who always means what he says, that you can believe.
An educated person to whom you can look up.
The person you feel you know really well.
A person you would like to have as a friend.
A very good-hearted person.
Like someone in your family, or living in your street.

Generally, we can do no more than roughly sketch in some of the children's attitudes to and perception of television personalities. But our findings do at least raise a number of queries to which answers would be useful: the importance, for instance, of intimacy appeal, of model value, realism, role playing contrasted with appearing as oneself, and the extent to which aspects of a character cling to an actor's personality as perceived by children.

PART IV

Reactions to Conflict, Crime, and Violence on Television

13

Outline of the Content of Television Programmes

FROM the findings presented so far, we have learned four things about the children's tastes. First, they were so varied that even the most favoured programme received only 30 per cent of the votes. Second, from the age of 10 (and we suspect even earlier) children preferred adult programmes to those specifically designed for them. Third, children with access to both channels more often watched ITV rather than BBC. Fourth, that supply affected taste; it lies, to some measure, within the power of television to broaden or narrow children's taste, to make it more, or less, mature.

What, then, does television offer? What are the elements making up television entertainment? In the chapters that follow we shall describe the themes, values, and characterisation contained in several principal and popular types of programme: adult plays, Westerns, and crime and detective programmes. But first, we need to look at both children's and adult television in broad outline, to see what proportion of time was devoted to different types of programme. It is argued (55) that the impact of television is cumulative. The number of programmes shown of a given type, therefore, needs to be taken into consideration in evaluating its effects; consequently we tried to find out, among other things, how many and what types of plays children could see on television, and how much information, and of what type, was available to them.

In looking at evening television, a distinction was made between programmes that children of 10–11 and 13–14 would be able to see before going to bed, and those which occurred after their bedtime.[1] This content analysis, which was carried out in the course of 1956, included both ITV and BBC programmes.[2] ITV was represented here by the two programme companies which transmit in London (Associated-Rediffusion from Mondays to Fridays, and Associated-Television on Saturdays and Sundays).[3]

Since the pattern of television programmes changes over time, we carried out a *trend* analysis by examining the monthly programme patterns of the two channels, first in February 1956 (when ITV was still relatively new) and then again in November 1956. By this time, ITV had developed its own characteristic style and the BBC, too, had adjusted itself to its competitor. For some analyses, July was included as an intermediate month, also as being representative of summer television.

CHILDREN'S TELEVISION

BBC *Children's Television* and ITV *Children's Hour* were on the air between 5 and 6 p.m. each day. The programmes were divided into four broad categories:

1. Plays (the largest single group).
2. Other entertainment programmes (including variety, light music, and quiz programmes).
3. Information programmes (including newsreel).

[1] The diaries had shown that few children viewed before 5 p.m. and that the majority of 10–11 year olds had gone to bed by 9.30 p.m. on week-days and by 10 p.m. on Saturdays. The times for the 13–14 year olds were 10 and 10.30 p.m. respectively.

[2] Although the main survey and the Norwich study had been confined to BBC programmes, we decided to include ITV in the content analyses so as to give a more representative picture of television entertainment today.

[3] In view of the frequent exchange of programmes between commercial television companies, the programme content of these two companies was probably fairly representative at that time of commercial television as a whole. Within the common pattern, each company has, of course, its distinctive programme balance, interests, and production techniques.

4. Puppet shows and stories with animated drawings, and other programmes aimed at the younger viewers.

Appendix Table 18 gives the number of hours per week devoted to each of these four main types of programme for February, July, and November. In February the BBC gave about a third of its time to plays, a third to information, and the remainder to different forms of light entertainment. In the same period, ITV allotted half its time to plays and one-fifth of its time to information.

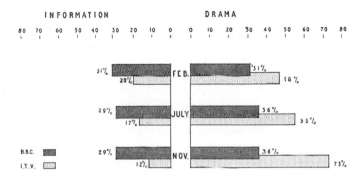

FIG. 6. Proportion of weekly time devoted by BBC and ITV children's television to information and drama. The figure presents the proportions for February, July, and November 1956

By November 1956 the picture had dramatically changed—ITV devoted three-quarters of its time to plays and no more than one-tenth to information programmes; it was no longer offering a varied set of programmes to the children. In the same period, BBC children's television had undergone little change (Fig. 6).

Children's plays

The true nature of this allocation of time is disclosed when these percentages are translated into the number and type of plays offered in one month. In September, October, and November 1956 we found that, on an average, the BBC showed twenty-three and ITV forty-nine plays for children per month. Adventure plays were the type most frequently shown on both channels. The proportion for ITV was surprisingly high (96 per cent); the majority of the adventure plays were Westerns and animal adventure series produced in America. Of BBC children's plays, some 74 per cent dealt with adventure, but these plays less often formed part of an American series. Fig. 7 gives the proportion of Westerns and other adventure plays shown by the two channels on children's television.

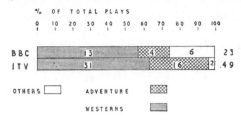

FIG. 7. Percentage of different types of plays shown per month (Sept.–Nov. 1956) on BBC and ITV children's television. The figures inside the bars indicate the actual number of plays

Children's information programmes

The BBC children's television information programmes[1] occupied almost as much time as plays. Not only did the BBC devote about twice as much time to these programmes compared with ITV, but the two channels differed also in the diversity and type of subject-matter covered. The detailed picture is presented in Appendix Table 19. During the period from September to November 1956, BBC information programmes gave more prominence, in particular, to 'doing and making' programmes (13 per cent of information time); to history and archaeology (5 per cent of information time); and to describing the way of life of people in other countries and in various walks of life (29 per cent of information time).

A child viewing BBC children's programmes, then, during the period we studied, could see about two hours of information programmes a week covering a fairly wide range of topics. Once or twice a week he could learn something about nature and animals. Once a week there was generally a newsreel and at least one feature about life in other countries, another on careers, or a general quiz. From time to time there would be history and archaeology programmes and occasionally some sports coaching or science.

The child, looking at ITV only, would see about as many animal programmes, dealing more specifically with domestic and zoo animals, and could learn something about the care of animals. Each week there would be a very short newsreel and one other information programme (at the time we were investigating it was giving a series of programmes on outer space (*Space Club*)), as well as fairly regular sports coaching. Every other week there would be a programme on gardening, and occasionally a book review.

---

[1] For this analysis we drew on two three-month periods, May to July, and September to November 1956. In defining information (as widely as possible) we excluded only programmes meant primarily to entertain. A child, as we shall see later, learns a lot from drama, also from quiz programmes, which are an important feature of children's variety shows. But for practical reasons we had to draw a line somewhere. This meant leaving out all 'give-away' programmes, children's variety shows, and also the semi-documentary type of plays.

EVENING TELEVISION

What types of programme could these two groups of children view? In a week, *a 10–11 year old*, watching continuously from the beginning of evening transmission until his bedtime, could get thirty minutes of information a week if he watched ITV exclusively, and around ninety minutes if he watched BBC. The ITV viewer, compared with the viewer of BBC programmes, would see less sport and hear less serious music, and instead watch more drama, light music, film news, and 'give-away' programmes.

A 13–14 year old could see on ITV more plays, variety, and films compared with the younger child; if he watched BBC he could gain an extra hour of information programmes. The distribution of different types of programme is given in Appendix Table 20.

In adult television, as distinct from children's television, the difference in style between ITV and BBC emerged as early as February 1956. There was only one important subsequent change—the introduction of American-type 'give-away' programmes. These were put on four or five times a week fairly early in the evening, each programme lasting thirty minutes.

Adult information programmes

Appendix Table 21 shows that adult information programmes differed considerably in content as between the two channels. Principally, however, they differed in the times at which they were shown. BBC information programmes were spread more or less evenly over the whole evening, while on ITV they occurred mainly after peak viewing hours (well after the children went to bed). Before bedtime, the children who watched BBC could see programmes about people from foreign countries, and about the Commonwealth and industry. Those who watched ITV could only see a very short news programme and about one or two programmes a week on current affairs such as *This Week*.

The children missed many programmes which they might have enjoyed. For example, some of the early afternoon programmes for women which contained information, and 'doing and making' programmes, would have been of considerable interest to teen-agers. The children also missed the ITV science programmes, all of which were put on after 10 p.m.[1]

---

[1] There was a welcome small increase in ITV evening information programmes between the early summer and the winter of 1956: the diet became more varied, with more emphasis on foreign countries and current affairs—it hardly affected the children, however, since most of these programmes were still shown after 10.30 p.m.

Those watching BBC missed almost all art programmes, nearly two-thirds of the science and medicine programmes, and almost half the programmes dealing with industry and economics, because they occurred after their bedtimes. Appendix Table 22 lists the proportion of information programmes which were shown after the children had gone to bed.

Adult plays

ITV showed some eighty-four plays a month, the BBC forty-eight. Both channels devoted approximately one-fifth of their drama time to crime and detective series. For the remainder, BBC gave more time to comedy and problem plays, ITV to adventure. Indeed, on cursory inspection, it seems as if ITV considered the tastes of adult audiences to be very similar to those of teen-agers. Table 27 gives the distribution of different types of plays shown during six months of 1956, and a schedule of a typical week's drama on BBC and ITV is presented in Appendix Table 23.

TABLE 27. Distribution of different types of plays shown on evening television by BBC and ITV during the two three-month periods in 1956.

	BBC		ITV	
	May–July	September–November	May–July	September–November
Subject:	%	%	%	%
Comedies	30	30	22	22
Problem plays . . .	29	30	19	22
Family serials . . .	4	3	5	—
Crime and detection .	19	21	28	18
Swashbuckling adventure .	—	—	9	9
Westerns . . .	3	1	5	6
Adventure	3	4	4	16
Others	12	11	8	7

Before his bedtime, and in addition to the children's plays, an older child could view about 80 per cent of all adult plays shown, and the younger child over 70 per cent. If he decided to watch ITV only, he could see 15–17 plays a week dealing with crime and adventure alone.[1]

How representative are these findings of television entertainment today?

We could not carry out another extensive content analysis, but were able to do a spot check on one aspect of television entertainment which has been causing concern, namely, the frequency with

---

[1] Of necessity, the shorter plays, characteristic of ITV, have simpler plots, more stereotyped themes and characterisation than the longer plays more characteristic of the BBC.

which adventure and crime programmes were shown at times when children are likely to view.

The number of plays which dealt with law-breaking and retribution shown between the hours of 5 p.m. and 9 p.m. during the week 11–17 May 1958 was listed. Table 28 gives the weekly schedule.

TABLE 28. Crime and violence programmes shown on ITV and BBC in the week 11–17 May 1958, between 5 p.m. and 9 p.m.

	p.m.	ITV Programme	BBC Programme	Country of origin
Sunday:	5.10	Robin Hood	—	U.K.
Monday:	7.00	Sheriff of Cochise (W)	—	U.S.A.
	7.30	Shadow Squad	—	U.K.
	8.00	Wagon Train (W)	—	U.S.A.
Tuesday:	7.00	Ivanhoe	—	U.K.
Wednesday:	5.25	The Adventures of Long John Silver	—	Australia
	7.30	Boyd, Q.C.	—	U.K.
Thursday:	5.00	—	Wells Fargo (W)	U.S.A.
	7.00	Assignment Foreign Legion	—	U.S.A.
	7.30	Shadow Squad	—	U.K.
Friday:	5.25	Cisco Kid (W)	—	U.S.A.
	7.00	Mr. District Attorney	—	U.S.A.
Saturday:	5.00	—	Lone Ranger (W, R)	U.S.A.
	6.30	Sword of Freedom	—	U.K.
	7.00	Cheyenne (W)	Wells Fargo (W)	U.S.A.
	7.30	—	Duty Bound	U.K.
	8.00	Truth about Melandrinos	—	U.K.

(W) denotes Western, (R) repeat.

NOTE. All programmes lasted 30 minutes except *Wagon Train* (60 minutes).

It will be seen that eighteen such programmes were shown, seventeen of which could be seen by one person, with judicious switching from channel to channel.

In grouping these programmes we do not wish to imply that the differences between them were not important, for example violence features little in some, a great deal in others. However, despite all their differences, these programmes dealt with the same main theme —transgressions against the law and the tracking down and capture of the wrongdoers by wits, determination, or force. The week selected was by no means atypical since each programme formed part of a series.

A child confined to BBC transmissions could see four of these programmes, two of them children's Westerns of which one was repeated in the evening. A child who watched nothing but ITV could see fourteen such programmes, including two children's Westerns and three adventure series (*Robin Hood, Ivanhoe, The Sword of Freedom*); the remaining nine were either adult Westerns or crime, detective, or adventure series designed for adult tastes.

On the other hand, ITV's children's programmes have become considerably more varied than they were in 1956. They contain more information programmes and fewer adventure series. The proportion of plays has been reduced to about 50 per cent.

COMPARISON WITH AMERICAN TELEVISION

We had occasion to carry out two comparisons with American television. We compared the number and amount of time spent on plays featuring violence and aggression at times when children are likely to view, and also the proportion of time which was devoted to plays on children's television.

Amount of adventure and crime programmes shown

The proportion of time devoted to programmes featuring violence and aggression during children's peak viewing hours (5–9 p.m.) was found to be approximately 20 per cent in this country and the same in the United States.[1]

Comparing the figures obtained here in 1956 with those for New York television in 1953 (85), the proportion of time on children's television devoted to plays was lower for BBC and higher for ITV, compared with New York television. New York television gave 57 per cent of the time on children's television to plays, the BBC 35 per cent, and ITV 73 per cent.[2] It would seem, therefore, that the ITV's very high allocation of time to plays is not the inevitable consequence of having commercial television, since New York television has seven commercial stations competing for audiences and is therefore in a much more highly competitive situation than ITV in this country. Such allocation is more likely the necessary consequence of having to fill a daily hour of transmission with a small staff; filmed plays bought in series are clearly of great advantage here. In 1958 the reduction of the number of plays on ITV brings its percentage to a little below that quoted for New York television.

[1] The figures for the United States were computed from figures given in a report on television and juvenile delinquency published in 1956 by the United States Senate Sub-committee under the chairmanship of Senator Kefauver. It provides detailed monitoring charts of programmes of all television stations in Washington during one week in September 1954; figures which are similar to those obtained in other cities in the United States (53).

[2] The figures for BBC and ITV are taken from our 1956 November analysis.

IMPLICATIONS

This analysis has brought to light a number of important points. First, children with access to both channels, viewing up to their bedtime, could see some twenty-five plays a week, approximately sixteen of these being plays featuring violence and aggression.[1]

Second, the number of information programmes children are likely to see are on the decrease, because such programmes (put on either by BBC or ITV) are often shown concurrently with plays on the other channel which prove ready winners.

Third, the range of programme-content on ITV—to judge from the content analysis in 1956—has become more uniform and narrower than when it first began. This trend towards greater uniformity was particularly noticeable in children's television. Assessment of the merits or demerits of a particular type of programme must inevitably depend on the frequency with which it and other similar programme types are shown. One wonders here whether the Children's Advisory Committee set up under the Charter of the Independent Television Authority could not play an active part here—an essential prerequisite for which would be repeated content analyses of the kind outlined here.

Findings reported in Chapter 8 have clearly shown that children see a great deal of evening television. Here we have indicated the type of programmes they are likely to see. This raises the question as to how far programme planners of evening television should take this fact into account and also how far it should affect the planning of children's television programmes. Taking the second point first, it would seem to us that the producers of children's television should recognise the fact that in addition to whatever is put on between 5-6 p.m., the children will in any case see some eight or ten plays, designed for adults, which deal with violence and aggression. Perhaps, therefore, children's television should aim more than it does at present (in particular ITV) at putting on programmes dealing with other themes.

How to deal with the big child audience on evening television is a difficult question. We do not, of course, wish to suggest that all evening programmes should be geared to the maturity and needs of children. Much of it, anyway, can hardly be said to be above the intellectual level of a 13–14 year old; it is rather that the large number of plays with an emphasis on violence and on adult problems may not be suitable for children. Perhaps such programmes could be spread more uniformly over the entire evening or be placed in the

---

[1] It is not suggested, of course, that any child would actually exercise such a choice.

later part of the evening. This whole question of the extent to which the needs of children should influence the programme balance of evening television is a very difficult one. It is unrealistic to suggest that any such planning must be solely the responsibility of the parents (through the control of their children's viewing). Such control is very difficult if, as is often the case, the television set is in the only living-room, and the age range to be catered for in any one family is a very wide one. Moreover, the title of the play does not indicate whether it is or is not suitable for children. In the case of films, control is partially taken out of the hands of the parents, since 'X' certificates make it illegal for children to see the films whether accompanied by an adult or not. Inevitably, some responsibility in the case of television must remain with the programme planners, just as some vetting of films takes place before children can gain access to them. The present system of warning parents at the beginning of a programme that a play is not suitable for children is not effective, to judge from the many children in our survey who had seen the whole of such programmes. Parents often miss opening announcements through switching on late, and, if children hear the warning without any adult present, they are hardly likely to stop viewing on that account!

In this discussion more attention has been paid to ITV than to BBC, largely because the majority of children tend to watch ITV rather than BBC.

In part what we offer the children today will determine what they will expect and demand to see as adults. We have indicated the diet on which they are fed

Content of Westerns, Crime and Detective Series

WE made a special study of the themes, values, and characterisations contained in the 'crime does not pay' and 'whodunit' programmes. In view of the concern expressed about them, a special Senate Sub-committee on Juvenile Delinquency and Television in the United States had inquired earlier 'whether there is a causal relationship between repeated exposure to crime and violence and overt delinquent action of today's youth' (53). It reported that it could not obtain conclusive evidence about the lasting effects of these programmes. We hope that a more systematic content analysis of the way in which aggression, law, and the characterisation of the criminal are handled in these programmes might help to formulate more precise hypotheses about their likely effects.

A proper content analysis[1] involves the systematic inspection and description of the content of a communication, using clearly defined criteria so that another research worker repeating the study could arrive at similar results. Such an approach can be purely quantitative, like the one adopted by Smythe (85); he monitored all programmes put out in New York City during one week and found that as many as 7,065 acts or threats of violence were perpetrated.[2] In this quantitative analysis all incidents are treated as psychologically similar, which is clearly not the case. A similar count of British television programmes, we felt, would not help us to understand much about the effects unless we could relate these acts to the setting in which they occurred. We therefore adopted a qualitative approach—

---

[1] Berelson, in his book *Content Analysis in Communication Research*, defines content as 'that body of meanings through symbols (verbal, musical, pictorial, plastic, gestural) which makes up the communication itself' (12).

[2] On behalf of the National Association of Educational Broadcasters, Smythe and his research team monitored programmes of various American cities for one week every year, beginning in 1951. In New York only the study was done for four years running (84, 85, 86). In some cities this involved monitoring a number of channels; in others as, for example, in New Haven, only one.

one which would assess the way violence was presented, the production techniques that were used, and the extent to which the personalites of the heroes and villains and their motives were defined.

The content analysis for this inquiry was carried out by members of the research team, two viewing each programme. They made what notes they could at the time and, immediately after the programme, wrote down a short account of the themes and impressions conveyed. They then completed five schedules for each programme about the setting, theme, values, personalities, and the handling of violence.[1]

The technique of content analysis which we have developed and the schedules used are described in Appendix D.

The comparative analysis of children's Westerns, crime and detective series

The plays were drawn at random from those shown on BBC and ITV television during February and March 1956. Ten Westerns and ten crime and detective programmes were monitored.[2] All but two of the Westerns had appeared on children's television, so that the picture presented here is not so much of Westerns in general, as of Westerns designed for children.

THE WESTERNS

Children's Westerns are characterised by the extreme simplicity of their plot, by not developing complex motivation, by the black-and-white presentation of hero and villain, by the stylised presentation of violence, and by their unvarying endings. The children's Western presents a simple, uncomplicated struggle between good and bad. The bad motive is economic and personal gain—but it hardly matters whether for money, oil, cattle, or political control, since the consequences of gain are never differentiated. The good motive is the desire to uphold the law. In Westerns, men or 'sides' (sharply contrasted in character but near-equal in resources of physical strength, wits, and determination) are pitted against each other. In the final struggle the good defeats the bad.

---

[1] For the development of the schedules we drew especially on Smythe's studies of New York television in 1953 (85), on Head's analysis of some thirty-nine television plays (39), and on the value analysis by White (101).

[2] The ten Westerns comprised: two episodes from *Gun Law*, three episodes from *Hopalong Cassidy*, and one episode each from *Roy Rogers*, *Eddie Dean*, *The Lone Ranger*, *Cisco Kid*, and *Gene Autry*.

Characterisation and setting

The characteristics of the heroes, the hero's henchmen, and the villains are presented in Table 29.

TABLE 29. Range of characteristics of heroes, henchmen, and villains, taken from eight children's television Westerns

(Range over five-point scale)

Personality characteristics:	Hero	Henchman	Villain
Just–unjust . . .	1	—	4–5
Kind–unkind . . .	1–2	1–3	4–5
Assured–insecure . .	1	—	2–5
Polite–impolite . . .	1–2	1–3	4–5
Satisfied–dissatisfied . .	1	—	2–5
Honest–dishonest . .	1	2–3	5
Selfless–selfish . . .	1–2	—	5
Strong–weak character .	1–2	4–5	2–4
Warm-hearted–callous .	1–2	1–2	4–5
Happy–unhappy . .	1–2	1–2	4
Humorous–dour . .	2–4	1–2	3–5
Sane–neurotic/insane . .	1–2	2–4	2–4
Strong–weak (physically) .	1	2–5	1–5
Gentle–violent (physically) .	3–4	3–5	3–5
Courageous–cowardly .	1–2	1–3	1–4
Enterprising–unenterprising	1–2	2–5	1–2
Ingenuous–cunning . .	1–4	2–4	3–5
Intelligent–stupid . .	1–2	2–4	1–4
Determined–feeble . .	1–2	2–4	1–2
Appearance and dress:	Hero	Henchman	Villain
Good-looking–ugly . .	2	3–4	2–4
Clean–dirty . . .	1–2	2–4	1–4
Tidy–untidy . . .	1–2	2–4	1–5

NOTE. The characteristics were rated on a five-point scale. Example of rating scale: 1 = very just, 2 = just, 3 = neither particularly just nor unjust, 4 = unjust, 5 = very unjust.

The hero is kind, assured, polite, selfless, strong-minded, sane, and merciful. He is essentially a stylised creation, even in appearance. But *the villain's* personality-characteristics and resources are less uniform than those of the hero; occasionally he may be weak or cowardly.

In both behaviour and outward appearance the heroes and villains betray their calling. Table 29 shows that as with character so with dress, the hero's appearance is more stereotyped in looks, cleanliness, and dress than that of the villain.

In dress, black and white are not used to denote respectively villainy and virtue: Hopalong Cassidy, for instance, wears all black. It is rather smartness in dress which reflects the hero's character; by contrast, the villain's appearance is drab and dirty.[1] The hero is

[1] The only hero with drab clothes is the Marshal in the adult Western *Gun Law*, but he differs also in several other respects from the cowboy heroes of children's Westerns.

always clean-shaven (and nearly always newly shaven); the villain is often moustached and scarred.

In manner, the hero is preoccupied with the serious business of life; calm and authoritative, he is a faultless horseman who carries his guns well. By contrast, the villain has shifty movements and a shifty manner.

Thus much of the characterisation in Westerns is expressed in *visual terms*; and what is said is almost incidental. This is why so many children get the gist of a Western even when, owing to their youth, or bad acoustics, they cannot understand most of what is being said.

In some Westerns a *henchman* is introduced for comic diversion. He acts as an extension of the hero by virtue of his unswerving loyalty. At the same time he is the hero's foil (Table 29). The hero is neither distrusting nor ignorant, but the henchman is both, not merely to enhance the hero's superiority but also to provide through his questions a formal exposition of what is going on. The henchman is also a jester—transforming some of the violence into slapstick aggression.

The physical background reflects the qualities of the men and situations contained within it. The bare rocks and wide craggy plains emphasise the violent mode of life. It is a man's world. To the average child or adult viewer, the settings of Westerns are unfamiliar, symbolic—part of the Western myth.

Violence

The following devices were used in children's Westerns to take the edge off violence:

Stylised presentation. Menace, attack, and injury are, like the characters, presented in a stylised manner. Tight lips and steely eyes convey menace. There is a limited and stereotyped range of traditional responses to injury; injury from behind is indicated by throwing back the shoulders, jerking up the head, and tumbling to the ground; a shot from the front is conveyed by clutching the stomach.

The camera veers away from the dead—it shows the leap, stagger or fall that precedes death, but moves at once from the inert body.[1] Interest, in fact, is centred on the group, not on the unfortunate individual. Wounds are never defined and never cause serious disfigurement.

Stereotyped use of guns. At the centre of the preoccupation with violence is the gun. Everyone has a gun ready for immediate use—even the barbers and storekeepers, who are not cowboys. People in

---

[1] In the films viewed, there was only one death-scene and then only because the dying man had to give vital information.

Westerns take guns for granted. It would be impossible to learn any-thing from a Western about real guns and how they work. What is more, guns are generally ineffective; in one fairly typical Western we found that 149 shots were fired, yet no one was killed and only one man seriously injured, a second one slightly. Even when lethal, guns are aimed at a distance.

Finally, while guns are used mostly for fighting, they are also let off for fun. Nevertheless, guns spell power, they make people listen, and force them to do what is wanted.

Frequency of aggression by good and bad people. Villains use verbal threats more but, when it comes to real fighting by fist or gun, they wound and kill fewer people than the other side does. In fact, if good is to triumph, good people must successfully kill or wound. This may worry humane persons; for children it has less significance because the hero with whom they identify themselves is never in doubt about what to do, never sentimentalises over his victims, and never pays for victory. He is not even personally involved in the kill, since it is rarely his gun or his fist which wounds the villain, however much he has done to bring it about. Table 30 gives the incidence of acts of violence perpetrated by the hero's and the villain's side respectively.

TABLE 30. Incidence of threats and acts of violence in eight Westerns on children's television

	Number of occasions	
	Hero's side	Villain's side
Verbal threats or abuse . .	4	10
Seizure by arms . . .	1	2
Fisticuffs	6	6
Shooting matches . . .	9	9
Wounding	3	1
Killing	3	2
Total	26	30

NOTE. Each act of violence consists here of very many individual incidents. One shooting match may involve several people and fifty or more gun shots.

Disguise of violence with humour. While children's Westerns pass lightly over death they dwell on and emphasise the earlier stages of violence for their entertainment value. Here are two examples from different films:

1. Hero and henchman go to a shack where dangerous villains are hiding. A fight ensues in which the henchman, with his back to the wall, is repeatedly punched on the chin, falling back under each blow. During the fight this vignette is reproduced no less than four times—each time the situation was exactly the same. (This is where the humour of the situation is supposed to tell.) The henchman is being punched senseless, without mercy, against the back wall of the shack. Each time his expression is exaggeratedly foolish

(meant to provoke laughter) and he is hardly conscious. The villain punching him never slackens or stops. The henchman reappears later as right as rain.

2. This time the henchman is delivering the blows. It is precisely the same humorous situation, a little refined. The victim is propped up against the bar in a saloon. He is punched time and again with energy and precision, but as he leans against the bar he cannot fall down. At last the henchman stops, not for mercy, but to ask the hero why this cross-eyed unconscious man does not fall down. 'Try moving him away from the bar' the hero suggests. The already senseless man is stood away from the bar, punched again on the jaw, and collapses out of sight. With a smile the henchman turns to the hero for praise.

The humour of all this lies in the foolish expression of the victim, the regular delivery of punches, and the satisfaction shown by the aggressor. The impression they give is of adults at play; but there is an underlying element of viciousness, since these episodes are frills, unnecessary for the development of the plot.

Use of tension. Tension is created by the promise of more violence and conveyed by silence and slow and stealthy movement. It is relieved by the sight and sound of horses galloping. The object is to make the viewer believe that this time the hero is in such danger that he cannot get away unharmed. There is usually one such scene in each episode.

In general, then, violence in Westerns is abstract, stylised, and made readily acceptable because the hero never hesitates to apply it and none of its moral consequences are ever dwelt on. Despite moments of tension, violence is disguised to look remote and inconsequential—in fact, a game.

Morality and values

The central lesson of Westerns is that good triumphs over bad through violence—the manly, as well as the only, course of action. The villain's case is never stated, no sympathy is invited for him, and the hero never gains anything from his deeds. There is no suggestion of internal conflict or indecision.

Explicit mention is made of certain other values such as regard for justice, life, and property. A whole range of values, however, never finds expression in Westerns—those to do with family, work, education, and manners. The characters do not need them in their way of life; they are rarely encumbered by parents, wives, or children, and seldom eat or go into their homes; most of the indoor action takes place in the sheriff's office or in the saloon.

Adult Westerns convey something about the frontier civilisation with its rough-and-ready administration of justice; hardly any of this is conveyed in children's Westerns. *Gun Law*, the adult Western series shown at the time of the study, stands half-way between the simple, clear-cut children's Westerns and the more complex detective and crime programmes. The villain in this series resembles 'the mixed-up kid' of many detective plays. The Marshal in *Gun Law*, by contrast with the cowboy heroes of children's Westerns, is often worried or undecided, and his victory over the villain is achieved at a cost.[1] In other respects—the format, the setting, and its presentation of violence—*Gun Law* resembles Westerns designed for children.

CRIME AND DETECTIVE PROGRAMMES

For the analysis of crime and detective programmes we monitored at least three episodes of each of the three weekly series shown at that time: *Fabian of Scotland Yard* (BBC), *Inner Sanctum* and *Dragnet* (ITV).[2] *Inner Sanctum* and *Dragnet* were both imported from the United States. At the time of the study they were being shown before the bedtimes of even the 10–11 year olds. Later, *Inner Sanctum* was moved to a later part of the evening.

Crime and detective programmes, like Westerns, are concerned with apprehending criminals and upholding justice. They are shown in regular series, each programme with its characteristic opening and closing scenes. There is often a central character to provide a link between episodes. Here, however, the similarity ends. Compared with Westerns, their plots are more complex, their characterisation more varied. The settings are realistic, they have a two-level morality rather than a one-level one, and a quite different presentation of violence.

All Westerns followed the classic mould so closely that there was little need to refer to individual programmes; but this was not so with the crime and detective series. *Fabian* and *Dragnet* are detective programmes with emphasis on the police machinery for detection, while *Inner Sanctum* is a crime thriller.

Motives are more systematically explored in these programmes than in Westerns. There are generally two kinds of motive—the surface one and the underlying one. Superficially the crime tends to spring from gain or greed, but this is rarely the genuine reason and the story is often designed to show that the real motive lies in the weakness or neurosis of the criminal, suggesting perhaps that he could not help

[1] Characteristically each episode opens with the hero standing on a graveyard, ruminating about the consequences of crime, rather like the narrator of a fable. Each time he selects the inhabitant of one grave as the villain of the story, so telling viewers at the outset that the story will end in death.

[2] The titles of the episodes are given in Appendix Table 24.

himself. This occurred, for example, in the four *Dragnet* stories that we monitored; in the first the criminal never intends to kill his victim, but does so in a panic; in the second the criminal is a transvestist; in the third a youngster of eighteen commits a purposeless crime (he runs over a pregnant woman) and is depicted as a friendless, uncared-for psychopath; and in the fourth an old, insane, one-time film producer distributes pornographic literature to teen-agers.

Fabian and especially the *Dragnet* series stress the 'psychological angle'. Unlike the Westerns, they implicitly enlist viewers' sympathies for the criminal—the situation is one not of 'black' and 'white' but of different shades of grey. It is not specifically suggested that these conditions excuse or explain the crime; but this is implied by the detective's attitude towards the criminal, which is sometimes distinctly sympathetic.

In *Inner Sanctum*, a crime thriller, the machinery of the law plays a very small part, and the series makes its impact by portraying the fears, conflicts, and struggles of the characters in it. It carries the 'appearances are deceptive' theme to even greater lengths than the other two series.

Appendix Table 24 lists the themes for the ten programmes we monitored; it also briefly describes the criminals and their motives.

Characterisation and setting

The hero in both *Fabian* and *Dragnet* is the detective. In *Dragnet* it is Friday, a detective of the Los Angeles police force; in *Fabian*, an inspector of Scotland Yard. In both series there is much emphasis on the machinery of the police; the detective represents the law and is backed by all its power; the balance is heavily weighted against the criminal. Table 31 lists the characteristics of the two detectives (Fabian and Friday) and those of the criminals.

Comparison of this table with Table 29 points to two main differences between the heroes of crime and detective programmes and those of Westerns. In the latter, the hero is sharply differentiated from the villain, he is always very just, never callous, and always very honest, whatever the excuse or provocation for dishonest manœuvres might be. Not so in the case of the detective; he can be unjust, callous, and stoop to dishonest means. This difference is brought out clearly in Fig. 8 on p. 188, where the range of ratings of six characteristics of heroes of Westerns, of *Dragnet*, *Fabian*, and of *Inner Sanctum* are presented side by side.

It will be seen that in the crime and detective series it is not nobility of character which decides whether the detective-hero will achieve his goal: he need not be idealistic or unselfish, but he must be efficient, almost machine-like. He achieves his end because of his infinitely superior resources; in some way the police machine becomes the romantic figure rather than the detective. Secondly, the detective-hero is not as stylised as the Western hero. Fabian and Friday share only one characteristic, that of ruthless determination to persevere to the end. The criminals, too, vary more than the villains in Westerns, largely because they are described at two levels which arouse conflict: as someone committing a serious, often shocking, crime, and as lost and broken persons.

TABLE 31. Range of characteristics of heroes and villains in ten crime and detective programmes

(Range over five-point scale)

Personality characteristics:	Inner Sanctum		Fabian and Dragnet	
	Heroes	Criminals	Heroes	Criminals
Just–unjust	1–2	1–5	1–4	4–5
Kind–unkind	2–5	5	2–3	4
Assured–insecure . . .	4–5	1–5	1	4–5
Polite–impolite	2–4	2–4	1–2	2–4
Satisfied–dissatisfied . . .	4	2–4	3	5
Honest–dishonest . . .	2–4	5	1–4	5
Strong–weak character . .	2–4	1–4	1	3–5
Warm-hearted–callous . .	2–4	5	3–4	5
Happy–unhappy . . .	4–5	2–5	3	5
Humorous–dour . . .	4–5	2–4	2–4	2–5
Sane–neurotic/insane . .	2–4	3–5	2	3–5
Strong–weak (physically) .	—	—	2	2
Gentle–violent (physically) .	1–5	5	1–5	1–5
Courageous–cowardly .	1–4	2–5	1–2	4–5
Enterprising–unenterprising .	1–3	1	2	1–3
Ingenuous–cunning . .	1–5	4–5	2–4	3–5
Intelligent–stupid . . .	1–4	1	2	1–4
Determined–feeble . . .	1–4	1	1	1–5

NOTE. The characteristics were rated on a five-point scale. Example of rating scale: 1 = very just, 2 = just, 3 = neither particularly just nor unjust, 4 = unjust, 5 = very unjust.

The detectives, like the Western heroes, have great physical presence. Both Fabian and Friday have expressionless faces and an air of menace, even when they are being most polite. Friday, in addition, uses crisp monosyllabic speech. By contrast, the criminals convey their neuroticism in their mannerisms and the way they look.

Once again dress plays a part; the detectives are smart, the criminals tend to be shabby or flamboyant in their clothes. Here the distinction is almost as clear-cut as in the Westerns.

In *Inner Sanctum* the theme is deception—the good turn may turn out to be bad, the innocuous to be dangerous. The good characters are generally not differentiated from the bad until the end. The hero is not the detective, but some character in the story who happens not to be wicked, though he may be weak and callous.

All this is more difficult for children to assimilate than the clear-cut characterisation of the Westerns, doubly so because the heroes change from episode to episode and because there is so little to dis-

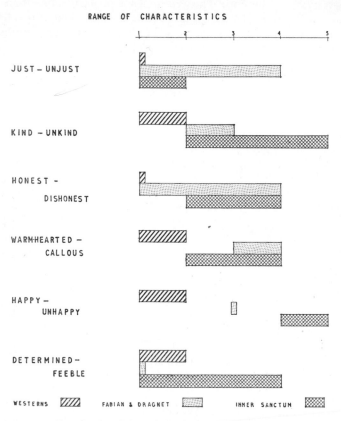

FIG. 8. Personality characteristics of the heroes of children's Westerns, of the detective series *Fabian* and *Dragnet*, and of the crime thriller *Inner Sanctum*

tinguish them from the criminals. Indeed, when it comes to resources, the criminal is generally more intelligent and enterprising and deter-mined than the hero—he is, in fact, better equipped for villainy than the hero is for heroism. There is a similar lack of differentiation in their dress.

In *Dragnet* and *Fabian*, unlike the Westerns, realism of atmosphere is greatly stressed. *Fabian* presents recognisable parts of London, while *Dragnet* gives a panorama of Los Angeles. The settings are urban, the office of the detective and the homes of the criminals are shown in great detail. The emphasis on realism is shown by the opening and closing shots.

Dragnet opens with the detective's voice saying something along these lines:

> This is the city of Los Angeles, California. I work here. My name is Friday. I am a cop.

It ends with an announcement thrown on the screen:

> 'On such and such a date, trial was held in such and such a court . . . in a moment the results of that trial will be made known.' A police photograph of the criminal is then shown and a voice announces that 'Joe Smith is now serving five years in such and such a penitentiary'.

Similarly, all *Fabian* episodes begin with the detective announcing himself through the microphone: 'This is Fabian of Scotland Yard. . . .'

In *Inner Sanctum*, however, the settings are as deceptive as the characters. The rooms look ordinary from the outside, but trap-doors are generally concealed underneath the carpet, or book-shelves open to reveal secret passages. In the opening scene a door slowly opens with a creak and an eerie voice speaks the opening sentence. In the closing scene the camera moves back to the door, which closes very slowly.

Violence

It is in the handling of violence, however, that these programmes differ most from children's Westerns and from one another. In detective and crime plays, violence is made to look realistic and personal. It is not conventionalised.

First, there is no attempt to evade the consequences of violence, the camera stays with a man who has been hit; we see blood on his hands and beads of sweat on his face; we hear him gasp for air. *Dragnet* shows detailed expressions of physical pain, expressions which vary from one incident to another. The camera, the music, the effects all underline the realism. The viewer is in no way helped to believe that what he sees is only part of a story.

In Westerns the impact of violence is dulled because there are no close-ups at the kill and also because the emphasis is on opposing sides, rather than on individuals. In *Dragnet*, violence becomes a personal thing—and whenever a gun is fired, a knife aimed, or a fist shot out, it is always effective. In two out of the four *Dragnet* episodes there were incidents of vicious violence and gratuitous horrors.[1]

[1] For instance, the ankles and arms of a dead girl in the *Big Trunk* were twice shown with the rope biting into her flesh, while in another episode there was a realistic close-up of a quivering lower arm, with blood running down it.

Violence in *Dragnet* is there to create sensation; it does not further the plot. In each of the episodes of *Inner Sanctum* there is at least one incident of excessive violence.

The episodes of *Fabian* that we monitored contain no murders, those of *Dragnet* two, and of *Inner Sanctum* three. Similarly, *Fabian* has on average four, *Dragnet* five, and *Inner Sanctum* six incidents of violence in one programme. The nature (as well as the amount) of violence is less serious in *Fabian* than in the other two.

Morals and values

There are three main types of explicit values in these series. First, that crime does not pay, because the law has vast resources. Indeed, the criminal pays heavily for his crime. In *Dragnet* much is made of the fact that each programme reports on a crime and ends with the court sentence.

Second, that the activities of criminals and of the law are not in fact dissimilar. Both sides bully and cheat if necessary.

Third, that appearances are deceptive; a person may look harmless and yet be a criminal (though hardly ever the other way round). The main idea, implied rather than made explicit, is that man is often not responsible for his deeds, that he cannot help himself. While the law must be upheld, the criminal can yet evoke sympathy.

Implications derived from the comparative analysis of children's Westerns, crime and detective programmes

The comparative analysis of children's Westerns, crime and detective series has brought out a number of points:

First, Westerns present a simple situation in which the permutations of plot, characterisation, motives, and presentation of violence can readily be learned. On these grounds alone, we would expect children, once they have learned the choreography of the Westerns, to cease to be disturbed by the violence contained in them. On the other hand, the crime and detective programmes (which after all are designed for adults) are more difficult to predict; the motivation is more complex, the characterisation less clear-cut. Particularly since the presentation of and the setting in which violence occurs varies from episode to episode, the format cannot readily be learned. This is especially true in crime thrillers like *Inner Sanctum*, where there is not even a central figure like a detective who recurs from episode to episode to provide the reassurance that comes with familiarity.

Second, Westerns are studies in black and white; crime and detective stories, studies in grey. In the Westerns, the villain has no identity; sympathy with his fate is not invited. This is not the case in crime and detective series where the complex motives of the villain are often expressed and with it sympathy for him invited. In this way a conflict of identification is set up in the child's mind and makes it more difficult for him to experience relief when the criminal is apprehended; in the case of children's Westerns this relief is complete.

Finally, the extent to which violence on television will prove disturbing to the child cannot be measured by the number of shots fired or the number of aggressive episodes contained in any one programme. It depends far more on the setting in which the violence occurs, on the manner of its presentation, and on the complexity of the characterisation of the two sides in the struggle.

On all these counts, violence is seen as little disturbing for the child familiar with Westerns, but in the case of the crime and detective series the extent to which it arouses tension will depend on the particular manner in which the theme, characterisation, and violence are handled in any given episode.

15

Reactions of Anxiety and Fear

So far we have looked at the content of Westerns, crime and detective series from an adult observer's point of view. Here we shall consider the children's reactions, how much they understood of these programmes, and how much they were disturbed by them. We shall also consider other programmes, whether presenting fictional or real events which have frightened children, in an attempt to establish some general principles about the types of situation that arouse fear and the type of child most affected.

In a survey of this kind we cannot, of course, tap unconscious responses; we can only ask children directly or talk to parents or other adults concerned with children about the fears they remember experiencing. Such a picture is inevitably incomplete, partly because the children may not be consciously aware of or remember feeling frightened, and partly because, especially as they grow older, they may not be prepared to admit to fears. On the other hand, it is most unlikely that a child will overtly confess or admit fears which he has not actually experienced. Our interest lies not so much in establishing the precise number of children who have been frightened by things shown on television as to learn about those incidents which cause a good deal of anxiety and those which cause little.

What frightens children may be very different from what adults consider to be disturbing to a child. It is perhaps because this has been insufficiently appreciated that there have been so few studies of the children's own reactions.[1]

The thesis we shall examine is that the child's reactions to scenes of violence and disaster may depend not so much on the extent of the violence and its consequences in terms of injury or loss of life as on the context, real or fictional, in which they occur. We begin with a more detailed examination of the effect of Westerns, not only because so much has been written about the violence contained in them, but

[1] Relevant studies are: Herzog's inquiry into children's radio listening (40), Dysinger and Ruckmick's study of children's reactions to films (29), and the BBC inquiry into *Dick Barton* and Juvenile Delinquency (15).

also because, at the time of the survey, they were the only children's programmes shown which featured violence. A study of the reactions to children's Westerns will also afford an opportunity to test our hypothesis that anxiety lessens or disappears once the format is learnt. We shall then discuss other types of programme arousing fear, and finally shall examine Klapper's contention that through seeing so many adult plays, children may become anxious about the difficulties of adult life (55).

Methods of inquiry

Much of this chapter is based on qualitative, not quantitative, material, obtained in the following way:

1. Observation of groups of children, of which one group was watching a Western, and the other a nature programme about polecats, which contained scenes of animals attacking each other.
2. A series of nine meetings with a group of 10–11 year olds. A good deal of the time was spent discussing their reactions to different programmes, especially to Westerns, detective, and murder plays.
3. We made use of the material obtained from individual interviews with 9–10 year old children reported earlier.
4. In the Norwich study we included questions to test the child's knowledge of the build-up of Westerns.
5. Both in the main survey and in Norwich, children were asked to say if they had ever been frightened by anything seen on television. Similar questions about films, radio, and books were included in other parts of the survey.
6. For reactions of young children we relied on the reports of the mothers who filled in the week's diary, and also on those teachers who had television at home and could comment on the reactions of their own children.
7. Finally, we devised a special questionnaire (a reaction list) to determine how far children's reactions to potentially disturbing incidents varied with the context, real or fictional, in which the incidents occurred. The reaction list is described in Appendix E.

CHILDREN'S REACTIONS TO WESTERNS

We are trying to answer two questions here. How far and at what age do Westerns prove disturbing? And how far are children of the ages we tested aware of the build-up of these programmes?

Relation of fear to knowledge of the format

According to the mothers' reports, children under 6 were quite often frightened by the individual acts of violence and the noise of shooting in Westerns. They would hide behind chairs, rush out of the room, or, if the anxiety was not too great, climb on to their mothers' laps and from there continue to watch. Finding that the hero was still all right at the end, and that the others watching the programme had enjoyed it, the young child might look again on other occasions. Gradually the stereotyped pattern of the Westerns gets understood—not in detail, but in broad outline. At the same time, the children, boys in particular, rehearse the main elements of Westerns in play as is shown in this account from a mother of a boy of 6:

> It is interesting to note his development from running behind the chairs whenever there was a Western film to his complete absorption in them now. He often plays at being Hopalong Cassidy, complete with gun.

In general it seems that the process of learning is related to the child's mental rather than to his chronological age and that round about 6 or 7 the majority of children cease to be frightened by Westerns. Girls tend to be a little 'backward' here, not for want of intellectual understanding but because of different interests and different play experiences. Girls play Westerns less often than boys, and when they do, are rarely cast in the glorious and ultimately secure role of the cowboy hero. By about 9 or 10, girls proved almost as interested in these programmes as boys.

There were many individual variations, due to differences in temperament rather than in intellectual ability. For some, anxiety lessened with understanding; others never experienced it at all. Here is a mother's account of the very different attitudes towards Westerns which her two children showed:

> For a long time Michael (aged 5) was frightened of the cowboy pictures, though having an armour of his own. Judy (aged 9) loved them, and Michael has gradually come to like them—I would not like to say why. Perhaps because the bad men never win, perhaps because he has some idea of the general pattern of the story and can follow it better; but he does seem to enjoy them now. I think there is something in the idea of his anxiety being linked to a lack of understanding, since he dislikes many period pieces, e.g. *Tom Brown's Schooldays*, Billy Bunter, the Children's Hour serial play about a French nobleman imprisoned in an Edinburgh castle. Judy, on the other hand, will watch anything, and obviously doesn't bother if she cannot understand.

Anxiety about Westerns were rare, well before the age of 10. In our survey, only seven children out of a thousand mentioned a Western when asked *Have you ever been frightened by anything you have seen on television?* Five of the seven were girls, and all seven were between 10 and 11 years of age, of below average intelligence, and—most striking of all—more beset by fears than other viewers of the same age.

The following observations, made on a group of 6–10 year old during the showing of an episode from *Cisco Kid*, illustrate children'

---

[1] This assessment was made on the basis of their responses to the inventory of fears which is described in Appendix A.

reactions to Westerns: intense involvement during the showing of the programme with complete release of tension at the end.

Film sequence:	Children's comments:
Cisco appears.	Cisco! (completely absorbed again when Cisco reappears).
	I *love* Cisco! (girl).
Cisco is knocking them down.	Good old Cisco! (boy).
Fist-fighting.	Cisco!
	Cisco!
	Cisco!
	Cisco always gets away, doesn't he.
Cisco held up at gun point.	Don't let him!
Bad man shoots at Cisco.	Oh no! Cisco!
	I could *cry* for Cisco, because I like him (she sucks her thumb).
Cisco on a roof, challenging the villains.	(Absorbed attention.)
A villain is shooting at Cisco. His gun jams and he can't fire.	(Pleasure, excitement, laughter.) Clever cock, ain't he, clever old cocky. Cisco's the best.
Cisco and villain fight in a stream.	(All gasp) Oh! Oh! Oh! Oh!
The fight is over and the villain dispatched. The stooges are talking and joking.	(Children abruptly relax. Some of the older ones giggle together, some start talking among themselves about where to put the toffee paper.)

Even during the showing, attention was aroused only by action sequences and not by dialogue.

Any residual tension that younger children may experience due to the fact that they are more involved, tends to be worked off in play. It is interesting that in such games a child may frequently change sides, being first the hero and then the villain. Here is a description of such a game played by a boy of 9:

> He will jump up and shoot somebody with an imaginary gun and appropriate sounds. Then he in turn will be 'shot' and he will spin round and fall on the ground.

The same idea is elaborated by a 10-year old boy describing the game he played with his friends:

> We usually play attacking each other. Some people get on one side and the others get on the other and we attack each other. . . . We've made up a new game. See, three men get gunned at, and the best to fall down dead when the gun is shooting at them is gunner, see? We have lots of fun in our gang.

These are not games of uncontrolled aggression, but are only versions of chasing and being chased—of cowboys and Indians, of cops and robbers—the oldest of childhood games, which were, of course, played long before television was thought of. They express the child's ingrained fondness for rules and for a clear differentiation between good and evil. The conventional cowboy films with their straightforward rules and straightforward sides suit the play needs of children between 6 and 10, when they are testing out ideas about fair play and about friendship.

Tension, then, is resolved at the end of the programme or worked off in play. It is characteristic, therefore, that when children were asked whether there was a programme which they 'could not get out of their minds', they would mention adult plays or thrillers, but not Westerns. These made no lasting impact.

Enjoyment of Westerns is at its height where the format has been learnt sufficiently for tension not to mount too much, but where, at times during the showing, some element of doubt remains, as the following account of a girl of 10 shows:

> Well, you know the good ones are going to win, but sometimes it's so exciting that you wonder at the time. Well, I wonder, you know, if the good ones really are going to win. Only it's silly really because I *know*. Only I'm just excited.

When children are 8 to 10 years old they become increasingly aware of the unreality and sameness of Westerns:

> But what puzzles me is—things don't always end up like that in real life (pause) *do* they? I think I like the goodies winning best, because then it's a happy ending (girl of 10).

Because children know that the ending will be happy, with no harm done to the hero, the violence does not matter. They gain security from the lack of variety in plot and solution, they enjoy being 'in the know'. When they stop playing at cowboys and similar games with clear-cut rules of good and evil and even the momentary doubt during the showing has gone, they lose interest in Westerns, and criticise the stereotyped presentation which at first appealed to them so much. Then they switch their allegiance from Westerns to more lifelike equivalents, such as the detective series *Fabian of Scotland Yard*.

To illustrate our hypothesis of the relationship between anxiety and lack of comprehension, here is a 10-year old girl's account of her own experience with Westerns:

> It happened when I was about eight or nine, I can't remember. Only I really was so frightened . . . and then if I did see it, then I'd dream of it, you know. I used to think it was *dreadful*. Only then you know that a bad man hardly *ever* shoots a good one, only perhaps he does it on the corner of his arm, and you see so many bad people being *shot*—well, when they fight and hide behind rocks and go like that (demonstrates firing), even though the person may be like this and then duck (demonstrates), he never gets, you know, shot.

Perception of heroes and villains in Westerns

We have seen that children learn the broad format of the Western; we also know that they listen little to the dialogue. How far then is their knowledge of the characters built on the visual cues provided? To test the children's awareness of these cues, the following question was asked of sixty 13–14 year olds and thirty 10–11 year olds.

> In cowboy and Western programmes, some people are good and some are bad. If you had to tell someone who had not seen a Western before how to pick out the good people and the bad people, what things would you tell him to watch for?

Since we worded the question to invite contrast, the children generally described villains by reversing the criteria used for heroes. Our interest lies in the nature of the criteria used. The following are examples of the type of answers obtained:

The good people:

The clean-shaven, the men in the cleanest clothes. The men with the best horses and the handsome ones.

They are mostly good-looking and kind to ladies, and usually make eyes at the women.

They always have a partner each. They go around in twos. They also do not go into bars drinking very much.

They usually wear neat clothes and are clean-shaven. They have pearl-handled guns, &c.

The bad people:

The men with dirty faces and clothes, and the men who treat their horses badly.

They are usually playing cards or gambling. They like to go about in groups and to start a fight.

They are always going into bars drinking, and also start fights and always go about in gangs.

Rough-looking men. Ladies are smart, wear fancies like long pearl ear-rings and have small private rooms.

Table 32 shows the main criteria used.

TABLE 32. Frequency of mention of the different criteria used to describe the characteristics of Western heroes and villains

	13–14 YEAR OLDS		10–11 YEAR OLDS	
	Heroes %	Villains %	Heroes %	Villains %
Appearance and dress (nice looking or dirty)	28	40	20	33
Facial expression (looks sly, kind) .	12	25	7	30
Activities (robs banks, gets hurt).	10	33	47	53
Position relative to the law (sheriff, law-breaker)	20	3	7	—
Character qualities (bad, truthful, or willing to help)	8	20	10	13
Speech (talks loud or whispers) . .	5	10	—	10
Manner (rough or polite) . . .	20	20	7	13
Social habits (drinks, gambles, doesn't drink)	12	20	3	17
Skill (good shot, good rider) . .	3	3	20	—
Guns (mention of guns; skill as a shot)	13	13	10	3
Total cases	60	60	30	30

NOTE. The totals exceed 100 per cent, since most children mentioned more than one characteristic.

As predicted, appearance and facial expressions were mentioned by and large more often than any other criteria. This was particularly so in the descriptions of the villains. Next came activities—like robbing a bank or helping people; in these descriptions villains came alive more than heroes. This is in line with our observation that Westerns permit a wider range of behaviour and appearance to villains than to heroes (Chapter 14). Age differences were remarkably few. The older children more often mentioned the hero's status, the younger ones his skill as a good shot.

Reactions to the scenes of violence contained in Westerns

The reaction list described in Appendix E made it possible to look more closely at the children's reactions to the different aspects of violence shown. For each incident the child would choose one of three possible answers: 'I like it', 'I dislike it', or 'I neither like nor dislike it'; then he was asked, for the same incident, to select one from another set of answers: 'I am always interested to watch this', 'I am bored watching this', or 'I do not mind watching this'.

On the whole, liking and interest went together, as did dislike and lack of interest. The pilot inquiry had shown, however, that another category was needed, one of ambivalence, where liking went with boredom, or dislike with great interest in watching the programmes.

Table 33 shows how the answers of seventy-five 11–12 year olds were distributed.

Guns, as we have seen, are very important in Westerns; they are almost symbolic weapons, signs of potency, and a person deprived of his gun is rendered helpless—or impotent. While surprisingly ineffective (149 shots resulting in just one injury), yet they remain in Westerns the only instrument of violence which injures, kills, or brings the criminal to justice. Fist-fights achieve nothing.

Children enjoyed shooting matches and also fist-fights and fights on the ground. They were made uneasy though by incidents which implied criticism of the hero or in any way threatened his inviolability or majesty. For example, 31 per cent disliked and a further 21 per cent felt ambivalent about seeing the sheriff rebuke the good cowboy for not catching the villain quickly enough; yet only 4 per cent said they would not like to see cowboys shoot at one another. Chases, fist-fights, and shooting are all part and parcel of the Western and are therefore enjoyed. Any deviation from the stylised pattern is disliked, as it upsets the sharp distinction between hero and villain, and reduces the hero to ordinary dimensions.

TABLE 33. Reactions of seventy-five 11–12 year old viewers to twelve incidents in television Westerns

	Liking %	Indifference %	Dislike %	Ambivalence %
When cowboys have gun battles among the rocks or on the prairie	81	9	7	3
When at last the bad man is tracked down and caught . . .	80	6	8	6
When everyone draws their guns to start shooting . . .	79	5	6	10
When cowboys fight on the ground and roll about in the dust	75	10	8	7
The noise of horses galloping and guns firing	73	10	9	8
When there is a fist fight between two cowboys	71	14	9	6
When cowboys shoot at one another	66	17	4	13
When cowboys get angry and begin to shout	63	21	15	1
When one cowboy is made to look silly and foolish the whole time	43	12	27	18
When the good cowboy is getting the worst of the fight . .	37	9	25	29
When the sheriff tells the good cowboy off because he is not catching the bad man quickly enough.	30	18	31	21
When cowboys look dusty, dirty, untidy, or unshaven . .	25	28	22	25

What happens when children see shooting in other contexts, in detective plays where injury and death are shown more realistically, and in real life situations? Appendix Table 25 shows that even in newsreels, shooting and rioting are disliked by very few. The concept of shooting as a game is taken over into actualities. This is not because children cannot differentiate between the real and the fictional on television—we shall show later that they can—but it seems that Westerns, through the stylised presentation of violence, while preventing the child from being disturbed by the shooting, also fail to convey its serious consequences.

REACTIONS TO CRIME AND DETECTIVE PROGRAMMES

In the light of the content analysis, we may assume that crime and detective programmes will prove more disturbing to children than Westerns because violence is specific, personal, and made to look realistic, the characterisation is 'grey' rather than 'black and white' (thus inviting sympathy with the criminal), and the settings come much nearer home. Although each episode has a similar theme, each differs substantially from the others in setting, type of crime, and violence depicted. For all these reasons the format is not easily learned and each episode makes a fresh impression.

Extent of disturbance

An 11-year old girl, asked if there was any programme which she thought was bad for children to see, wrote: 'A murder play with too much murdering' and almost in the same breath listed among the types of play she liked best, family serials and a play about cowboys, 'they are good with their guns and I like seeing the cowboys kill each other'. She had learnt to tolerate and enjoy aggression in the stylised way of the Western, but was disturbed by it when presented in more realistic form.

Ninety-five children named murder plays and thrillers when asked if they had been frightened by something seen on television; one-third of the children were 13–14 year olds. Unlike the seven who had been frightened by Westerns, these children were of all levels of intelligence and were no more anxious than other children in their age group. Their fears were stimulated by the programmes rather than by their own anxieties.

Answers to other questions supported these findings, as for example: *Are there any things on television which you yourself think are bad for children to see?*

If yes, what sort of things? What makes you think they are bad for children to see?

Nineteen per cent of the older, and 17 per cent of the younger, children thought that there were things on television which were bad for children to see. Most of them instanced murder, horror plays, and thrillers because 'they frighten you and give you bad dreams'. These programmes are generally shown just before children's bedtime. One 11-year old girl, explaining why television had more impact than films, said: 'Well, in the pictures I have time to walk home.'

In detective series, to have no sympathy with the criminal is made more difficult than in Westerns. In one of the group discussions, the children talked about an episode of *Inner Sanctum* (ITV) in which a deaf and dumb man proved to be the murderer; they all agreed that they did not like it, 'because it's not very nice taking a deaf and dumb man, really. He's got to be punished, but you can still feel sorry for him.' This situation is much more difficult for children to accept than the black-and-white differentiation of the Westerns.

The content analysis showed that *Fabian of Scotland Yard* was less violent than the other two series (*Inner Sanctum* and *Dragnet*) which we monitored (Chapter 14). Children in the main survey had access to BBC programmes only, and, individual murder plays apart, could have seen only two series—*Fabian of Scotland Yard* and *Tales of Soho*.[1] If our analysis is correct, we might expect that, if these children had had access to ITV as well, the number of frightening incidents reported would have been substantially higher.

The particular incidents mentioned ranged widely; two were given by a number of children. The first, an episode from *Fabian of Scotland Yard*, concerned the murder of a woman in a bath; this may have frightened children by the very ordinariness of the setting in which it occurred; or may have touched on unconscious fears of drowning. The second incident mentioned related not so much to the sight of the crime being committed as to the signal that preceded it. The following description of it was given by an 11-year old boy. (The incident occurred in a play called *The Little Red Monkey*).

> There was a tune that goes (Boy: whistles cheerful tune; second boy begins whistling). It was about a monkey and everywhere it went a certain murder happened. Oooh, it was terrible! And my heart beat! I used to run—to run away when I heard that tune—it was *so* haunting that I used to be ever so frightened until Jimmy Edwards wrote a comic programme about it (other boy starts to whistle tune again) . . . in *Take It From Here*, a skit on it. Yes, it was the same tune, but they all started, they were talking, they were singing it . . . about the Little Red Monkey.
> Investigator: Did they make fun of it?
> Boy: Yes.
> Investigator: And then what happened?
> Boy: Well, I didn't get frightened at the tune any more.

This account shows two things: first, that sound effects can make a strong impact, and second, that by changing the context with which the child associates the sound, fear is removed. In this instance, it was done through persiflage; it can equally well be done through comment and discussion.

Sound effects were often mentioned, especially music and also the creaking door in *Inner Sanctum*. Despite the pictorial character of television presentation, it is often the sound that haunts the child rather than the picture. This is interesting in view of the popular view that the emotional impact of things seen tends to be stronger than that of things heard. This may not be so; we found, for instance, that among the controls, as many children were frightened by murder plays on the radio as were viewers by murder plays on television.

---

[1] We also monitored this series and found it the least violent of the four, depending for effect on battles of wits rather than on physical acts of violence. The action took place entirely in the Soho world of petty criminals; a distinction was made between good and bad criminals, the former being rarely brought to justice. The story revolved around the unorthodox police inspector, Charlesworth.

REACTIONS TO OTHER PROGRAMMES

Crime and detective programmes, while more complex than Westerns, have a known end and a known theme. On the whole they proved rather less disturbing than three other programmes the children saw: *The Abominable Snowman*, a science fiction programme called *Quatermass*, and George Orwell's *1984*. The BBC warned parents that these last two programmes might not be suitable for children; yet *Quatermass* was shown very early in the evening and was evidently watched by a large number of children. One hundred and thirteen children mentioned these programmes as being frightening.

Our group discussions took place several months after the programmes were shown, so that they were little referred to; but they occurred soon after the showing of *Jane Eyre* and of a dramatic life-story of Edgar Allan Poe. These programmes aroused in some children a feeling akin to terror; the second had again been described by the BBC as unsuitable for children. One boy of ten said of it:

> I was scared, I went straight to bed, I was scared for the day . . . I kept thinking when I get out of bed something from underneath will grab me. . . .

Another well-adjusted, highly intelligent boy of 11 described the presentation of Poe's own nightmare as follows:

> It showed you the coffin, it showed you—*you* were supposed to be inside the coffin and there was a glass top to the coffin and you could see them turning the earth on top of it and he kept on shouting 'No! No! It's not safe! I'm alive!' And they take it away and you kept on seeing the earth being poured in (pause). Horrible.
> Investigator: Did you think about that afterwards?
> Boy: Yes! I went to bed with my head—with my dressing gown over my head so I won't hear the ghosts.

Jane Eyre aroused fear too—fear because of the madness of the wife and the neglect of the child. The following account by a parent shows how an initial stimulus was transformed (this time enhanced) because of the way in which one child played on another's fear.

> When the *Jane Eyre* series was on, Pauline (aged 10) and John (aged 6) were so interested and eager to see it each Friday and yet they were always terrified to go to bed, when they were in their rooms they'd shout to each other 'Jane Eyre' really loud and scare each other to death. In fact I threatened to stop them viewing it but they used to promise not to scare each other, but of no use; as soon as it was dark they'd start and one night in particular they were going to bed and I was busy, and suddenly there was such a scream of terror, that I rushed up to the landing. Both were petrified. Apparently Pauline said 'Jane Eyre' very quietly and John thumped her and screamed. It ended by a wallop each and a promise of no more scaring plays late at night and if I heard either mention Jane Eyre late at night again I'd stop the pocket money.

Extent of impact of non-fiction programmes

Asked whether they had seen anything on television which frightened them, only 14 children mentioned non-fiction programmes; some referred to floods and fires seen on newsreels, others to hospital scenes; a small response rate when set against the 200 or so who had been frightened by fictional programmes. We found that injury to animals also does not necessarily disturb when these are portrayed in a nature programme. Children watching such a programme were quite unmoved by the scenes of polecats attacking and devouring different animals, a sight which the adult observer found rather too vividly presented. Here is an extract of her observations of a group of 9–10 year old children:

> One of the highlights of the programme—a battle between a polecat and a snake—did catch the attention. The pictures were very dramatic from the beginning—the snake's head raised venomously, the polecat vicious and ready to spring—and they were treated with very noisy, though varied consideration, including comments, cheers, and laughs. The children followed the struggle like a boxing match until the snake was killed. Then a roaring cheer went up. The snake was dragged back to the small polecats and they literally tore it to pieces, stretching, pulling, tugging, and swinging. Everyone, except one little girl, seemed to think this was extremely funny.

Undoubtedly viewing in a group increased the enjoyment of this programme, but similar observations were made of a boy of five who watched it with his mother: 'He was very interested and laughed and clapped his hands at baby polecats pulling a snake in two opposite ways over the root of a tree.' This same boy had been described as readily frightened by some of the plays shown on children's television.

This lack of concern contrasts sharply with the anxiety children express at any threat to the dogs in *Lassie* and *Rin-Tin-Tin*. This is partly because of their love for dogs and partly because of the near-human build-up that the dogs are given in these two adventure series.

Whether an incident will disturb depends less on whether it is fictional or real than on whether it comes within the child's experience and is one with which he can identify himself.

COMPARATIVE STUDY OF CHILDREN'S REACTIONS TO
DIFFERENT FORMS OF VERBAL AND OF PHYSICAL
AGGRESSION

Incidents may arouse enjoyment or boredom, fear or unease. So far we have looked at incidents which aroused fear; here we shall examine how far given incidents may arouse unease and discomfiture, using for the purpose the reaction list described earlier.

Appendix Table 25 gives the children's reactions of like, indifference, ambivalence, and dislike to different acts of physical violence: fist-fights, fighting on the ground, fighting with weapons such as daggers, swords, and guns. Each type of aggression was examined separately for Westerns, detective plays, other plays, and news. Further, we investigated the children's reactions to different kinds of verbal aggression: reprimand, ridicule, and also anger and grief; once again as they occur in the various fictional programmes and also in panel games, discussions, and newsreels. The children's reactions to these incidents are given in Appendix Table 26.

First, as we have seen, no form of fighting in Westerns or in detective plays aroused much unease—secondly, piercing weapons like daggers were more disliked than guns, fist-fights, or fights on the ground.[1] Thirdly, and this was largely unexpected, children at that age are more sensitive about acts of verbal than of physical aggression. In the case of verbal aggression, they made a very clear distinction between fictional and non-fictional programmes—the strongest dislike, for instance, occurred in connexion with anger or rudeness shown in panel games.

The technique of examination adopted here has many limitations: it fails to distinguish between degrees of dislike; it equates dislike with unease or disturbance; it does not go into the many reasons behind dislike or ambivalence. Yet, despite these limitations, it provides a useful picture of the type of incidents in television which disturb children.

Children differ from adults in what they perceive as disturbing. Adults are more inclined to react to aggressive incidents in terms of damage done or vividness of presentation, children more in terms of self-identification with the situation portrayed. Sudden disasters are beyond their comprehension, so are rioting and warfare; consequently they view these situations with the protective glasses provided by fiction. But they remove these glasses either when fictional heroes with whom they identify themselves are threatened or when real characters find themselves in threatening and embarrassing situations which mean something to the child—when, for instance, they are reprimanded, or lose face, or have angry arguments.

[1] We found little support for the view that seeing fighting on the ground disturbs children.

AGE AND SEX DIFFERENCES IN SUSCEPTIBILITY

Age differences

The younger the children, the less easy it is to predict what types of incident will frighten them. The noise and shooting of Westerns disturbed many children (until they had learned the format), but other frightening incidents varied greatly from one individual to another. One child, for instance, was frightened by the Royal Tournament, yet enjoyed Westerns and *Robin Hood*. A mother wrote about her 3½ year old girl:

> Westerns she loved and did not mind the shooting noise at all. She even comforted her 6 year old sister and held her hand when she was alarmed. Slapstick, however, upset her greatly and Billy Bunter and Peter Butterworth she could not bear and left the room. . . . Being a very 'moral' child she was horrified by any wanton destruction . . . and once in a play when the children took a new bicycle to pieces and sold the parts, she was very upset. Gradually fact and fiction were separated in her mind.

The girl in our example reacted to the activity just as if it was happening to her at home; she could not look at it in its fictional context. Studies by Dysinger and Ruckmick (29) and Franck (34) throw further light on this subject by showing that young children react to individual episodes and can neither link scenes together nor comprehend the story as a whole. Franck showed that incidents they remember and react to are those most closely linked with their daily lives.[1]

The young child, then, reacts strongly for four reasons: first, he reacts to the episode by itself—without relief from the context in which it occurs; secondly, he has little accumulated experience of television to use as a standard; thirdly, he cannot at this stage in his development make a sharp distinction between reality and fantasy; lastly, he may react keenly to incidents of aggression because at his age he is bothered by his own hostile feelings.

This is also the time when phobias and dislikes occur in all aspects of the child's life. What he enjoys one day he may dislike intensely the next. This is as true of television programmes as of other features in his life. This mother wrote about her 3½ year old son:

> My younger son up till three weeks ago would watch any programme quite happily, but now as soon as there is a Western or anything with shooting, he runs out of the room and will not return till it is finished. He won't watch Roy Rogers or any other cowboy, and *Robin Hood* he loved to view. I think the trouble

---

[1] Piaget's developmental study of the moral judgement of the child is of relevance here (74). He found that young children judge an act in terms of the amount of damage done, not in terms of the motives which prompted the performance of it.

started one week when in *Rin-Tin-Tin* the dog got hurt. Neil was so upset, he rushed out of the room. I made him go back right at the end to show him that the dog was well and happy. And he then said: 'I don't like them hurting the animals.' The dog had been hit on the head by a gun. But that is the end of his viewing *Rin-Tin-Tin*. I have to take him into another room while the other children view it.

This child also reacted to other programmes in an almost phobic manner for fear that the disturbing incident might be shown again. The fact that the dog was well again at the end of the programme did not give the child sufficient reassurance.

The young child expresses his emotions freely, so that it is easy to know when he is frightened. Older children are more reluctant to express such feelings. Yet in direct questioning, a large number of 10–11 and 13–14 year olds admitted to fear of things seen on television—one boy in four and one girl in three. If anything, the older children were more often frightened than the younger ones (Table 34).

TABLE 34. *People feel differently from one another about things they have seen, read, or heard. Have you ever felt frightened by anything you have seen on TV? (Read about? Heard on the radio? Seen in a film?)*

(Distribution of affirmative answers by age and sex)

| | 13–14 YEAR OLDS | | | | 10–11 YEAR OLDS | | | |
| | Boys | | Girls | | Boys | | Girls | |
	v %	c %	v %	c %	v %	c %	v %	c %
TV . . .	25	—	44	—	27	—	30	—
Reading . .	10	11	19	16	10	6	12	9
Radio . . .	11	16	19	34	3	12	10	19
Film . . .	22	21	34	34	14	19	21	23
Total cases (weighted)	252	252	252	252	252	252	252	252

We have no evidence as to why this should be so, but suggest that the greater maturity of the older children enabled them to become identified with more situations, to respond to motives as well as to actions. They are therefore exposed to a greater range of potentially disturbing experiences.

Sex differences

Girls were more readily disturbed than boys by what they saw on television. More girls than boys thought a lot about programmes they had seen and they were more often made sad by them (Tables 34 and 35). This difference extended to radio, films, and books and was found among controls as much as among viewers.

TABLE 35. (a) *People feel differently from one another about things they have seen, read, or heard. Have you ever felt sad about anything you have seen on TV? (Read about? Heard on the radio? Seen in a film?)*

(b) *Have you ever seen anything on TV that you couldn't get out of your mind—that you have been thinking about a lot?*

(Distribution of affirmative answers by age and sex)

	13–14 YEAR OLDS				10–11 YEAR OLDS			
	Boys		Girls		Boys		Girls	
	V %	C %	V %	C %	V %	C %	V %	C %
(a) *Sad:*								
TV . . .	24	—	57	—	21	—	40	—
Reading . .	14	12	38	48	7	11	17	27
Radio . .	7	10	9	17	4	5	4	13
Films . .	25	33	48	54	11	17	23	24
(b) *Could not get out of your mind (TV):*	19	—	26	—	7	—	16	—
Total cases (weighted)	252	252	252	252	252	252	252	252

The difference became more marked with the approach of adolescence. Among the 10–11 year olds, girls were a little more responsive than boys, but among the 13–14 year olds markedly so. By that age they had experienced most of the physiological changes of adolescence and their emotional life and needs were similarly changing more noticeably; they were at a particularly sensitive and uncertain period in their development.

DISTINCTION BETWEEN SUSPENSE AND FEAR

Undoubtedly children enjoy suspense; the plays most often named as favourites were mystery and murder plays. The point at which pleasurable tension becomes fear depends on the maturity and emotional balance of the child as well as on the nature of the programme.

Television offers means by which frightening incidents can be enjoyed; viewers are secure in the knowledge that the aggressor will be punished, that the hero and heroine are only temporarily in danger, and that they are viewing fiction, not reality. When these devices are understood and emotionally accepted, children can watch without feeling too much threatened.

Part of the appeal of these programmes lies in the relief that follows the lifting of fear. Indeed, this relief through contrast underlines the security of the child's own life, just as in the game of 'peep-bo' the mother's presence is rendered more pleasurable and reassuring by the momentary fear that she had disappeared. A startled child, or even adult, laughs with excitement and pleasure once the danger has passed.

The effects of real fear, unlike those of tension, can last quite a while. A boy of 10 who had been terrified by the dramatic life of Edgar Allan Poe (*Nom de Plume*, BBC) said:

> I was ever so scared that night; because I used to sit up until my Mum used to go out, then come back—because she said I could sit up reading comics. But it was still in my head and wouldn't go away.
> Did it go out of your head the next day?
> Yes, I forgot about it then. . . . Well, I didn't forget about it—I told the kids. I don't know why, but I just had to go and tell the kids about it. And I didn't even like it!

The children themselves distinguished between frightening and exciting programmes. In Norwich we asked two questions: *What would you do to make a programme exciting?* and later *What would you do to make a programme frightening?* (Table 36).

TABLE 36. *What would you do to make a programme exciting?*
What would you do to make a programme frightening?

(Distribution of types of programmes mentioned in the answers)

	14–15 YEAR OLDS %	11–12 YEAR OLDS %
What would you do to make a programme exciting?		
Miscellaneous	13	10
Sport, games	—	5
Plays	13	17
Western	8	9
Crime, murder	13	17
Mystery, adventure	5	5
Variety, circus	3	8
What would you do to make a programme frightening?		
Space travel	5	2
Mystery, horror	13	9
Ghosts	6	19
Quatermass	3	12
Crime	3	7
Total cases	64	123

NOTE. The percentages add up to less than 100 per cent as many children answered 'I don't know'. The questions were given to the children in 1956.

Mystery and horror plays and horrific space fiction programmes like *Quatermass* tended to be seen as frightening more often than exciting. Here are the answers of three children to these two questions side by side:

A frightening programme:	*An exciting programme*:
Frankenstein	Mystery
Crime thriller	Murder
Murder	Cowboy

There is a downward progression here: the child with a strong digestion found programmes like *Frankenstein* frightening and mystery plays exciting; the one who found mystery frightening named murder plays as exciting; and finally, one for whom murder and detective programmes were frightening selected Westerns as exciting. All these programmes contain elements of suspense, danger, uncertainty, eeriness, and violence, they differ from one another in the emphasis given to each of these aspects and in the presence or absence of strong heroic figures. These differences may well determine whether a programme is enjoyed for its tension (and subsequent release of tension) or feared for its terrifying elements.

CONCLUSIONS

What frightens children depends on both the stimulus and the child, his intellectual and emotional maturity, his needs and conflicts of the moment.

Only the very young were frightened by the noise and shooting of Westerns; most children of 6 or 7 enjoyed them and only a few dullish, fearful 10 year olds were still disturbed by them. Fear, it seems, disappears as children learn the format of Westerns; the very simplicity of plot and characterisation facilitates identification with the hero and rejection of the villain, while the stylised portrayal of violence protects the child from the consequences of violence.

It follows that, where the format is less clear cut, identification with the hero is less easy, and where violence is specific and personal, fear is more readily aroused. This is the case for both age groups with crime and detective plays and with thrillers. Nevertheless, some things in these programmes are predictable—the catching of the criminal, the cleverness of the detective, the power of the police. Where this is not so, in an individual play or in a situation of which the child has little prior knowledge, he can easily become disturbed.

Children are disturbed by things which are uncanny and fantastic and resemble nightmares—but equally by things with which they become readily identified. For instance, situations where people are made to feel uneasy or are told off or become angry often disturb children more than scenes of mass destruction which have little meaning for them. Children fortunately have no direct experience of war and so react to its portrayal in much the same way, whether it be in newsreels or in plays. But when they can identify themselves with situations, they find them more disturbing on the screen if they concern real people rather than fictional characters.

By the age of 11–12 children often seem more disturbed by displays of anger and distress than by scenes of shooting, even when they happen in the news. We suggest that the cushioning of violence —so much a feature of Westerns—by hiding the consequence of death and injury has made all shooting seem like a game. This reaction is not confined to viewers; controls showed it to almost the same extent (when asked about the same incidents in the cinema).

Television makes more impact on girls than boys—on young adolescent girls especially.

Some of the common stereotyped ideas about what frightens children have little foundation in fact. The number of injured and the number of shots are less important than the manner in which the injury occurs. Shooting is not very disturbing, nor fighting on the ground, but injury by knife or dagger is far more so; swords and other weapons occupy an intermediate position.

The impact of television does not lessen with time and veteran viewers are as frightened as recent ones. A child gets more frightened when he views alone or with children of his own age (with no adult present). Viewing in the dark, where familiar surroundings are obscured, makes more impact than viewing with some lights on.

A child enjoys being frightened just a little bit, but not too much. He likes the suspense for the pleasure of the relief that follows it (this partly explains the popularity of eerie programmes and thrillers); the boundary between tolerable suspense and fear is almost invisible, but the more structured and predictable a plot the less likely is it to cross the line.

16

Appraisal of Westerns, Crime and Detective Series

So far we have looked at the content of these programmes, which are so popular with children, and have examined how far they frighten and disturb. Here we shall consider their other effects.

We shall draw on the results of our own survey and also on the comprehensive report on television and juvenile delinquency made in 1956 by a United States Senate Sub-committee under the chairmanship of Senator Kefauver (53). The recommendations of this committee are based on two sets of evidence: a series of monitoring studies and the testimony of expert witnesses. How far are they relevant to this country? Many people in this country believe that events in the United States cannot happen here, or can happen only on a very reduced scale. What are the facts?

Amount of violence

In Chapter 14 we have shown that the proportion of time devoted to these programmes between the hours of 5 and 9 p.m. is the same for both countries, amounting to approximately 20 per cent.

Type of violence

It is more difficult to make a comparative assessment of the types of violence. It may well be that the incidents of sensational violence are rather less in this country than in the United States, but British programmes are certainly not devoid of scenes of viciousness and brutality. Here are two shown recently at peak viewing times:

> *Boyd Q.C.* (ITV). The episode contained a long drawn-out scene where a man attacked a young girl as she entered her home, seized her face and slashed it. Although the insertion of the knife was not seen, the whole episode was very realistically presented and the effect enhanced by the cries of the victim. The whole scene seemed long, and entirely unnecessary for the development of the theme— a piece of pure sensationalism. Other dramatic techniques could easily have been used to convey the savageness of the crime. The episode was shown at 7.30 p.m. when children of all ages view.
>
> *Shadow Squad* (ITV), another British production shown twice weekly at peak

viewing time, contained on several occasions scenes in which the detective's henchman was beaten up—once, for instance, by a slow-witted helper of a criminal gang, whose sadistic enjoyment of his task was revealed in a close-up. In each instance the face of the victim showed realistically the effects of the attack.

Type of crime

The well-written adult crime and detective series attempt characterisation, exploration of motive, and the 'psychological angle'. More complex characterisation may prove as disturbing to children as any overt act of violence. For example, in an episode in *Boyd Q.C.* (*The Other Half*) there was a sympathetic portrayal of the way in which the whole machinery of justice was set in motion to help a mother who tried to murder her child and then to commit suicide. The child viewer could carry away an image of the humanity of the law, but also a profoundly disturbing image of a mother injuring a child whom she loves.

It is against the background of television violence and crime of this amount and type that discussion has to be conducted. It seems that the situation in this country is sufficiently similar to that in the USA for the findings of the Kefauver committee to be of relevance here.

DO SUCH PROGRAMMES HAVE ANY DESIRABLE EFFECTS?

It is said that these programmes have two main desirable effects; they teach the lesson that crime does not pay; and they provide a harmless outlet through fantasy for the child's hostile feelings. We shall take issue with both statements.

Certainly the lesson that crime does not pay, that the criminal is always apprehended and the punishment always severe, does emerge clearly from these programmes. The reasoning would seem to run along these lines: from this welter of adult crimes, the child singles out the lesson that people who break the law are found out and punished; he applies it to his own daily life, and it acts as a deterrent against unlawful behaviour, a lesson which is of course taught in more everyday terms by parents and teachers as a basic part of the process of *socialisation*. The lesson as taught in these programmes is entirely negative (it is best not to offend against the law); they do not convey the positive lesson inculcated by parents and teachers, that good actions bring pleasure and reward. To present such a one-sided view, repeated week after week, is contrary to the recognised educational principle that a moral lesson, to be effective, must teach what should be done as well as what should not be done.

More serious is the fact, shown in Chapters 15 and 20, that the child may equally well learn other, less desirable lessons from these programmes; that to shoot, bully, and cheat is allowed, provided one is on the right side of the law; and that relationships among people are built not on loyalty and affection, but on fear and domination. In these circumstances the 'crime doesn't pay' lesson, as well as being morally rather dubious, seems to be taught at too great a cost.

The second argument is that these programmes serve a useful purpose in providing a harmless outlet for aggressive feelings. The child, it is argued, by identifying himself both with the criminal and, much more, with the hero-detective or hero-cowboy, finds an outlet in fantasy for his pent-up aggressive feelings, which in real life he has little opportunity to discharge. Maccoby, testifying before the Kefauver committee, raised some questions with regard to this argument:

> Basically, the idea is this: if a person is thirsty, and takes a long drink of water, there is a period of several hours when he won't want a drink of water again. His need has been satisfied. Similarly, the theory goes, when a person is frustrated and angry, if he does something aggressive, this will discharge his anger and he will be more quiet and peaceful afterwards. The next step in the theory is that it is possible to discharge one's anger vicariously, by watching a prizefight or a gun battle on TV. Now a number of questions come to mind about this point of view: First, if it is true that a child can get some discharge of his aggressive feelings by viewing aggressive activity on TV or other media, how long does the relief last? (53).

She also points out that this discharge in fantasy alters nothing in the child's real life and so has no lasting value. Again, not every child who watches television does so out of frustration; he is as likely to watch for other reasons, and aggressive feelings may be aroused in him, rather than quietened. What is more, when these feelings exist they are not as a rule discharged on viewing crime and violence. We cite three sets of data dealing with different facets of the problem; they all show that aggressive feelings are just as likely to be aroused as to be lessened through viewing these programmes—indeed, this seems more often to be the case.

The mothers of small children who kept a diary of their children's viewing, were asked to describe the children's behaviour following viewing. A considerable number instanced examples of aggressive play after watching Westerns.

An experiment, bearing on this topic, was described by Maccoby, who showed how far memory for aggressive content varied with the child's emotional state at the time of viewing. She found that those emotionally upset while viewing an adventure film would, a week later, remember a greater number of aggressive scenes than did those who watched the film in a more settled frame of mind. The effect of these programmes is not, therefore, a constant one.

> This means that the very children who are presumably using the movie as an outlet for their aggressive feelings are the ones who carry away the aggressive content in their memories, for how long we do not know (53).

The third set of data comes from Albert (2). He examined how far the ending of the film determined whether aggressive feelings were aroused or quietened; also the extent to which a child's own aggressiveness determined the effect of the programme. He examined the reactions of some 220 8–10 year old children, matched for age, sex, and intelligence, who had given different responses to a projective test of aggression.[1] The children were divided into high, medium, and low aggression groups on the basis of their test results and then divided into three groups, each containing the same proportion of children with high, medium, and low aggressive scores. One group was shown a conventional Western (an episode from *Hopalong Cassidy*), the second a doctored version where the villain was successful, and the third an incomplete version where there was no resolution of conflict. After seeing the films, the children were retested. Table 37 shows the percentage for each type of child and each type of film.

TABLE 37. Change in aggression scores of 8–10 year old children after seeing a *Hopalong Cassidy* film with (a) a conventional ending, (b) a doctored ending in which the villain wins, and (c) the ending removed

	Conventional Western ending			The villain wins			No ending		
	In-crease	No change	De-crease	In-crease	No change	De-crease	In-crease	No change	De-crease
Aggression group:	%	%	%	%	%	%	%	%	%
High . . .	44	11	45	37	11	52	20	30	50
Medium . . .	39	22	39	53	20	47	29	21	50
Low . . .	36	43	21	50	41	10	48	43	9

Once again we see that the degree of aggressiveness of a child determines how he will react. We also find that over one-third in both high- and low-aggression groups were more aggressive after seeing the conventional cowboy film. Clearly then, at the fantasy level at least, children's aggressive feelings may be as often aroused as reduced through the showing of these conventional programmes.

It is often claimed that tension is reduced only because the villain is punished. This is not so. Albert found that, in the high-aggression

---

[1] The scores were derived from responses to the Rosenzweig picture-frustration test administered a week before the showing of the film.

group, the doctored and incomplete versions of the film reduced aggression more than the version with a conventional ending.

The findings of Maccoby (53), Albert (2), and our own show substantial agreements, disproving the arguments which are sometimes advanced to explain why these programmes may be desirable for children.

HARMFUL EFFECTS

It is suggested that crime and violence programmes increase tension and anxiety, increase maladjustment and delinquent behaviour, teach children techniques of crime, blunt their sensitivity to suffering and, related to this, suggest to them that conflict is best solved by aggression. We add two more to this list; the inadequacy of the model offered to children for self-identification and the one-sided view presented of the problems of life.

In Chapter 15 we have shown that these programmes can and occasionally do produce tension and anxiety in a number of children, though not in all; in those who are well adjusted as well as in the emotionally more labile.

In our survey we found no more aggressive, maladjusted, or delinquent behaviour among viewers than among controls.[1] Seeing violence on television is not likely to turn well-adjusted children into aggressive delinquents; there must be a predisposition for them to be affected in this way. Nor do children as a whole translate television experience into action. It may happen in extreme cases where children have a strong desire to be aggressive or to perform a delinquent act, and for whom constant watching of programmes with an explosive content may be the last straw.

Even in extreme cases, the influence of television is small. The child's emotional make-up and the total of his environmental influences determine his behaviour.

Our findings and those of Maccoby suggest, then, that these programmes do not initiate aggressive, maladjusted, or delinquent behaviour, but may aid its expression. They may not affect a stable child, but they may evoke a response in the 5–10 per cent of all children who are disturbed or at least emotionally labile—'a group to be reckoned with by all the responsible people in the field of mass communication' (53).

Glueck, an eminent criminologist, asked for his views by the Kefauver committee, remarked:

A consistent hammering-away influence of an exciting or salacious crime, day in day out, must have an erosive effect on the mind of the youth (53).

[1] This assessment was based on teachers' ratings and on the children's answers to the personality inventories.

Facts on this aspect of the matter are difficult to come by; we do not know how children who have seen much television react to suffering compared with those who have not. But some evidence can be gained indirectly from our own findings.

Violence on television may make children not so much callous as apt to consider all violence, even in newsreels, as if it was occurring in a fictional context. We saw in Chapter 15 that children are apparently little disturbed by rioting, shooting, and warfare in newsreels—hardly more than by similar scenes in Westerns. Yet we also showed that children are quite capable of distinguishing between the real and the fictional on television, and wherever they can readily identify themselves with a situation they are more disturbed by the real. But shooting, first in Westerns and later in crime and detective stories, has become so much of a game that this play attitude enters into their evaluation of the real situation, even though books, plays, and talk at home must have given them some general idea of the tragedy of war and fighting. By the age of 11–12 they should be able to separate more clearly in their minds the tragedy of real violence from its inconsequential character in fictional programmes. We suggest that this distinction may be retarded through the steady stream of fictional violence, especially shooting, that they witness.

A related view is that in these programmes, according to Klapper, a 'seal of social acceptance' is placed on aggression. It becomes the manly, the normal way of dealing with conflict. Once again we can cite only the indirect evidence provided by our study of the effects of television on children's values and outlook (Chapter 21). On the basis of several different tests, we have been able to demonstrate that under certain conditions, ideas and values which form part of the underlying entertainment pattern do influence children's attitudes, not because they differ from the content of other mass media, but because they are repeated and seen much more often. We have no reason for assuming that respect for violence and aggression—a basic feature of the popular dramatised programmes under review—should have a smaller effect than other scenes on television. To test changes in the acceptability and respectability of aggression is difficult and, we think, unlikely to be successful. However, it is perhaps permissible to extrapolate from our findings about attitudes to other matters. Extrapolation suggests that these programmes may indeed shift a child's views so as to make aggression seem more normal and acceptable, especially if the child is particularly concerned with the expression and control of hostile feelings.

Inadequacy of the model offered. Here we offer no evidence—only value judgements, which take into account the frequency with which programmes of crime and violence are shown. The only characters who occur often enough to serve as models to children are detectives and cowboys. They are courageous, incorruptible, and efficient. These heroes, though admirable, are insufficient to serve as suitable models, since they exclude all the gentler and more compassionate virtues.

One wonders why children are not offered heroes who fight the injustices of today, as well as the Robin Hoods, Ivanhoes, and Medicis—or heroes who wrestle with physical obstacles or scientific problems. There is also a need for characters with whom girls can identify themselves.

Because these programmes take up a great deal of time, they leave insufficient time for other dramatic programmes which might provide an effective antidote to the generally violent mood of modern society.

The programmes also have a fixed framework, which is becoming more and more familiar to child viewers. Once children and adults become blasé about them, producers will have to devise some new twist to hold their interest. The most likely ways of doing this are to make the characterisation more psychological and complex and to increase the diversity and impact of the crimes. Both these methods are undesirable from the standpoint of child viewers.

ARE CRIME AND VIOLENCE PROGRAMMES INEVITABLE?

Is the public demand for crime plays and Westerns so great and so insistent that television companies cannot withhold them? Certainly these programmes are very popular with children, but much more so with children with access to two channels than with those who have access to one channel only. Of the latter group (with experience of Westerns and two crime series, *Fabian of Scotland Yard* and *Tales of Soho*), 29 per cent mentioned a crime programme as one of their three favourites. This was true, a year later, of 47 per cent[1] of children with access to BBC and ITV. These children had seen more programmes containing violence than those watching BBC only.

Does this difference mean that television companies have met a previously unsatisfied demand? Not necessarily: an equally plausible explanation is that television itself has created the demand. On the whole, children like what has become familiar. It must also be remembered that 71 per cent and 53 per cent respectively never

---

[1] This figure was somewhat inflated, since children who liked this type of programme were now able to give their second and third choice in the same category.

mentioned these programmes at all as one of the three best liked. Moreover, among those children in the survey who named plays they disliked, 16 per cent of the 13–14 year olds and 35 per cent of the 10–11 year olds listed plays about crime and detection. These programmes are, therefore, popular with many and disliked by some.

Television planners can greatly influence children's taste; they have it in their power to build a taste for more worth-while programmes, and equally to build on and strengthen the existing popularity of crime and violence. What do the children themselves feel about all this; can they envisage being entertained in other ways? In Norwich we asked children what kinds of programme they would put on if they could arrange one evening's television from 7 p.m. to bedtime (Table 38).

TABLE 38. *Now imagine you could arrange evening television for one evening after 7 o'clock. What sort of programmes would you put on during all this time before going to bed?*

(Distribution of answers from children in Norwich, 1956)

Types of programme mentioned:	14–15 YEAR OLDS %	11–12 YEAR OLDS %
Crime	3	19
Westerns	2	2
Adventure and mystery	2	5
Variety	20	24
Comedy	13	13
Family comedy serials	7	36
Music and singing	8	7
Dancing and ballet	2	3
Sport	6	14
Documentary	3	3
News	14	7
Panel games	5	13
Miscellaneous	17	14
Total cases[1]	67	134

[1] The totals exceed 100 per cent because some children mentioned more than one type of programme.

Crime, Westerns, adventure, and mystery programmes taken together were mentioned as part of an ideal evening's entertainment by *only* 9 per cent of the adolescents and 26 per cent of the younger children. The demand is therefore far from overwhelming.

It would seem, then, that other programmes could well be found to replace some of the crime and detective series without losing child, and possibly even adult, audiences.

RECOMMENDATIONS OF THE U.S. SENATE
SUB-COMMITTEE

In view of their relevance, the main conclusions of the hearings are presented here.

This sub-committee, though unable to prove a direct casual relationship between viewing and performing acts of crime and violence, felt that 'there is a calculated risk'. It therefore made the following recommendations:

1. A citizen's listening council should be set up, composed of responsible unbiased adults keeping a watchful eye on the relevant programmes.

2. The Federal Communications Commission, which had so far concerned itself solely with the technical and financial aspects of radio and television, should enlarge its function to include standards of content in programmes. It should first develop minimal standards 'both in terms of prohibiting the presentation to children of certain materials in such manner as to be damaging to them and in setting forth criteria as to what constitutes, in minimal terms, balance in programming'. For this purpose it should consult with educators, psychologists, and others concerned with children. Secondly, the Commission should do more monitoring of programmes and more fact-finding. Thirdly, it should consider its standards and findings when looking at requests for renewal of licences.

3. All television companies (instead of 60 per cent) should join the National Association of Radio and Television Broadcasters, since eventually the industry itself should determine its standards. The Association's code of practice should be expressed in more definite terms and ought in particular to ensure that there is no 'excessive presentation of crime and violence materials during children's viewing hours'—in films as well as other television programmes. To do its job more effectively, the Association should increase the scale of its monitoring.

4. There should be immediate legislation to set up a presidential commission, first, to study all mass media as they affect, or may affect, children and young adults in the United States; secondly, to report periodically to the President, Congress, and the public on practices and material which may have detrimental effects on children; and thirdly, to stimulate basic scientific research by public and private agencies and organisations.

These are far-reaching, precise recommendations—which appear to provide a useful working basis for action in this country. We shall consider them in the wider context of our own recommendations.

CONCLUSIONS

We have spent a great deal of time on what may appear a pedantic analysis of the problem in its various aspects. We have done so because we think the evidence is sufficiently strong for action. We have not proved any causal relationship between seeing these programmes and behaving undesirably; but what relationship exists we have shown to be more likely to be harmful than desirable. We find little evidence that these programmes are desirable as a means of discharging tension (they often increase it), but do find evidence that they may retard children's awareness of the serious consequences of violence in real life and may teach a greater acceptance of aggression as the normal, manly solution of conflict. The main negative or harmful effects of these programme lies in preventing, by taking up so much time, the development of alternative, more worth-while programmes. Just as a nation improves public hygiene when the evidence suggests, without necessarily proving it, that harm may otherwise result, so, we think, there is need for remedial action here. The same conclusion was reached by the U.S. Senate Sub-committee, whose recommendations we have presented above.

We feel that our evidence is sufficient to warrant:

1. a reduction in the number of crime and violence programmes shown at times when children are likely to view;
2. far more supervision of the vicious, though often short, episodes of violence and aggression in these programmes; and
3. research, not merely into whether these programmes really do harm—this we think has been sufficiently explored—but into the more important question of how to devise programmes which incorporate the successful ingredients of the crime, detection, and Western programmes and yet present themes and characterisations which are morally and socially more worth-while.

PART V

Effects on Values and Outlook

17

Content of Adult Television Plays

In order to gain an impression of the view of life and of the values contained in adult television plays which children see in large numbers, we carried out a content analysis of a random selection of BBC and ITV straight plays shown in February and March 1956.[1] Five BBC and eight ITV plays were viewed and analysed.[2] It is not our intention here to make a comparative analysis of the plays shown on the two channels, but rather to look at the two together and see to what extent there is uniformity in the values and views they offer; once again we shall be dealing with implicit as well as with explicit values. Comedies were left out even though they comprise, particularly on BBC, a considerable proportion of the plays shown. As time was so limited, it seemed best to concentrate on the type of drama which might present an unfamiliar and possibly a disturbing view of adult life. As before, we shall briefly outline the themes, characterisations, and values contained in these plays.

Themes and settings. The majority of plays take place in post-1939 England and in an urban rather than rural setting. Each play contains about two themes; the longer ones three. As in popular

[1] The technique of content analysis is described in Appendix D.
[2] We monitored more ITV than BBC plays because ITV plays were so much shorter; in this way the amount of drama time covered for each channel was the same.

magazines (51) and films (50), love is, of course, the most frequent theme. (It featured as the central one in eight plays.) What is, however, surprising, considering that we had excluded all crime and detective series, is the frequency of murder as the central theme (seven plays). In addition, six plays deal with justice, six with the acquisition of wealth, and six with various personality problems.

The character's age, nationality, occupation, and social class

Youth does not make good television drama, it seems. The majority of characters are in their thirties; in BBC plays almost a third are over fifty. Head (39) showed that the trend for American television plays is the same, although less pronounced than in this country.

In American television plays, four out of every five characters are American-born white; British plays seem less nationalistic (only one in two is British).

Rather striking is the restricted social and occupational range from which the characters are drawn. This is especially true of ITV plays. Three-quarters of the characters from both channels belong to the upper-middle and upper classes; only 7 per cent to the working class.[1] Politicians, state officials, dictators, high-ranking officers, doctors, and other professional people feature often. Lower-middle and working-class characters tend to be servants or policemen, and to take subsidiary roles.

The standard of living is comfortable, even luxurious; the rooms are large, often have chandeliers, expensive period furniture, and thick carpets. The characters themselves are well dressed, clean, and neat. Unlike detectives in crime programmes, the characters in these plays are often seen eating or drinking—pouring tea out of silver teapots or serving drinks—whisky, brandy, or sherry rather than beer. Sometimes drink is taken because an individual is under stress, but more often it is offered as an automatic sign of hospitality.

Seen from the child's point of view, the adult television plays afford a glimpse into a way of life and into types of people with whom he is little familiar in his own environment.

Heroes, heroines, and villains

Within this world there is a variety of adults with whom the child can identify himself. We have divided them into three main types: heroes and heroines, villains, and supporting characters. These terms

[1] Their social level was judged by their occupation, dress, appearance, and speech.

are slightly misleading since many of the central characters are part-hero and part-villain, but we have used them for want of better ones and to avoid the more elaborate terms, 'protagonist' and 'antagonist' (39).

The heroes and heroines of these plays, compared with the villains, are more often British, hold more of the glamorous and high-powered jobs, and enjoy a higher social status. This is particularly true of ITV plays. Only the heroines have to be young (Table 39).

TABLE 39. Percentage of heroes, heroines, villains, and supporting characters in thirteen BBC and ITV plays who were British, held glamorous jobs, and belonged to the upper-middle and upper classes

	Heroes and heroines %	Villains %	Supporting characters %
British nationality	60	37	64
Upper-middle and upper class . .	93	55	72
Glamorous and high-powered occupations .	70	55	49
Total cases	27	11	43

The main difference between heroes of adult plays and those of Western, crime and detective plays lies in the greater diversity of their behaviour and personality. They are idealised, it is true, especially in looks and such virtues as selflessness and loyalty; yet they are generally dissatisfied and unhappy and take life rather hard. The hero's main distinguishing feature is the strength of his personality; he has enterprise, courage, and self-assurance.

The villain is almost equally, though not quite as well, endowed with all these qualities; what makes him different is his callousness, his lack of honesty, and his deficient sense of justice. In fact, the villains in these plays tend to be more stereotyped than the heroes, an interesting reversal of what happens in Westerns and detective plays. The supporting characters are less clearly defined.

Unlike the characters in children's Westerns, those in adult plays are not all of a piece. Heroes can be mean and unkind, villains gentle and courageous (Appendix Table 27). We have already seen that in crime and detective programmes the lack of clear differentiation between hero and villain creates problems of identification and of loyalty for the child viewer.

Values

On the whole, the values supported by television drama are socially sanctioned values: social graces, solidarity of family and marriage, unselfishness, loyalty, patriotism, and so on. Individual values stressed are love, independence, ambition, and the desirability of having money and comfort.

Let us examine what picture these values offer to a child as yet little familiar with the problems of adult life. He finds that values contradict each other, both between plays and within the same play, and that the goodness or badness of an act depends largely on who performs it. While the villain may not kill and get away with it, the hero may do so and may even be commended for it. Neither victim nor villain is mourned, only the hero's life is sacrosanct. This duality applies equally to stealing and lying and to patriotism; the last is valued only as long as it is directed towards the right country. In these plays, just as in Westerns, villains threaten more than heroes, but kill less often.

Certain values may have particular significance for the young viewer, notably those on sex and marriage. While in general the plots uphold the desirability and sanctity of marriage, five out of the nine marriages depicted were unhappy. Extra-marital relations are disapproved of unless they occur between hero and heroine. *The Death of the Heart*, a BBC play about adolescent love and development from the novel by Elizabeth Bowen, illustrates these different sets of standards very well.

Table 40 shows how values fare in television plays.

TABLE 40. Number of times given central values were rewarded in thirteen adult television plays

Values:	Rewarded	Unrewarded	Total
Love	7	4	11
Loyalty	3	3	6
Love of children	—	1	1
Trust	3	1	4
Unselfishness	1	1	2
Innocence	2	—	2
Honesty and truthfulness	1	1	2
Patriotism	4	1	5
Courage	2	1	3
Brains and ability	4	1	5
Determination	6	2	8
Ambition	—	4	4
Hard work	2	2	4
Effort	4	1	5

Love, brains, drive, and patriotism tend to be rewarded often; goodness less often. Once again these adult plays convey a view of life which may contrast with that taught to children of the age of 10, where, on the whole, parents, teachers, and the books children read at that age try to convey that good behaviour leads to contentment.

Chance

Chance plays a major part in five out of the thirteen plays. An example of this is given in the play *Bamboo Bar* (ITV), where a man suffering from amnesia is told he committed a murder before he lost his memory; he is saved through his fortuitous rescue from the jungle by a company commander who knew him and could testify to his innocence.

About one-third of the plays provide no solution for the problems raised, especially for those of personal relationships. This is more true of the longer BBC plays than of ITV playlets, which are more like magazine stories (Table 41).

TABLE 41. Number of problems which are resolved, partially resolved, and unresolved in thirteen adult television plays

Type of problem:	Resolved			Partially resolved			Unresolved		
	BBC	ITV	Total	BBC	ITV	Total	BBC	ITV	Total
Personal relationships	1	3	4	1	1	2	6	2	8
Personal choice.	—	3	3	—	—	—	1	1	2
Abstract .	1	—	1	—	—	—	—	—	—
Technical	1	4	5	2	—	2	—	—	—
Total number of problems	3	10	13	3	1	4	7	3	10

General view of adult relationships

Klapper suggests that television provides for the children an adult world which they would otherwise 'see and enter far less often, far less freely and perhaps under adult guidance', and that this may make them anxious about the difficulties of becoming adult.

Much the same is true of British television. Good and sympathetic characters, despite their strong personalities, are often unable to control their own lives. In only one play out of the thirteen is the hero fully responsible for a satisfactory outcome. In the other twelve, either the main character is aided by chance (five plays), or his fate changes little (two plays), or his efforts get him nowhere (five plays).

Relationships between adults and children are only rarely portrayed. When they are, they tend to be unhappy. (There are only two children below 14 in all the plays monitored, of whom one is shown watching an old woman die who was acting *in loco parentis* to him (*The Seddons*, BBC). Of the five young adolescents in the thirteen plays, only one has a satisfactory relationship with the adults; the others are at odds with the world around them and have distinctly unhappy relations with parents or parent substitutes.

Violence

In assessing how much violence children see, it must be re-membered that in addition to the crime and detective series violence features very often in the straight plays. It is an important element in nine out of the thirteen.

Production techniques

Apart from close-ups of love-scenes, techniques of lighting, music, close-ups, and semi close-ups are used almost exclusively to empha-sise unpleasant emotions. ITV favours the close-up; the BBC the semi close-up. Pleasant emotions are conveyed through close-ups in 8 per cent of the cases; unpleasant ones in 74 per cent of them. From a dramatic point of view, in straight plays, tension and grief are, of course, more important moods to convey than happiness. But from a child's point of view, it means that these emotions will make the greater impact.[1]

Great emphasis is laid on preparation for death, on showing the killer and his weapon. When death occurs there is generally a close-up of the wound and prolonged close-ups of the dying victim's face.

CONCLUSIONS

A content analysis of straight adult television plays was carried out. From the point of view of the play's potential impact on children, the most important feature that emerged is the consistency of the view of life and of values offered. They portray essentially an urban upper-middle and upper-class society. From television drama, the child might learn what the homes of upper-middle and upper-class people look like, and how the people themselves behave and dress; that the professions, big business, and journalism are desirable occu-pations which good people hold more often than others; that manual workers lead less exciting, more humdrum lives. They may also learn that being good does not necessarily lead to happiness; that things rarely turn out all right; that the end justifies the means. The most important qualities for success are determination and will-power; kindness and unselfishness are of lesser consequence. Further, these plays convey that marriages are often unhappy, that parent–child relationships (especially between adolescents and their parents) tend to be difficult. Finally, the child may learn that violence is

[1] Another production device used to convey tension is that of moving the camera away from the main character to the anxious expressions of the supporting charac-ters, or of showing in close-up the victim's face registering horror and staring fixedly at a source of danger unseen by the audience.

often committed by good people, and that it is frightening for adults as well as for children. Impressions that life is difficult and that adults are unable to deal with it are conveyed strongly also through the production techniques used to underline tension and anxiety.

Within this framework, ITV represents a somewhat sharper differentiation by occupation between the good and the worth-while and the less worth-while people; its society is more exclusively upper-middle and upper class. Compared with BBC, ITV uses close-ups and other production techniques more heavily to create an atmosphere of tension. On the other hand, more of its playlets, which comprised at that time the major part of ITV drama, offer a resolution to the main problem raised by the play; this is not so with BBC plays. In that respect plays on BBC may well prove more disturbing to children than those on ITV.

The view of life conveyed in these plays may be fairly realistic, but it contrasts sharply with that presented to 10–11 year olds, or even 13–14 year olds, in their books or by their teachers and parents. Even films romanticise life rather more than do these plays. The overwhelming impression which they convey is of the difficulties and unfairness of life—a picture which may well bewilder and prove disturbing to the young viewer.

18

Television and Values: Introduction

OUR problem was to study the impact of a medium whose first aim is to entertain, not to convert. Apart from commercials and a few atypical programmes, television has no explicit, intentional message. Its influence, if any, comes from the consistency of the values it offers, from its prevailing entertainment pattern. In the preceding chapter we have shown that the values in adult television plays are surprisingly consistent and have suggested ways in which these might influence children. The correctness of these hypotheses will be investigated in the next two chapters. First, however, we should like to consider the problem in general outline, drawing, wherever possible, on relevant studies in the field of communication.

Communication research, in the main, has been concerned with factors which determine how far propagandist programmes achieve their aim, whether it be in effecting the purchase of a product or the acceptance of a point of view. Our inquiry is concerned more with gradual, almost imperceptible, cumulative impact.

In content, television shows little which is not offered by films, radio programmes, or magazines. It may yet make a distinctive impact on the viewers, simply because they will be exposed to these values more often through the many plays on television than the controls will through the other media to which they have access. The young viewers therefore come into contact with a larger slice of adult views and behaviour. What effect does this have?

Let us first look at the way a child is likely to build up his attitudes and values and see what place television might have in this process. A child, faced with the bewildering array of impressions around him, organises these into some kind of framework *scheme* (4), initially dividing people and things simply into good or bad, useless or useful. These are broad classifications; as he gains experience he makes finer sub-divisions and sees people and things as belonging to different frameworks, depending on the context in which they appear.

This process of acquiring skills, insight, and attitudes is continuous and largely unconscious. It involves feelings as well as intellect, and learning by identification as well as by imitation. The child uses models in the process of learning—people in his environment to whom he is attached and whose behaviour, outlook, and attitudes are accepted and absorbed; first the parents, then the peers, the teachers, later the heroes of the mass media. New views are imperceptibly added to existing ones. New stimuli which tally with what is already accepted are readily absorbed; those which go counter to it may go unperceived or be rejected. When they impinge on the child again and again, they can gradually modify his existing views.

Television is *one* further source of information—probably an important one, because it fulfils three conditions for effective learning. First, the child enjoys it and so is favourably predisposed to what is put over. Secondly, he spends a lot of time watching and, since the views and values presented are fairly consistent, he receives many cues pointing in the same direction thus reinforcing one another. Thirdly, television affects two senses at once and so might offer the child more than the same material would offer if it was heard on the radio or read in a book. Examples are the dress or appearance of people in a play, the expressions on their faces, and the settings in which they move.

Despite these favourable conditions, it is extremely hazardous to predict from the content of the communication to its effects. Indeed, in view of this, it is surprising how rarely television producers ask for research to be done to check whether the points they have wanted to make have in fact got across to the intended audience. Being a producer, a teacher, or a parent may give one a greater confidence in one's hunches; it does not, however, mean that these hunches are any more valid. Nor are popularity ratings a valid indicator of effectiveness.

Communication research has shown that the effect of a communication depends on the existing knowledge, attitudes, and background of the reader and viewer, as well as on the way in which the communication is put over. Described like this, it sounds very obvious, and yet how rarely do those concerned with communicating ideas take account of these factors. The main variables which have been isolated in communication research and which are of particular relevance to our inquiry are presented below:

1. *Selective perception*. An individual listening to a talk or seeing a film picks out and recalls different items according to his interests and viewpoint (46).

2. *Belief in the source of communication*. The most dramatic

example here was Cantril's study of people's reactions in the United States to the Orson Welles broadcast *Invasion from Mars* in 1938:

> Long before the broadcast had ended, people all over the United States were praying, crying, fleeing frantically to escape death from the Martians. Some ran to rescue loved ones. Others telephoned farewells or warnings. . . . At least six million people heard the broadcast. At least a million of them were frightened or disturbed (82).

The performance took the form of a series of news reports interrupting what appeared to be regular programmes. Cantril attributed the people's panic reactions in part to faith in the reliability of the radio and to acceptance of it, especially the news-service, as the official means of telling people of what is going on. Moreover, the introduction of fictitious scientific experts increased general acceptance of the message.

'I believed the broadcast as soon as I heard the professor from Princeton and the officials from Washington.'

Children, we have seen, have great faith in the authority of television, thus predisposing them towards believing in the views it offers.

3. *Boomerang effects*. These are effects produced by a communication which are different from the intended ones (66). This type of effect may readily occur with children watching a play written for adults, and was actually produced (among adults) by a BBC television programme, *Bon Voyage* (8), designed to give intending travellers to France useful tips about travel and some knowledge of French; this programme achieved its primary aim, but also made people more aware of the difficulties of foreign travel and so less keen to go to France.

Differences in intellectual maturity, leading to differences in perception and recall, were shown particularly clearly by Franck (34), who studied the ability of 6–14 year old German children to recall a ten-minute film based on Beatrix Potter's *The Tale of Johnny Town Mouse*. For purposes of analysis the film was divided into twelve scenes. The order, quantity, and type of material remembered by the different age groups was recorded. The 6 year olds had no awareness of chronological sequence; they remembered familiar scenes of dressing and eating, but neither linked scenes together nor understood the theme or the motivation of the characters. Indeed, when close-ups of the mouse were shown, the children thought it was a different, older animal because it was larger. After viewing the film a second time recall was improved;

the 6–7 year olds gave answers characteristic of the 8–9 year olds and so on.

The effect of a television programme for children may therefore depend not on its overall theme, but on the individual episodes contained in it.

Audiences differ not merely in intellectual and educational maturity but also in needs, interests, and previous attitudes. The adolescent's needs differ substantially from those of a 10 year old; he is about to enter an adult world and wants information about personal, especially heterosexual, relationships. These are of less concern to the younger child, who seeks in drama excitement and action rather than an interesting interplay of personalities. Consequently, the content of adult plays may assume a different meaning for the two age groups.

4. *The sleeper effect.* This effect, described by Hovland (47), is one in which the communication may make a stronger long-term than short-term impact,

> so that the individual has a greater tendency to go beyond the facts initially learned. . . . Any opinions that dealt with specific contents would show a decrement with time, whereas those dealing with generalisations beyond the evidence would show an increment with time.

With children, this is important; they may receive many impressions which will have an effect only when they are touched off by some happening in the child's life or by some comments made by a person in his surroundings. It becomes difficult, therefore, to decide at what point in time the effects of a communication should be assessed.

Because so many variables enter into the effects of a communication, the results of intensive research with small numbers would be indeterminate and confused. The effects are very likely to vary with the child's intellectual and social maturity, his needs and interests, his home background and past experience, as well as with his general liking for television. This meant abandoning the intensive studies as a first approach and designing other techniques which, though as projective and non-directive as possible, could be applied to the larger samples used in the survey.

In many respects our study differs from those used to isolate the variables just described; for one thing, instead of using 'captive' audiences brought together especially to hear or view a particular communication, we were studying the effect on children viewing in their own homes, where other things may be going on in the room at the same time. The beginning may be missed, or they may hear adverse comments from others. All this will influence the impact that programmes will make.

In the chapters that follow we shall examine how far programmes designed to entertain, slowly and over time make an impact, and how far we can formulate certain general principles about the way such cumulative impact is likely to make itself felt. The areas selected for examination were chosen to represent the range of views put over on television; they are in no way intended to represent all that television has to offer. The following criteria were adopted in making a choice: the views had to occur frequently on television; they should not be too trivial; their impact should be amenable to assessment by quantitative techniques; and, finally, they should form part of the prevailing entertainment pattern rather than have been given special prominence by the producer.

In Chapter 19 we look at the way television has influenced the child's view of society: his ideas about the world of work; about his own future career; about how people behave in other walks of life; his awareness of the symbols of social status; and his views on the factors that make for success.

In Chapter 20 we consider the influence of television on the child's assessment of the importance of school and education; on his views about marriage and about the type of person he would like to be when he is grown up; on his credulity (his ability to differentiate between fact and fiction); and, finally, on his attitude towards foreigners.

In Chapter 21 the findings will be brought together in an attempt to describe the general principles which govern the cumulative effect of television content on children's outlook.

19

Effects on the Child's View of Society

THE CHILD'S VIEW OF THE WORLD OF WORK

TELEVISION provides a great deal of indirect information about jobs—in plays, newsreels, interviews, panel games, and discussions.

Our content analysis has shown that adult television plays highlight the prestige and the way of life that goes with upper-middle-class occupations. In addition, it invests certain occupations with glamour, notably entertainment, detective work, and journalism.

We studied the influence of such bias in two main ways: first, to see how far it affects the child's knowledge of various types of jobs, and, secondly, how far it affects his expectations and dreams about his own future career.

Knowledge about jobs

We thought that television's influence might show itself when children were asked to name occupations which they believed were either very well paid or glamorous, both types of jobs much brought to the fore by television. They were asked: *Now think of all the jobs you know or have heard about. What would you say is a job that is very well paid? . . . and what would you say is a very glamorous job?*[1] The uniformity of replies given by viewers and controls about the glamorous job was overwhelming. Nearly every child mentioned fashion modelling or some job connected with the world of entertainment. Clearly, the 'glamour' of these jobs had already been sufficiently underlined by films, weekly magazines, and the press for television to add little that was new.

Knowledge about really well-paid jobs is obtained in a more incidental manner. Here television exerted an influence on the viewers in both age groups. Compared with the controls, viewers drew less often on their own local experience (mentioning jobs in the local boot or shoe factory) and more often mentioned white-collar jobs (67 per cent of the older, 75 per cent of the younger

[1] This question was asked only during the repeat testing in Norwich.

viewers, compared with 50 and 59 per cent respectively among the controls).

Job expectations and job fantasies

Here we are trying to see whether television has affected children's ideas about their careers, about the jobs they expect to do, or about the jobs they dream about. We are looking at the effect of television at two levels then: in terms of expected job choice, and in terms of the children's hopes. To trace such effects is useful in its own right, since we want to understand the influences which shape a young person's choice of job; it is also useful in showing whether information subtly conveyed, as a kind of background, can yet make an impact. If this is so, it should then be possible to extrapolate from such findings to other areas.

For most 13–14 year olds, job choices are of immediate relevance and importance; not so for the 10–11 year olds. We shall therefore consider the two age groups separately. If we can show that the impact of television varies for the two age groups, this has a bearing on theory, on showing how the cumulative impact of incidental background information depends on the need of the individual to search for such cues (i.e. depends on *selective perception*, to use the psychologist's terminology).

We asked the children two questions which had been found useful in a previous inquiry (41): *Write down the job you think you will do when you leave school,* followed by, *Now supposing you could be anybody, go anywhere, or do anything—what sort of work would you most of all wish to do when you are grown-up?* The first question gives us his *expected job,* the second his *wish job.*[1]

Wish jobs differed greatly from expected jobs. The son of an hotel proprietor going into the family business wanted to be a fur trapper, an intending typist to be Doris Day, a future bank-cashier to be a veterinary surgeon. An intending plumber wanted to become manager of a football team, having seen one on television, and a future decorator wanted to emulate his father and be a signaller in the Navy. (Sample answers may be found in Appendix F). The answers were analysed in three ways:

1. To see how often jobs glamorised on television were mentioned by the children.

2. To see how far the emphasis given to the professions and to big business on television found reflection not so much in their actual job choice, but in the level in which they thought about jobs. This was done by classifying expected- and wish-jobs in terms of a threefold prestige-classification consisting of manual

[1] The order of the questions was arrived at as a result of the pilot work. It was found that when the question about the wish job was put first, the child tended to reply with the job he intended to take up.

work, routine white-collar jobs, and other non-manual jobs of a more responsible kind, such as executive and professional jobs (38).

3. To see how far viewers, compared with controls, showed a greater discrepancy between the job they expected to take up and their fantasy job. This would be the case if television influenced the child's wishes but not his perception of the reality situation.

In line with previous studies, we found sharp differences between grammar and secondary modern school children. We also found differences between children from different socio-economic backgrounds in the same type of school (Appendix Table 28). More middle-class than working-class children expected, and wanted, to do white-collar work (usually professional work in the case of grammar school pupils). Finally, future viewers, within each type of school and class, tended to be less ambitious than the controls— to expect and want manual work more often than to enter the professions. While 25 per cent of the controls chose manual work and an equal percentage the professions or business, the corresponding percentages for those who acquired television sets early were 37 and 16 per cent respectively. This is a further instance of the association between greater purposiveness and striving and delay in acquiring a television set (Chapter 7).

The adolescents' expected job choices. The Norwich results indicate that television has had an effect; it has made the viewers more ambitious in their expected job choice and also in their dreams about jobs. As a result, the original discrepancy between future viewers and controls disappeared. More precise information can be gained by comparing answers given in 1955 with those given in 1956. Viewers, compared with controls, more often changed the expected and wish jobs they named and also selected more often for their 1956 choices jobs which carried a higher prestige than those given in 1955 (Table 42). Television here seems to provide for viewers something that the controls obtain in other ways.

TABLE 42. Percentage of 13–14 year olds in Norwich who changed their choice of jobs between 1955 and 1956[1]

	13–14 YEAR OLDS	
	v	c
	%	%
Expected job:		
Change in choice of job	56	41
Change to job of higher prestige . .	26	9
Wish job:		
Change in choice of job	92	83
Change to job of higher prestige . .	46	22
Total cases	24	23

[1] This question was asked only in the Norwich study and was not repeated in the grammar school.

The main survey suggests, however, that this 'boost' in enterprise is not sufficient to offset completely the pre-existing differences between viewers and controls (Appendix Table 28). Within each type of school, children from homes with television sets (and especially those from working-class homes) tended more often than their controls to choose manual work and less often to expect to enter the professions. But for the knowledge that the difference already existed in Norwich between future viewers and their controls it would be tempting to suggest that television made adolescents less ambitious.

Length of ownership or amount of viewing did not seem to affect the choice of job. On the other hand, viewers did not mention any more frequently than controls the jobs which appear so often on television: medicine, science, the world of business, work with animals.

The impact of television lay more in subtly raising their level of ambition rather than in directing their job choice into specific occupations. For the job they expect to take up, children draw for ideas on their immediate environment. 'Seeing men coming to our house to do the job' or 'My brother is in it' were the type of answers given to the question as to how they came to hear about the job.

The adolescents' wish jobs. Here the situation was different; ideas, according to the children, were derived not only from parents and friends, but from books, films, and television. The boy who wanted to be manager of a football team got the idea from television; the girl who wanted to be Doris Day had seen her in a film.

In this realm of fantasy, television made an impact in several distinct ways:

1. It led to a shift in the type of job through which boys would express their love for adventure (Table 43).

TABLE 43. Types of adventurous wish jobs chosen by 13–14 year old boys

	v %	c %
Job to do with sea and air . . .	11	26
Detective, journalist, big-game hunter, sportsman	21	13
Total cases (weighted)	252	252

Those without television wanted to go to sea or to be pilots; but viewers tended to choose the adventurous types of job made popular by television—crime detection, journalism, big-game hunting, or some form of sport. These differences were found to be significant at all levels of intelligence and in both social classes.

2. Television also seemed to make viewers more ambitious to take up a profession or executive job rather than manual work. A significantly higher percentage of viewers than controls chose a wish job that carried more prestige than their expected job; this was true especially of girls and of the less bright children in secondary modern schools. Of viewers with I.Q.s below 100, some 37 per cent chose a wish job of a higher prestige than their expected job; the corresponding figure for the controls was 26 per cent.

3. Among the girls, more viewers than controls chose more glamorous wish jobs than their expected job (Table 44).

TABLE 44. Percentage of children whose wish job differed in various ways from their expected job

13–14 YEAR OLDS

	All		Boys		Girls		Middle class		Working class	
	V %	C %	V %	C %	V %	C %	V %	C %	V %	C %
Different type	62	57	53	54	72	60	65	57	62	57
Higher prestige	35	29	28	27	42	30	40	31	31	26
More glamorous	31	25	25	23	38	27	36	27	26	23
Total cases (weighted)	504	504	252	252	252	252	252	252	252	252

The effect was the same for heavy and occasional, for recent and veteran viewers. There was one exception: children of average and below-average intelligence, who had had television for a year or more, showed the features just described to a more marked extent than did recent viewers.[1]

What makes a job attractive or unattractive to adolescents?

To find out whether television had affected the adolescent's ideas as to what makes a job attractive, he was asked to select one from each pair of a series of mutually exclusive alternatives concerning different aspects of job choice:

> *When you grow up, which of these jobs would you rather have:*
> *A job in which you work mostly with your brains?*
> *A job where you work mostly with your hands?*

[1] A comparison of 29 veterans with 32 recent viewers, all with I.Q.s of below 100, showed that 51 per cent of the veteran viewers chose wish jobs which differed in type from the work they expected to take up, and 31 per cent chose one which carried a higher prestige than did the expected job. Percentages for the recent viewers were 31 per cent and 19 per cent respectively.

The other four paired choices were: intellectually challenging work against routine work; security against opportunity and risk; greater against lesser importance of good appearance; further study against going straight into a job.[1]

Because television stresses the rewards of professional work and of brain work, we expected viewers to plump more often than controls for further training, for brain work, work requiring initiative and independence, for good appearance, and for work in which lack of security was balanced by the scope offered to ambition.

As in a previous study (41) we found that the grammar school children and, within each type of school, the middle-class children, made these choices more often than secondary modern or working-class pupils. They represented, in fact, essentially middle-class values.

Future viewers in both the grammar and the secondary modern schools showed less of a middle-class outlook when faced with three of the five choices. They chose manual work more often, went less often for jobs offering chances of advancement with risk, were less often attracted by jobs requiring high standards of dress. This difference links well with the lower level of ambition in their expected job choice. What change did television bring about? On the whole our hypothesis was confirmed. First, the values put over in television drama were partly absorbed by children from both grammar and secondary modern schools. This influence showed itself less in significant differences between viewers and controls in the main survey than in the fact that the differences between future viewers and controls shown in 1955 had disappeared. Compared with controls, viewers now more often stressed brain work and having to be nicely dressed (Appendix Table 29). The change was not sufficient, however, to reduce existing school or class differences.

Once again television made its maximum impact on adolescents of I.Q.s below 100 (those in the lower streams in the secondary modern schools).[2]

Differences in impact of television on the two age groups

So far we have considered the adolescents, the group most

[1] The questions were taken from an earlier inquiry into social-class differences in outlook and values of 13–14 year old boys. Differences were found between pupils of grammar and secondary schools and within each type of school, between children from middle- and working-class homes (42).

[2] In the main survey, the choices of those whose I.Q. was below 100 were as follows: 'you work mostly with your brains', viewers 33 per cent, controls 18 per cent; 'you have to think things out for yourself', viewers 24 per cent, controls 15 per cent; 'go to the university or college', viewers 57 per cent, controls 40 per cent. For all five paired choices, as one descends the intellectual scale, fewer middle-class choices are given.

interested in jobs. With them, television has had a subtle influence, in terms of the aspects which they considered important in choosing their jobs, in terms of their ambitions, and in the way in which, in fantasy, they express their longing for adventure. Among this age group, television has had its maximum effect on the less intelligent children and, irrespective of intelligence, on girls. It has reduced differences due to intelligence, but not differences in job expectations and fantasies due to social background; children from middle as well as from working classes seemed influenced by television's 'ethos'.

The 10–11 year olds were not yet very interested in the world of work; they might like its glamour and adventure, but were not yet attuned to subtle social differences.

The job choices of the 10–11 year olds (both expected and wish jobs) did, however, reflect differences in socio-economic background and in intellectual maturity. This came out clearly both from the Norwich study and in the main survey (Appendix Table 30). (Examples of their choices are given in Appendix F.)

Home background and intellectual maturity play a part; television does not; the information presented on television consists in the main of background cues, noticeable only to those who have a special stake in them.

The considerable impact of television on the young adolescent's view of the world of work and the lack of impact on the 10–11 year old illustrates the need for correct *timing* of the presentation of ideas; the more the ideas link with the prevailing interests of the audience, the more likely are they to be noticed and absorbed.

AWARENESS OF SOCIAL-CLASS DIFFERENCES

The content of adult plays presented in Chapter 17 has shown how the social level of the character is indicated by a series of standardised patterns of speech, dress, and décor. To the adult, these may appear hackneyed, but to the child viewer, they may convey information about how people in other social levels live. How much of all this is absorbed?

Dress and speech as symbols of status

Television has made viewers, especially the younger ones, more aware of dress and speech as symbols of status.

We put the following two questions: *Do you think you can tell how important a man is by the way he speaks? Do you think you can tell how important a man is by the way he is dressed?* Children were asked to tick one of the following: *usually; sometimes; hardly ever.*

Speech. Apart from cues provided by their own environment, both viewers and controls were already familiar with speech as a symbol of status through radio programmes; any effect of television would therefore be due to their seeing more adult plays and other programmes than controls hear. No differences were found in the main survey. In Norwich, however, young future viewers seemed less aware of speech as a status symbol than the controls. After one year's viewing they were equally sentitive to it (Appendix Table 31).

Dress. The younger viewers, especially the girls, had become more aware of dress as a status symbol; this was found both in the Norwich study and in the main survey; a difference which did not exist between future viewers and their controls (Appendix 31 and Table 45).

TABLE 45. *Do you think you can tell how important a man is by the way he is dressed?*

| | 10–11 YEAR OLDS | | | | | |
| | All | | Boys | | Girls | |
	v %	c %	v %	c %	v %	c %
Usually .	38	29	34	28	43	30
Sometimes .	46	55	50	58	42	52
Hardly ever .	16	16	16	14	15	18
Total cases (weighted) .	465	471	233	238	232	233

There was no difference between older viewers and controls, presumably because they were anyhow fairly familiar with these symbols.

The way other people live

How far do the settings of television programmes influence the child's view of how other people live? We have considered this question in two parts—the appearance of the homes shown in television plays and the way of life of the families portrayed in these plays.

The children were asked: In these questions, you are asked to imagine what other people are like and how they live. Try to imagine a house in which a *really rich family* lives. Think of the living-room. Say what it looks like and what it has in it.

A few questions later they were asked to describe the living-room of a *perfectly ordinary family.*

Here are examples of the way children of different ages and intelligence described *The living-room of a really rich family*:

10–11 year old children:

> Large, all well painted, nice covers to the chairs, a settee, a bookcase, a coffee table, a bell for the maid, a valuable clock. (Boy I.Q. 115.)
> A television, wireless, telephone, a rich coloured carpet, a group of light French windows. (Boy I.Q. 100.)
> In a house where a rich family lives the house is clean and has got quite a lot of things in it. (Girl I.Q. 90.)
> It has crystal chandeliers with a grand piano in one corner furnished with a beautiful suite of furniture. (Girl I.Q. 115.)

13–14 year old children:

> It would have two large armchairs, a lot of animal trophies on the wall, a lot of carpets and animal rugs, and a large fire. (Boy I.Q. 110.)
> Radiogram, cocktail cabinet, a TV., piano, big armchairs, some mirrors, a large bookcase. (Boy I.Q. 118.)

The emphasis was on cleanliness, costly objects, highly polished surfaces, and soft carpets. Some children referred to particular objects, others used adjectives like 'rich', 'soft', and 'beautifully patterned'. One child put two television sets in the living-room, another crowded into it all the expensive objects she could think of: 'large brilliant carpets, a television set, a radiogram, a chandelier, a washing machine'.

On the whole rooms like these were admired. The few criticisms tended to equate wealth with coldness and distance—'a large fussy room, no comfort at all', 'a cold, damp room'. One 11 year old conveyed her feeling of coldness rather differently: 'It has beautiful furniture and a big fire. The man of the house is sitting by the fire reading, the lady is biting her finger-nails. No one speaks.'

These highly individual descriptions were classified so that the influence of television over and above that of other media could be measured.[1] This analysis proved so time-consuming that we confined ourselves to the Norwich sample only.

Television influenced the descriptions of younger viewers. Their descriptions tended to become fuller than those of the controls and contained more frequent mention of television's hallmarks of

---

[1] Of the code categories, the first assessed the fullness of responses. Answers which gave more than two items over and above the standard set of furniture, television, radiogram, and wireless were classified as full replies. Secondly, we analysed the frequency of mention of chandeliers, big fireplaces, glass cupboards, and French windows, &c. Thirdly, we noted the frequency with which visual versus tactile adjectives were used—comments on brightness would be examples of visual responses and references to rich velvet and soft carpets examples of tactile responses.

wealth, such as chandeliers, glass-fronted cupboards, and grand pianos (Table 46). The difference was more marked among working-class than middle-class children.[1]

TABLE 46. Frequency with which certain objects were mentioned in the descriptions of the living-room of a really rich family

(Answers of 10–11 year olds from Norwich)

	Viewers		Controls	
	1955 %	1956 %	1955 %	1956 %
Show-cases, glass cupboards, big fire-places, chandeliers . . .	5	9	5	3
Full list of objects	17	22	16	10
Total cases	69	96	67	83

But since our sample was small, the difference, though consistent, was not statistically significant. Contrary to expectation, television did not increase reference to visual attributes.

The living-room of a perfectly ordinary family. Where ideas are drawn from everyday experience, television does not appear to exert any influence. Children seemed to be describing their own familiar surroundings. Those who had a television set at home included it in their descriptions; while those who had no television set listed a radio instead. Here are a few examples:

10–11 year old children:

A settee, fireside chairs, bookcase, a cupboard, a clock, and fireplace. (Boy I.Q. 120.)

It is a shabby room. People with hardly any money. It has an old table, torn chairs, and a broken lampshade. (Girl I.Q. 100.)

It has a tweed sofa with an oak table and chairs and sideboard, a twelve-inch television, and rather a small old wireless. (Girl I.Q. 105.)

13–14 year old children:

Armchair next to the fire, a chest of drawers, a table, a large fireplace, a wireless on chest of drawers. (Boy I.Q. 110.)

Room quite small and floor covered with mats. Three-piece suite. Small television and a machine. Small table for meals. (Girl I.Q. 95.)

Large battered table with homework on it. Large window with thick curtains. Looks out on to neat front garden. Not a very new carpet. Some reproductions of the more cheerful Old Masters on the wall. Brick fireplace, straight-backed chairs up to table. Leather armchairs against the wall. Radio stands on bookcase. Untidy pile of magazines by the window. Mecanno model—library books—vase of heather and primroses. (Girl I.Q. 120.)

The fact that they had just described the living-room of the very rich family no doubt influenced the children's ideas. The rooms

[1] Of the working-class viewers, 4 per cent mentioned them in 1955 and 10 per cent in 1956 compared with 7 per cent and 4 per cent for the controls.

were small, not large; the chairs ordinary and not decorated; the fitted carpet became a rug, and the twenty-two-inch television became a twelve-inch set.

The way of life of people of different social levels. The children were asked, 'What does the father of this rich family spend his time doing?' and later, 'How does the father of this perfectly ordinary family spend his time?' Once again the answers were colourful:

Many saw the rich man as someone who 'smokes cigars and rides horses', and as 'looking around the house, smoking and drinking'. Only a few referred to his work—'a bank manager and very strict' or 'doing reports at his office desk'. The emphasis on smoking, drinking, playing golf, or hunting occurred as frequently among the controls as among viewers.

By contrast, the father of the ordinary family was seen essentially as a working man: 'goes to work from 8 to 6' or 'works as a gardener'. When his leisure time was described, work was always mentioned first: 'works all day, home in the evening', or 'working; when he comes home sitting with his feet up'. Children were drawing largely on their own family; indeed, several of them made direct reference to their fathers: 'Father spends his time healing people.' One girl described her father as 'backing horses, doing football pools'. One 10–11 year old (I.Q. 90) wrote just one word: 'drinking'. Evening activities formed a limited range in which television, the pub, and gardening featured prominently.

Answers to questions about the mother of the two families followed the same pattern. The mother of an ordinary family, it was said, 'keeps the house clean, cooks and bakes', and perhaps was seen 'mending and looking after the children'. The mother of the rich family was seen as either 'ordering the servants' or 'sewing or playing the piano'. One child expressed this comparative leisure as 'working very slowly'. There was a good deal of emphasis on spending: 'buying new clothes or titivating herself up'.

The answers have been quoted fairly fully because they throw an interesting light on the children's perception of the way of life of different social classes. They are well worth further analysis in terms of social-class differences and in relation to the children's own vocational wishes. Seen from the point of view of the influence of television, no differences were found. This may be because the way of life of the ordinary family is anyhow drawn from the children's daily environment and that of the really rich families may come as much from films and magazines as from television. Here may be another instance where television does not add information to that which the children have already acquired from other sources.

How to get on in the world

The content analysis of adult plays has shown that independence, initiative, and personal effort are rewarded by success. This is essentially the ideology of a competitive society. High moral qualities, while no impediment, are not enough: they must be backed by strong personality, self-confidence, and willingness to take risks.

We have already seen that this ideology is partially reflected in viewers' preferences for different facets of work. What are the wider effects?

Two questions bearing on this were asked in different questionnaires. The first question was open-ended: *What do you think are the three main things that help a man to get on in the world?* During the later testing, the children were offered a similar question with several ready-made answers to choose from: *Here are ten things which may be important in helping a person to get on in the world. Tick the one which you think is the most important.* Nine of the ten characteristics were chosen from the qualities mentioned by adults in another survey: *good character, people known to your family, brains, money, hard work, good luck, good dress and speech, having the right friends, education* (41). The tenth characteristic, *not being afraid,* was added, because it seemed to represent more sharply a characteristic of television ideology.

In Norwich the answers of future viewers did not differ from those of controls, so that any differences between viewers and controls may confidently be associated with viewing.

Before discussing differences between viewers and controls, it may be of interest to note the responses of children of different ages.

In reply to the closed question, one in three of the 13–14 year olds thought *good character* the most important factor; one in four selected *education*, one in five *hard work*. Only one in ten chose *brains* (Appendix Table 32).

The only difference between children from grammar and secondary modern schools was that the latter gave precedence to education over hard work. Each group, in fact, looked at social mobility from its own frame of reference. Since grammar school children found education less of a barrier to success than did children from secondary modern schools, they mentioned more often characteristics like hard work which would affect their own future progress.

The younger children, being still at primary school, differed from the adolescents in their choices. Almost a third of their votes went to *education*, a quarter to *brains*, and only about a fifth to *good character*. Education was an important issue for them because they had just taken the 11-plus examination but had not yet had their results. They were well aware that different types of secondary school provide different opportunities for getting on in the world. But children aged 11–12 (those retested in Norwich) already gave answers in line with those of adolescents.

Our predictions derived from the content analysis were fulfilled viewers mentioned *brains* and *not being afraid* significantly more often than controls. First place was more often given to *not being afraid* especially by girls. The same difference held for the younger age group, though it was less marked. On this occasion it was the more intelligent child who showed it most clearly.

Replies to the open-ended question confirmed the difference revealed by the closed question. The adolescent viewers, boys and girls, and the highly intelligent among the young viewers, mentioned *brains, drive, self-confidence* significantly more often than the controls did (Appendix Table 33).

Heavy viewers seemed more influenced than occasional ones, but veteran viewers no more than recent ones.[1]

CONCLUSIONS

We have looked at the impact of television on the child's view of some aspects of the social structure of our society. These fall into two broad parts: those which might be described as visual information provided by the dress and setting typical for people of different walks of life, and those which relate to more abstract information in the form of value judgements.

The visual information provided only the younger viewers with new information: it made them more aware of social-class differences.

Our findings reinforce the conclusions reached by Franck (34) on the capacity of different age groups to absorb values. Cumulative effects occurred only with the older viewers or with the 10–11 year olds whose mental age was above their chronological age. Sensitivity to cues about jobs seemed to be related not so much to intellectual maturity as to social maturity. In the case of values it was intellectual rather than social maturity that determined the amount of impact.

We believe these findings to be of considerable importance because they clearly show the influence of television plays on the child's view of society. The influence is not overpowering, but it is solid and consistent.

[1] In a comparison of answers of groups of 37 heavy, 37 moderate, and 37 occasional viewers, matched for intelligence, age, sex, and social class, mention of moral qualities as a way of getting on in the world was made by 21 per cent of the heavy viewers compared with 54 per cent of the occasional viewers.

20

Effects on Other Attitudes

DOES television, by providing strong counter attractions, cause children to have a lower opinion of the importance of education and to grow impatient with school?

One might think that television, by showing the child varied and exciting ways of life, could make school appear drab and uninteresting; cowboys, detectives, and film stars rarely reach their position through application to school work. Indeed, this is one of the fears frequently voiced by those who are convinced that television is harmful. On the other hand, television drama shows up the rewards of the professions, and appears to have made the children more ambitious, at least in fantasy.

The findings show that television has not affected the importance children attach to education. Five different techniques were used to study what children felt about school, schoolwork, their relationship to their teachers, and the importance of school marks and attendance. The measures used are given in Appendix G. Neither the main survey nor the Norwich study showed any differences between the groups.

In addition, we obtained corroborative evidence from the teachers themselves, who found no difference between viewers and controls in their interest both in school and extra-curricular activities. Teachers also found no difference between viewers and controls when they assessed each child as to whether he generally liked school, was indifferent, or even resented it.

A child may enjoy school, may even consider education important to his future, and yet be impatient to leave school because of the many counter attractions offered by the outside world. Children were asked: *If you were free to do as you liked, at what age would you leave school?*

As in previous studies (42), significantly more middle-class than working-class children in both age groups chose to stay at school beyond the school-leaving age (Appendix Table 34). Television viewing made no difference here.[1]

[1] These findings are of general interest. They show clearly that, even when intelligence is held constant, children's ideas about school-leaving depend on their social background, and that social-class differences in this direction show themselves by the time children are 13 to 14 years of age.

IDEAS ABOUT MARRIAGE

Television drama presents two very different pictures of marital relationships. The family serials: *The Groves, The Appleyards,* and the American husband–wife serials, *I Love Lucy, I Married Joan, The Burns and Allen Show,* all depict the ups and downs of marriage within a framework of a united family and of mutual love and affection.

But just as often, as the content analysis has shown, other plays depict strained marital relationships where the prevailing atmosphere is one of hostility, disloyalty, of being 'caught' or 'misunderstood', and so on. Such plays show that marriage can be complicated or unsatisfactory. Again it should be emphasised that these plays, although hackneyed for the adult, may present a disturbing and novel view of adult relationships to the child.

To test the degree to which these plays affected children's ideas on marriage, they were asked: *Not everyone gets married when they grow up. When you are old enough to marry, what would you rather do?* The answers showed no differences between viewers and controls. The great majority said they wanted to get married.

Then, in a list of statements, we included: *Once people are married, they are sure to be happy,* and asked children if they agreed, or disagreed, or were not sure. Once again there was no difference between viewers and controls. About 15 per cent in both groups agreed and 65 per cent disagreed with the statement.

We also tried to find out whether television affected the child's ideas as to what makes a good husband or wife. The children were asked to complete the following two sentences: *A good husband is a man who . . .* and *A good wife is a woman who . . .*

In adult television plays, other than family serials, there is less emphasis on the partnership aspect of marriage and more on the personal relationships. We therefore expected viewers, rather more than controls, to stress qualities of personality. This was so in the case of adolescent girls. They stated more often than controls that a good husband is one who is 'loyal to his wife and kind to his children', or who 'has a good nature and is not jealous'. Conversely, more of the controls mentioned the partnership aspect—that a good husband is one who is a good provider, 'takes his wife out, gives her his wages' (Appendix Table 35).

No such difference was found in answers about what makes a good wife; viewers and controls were about evenly divided between domestic virtues ('is a good cook') and personality qualities ('is kind and loving').[1]

[1] One grammar school boy wrote: 'is a female who devotes her attention to her husband only'.

On all questions about marriage there were no differences in Norwich between future set owners and controls.

* * * * *

Television appears to have only a negligible effect here—for two reasons: first, children get their views about family life chiefly from home; and secondly, television, by stating two conflicting views, may well destroy the potential impact of its plays.

THE CHILD'S IDEAL OF A GROWN-UP

The following question was asked: *Write down what sort of person you would like to be when you are 25 years old.* Answers were classified under the following headings: love, marriage and home; work; material circumstances; appearance; moral qualities; and fame.

No differences were found between future viewers and controls in Norwich and, contrary to expectation, television did not make children more interested in appearance or in fame and glamour. But it did make them (especially the adolescent boys) more interested in the things they would like to own, such as cars and houses, than in the work they would like to do.

Among 13–14 year old boys, 38 per cent of the viewers mentioned material things (as compared with 27 per cent of controls). Only 30 per cent of viewers described the work they would be doing (as against 37 per cent of controls). This more materialistic outlook fits in well with television's success ideology. The longer the access to television, the more pronounced it became.[1]

* * * * *

To learn more about the children's aspirations we asked them: *If you were told you could meet anyone you liked in the whole world, whom do you think you would choose to meet?* The answers fell into four main types: film, stage, and TV stars; sportsmen; members of the Royal Family; and a small group of other famous people such as scientists and statesmen.

Television here had an effect on both age groups (Table 47). Viewers wanted to meet film, stage, or TV stars and sportsmen more often than did the controls, while controls more often mentioned members of the Royal Family. The occasional appearance on the screen of explorers, statesmen, or scientists had clearly made little impression. Exceptional personalities apart, individuals have to be

[1] Comparing matched groups of veteran, experienced, and recent viewers we found that 28 per cent of the veteran compared with 18 per cent of the experienced and 17 per cent of the recent viewers mentioned material possessions.

'sold' to the public in much the same way as commodities if they are to make an impact.

TABLE 47. *If you were told you could meet anyone you liked in the world, whom do you think you would choose to meet?*

(Distribution of answers by age and sex)

| | 13–14 YEAR OLDS All | | 10–11 YEAR OLDS All | |
	v %	c %	v %	c %
Miscellaneous	7	16	8	18
Film, television, and stage stars . .	42	30	39	32
The Queen, members of the Royal Family	24	24	22	33
Sportsmen	17	11	18	10
Relatives, friends . . .	1	2	3	3
Scientists, artists, explorers . .	4	11	2	1
Sir Winston Churchill . . .	5	6	8	3
Total cases	134	132	132	135

IMAGE OF ADULT LIFE

Klapper (55) pointed out that through television young viewers obtained an earlier and more frequent view of adult life, in which adults are troubled, than do children who only go to the cinema and listen to the radio. He suggests that this may well make young viewers anxious about their own competence in facing the demands of adult life.

After all, as we have seen, adult television plays leave few of the comforting black and white philosophies of childhood intact; fewer viewers than controls, for instance, believed the statement to be true that 'good people always come out all right in the end'. Television seemed to produce an earlier intellectual awareness of the complexity and essential unfairness of life. Here, then, we examine how far this awareness disturbs the child.

Our data show that, compared with controls, adolescent viewers, especially girls, were more worried, indeed were even frightened about growing up, leaving school, leaving home, taking up their first job, and getting married. For evidence we draw on two personality inventories, the 'worries' and the 'fears' inventories.

In the inventory of worries, fifty-two items were presented and the child was asked to tick each one to indicate whether it 'worries me a lot', 'worries me a little', 'hardly ever worries me'. Seven areas of concern were covered: school and school performance; moral standards; feelings of social insecurity; rejection by other children; parents' attitude to child; material aspects of home life; and growing up.

Table 48 shows that 13–14 year old girl viewers were more worried about growing up than the controls. The difference was very significant. With adolescent boys the difference was small, but consistent for four out of five items.

TABLE 48. Percentage distribution of answers, by age and sex, of 'worries me a little' and 'worries me a lot' to items about growing up contained in the inventory of worries

| | 13–14 YEAR OLDS | | | | 10–11 YEAR OLDS | | | |
| | Boys | | Girls | | Boys | | Girls | |
Worries associated with adult life:	v %	c %	v %	c %	v %	c %	v %	c %
The thought of marrying .	33	35	32	23	34	37	35	28
The thought of having to leave school	31	25	37	23	33	36	36	34
The thought of having to leave home when I grow up .	45	37	55	45	58	54	65	63
The thought of going to work later on	31	24	36	20	31	35	36	34
Finding a job when I am older	42	36	47	39	41	40	40	43
Total cases (weighted) . .	130	135	157	158	182	180	170	167

The viewers' greater concern about growing up, compared with that of the controls, cannot be dismissed on the score that viewers were emotionally more labile; they were not. When we looked at the total score on these inventories, and on the incidence of attendance at child-guidance clinics or of psychosomatic symptoms, no differences between viewers and controls were found except in two respects; viewers were less concerned about their parents' attitudes to them and about the material deficiencies of their home.

Thus worry about growing up occurred among children who otherwise differed little from their controls. The 'fears' inventory lent further support to this by revealing the same type of difference for adolescent girls.[1] Again, for girls the difference was very significant (Table 49).

Appendix Table 36 lists fears commonly found among sensitive and emotionally somewhat labile children. Apart from one item—being made to look silly—the incidence was much the same for viewers and controls. This is a further support of the specificity of these anxieties.

---

[1] Not for boys this time. Boys of that age in particular were reluctant to admit to any fears, so that the effect would have had to be very considerable to make itself felt.

TABLE 49. Percentage distribution of answers, by age and sex, of 'frightens me a little' or 'frightens me a lot' in the inventory of fears

| | 13–14 YEAR OLDS | | | | 10–11 YEAR OLDS | | | |
| | Boys | | Girls | | Boys | | Girls | |
Fears associated with adult life:	V %	C %	V %	C %	V %	C %	V %	C %
The thought of having to leave home when grown up .	42	32	49	39	43	43	56	55
Growing up . . .	9	9	25	15	14	9	16	19
The thought of marriage .	16	22	25	9	12	19	21	20
The thought of my first job .	43	43	54	45	29	26	41	33
Older boys. . . .	18	14	34	20	18	19	35	30
Older girls. . . .	7	4	15	10	5	7	11	13
Total cases (weighted) . .	135	133	154	159	191	183	169	172

Greater anxiety about growing up occurred only among adolescents, particularly girls. The secondary modern girls were more strongly affected than girls from the grammar school, especially those from middle-class homes. These girls, just about to leave school, are emotionally in an in-between stage. Television drama is not so much frightening by adult standards, as unable to provide the positive reassurance needed at that period. We have already shown that adolescent girls, both viewers and controls, were far more susceptible than other groups to the emotional impact of mass media. Emotionally responsive, they selected from television whatever reinforced their feelings of insecurity. This was an easy task, since television offers so few characters who are confident, good, and happy and so serve as suitable positive models for the child. We suggest that middle-class children may be more affected because the adults around them may be more zealous in sheltering them from problems of adult life and may make more effort to present a competent and united front. If this is so, then television possibly shows them a side of adult life of which they have had less experience than working-class children. That the grammar school girls were little affected is in line with all our other findings: in any case the problems were less immediate for them, because they would be staying at school for some years longer.

The results are interesting, because they show, first, that it is possible to test psychological hypotheses about long-term effects by means of a survey, and, secondly, that any generalisations such as 'television makes children anxious' are oversimplified. The effects on personality we found were specific and depended on the intellectual maturity and emotional needs of the child. Once again there was an *optimal age of emotional responsiveness*. On the face of it, it would seem more plausible to argue that anxiety about adult life showed itself more among younger children with less direct experience of adults and less knowledge of the world gained from films and newspapers. Yet this was not the case: partly because children saw rather less adult television, but mainly because they were not looking for this type of information.

ABILITY TO DIFFERENTIATE BETWEEN FICTION AND REALITY

Instances are often quoted of children accepting as true a purely fictional piece of television drama. Does the screen possess some compelling authority superior to that of the spoken or printed word for children? Does this make it more difficult for them to distinguish fiction from reality, drama from news or information programmes?

To study this credulity we first chose the subject of space travel, since the BBC has had an information programme on outer space as well as a fictional serial called *Quatermass*, which dealt with Martians.

The following statements were presented to the older children: two dealt with space travel, two with the Martians.

> Flying saucers are space ships from Mars.
> There are people living on Mars.
> We can now visit the moon in a space ship.
> We are being watched from Mars.

Most children knew these statements to be untrue (Appendix Table 37). Throughout, the least-informed group were the girls from secondary modern schools. This was the only group where differences were found between viewers and controls, differences which we believe can be traced to the impact of specific programmes. The first concerns the visit to the moon in a space ship; significantly more girl viewers knew these statements to be untrue compared with their controls, probably as a direct result of the information programmes on this topic. At the same time, they were less certain than the controls that the statement *There are people living on Mars* was untrue— possibly a reaction to the strong impact made by the science-fiction series *Quatermass*. We suggest that the impact is noticeable only in girls because they have less science fiction in their comics and listen less often to space serials than boys, who are more informed on these issues and so less influenced. For the girls, on the other hand, factual and fictional programmes may have provided novel information.

IDEAS ABOUT FOREIGNERS

Television provides many opportunities for children to see how foreigners live and what their outlook and attitudes are. The BBC ran, at the time of testing, *Children's International Newsreel* and other types of programme designed to bring young viewers in contact with European countries. How far has television given children a better understanding of other people's ways of life? How far has it made foreigners and foreign countries more attractive to them?

We asked the children: *Suppose you could choose to be born again anywhere. Which country would you choose?* They were given two sentences to complete: *I would choose to be born in* . . . *I would choose this country because* . . . The question was deliberately worded so as to encourage children to name countries other than their own.

Television, we found, made viewers somewhat more interested in other countries; 51 per cent of the older children (as against 45 per cent of the controls) and 46 per cent of the younger viewers (as against 39 per cent of the controls) chose countries other than England. The difference, while consistent, was not, however, significant.

Of countries outside the Commonwealth, the United States received the highest mention by viewers and controls alike (about 18 per cent). There was a tendency for more viewers than controls to name European countries. This was especially so with the 10–11 year olds (18 per cent as against 10 per cent of the controls; the figures for the 13–14 year olds were 17 and 12 per cent respectively). This greater interest probably reflected the greater familiarity with the life in these countries brought about by television programmes. The data from Norwich showed no differences between future viewers and controls.

The preference for European countries increased the longer children viewed. Twenty-one per cent among veteran viewers mentioned them, compared with 13 per cent among the recent viewers.

We next compared the descriptions given by viewers and controls of different types of foreigners who had appeared on television in newsreels or plays. A sentence-completion test was used as follows: *Here is a list of different kinds of people. How would you describe them to a friend? Finish each sentence to show how you would tell your friend something about them—not what they look like, but what sort of people they really are.* The instructions were worded so as to avoid answers like 'Germans are people who live in Germany', and to encourage less stereotyped descriptions. Six groups of foreigners were included in the list. Two of these six were traditional 'out-groups', Jews and Negroes. Jews

named as such occasionally feature in plays; Negroes are often seen
in dance bands and variety shows. The French and the Americans
were included as peoples towards whom most English people are
generally well disposed. The remaining two, Russians and Germans,
were peoples towards whom the general attitude might be neutral or
hostile.

Answers were classified into four main categories to show whether:
(1) children had gone beyond bare definition; (2) they referred to
the way of life, the appearance, or the character of the people concerned; (3) the answers showed a neutral, non-evaluative, or a biased
attitude; and (4) any descriptions given by viewers differed systematically from those given by the controls.

The Norwich data showed no difference between future viewers
and controls.

As we expected any influence to be slight, we had to make our
measuring instruments as sensitive as possible. Consequently in
Norwich we worked out a change score for each child whereby the
answers given in 1956 were compared with those given a year earlier
—before television had come to the city (Table 50).

TABLE 50. Percentage of children in Norwich who changed from value judgements
in 1955 to non-evaluative descriptions

	13–14 YEAR OLDS		10–11 YEAR OLDS	
	v	c	v	c
Description of foreigners:	%	%	%	%
Negroes . . .	6	4	13	5
Jews	19	10	16	7
Russians . . .	34	10	24	3
Germans . . .	46	27	22	18
French . . .	31	20	16	8
Americans . . .	13	14	19	9
Total cases . . .	32	29	68	74

The analysis proved so time-consuming that while we coded all
the Norwich cases, we coded only a smaller random sample from
the main survey. The numbers were therefore relatively small and
differences were not always statistically significant; nevertheless they
were too consistent to have come about by chance; in each instance
they showed difference between viewers and controls in line with the
trend just noted.

This test showed that television influenced children's attitudes to
foreigners in two ways. First, the Norwich children, after one year's
viewing, made more objective and fewer evaluative statements.
They would describe aspects of foreigners' lives rather than pass
value judgements, even though the wording of the question encour-

aged the latter. For example, more children said that Jews are people who 'believe in God, not Christ' or that they are 'religious', than called them 'pleasant' or 'swindlers and misers'. More of them mentioned that Negroes are 'black people' or 'dark skinned', than that they are 'cunning' or 'unhappy'. Television seems to have produced in the child a more detached, objective attitude.

Secondly, in describing different sets of foreigners, the younger children were influenced by how the people had been presented on television. In the main survey more viewers than controls mentioned, for instance, that Jews were religious or carried out certain religious practices. This derives directly from television drama, for when Jews are identified in the plays as such there is usually some reference to their religious practices. More viewers than controls described the French as gay and witty, reflecting the fact that nearly all the French people they see on television are cabaret artistes. Among younger children at least, more viewers than controls saw the Germans as arrogant and vicious—again, a reflection of television drama, where Germans are mainly presented in the role of Nazis (Table 51).

TABLE 51. Percentage of children who gave the following stereotyped views about foreigners

	13–14 YEAR OLDS		10–11 YEAR OLDS	
	v %	c %	v %	c %
French: gay, witty .	14	8	6	1
Germans: vicious, arrogant . . .	14	14	14	7
Jews: religious, practise their religion . .	14	9	11	7
Total cases . . .	144	144	144	144

Viewers and controls gave the same stereotypes for Americans, Negroes, and Russians.

Horowitz (45) has shown that attitudes to foreigners, especially 'out-groups', become more fixed and so less amenable to change as the child grows older. This matches our own findings, which show the influence of television to be more marked for the younger viewers than for adolescents.

Attitudes to foreigners in general

Next, in the list given to the older children, we included three statements with a bearing on xenophobia: *My own country is always right. You can't trust foreigners. We can learn a lot from foreign people.* They were asked for each statement to check one of three responses: *I agree, I disagree, I am not sure.*

We found differences in respect to one question out of the three. Significantly more viewers than controls disagreed with the statement *My own country is always right*. Appendix Table 38 gives the results by type of school; the interest lies in the markedly greater insular attitude of secondary modern compared with grammar school pupils.

A great deal of what we have examined in this chapter consisted in tracing the effects of a rather one-sided view of society on the child. Here, we have done the opposite—traced a broadening influence. The impact is limited, but nevertheless clearly discernible. The children we tested had seen BBC television only, where much thought is given to the presentation to children of the way of life of other countries.

If the children had had access to ITV only (which shows foreigners more often in the role of the criminal) the influence might well have been in the opposite direction, namely, that of increasing prejudice against specific 'out-groups'.

There is great scope here, through newsreels, and even more through drama, to acquaint children with the way of life of other countries and of other social groups.

Television and Values—a Summing Up

IN the previous chapter we have traced the cumulative effect of television on the child's sense of values and his outlook on life. Here we shall look at the findings as a whole. We first look at the negative findings.

WHERE TELEVISION HAS NO APPARENT INFLUENCE

First, let us stress what television does not do. It does not have a high direct *model value* for children, i.e. the child viewer does not develop any great desire to be famous or to be a great star, or expect to take up any of the numerous jobs glamorised by television. He identifies himself with television personalities only in his wish-dreams about jobs and as a way of expressing his longing for adventure.

Television has no apparent influence on children's views on marriage or (with one exception) their view of the role of a good husband or wife. This probably is, first, because there is usually no shortage of data in his real-life environment, and, secondly, because television here does not present a consistent point of view. The family or husband–wife type of serial stresses family unity and affection, but many of the adult plays show marriage and family life in jeopardy.

Children do not find everyday life drab and uninteresting when they contrast it with the edited version of life they see on television. It has not made them less interested in school or more anxious to leave school early.

Nor has it blunted the older children's ability to differentiate between fact and fiction. They do not become more gullible; indeed, in certain respects they become more sophisticated. Much exposure to adult plays and to documentaries influences many of them to reject the comforting black-and-white philosophy of childhood tales. This is an interesting finding, particularly since television writers and producers always give children's programmes happy and just endings.

WHERE TELEVISION MAKES AN IMPACT

Where television has made a positive impact it is subtle and consistent. On the whole it bears out the hypotheses derived from the content analysis.

Television influences the way children think about jobs, job values, success, and social surroundings. It stresses the prestige of upper-middle-class occupations: the professions and big business. It makes essentially middle-class value judgements about jobs and success in life. It stresses initiative and good appearance, and suggests that success in life depends not only on moral qualities but on brains, confidence, and courage. This influence shows itself in two ways. First, it broadens the child's knowledge of different occupations and leads him to a more adult awareness of the prestige attaching to them. Secondly, it affects his value judgements; more of the viewers than the controls come to believe that the most important qualification for 'getting on' is not being afraid. Such a child would prefer a job which requires brains and independent thinking, and where neat dress matters. As regards wish-jobs, he thinks more in terms of upper-middle-class occupations, so that in fantasy at least television has made him more ambitious; he is also more attracted by glamorous occupations.

Viewers seem to be affected by the materialistic outlook inherent in many television plays. When considering what sort of adult they themselves would like to be, they tend to think more of the things they would like to own than of personal qualities or the work they would like to do.

Television has also provided young viewers with a visual education on social-class differences, on which they draw when judging a person's importance by his dress or describing how people in other social classes live.

The difficulties of adult life which form the principal theme of so many television plays seem to have influenced the adolescent viewers, making them more anxious than the controls about their competence in dealing with adult life, more reluctant to leave home and school, and more worried about going out to work and about marriage.

The BBC's policy of presenting foreign countries (especially European) to children has led many viewers to consider foreigners with more detachment and to make fewer value judgements about them. The children tended to reproduce an image of foreigners which was influenced by the way they had appeared on television.

HOW THE EFFECTS VARIED DEPENDING ON THE TYPE
OF CHILD

The influence of television on the 13–14 year old grammar school children is negligible; their views are more formed, and they have more access to alternative sources of information. Further, they see television rather less frequently than the other groups and are generally less responsive to it.

In general, it seems, the groups most influenced are children from secondary modern schools, especially those of only average and below average intelligence. They read fewer books than other groups, and if they have no television they obtain knowledge of the world from comics, films, and the BBC Light Programme. For them television provides an important source of additional information.

The younger child, the 10–11 year old, is more influenced by visual information. He does not as yet respond much to values. This requires powers of abstraction and comprehension of themes that are beyond him. On the whole this study, and that of Franck (34) described earlier, show that the comprehension of themes and of psychological motivation only begins at a mental age of about 11 or 12. Consequently, only the most intelligent of the younger children are influenced by value judgements.

The younger children are also not influenced by the picture television gives of the world of work. Information about jobs which may form part of the background to the story is noticed only by those children who have a special interest in these cues. The process of selective perception is at work here.

Television does not reduce differences in outlook resulting from social class. It does, however, make the child of below-average intelligence look at things rather more in the manner of the intelligent child: it provides him with information and ideas that the latter has already picked up in other ways.

The effect of television differs for boys and girls; we have already noted that girls react to viewing and other forms of mass communication more than boys. They are more interested in people, dress, and settings, and are thus a more responsive, more readily influenced, audience. In particular, however, they seem more disturbed by the anxiety-laden view of life presented by adult plays. We suggest that this may be because television offers so few positive models for girls, either in children's television or in adult plays. Unhappiness seems to be the common lot of television heroines and there are no female equivalents to cowboys or detectives to provide the reassuring counterpart.

These findings have general implications; even though some of them lack statistical significance, they are too consistent to have arisen by chance. Our test was stringent: we took only values which were put over incidentally, not those which were specially brought to the fore; we tested children whose viewing was restricted to BBC programmes, even though of the two channels BBC plays present more diverse views. Finally, we chose children old enough to have picked up information and views from all sorts of other sources.

A GENERAL FORMULATION OF THE MANNER IN WHICH TELEVISION AFFECTS CHILDREN

We draw here on our findings and those of other studies mentioned in this chapter. We have noted the following seven factors:

Television exerts an influence only where the views are put over repeatedly, preferably in dramatic form. Because television entertainment is built on contrast and the child sees many programmes, the effect of a single programme on outlook is likely to be slight. But the more the views are repeated—the more, for example, different serials on television present, with minor variations, the same values, the same attitudes about people—the more effective will their influence be.

Television exerts an influence only where views are not already firmly fixed, or where it gives information not already obtained from other sources. This is not as obvious as it seems; it underlines the need to relate the effect of television to the intellectual and social maturity of the viewer. For example, the attitudes put over on Westerns are not likely to make much impact on teen-agers, but may well do so on a considerably younger age group.

There is an *optimal age of responsiveness* for each attitude or topic presented. If the child is too young he does not take up the cues; if too mature he already has fixed attitudes or has found other ways of becoming familiar with the attitudes presented.

The responsiveness depends on emotional and social maturity as much as on mental age. The greater the child's interest in a theme and the greater his need for information on it, the more receptive he will be. Among older children, especially girls, views about heterosexual relationships may well be picked up from cues which make no impact on a younger, less concerned age group. By contrast, younger children (the 5–7 year olds who are concerned with problems of right and wrong and with the control of aggression and hostility) may absorb views which would have far less significance for the older child.

The more a child is emotionally responsive to the medium, the more likely he is to be influenced by it. We found that girls generally were more influenced than boys, especially the 13–14 year old of average intelligence.

We made no special study of disturbed children, or of children with some specific problem. Our findings would suggest that these children, while not necessarily more responsive in general, would be highly susceptible to ideas bearing on their problem. This would explain the few instances, like those mentioned in the Kefauver report (53), where disturbed children have copied the ways criminals behave in a crime programme. But effects like these are due far less to the television programmes than to the psychopathology or over-receptiveness of the viewer.

There is a minimum mental age, probably at least 11, below which children tend to have a low capacity for abstraction and for understanding psychological motivation. They can comprehend broad themes only if these recur in identical format in a series of plays, e.g. Westerns. They tend to respond to individual episodes rather than to a story as a whole. The effect of a programme, or a series of programmes, will therefore depend on the subsidiary themes of the short episodes.

The following are suggested as criteria from which to predict the likely cumulative influence of television on children's outlook:

They are more likely to be affected:

1. the more the views presented are stereotyped;
2. the more they are dressed up in dramatic form;
3. the greater the viewers' interest in that type of information;
4. the less complete their knowledge from other sources;
5. and the more responsive they are to the medium in general.

It is possible from these findings to extrapolate to the likely effect of crime and detective programmes on children. The attitude to violence and the various other values which they contain and which we have described in Chapter 14 are conveyed repeatedly and in dramatic form to children interested in the subject; there is therefore no reason to suppose that these programmes will not have their cumulative influence especially on those concerned with their own feelings of aggression and hostility. Similarly, the results have shown that giving children at the appropriate age a view of the way of life of other people and other social groups, can have a broadening effect.

Television's powers are very considerable in shaping children's outlook as well as taste. This shows the need for greater diversification of themes and values, and for doing repeated content analyses to see that a proper programme balance is preserved. A producer may argue that his plays are good for children because the themes represent socially sanctioned values. But, as we have seen, subsidiary touches used to bring characters to life may influence children as much as the main theme.

There is need, therefore, for continuous research of three types: content analyses, especially of programmes which occur repeatedly; studies of the effects on children for whom the programmes are specially intended; and studies of the effects on those child-viewers who are too young to grasp the main themes.

The results, too, have a bearing on communication theory. They show first, that cumulative effects can be measured, and secondly, that the factors which determine cumulative impact tend to be much the same as those which determine impact of individual programmes designed to convert. Through using children of different emotional and intellectual maturity, and boys and girls with different interests, it was possible to spell out some of the factors that make for impact rather more clearly than would have been possible with a more homogeneous or less clearly defined adult group. Above all, we have shown here that the effects operate even though viewing is casual.

PART VI

Effects on Knowledge and School Performance

22

General Knowledge

INTRODUCTION

MUCH of the controversy concerning the effects of television has been concerned with its impact on the child's general knowledge and interests, and we have devoted much time and effort to this problem. In the next few chapters we shall deal with the several aspects of it in detail. Here we need to outline some of the questions involved, and to give a general framework for the studies which we undertook.

For a start we may give here the opinions of a group of teachers who had children of their own. As part of a wider study of their attitude to the new medium (see p. 87) those teachers who had a television set were asked:

Have your children picked up information from television?
If so, please give examples.

Here are some of the responses:

Very much. George Cansdale's programmes. *Look* (Peter Scott). Historical programmes (*The Fire of London*). The Queen's tours. (Son of 11 years.)

Yes. Facts about famous people, e.g. in '*Nom de Plume*' plays, '*Buried Treasure*', science reviews, quiz, and general knowledge programmes. (Daughter of 14.)

Yes. Zoo films; how to make various articles, e.g. dancing dolls; how people in other lands live; how to look after pets, &c. . . . increased their thirst for knowledge. (Daughters of 5 and 7 years.)

Yes. Knowledge of sport. How to play cricket, water skiing, tennis, skating, horse jumping, &c. Knowledge of puppetry. Have learnt to recognise lots of birds and animals. Recognise musical instruments. Historical facts from plays. (Daughters of 3 and 7 years.)

Found the series on the Lost World of Kalahari very helpful to him during geography periods. (Son of 13 years.)

The most frequently mentioned programmes were those dealing with animals and nature talks, while travel and sports programmes were also prominent.[1]

Very similar types of responses were obtained from other parents of different social background and with children of all ages. More rarely parents mention an occasion when the child remembered seeing something on television *a long time* ago, when something in the immediate situation acted as a reminder.

THE MAIN ISSUES

We have concerned ourselves with four main questions in this part of the study. The first arises from the fact that we are dealing with spontaneous viewing for entertainment. Any information which is picked up is absorbed *incidentally*, without any special effort at retention. This is very different from the effect of educational television in the class-room, or the effects of instructional films or radio programmes; for the child is not at school, and is not specifically stimulated to acquire new knowledge, nor is he supervised by teachers who follow up the programmes with lessons and homework. While there have been a number of studies showing the efficacy of film or instructional television in the class-room, none have so far dealt with the efficacy of information programmes when they are merely part of the child's general leisure activities. How much, if anything, is retained by children when they are presented with such programmes at home?

Secondly, it is evident from the comments of parents and teachers that children may learn something not merely from the documentary and information programmes, but from many other types of programmes as well. Most plays, for instance, contain details of plot and setting which may be instructive. In such programmes the transmission of information is not deliberate, yet to the child they may be highly valuable. Moreover, it has often been noted that dramatic presentation helps children to absorb and retain knowledge. In our

---

[1] Many teachers found it difficult to answer this question, sometimes because they felt uncertain about the effects of television in this respect, but occasionally also because they found it hard to enumerate a long series of small, isolated items.

work, therefore, we had to consider *all* types of programmes, not merely newsreels and documentaries.

In the third place, it should be realised that a child may acquire much more than factual knowledge from seeing a television programme. For instance, even if many of the facts escape him, he may still gain an interest in the subject-matter or a feeling of ease and familiarity with the contents. He may gain a sense of participation with events in the outside world from an information programme, or new values and attitudes. Any of these developments may in turn lead to more and better reading on the subject, or possibly to a visit to a museum or exhibition, or it may stimulate questions at home and in the class-room. It may well be that these attendant effects are almost as important as the acquisition of knowledge itself.

Last but not least is the effect of television on the child's performance at school. How much of the information offered to him on television is of educational value? Does any of it lead to greater interest and to an improvement in particular school subjects—such as geography, nature study, or current affairs? Or do viewers fall behind their controls in school marks because viewing takes too much time away from reading, homework, &c.? Obviously the net outcome will be the result of several tendencies, some working in opposite directions.

We have found generally that the effects of television are best thought of in terms of gains and losses. For every favourable argument, there is also a negative one, often due to the time which viewing takes away from other interests. *On the credit side*, parents and teachers report that children gain knowledge from viewing, particularly in certain subjects; television may give children a sense of familiarity even where it does not instruct, it may broaden the child's horizons and stimulate his intellectual interests; much of the material offered on television may act as a stimulus to further activity, e.g. reading, visiting of museums, an interest in archaeology; all this may lead to improvement in schoolwork, especially in certain subjects. But *on the debit side*, it is suggested that the level and quality of the programmes is not high enough to benefit any except the youngest or the very dull; teachers often argue that the information absorbed is of little value since it consists of snippets of information, which are not integrated into a meaningful whole; viewing may lead, not to heightened intellectual curiosity but to a narrowing of interests and to a depreciation of the value of knowledge in the eyes of the child; it may also curtail the time available for various kinds of hobbies and creative activities, homework, and reading; and due to these displacement effects, schoolwork will also suffer. In this context it was our task to *draw a balance*.

We see now, too, that the usual way of posing the question (e.g. do children learn anything from television?) is incorrect. What we really need to know is whether the gain in knowledge due to television is sufficient to offset the undoubted losses caused by the displacement of other sources of information. Can television, even in the ordinary circumstances of casual viewing at home, show a profit to the child?

Our first task was to find out how much and what kind of informational material was being shown on each television channel in an average week, before the children's bedtime. In the section on content analysis (Chapter 13) we have paid special attention to information programmes, and from this it is possible to suggest in which subjects and to what extent one would expect viewers to gain. These and other hypotheses have been examined by means of a set of specially designed tests of general knowledge. The tests can also tell us whether television benefits one type of child more than another, and whether more viewing leads to greater gains, or not. In this chapter we also report on our attempts to explore whether viewing gives a child a sense of familiarity with a variety of subjects, and how far a sense of familiarity would show itself in a test of 'broadened horizons'. At the end of the chapter we supplement our tests of the children with the views and comments of teachers, as obtained in an attitude survey.

The transmission of information depends in the first place on whether or not the child can understand the programme. We took three selected programmes: a children's documentary, an adult information programme, and a dramatisation of the life of Jesus, to study the way in which these programmes 'get across' to the child. In another study we attempted to find out which methods of television presentation were more effective with children (Chapter 23).

The general effects of television on the child's leisure interests are dealt with in Chapters 27–32, but in the present context we have concerned ourselves with his intellectual and cultural interests (Chapter 24). Among other things, we have made a special study of the stimulation effects of one particular programme featuring exhibits from the Ashmolean Museum in Oxford.

Finally (Chapter 25), we have examined the whole problem of television's effects on school performance.

GENERAL KNOWLEDGE

Does television give a child a better background of general knowledge than he would have without it? Or does it, by taking up time he could spend on other things, prevent him from acquiring as wide a range of information as he might otherwise have obtained? We tried to answer these questions with a set of specially constructed general-information tests covering different fields of knowledge. They were simple, straightforward tests of knowledge, bearing no particular relationship to the kinds of programme that may provide children with knowledge or to the other effects the programmes may have.

Techniques. Our purpose was to test the amount of general knowledge which children (in the main survey and the Norwich study) had in different subjects. They were given a limited number of test items, which were representative of each area of knowledge and accurately graded for level of difficulty.[1] We defined 'general knowledge' for children as the aggregate of 'specific' knowledge corresponding largely to the kind of information taught and valued at school. We then took up to eleven subjects systematically and covered each with an equal number of items in random order; we made our selection of items as representative as possible of all the information normally available to a child in each subject. In order to achieve a good spread of scores and the appropriate level of difficulty we carried out several pilot studies. Separate tests were constructed for children in grammar, secondary modern, and primary schools, respectively. Each test consisted of five items in each of the following subjects: English literature, history, geography, science, nature and rural studies, sport, current affairs,[2] art and architecture,[2] handicrafts and housecrafts, music, religion.

Every item took the form of a question with a choice of four possible answers, only one of which was right. For instance, the following questions were asked on geography:

Grammar school:

Which is the largest ocean? (Atlantic, Pacific, Southern, Arctic.)
Which is the largest city? (Paris, Moscow, Berlin, New York.)
A narrow neck of land connecting two land masses is called ... (An archipelago, an isthmus, a peninsula, an atoll).

---

[1] During the construction of these tests we received valuable help from Professor P. E. Vernon of the University of London Institute of Education. Altogether, we tried out eight different versions before we were satisfied that we had tests capable of fulfilling their function.

[2] Not given in primary schools.

Which coast of the British Isles receives the heaviest annual rainfall? (North, south, west, east.)

What is the longitude of the Greenwich Observatory near London? (o degrees, 90 degrees east, 150 degrees east, 180 degrees west.)

Secondary modern school:

Which is the largest island? (Borneo, Madagascar, Greenland, New Guinea.)

In which country would you find geysers made by nature? (Norway, New Zealand, Japan, Russia.)

Where is Brazil? (North America, South America, Africa, Asia.)

The largest number of English cotton mills will be found in . . . (Lancashire, Derbyshire, Nottinghamshire, Shropshire.)

Which country is England's chief supplier of wool? (Australia, U.S.A., Argentina, New Zealand.)

Primary school:

Where is the Suez Canal? (Panama, Greece, Egypt, Syria.)

Which is the largest continent? (Africa, North America, Europe, Asia.)

Which one is an important port? (Liverpool, York, Guildford, Leeds.)

The capital of Russia is . . . (Moscow, Leningrad, Berlin, Warsaw.)

Which people live in the coldest country? (Laplanders, Negroes, Chinese, Red Indians.)

The full set of test items can be obtained on application.[1]

Any difference in scores between viewers and controls is the result of two opposing trends: on the one hand, gains due to the information content of television programmes, on the other, the lost opportunities of gaining knowledge from more conventional sources. The question is not whether children gain general information from viewing— they do—but whether television makes children better informed than they would have been without it.

General results

On the whole, we found that television mainly benefited the younger, duller viewers. Grammar school viewers, on the other hand, did somewhat less well than their controls.

First we studied the distribution of scores among the controls, where we could see the pattern of general information before the advent of television. Almost invariably, there was a marked and regular rise in scores with increasing intelligence. Boys scored higher than girls[2] in all subjects except two: art and architecture, and music.

---

[1] Although we have scored only the cases required by our study, we have given these tests to over 7,000 children in different parts of the country. They could yield data of considerable value to educationists. In Norwich, the tests were given twice —with an interval of twelve months—thus making it possible to study gains and losses in general knowledge.

[2] This finding is usual in most information tests.

There was a less marked (and sometimes reversed) trend towards higher scores among middle-class children, who often have better access to books and other sources of knowledge. This trend was most marked in two subjects—nature study, and handicrafts.

Next, we examined the effects of television, by studying the differences between the scores of viewers and controls.

In no subject did viewers as a whole score significantly less than controls.

Viewers as a whole scored significantly *higher* in five subjects: geography, science, sport, music, handicrafts and housecraft.

Viewers as a whole made *no significant gains* in the following subjects: English literature, history, nature and rural studies, art and architecture,[1] current affairs,[1] religion.

Finally, we explored the scores of both viewers and controls more carefully, to see whether some viewers gained or fell behind more markedly than others.

We found that where viewers as a group gained significantly, this happened almost exclusively in the primary schools and especially among the duller children. The 13–14 year olds often fell a little behind their controls. Grammar school viewers showed a slight drop in all subjects except sport, and handicrafts and housecraft. The younger children tended to gain in nature and rural studies, but not the older ones. Boys tended to gain more than girls in sport, especially grammar school boys and the less intelligent boys from primary schools. Social class hardly affected the results at all.[2]

Appendix Tables 39, 40, and 41 give, as an example, the detailed results obtained for one subject (English literature), and the main results for each area of knowledge.

To obtain a further appreciation of the size of the gains recorded for the viewers, it may be useful to offer some standards of comparison. For the main sample overall results (Appendix Table 41) we computed the following average difference scores (viewers minus controls) for the entire test:

Secondary schools --0·202
Primary schools   1·635

How large is a gain of 1·635? Compared to the maximum possible score, it amounts to just under 4 per cent. A normal annual increment in information amounts to some 10 per cent, as the Norwich results show (see below). A gain of 1·635 could thus be regarded as

[1] Not given to primary school children.
[2] We are aware, of course, that with only five items for each information area the element of chance is not ruled out. There is no reason to suspect, however, that this has biased the findings.

the equivalent of about 4 months' normal development in general knowledge. It is also no more than a quarter the size of the differences found between the scores of the brighter and the duller children (16–20 per cent).

The effect of intensive viewing

If viewing adds to the child's store of general knowledge, then the more he views the higher one should expect his score to be on the test. On the other hand, the more he views, the less time remains available for the absorption of information from other quarters. To what extent does the additional knowledge gained from viewing compensate for this?

Two consistent, though slight, trends emerged from the detailed analysis: for the older children, the more evening television they viewed, the better were their scores; for the younger age group this was not so, and heavy viewers of children's television tended, if anything, to have *lower* scores than the rest. When each of the information areas was studied in turn, no regular trends emerged.

This suggests one tentative and unexpected conclusion: that the information programmes on children's television do not add much to the child's knowledge.[1]

The benefits of the evening programmes were confined to the older children who had sufficient time to view and to use other sources of information as well. The younger ones were not able to watch very many of the evening programmes, but viewing left them with comparatively little leisure time in which to gain information from elsewhere. Again we see how important it is not to generalise, but to study the effects on different sub-groups.

Are the effects cumulative?

If the effects of television on general knowledge are cumulative, the process starts fairly late, since results of our analysis by length of set ownership suggest that children under 10 years old, when exposed to information programmes on television, do not seem to retain and accumulate the kind of general knowledge demanded by our test. In any case, so young a group will see mainly children's programmes, and these, as we have seen, do not tend greatly to increase their store of general knowledge.

---

[1] This was corroborated by a study of items specially selected from programmes which had been presented on children's television shortly before the time of the test.

TABLE 52. Mean information test scores of recent, experienced, and veteran viewers

| | 13–14 YEAR OLDS | | | | 10–11 YEAR OLDS | | | |
| | | | Secondary modern | | | | | |
	All	Grammar	I.Q. 100–114	I.Q. below 100	All	I.Q. 115+	I.Q. 100–114	I.Q. below 100
Recent viewers	28·6	29·2	29·2	27·3	26·5	29·2	27·7	22·6
Experienced viewers .	29·5	29·3	31·9	27·4	26·4	29·8	27·9	21·4
Veteran viewers .	30·3	29·6	32·5	28·7	26·5	30·0	27·6	22·0
Total cases .	337	148	111	78	295	115	116	64

Among the older children (mainly those with I.Q. 100–114) our analysis (Table 52) showed somewhat higher scores with longer set ownership, but we found no such relationship in the scores of primary school children, except among the brighter ones. This suggests that most young viewers have not retained much of the information presented to them on television at an earlier age. Possibly children's information programmes may be inadequate, or children may not understand what they see, through lack of interest or of the necessary frame of reference.

The Norwich results

Our main aim in Norwich was to find out whether the sample of future viewers had been generally better informed than their controls even before the advent of television.

TABLE 53. Mean general knowledge test scores for viewers and controls in Norwich in 1955 and 1956 (before and after viewers received their sets)

| | | | | 13–14 YEAR OLDS | | 10–11 YEAR OLDS | |
Year:				v	c	v	c
1955 .	.	.	.	29·3	32·0	28·9	28·7
1956 .	.	.	.	37·2	37·4	32·1	33·2
Gains .	.	.	.	7·9	5·4	3·2	4·5
Total cases .	.	.	.	52	52	120	120

Taking all subjects together, the results (given in Table 53) of the 1955 scores of future viewers and controls were very similar. By 1956 the controls had improved their scores by approximately 10 per cent of the maximum possible score; the older viewers did only slightly better (14 per cent up) while the younger viewers did slightly worse (7 per cent). As in the main sample, the duller viewers gained most.

However, none of the Norwich viewers had had their sets for long. Since longer set ownership tends to improve the scores of secondary modern school children, the younger age group in Norwich, after initially falling behind, may be expected to improve their scores, especially the brighter children in secondary modern schools.

CONCLUSIONS

Except in the grammar schools, television does not seem to have lowered the level of general knowledge, as measured by our tests, and in a number of subjects it has produced significant gains. Thus, most children get at least as much information from television as they might have obtained elsewhere.

Gains in knowledge were recorded primarily for the younger, duller viewers, while the grammar school viewers often showed a slight fall, compared with controls. Viewers scored significantly higher than their controls on geography, science, sport, music, and handicrafts and housecrafts. They did not score significantly higher on English literature, history, nature and rural studies, art and architecture, current affairs, and religion. Social background hardly seemed to affect the results at all. For example, it is not true that children in middle-class homes are better able to use the information provided by television. Nor does television mainly benefit the older, brighter child; indeed, it has comparatively little to offer him. On the whole, the benefits of television are confined to the younger, less intelligent children, whose access to other sources of general information is restricted.

Some of these results are expected, others are not. Our analysis of programme preferences and viewing times and of the content of information programmes suggested that gains might be expected in geography, handicrafts, and sports; these expectations were confirmed. We had expected few gains in science because science programmes usually were put on too late in the evening and were not very popular, but appreciable gains in knowledge were recorded. We had expected gains in history, but the historical content of some television programmes is evidently not precise enough to increase factual knowledge of history, and the same may well be true of English literature. Although nature programmes are plentiful, few gains were recorded in this subject, possibly because the programmes tend to deal more with particular animals or plants than with the broad aspects of botany or zoology. The lack of gains in current affairs in unexpected, since television excels in providing this type of information. The information offered by television may perhaps be too limited and too specific, making it difficult for the child to integrate and remember what he has seen, and to answer broader questions about it. Swanson and Jones (90) in Minneapolis have found adults from television homes to be less knowledgeable than others about current affairs.

There may, however, be a more general explanation for these unexpected findings: *a child may gain valuable knowledge from programmes* <u>other</u> *than those that are deliberately instructional.* Learning from television is incidental to being amused or excited, and most programmes contain details of plot or circumstance which are authentic and which accumulate in time and are remembered, partly because they have been embedded in interesting or exciting programmes.

These effects of television are cumulative. The longer the television set has been in the home, the greater is the store of general knowledge. However, this applies only to older children, especially those of medium intelligence. Younger children only start to accumulate the kind of information relevant to our test at about the age of 10, and in any case they see mainly the early evening and children's television programmes which, as we have seen, are not likely to improve their score.

Similarly the more the child views, the better his score on our tests—in spite of the fact that increased viewing gives less time for collecting information from other quarters. Again, this applies only to older children, and to the viewing of adult programmes. Heavy viewing of children's television, though a third of it may be information, does not help much; the information is not of a sufficiently high level for the older children, and the younger ones score better if they can devote more time to other sources of knowledge, irrespective of intelligence.

Among new viewers the older children gain and the younger ones at first fall behind, though they are likely to catch up.

Television to some extent acts as an equaliser in that it reduces the differences between the brighter and duller children, but this is hardly ever sufficient to upset the basic pattern (a regular rise in score with increasing intelligence, and usually a higher score for boys than for girls). For instance, among the younger children intelligence differences amount to some 16 to 20 per cent of the maximum score, whereas average gains are in the neighbourhood of 4 per cent.

We may compare gains due to viewing with the normal development of a child's general knowledge in the course of time. The Norwich data indicate that in a year the average child gains about 10 per cent in test score. The average gains in the primary schools therefore amount to four to five months' of normal growth, while in some areas and in some sub-groups gains equivalent to some eight months of normal growth have been recorded.

FAMILIARITY WITH SUBJECTS

It is sometimes claimed that, while television may or may not be a good medium for providing information which is accurately retained, it does give the child an easy and entertaining introduction to a subject, makes him more familiar with it, and thus more ready to absorb information when he comes across the subject another time. We made two attempts to study children's familiarity with various fields or items of knowledge, and the extent to which television broadens their horizon.

The familiarity test

We first asked each child to tick one of four statements against each item in a list:[1]

I know enough (about it) to give a short talk or write a brief essay;
I know enough to talk about it to my parents or friends;
I have heard something but do not remember much about this;
I have heard nothing about this.

This list contained subjects which are often featured on television, such as famous people, country houses, the weather, and also subjects about which there is as much information elsewhere, such as the Royal Family, the Olympic games, news, and the instruments of the orchestra.

The list was completed by 240 children of 11–12 years in Norwich in 1956. The pattern of scores among controls was similar to that shown on the general-knowledge tests: familiarity increased with intelligence, and middle-class did better than working-class children. Television did not greatly change the pattern. The average score of viewers was a little higher (26·7 compared with 22·8 for the controls), but for most items the difference was small. Once again the duller children gained more than the brighter ones.

Fig. 9 shows that controls felt most confident about their knowledge of the life of Jesus, the Royal Family, and life on a farm; they claimed less knowledge of the other subjects. The order was much the same for viewers, with one major exception: *Jane Eyre* was given a very high familiarity score by viewers and a very low one by the controls. This was a direct effect of the recent dramatisation of this book on television. We can trace smaller increases in familiarity with

[1] We scored the items numerically by arbitrarily giving them weights from 3 to 0.

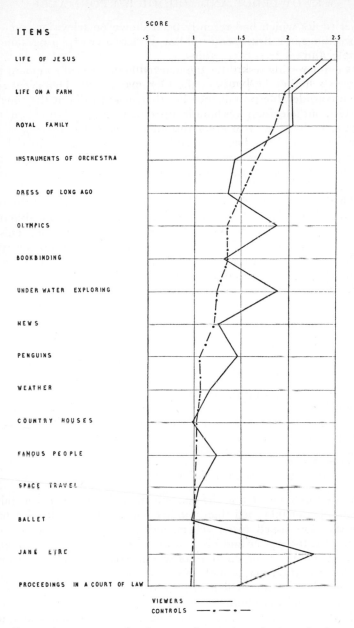

ITEMS

SCORE

LIFE OF JESUS

LIFE ON A FARM

ROYAL FAMILY

INSTRUMENTS OF ORCHESTRA

DRESS OF LONG AGO

OLYMPICS

BOOKBINDING

UNDER WATER EXPLORING

NEWS

PENGUINS

WEATHER

COUNTRY HOUSES

FAMOUS PEOPLE

SPACE TRAVEL

BALLET

JANE EYRE

PROCEEDINGS IN A COURT OF LAW

VIEWERS ———
CONTROLS — • — • —

FIG. 9. Average scores for viewers and controls on the items in the Familiarity Test. The items are arranged in descending order of the scores for the controls

other topics which had recently been shown on television, such as proceedings in a British court of law, underwater exploring, famous people, and the lives of penguins.

One interesting result was the marked increase in the amount the viewers felt they knew about the Olympic games. This event was given considerable prominence in other mass media at the time of the test, but television was handicapped by having no films about the games. Perhaps the reason for this effect was that television, as we have seen elsewhere, has made children more knowledgeable about sport, so that they were probably more interested in the descriptions of the games, even though these were not supported by actual films.

There was practically no difference in the familiarity of the two groups of children with the weather forecasts and the news, although considerable time is devoted to these topics on television. This is probably because such programmes were not very popular with children. There was also no difference in respect of the life of Jesus, despite the series of dramatic programmes in children's television which had been televised three months earlier. This is probably because the Bible story was already very familiar to all the children in the sample and scores were already very close to the maximum.

The breadth of knowledge test

Do children pick up knowledge about the world around them from television? To examine this, we gave 130 pairs of 14–15 and 11–12 year old children taking part in the retest in Norwich a sheet of paper headed as follows:

So much is happening in the world today. Think of as many events or happenings as you can and write them down one by one below.

With this type of test the judgement as to whether one pupil seemed better informed than another had to be a qualitative one. We therefore asked two teachers, independently, to compare the answers of the viewer and his control twin, and to indicate whether they were of the same standard or whether one was better or worse. All identification marks had, of course, been removed so that the teachers did not know which script belonged to the viewer and which to the control.[1] The children's answers were rated for general breadth of information, for frequency of reference to national and inter-

---

[1] There was 90 per cent agreement between the teachers on overall assessment; where they disagreed, a third teacher gave the casting vote.

national events, to science and to sport (the areas frequently featured on television).

The results were on the whole negative. Television, it seems, does not increase the children's breadth of knowledge; the few instances where viewers scored higher than controls were almost all confined to older children of below average intelligence. Moreover, the frequent showing of international events made no difference here—the proportion of national to international events mentioned was much the same for the two groups. One exception was found—viewers more often mentioned sports events (116 such mentions compared with 86 among the controls). This is not surprising since the survey was conducted at a time when a great deal of tennis and cricket was being televised. It would seem that for television to make an impact it must build on existing interests. Seeing national and international events in newsreels, in which children are little interested, does not lead to a widening in knowledge.

OPINIONS OF TEACHERS

We also obtained the personal views and opinions of 520 teachers about the influence of television on knowledge and school performance (see Chap. 6).

The questionnaire opened with a very general question about the effects of television, harmful and beneficial, on children whom they taught. The beneficial effect most often mentioned was that viewing increases the child's general knowledge. Mentioned by one-third of the teachers, and by an even higher proportion of those who had television at home, this view tended to be expressed as part of a more general comment—that television stimulates the child's general interest in new topics and broadens his experience. Rural teachers stressed this significantly more often than urban teachers; those in the more isolated districts sometimes saw in television an antidote to parochialism. Several teachers said appreciatively that viewing presented children with subjects they could not possibly encounter at school, or that through television children gained an insight into the way people live in other lands.

A fifth of the teachers in secondary modern and junior schools, but only about a tenth of the grammar and infant school teachers, claimed that viewing stimulated interest in some specific school subject, notably nature study, religious instruction, geography, and history. They said that teaching could be more successful if preceded (or preferably followed) by television programmes dealing with a similar subject. Such programmes, they added, help to bring subjects alive for pupils.[1] Here are some fairly typical comments:

> Television lights up for the child much of my nature study lessons. A quickening of interest is very apparent when I mention something which television has dealt with.
>
> (A junior-school teacher.)

> Where I have asked them to look at programmes which have a bearing on the teaching matter, lessons have been more successful—better response to questions and more volunteering of information.
>
> (A secondary modern school teacher.)

Some of the alleged harmful effects of television were less often mentioned than might be expected. Thus, only 12 per cent of the teachers held that it reduced reading, only 2 per cent that it gave children false impressions, and only 1 per cent that it made children too sophisticated. As regards other, beneficial effects, a mere 6 per cent of the teachers said that dramatisations of books aroused a desire to read good literature.

We also asked for more particular observations by means of a question aimed specifically at the problem of general knowledge:

> There has been much discussion as to whether or not children gain information from television, and if so, what kind of information is acquired and how long it is remembered. What are your observations on this matter?

Just under a quarter of the teachers did not attempt an answer; this could imply that they had not noticed any gains in information. But over two-thirds of them said they had noticed at least some gains in information among viewers and only 6 per cent stated that they had noticed no gains at all.

There is no real contradiction between the teachers' observations and the results of our survey. Two different issues are under consideration: whether children learn anything from television (this can scarcely be doubted); and whether they learn more in this way than from other sources. Since no comparisons were made, the teachers' responses cannot tell us whether television is in any way superior to such other sources. On the other hand, our survey was designed with precisely such comparisons in mind.

The group of teachers who thought there had been at least some gains in information contained an unusually high proportion of set owners. This suggests that personal viewing experience, and a comparatively favourable attitude to television, had rendered these

---

[1] This view was held even by teachers who did not have sets of their own.

teachers more alert to gains in knowledge from television. This was especially true of grammar school teachers (Table 54).

TABLE 54. Percentage of teachers answering the question who thought there had been definite gains of information

					Set owners	Others
					%	%
Type of school:						
Grammar	.	.	.	.	79	49
Secondary modern	.	.	.	82	77
Junior	.	.	.	.	86	79
Infant	.	.	.	.	74	68
Total cases	.	.	.	.	186	214

These are typical comments:

Children definitely gain information from television, especially about nature and geography. Some children are very keen in contributing their added information whenever the lessons permit. They retain information obtained in this way and show interest, especially when they know they may be asked to tell the other children what they saw on television.

(A junior-school teacher.)

Information gleaned when watching television alone suddenly falls into place when the subject crops up in class and is fully explained. Information interesting to the child, for example on wild animals, in travel series, is readily absorbed and remembered.

(An infant-school teacher.)

The best aspect of children's watching television is their increased appreciation of animals through being able to see them moving and playing in their natural surroundings.

(A junior-school teacher.)

A few teachers (up to 6 per cent) suggested that more information would be gained if any of the following conditions were met: if the subject appealed to the child; if the child were intelligent; if the subject linked up with school work; if the teacher followed up in class the child's previous viewing; if the child were guided in his viewing; and if the subject had been dramatised.

On the other hand, 12 per cent of the teachers were not satisfied with the type and quality of some information which, they said, their pupils had acquired—disconnected, odd scraps of superficial and sketchy information, a rag-bag of startling or trivial facts. Another 3 per cent felt that false or inaccurate impressions were sometimes gained through the children's lack of understanding. A junior-school teacher said, for instance: 'They remember a few useful facts . . . though often they get wrong impressions through lack of background knowledge.' And a teacher in a grammar school commented: 'They often get very muddled—probably the medium moves too quickly for some of them.' Another junior-school teacher contended that the viewers appeared to have acquired snippets of information, mostly unrelated to each other and extending over a greater range of human activities.

Table 55 shows how far teachers thought different subjects benefited from the general gain.

TABLE 55. Percentage of teachers who mentioned these specific subjects, as areas in which the children seemed to have gained information

	%
Nature study (especially Peter Scott programmes) . .	18
Scripture (especially the life of Jesus series)	12
Current events	8
Geography, travel	8
History	6
Literature, drama.	4
Physical education, sport	4
Science	2
Art, architecture, music, ballet	2
Craftwork	2
Dress, costumes, fashion	1
Total cases	520

In addition, 10 per cent said that child-viewers either obtained knowledge directly related to school work (without mentioning a specific subject), or showed greater interest in a given school subject.

Over half the respondents commented on the length of time over which information was retained, and on the quality of what was retained. Of those who commented, almost two-thirds made positive statements, indicating that information gained from viewing was well remembered (though only very few definitely considered television superior to other sources of information in this respect). The remainder commented adversely, suggesting that not much was remembered for any length of time, or that too many facts were presented too quickly for effective retention.

CONCLUSIONS

What conclusions can we draw from relating teachers' opinions to the results of the various tests used?

The teachers' views give much additional support to the belief that television is a valuable and effective medium of instruction, although some teachers feel that the information it gives is too scrappy and superficial, and only a few suggest that television is superior to other mass media in this function.

The general-knowledge tests have shown that, while television is of only limited value to adolescents, it has a greater effect in the primary schools. The teachers' responses seem to confirm this for both junior and infant schools. Similarly, our data suggest that television is more often effective among the duller children; many teachers said this too, and spoke of its value even among children who are educationally sub-normal.

Our findings do not suggest that television is more effective than other media in arousing new intellectual interests or in broadening the horizons and general awareness. Teachers' views suggest, however, that if children from more isolated areas were to be tested, the findings might be more favourable to television.

Our tests were perhaps unduly narrow and restricted because we had to make careful statistical comparisons between matched samples; but the teachers' comments suffered from over-generalisation and were inevitably coloured by their general attitude to television.

Teachers' opinions varied as to how long information is retained; our own tests indicated that the effects of television do not begin to accumulate until the child is about 10 years old. Before that age little information is absorbed or retained for long. Even so, the quality of information that comes from television is not sufficiently high to compensate the brighter adolescents in grammar schools for the expenditure of time which it requires.

23

Recall of Information

WHY is it that certain pieces of information stick in a child's mind, while others are forgotten? Is it because of the subject or the method of presentation? For how long afterwards are various kinds of item remembered? Could an experienced teacher or producer look at a programme and predict with some accuracy which items would be retained and which forgotten?

Two special difficulties are met in a problem of this kind: that of applying laboratory findings to the casual way in which people learn from television; and the need to deal with a number of variables all operating at once.

American investigations dealing with visual aids or educational television in the class-room (49) have helped to throw light on what determines effective recall. In this country valuable work has been done by Burt (20), Kay (52), P. E. and M. D. Vernon (97, 96), and the BBC investigators Belson (6) and Trenaman (94). They have used a variety of subjects, materials, methods, and periods of time. Some of the results have been related to age, intelligence, and other background factors. It has proved difficult to attribute particular importance to any one determinant, yet one point has emerged repeatedly—the strong impact of dramatised material. As Kay (52) sums it up:

> It would seem that a dramatised version as compared with a talk can make a more definite and permanent impact upon listeners, but whether the relevant or irrelevant items are retained depends upon the skill with which scenes and subject-matter are inter-related. The dramatisation runs the risk of overplaying its illustrative material and underplaying its essentials.

Many of these studies have been made under laboratory conditions, and only a few investigators, notably Stoddard (43), have tested how much (or how little) respondents knew about a topic *before* being presented with a film or television programme dealing with it. We must then ask how far the knowledge scores are due to the experimental stimulus and how far to previous knowledge.[1]

[1] Belson (7) has gone some way towards meeting this objection by employing a 'stable correlates' technique, which allows him to compute a respondent's initial score without having to subject him to a before-and-after testing procedure.

Retention test used in this inquiry

In our own investigation we confined ourselves to scheduled television programmes, viewed by the children in normal home conditions, and we made every effort to isolate previous knowledge from that gained from a given programme, by studying controls alongside viewers. We hoped that this study would give some measure, however rough, of how effectively information comes across on television and is retained in different types of presentation.

To find information that would meet our requirements, we monitored the children's television and many of the early evening programmes for several months prior to the main survey. We thought that the items finally selected would avoid trivialities, and be less familiar to the controls, and that they were items which few viewers would previously have known. Separate tests of 23–24 multiple-choice items were given to grammar, secondary modern, and primary schools during the main survey.

Our aim was to examine the effect of television by looking at the difference scores between viewers and controls, assuming the latter's score to indicate how much the viewers would have known even without television. Once the various difference scores had been computed, we examined them in relation to the child's age, sex, intelligence, social background, general knowledge, programme preferences, and spare-time interests. In addition it was intended to relate them to manner, frequency, and saliency of presentation and to the type of subject-matter.

The results of the test showed, however, that on nearly every item the controls had scored as high as the viewers (the viewers' average gain was only about 6 per cent). This meant that, a few exceptions apart, we had not been able to find items with which children without access to television were not also familiar. It illustrated that the topics touched on by television tend to be much the same as those covered by other mass media or those taught in schools. By far the greater part of the viewers' scores was due to previous knowledge, rather than to having seen the programme concerned.[1]

In spite of the smallness of the difference scores, we did analyses for the following variables:

time elapsed between programme and testing;
area of knowledge;
children's television or evening television;
scholastic or non-scholastic information;

[1] The findings indirectly confirmed the results of the general-knowledge tests. The distribution of scores was very similar, with the highest gains among younger, duller children. The area in which most gain was noted was geography.

of special interest to boys or girls;

pictorial, or verbal, or verbal and pictorial presentation;

mentioned once or mentioned repeatedly;

single programme or serial;

salient or subsidiary emphasis;

dramatisation or documentary;

predicted outcome (weighting and combining these various factors intuitively).

The results showed a series of contradictory trends, which could not be used in support of any hypothesis.

A second attempt was made in Norwich (1956), using a test of thirty-six multiple-choice items. Again we took great care in our selection of items from recent television programmes, but once again the difference between viewers and controls was very small. The younger viewers gave on average 16 correct responses, the controls 14·8, and the difference was no greater among the older children. Careful analysis of successes against our own predictions and against a number of other hypotheses about methods of presentation revealed no consistent trends. This was an inevitable result, it would appear, due to the nature of the topics covered by television, and to our refusal to test for trivialities.

There were, however, a few exceptions where substantial gains were recorded.

Two more specialised items had been included in this repeat test:

Which of these birds originally came from India?
(Bar-headed geese, black swans, pintail ducks, chaffinches.)

Good underwater photographs have been taken with the help of . . .
(Magnesium flares, acetylene lamps, flash bulbs, searchlights.)

In both instances we were dealing with knowledge which controls would not readily pick up from other sources. It will be seen that in both cases, viewers gave significantly more correct answers than controls:

	Viewers %	Controls %
Correct answer about origin of birds .	35	18
Technique of underwater photography	51	29

Apart from these, a recent series of fictitious court cases presented on television led to some increased knowledge of the proceedings in an English court of law. Viewers also scored significantly better than controls on two questions derived from a serial dramatisation of *Tom Brown's Schooldays*; however, other dramatisations did not yield such gains.

These few items illustrate the fact that considerable difference scores can be obtained when dealing with trivial or highly specialised knowledge. Our concern, however, was with information that would be of general educational value to the child.

Comparison of viewers and controls who had seen a particular programme

So far we have compared viewers and controls on the assumption that at least some viewers would have seen the programmes in question, particularly since the items were selected from children's television or early evening programmes, all of which had substantial child audiences.

However, when the differences turned out to be small, we had to introduce a greater degree of precision, namely, by studying only those viewers who had actually seen the programmes from which each retention test item was derived, but who had not previously known the correct answer. Our first problem was how to obtain this estimate of previous knowledge.

We could not give a pre-test of knowledge—which would in any case have alerted the children to the particular demands of the programme. Instead, we estimated previous knowledge from the scores of their controls,[1] discarding on each test item in turn all viewers whose controls scored correctly and dividing the remaining viewers into those who answered the test item correctly and those who did not.

Our second problem was to find out which viewers had seen a particular programme from which information test items had been taken. By means of the 1955 programme-recall lists we were able to find out which viewers had actually seen each programme in one particular week.

The results for the eighteen programmes from which items were taken are given in Appendix Table 42. All the items were shown in the same week, which means that the interval between seeing the information on the screen and being tested as part of our main survey was approximately the same for all.

Comparing those viewers who had seen a particular programme to their controls, we noted higher scores for viewers on seven of the items, but the differences followed no consistent pattern. The largest

---

[1] Strictly speaking, we cannot be sure of the quality of this estimate since we do not know to what extent the matching criteria used were relevant to these information scores, although the relationship is likely to have been fairly good. Also, there was less time for viewers to gain access to other sources of information, and so the controls' scores were likely to have been an overestimate of the viewers' previous knowledge.

single gain concerned a serial on the life of Stanley; viewers who did not see this particular programme also scored much higher than their controls, presumably as a result of having seen previous episodes. The method, however, was precise enough, and yielded appreciable difference scores. If viewing data had been available for more items, some broader trends might well have emerged from the analysis.

COMPREHENSION OF
THREE INFORMATION PROGRAMMES

We now consider the effects of specific programmes under conditions of normal home viewing. Three programmes were selected so as to bring out the role of television under three very different conditions.

The first was a nature documentary about polecats and formed part of a series of animal programmes presented by Peter Scott under the title of *Look*. In this case we tested how far the children understood a programme with some dramatic content, which gave detailed information about a particular animal of which most children had no previous knowledge.

The second programme dealt with intelligence testing, about which most of these children had ideas as well as personal experience, though many of these ideas might be incorrect. This programme, which was put on primarily for adults, gave an account of the nature of intelligence, the ways in which intelligence tests work, and their use in the eleven-plus examination. Here we were particularly interested in seeing how far comprehension differed for the older and the younger children. Both age groups had taken intelligence tests at school, and the older ones had already been allocated to different secondary schools on the basis of their results in this and other tests.

The third programme consisted of a dramatised series on *Jesus of Nazareth*—a topic about which all the children had received a great deal of instruction. Here we were concerned with how much of the attitudes, values, and detailed information that were contained in this series the children had absorbed.

In the case of the first two programmes, the children were interviewed the next morning and given specially designed comprehension tests which had been developed the day before, immediately after seeing the programme.[1] The results measured incidental learning, the short-term impact of these programmes when viewed under normal home conditions.

[1] Questions on the *Jesus of Nazareth* programmes were given as part of our repeat study in Norwich.

A children's documentary film

We gave a questionnaire to twenty-three primary school children who had seen the programme on polecats. There were eighteen factual questions, and six others dealing with reactions and with earlier programmes in the series. Here are a few typical questions and answers:

Question	Correct answer	Number out of 23 who gave the correct answer
In what country was the film on polecats made?	Germany	21
In what type of home do polecats live?	Burrow	14
What is the most important thing about the play of young polecats?	It trains them to get their own food	17
How did the male polecat take his mate to the nest?	By the scruff of the neck	20
Polecats have: very good eyesight short sight long sight	Short sight	14
In what special way did the mother polecat kill the snake?	By biting it at the back of the neck	15

All the children said they had never heard about polecats before this programme, but sixteen of them had seen at least a few other *Look* programmes. All but one liked the programme, fourteen liked it 'very much'. When asked: *What did you find most interesting in the programme?* twelve mentioned the fighting and catching of prey.

These results suggest that, when a subject which interests the children is dramatically presented with vigorous action sequences, children pick up a good deal of accurate information and retain it at least over a short period. Evidence from group-viewing sessions confirmed this finding.

An adult programme about intelligence tests

This programme was presented entirely for adults, with the aid of a panel of experts. It tackled such issues as the constancy of the I.Q., the value of coaching for intelligence tests, different types of test items (examples were shown), the ratio between mental and chronological age, and the meaning of different scores in terms of educational capacity. The programme ended with a scene in which Gilbert Harding and a grammar school boy discussed their experiences in trying to complete the same intelligence test.

None of the child viewers of the *Look* programme knew anything about polecats beforehand and so their scores could be attributed to the effects of the programme. However, most children know something about intelligence tests, and the effects of this programme could only be gauged by comparing children who had seen it with children who had not, while controlling for age, sex, type of school, and intelligence.[1]

Children were first asked to write an essay (*Write all you know about intelligence tests and the uses to which they are put*), and were then given a comprehension questionnaire. As expected, even children who had not seen the programme were fairly well acquainted with the subject.

On the whole, the detailed analysis of the results suggested that the programme was more effective with the older children of at least average intelligence than with the younger ones. This is partly due to their age and intellectual development, and partly to the fact that they had not only been through the eleven-plus examination, but had also gained some idea of its consequences, whereas the younger children, even if they had already done the eleven-plus examination, did not yet know the results and had not yet been moved to a different school. Typical of the younger age group were fourteen children from primary schools who had just taken the eleven-plus examination; most of them had misunderstood the aims of the tests in one way or another, even though they were familiar with the procedures. Five of them thought it helped 'to get good jobs', nine said 'to get on in school', and two said 'to get on in life when you are grown up'. They all favoured coaching because, they thought, it would help them not only in the examination but also in the next school. On the whole the younger children tended to gain very little useful information from the programme, and to persist in their misconceptions.

Interviews with the younger children also showed that, although they had wanted to watch the entire programme and often knew what had happened on the screen (various professors had appeared, test items had been shown, and Gilbert Harding had done a test too), they had not taken in what was being said and so had missed the point of the demonstrations.

At the other extreme the older grammar school pupils had gained both understanding and a more sophisticated vocabulary about intelligence testing. They also showed more understanding of the techniques of test construction. On the other hand, they often failed to link these tests with the eleven-plus examination.

It would seem, therefore, that adult documentary programmes containing much verbal material and little action are not very effective with children unless they are old enough, intelligent enough, and have a personal interest in the subject-matter.

---

[1] It proved difficult to find enough pupils who had seen this programme in the few schools which we could visit the next day. It was also difficult to find controls—similar children who had not seen the programme. Altogether, we tested 108 children.

A serial on the life of Jesus

Jesus of Nazareth was shown every Sunday for several weeks before Easter 1956. The BBC did all it could to make the programme realistic to children and to give them some idea of contemporary events and conditions.[1] The visual and dramatic presentation in itself probably brought home to the viewer the type of life which Jesus and his disciples would lead, the practical difficulties they would meet, the clothes they would wear, the countryside in which they would travel, the people with whom they would have to deal, and the practical consequences of becoming a disciple.

TABLE 56. Questions about *Jesus of Nazareth* with multiple choice answers

(Proportion of 11–12 year olds who gave the correct answers)

	Choice of answers with correct one in italics	Proportion who gave correct answer	
		v %	c %
Jesus lived in Palestine. In which part of the country did he grow up?	Judea Kerioth Samaria *Galilee*	81	77
About how old was Jesus at the time he was crucified?	He was a youth *He was a man of about thirty* He was a middle-aged man He was an elderly man	76	68
What language did Jesus speak?	Greek Arabic *Hebrew* Latin	81	78
	Total cases	112	112

Thus this information programme, like many others, was also likely to create subtle changes in attitude. This we tried to test,

[1] The question of the degree of 'realism' in a film or television programme is difficult to assess. From the most candid documentary to the Western, realism and make-believe are mixed in different degrees. Much of the quality of realism lies in the mind of the beholder, especially with children, and directors and producers have become skilled in portraying events like murders, car crashes, fist-fights, and falls from high buildings with ever-increasing realism, employing the various subterfuges of sound track, cutting technique, and the use of stunt men and models. In the case of *Jesus of Nazareth*, since documentary reconstruction was out of the question, realism was invoked rather than produced. Jesus was made to speak in language which we have learnt to recognise as 'biblical'; film sequences were shot on the sea of Galilee and in the surrounding hills. The disciples were given regional accents, though they all spoke in English. Paradoxically, some of the miracles lost realism because cinema techniques make it relatively easy to create the appearance of supernatural events.

realising, of course, that the gospel story was in any case well known to the children long before the programmes.

We tried a number of approaches in a pilot survey, as a result of which we incorporated five questions in the second stage of the Norwich study. The three factual questions for 112 pairs in the younger age group (11–12 year olds) showed a slight gain for the viewers (Table 56).[1]

Since all the main aspects of the life of Jesus were well known to viewers and controls alike, it was difficult to choose questions which were neither trivial nor too familiar. Also, the differences between the two groups might have been greater if it had been possible to test for the effects of individual episodes, using only those viewers who had seen the particular programme.

The remaining two questions were of the free-answer type, and were intended to probe for changes in attitude.

> If you had been chosen to become one of Jesus' disciples, you would probably have found it both easy and difficult.
> (a) Why do you think it would be easy?
> (b) And why do you think it would be hard?

The results (Appendix Table 43) show first of all that a few more viewers than controls were able to answer this question because the programme had succeeded in conveying to them ideas about a disciple's life. Moreover, the programmes taught the children to look at the life of Christ in a different way. In the answers to the question *Why do you think it would be easy* (to be a disciple)? viewers more often than controls referred to practical assistance to be obtained from Jesus, and to His humanity and understanding.[2] The duller children showed the influence of the visual presentation of *Jesus of Nazareth* by sometimes giving naïve answers such as 'You only need to leave your home and follow Jesus', or 'You need no education, only will-power'. When these shifts in attitude are combined (36 per cent *v.* 25 per cent) the difference just reaches statistical significance.

Viewers also gave more realistic answers to the question *And why do you think it would be hard?* They referred more often to the difficulties of leading a highly moral life and to everyday difficulties— like the walking and all the hard work involved—and the loss of home, job, and material possessions. Controls more often referred to the difficulties of preaching and to the possibility of opposition and

---

[1] These viewers comprised all those children who had a television set at home, irrespective of which of the *Jesus of Nazareth* programmes they had watched, since the children were not always sure which episodes they had seen or missed, and since the correct answers could be learnt from several of the episodes.

[2] 18 and 10 per cent—a difference which was, however, not significant.

persecution—to the religious aspects rather than to practical every-day life. Again, if we combine these small changes in attitude (37 per cent *v.* 25 per cent) the difference is statistically significant.

CONCLUSIONS

We were not able to find a sufficiently large number of information items (despite careful monitoring of children's and early evening television) which, without being trivial or abstruse, were not also known equally well to the controls—a further indication of the essential similarity of the material put over by the different mass media. As a result we could not find, as we had intended, what topics and what manner of presentation make for effective learning. One or two items of rather specialised information included in the test showed that the viewers do pick up information—but their number was too small to permit more detailed analysis. If such studies are to be more rewarding, they need to be done in large numbers and in collaboration with producers, so that one can purposely select useful information little known to children of that age and then systematically vary the manner of its presentation on television, using as subjects only viewers who have seen the programme, and obtaining an estimate of their previous knowledge from matched controls.

The testing of children's comprehension of three specific pro-grammes suggests the following tentative conclusions:

Children aged 10 and over had no difficulty in absorbing and remembering, at least for a day or so, a typical documentary pro-gramme on children's television. There is evidence that interest in such programmes may best be captured by action sequences.

An adult information programme, even when the subject in-terested children, did not increase factual knowledge, except among the brighter adolescents. The younger children often remembered it well, but they did not understand what was being said, or what point was being made.

A dramatised information programme was able to bring about subtle changes in the child's attitude, even when he already knew the material well from other sources.

24

Effects on Cultural Interests

IT has often been suggested that television stimulates the child's interests, widens his horizons, creates a hunger for further information on topics as unexpected as archaeology, and encourages him to make or do certain things for himself. On the other hand, others think that interest aroused by television seldom becomes permanent or leads to action; that in the end it leaves the palate jaded or, at most, accentuates existing patterns of interest. Moreover, television, by catering for these interests in ready-made programmes, often tends to inhibit the child from acting on the interests himself.

In examining these opposite views we have asked not merely whether television can stimulate and widen children's interests, but whether it can do so better than alternative sources whose time it takes up. We have also explored its effects on children's interests and activity patterns according to age, sex, and intelligence, paying special attention to cultural or creative interests and activities. Finally, we have asked whether it can be shown that increased interest in a subject leads to increased knowledge of it, and increased activity around it.

In Chapter 31 we shall examine how far television does make children mentally lazy or passive and how far it stimulates them to take up new hobbies and interests. Here we concentrate on the effect on *cultural* interests and pursuits.

CULTURAL INTERESTS AND ACTIVITIES

Three sets of data are presented here: a special study of how the showing of exhibits from a museum affected children's subsequent visits to that museum; a comparative analysis of the frequency of visits to museums and art galleries by viewers and controls; and a comparison of the more creative hobbies and cultural interests of the two groups.

The Ashmolean Museum study

This museum houses the chief art and archaeological collections of Oxford University. Part of the Cretan collection normally exhibited there was the subject of a children's television programme in the BBC *Treasure Hunt* series. Did this programme stimulate children to visit the museum and, if so, what did they want to see?

Two other local museums had previously had some of their exhibits featured in *Treasure Hunt* programmes, namely the Castle Museum, Norwich, and the museum at Ipswich. We asked the curators for information and both responded with interest, although it was difficult for them to be precise since naturally they had kept no records of the number of child visitors or types of question asked. The curator at Norwich had noted a quite considerable surge of interest among the local children after the programme which included local exhibits. The children mostly came by themselves, not in school parties, and they definitely asked to see the exhibits mentioned on television. The curator at Ipswich, on the other hand, did not believe that children had been stimulated to come to see the local exhibits; however, he attributed this to the poverty of television reception in his area.

We had wanted to undertake studies like this in order to explore the stimulus of specific programmes, but we had refrained from carrying them out because they seemed unlikely to give enough precision.[1] The basic problem was how to gauge the strength of the inner 'demand' created by a programme. Direct questioning of the children soon afterwards would draw attention to the programme and bias the results. The alternative was to measure the expressed demand and, as market researchers well know, the question whether any demand set up is expressed in action (say, the purchase of an article) depends largely on how soon that object is available. In short, to assess the actual stimulus of a programme, we needed a fairly closed area in which the demand could be satisfied and measured at the same time. The measurement would have to continue for some time before and after the programme and it would have to be analysed by age, sex, and possibly other determinants. Also the method should not interfere with the free flow of demand, either by heightening it or by slowing it down.

In framing our museum study we regarded Oxford as a relatively

[1] Investigations have been made of children's library-borrowing habits, and in some of them certain changes over time have been noted. The weakness of such investigations lies in attempts to explain such changes in terms of concurrent trends, like a rise in comic reading, juvenile delinquency, or television viewing, or a decline in Sunday school attendance. This procedure seemed to us to lack scientific rigour.

closed area, within which the museum was well known and readily accessible. We could see what the immediate and local effects of the programme, if any, would be. Other factors also favoured the experiment. The *Treasure Hunt* series had been going for some time and was thought to be fairly popular with the children. Museum visiting is perhaps less difficult to measure than the demand for a particular book. In Oxford, the stimulus of the programme was expected to be at its highest since the local museum had been featured. Finally, the programme appeared on 30 July 1956, just after the beginning of the summer holidays.

We decided not merely to note the frequency of children's visits to the museum before and after the programme, but also to ask them whether they had seen the programme and whether seeing it had brought them to the museum at that particular time. More important, we wanted to know why the children had come to the museum after seeing the programme, since on this question there was room for doubt. It might be that the objects, including the famous head of a bull, would look rather abstract and lifeless on the screen, and that children would like to see them in reality and in colour; or that the objects shown on the screen might be taken for granted, but that children would now want to see what else the museum had to offer. They might also come merely to see a local phenomenon which had acquired sudden fame—without being concerned with any particular aspect or feature. We were, therefore, interested to find out exactly why the children had come, what they had seen, and how they had reacted to the Cretan exhibits and to other parts of the museum. We also needed to know their general background—age, sex, school, social class— whether they were interested in archaeology or museums of any kind, or had previously been to this museum. Finally, we wanted to know their reactions to the television programme and how well the objects seen 'in real life' compared with the objects seen on the screen.

Observations had to start several days before the programme, in order to gain some idea of the normal frequency of child visitors, and had to be extended to include the following week-end, the programme being shown on a Monday afternoon. A great deal of time was spent in careful preparation.[1] Even so, the results could by no means be regarded as typical of what such programmes regularly achieve in the long run. We expected a fairly marked, observable local effect, and in our preparations we were trying to make sure that none of

---

[1] We prepared a short questionnaire which the older children could fill in by themselves, and used it as a *pro forma* for interviews with the younger children. The questionnaire had to be tried out and revised, interviewers had to be engaged in Oxford and briefed: they had to cover the opening hours of the museum (10 a.m. to 4 p.m.). The Curator of the museum and his staff were most helpful and co-operative in all this. We had to take care that the interviewers would be so placed as to be unobtrusive to children entering the museum, yet sufficiently near the exit to interview every child as he went out. Arrangements had to be flexible, in case there was a sudden influx of children at particular times, such as Saturday afternoon. A special effort was made by the programme organisers to get the borrowed objects back in their place at the museum as soon after the programme as possible. We received much helpful co-operation from the BBC, and from the programme organisers personally, in making arrangements for this study.

the immediate and obvious effects escaped our attention. We even sought to maximise the potential effects of the programme by asking the BBC to mention the name of the museum both at the beginning and at the end of the programme. Thus, while this case-history was not perhaps very representative, we hoped it would provide valuable qualitative information, and that it might be followed by several others, each devoted to a different aspect of the problem.

The number of children attracted to the museum did not increase as a result of the programme. During the week after the programme, including the week-end, 145 children were interviewed at the museum—not noticeably more than before the programme. Of these, only fifteen had seen the programme—and most of these went to see other parts of the museum and not the Mycenaean gallery.[1]

Only three of the fifteen children said they had come because their interest had been aroused by the programme, and only two of the three actually saw the exhibits. Three other viewers had come to the museum for other reasons, but went to see the exhibits too, though one (a girl of 9) could not find them. Having seen the objects on television, three boys thought them much more interesting in the round ('more detail than on TV', 'can't see colours on TV'); but a 12 year old girl had found the programme 'boring' and thought the exhibits 'not quite as interesting' as she had expected. All but one of the children who had seen the programme had liked it, especially the bull's head and the swords and cups of gold. On the whole, however, the impact of the programme was slight.

We believe that this is the first 'direct effects' study of its kind, in which children were not asked whether television had stimulated them but the stimulation was directly measured and related to the viewing of the programme. We have described it in some detail because it shows the difficulties and hazards, even under favourable conditions, that face this kind of action research.

The results were largely negative, yet they show how important such studies are as correctives; for increases in, say, museum attendance are all too readily attributed to television when they may stem from other sources.

Visits to museums and art galleries

These observations may tell us little of the effects of one programme, but we have data on the frequency of museum visiting in general. In the main survey and the Norwich study we asked children

---

[1] In part these disappointing results may be attributed to the fact that, in spite of our request, the name and locality of the museum were mentioned only at the beginning of the programme and not at the end as well.

whether they had ever been to a museum or art gallery and, if so, how long it was since they last went. In addition they were asked to write down their reasons for going, so as possibly to throw light on any influence by television.

One-third of the sample said they had been to a museum or art gallery within the last three months; roughly two-thirds—rather more of the older, but rather fewer of the younger children—said they had been within the preceding twelve months. Neither sex, social class, nor intelligence made much difference to the results.

There was a slight, but not significant, tendency for viewers to visit these places more often than their controls. But this difference cannot be attributed to the effects of television, since it also existed in Norwich between future viewers and controls in 1955. In Norwich, after a year's interval, there was no discernible increase in museum or art-gallery visiting which could be attributed to viewing. When giving reasons for going to museums and art galleries, children seldom mentioned the effects of any television programme.

Other evidence of stimulation

We now briefly consider some of the other evidence at our disposal.

First, in a questionnaire designed to find out whether children would prefer to see certain things and events in real life or on television, an opportunity was also given for each child to indicate whether he was interested in seeing these things at all. The relative preferences for seeing things in real life or on the screen are discussed in Chapter 31. Here we are concerned with this instrument as a measure of 'interestedness'. It contained several cultural items such as visits to an exhibition, a museum, and an art gallery. In general, viewers were interested in a greater number of things than controls; with regard to these particular items, however, there was no difference.

Second, the inventories of interests and activities (see Appendix A) also had sections on cultural and intellectual interests—such as going to a concert, opera, ballet, or play, discussing politics, reading books (apart from school books), and writing a story, play, or poem. Again, there is no evidence that these interests were particularly affected by viewing.

Third, we have diaries kept by children for a week (see Chapter 6). When classifying the leisure activities recorded, we paid special attention to cultural or creative interests. We assessed the amount of time each child had spent during the week on such activities as writing, drawing, painting, and making scrap books (but not including manual efforts of a more technical kind, such as model making, constructional work, or doing repairs). In terms of both time and frequency viewers actually obtained slightly lower scores than controls. This difference in frequency was significant among the younger children. Far from stimulating this kind of activity, television tended to displace it.

Lastly, there are the data obtained by means of the following question (see Chapter 9 and Appendix Table 8):

> There are sometimes discussion groups on TV where young people talk over different problems. What would you like them to talk about?

Broadly speaking, the results showed that viewers and controls had a similar range of cultural interests. The few consistent differences between them were on non-cultural subjects.

To sum up, our answer to the question *Does television encourage cultural interests and activities among child viewers?* must be cautious. There is some evidence that it can give this kind of stimulus, for instance in broadening tastes in reading (see Chapter 28). For the most part, however, television stimulates viewers no more than other mass media and the other social influences which stimulate controls. More could be done to turn the interest aroused by television programmes into action—for instance, by developing the appeal of such programmes as the *Treasure Hunt* series to persuade more children to visit their local museums.

Interests and knowledge

It is often assumed that interest leads to knowledge. If television stimulated certain interests, viewers might try to obtain further knowledge in those fields, in which case the benefits of television would be twofold. But the opposite may well be true; a child may only develop an interest in a subject when he knows something about it. Or there may be an interaction between the two processes. We decided to look into the relationship between knowledge and interest derived from television.

One easily examined aspect of this question is the child's liking for certain school subjects, which can be affected by actual programmes, or by selective viewing of certain types of programmes. It is relevant to compare the preferences and dislikes of viewers and controls so far as these subjects are concerned. We gave the children the following questions:

> Write down the school subject that you like best of all.
>   I like this subject best because . . .

Is there any school subject that you *really* dislike? Yes . . . No . . .
If *yes*, what subject is it? . . .

   I do not like it because . . .

If there is no subject you really dislike, write down the one you are not so keen on.

   I am not so keen on this subject because . . .

Later we asked each child to indicate by means of a tick the degree to which he liked or disliked each of a given list of 20 school subjects, or (where appropriate) to tick 'I do not do this subject'. He was asked to add to the list any other subjects he was being taught at school and to indicate whether he liked or disliked them.

The results revealed no significant differences between viewers and controls. Such interests as are stimulated by television do not extend the desire for knowledge in particular school subjects.

We next related the interests expressed by children to their general knowledge of those subjects by analysing the children's scores on the general-knowledge tests (see p. 267) in relation to their interest scores (see p. 148), wherever the two techniques covered similar subjects.

There were only three areas of knowledge which lent themselves to this type of analysis: music, nature and rural studies, and current affairs. The results showed that among controls a rise in the information score very often went with a rise in their interest score. However, among viewers this relationship was absent and sometimes the opposite happened. From this we may conclude that learning from television, unlike learning from other sources, is not necessarily accompanied by interest in the subject. Television can teach even the bored or the antipathetic as well as the genuinely interested.

Naturally, we must be cautious in drawing conclusions from this evidence, since it is derived from only three school subjects and the trends were not particularly marked. Fuller investigation would quite possibly modify some of our interpretations. For the moment, however, we conclude that television affects neither viewers' interests in particular school subjects, nor their performance in any given subject at school; but there are signs that it can upset the usual relationship between interest and knowledge, in that viewers may learn even though they are uninterested, and increased interest is not necessarily accompanied by increased knowledge.

CONCLUSIONS

On the whole, we have found that (with the exception of broadening taste in reading) television does not markedly stimulate the child's cultural, intellectual, or creative interests. On the other

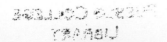

hand, television has not made the child's interests more narrow or limited nor, as we shall see, has it turned him into a passive consumer of the ready-made. There is evidence that television does, on occasion, stimulate the child to certain activities such as museum visiting (though probably no more often than other mass media do), but a great deal depends on the ready availability of an outlet for the new interest which may be aroused. There is need for more research to study the processes by which such newly stimulated interests can best be turned into some form of activity and become consolidated.

There is no indication that any specific interests aroused by television carry over into a heightened liking for particular school subjects. On the other hand, we have seen that children can assimilate knowledge from television without necessarily being interested in the subject.

Altogether it is evident that much more effort will be required on the part of research workers, producers, parents, teachers, and other members of the community, such as directors of galleries or curators of museums, before the potentially stimulating capacities of television are likely to be turned by child viewers to their own cultural advantage.

25

Television and Schoolwork

IN one school week the average child viewer spends over one-third as much time watching television as he spends in class. The grammar school child spends more time on television than on homework. It is not surprising therefore that the effect of television on school achievement is so often discussed by both parents and teachers.

Two sets of views are generally put forward. On the one hand, it is said television may interfere with homework and serious study; it distracts children from reading and other educational pursuits; and when children go to bed late and lose sleep they cannot concentrate on their schoolwork. On the other hand, it is said that certain television programmes have educational value and may help children in their schoolwork. Also television may encourage new interests, and so may make the child more willing to take certain school subjects more seriously. (Critics of this argument point out that the new viewer, for the first few weeks at any rate, tends to drop everything and spend most of his waking hours in front of the television set, while his position in class falls sharply.)

Our task was to see how far these various influences are revealed in school performance. American research, especially by Witty and his colleagues (104), has not found any significant differences in performance. Remmers found that 30–40 per cent of one age group admitted that television interfered a little with their schoolwork (76), while 31 per cent of another group claimed that television helped them with their schoolwork (103). In Britain, Middleton (68), working in a Lincoln grammar school, reported little difference in school performance between unmatched viewers and controls, except that among the most recent set owners performance dropped temporarily, though half had regained their position in class within a year. Duggan (27), reporting on a London grammar school, found no differences in bedtimes or in time spent on homework; differences in examination marks, if anything, favoured the viewers. A very slight difference has been reported from a Manchester secondary modern school by Mitchell (70), who also noted that viewers more often chose science subjects as their favourites in school. In this study viewers were carefully matched with non-viewers.

Teachers' opinions

The teachers whom we questioned were divided in their views. Only 16 per cent spontaneously mentioned that television helped with schoolwork; 12 per cent, on the contrary, thought it a hindrance because it interfered with homework (a third of these were grammar school teachers). Some 15 per cent, mainly from secondary modern and primary schools, felt that television had created fresh interest in subjects like nature study, religious instruction, geography, and history. Another 9 per cent, mostly in junior and infant schools, said that viewing had enriched the children's vocabulary and given them something to talk about, so improving their capacity for verbal self-expression.

Comparison of school marks

To compare viewers with controls in respect of their school performance, we used teachers' assessments based on school marks and test results.[1] Restricting our comparison to children from the same class-room, we gave each class teacher a form on which the viewers and controls in their own classes were listed in pairs (as 'A' and 'B'), and then asked the teachers to indicate for each pair, in respect of a number of school subjects, whether A was:

> much better than B,
> a little better than B,
> about the same standard as B,

[1] We decided against the use of standardised attainment tests, mainly for practical reasons, since we wished to study the school achievement of those children who were already part of our main sample and on whom we had a great deal of other relevant information. We were forced to rely on teachers' assessments because we often needed to compare viewers and non-viewers from different schools, sometimes even from different cities, and it soon became evident that there are considerable differences in systems of marking and standards of comparison from one school to another and from one city to another. In addition, not all children in the same age group are taught exactly the same subjects, nor are all children tested with equal frequency. Where only rank order within class was available, there was the additional difficulty of different universes of comparison. In these circumstances we decided, in order to preserve our comparisons from bias due to any of the above factors, that we would need to restrict these comparisons to children from the same class-room, taught and assessed by the same teachers. This appreciably reduced the number of cases on which we could obtain information, but it considerably enhanced the quality of the comparisons.

a little below the standard of B,
very much below the standard of B.[1]

The teachers were not told which of the two was the viewer. They were asked to use marks and test results as much as possible and only to give their own impressions or assessments when no other objective information was available. They were also asked to give an independent general assessment.

The class teachers' response to this rather formidable request was excellent. Altogether we obtained assessments for 172 pairs, 46 in grammar schools, 65 in secondary modern schools, and 61 in primary schools. For most of these we obtained comparisons on up to seventeen school subjects, as well as the independent overall assessments.

The results suggest that, on the whole, school performance of viewers was level with, or slightly lower than that of their controls.

The distribution of the overall assessments for all the pairs was as follows:

	%
Control child much better than viewer	24
Control child a little better than viewer	23
Control child and viewer much the same	17
Viewer a little better than control child	23
Viewer much better than control child	13

Altogether 47 per cent of the controls were doing better than viewers matched with them, and 36 per cent of the viewers were doing better than their controls. There was a trend, not statistically significant, towards better school performance on the part of the controls.

Table 57 shows that in most subjects there was little difference between viewers and controls in the grammar schools, though the trends favoured the controls. This superiority of controls in some

[1] The teachers were not told the purpose of these paired comparisons, but they may have guessed it, knowing the general object of the inquiry. Furthermore, some teachers may have known which members of some pairs had a television set at home. Their assessments and comparisons, though based on their mark sheets and test results, may have been biased by their own views on the influence of television, though in which direction we cannot say.

To prevent misunderstanding it should be made clear that these assessments were made by the children's own teachers and that the teachers to whose opinions we have made reference earlier were quite a different group, in different parts of the country. Altogether we attach much more weight to detailed, 'blind', paired comparisons using examination results subject by subject, dealing with not more than two children at a time, than to opinions and impressions given in general terms.

subjects was even smaller in the secondary modern school, where viewers scored significantly better in spoken English, music, and geography. Among primary school children there was no appreciable difference in half the subjects; in a few subjects the controls scored a little higher, but viewers scored significantly higher in handicrafts. Again and again, however, we find that the children were most often rated as level.[1]

TABLE 57. Class teachers' assessments of 172 pairs of viewers and control cases from the same class-rooms

(Entries in the table are *raw frequencies*)

Subjects:	Grammar			Sec. mod.			Primary		
	Controls better	Same	Viewers better	Controls better	Same	Viewers better	Controls better	Same	Viewers better
Reading in class	13	8	12	19	22	22	30	16	15
Spoken English and Drama . .	12	9	16	15	17	26	23	20	18
Written English .	21	10	11	26	9	30	30	14	17
Physical training, sports, games .	14	11	16	24	18	20	19	17	24
Music, singing .	11	21	3	12	18	23	18	29	11
Arithmetic or Mathematics .	24	7	14	23	17	24	24	9	28
History . .	20	7	16	21	17	24	17	24	20
Geography . .	19	14	13	19	18	27	19	25	17
Current affairs .	4	6	3	5	5	6	10	9	10
Art, modelling .	15	13	12	20	18	19	20	16	24
General science .	13	16	15	21	16	14	—	—	—
Religious instruction .	15	17	7	23	15	19	18	33	7
Domestic subjects	4	3	1	14	7	17	—	—	—
Needlework .	1	4	3	19	10	6	13	10	8
Handicrafts, including wood and metal work .	2	3	5	9	12	12	5	8	11
Nature study, botany, biology, zoology . .	5	9	8	7	3	14	17	26	13
Foreign languages	21	3	22	8	3	9	—	—	—
Overall assessment	23	8	15	29	9	27	29	12	20

The viewers' school attainment was occasionally a little poorer; there were hardly any sharp differences in the pattern from one school subject to another. Viewers did not score consistently lower

[1] In assessing the statistical significance of these results, the sign test was employed, simply comparing 'controls better' categories with 'viewers better' categories. This gives slightly misleading results since it ignores the sometimes quite considerable central 'no-difference' category. For instance, on the subject of music the scores for the grammar schools are 11–21–3; the difference between 11 and 3 is significant at the 5 per cent level of confidence, but this ignores the fact that no difference was reported for over half the number of pairs.

in any subject (except possibly in religious instruction), nor did grammar school children suffer disproportionately because of interference with homework.

Use of intellectual capacity. We also asked teachers to mention any subject in which a child was unexpectedly above or below his general standard of attainment.[1] Again the differences were slight; a viewer was reported to be doing exceptionally well on 137 occasions, a control on 146. For unexpectedly poor performances the respective figures were 39 and 37.

It is sometimes suggested that television enables a child to make the most of his intellectual capacity. We asked teachers to assess the children in their classes, saying whether they were working above, up to, or below their estimated intellectual ability. Altogether such assessments were obtained for 434 viewers and 460 controls. Again there was hardly any difference between the two groups; this was true of both sexes and all three types of school.[2]

When asked to report any instance where a child's schoolwork or behaviour was influenced in any way by out-of-school conditions, teachers mentioned favourable conditions for 26 viewers and 24 control cases and unfavourable conditions for 28 viewers and 55 controls. (More controls came from exceptionally poor homes, or homes where the child had to help a lot, or from broken homes or orphanages.)

We conclude, therefore, that neither marked physical disability nor poorer home circumstances help to account for the viewers' slightly lower achievement.

Children's self-assessment

We tried to find out how far viewers themselves felt that television had taught them something about various school subjects.[3] Not surprisingly, children felt that they had learnt a good deal. The highest figures were obtained for animals, other countries and other people, cooking and housecraft, people or happenings in history, science, and nature study. The lowest results were for English (poetry and literature) and foreign languages. The results are set out in detail in Appendix Table 44.

In most subjects these views bore little relation to the teachers'

[1] We obtained this information, not merely for the 172 pairs mentioned earlier but for 441 viewers and 474 controls.

[2] Also, teachers, when asked whether any child's work was affected by physical disability, illness, or stress, mentioned only 33 viewers and 40 controls.

[3] The actual question asked was: *Some children feel they have learnt something from television, while others do not. Here is a list of subjects. Tick 'yes' or 'no' to show whether or not you have learned something about them that you did not know before.*

assessments of attainment—a further indication of how little self-assessments can be relied on for accurate and valid information.

The influence of intelligence, viewing frequency, and length of set ownership

What kinds of children do better or worse in school because of television? The teachers' assessments showed that boys were no more affected than girls, and older children no more than younger children (in spite of the homework problem). But the brighter children were affected somewhat more than the duller ones—in both age groups. It seems that, given the level of performance expected from these brighter children, television has very little new to offer them; but viewing can take time from other ways of learning (Appendix Table 46).

Amount or frequency of viewing affected the results very little.[1] New set owners in primary schools tended to do slightly less well at school than controls, but veteran viewers did not necessarily do much better. Our results do not substantiate Middleton's findings (68) that, when television arrives, the child's school performance declines rapidly at first but subsequently recovers; indeed, the data from secondary schools showed that the more recent viewers particularly tended to score better than controls. Middleton's study did not use matched samples, which may account for the discrepancy.

Television and homework

While the precise relationship between the amount and quality of homework and a child's school performance is unknown, the two are generally thought to be closely linked, especially among older and more intelligent children. It is therefore important to know how far television affects homework.

In our sample nearly 90 per cent of the primary school children and nearly 40 per cent of the 13–14 year olds claimed to do no homework. We confined our attention to children in secondary schools—especially grammar school children, 80 per cent of whom said they did some homework every day.

The children were asked: *How much time do you spend on homework each day?* and were given a choice of answers ranging from '15 minutes or less' to 'more than an hour'. The results (Table 58) show that among grammar school children, whose homework was regular and considerable, the time spent was not curtailed by television. There

---

[1] Data were available for 130 pairs (83 pairs of children aged 13–14 years and 47 pairs of children aged 10–11 years).

was, however, a slight effect in secondary modern and primary schools; those who had television, according to their estimates, spent on average 6–8 minutes less on their homework each day than controls did.[1]

TABLE 58. *How often do you have to do homework? How much time do you spend on homework each day?*

(Distribution of answers by intelligence)

13–14 YEAR OLDS

	Grammar		I.Q. 100–114		Sec. mod. I.Q. below 100	
How often:	v %	c %	v %	c %	v %	c %
Don't have to do it	—	—	40	41	75	70
Do it once a week	—	—	17	16	6	8
Do it most days	18	22	35	41	16	19
Do it every day	82	78	8	2	3	3
Total cases (weighted)	168	168	167	185	165	151
How much time each day:						
15 minutes or less	2	—	24	9	5	—
About half an hour	5	8	37	25	55	36
About three-quarters of an hour	15	14	17	37	10	34
About an hour	29	28	14	21	23	17
More than an hour	49	50	8	8	7	13
Total cases (weighted)	168	166	99	92	40	47
Do homework:						
Sometimes with television on	19	—	23	—	6	—
Sometimes with radio on	27	37	30	26	12	20
Total cases (weighted)	180	180	180	180	180	180

What happens when television and homework clash? The children were asked: *Do your parents make you finish your homework before you can look at television or listen to the wireless, or do they let you do as you like about it?* and then could tick one of two answers: *They make me finish my homework first,* and *They let me do as I like.*

Of older children who did homework, 60 per cent of the viewers and 56 per cent of the controls said they were made to finish it first; figures for grammar school children were even higher—their homework tended to be taken more seriously by the parents. Viewers' parents were about as strict as those of controls; strictness, in fact,

[1] In studying displacement effects we do not have to accept the children's self-estimates as accurate or unbiased, since we are only studying viewer-control differences and are principally concerned with *relative* figures. All we assume is that inaccuracies or biases are equally present among viewers and controls. In fact, however, these estimates correlate well with our own calculations from the children's diaries.

seemed to depend on the attitude of parents to homework, irrespective of whether they owned a television set.

It would appear that viewers did their homework regularly, although it might sometimes be delayed or interrupted. This was confirmed by the children's diaries, which also showed that homework was rarely interrupted, once started. Children, when permitted, tended to view or listen in to programmes they particularly liked and do their homework afterwards.[1]

Only a few children seemed to be disturbed while doing homework by having radio or television on; 19 per cent of the grammar school viewers and 37 per cent of the controls ticked *I do my homework* as one of the things that 'sometimes' went on in the same room while television or radio was on (Table 58). In the older age group a further 10 per cent 'usually' did their homework with the television set turned on in the same room. Also 11 per cent of the viewers and 23 per cent of the controls 'usually' did their homework while the radio was on. All these viewers and 15 per cent of the controls said there was another room in which they could do their homework while the radio or television set was switched on, so that they must have *chosen* to do their homework with television on in the same room.

The children were further asked whether television or radio *makes it harder or easier to do your homework—or doesn't it make any difference?* In the case of radio, three-quarters said it made no difference, and 11 per cent thought it made it easier. Most of those who said it made it harder were grammar school children.

There were no children who said that television made homework easier, and only 57 per cent said it made no difference. This difference between radio and television is to be expected, in view of the different demands they make on the attention.

Reports from the United States also indicate that a small minority of children do their homework while watching television, or at least with the set switched on in the same room. Also many children complete their homework while the radio is on. These findings raise some interesting problems—fluctuations of attention, background noise as an aid to concentration, the capacity to follow a television programme by ear alone, and the effectiveness of homework in improving the child's school performance.

---

[1] Since our data were collected both the BBC and ITV have abandoned the close-down period between 6 and 7 p.m. This is likely to have made it more difficult for some of the older children to do their homework—those (one-third) who are not expected by their parents to finish their homework before viewing.

CONCLUSIONS

Thus the possession of a television set appears to be neither a distinct advantage nor a severe handicap as far as the child's performance at school is concerned. Viewers in the same class-room, on average, tended to do a little less well than controls, but no distinct influence can be seen on particular school subjects. Moreover, television does not lead to either over-achievement or under-achievement. The effects of frequency of viewing and length of set ownership proved to be slight, as also were, for the most part, the influences of age, sex, and type of school; but television appears to be more of a hindrance than a help to the brighter children in both age groups.

About two-thirds of the children who were given homework to do were made to finish it by their parents before being allowed to view. Some viewers (but not the grammar school children) spent slightly less time than controls in doing their homework. They were not often interrupted by television, but some of them chose to do their homework while television was on in the same room.

26

Television and Knowledge—a Summing Up

THE question we raised was: Does television give a child a better background of general knowledge than he would have had without it? Or does it, by taking up time he could spend on other things, prevent him from acquiring as wide a range of information as he might have obtained otherwise? In answering this question, we have to try to balance gain and loss against each other.

Information programmes on children's television. It would seem that children's information programmes, though moderately popular, readily understood, and well remembered (especially when they contain action sequences) do not much improve the viewers' knowledge relative to that of the controls. There would seem to be three reasons for this: first, much of what is offered on children's television is already known to children of that age group or else readily available to those with more time to spend on other sources of information. Many of these programmes fail to break new ground, and their level is often too low even for the younger children in our sample. In the second place, information conveyed in these programmes is not retained for long by children below the age of 10–11, and after that age watching children's television becomes less frequent. At this age the veteran viewer (the one who had acquired a set at the age of 6 or 7) proved no more knowledgeable than the one whose parents had acquired a set more recently. There is thus little storing of information. The third reason lies in the specificity of much of the information put over. For example, the child may gain specific knowledge about particular animals and plants but he would not acquire more general knowledge of the kind that would be tested in school work or in information tests.

Information programmes on evening television. Adult information programmes, on the other hand, might make a real contribution when they deal with subjects in which the children are interested, but for the fact that children often miss the essential points. The usual method of presentation—drawing on a panel of experts and using short film or action sequences—is effective only with the older and brighter adolescents. The younger and less intelligent children may recall the events which took place on the programme, but they take in little of the spoken word and so lose the trend of the argument. Of course, many of the informative evening programmes (such as science programmes, which through their dramatic quality might well appeal to children) are shown too late for the majority to watch, while others (for instance, current-affairs programmes) are of little interest to children and have small audiences.

Other evening programmes. Paradoxically, perhaps the most effective sources of useful information to children are those evening programmes which do not deliberately set out to instruct. We infer this from the fact that we have found viewers better informed than their controls in a number of unexpected fields of knowledge, while in other fields, where content and preference analysis of information programmes would lead one to expect clear gains, such gains have failed to show up on our tests. Many dramatic productions, for example, may contain informative detail in plots and settings which would give viewers an advantage over their controls—a process of incidental learning seems to be at work, which is assisted by the dramatic impact of the programme as a whole.

If this conclusion is valid, then it is of the greatest importance for viewers of the future. As we have seen, for different reasons children's and adults' information programmes do not make children more knowledgeable than they otherwise would have been. More important, in the two-channel home the child tends to switch from channel to channel pursuing his first or second favourites, so that consequently audiences for information programmes have dropped from an average of around 45 per cent to somewhere nearer 15 per cent. From this one might be tempted to predict that in future viewers would steadily lag behind non-viewers as far as their general knowledge is concerned. However, it now seems more likely that the situation will remain roughly where it is now, since viewers apparently do benefit considerably from non-informational programmes. Much will therefore depend on the quality and range of these programmes.

Television and schoolwork. On the whole we find that viewers are more or less able to hold their own, generally scoring just a little below their controls in the same class-room. This seems to be true for all sub-groups of age, sex, class, and intelligence, except for the brighter children. In both age groups these seem to fall behind just a little more often.

Television had not led viewers to take a special interest in any one school subject; nor were they markedly better or worse at one subject rather than another. The very frequent showing of information programmes about nature, other countries, and current affairs had made little impact here; the viewers' performance at school in these subjects was no better than that of the controls. Television seems to be of no particular help to the child in making the most of his intelligence: it causes neither over- nor under-achievement. We feel particularly confident in our conclusions regarding school performance since we have used measures specially designed for the inquiry, and since American findings, on the whole, have been similar.

Television and homework. As a social problem, the effect of television on homework is slight. It concerns only a small proportion of the older children to any marked degree, namely those 15–20 per cent who go to grammar schools, and almost two-thirds of these are under parental injunction to finish homework first. The remainder were most often found to postpone their homework until after viewing, and a few did it in snatches, in between watching. Quite a number who did homework in the room in which the television was on, did so from choice rather than from lack of alternative accommodation.

The amount of time spent on homework by grammar school pupils was the same for viewers and controls. It must be remembered, however, that we carried out our inquiry in the summer and that there was still a gap in transmission between 6 and 7.30 p.m.

Television and cultural interests. Television can act as a stimulator of cultural and creative interests and activities, but no more so than other influences. Archaeological, artistic, or 'how-to-make' programmes arouse interest, but this is not often turned into activity by the child. Television has the capacity to familiarise the child with out-of-the-way subjects, especially when dramatised; however, on the whole increased familiarity goes hand in hand with—and not in advance of—increased factual knowledge. A vivid example at the time of our survey was the serialisation of *Jane Eyre*, which made a considerable impact on the viewers and in that respect gave them a clear advantage over their controls. When such influences are averaged out, however, the results of viewing are not, in the long run, superior to those of reading or listening to the radio. We have found elsewhere, however, that television can broaden the viewer's taste in reading.

In offering dramatisations, even of well-known material, television does not merely convey knowledge and a feeling of acquaintance; it can also create changes in the child's attitude. The effects of visual and dramatic presentation can be both subtle and lasting.

Who gains? Parents as well as teachers (especially those owning television sets) testify that children gain knowledge from viewing. While this is undoubtedly the case, we must ask whether such knowledge can compensate the child for the time viewing takes from reading, radio listening, and other sources of information. Our findings indicate that among the children we examined there was one group which really benefited from viewing in this respect, namely the duller, younger children, whose access to other sources of information is restricted. To most other children viewing offers about as many advantages as disadvantages, while for the grammar school children the loss tends to be greater than the gain. Thus, television is at its strongest where other media fail.

PART VII

Effects on Leisure and Interests

27

Television in the Pattern of Leisure

VIEWING takes up about one-third of the child's leisure time, a little more for some days and less for others. How does he find the necessary time for viewing? Does he manage this by giving up one or two activities completely, by reducing them all proportionately, or by cutting down some a great deal, others very little?

To a large extent the way a child divides his time will depend on the relative needs served by television on the one hand and competing pastimes on the other. Radio, for instance, gratifies the same needs as viewing, but less effectively; as a result, it cannot compete with television. At the opposite extreme, a day by the sea would cater for very different needs and hardly come into conflict with television. But most leisure activities fall somewhere between these two extremes. A child has to strike a balance between the claims of television and those of other ways of spending his time.

It would be misleading to consider the effects of television as static. Some of them occur immediately, others only after a period of viewing; some come to stay, even growing more pronounced as time goes on; others prove only transitory. A child's interests change and develop, and the time he takes to adjust himself to television must vary according to what kind of child he is.

We also have to distinguish differences due to television from those which existed before television became available.

Some research has been done in this country, and a great deal in the United States, on the effects of television on children's leisure. The results, which will be discussed as they become relevant, point to considerable changes due to television. Many of the surveys are thorough and comprehensive, but many also suffer because of inability to take account of the factors outlined above. Our survey, whatever its limitations, did at least incorporate safeguards which helped us to disentangle some of these complexities.

It was clearly impossible to cover all the leisure activities and interests of a child; in our inquiry, however, we were able to draw on children's diaries for detailed accounts of how they had spent their time; this was particularly useful in showing us how much the less organised activities ('doing nothing in particular') were affected by television.

Before going on to discuss television's effect on specific types of activity, we shall show what part it played in children's leisure, how much it meant to them, and what were its main competitors.

THE ROLE OF TELEVISION IN CHILDREN'S LIVES

The average child in the survey viewed for an hour and three-quarters a day. He spent about a third of his leisure time viewing on week-days, although not so much at week-ends.

The younger child, although he went to bed earlier than the adolescent, fitted in as much viewing and therefore had less free time available. On the other hand, the duller child, who viewed more than the brighter ones, also went to bed later and so had at least as much time left for other things.

Interest in viewing

Television takes up a great deal of time, but does it command as much interest? The children's answers to three questions suggested that it did not: many were only moderately interested in television. The first question was: *How much would you miss your television set if you had to do without it?* (*Very much. Quite a lot. Not very much.*) (Table 59.)

It will be seen that only half the children said they would miss television very much, and as many as 15 to 20 per cent would not miss it much at all. Least interested were the grammar school children.

By drawing attention to television, this question could give an exaggerated measure of interest in it. For a more accurate assessment we sought spontaneous references, elicited very early in the survey —long before we made any mention of television: *There never seems to be enough time to do all the things one likes doing. Write down the three things you like doing best, that is, in the time after school.* Even among the younger children, whom we knew to be the keener viewers, only 19 per cent gave viewing as their first choice and over half did not mention television at all (Appendix Table 45).

TABLE 59. *How much would you miss your television set if you had to do without it?*

(Distribution of viewers' answers by age and intelligence)

13–14 YEAR OLDS

Would miss television set:	All %	Grammar %	Sec. mod. I.Q. 100–114 %	I.Q. below 100 %
Very much	49	34	56	58
Quite a lot	32	39	32	26
Not very much	19	27	12	16
Total cases (weighted)	532	178	175	179

10–11 YEAR OLDS

Would miss television set:	All %	I.Q. 115+ %	I.Q. 100–114 %	I.Q. below 100 %
Very much	59	53	60	64
Quite a lot	28	31	31	22
Not very much	13	16	9	14
Total cases (weighted)	534	180	175	179

Answers to this question may, however, have underestimated the everyday impact of television, since it had to compete with the whole range of desirable leisure-time activities. We therefore asked a third question, in which the attractiveness of television was weighed against other things which the child had actually done on that day. Every day for a week, after completing their diary, children were asked to think over what they had done the previous afternoon and evening and to write down the three things they had most enjoyed (Table 60).

Almost 30 per cent did not mention television at all. At the other extreme there were about 5 per cent who listed it as the thing they most enjoyed, on six or seven days of the week.

TABLE 60. *Please think back again over everything you did yesterday afternoon and evening. Write down the three things you really enjoyed.* (Frequency with which viewers mentioned television as the most enjoyed activity)

Television mentioned on:	13–14 YEAR OLDS %	10–11 YEAR OLDS %
6 or 7 days . . .	5	4
4 or 5 days . . .	14	17
2 or 3 days . . .	33	29
1 day	20	21
No day	28	29
Total cases (*weighted*) . .	132	132

Taking all three of these questions together, here—very broadly— is the overall picture:

1. About 5 per cent appeared to be dependent on and interested in television to the exclusion of almost everything else.
2. About 15 per cent appeared to be fairly dependent on television (on most days they were more interested in it than in anything else).
3. About 30 per cent made television one of their favourite pastimes but not their first (on most days they enjoyed something else better).
4. About 20 per cent were little dependent on television and only on occasional days derived their greatest pleasure from it.
5. About 30 per cent were in no sense dependent on television and hardly ever enjoyed it more than any other of the day's events.

On all these questions younger children showed more interest in viewing than adolescents, and brighter ones, especially those attending grammar schools, showed least interest. Working-class children were no more interested than children from middle-class homes; boys no more than girls.

Limiting children's concern with television is their interest in other activities, especially outdoor play and (among older children in particular) social pastimes that bring them into contact with friends of their own age. The answers to the questions inquiring into their favourite leisure pastime throw light on these points. The older boys mentioned outdoor play four times as often as television; the others, rather less sport conscious, about three times as much. Only among the younger girls did viewing begin to compete seriously with outdoor interests. Among girls and the brighter children of both age groups reading was about as popular as television. Among the older children of either sex, cinema visits (including a few theatre visits) were at least half as popular as television. Only among the duller children was viewing equally or more popular than the sum of other home activities (Appendix Table 47). Appendix Table 48 lists the frequency with which, during the diary week, the different activities were mentioned as having been much enjoyed.

With adolescence, social activities—visiting friends, going to clubs and the cinema—become a stronger challenge to television. Television has then two major competing rivals: outdoor play and activities outside the home.

Activities that interest children most are not necessarily the most time-consuming, and viewing tended in the majority of cases to consume more time than interest.

But all this is a matter of averages and trends. Behind the percentages, and too easily forgotten, are the individual children. Three extracts from their diaries have been chosen to illustrate differing degrees of viewing interest, and different factors which curb the importance of television.

A keen viewer also keen on sport. A 13 year old secondary modern school boy of average intelligence, the son of a skilled worker. He had two brothers. He played football or cricket whenever it was fine, but also watched television unvaryingly except on his club evenings. Sport and television took up all his leisure time apart from occasional breaks for reading and social activities, the cinema, his club, visiting a friend, and going to Sunday school. Once home from playing out of doors, he viewed continuously, and only on one evening did he break off to read the paper for fifteen minutes before going to bed. Nevertheless, it is significant that he was usually home too late for the early part of evening television, and on two occasions went out before children's television was over. Generally, it seems, viewing and sport were for him two conflicting interests, with the scales tipped slightly in favour of sport. But they partly overlap; he enjoyed watching television programmes best on three days out of seven; on two occasions these were sports programmes. Here is his Thursday's diary:

> I went home and read a comic called *Eagle*. I watched TV till 5.15 and then had tea. At 5.45 I went round to call my friend. We rode up Rodney Park and played cricket with nine other friends. Played until 7.30, rode home with my friend, and then watched TV. Watched till 9.5 then washed and read *The Evening Post*. Went to bed at 9.30 and read a book called *William in Trouble*.
>
> *Enjoyed most*: watching *Sportsview* on TV.
> *Next most*: cricket at Rodney Park.
> *Third most*: *Find the Link* on TV.

Viewing as a stopgap. For a 13 year old grammar school girl, from a working-class home, television was largely a stopgap. It was her first choice on only two days out of seven; her greatest pleasure came from social activities, of which she had fewer than she would have liked. This was her Tuesday's diary:

> I went out with my friend. I had my tea. After I had finished I watched *Children of the New Forest* on TV. I did my homework, then climbed trees with some boys and girls. After that I went home and did my half hour's practice with my elder brother who helped me. I read my *School Friend* and read the paper. I tidied my needlework box and my brother's toy cupboard. When my father came home I showed him Mummy's birthday present and watched *Newsreel* on TV. I had my supper and went to bed.
>
> *Enjoyed most*: climbing trees with the boys and girls because it was a change for me.
> *Next most*: tidying my needlework box.
> *Third most*: I love reading my *School Friend*.

A television addict. An 11 year old working-class boy of slightly below average intelligence showed a more marked interest in television than others of his age. On five out of the seven days he watched children's television in its entirety. He also viewed every evening from the beginning of transmission at 7.30 p.m. right round to his bedtime. Apart from Tuesday, when he sacrificed children's television to visit his friend, and Sunday, when he was too busy playing on Greenwich Pier to watch any television at all, he gave viewing total priority over other activities, all of which ceased promptly at television time. Moreover, viewing conditioned, as well as displaced, his other spare-time interests. On Saturday he returned from the park for the sake of a motor-cycle programme, which inspired him to 'make himself' a motor-bike; but even this absorbing activity stopped with the start of children's television at 5 p.m. He enjoyed his viewing more than anything else on five days out of seven; it was, in fact, his main preoccupation. He played with his friends only when there was no television to watch; his reading he did almost exclusively in bed. This was his Thursday evening:

> I ran home from school and when I got home we had a game with a water pistol; I done it with my brother and my friend. At 5.0 I saw TV, at 6.0 it ended and then I had my tea. My Daddy asked me to go and get him some cigarettes. Then I played out, with a lot of people, and at 7.30 I looked at TV until 9.15 when I went to bed and read a book called *Tom Brown's School Days*.
>
> *Enjoyed most*: TV.
> *Next most*: My game.
> *Third most*: TV.

PRELIMINARY PICTURE OF THE GENERAL EFFECTS OF
TELEVISION ON CHILDREN'S LEISURE

The ramifications of children's leisure are too numerous to be covered in detail in this survey. Some activities, notably the mass media, outdoor play, and social activities were dealt with thoroughly, others only touched upon.

Much research has already been done on this subject among adults in this country (9) and the United States (19, 27, 63). The results show, with some variations, that all the other mass media are affected—radio dramatically, cinema-going considerably, and reading moderately. Viewing also cuts into the group activities that take adults out of their homes, but there is little effect on viewers' social life in the home.

What happened in the case of children? We shall examine the effects of television on the major leisure activities, in the following chapters. Here we give a brief preliminary outline of our findings, to provide a background against which to set the more detailed results.

Chapter 7 has shown that the future viewers in Norwich, even before they got their television sets, were more interested than other children in films and radio, and also read comics more often—without being generally more interested in reading. Their tastes in these media were rather narrow. When the future viewer got television he could indulge his need for entertainment to the full. He spent four times as long on viewing as the controls spent on listening to the radio, and as a result gave less time to almost all other activities. The pattern of leisure activities which he developed remained about the same, but a little less time was spent on each, with the single exception of radio listening, which almost disappeared (Appendix Table 49).

Studies in this country and in the United States suggest that the effects of television on the leisure life of adults persist for some years; Belson (9) has shown, for instance, that the return to the former pattern varies according to the activity concerned and may take four years or more. Our study with children shows that much of a good deal of the revival of interest occurs during the first year.

Among recent viewers in Norwich, none of whom had been viewing for more than a year, over a third mentioned television as their favourite spare-time interest, compared with only a sixth among the experienced and veteran viewers. This initially high interest in viewing took a drastic toll of other interests. Both radio and cinema all but disappeared from the list of first preferences, general outdoor activities lost about a quarter of the interest they had previously attracted, and even sports were heavily affected.

Once the novelty of television had worn off, interest in other activities revived. In the general pattern of leisure interests, the long-term change was very slight indeed. The adaptability and resilience of children in this respect would appear to be greater than that of adults.

Since viewing was most important to the less intelligent children, changes in leisure activities were at their most marked in this group. By contrast, neither sex nor social background had any decisive influence.

28

Effects on Reading

MANY thoughtful people today are anxious about the effect of television on children's reading. Does viewing force reading into the background? Does it strengthen a child's preference for comics and magazines, which he can read quickly in odd moments, and discourage the reading of books which require prolonged concentration; or do book reviews and dramatisations, and programmes dealing with specialised topics such as science, actually stimulate and widen the scope of children's reading?

American surveys among adults (19) have shown that television reduces time spent reading books and magazines but that newspaper reading is not affected, because it is a firmly established habit. In this country, Belson (9) has found that the amount of book reading among adults is reduced by television.

It is reasonable to expect the same to hold for children, yet the teachers we questioned showed little concern; only 12 per cent listed a decline in reading among the changes they had noticed — a small number when set against the 51 per cent who mentioned late nights.

It has been suggested that the importance of reading may be overstated, represented as something desirable for its own sake, irrespective of what is read. Consequently, before discussing the changes which television has brought about, it is worth-while to consider what is the significance of reading to the child and to examine the reading of children of these two age groups before television came on the scene. Only against the background of these considerations is it possible to evaluate adequately the effect of television on children's reading.

The value of reading

For adults the value of reading must, in the last resort, depend on the quality of the reading matter. They have already acquired reading skill, and reading as such has no intrinsic value. But children need a great deal of practice in reading, especially the less intelligent ones. The following comments from the pamphlet on standards of reading published by the Ministry of Education in 1957 are pertinent here.

> . . . Some of these good readers seemed to have thrived on what might be regarded as a somewhat deleterious fare, but there was enough of it. Others had formed, or accepted, a higher standard of taste. Popular technical journals were frequently read by the older boys, and the better sort of juvenile fiction by both boys and girls, but comics and the lower order of magazine were also mentioned. The inference to be drawn is not that it is a mistake to try to form a child's taste in reading—but that it is even more important that he should have access to a wide range of reading matter. One child's ice cream is another child's cold sago pudding (69).

Children also have to acquire the habit of referring to books, of turning to them for their enjoyment. All this depends to a great extent on the number of books read; it is important, then, that the level of book-reading be at least maintained, especially among those children who read fewest books to start with: that is (as will be shown later) boys, the less bright children, and those coming from working-class homes.

The best reading material can offer a greater wealth of experience than any other medium. But this variety only benefits children who take advantage of its scope; those who read mainly comics, or merely one style of novel, will gain no more than those who confine their interest to one type of film or television programme.

Moreover, any children's library contains a large selection of books appropriate to all stages of development and maturity, while television, radio, and cinema cater mainly for adult tastes and experience.

On the other hand, reading, like any other medium, offers children a certain amount of material which would be no help to them, and some of the crudest and most facile of the comics, especially, may in fact debase children's tastes.

READING OF CHILDREN WITHOUT TELEVISION

Even children with no television gave, on average, relatively little time to reading. Their diaries suggested that, between leaving school and going to bed, the average adolescent read for about two and a half hours a week, the average younger child for about two hours. This was probably an underestimate,[1] but even if the true figure was four to five hours a week it would still be low.

[1] Partly because the diaries were kept in summer, when reading was likely to be less, and partly because it also excluded reading earlier in the day and after going to bed.

Reading time was divided between books, comics, and, for the older children, adult newspapers and magazines. Both age groups gave roughly twice as much time to books as to comics, and the older children spent nearly as much time on books as on comics, newspapers, and magazines put together (Figure 10 on p. 326).

Books. Children were asked how many books they had read during the previous four weeks. Appendix Table 50 shows that, on average, this amounted to two to three books; about 20 per cent from each age group had read only part of a book or, more often, had done no book-reading at all.[1] At the opposite extreme, about 14 per cent claimed to have read six or more books. Girls read more than boys, younger children more than adolescents (their books may be shorter), and those of high intelligence more than the less intelligent. Since book reading was also greater among children from middle- than from working-class homes, the most avid book-readers were the intelligent children from middle-class homes.

Comics. The average child also claimed to read between three and four comics a week;[2] about 5 per cent read none and 17 per cent read seven or more. The younger children, the less intelligent, and in the younger group those from working-class homes, were the keenest readers of comics as well as reading the smallest number of books (Appendix Table 51). While many children did little reading of books or comics, a few managed to read a good many of both.[3] The children's diaries showed how books, comics, and some adult newspapers and magazines were interlaced; they also showed how the quality of reading matter varies directly with intelligence.

Quality of reading matter. The books the children read were mainly adventure stories and, among older children, thrillers. As far as comics were concerned, those most often read were the crudest in type; we discovered this by asking children to indicate on a list which of the comics and children's magazines they read frequently. These were then classified into four similarly sized groups:[4]

1. The now-defunct junior national weeklies (*Mirror*, *Sketch*, and *Express*) and

---

[1] To ensure that the children really answered in terms of books, the questionnaire on reading began with the heavily stressed instruction *When we talk of books we mean real books, not magazines or papers*. To make it clear that we were not interested in the books they read in school the questions were prefaced with: *Apart from your school books* . . .

[2] This figure coincides closely with the results of a small-scale American study which found that the average child without television read over three comics a week (36).

[3] Thirteen per cent of each group read no more than one book and two comics a month, but nearly as many read one book and at least five comics a week.

[4] This classification was carried out with the help and advice of Mr. David Pickard of Research Services Ltd.

     well-produced and informative magazines like *Young Elizabethans, Children's Newspaper, Boy's Own Paper,* and *Mecanno Magazine.*

2. Well-produced comics, specialising in straightforward adventure stories, like *Eagle, Girl, Swift,* and *Robin.*

3. Comics which are less well produced and offer stories of tougher and somewhat exaggerated adventure.

4. A group comprising American comics and their nearest British equivalents, which give coarse exaggeration and crude pictorial content.

In each age group, children read far more comics of the lowest (fourth) group than of any of the other three groups[1] (Table 61).

TABLE 61. *Which of these comics do you often read?* (Average number of different groups of comics read by controls)

	13–14 YEAR OLDS	10–11 YEAR OLDS
Average number read in each group:		
Group 1	1·2	1·5
Group 2	1·6	1·9
Group 3	2·3	2·1
Group 4	3·8	3·7
Total cases (weighted) . .	450	450

Although the average child spent longer on books than on comics, much of children's reading time was in fact spent on comics, from which they could derive little benefit but reading practice. In general it is clear that the quality and amount of children's reading, even when they had no television sets, was not such as to demonstrate automatic superiority to what they would see on television. Equally, time spent on reading was not so great as to be able to afford much encroachment from viewing.

READING HABITS OF FUTURE VIEWERS

Television's effects on children's reading (even more than on other aspects of their lives and behaviour) cannot be looked at merely in terms of differences between viewers and controls. Already, before they got their television sets, the future viewers differed in their reading habits and tastes from children whose families only acquired television much later (cf. Chapter 7).

There were three main facets of these differences: the future viewers were particularly voracious comic-readers; they read less

---

[1] Children who read *any* group 4 comics totalled an average of four to five comics a week; children who read comics of groups 1, 2, or 3, read between two or three a week.

mature books; and they were less interested in non-fiction subjects.

Irrespective of sex and class, the future viewers read a greater number of comics than their controls, and they more often claimed that they spent most of their reading time on comics. There is probably a common factor in the needs gratified by comics and television. Interest in books, on the other hand, appears to be unrelated to the desire for television; before they had television sets, future viewers read as many books as controls. But this was not true of every kind of book.

The reading tastes of future viewers tended to be more immature than those of the controls. More among them, for instance, named one of Enid Blyton's stories as their preferred book[1] (stories which are more appropriate for a younger age group than the one we tested). Asked to indicate the extent of their interest in a list of fiction and specialist subjects, future viewers showed less interest than other children in more specialised reading but were just as interested as the controls in most fiction subjects—such as horror stories; crime and adventure stories; school stories; serials and stories about Westerns.

Their choice of favourite newspapers and magazines reflects the same tendency for enjoyment of general rather than specialised reading. This, of course, represents their parents' tastes as much as their own.

The effects of viewing

Under pressure from television, children may read less than before; they may also read at different times of the day. The children were therefore asked to indicate on a list at what times of the day they did most of their reading. To some extent, viewers adapted their day to fit in both reading and television. The viewers read significantly less often during television transmission times (5–6 p.m. and 7.30 until their bedtime)[2] and also read less often in bed.[3]

---

[1] Sixteen per cent of the future viewers compared with 5 per cent among the controls.

[2] Since the completion of the field work the gap in television transmission between 6 and 7.30 has been closed. With each fresh demand made by television, reading may lose increasingly. Even two or three years ago the last ditch may have been reached, at least by the 13–14 year olds. Moreover, if the child fits his reading in at odd times, he may read more in snatches, so that he may not develop the concentration needed for sustained reading.

[3] Thirty-three per cent of the older controls did most of their reading during television times compared with 16 per cent of the viewers. Among the 10–11 year olds, the percentages were 25 and 18 per cent respectively. Fifty-four per cent of the 13–14 year old controls did most of their reading in bed, either in the morning or evening, compared with 42 per cent of the viewers; the percentage for the younger age group was 60 and 53 per cent respectively.

There was little variation here, except with age. The 13–14 year old viewers more than the 10–11 year olds lost time previously spent reading in bed or during television hours, and less often made it up by reading at other times.

The diaries show that reading dropped by about a quarter in both age groups once television arrived—the drop was rather heavier among the older children, rather lighter in the younger age group. Book-reading suffered most, being reduced in both age groups by a third. The 13–14 year olds cut down their reading of comics, magazines, and newspapers by about a fifth, but the 10–11 year olds seemed to find time for nearly as much as before. Thus the relative proportion of books to other forms of reading matter declined in both age groups.

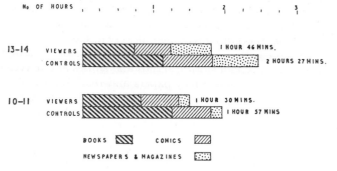

FIG. 10. Estimated average number of hours spent in one week (between 4 p.m. and bedtime) on various forms of reading. The times are taken from the diaries

Fig. 10 gives the estimated average number of hours spent on various forms of reading.

This result was not unexpected. Book-reading requires prolonged attention, while comics, newspapers, and magazines can be more easily fitted into odd moments—or even read during the television programmes.

Unexpectedly, the total time spent on reading did not vary with time spent on viewing. The diaries showed that those who viewed most spent the longest time on comics, newspapers, and magazines, but they also spent the *shortest* time on books, and these two trends cancelled each other out.[1] It seems that comic-reading and viewing can go hand-in-hand, but book-reading and viewing compete for a child's time.

[1] The groups involved are small, but the trends marked and consistent.

Amount of book-reading

When we examined the effect on book-reading in detail, a good deal of difference between groups emerged. In Norwich we looked at the changing habits of individual children during the twelve months after acquiring television. In both age groups a proportion of viewers managed to read more books despite television; the initial decline in reading was only striking among the 13–14 year olds, and was barely perceptible in the younger age group (Table 62).

TABLE 62. Change in number of books read by Norwich children after one year. (Comparison of the number of books read during one month, in 1955 and 1956)

	13–14 YEAR OLDS		10–11 YEAR OLDS	
	v	c	v	c
Compared with *1955*:	%	%	%	%
More books in 1956 . .	13	29	22	28
Same number in 1956 . .	37	42	33	30
Fewer in 1956 . . .	50	29	45	42
Total cases . . .	38	45	110	113

The main survey also indicated that the heavier cuts in book-reading were made by the older children; and in both age groups by boys and by children of average intelligence (Table 63).

TABLE 63. Average number of books read during a four-week period

	13–14 YEAR OLDS		10–11 YEAR OLDS	
	v	c	v	c
I.Q. 115+ . . .	2·8	3·0	3·3	3·1
I.Q. 100–114 . . .	1·9	2·7	2·4	2·9
I.Q. below 100 . .	2·0	1·9	1·9	2·2

A fuller table is given in the Appendix (Appendix Table 50).

This means that on the whole television cuts down book-reading where it can be afforded least.[1] Once television arrived, the proportion of older boys and older children of average intelligence reading no books at all nearly doubled. Those who read fewest books before having television were, it seems, the most affected by viewing— possibly because they were less interested in reading books they were especially inclined to give them up. There was one exception here—

[1] Without television 40 per cent of the older boys read only one book or less a month; with television the number rose to 56 per cent. Without television 31 per cent of the children of average intelligence in secondary schools read one or less; with television 46 per cent did so. Without television 29 per cent of primary school children of average intelligence read one book or less, compared with 39 per cent of those who watched television.

the children of below average intelligence, who read few books before they got television sets, and continued to read few afterwards.

Understandably, the more children viewed, the fewer books they read.[1] Moreover, the girls and the brightest children, who were more interested in books, spent less time viewing and so were doubly protected against encroachment on their reading time.

Reading tastes

The evidence of this survey suggests that television widened children's tastes in reading. We have seen that the future viewer read more books of a relatively immature level and that he showed less interest in the reading of non-fiction subjects. After some years of viewing, however, his tastes became as mature as the tastes of the control children, and his interests outside fiction were even wider.

These results come from two main sources. Children were asked, both in the main survey and in Norwich, what sort of books they liked reading best. The greater preference for Enid Blyton stories which characterised the future viewers disappeared—if anything children with television mentioned her books less frequently than the controls. In general, there were only negligible differences in reading preferences between viewers and controls, whatever their sex, intelligence, or social class (Appendix Table 53).

This method could only show shifts in relative emphasis from one subject to another. Children were therefore asked to indicate the extent to which they would like to read about forty-four different kinds of subject.

It has already been seen that the Norwich future viewers showed a relative lack of interest in almost all the non-fiction subjects; but their interest in fictional subjects was well up to standard. A year's viewing had a marked influence. After twelve months with television viewers actually became more interested than controls in some non-fiction subjects, significantly so in reading about animals and birds, which were much featured on television. Teachers, in their capacity as parents, corroborated this finding. One remarked about her daughter of 7: 'She has requested stories of real people who lived long ago or have travelled through jungles.' Another commented: 'Good effect. They (boys aged 8 and 9) refer to my books to find out things connected with the programmes.' This shift was also evident among fictional subjects, resulting in greater interest in some of those stressed by television—cowboys in particular, and to a lesser extent horror, serials, crime, and ordinary families.

---

[1] Fifty-four per cent of the heaviest viewers had read one book or less in the last month, but only 43 per cent of those who view relatively little.

So much for the immediate effects of viewing, as shown by the Norwich results. The main survey showed the long-term pattern of differences (Appendix Table 54). Viewers showed more interest than controls in a large number of fiction and non-fiction subjects; in only a very few subjects did non-viewers still keep the lead.

The broadening of interest occurred particularly among the less intelligent 13–14 year olds and among the more intelligent 10–11 year olds. It looks, therefore, as if actual mental age, not intelligence (i.e. the relation of mental to chronological age), determines how much children benefit from television in this way.

Comics

The future viewers, before they got television, read *more* comics than other children; after a period of viewing they read, if anything, *fewer* than their controls. Although the end-results showed, therefore, little difference between the two groups, some considerable shift had in fact taken place.

Norwich trend results (Appendix Table 52) showed that comic reading fell off more among viewers than controls in both age groups (it declines anyway with age). The main survey confirmed that a shift had occurred; in all groups television had ironed out the earlier differences between future viewers and controls (Appendix Table 51).

In this way television reduced children's need for comics. The heavy viewers proved an exception here: their need for ready-made entertainment seems particularly strong.[1]

This change from unusually heavy comic reading among the future viewers, to a position where they at least read no more comics than the controls, did not apply to the relatively high level children's newspapers and magazines (group 1); these were unchanged. Here the effect of television would seem to have been a beneficial one.[2] (See page 324 for definitions.)

Magazines and newspapers

American research among adults has shown that magazines, like books but unlike newspapers, suffer considerably from the inroads made by viewing. According to Bogart (19) the women's magazines and non-specialist magazines that provide largely fiction and enter-

---

[1] Three-quarters of the heavy viewers said they read comics often, compared with only half the occasional viewers.

[2] Forty per cent of future viewers read seven or more comics of group 4, compared with 27 per cent of the controls; a year later, the figures were 26 and 23 per cent respectively.

tainment suffer most, while the more informative magazines are relatively unchallenged.[1] He suggests that, with competition from television, American magazines are growing more specialised and giving more information.

In Britain, readership statistics indicate similar tendencics (48). Between 1949 and 1957 *Picture Post* lost more than half its readers and in the end ceased publication. *Everybody's* and *Illustrated* also suffered readership losses. These weeklies have an all-round appeal, similar in many ways to that of television. By contrast, the *Reader's Digest*, which lays stress on information, slightly increased its readership, together with specialised monthlies with small circulations, such as the *Ideal Home* and farming and photographic magazines. *Reveille* was not affected. Unlike the American women's magazines, women's papers in this country went from strength to strength, and in the winter of 1957–8 two new ones were successfully launched.

It has already been seen that child-viewers also became more interested in more specialised reading, although with certain differences. The Norwich future viewers tended to read *Reveille* and *Picture Post* more frequently than the controls; once viewing began, it captured a share of this interest, and both magazines lost child readers to television.[2] There was a similar change with *Woman* and *Woman's Own*; before television came they were read equally by future viewers and controls; then among viewers their popularity declined. The children's appetite for these papers would seem to be less strong than that of adults and so more readily reduced.[3]

Viewers and non-viewers showed no difference in the newspapers they preferred, their choice being largely dictated, of course, by what papers came into their homes.

TELEVISION AS A STIMULUS TO READING

Television can exert a beneficial influence by stimulating interest in a wider range of reading. This may be done indirectly, by arousing curiosity about certain fields of interest, or directly, by dramatising or reviewing books.

[1] In more precise terms, circulations tend to increase, but only for the relatively specialist or 'cultural' magazines; the effects of television are mainly seen on those magazines (mentioned above) which fail to increase their circulations.

[2] No really thorough attempt could be made to measure children's newspaper- and magazine-reading because many children (as well as adults) skim magazines and newspapers and also because children have little free choice in the magazines or newspapers they see, so that their reading is more likely to reflect their parents' taste than their own.

[3] Twenty-seven per cent of the 13–14 year old viewers named *Woman* or *Woman's Own* as one of their favourite magazines, compared with 37 per cent of the controls. Among the younger age group the percentages were 22 and 30 per cent respectively.

The survey of teachers' opinions offered evidence of this stimulation:

> Some of our lowest intelligence range have been attracted to classics after seeing TV productions. *Lorna Doone*, I think, was one instance of this.
>
> (Secondary modern school teacher.)

> Children usually acquire copies of any books which have been serialised, and, because the plot has already been simplified for them, and the characters are familiar, are able to enjoy books rather beyond their reading age.
>
> (Primary school teacher.)

Children's librarians have had similar experiences in public libraries. One public library reports:

> Perhaps the most encouraging feature of the issue figures over the past decade is the steady rise in children's reading. In the last few years, in spite of the fears expressed in many quarters that the growth of television would have a disastrous effect on reading, the rate of increase has accelerated. . . . Another notable point is that of the record total of . . . books issued from the Junior libraries . . . almost 50 per cent of which were works of non-fiction, in spite of the fact that all tickets issued to children are now general tickets, available for any type of book, as in the adult libraries (81).

It also mentions the direct stimulus:

> Radio and television, particularly the latter, have a tremendous influence on what is being read; the serialisation of a children's classic brings an immediate increase in the demand. The 'Jennings' stories have led to a revival of the boy's interest in school stories; a year or two ago boys rarely asked for school stories, but now the demand is brisk (80).

In the early summer of 1956 we asked children in Norwich to indicate which books on a list of 16 they had read since the previous summer. In that period 6 of these books had been dramatised on BBC television, and another 6 on sound radio, while 4 had been reviewed on both radio and television. In content, dramatic form, and the time of day at which they were broadcast, the television dramatisations were chosen so as to be as similar as possible to those broadcast on sound only. All the dramatisations except *Jane Eyre* and *Cranford* were in children's programmes on radio or television, and all were serialised except *Alice in Wonderland*.

Television dramatisations

Book	Author
Jane Eyre	Charlotte Brontë
St. Yves	R. L. Stevenson
Children of the New Forest	Captain Marryat
The Prince and the Pauper	Mark Twain
Rex Milligan	Anthony Buckeridge
Alice in Wonderland	Lewis Carroll

Radio dramatisations

Book	Author
Cranford	Mrs. Gaskell
The Box of Delights	John Masefield
Nicholas Nickleby	Charles Dickens
Carbonel	Barbara Sleigh
Jennings at School	Anthony Buckeridge
Winnie the Pooh	A. A. Milne

Books reviewed on both radio and television

Book	Author
Harriet and her Harmonium	Alan Lomax
Man Must Measure	L. Hogben
The Borrowers Afield	Mary Morton
Swarm in May	W. Mayne

Table 64 gives the percentage of viewers and controls in Norwich who claimed to have read each book since the previous summer.[1] Book *reviews* did not encourage children to read. Some dramatisations were also relatively unsuccessful; they may have achieved more with much younger or older children than the ones tested; but others, particularly those on television, greatly stimulated reading of the books concerned.

Among radio dramatisations, only *Jennings at School*, *Nicholas Nickleby*, and—for younger children—*Winnie the Pooh* had a substantial effect: *Jennings at School* was especially successful among the boys, *Nicholas Nickleby* among the girls. Understandably, it was those who were potentially most interested in a book in the first place who were most influenced. The least successful dramatisations—*Cranford*, *The Box of Delights*, and *Carbonel*—were based on books which (judging by the control figures) apparently had little interest for children.

As many as one child in five of both age groups read *Jane Eyre* as a direct result of seeing it dramatised on television; among younger girls the figure was one in three or four. *Rex Milligan* was also particularly successful among the younger girls. On the other hand, the success of *Children of the New Forest*, *St Yves*, and *The Prince and the Pauper* was evenly spread. Only *Alice in Wonderland* had little effect: it was probably too well known for the older children and already popular with younger ones.

---

[1] There was some confusion in children's minds about how long ago they had read these books. But this bias should be constant for both viewers and non-viewers.

TABLE 64. Proportion of viewers and controls in Norwich who said they had read the following books since the summer of 1955[1]

	14–15 YEAR OLDS[2]			11–12 YEAR OLDS[2]		
	V %	C %	V *minus* C[3] %	V %	C %	V *minus* C %
Books dramatised on television:						
Jane Eyre	34	13	+21	29	7	+22
St. Yves	10	6	+ 4	13	3	+10
Rex Milligan . . .	18	9	+ 9	32	10	+22
Children of the New Forest . .	21	13	+ 8	34	23	+11
The Prince and the Pauper .	21	9	+12	30	21	+ 9
Alice in Wonderland . . .	13	11	+ 2	37	34	+ 3
			C *minus* V			C *minus* V
Books dramatised on radio:						
Nicholas Nickleby . . .	5	23	+18	10	15	+ 5
Jennings at School . . .	3	23	+10	22	30	+ 8
Winnie the Pooh . . .	3	6	+ 3	10	22	+12
Carbonel	—	4	+ 4	2	5	+ 3
Cranford	5	—	— 5	—	3	+ 3
Box of Delights . . .	5	2	— 3	3	9	+ 6
Books reviewed on television and radio:						
Swarm in May . . .	—	4		1	—	
Man Must Measure . .	3	—		1	3	
Harriet and her Harmonium .	—	2		2	3	
The Borrowers Afield . .	3	4		7	2	
Total cases	38	47		115	116	

[1] The question was put in June 1956.

[2] These children were aged 13–14 and 10–11 in 1955.

[3] For books dramatised on television, the control figures were used as base-line, indicating the number of children who would have read these books in any case. For books dramatised on sound radio, the figures for the viewers were used as base-line. Thus, in the columns headed 'V *minus* C' or 'C *minus* V' a plus figure indicates the percentage of children whose reading of this book can be attributed to television (or to sound radio). For book reviews, which appeared both on television and radio, this could, of course, not be done.

The teachers gave numerous examples of the stimulus provided by television to their own children. Here are some of their comments:

After seeing *Anne of Green Gables* and other stories dramatised she has been eager to read the books. They widened her scope and made a step between Enid Blyton and more advanced books. (Girl 13.)

They have asked to be allowed to buy books, e.g. *Heidi*, *Jane Eyre*, and have read them and have brought other books from the library. (Girl 13.)

They have several books about TV characters—*The Flower Pot Man*, *Andy Pandy*. My older child has read books of the plays seen, e.g. *Swiss Family Robinson*. (Boy 9, girls 7 and 4.)

Four points emerge. First, dramatisations are much more effective than reviews, which do not seem to interest children. Secondly, television provides a more powerful impetus than sound radio.

Thirdly, success in either medium depends on the intrinsic appeal of the dramatisation combined with an appropriate choice of book. Finally, the most successful dramatisations are based on books which normally are not widely read but which have a potential appeal for children.

HOW LONG DOES THE INFLUENCE OF TELEVISION LAST?

Some leisure activities that are at first reduced by viewing later regain favour. American surveys among adults suggest that the same may be true of reading. For example, Cunningham and Walsh (25) and also Coffin (24) have found that magazine-reading recovered some lost ground. An investigation into book-borrowing showed that viewers initially made less use of libraries, but after viewing for about a year they showed signs of a revival of interest (19). On the other hand, Belson, working in this country, did not find any such parallel even after five or six years' viewing (9). But this could be due to differences in book-reading habits between Britain and the United States, as well as between children and adults.

We investigated how long the following effects of viewing lasted: the decline in book-reading; the reduction in comic-reading among early viewers; and the eventual maturing of viewers' book-reading tastes.

Book-reading. Appendix Table 55 shows that after about three years viewers again read as many books as controls, even those children of medium intelligence whose book-reading was at first hardest hit by television. There are signs that among 13–14 year olds below average in intelligence, viewers actually overtook the controls. This trend, statistically insignificant because of the small numbers involved, supports an earlier finding—that the duller 13–14 year olds responded more profitably than others to the stimulus of television.

We have seen that Norwich future viewers, before having television sets, read as many books as other children. Once viewing started, viewers read fewer books probably through sheer lack of time. But it seems that viewing is too different from book-reading to satisfy the appetite for books; after a few years children found time for both activities.

Comic-reading. Here we found no sign of reversion. No matter how long they have been watching television, viewers no longer read more comics than controls. In fact, after three years, 13–14 year old viewers might even be reading *fewer* comics than controls.[1] It seems

[1] Among the 13–14 year olds, 53 per cent of the veteran viewers read comics frequently, compared with 65 per cent of the controls. For the 10–11 year olds the figures were 72 and 71 per cent respectively.

that viewing could permanently satisfy some of the children's appetite for comics.

Maturity of taste. Interest in Enid Blyton stories continued to decrease (Table 65). Viewing either raises the maturity of children's tastes, or else provides an alternative means of satisfying the need for stories of this kind which are aimed primarily at a younger age group than those we studied.

TABLE 65. *What sort of book do you like best?* (Number of controls, recent, experienced, and veteran viewers who named a book by Enid Blyton)

		Controls	Recent	Experienced	Veteran
				Viewers	
13–14 YEAR OLDS .	.	5	8	2	—
Total cases .	.	456 (*weighted*)	74	145	76
10–11 YEAR OLDS .	.	12	13	5	2
Total cases .	.	456 (*weighted*)	76	100	78

CONCLUSIONS

The less intelligent children and those from working-class homes do not read much even when they have no television. Any reduction in reading time can therefore be serious; children need to learn to read without effort as early as they can and so develop the habit of reading. On the other hand, reduction of certain types of reading, such as comics, is likely to matter less. On these criteria television may on balance do more good than harm, for several reasons.

Under the influence of television, children initially read less. Books suffer most; comics simply drop from an unusually great interest to a normal one. The better children's papers and magazines are apparently not affected. After a few years of viewing book-reading returns to its original level, but the loss in comic-reading remains. The proportion of books to comics read by viewers therefore increases.

In the interim period, the loss in book-reading is greatest among boys, and among children of average intelligence, in both cases children who tend to read less to start with and so are less able to afford the loss. After several years' viewing their book-reading revives and finally gains slightly on that of non-viewers. But meanwhile they lose badly needed reading practice for a few, perhaps crucial, years.

The results of other research on this matter are conflicting. In a Manchester study heavy and light viewers in a secondary modern school (matched for intelligence and home background) were compared for reading ability; the results showed a lower level of reading skill among heavy viewers (70). But a similar study carried out in the USA showed no such effect (19). It may be that the average viewer maintains his reading ability in spite of a temporary reduction in reading practice, while some of the slower learners may be seriously handicapped by this break.

This loss is unlikely to affect later generations of school children; in six or seven years' time television may be as commonplace as radio is today, and children born into homes with television may well take it in their stride.

Viewing encourages new interests and reinforces old ones. It can extend the range of children's reading into non-fiction: whereas the future viewer is disinterested in non-fiction topics, the experienced viewer becomes unusually interested in them. This stimulus is strongest among the duller adolescents, who are most in need of it.

Among younger children, the brighter ones respond most to the new ideas television can provide. In other words, response to the stimulus is greatest at a given stage of intellectual development— that of the brighter child aged 10–11, and the less bright child of 13–14. The less intelligent child of 10–11 needs more maturity before he can profit to the full. At the other extreme, the grammar school child does not need the stimulus of television.

There is no evidence that television changes the broad shape of children's reading interests in fiction. Sometimes, however, it does stimulate the reading of the books it dramatises; whether it does depends a good deal on the manner of dramatisation and the choice of book. Where television has been successful, the gain is very considerable.

The effects of television cannot be considered statically; they form part of a dynamic process. We have tried to foreshadow what might be the state of affairs some years from now when most children will have grown up with television. Until that time, it is especially important for teachers to encourage the habit of reading and of enjoying books among their less intelligent viewers. Parents can help in a similar way. Finally, the producer's role is an important one, in selecting the right books for serialised dramatisation, and in using dramatised excerpts when reviewing books for children.

29

Effects on Cinema and Radio

IN this chapter we shall discuss the extent to which television has ousted the cinema and radio from their former positions as major sources of entertainment for children.

TELEVISION AND THE CINEMA

The impact of television on the cinema has been dramatic. In the United States, average weekly cinema attendance dropped from about 90 million in 1946 to 46,500,000 in 1955. In this country, between the end of 1955 and the end of 1957, 295 cinemas out of 4,437 were closed (93). Television undoubtedly played a considerable part in bringing this reduction about; for many adults it is an effective substitute for the cinema.

How far is this true for children? How far does television reduce cinema attendance and lessen children's interest in the world of the cinema? Further, can television influence the children's taste in films?

CINEMA ATTENDANCE

Frequency of cinema visits of children without television

Appendix Table 56 shows how frequency of cinema-going varied significantly with age, sex, social class, and intelligence. The older children, as one would expect, went more often than the younger children (64 per cent had been within the past seven days compared with 44 per cent of the younger children). Among the 10–11 year olds, boys went more often than girls, working-class children more often than middle-class children.[1]

It is intelligence more than social background which determines

---

[1] Our findings show the same variation as do surveys by the BBC (16) and by the Social Survey (100). Among the 13–14 year olds there was no social-class difference in frequency of attendance.

how often a child goes to the cinema. The difference between duller and brighter children was very marked, as shown in Table 66. There

TABLE 66. Percentage of controls who had been to the cinema *within* the last two days

Intelligence level:				13–14 YEAR OLDS %	10–11 YEAR OLDS %
I.Q. 115+[1] .	.	.	.	13	6
I.Q. 100–114.	.	.	.	21	12
I.Q. below 100	.	.	.	36	29

[1] Among the 13–14 year olds this group comprises the children attending grammar schools.

was no difference in frequency of cinema visits between future viewers and their controls.

The effect of television

Data from both Norwich and the main survey showed that with viewing cinema-going was reduced, particularly among the younger children (Appendix Table 56). The groups who were most affected in this way were boys, the duller children, and children from work-ing-class homes, i.e. the very groups who initially had been the most frequent cinema-goers. Not only did the effect differ for the older and the younger children, but it also wore off at different rates. For example, after only one year's viewing the older viewers went almost as often as before, while for the younger children, even after three years of viewing, the effect still made itself felt.

The duration of impact varied not only with age, but with intelli-gence. Once the novelty of television had worn off, all except the very intelligent children stepped up their cinema visits once again. The very intelligent children did not change back for some years, even though initially they went less often than the others. It seems that this type of child will spend only a limited amount of time on spectator entertainment, and that neither television nor the cinema is allowed to encroach on his other interests.

By contrast, after one year, the duller children went as frequently to the cinema as before, combining it with heavy viewing. These are children with fewest resources of their own. Characteristically, the dull children, more than others, were inclined to think the best thing about television was that 'It gives you something to do', or 'You are no longer bored'.

The difference in the effect of television on the cinema visits of older and younger children is of special interest here; it tells us of the extent to which the two activities are functionally equivalent. The extent to which one activity can be effectively substituted for the other depends, then, not so much on the similarity of the two media as on the extent to which they satisfy the same needs. Both age groups considered television to some extent as a substitute for the cinema. Answers to the question *What is the best thing about television?* make this clear: 'You have to pay to see the pictures, but you don't have to pay to see television', for example, or 'It saves going to the pictures'. But this was the case far more for the younger children who seek in television primarily entertainment; this television can satisfy as effectively as the cinema with the added advantage of constant availability at no cost. The adolescent wants entertainment too; but in addition, cinema visits are important for him as social occasions, and for this television is no effective substitute. So he makes time for both at the expense of some other leisure activities.

Time of attendance. Going to the cinema becomes a more casual affair for the viewer. When asked to tick on a list the days and times they usually went to the cinema, viewers compared with controls more often marked 'no special day' or 'no special time'.[1] Among the 10–11 year olds there was also a shift from Saturday to other days of the week, because two of their favourite television programmes appeared on that day—the Westerns in the afternoon and a variety show in the evening.

INTEREST IN THE CINEMA

Reduced attendance ran parallel with reduced interest. When children were asked *Would you like to go to the pictures more often than you do now?*, no differences were found in the younger age groups, but among the older children viewers were significantly more often satisfied than controls. Interest in going more often, however, revived more quickly than increased attendance (Appendix Table 57).

Hero-worship of film stars

Hero-worship of film stars has certainly not been eclipsed by television. When the children were asked: *If you had to be one of these four people who would you rather be? A famous author, a famous wireless*

---

[1] 'No special day' was ticked by 31 per cent of the older and 41 per cent of the younger viewers; the figures for controls were 25 per cent and 35 per cent. 'No special time' was ticked by 37 per cent of the younger and 55 per cent of the older viewers, and by 32 per cent and 41 per cent of the controls. Thirty per cent of young viewers chose Saturday, compared with 41 per cent of the controls.

star, a famous film star, or a famous television star?,[1] the film star easily topped the poll among both viewers and controls. Viewers mentioned television stars more often than controls did, but at the expense of authors and radio stars—not of film stars. In this respect there was no difference between brighter and duller children, or between boys and girls (Appendix Table 58).

The next question permitted a better measure of the model value of film stars: *If it were possible, would you like to be a film star when you are older?* In reply, more viewers than controls said 'yes'.[2] However, Norwich data showed this difference to have existed already between future viewers and controls, a difference in line with their generally greater interest in light entertainment described in Chapter 7.

In a way, television enhances the appeal of the film star for the viewer. He sees him being interviewed, he learns about his plans, his life and interests; the star becomes more of a person to him.

Emotional impact of films. Another indirect measure of interest consisted in seeing how strongly children reacted to the films they saw. Future viewers whom we knew to have a strong interest in spectator entertainment more often gave affirmative answers to the following question: *After seeing a really exciting film, do you sometimes want to do any of these things?* (cf. Chapter 7).

Yet once children had television, with its rapid succession of programmes, the difference had disappeared, and in fact, among the older children, fewer of them wanted to think about the film or see the film a second time (Table 67).

TABLE 67. Proportion of viewers and controls who said they wanted to do any one or other of the following things after seeing a really exciting film

	13–14 YEAR OLDS		10–11 YEAR OLDS	
After seeing a really exciting film, do you sometimes want to do any of these things?	V %	C %	V %	C %
Do something brave and daring	10	16	13	21
Think about the film	32	42	28	31
Talk to others about the film	64	58	46	42
Start an exciting game	3	3	15	18
See the film a second time	33	45	32	34
Do none of these things	13	10	14	14
Total cases (weighted)	480	480	480	480

NOTE. The percentages total more than 100 because some children ticked more than one reaction.

---

[1] To avoid over-weighting the replies in favour of the cinema or any other medium, the question was placed with other 'choice' questions in a separate questionnaire entitled *Which do you choose?* This questionnaire was given to the children before any questionnaire dealing with the various mass media.

[2] Thirty per cent among the older and 30 per cent among the younger viewers, compared with 29 per cent and 24 per cent among the controls.

That films seemed less important and interesting to the viewers was also seen from their answers to the following questions, where viewers gave fewer positive replies compared with controls.

> Sometimes, after seeing a film, people try to act or make up games about it. Have you ever done this? Please tell us what the game was about.
> After seeing a film some people pretend to themselves that they are like someone in the film. Have you ever done this?
> Is there any film that you have not been able to get out of your mind, that you have been thinking about a lot?

Television, then, has quite marked effects on children's attendance at the cinema, on their interest in going, and on the emotional impact that individual programmes make. Has it also effected a change in taste?

TASTE IN FILMS

Even the most enthusiastic film fan would hardly claim that films present the child with an accurate or many-sided view of the world. The Wheare Committee, set up jointly by the Home Office and the Ministry of Education, stresses this point very strongly (44).

Television, compared with the cinema, while it has taken over Westerns, thrillers, and many other sure successes of the screen, offers a much wider range of material, including daily children's programmes and information programmes. At the time of our survey the children had access to BBC television only, with its stress on these types of programmes. We found few children switched off even when an information programme came on; they therefore saw some programmes which, if they had had a choice, they would probably have avoided.

How is the child's taste in films affected by having access to a more varied diet on television? To examine this, two open-ended questions were asked: *What sort of film do you like best?* and *Which of all the films you have ever seen did you like best?* In addition the children were presented with a list of types of film headed *What kind of film do you like to see?* Three possible answers were provided—*I would like to see it; I would not mind whether I saw it or not;* and *I would not like to see it.*[1]

We classified answers according to the three types of subjects dealt with below and listed in Appendix Table 59.

---

[1] The list included film subjects corresponding to the subjects of television programmes and each item was described as *films about . . .*; for example, *films about happenings in history.* (The names of actual television programmes were, of course, not given.)

Fiction subjects common to both media: such as Westerns, detective stories, and thrillers. Answers to the question *What sort of film do you like best?* suggest that the film tastes of viewers moved in the direction of films shown on television (Appendix Table 60). The older viewers, boys especially, chose detective and gangster films more often than the controls; the 10–11 year old viewers preferred Westerns, irrespective of sex. These differences were small but significant, and found confirmation in the Norwich results. The shift in taste became more pronounced with length of exposure—at least in the older age group—where 29 per cent of the veteran viewers chose gangster and detective films, compared with 20 per cent of the recent viewers. Among younger children, the picture was less clear cut.

Fiction subjects characteristic of television rather than the cinema: such as serials, programmes about famous people, ordinary families, or programmes with children. Appendix Table 59 shows that significantly more viewers than controls would like to see such subjects for films in the cinema, especially serials and films with children. Television here exerts a marked influence on taste in the direction of its own subject-matter and style.

Information subjects as shown on television but not, on the whole, in the cinema. Have these programmes made any impression? Have they stimulated interest and so become more acceptable to children as entertainment? We included in our list subjects of intrinsic interest to children, such as sport and flying, and more educational subjects like science, animals, and birds (Appendix Table 59). Significant differences were found, especially among secondary modern school children of average and below-average intelligence. Compared with controls, viewers in these groups were more interested in twelve out of the fourteen non-fiction subjects.

In the case of grammar school viewers (who had less interest in television and more alternative sources of stimulation) there was only one difference—films on science; the viewers seemed more interested in these, very probably as the result of seeing the excellent and often dramatic BBC science programmes.[1]

On the whole, the 10–11 year olds were not affected, not even the brighter among them. Three reasons come to mind why the younger viewers responded so little. The younger children saw, of course, fewer such programmes on television, since many were put on after their bedtimes. Some of the topics, such as films about animals, dealt anyhow with subjects in which both viewers and controls of that age were interested, so that the additional stimulus of television was not needed here. It is, however, very likely that for television to

---

[1] Forty-seven per cent of the viewers among them would like to see a film on science compared with 29 per cent among the controls.

stimulate effectively there must be reasonably complete understanding of what is presented; at present even a bright 10–11 year old
cannot sufficiently take it in.

TELEVISION AND RADIO

Almost all radio surveys in this country (31) and America (19)
have shown that television hits radio listening more than any other
activity. In 1955 (when most of the fieldwork for this survey was
done) television, compared with broadcasting, still had no alternative programme, nor continuous programmes throughout the day.
Today programmes are continuous from at least 5 p.m. onwards and
ITV has provided a second channel. Radio has little to offer viewers
and, with the rapid spread of television, listening must ultimately
become very much less important—or else must take on a different
role. Our interest in the impact of television on radio, then, lies in
the amount of listening that continues among viewers, and the nature
of its changing role.

BBC figures for adults show that in 1954, during times when
television was on the air, the average audience for radio was one-
fifth as large among viewers as among non-viewers; when television
was off the air it was half as large. The figures for viewers were 4 per
cent and 17 per cent respectively. Radio had receded so drastically
into the background for the television public that even when there
was no television transmission only a few turned to the radio (31).

For children the trend seems to be the same. In Norwich, future
viewers were keener listeners than controls. Once television came
on the scene the picture changed dramatically: controls spent five
times as long as viewers listening-in.

Radio listening did not cease completely—about half the older
and a third of the younger children still spent some time on it. For
the majority this amounted to about one hour a week, a remarkably
small amount of time considering that, at the time of the survey,
there was no television transmission between 5 and 7.30 p.m.[1]

Although children made so little use of radio, one in three said
that if they had to do without radio they would miss it quite a lot;
in explanation, they either mentioned some specific programme
which they enjoyed, or else said they were used to the radio—rather
the attitude that one might adopt towards a familiar (but not
necessarily useful) piece of furniture.

[1] The figures may somewhat underestimate the actual time, since when (in
the diaries) two activities were mentioned as occurring simultaneously, half the
time was allotted to each.

Children who had been watching television for several years listened a little more often. This sign of a revival is in line with that reported for adults (9); during television transmission the average evening audience for sound radio barely increased from 5 per cent among viewers of one year's standing to 8 per cent among those who had had their sets for five years or more; in the first group, ten times as many viewers watched television as listened to the radio, but among the long-established viewers only five times as many.

The changing role of radio

The slight revival in listening is due less to a revival of interest in radio generally, than to the appeal of specific programmes. When asked: *Of all the wireless programmes you have heard, which three have you liked best?* viewers mentioned plays, including adventure and space serials, less often than controls, but equally often stressed programmes such as sport commentaries, panel games, and discussion programmes, and music was mentioned even more than among controls. This shift in interest was more marked for viewers of some years' standing.

Even plays can continue to be interesting on radio if they are familiar favourites in the first place, especially if presented at a time when there is no competition from television. At the time of our survey the family serial, *The Archers*, met both these conditions. The children with television listened to it much less than controls, but even so 10 per cent of the older viewers and 19 per cent of the younger viewers claimed to listen to it often, and about 50 per cent in each age group at least sometimes.

CONCLUSIONS

Many children, especially the 10–11 year olds, find in television an effective substitute for the cinema, and so go to the pictures less often even when they have had a television set for some time. For 13–14 year olds, however, the new medium cannot satisfy the need to meet friends away from home. These children do not reduce their cinema visits as much as the younger ones; after one year, they go as often as the controls.

As attendance at cinemas declines, so does interest in films and the impact made by individual films. Film stars, however, retain their glamour and model value. This may be another example of the effect of television's cult of personality.

Viewers, compared with controls, became more interested to

see a wider range of films, notably films on topics with which they have become familiar through television. This applies in the case of the older children (especially the less intelligent among them), also to interest in documentaries and non-fiction programmes generally.

Three points emerge. First, children are not insatiable spectators of screen drama; given enough of one medium, they will want less of the other. Secondly, how far one medium will replace the other depends less on their technical similarity than on whether they satisfy similar needs. Television meets the younger child's need for entertainment as effectively as the cinema, but for the older child its effect is slight and transitory as it cannot satisfy the second, equally important, social need, that of meeting friends away from home. Thirdly, film producers might reconsider in the light of this evidence whether the interest stimulated through television could not be used to introduce into the cinema a wider range of subject-matter, including non-fiction films.

The radio cannot hold children once television arrives. Exceptions apart, its role becomes a specialised one. By and large its plays cannot compete with plays on television. It remains, however, a medium to which the children may turn for certain specialist types of programmes—panel games, discussions, music, and sport commentaries. Radio, then, has at least a chance of holding listeners who are interested in these particular programmes and subjects.

30

Effects on Other Leisure Activities

OUTDOOR LIFE

From the children's diaries we obtained a measure of the total amount of time spent out of doors during one week of really fine weather in May 1955. We also looked at the different ways in which this time was spent, whether in carrying out or watching some sport, in walking, cycling, gardening, or in just kicking a ball around and doing nothing in particular.

The picture was clear cut. Television effects a small reduction in time spent outdoors, particularly so in the case of the younger children with less free time at their disposal. Our assessment included weekdays and weekends, and taking seven consecutive days the following differences were found:

	13–14 YEAR OLDS		10–11 YEAR OLDS	
	V	C	V	C
	%	%	%	%
Spent more than 12 hours out of doors . .	25	32	16	30

The full table is to be found in the Appendix Table 61. As is to be expected, the more any one child viewed the less time he tended to spend out of doors. The effect, however, was not drastic. Seventy per cent of the younger and 50 per cent of the older viewers appeared to spend at least one hour a day out of doors.

The unorganised activities such as walking and just being outdoors with friends suffered most inroads from television. Sport and watching sport were much less affected. Participation in competitive sports held its own with younger children, and even with the adolescents the loss was barely significant. These types of outdoor activity were better protected from encroachment by television, because they are so very attractive to children, and also because television can actively stimulate interest in sport. Our information tests showed viewers to be more knowledgeable about sports than controls. Belson (9) similarly found among adults that television increased interest in sport.

SOCIAL ACTIVITIES

When television first came on the scene many people predicted that this would mean the end of clubs for children. How far has this taken place and if so does it apply to all clubs or only to certain ones? And apart from clubs, in what ways has television made inroads into the social life of young people? How far, for instance, has television affected the time children give to visiting and entertaining friends? How has it affected the unorganised but equally important social activities, such as going for walks, window shopping, or just standing around at street corners? Our main source of information was again the diaries, where children were asked not only to state what they were doing but also with whom they did it.[1]

American research on adults (91, 24) points to a decline in social activities outside the home, such as going to concerts or theatres and, less markedly, visiting other people's homes. In this country, Belson (9) has found a more complex picture, again among adults: a substantial loss in cinema- and theatre-going which persists even after some years, and a moderate and transitory reduction of what he calls 'sociability'—making new friends, visiting people, playing cards, and going to clubs and sporting events. Club attendance alone showed no difference; in fact, so far as interest in club membership was concerned, there was even a small gain over non-viewers after five to six years' viewing.

Club membership and attendance

Children were presented with a list of nine different types of clubs and organisations, and asked to tick all those to which they belonged and to indicate how often and on which days they attended; they were also given the opportunity to mention additional clubs that we had not specified.

Among the controls, three-quarters of the adolescents and two-thirds of the younger children belonged to at least one club; the average lay between one club and two. The younger children most often belonged to Cubs and Brownies, then cinema clubs, but relatively few mentioned the others. Among the older children, youth clubs predominated, followed by Scouts and Guides, church clubs, sports clubs, and cinema clubs (Appendix Table 62).

The more intelligent children preferred Scouts, Guides, Cubs, and

[1] A special layout of the diary was designed in such a way as to draw the child's attention to this and to ensure that the children complied with the request (Appendix A).

Brownies, hobbies and music clubs; the less intelligent, cinema clubs.[1] Intelligence was not, however, a factor in determining whether the child became a member of a club or how many clubs he joined. Rather contrary to our expectation, there were in this respect no social-class differences.

THE EFFECT OF TELEVISION

Future viewers had been more club-minded than their controls. This was the trend in both age groups, among both boys and girls, and among children of different intelligence levels and social background. A year of viewing effected little change with the adolescents; the younger viewers (now 11–12) did, however, go rather less often, so that their controls and not they were now the more frequent club-members (at both ages, one year should step up attendance).

TABLE 68. *Which of these clubs do you belong to and how often do you go to them?* (Index of attendance among children in Norwich)

	13–14 YEAR OLDS			
	1955		1956	
	Future viewers	Controls	Viewers	Controls
Mean index of attendance	2·9	2·1	3·3	2·8
	10–11 YEAR OLDS			
,,	2·0	1·7	1·9	2·2

NOTE. Since some children belonged only nominally to any one club, we obtained a weighted composite measure of membership and attendance. A club which the child attended 'often' was given a weight of 3, 'sometimes' a weight of 2, and 'hardly ever' a weight of 1. Each child's index of attendance consisted of the sum of these scores.

Inspection of the type of clubs most affected showed that fewer of the younger viewers (now 11–12 years old) were members of the Scouts or Guides. Otherwise there was no difference between viewers and controls. Since this pattern did not hold for the main survey, it may have represented a temporary delay in joining such clubs, for which they had just become eligible.[2]

The main survey showed only a faint drop in interest, among the 10–11 year olds, which was almost entirely accounted for by the fall-off in attendance at cinema clubs.

Another indication of the slight impact of television on club at-

[1] These clubs provide special film shows on Saturday mornings.
[2] In the main survey, the mean index of attendance was 3·0 for the older and 2·4 for the younger viewers; for the controls the figures were 3·0 and 2·5.

tendance is provided by relating our findings to an inquiry carried out seven years earlier by Social Survey (99), at a time when not many children had television. Their figures and ours agree closely, despite the fact that the Social Survey figures were drawn from a national sample and that their inquiry was conducted in the winter when club attendance may well be higher. It is likely, in fact, that the only lasting change is the reduction in attendance at cinema clubs. This is specially interesting since cinema clubs are held on Saturday mornings when there is no television transmission, so that children could attend without missing any programmes. Once again it is clear that a child's thirst for spectator entertainment is not insatiable; with a sufficient dose of it at home, he demands less of it outside.

The National Association for Group Viewing has reported on an interesting attempt to bring television into the youth club. In some youth clubs and social centres television has been installed on the understanding that it is put on only for certain programmes of special interest, and that when these programmes are over the set is turned off and the programme discussed. In some clubs, the boys watch sports commentaries with their coach; in others they may watch a play or documentary programme. The club leaders have reported that there is no difficulty in enforcing the rule that television should be turned off at the end of the programme, and also that many children who have television at home still prefer to come and watch in a group. This is an interesting experiment well worth following up, and provides further evidence that television need not seriously threaten youth clubs.

Church-going and Sunday school attendance

Church and Sunday school are not, of course, primarily social occasions, and they are considered here largely for want of a more appropriate niche. There was no difference in church-going between viewers and controls, but there was a greater irregularity in Sunday-school attendance among the viewers.

TABLE 69. Percentage of children who attended Sunday school

	13–14 YEAR OLDS		10–11 YEAR OLDS	
	V	C	V	C
Attendance at Sunday school:	%	%	%	%
Every week or every other week .	33	36	48	53
Some weeks only	18	8	21	16
Does not attend	49	56	31	31
Total cases (weighted) . . .	380	384	445	447

It would be tempting to ascribe this difference to the materialistic pleasure-loving impact of television; yet, as shown in Chapter 7, these differences existed already before television came on the scene.

Visiting other children's homes and entertaining friends

The question *How often do you go to the homes of your friends?* showed no difference between viewers and controls either before or after the viewers had got their sets; a better measure of the effect is found in the amount of visiting that actually took place during one week in which children filled in diaries. These showed no difference between the younger viewers and non-viewers, but among the 13–14 year olds there were signs of a fall in the time spent visiting (Table 70).

TABLE 70. Percentage of children estimated as spending various lengths of time visiting friends (between 4 p.m. and bedtime)

	13–14 YEAR OLDS		10–11 YEAR OLDS	
	V %	C %	V %	C %
No mention made of this activity .	61	49	56	58
Less than two hours . . .	22	31	30	28
Two hours or more	17	20	14	14
Total cases (weighted) . . .	84	84	84	84

Visiting, like other social activities, increases as children enter adolescence: the effect of viewing here was to retard this development, so that the older viewers spent no more time visiting than the younger controls. This effect increased in proportion to the amount of viewing children did.

As regards entertaining friends, the diaries showed no difference for the older children, but the younger viewers spent longer than controls (Table 71).

TABLE 71. Percentage of children estimated as spending various lengths of time (between 4 p.m. and bedtime) entertaining, playing or viewing with friends at home

	13–14 YEAR OLDS		10–11 YEAR OLDS	
	V %	C %	V %	C %
No mention made of this activity .	80	78	74	82
Less than one hour	8	8	8	11
One hour or more . . .	12	14	18	7
Total cases (weighted) . . .	84	84	84	84

Finally, in respect of general social activities, Appendix Table 61 shows the amount of time children spent 'aimlessly' out of doors—

on shopping expeditions, wandering, talking, loitering, doing nothing in particular but doing it often with friends of their own age. It was the older (and therefore more socially minded) children who most often reported this kind of activity, and who allowed it to be most severely affected by television. As with visits to friends, the increase in social activity that should have come with age was delayed by viewing.

CONCLUSIONS

Television appears to a fairly small extent to reduce the time children spend outdoors. This effect was more marked for younger children and for those who view heavily. But in sheer amount the loss was on average no more than a quarter of an hour a day. Clearly defined activities, such as sport, were less affected than the casual wandering about, meeting friends, cycling, and walking.

In social activities, too, the more clearly defined activities were the least affected. If club membership and club attendance were much affected at all, this was largely a matter of reduced attendance at cinema clubs among the younger children. It would seem that clubs which offer children scope for activity can well hold their own against television. If a club announces that it has to close or is losing members because they prefer to stay at home to watch television, one should treat this claim with extreme caution. It is much more likely that something in the running of the club or in the activities it offers is failing to hold the members, many of whom will, of course, have television at home.

The introduction of television into the club has been successfully adopted by some youth centres, where the set is put on for specific programmes only. By following these programmes with a discussion, a more active use can be made of the stimulus that certain documentaries, plays, or sports programmes provide.

Although entertaining at home increases, television does tend to reduce spontaneous social life outside the home. Viewers visited other children rather less and spent less time with them out of doors. Among the 13–14 year olds in particular, viewing may have delayed the increasingly active social life that should come with adolescence.

31

Passivity and Stimulation

DOES TELEVISION MAKE CHILDREN PASSIVE?

MANY parents and educationists in the United States expressed concern about the possibility that television might make children passive, usually in such broad terms as:

> I just think it's dangerous. Just sitting around having things thrown at you without stirring a muscle is very bad for children in my opinion (55).

The survey of teachers' opinions in this country showed that 25 per cent of them felt much the same and rated passivity second in the list of television's harmful effects. About 11 per cent referred to physical passivity—doing fewer things, being less active—and 14 per cent to mental passivity:

> It makes children less inclined to think for themselves, or to undertake creative activities.
>
> Children are less self-reliant; it induces a lazy attitude of mind.
>
> It dulls the imagination.

Such criticisms were made significantly more often by teachers who disapproved of television and by those who rarely viewed. It is possible, then, that the belief that television increases passivity is merely a convenient way of expressing prejudice against television; conversely, rejection of the belief may conveniently follow from personal acceptance and enjoyment of viewing. It seems unlikely that either group of teachers consistently had more 'passive' children in their classes than the other.

What do people mean by passivity?

Five aspects are frequently mentioned:

1. Viewing itself is a passive mental activity—the child sits immobile, open-mouthed, and drinks in all that the screen offers —he absorbs the content of television like a sponge.

2. Viewing may lead the child to prefer an edited version of life to life itself. At the turn of a knob, entertainment, interesting personalities, and events are brought effortlessly to the child. This becomes so satisfying that he acquires a taste for seeing things second-hand rather than making the effort to see (or do) the real thing for himself.

3. Viewing leads to 'spectatorism' and loss of initiative. This argument is really an extension of the one above. It suggests that when television is not available, the child will turn to other forms of spectator entertainment—the radio or the cinema —rather than engage in active play.

4. Television leads to a jaded palate. The child is being bombarded by a great diversity of stimuli; one or the other may interest him, but he will not translate it into action because immediately afterwards something else is offered which diverts his attention.

5. Viewing dulls the imagination. It provides the child with ready-made fantasy material so that he makes less use of his creative imaginative abilities.

There is a fear that a group of apathetic spectators will succeed the pre-television generation of alert, active 'doers'. It is worth re-calling that anxieties about films and the radio were expressed in very similar terms. The criticism also equates physical inactivity with mental inactivity; and yet story-tellers and teachers know very well that children who sit still and listen spellbound are children who are responding intellectually and emotionally to what is being told. The mothers' diaries, too, show how a child who is interested in a programme and likely to ask questions about it afterwards is just the one who sits enthralled and will not budge while the programme is on.

The criticisms examined

'*The child absorbs television like a sponge.*' This assertion can be readily dismissed in the light of our findings about the effects of television on values and outlook (Chapters 19 and 20). There is no evidence whatever that viewing is of necessity a mentally passive affair. It is no more passive than watching a play in the theatre; it may be no more passive than reading a light book, once the process of reading has become automatic. But in both these instances the child or adult makes a choice; with television the choice is more limited and less physical exertion is needed.

'*Viewing leads the child to prefer an edited version of life to life itself.*' The evidence we gathered suggests that fears on this score are unnecessary. We devised a questionnaire entitled 'Ideas about TV' and asked the question: *Some people like to watch things and people on TV—others like to see the real thing for themselves. If you had the chance to see these people and places, how would you like to see them—in real life, or on TV?*

Twenty-seven places or personalities were listed and for each the child was asked to tick one of the following answers:

> I would best like to see this on TV.
> I would best like to see this for myself—the real thing.
> I am not interested in seeing this at all.[1]

We chose six groups of subjects for examination, each representing some particular advantage that television might offer in relation to seeing the thing for oneself.[2] Items were only included when we felt confident that the children could have seen something of the sort on television and so would have a basis for making their choices.

The first two groups—ceremonial and sports events—are events where the screen affords a closer and more detailed view than would be possible if actually present. The ceremonial events chosen were: Trooping the Colour, the Lord Mayor's Show, and the Coronation Procession, and the sports events were the Football Association Cup Final, the Boat Race, a boxing match, tennis at Wimbledon, and an ice-skating competition. The third group, plays and entertainment, consisted of a play, an ice show, a musical concert, a panel game, a puppet show, and a ballet. Here the choice lay between being an audience at home and being taken out to a theatre or concert hall.

The fourth group, famous personalities, included a politician, an explorer, a film star, famous people in their homes, and the Royal Family. Interest in personalities is great and we wanted to see whether here the real contact would be preferred to the screen contact. The fifth group, the exhibitions and art galleries, were the Schoolboys' Own Exhibition, Windsor Castle, a museum, and an art gallery. Except for the Schoolboys' Own Exhibition, these places do not greatly interest children of the two age groups with which we were dealing, and here we expected the convenience of television to win. In the final group (special places of work) were a fashion show, a motor-car factory, an airport, and Scotland Yard. Here, interest may be stimulated by television but not satisfied, so it was expected that the child would wish to see the real thing.

We calculated for each child six preference scores, one for each group. A child was given a positive score if he preferred to see on television more than half the items of a given group. Items in which

[1] By eliminating the items about which the child cared very little, we hoped to make the choice a more meaningful one.
[2] For instance, close-ups of tennis at Wimbledon.

he was not interested were excluded from this calculation.[1] Table 72 shows how much children prefer the real thing to seeing it on television.

TABLE 72. Percentage of viewers who would prefer to see more than half the items of each group on television rather than in real life

Class of items:	13–14 YEAR OLDS %	10–11 YEAR OLDS %
Ceremonial events	19	12
Sports events	20	22
Plays and entertainment . . .	48	39
Famous personalities . . .	10	4
Exhibitions and art galleries . .	23	18
Special places of work . . .	19	19
Total cases (weighted)	516	516

In five out of the six groups some 80 per cent chose to see events and people for themselves. In the case of famous personalities the percentages rose to over 90 per cent; only for plays, ballet, and concerts did the figures drop to 60 per cent. Where the choice is between watching entertainment in the theatre or concert hall and watching at home, the 'real thing' wins by only a narrow margin. But when it comes to going out to see processions, to visiting places, to seeing famous personalities, television is left far behind. Special mention must be made of sports events; here, too, the 'real thing' means sitting and watching a performance, but children's very strong interest in sport and hero worship of sports personalities lead them to prefer the actual event to the television version.

On the results of our findings, there is no difference between the intelligent and less intelligent, veteran and recent, or heavy and occasional viewers.

'*Viewing leads to "spectatorism" and loss of initiative.*' Those who make this criticism are advancing two related points: first, that the child will come to expect all his entertainment to be ready-made; and second, that this demand for the ready-made will eventually lead him to be less enterprising and resourceful generally. Our findings do not show that television induces a greater preference for ready-made entertainment, or that it renders viewers less active or less capable of showing initiative than controls.[2]

[1] The method of scoring is relatively crude. Finer gradations were tried, but gave much the same result. They would, moreover, have been very cumbersome to calculate since each child had a different number of items in which he was interested.

[2] The Norwich study also showed that there was no difference in this respect between future viewers and controls.

Previously we have shown that, where time has to be found for viewing, it is the other mass media, especially radio and the cinema, which suffer, and not playing with friends or taking part in some sport. Club attendance was hardly affected—with the possible exception of the cinema club (Chapter 30).

Two open-ended questions about interests were asked: *There never seems to be enough time to do all the things one likes doing. Write down the three things you like doing best, that is in the time after school*; and: *Imagine you were spending an afternoon with a friend. What would you both be doing?*

The answers of viewers and controls were very similar (Appendix Table 47); they both enjoyed the same sort of things—sport, playing, kicking a ball around, going for cycle rides, and so on.

We also devised an activity preference questionnaire entitled 'Which would you rather do?' Six different types of situation were presented, for each of which the child was offered the choice of taking part or watching. An example of a general question on sport was: *Which would you rather do: watch sport or games, or play in sport or games?* Specific sports such as swimming and skating, which are often shown on television, were similarly dealt with. In both, the active 'going swimming' or 'skating yourself' was contrasted with 'watching a swimming competition' or 'watching a skating contest'.

The other three situations were: learning to play a musical instrument (rather than 'listening to music'), making something (rather than 'buying it ready-made in a shop'), and finding one's way about with a friend (rather than being 'shown round a town by a grown-up who lives there').

TABLE 73. *Which would you rather do?*

Number of choices made in favour of doing things for oneself

(Maximum score = 6)

| | 13–14 YEAR OLDS | | 10–11 YEAR OLDS | |
| | v | c | v | c |
Preference for doing things for oneself:	%	%	%	%
Low (below 4)	20	23	17	18
Medium (4)	31	28	29	25
High (5 and 6)	49	49	54	57
Total cases (*weighted*) . . .	459	461	472	457

Table 73 shows once again that both viewers and controls preferred to do things for themselves. The one exception was learning to play a musical instrument—an activity which requires staying power, links up with schoolwork, and is, of course, related to a specific interest and ability. But here, too, viewers and controls behaved in much the same way (see also Appendix Table 63).

Finally, we sought the co-operation of teachers, asking them to rate each child on the following three-point scale: *Shows a great deal of initiative, shows some initiative, lacks initiative*. Again, there was no difference between viewers and non-viewers.

'*Television leads to a jaded palate.*' The findings do not support this opinion; if anything, the reverse is true: viewers were more curious, more ready to interest themselves in a wide diversity of things—a difference which did not exist between future viewers and controls in Norwich. The livelier interest of viewers was shown in their responses to three different questionnaires. Children were presented with lists of different types of films and books,[1] an inventory listing eighty different types of interests, and the 'preference for television versus real life' questionnaire which enabled them to say whether they were at all interested in seeing any of the items listed (Table 74 and Appendix Table 64).

TABLE 74. *How would you like to see them—in real life or on TV?*

Number of items out of 27 ticked as 'I am not interested in seeing this at all'

(Distribution of answers by age and intelligence)

13–14 YEAR OLDS

		All		Grammar		Sec. mod. I.Q. 100–114		I.Q. below 100	
		v %	c %	v %	c %	v %	c %	v %	c %
Not interested in:									
Less than 4 items	. .	37	36	35	39	31	35	42	34
4–9 items . .	. .	48	46	47	49	56	48	43	50
10 or more items	. .	15	18	18	12	13	17	15	26
Total cases (weighted) .	.	502	503	169	168	171	171	162	164

10–11 YEAR OLDS

		All		I.Q. 115+		I.Q. 100–114		I.Q. below 100	
		v %	c %	v %	c %	v %	c %	v %	c %
Not interested in:									
Less than 4 items	. .	40	31	33	31	47	34	40	30
4–9 items .	. .	45	41	56	44	37	39	40	42
10 or more items	. .	15	28	11	25	16	27	20	28
Total cases (weighted) .	.	505	502	170	166	170	171	165	165

Once again, we found that the influence of television depended on how receptive the child was and what alternative sources of stimula-

[1] Cf. Chapters 28 and 29.

tion were within his reach. Differences between viewers and controls were particularly significant among the dull adolescents and the bright 10–11 year olds. These children, despite their differing ages, were at much the same stage in intellectual development—a stage when the encouragement that television offers appears to fall on particularly fertile ground. It will be remembered that similar results were obtained when assessing the effects of television on values, attitudes, and knowledge.

'*Viewing dulls the imagination.*' This view is difficult to assess adequately by means of questionnaires, so we relied on information from the teacher. The children were rated on a three-point scale: 'Unusually imaginative; moderately imaginative; unimaginative.' Once again no differences were found between viewers and controls.

It is, however, likely that television influences the type of fantasy material produced much more than its quality or diversity. The younger viewers will now play at being the heroes of television Westerns or *Robin Hood*, just as those without television may identify themselves with other types of Westerns and with heroes of books or radio plays.

It has been suggested that with both sound and vision provided, nothing is left to the imagination. But this argument would equally mean that radio plays and books are better stimulants for the imagination than the theatre, a point of view that is clearly untenable. It may be that some critics who use the argument are against television not because it occupies both eyes and ears, but because in their opinion much of what is presented is banal and stereotyped. The sophisticated adult may indeed find it so; but not the child, who is still trying to discover all he can about the rather bewildering world of adults and their relationships and problems.

There is, however, one small group of viewers—the television addicts—who showed signs of *spectatorism*, or lack of initiative and interest. But these children differed too much in other ways from the average viewer for their behaviour to be readily explained as an effect of television. (For more detailed investigation of this, see Chapter 35).

DOES TELEVISION ENCOURAGE CHILDREN TO BE MORE ENTERPRISING?

Our findings show that viewers were no more passive than controls; some viewers in fact seemed readier than the controls to be interested in a wide range of ideas and topics. Teachers often felt that children had become more receptive to new ideas.[1] Is it then possible to go further and claim that television encourages a child to take up new interests for himself?

Making things as a result of viewing

Over 70 per cent of the viewers had seen BBC competition programmes asking them to make models and drawings and to send them to the Television Centre.

We asked the children whether they had tried to make any of the things suggested, and also whether they had finished anything and sent it to the Centre. The answers were as follows:

	13–14 YEAR OLDS %	10–11 YEAR OLDS %
Finished something and sent off	2	3
Finished something but not sent off	6	10
Started something but not finished	9	19
Had not tried to make any of the things shown . . .	83	68
Total cases (weighted)	387	399

It will be seen that only 3 per cent even of the 10–11 year olds had gone as far as finishing a model or drawing and sending it in. The figure for the older children was somewhat lower. Even in Norwich, in the first excitement of having television, the response was no greater; only 3 children out of 120 sent models to the Centre.

We allowed the children to interpret 'started to make something but not finished it' in the most lenient way possible; they were not restricted to any one programme, nor did we stipulate how much they need have done. Even then only 19 per cent of the younger and 10 per cent of the older children answered in the affirmative.

Neither intelligence nor social background distinguished those who attempted or completed models from the remainder of the viewers. The relevant factors seemed to be an interest in hobbies, in specific crafts such as woodwork and modelling, and also a general 'interestedness'.

> Brian R., a 10 year old member of our group interview session, was a good example. He had sent a model in; and, characteristically, he had also responded to an invitation from another programme to send in old coins for identification. This is a boy with wide interests who responds to stimulation, from television as from other sources. The interviewer reports that he is well balanced and a highly intelligent child; television represents one item in a very full life.

---

[1] This was mentioned as one of the three most important effects by 21 per cent of the teachers.

Others sent models in because the topic offered on television fitted the children's established special interests.

One 10–11 year old boy had sent in a model aeroplane and also built a cutter. Asked what programme he could not get out of his mind, he mentioned a programme featuring model aircraft, and when asked what wish he would like Wilfred Pickles to grant, he said he would like to meet Neville Duke, the test-pilot.

Taking up new hobbies

Even among children of professional parents who encourage any sign of interest in a hobby, television appears to have very little effect. In their capacity as parents, ninety-four teachers were asked: *Has watching led your children to take up any new hobbies or interests or to give up any old ones?*

The ages of the children were from 2 to 16, and Table 75 below gives their replies separately, for two groups of children, the under-nines and over-nines. Apparently no hobbies were abandoned and very few were taken up as a result of viewing—apart from an increased interest in sport and athletics among the teen-agers (for which we have cited evidence throughout this report).

TABLE 75. Reports by teachers on hobbies or interests which their own children have taken up as a result of viewing

	UNDER 9 YEARS OLD	OVER 9 YEARS OLD
Hobbies or interests given up . . .	—	—
No new hobbies or interests developed .	25	30
Hobbies taken up:		
Miscellaneous	5	2
Model making	1	4
Puppetry	2	—
Paper cutting, wire models . . .	2	1
Collecting things . . .	1	—
Sketching, painting . . .	2	2
Interests developed:		
Interest in wild life, bird-watching .	2	—
Music and ballet . . .	1	—
Increased interest in sport . . .	1	13
Total cases	42	52

(The figures represent actual cases, not percentages)

Visits to places of interest

An equally poor response was apparent from a study of a series of BBC children's programmes entitled *Treasure Hunt*: we carried out an inquiry into the frequency of visits to a museum following the display of its exhibits on this television programme. (Chapter 24 gives detailed results.)

Reading

Reading is the only activity which appears to have been encouraged by television. It has been shown that quite a number of children read books that have been dramatised on television (see Chapter 28). Here we were able to compare the relative effectiveness of radio for controls and television for viewers; among both younger and older children television emerged as the more potent stimulus.

CONCLUSIONS

Passivity. There is no evidence that viewing makes children passive. Using a variety of measures, we examined different ways in which such passivity might express itself. None showed a difference between viewers and controls. Viewers appeared to have as much initiative, imagination, and pleasure in active play as controls. Indeed, the activities they dropped to make room for viewing were in the main other forms of spectator entertainment: the radio and the cinema.

These findings differ from those of Belson on adults (9). He found that in some areas a restriction of interests took place during the first few years of viewing. Among children not even recent viewers responded in this way. Enjoyment in doing things is too integral a part of childhood to be readily ousted by television.

Stimulation. Many children read books that have been dramatised on television, and also gain a sense of interest in the subjects of nonfiction reading. But there were few signs of such interests translated into activities; nor did viewers go in more for hobbies, making things, entering for competitions, or visiting interesting places. Why, then, is television not more effective? Part of the difficulty lies in the nature of televised entertainment. The rapid succession of programmes makes it difficult for the child to stop and think about what he has just seen: his attention is at once diverted by the next programme. For this reason, television preaches mainly to the converted, to the child who has a strong interest and so needs little encouragement.

Serialised dramatisations of books may be more effective because each episode ends on a note of suspense. Psychological experiments on memory have shown that this technique, which avoids satisfying closure, and does not round events off, is an aid to retention and interest.

However, television has been successful in making adults *actively* interested in such unlikely subjects as archaeology. It would therefore be useful to know why viewing is not equally stimulating for children. Do programmes fail because the wrong topic is chosen, because they are poorly presented or because they require materials that are not readily available in the home? There is scope here for research to determine what activities are suitable and what are the most effective ways of getting them across. Such research should include details of exposition and display and determine what kind of person is particularly effective with the young viewers; how clear the instructions are, and how far the speed of giving instructions is suited to the age group for which the programme is intended.[1]

Until such studies are carried out, it would be premature to say that television is not a suitable medium for encouraging children to become more enterprising—all we can say is that at present its effects are negligible.

[1] One of the authors of this report was asked by her 9 year old daughter to take down the questions at the end of a BBC children's programme on astronomy. Forewarned, with pencil and paper at the ready, and a university degree behind her, she was able to record three of five questions in full and one in part. One had to be omitted altogether. They were dictated at top speed, even though specialised terms were used.

32

Television and Leisure—a Summing Up

CERTAIN themes are common to all the effects which television has on children's leisure hours. Television absorbs a great deal of a child's free time, but takes up less of his interest. As a result it has definite *displacement effects*—the child no longer has time for all the things he used to do.

Television makes its strongest appeal to children who, even before their family get television, have a strong need for ready-made entertainment and for external stimulation—in this they resemble Riesmann's 'other-directed' type of individual (77). This need expresses itself in unusually strong radio interest, and unusually frequent comic-reading and club attendance.

Television satisfies part of this need to be entertained. Since it certainly does not stimulate it further, the child can now dispense with some of the other ready-made entertainment to which he previously turned: time spent listening to the radio dwindles to almost nothing, cinema visits are at first heavily reduced, and comic-reading comes down to about the average level. But as always, it is important to emphasise the range of individual variations, particularly those dependent on age and intelligence—social background is far less important here.

For the younger child, who goes to the cinema to be entertained, cinema and television are practically interchangeable; consequently he cuts down on cinema visits, preferring the readily available, free entertainment that he can get at home. For the older child, the cinema serves in addition a social need: it is a way of meeting and being with friends away from home. Since television cannot compete in this respect, older children reduce their cinema visits relatively little—one example of the way in which the same medium can serve different needs for children of different ages. The extent to which one medium is allowed to replace another provides a measure of their *need equivalence*.

Activities which can offer something over and above entertainment tend to be taken up again once the initial enthusiasm for television has worn off; those which can be fairly adequately replaced by television remain in the background. Comic-reading, for instance, does not revive: even after several years of viewing television, children read only about the same number of comics as the controls (although before they had television, future viewers read considerably more comics than other children). The cinema, on the other hand, comes into its own again, because it is part of the social life of the older child. The duller child, whom we have seen throughout to be more in need of external stimulation, manages to fit both increased cinema visits and heavy viewing into his schedule. Radio listening shows only a slight revival after years of viewing, and then only for specialist programmes with which television does not compete.

Attendance at clubs is affected in much the same way as visits to the cinema, but with some important differences: future viewers went to clubs more than other children, and the younger viewer initially reduced his club-going. But in the case of the older children, clubs were too important a part of their social life to be affected; so ultimately, club attendance is not reduced by viewing.

The influence of television on book-reading is complex, though the basic principles on which change occurs remain the same. Future viewers showed no more interest in books than other children; nevertheless, viewing made fairly drastic inroads into the book-reading of the older children—not because television offers the same satisfaction as book-reading, but because it leaves little time for an activity requiring prolonged concentration. In the long run the greater diversity of content that books can offer brings about a revival of interest, and ultimately viewers read as many books as controls.

By and large, these are the negative effects of viewing, the outcome of an extra demand on a limited amount of leisure time. On the positive side, television acts as a stimulant. Book-reading suffers a temporary set-back, but in the long run comes back into its own, and among duller children even gains some ground—not only in the number but also in the range and quality of the books read. Many children follow up dramatisations by searching out the books on which they are based, and in this way their interest is extended to fiction beyond the relatively stereotyped cowboy and adventure stories. Curiosity about certain specialised subjects is often aroused by television programmes, and whereas potential viewers start off by being less interested than controls in non-fictional subjects, after several years of viewing they finish up more interested. The same is true in the case of the cinema—viewing makes children alert to the potential appeal of a wider range of informational films.

Such stimulation occurs especially among the duller secondary modern children (who come in the end to read slightly more books than the corresponding children in the control group) and the brighter 10–11 year old children. It seems generally that receptiveness to the stimulating effects of television is at its peak at a *mental* age of about 11 to 12—the crucial factor being a combination of intelligence and maturity rather than any one of these factors alone.

The increased interest in information subjects that comes from watching television does not necessarily mean a gain in knowledge. The information tests discussed in Chapter 22 have indicated only a slight tendency for children to increase their store of information as a result of watching television. Television stimulates interest and curiosity, rather than implanting facts.

On balance, then, the long-term results are not likely to be alarming. Children may increase the time they spend at home with their family, at the expense of time with their friends, and where previously they listened to the radio and read many comics, they will now tend to give their time to television.

The general social activities of teen-agers, which viewing tends to reduce, are likely to revive gradually because these children have a strong need for social interchange.

Equally, though at first television cuts down the time spent out of doors, our research points to the extreme importance which outdoor activities have for children and adolescents. In fact, here television proves the weaker rival because the children enjoy outdoor play so much. The outdoor activities which are most affected are those which are less specific and clear-cut and which lack immediate purpose, such as riding round on bicycles, or kicking a ball around.

Television may eventually keep children more busy and make their lives more organised than formerly; this is not, of course, necessarily a desirable outcome.

There is no evidence whatsoever that television makes children passive; viewers are as active, independent, and imaginative as controls.

The changes which occur in the way children spend their free time are often temporary, and are likely to affect only one generation of children—the generation which first encounters television at a crucial stage in its development. For these children there may be some regrettable loss in reading skill, and some delay in widening social contact outside the circle of their home and family, but little else. It is unlikely that children born to television, and growing up with the set as familiar a piece of furniture as the piano and radio, would be adversely affected in these ways.

The main positive value of television may be as a source of ideas, introducing the child to a wide range of subjects. Too much may be expected of it: the interest it stimulates is fleeting and not readily translated into action, and whether this interest is dissipated or developed will depend a good deal on the child's environment and the adults around him. It rests with parents, teachers, and youth-club leaders both to guide the child in his choice of programmes, to encourage him to follow up any new interests that may be stimulated by his viewing, and above all to provide opportunities for the child to engage in those activities which mean more to him than television.

PART VIII

Other Effects of Television

33

Effects on Eyesight and Night Rest

OPHTHALMOLOGISTS make two points: first, viewing itself may prove a strain, especially if continued over long periods at a time; and secondly, strain may occur more readily under certain viewing conditions.

Do children view under suitable conditions?

According to the magazine published by the Association of Optical Practitioners (92), there are three requisites for 'good viewing'. The distance between the viewers and the screen should be at least six feet, the screen should be at or below eye level, and to avoid glare there should be some light in the room. (The detailed recommendations are given in full in Appendix H.)

Without going into the children's homes, it was not possible to find out anything about distance, but questions were asked about angle and glare. The results show that 10 per cent of the older and 21 per cent of the younger children said they viewed sitting on the floor, in which case the screen would be above eye level; 25 per cent of the younger and 20 per cent of the older children said they usually viewed in the dark. In other words, a sizeable minority viewed under unfavourable conditions—and this occurred in middle-as well as in working-class homes and in the homes of veteran as well as of recent viewers (Appendix Table 65).

Defective vision and eyestrain

In the absence of a proper medical examination, we took the wearing of glasses as a sign of defective vision and the affirmative response to *Do your eyes ever hurt you?* as a sign of at least occasional eyestrain. The teachers listed all children who wore glasses. The findings derived from the teachers' replies agreed so closely with those obtained from the children that only the one set of figures will be presented.

	13–14 YEAR OLDS		10–11 YEAR OLDS	
	V %	C %	V %	C %
Do you wear glasses? . . .	10	16	16	15
Do your eyes ever hurt you? . .	13	20	19	25
Total cases (*weighted*) . . .	502	502	502	502

Neither teachers' reports nor the children's answers showed any significant difference between viewers and controls in the incidence of defective eyesight. In the case of eyestrain, more controls than viewers said their eyes hurt them. Among girls of both age groups the latter difference was statistically significant at the 1-per-cent level.[1]

If television does cause eyestrain, the heavy and the veteran viewers would be more likely to show signs of it than the occasional and the recent viewer. This was not so; the findings were uniformly negative. It is true that certain children with poor eyesight may experience strain and headache after viewing, but these findings suggest that if the same children spent the same amount of time reading, the results might well have been the same.

Our study shows that other sources of eyestrain need equal attention; for example, reading. (We know controls read more than viewers, especially in bed at night.) Faulty angle of book to eye, bad lighting, and poor-quality print may all be relevant factors here. Daish (26), for example, refers to the strain caused by the small print of just those comics on which our control children spent a good deal of time.

[1] Confirmation of these findings was obtained from the 'Wishes' questionnaire, where fewer viewers indicated that they sometimes or often wished 'my eyes did not hurt so much'. This questionnaire was administered in a different testing session and the eyestrain item had been placed among wishes dealing with a wide range of topics.

THE EFFECT OF TELEVISION ON SLEEP

In the study of teachers' opinions, they were asked what were the three main effects of television on pupils. More than half the teachers mentioned late nights and a consequent lack of concentration at school the next morning. This effect was mentioned very much more often by junior- and infant-school teachers than by teachers in secondary schools:[1] but overall, those teachers who were themselves unfavourably disposed to television mentioned late nights more often than those who were in favour of television (62 per cent and 45 per cent respectively).

Adequate sleep depends not merely on bedtimes but on time available for sleep, the time taken to go to sleep, and the extent to which sleep is disturbed by frightening dreams. Clearly, if night rest were drastically affected, children would be listless, concentrate badly at school, and so would work below capacity. We have tried to obtain evidence on all these aspects.

Bedtimes of children without television

On two occasions during the testing children were asked: *What time did you go to bed last night?*[2] In addition, when filling in the diaries each morning children wrote down the time they had gone to bed the night before. This made it possible to work out a *mean week-day* bedtime (for Mondays to Thursdays inclusive, days followed by school the next morning) and also the *mean week-end* bedtime (for Fridays and Saturdays, days not followed by school) (Appendix Table 66). Appendix Table 67 gives the bedtimes obtained from the questionnaire for boys and girls of different ages, intelligence level, and social background.

The mean bedtime of the *13–14 year olds* for week-days and week-ends was 9.40 p.m., but there was considerable variation.[3] Girls

[1] Late nights were mentioned by 70 per cent of the urban and 55 per cent of the rural teachers in junior and infant schools.

[2] The average bedtimes for the various groups obtained from the two questionnaires agreed well and so gave confidence in the reliability or consistency of the data. This consistency also makes it possible to present here tables based on the results of one questionnaire only.

[3] It is difficult to say whether the times taken from the questionnaire or those taken from the diaries were more accurate. The latter were less influenced by the happenings of any one day, since they were based on the mean bedtimes of four successive days. On the other hand, the diary results may be less reliable because they were based on relatively small samples. (Appendix Table 66). Sunday was excluded because it does not fit clearly into either the week-day or week-end categories.

went to bed much earlier than boys, grammar school earlier than secondary modern school children. Middle-class girls went to bed before working-class girls, but with the boys there were no class differences.

The mean bedtime of the *10–11 year olds* was 8.45 p.m.—with little variation—but bedtimes were later at week-ends. Once again, girls went to bed earlier than boys, and highly intelligent children (those of grammar school calibre) earlier than the less intelligent. In this group, the social-class differences were clear-cut for both boys and girls; middle-class children went to bed earlier than working-class ones.

What happened when television was introduced?

Future viewers, as we have shown in Chapter 7, came from homes with a less rigid discipline about bedtimes than did the controls. Their bedtimes were later, a difference which was accentuated once television came into the home. To ascertain the extent of the change, we calculated for each child the shift in bedtime as between 1955 and 1956, during which period television was introduced (using his 1955 bedtime as the base line, Table 76).

TABLE 76. Shift in bedtimes among Norwich children between 1955 and 1956

	13–14 YEAR OLDS		10–11 YEAR OLDS	
	V %	C %	V %	C %
Unchanged or ½ hour later . .	22	27	49	60
1 hour later	30	38	26	20
1½ hours or more later . . .	48	35	25	20
Total cases	27	32	88	91

As the children were a year older in 1956, most of them naturally went to bed a little later; but viewers much more so than controls.

More detailed information on a larger sample was provided by the main survey, showing that the postponement for both age groups in fact averaged only 10 to 20 minutes—not the dramatic difference that might have been expected (Appendix Tables 66 and 67). In an inquiry in Boston, Maccoby (58) obtained a very similar figure, as did the BBC Minors' Study carried out in 1954 (16).

At the week-end, with no school the next day, the difference between viewers and controls became more pronounced; of the younger viewers, 29 per cent went to bed after 10 p.m. as against 17 per cent among the controls.

The postponement showed itself most among those who, on ordinary week-days, went to bed rather earlier than the rest of their age group, namely, girls and middle-class children. But even there it did not, on average, exceed half an hour.

The 10–11 year old of grammar school calibre and the grammar school 13–14 year old both went to bed at much the same time as before, whereas the least intelligent were the ones who postponed their bedtimes most. We know that the more intelligent the child the less he viewed and the less interested he appeared in television. It is also likely that this applies not only to the children but also to their parents. In homes where television occupies a secondary role, it is easier to prevent it from affecting the general routine.

Unduly late nights occurred as often among those who had no television at home as among the viewers. Perhaps the most striking finding was that the number of children who went to bed particularly late (after 10 p.m. in the case of the younger and after 10.30 p.m. for the older children) was the same for viewers and controls. Television does not seem to be the dominant factor here, although, of course, a teacher will come across some children who go to bed at these very late hours and who have also spent the evening viewing. We suggest that these will belong to that small percentage who tend to go to bed late anyhow, but who happen to have a television set at home. In one American study (23) persistently late bedtimes were found to be associated with inadequate parental control, apathy, low intelligence, poor school performance and general behaviour. Excessive and late-night televiewing was part of this total situation, not its cause.

Not surprisingly, once bedtimes have been postponed they remain late. No difference in this respect was found between recent, experienced, and veteran viewers.

Do heavy viewers postpone their bedtime more than occasional viewers?

Since older children have more spare time than 10–11 year olds, they can fit in quite a heavy viewing programme without having to postpone their bedtime further. Thus among adolescents there was no difference in bedtimes between heavy and moderate viewers. The available time in the evening during which a 10–11 year old can view is much shorter. The 18–20 hours a week viewed by addicts can be fitted in only at the expense of an early bedtime. Hence the younger heavy viewers stayed up much longer than those who viewed less heavily. The diaries show that a third of the heavy viewers went to bed after 9.30 p.m. compared with 10 per cent of the occasional viewers.

How far does television affect hours of sleep, as distinct from bedtime?

Bedtime does not itself necessarily govern the amount of time children spend sleeping; it is necessary also to take into account the time spent between going to bed and turning out the light.

We asked in the diary each day: *Did you do anything after you went to bed?* Fewer viewers than controls said that they read, played, or wrote after going to bed.[1]

It seems, then, that the child without a television set may go to bed a little earlier, but he is more likely to spend longer between going to bed and turning out the light. The actual loss of sleep for the viewer may therefore be even smaller than the bedtimes suggest, or there may be no loss at all.

Young children between 5 and 10 years old

Very young children need a great deal of sleep, and so should have little opportunity of seeing any evening television. However, many nursery and infant school teachers referred to children's comments which clearly showed that they were familiar with evening programmes. Among the families who took part in the mothers' diary study there were two such cases. One was a working-class family with three children aged 3, 7, and 10 who watched television on most evenings until 9 p.m. and later. But such reports were rare; the bulk of mothers' diaries showed that the younger children watched children's television, and saw evening television for only about half an hour, if at all. Some selective factor may be at work here: mothers who took the trouble to complete the diary were likely to be equally conscientious about bedtimes and the welfare of their children generally.

Reliable information about the bedtimes of young children is not easily obtained from parents, since in giving it they must unconsciously be influenced by their ideas as to when the child ought to go to bed.

Conflict over bedtimes

Interviews with parents and comments in the mothers' diaries show that conflict over bedtimes—always a popular scrapping ground—sharpened once television arrived. Some parents were found to have little difficulty on this score; but others found it an unending source of wrangling. The mother of a nervous boy of 10,

---

[1] The mean incidence for the week was as follows: 34 per cent of the adolescent and 34 per cent of the younger controls mentioned that they either read or played, while corresponding figures for the viewers were 25 and 28 per cent respectively.

for instance, described how she was powerless to stop the children fighting over the set and spontaneously said that she had no control over the children's viewing when father was not there. 'They watched until late at night' . . . 'They got round me' . . . 'They know I am soft'. It transpired that the family had bought the television set because the children would rarely come straight home from school, or when they did, would rush in for bread and jam and run out again. For this family, television had restored order over mealtimes —but bedtimes were out of hand now.

Whether or not bedtimes become a ground for conflict seems to depend less on the attractions of television than on the general character of the home. The interview just quoted showed vividly how lax bedtimes were one facet of a generally weak home background. In families where the children have learnt that much may be gained by wheedling, they will exert all their powers of persuasion. In others where there is established discipline and settled policy, viewing simply takes its place among the many other reasons that a child finds for wanting to stay up late.

Television and disturbed sleep

To find out whether television led to disturbed sleep, the children were asked the questions presented in Table 77 on p. 374.

There was no difference between viewers and controls. Television viewing as such did not overstimulate, making it difficult to fall asleep, nor did it lead to disturbed night rest.

While this was true of viewing in general, we have a good deal of evidence that after certain programmes children have difficulties in falling asleep and report bad dreams.

As many as 20 per cent of the older and 30 per cent of the younger children agreed with the statement: *Sometimes the things I see on television make me lie awake at night*. This, of course, does not mean that a particular film, radio programme, or book may not have the same effect.

Some further evidence came from the answers to the question: *Are there things on television which you yourself think are bad for children to see? If yes, what sort of things, and what makes you think they are bad for children to see?* By asking the question about children in general, we hoped to get round the reluctance of older children to admit that they themselves might have been frightened by a programme Twenty-five per cent of the older and 21 per cent of the younger viewers answered 'Yes' to the first question, and of these about half said that television programmes were bad for children to see because 'They are frightening and keep you awake' or because 'They make you afraid and give you bad dreams'. Again, however, we have no comparable figures for the other mass media.

TABLE 77. Answers of children in the main survey to questions about ease of falling asleep, amount and type of dreams reported

	13–14 YEAR OLDS		10–11 YEAR OLDS	
	V %	C %	V %	C %
Some children go to sleep easily, others lie awake for a long time. Which do you do?				
I fall asleep:				
Easily	30	26	26	24
After a while	49	45	44	38
After a long time . . .	21	29	30	38
Some children dream a lot, others don't dream much. What do you do?				
I dream:				
Almost every night . . .	12	17	16	20
Sometimes	44	44	36	36
Hardly ever	44	39	48	44
Some people's dreams are happy dreams, others have dreams that make them wake up frightened or unhappy. What are most of your dreams like?				
My dreams are:				
Mainly happy	46	47	43	45
Some frightening, others not .	43	45	42	43
Mostly frightening . . .	6	5	10	9
Never dream	5	3	5	3
Total cases (weighted) . . .	494	497	499	504

These children were no more highly strung and had no more fears than the rest of the viewers, nor did they have greater difficulty in falling asleep or have nightmares. It is important that the number who were both disturbed and also claimed to be kept awake was much the same for both age groups. Being older does not protect from getting over-excited and from being frightened by certain programmes.

Television viewing as such does not make it difficult for children to settle down to sleep. What has to be avoided, however, are over-exciting and frightening programmes.[1]

Listlessness in the morning

The viewers themselves did not admit to feeling any more tired in the morning than did the controls.

[1] Freda Lingstrom, until recently Head of BBC Children's Television, speaks of the need for presenting a calming, more neutral programme after a very exciting one to counteract its anxiety- or aggression-provoking impact.

A more reliable measure comes from the teachers' ratings of these children. Once again there were no differences; the number described as working below par, or with diminished concentration or initiative, was the same for viewers and controls (Appendix Table 69).

There is thus no empirical evidence to support the anxiety of teachers that television viewing leads to listlessness or poor concentration at school. It must, however, again be remembered that we were dealing with children above the age of 10; anxiety may have a better foundation with regard to younger children. Moreover, there must remain many children who are, in fact, tired in the morning because of late viewing. Our results serve to set these instances in the proper context by showing that there may be as many children among the controls who, for other reasons, get inadequate night rest and whose school performance and concentration is below par.

CONCLUSIONS

Effect on eyesight. A sizeable number of children viewed under poor optical conditions: they looked up at the screen or else viewed in the dark. There is need here for parent and child education in the correct conditions for viewing. Parents could be informed through the medium of the *Radio Times* and *TV Times*, and the children through their teachers at school. Advice given should be clear-cut and specific, and represent the consensus of opinions of experts in this field.[1]

Despite the fact that conditions for viewing were often inadequate, we found no evidence of greater eyestrain or of defective eyesight among viewers compared with controls.

Night rest. The examination of the effect of television on children's bedtime habits showed that the amount of anxiety voiced far exceeds what is justified by the facts. Bedtimes were postponed—but on the average only by twenty minutes, and even this was frequently offset by viewers spending less time on reading and playing between going to bed and turning the light out. In any case some of these differences existed between future viewers and their controls before television came on the scene.

The postponement of bedtime, moreover, took place particularly among children who normally went to bed rather early. The most

---

[1] Klapper (55) in his study of the comments made on children and television found that many articles mentioned eyestrain, but only three gave sufficiently specific advice to be useful. He further mentions how often advice in one article was contradicted by that given in another.

significant finding was that really late bedtimes occurred as often among controls as viewers, such bedtimes reflecting the general home atmosphere rather than the lure of television. This finding is important from two points of view. First, it shows how readily a causal connexion is assumed of what may well be two aspects of a syndrome. A teacher might find a child is looking tired. The child tells the teacher that he watched television until late the night before. This association of events is registered as cause and effect, but not so the more varied reasons for which the control children stay up equally late. Secondly, it draws attention to the *real* problem; it forces us to ask why this child is up so late, compared with other viewers, so that we do not pass it off as yet another of the harmful consequences of television that we are powerless to influence.

It is worth noting in this connexion that teachers who held generally unfavourable attitudes to television mentioned late bedtime significantly more often than those who liked it.[1] It may well be that in a younger age group than the one we tested the postponement of bedtimes would have been more marked. While there was no evidence that generally children were over-stimulated by viewing, nevertheless a sizeable number said that they had been kept awake after one or other programme; and these were children who were no more highly strung or fearful than average. Older children mentioned this as often as the younger children. The type of programme that frightened them differed with the age of the child, not the frequency with which such fears occurred.

An invention as powerful and recent as television is blamed for many shortcomings. Here we have an instance where an empirical inquiry forces us to reassess the situation, in the case of eyesight to consider other sources of eyestrain, and in the case of the unduly late nights to seek for an explanation and consequently for a remedy in the home of the child.

---

[1] A neat demonstration of what psychologists describe as 'halo' effects.

34

Television and the Family

VIEWING is more of a family activity than listening to the radio or visiting the cinema. Eighty per cent of the children viewed in the evening with their parents, and almost half of them did so during the afternoon. For radio listening the figures were lower (Appendix Table 68). The role of television within the family, and the repercussions of its presence there, have occasioned much anxiety.

Television could disturb the home routine in many different ways —with discord, with the perennial conflicts over homework and bedtime, with the need for mealtime adjustments, and with the possibility of a stream of visitors coming to view. What in fact happens?

Bringing friends in to view. Only about 10 per cent said they could not bring friends home; a further 6 per cent did not want to, and, characteristically, there were more heavy viewers among this group than moderate or occasional viewers (cf. Chapter 35). Although children were allowed to bring friends home, they had to ask first— casual dropping in was the exception rather than the rule (Appendix Table 70).

Mealtimes. In the diaries the children were asked each day to say at what time they took their main evening meal. Table 78 gives the

TABLE 78. Distribution of children's evening mealtimes, as recorded in diaries

	13–14 YEARS OLDS		10–11 YEARS OLDS	
	V %	C %	V %	C %
Mostly 4–5 p.m.	34	23	22	30
„ 5–6 p.m.	34	28	49	39
„ 6–7 p.m.	8	11	21	9
„ 7–8 p.m.	2	—	1	4
„ after 8 p.m.	22	38	7	18
Total cases	84	84	84	84

distribution of times—these times are interesting in showing the wide variation in pattern even for the controls.

As far as the effects of viewing are concerned, some adjustment of mealtimes had been made, but much less than had commonly been supposed. Evening meals were sometimes shifted to conform with two demands: in order to get meals over before the start of evening transmission, and (mainly among the younger viewers) to have the main meal during the children's programmes (5–6 p.m.). The net result was that the main evening meal was in many viewing households eaten rather earlier than before.

Parental control

Bedtimes. Chapter 33 shows that viewers' bedtimes tended to be postponed, but only to a relatively small degree. The slightness of the postponement suggests a good deal of parental control of children's viewing, both in working-class and in middle-class homes.

The close agreement between the times children mentioned as the latest times they were allowed to view, and their actual bedtimes,[1] also suggests that the rules were usually adhered to.

Homework. To check on the degree to which homework routines were disturbed by television, we asked children (*a*) how much time they spent on homework each evening, and (*b*) whether their parents insisted on their finishing homework before they could look at television. The results of these questions (discussed in detail in Chapter 25) show that 60 per cent of those who did homework regularly claimed that they were made to finish it before they started viewing. This figure might well be exaggerated; nevertheless it gives some idea of the prevalence of rules about viewing and homework.

Banning of unsuitable programmes. A different form of parental control lies in the banning of programmes which parents believe to be unsuitable. Many parents did not recognise this need: even among teachers with television at home, only about one-fifth of the 106 parents included in the study of teachers' opinions said they forbade their children to view unsuitable programmes, and a further 15 per cent (mainly those with children under 9) allowed their children to view only children's television. This group of parents is, of course, a selected one, probably with more concern about television's effect on their children than is characteristic of most families. Personal interviews with mothers (this time using a sample in which working-class respondents predominated) showed even less awareness of the need for control. Most of them insisted that they did not direct their children's viewing.

Control, then, is rare, and where it exists, it is aimed at preventing

---

[1] As given in the diaries and also in answer to the question: *What time did you stop viewing last night?*

the child from watching horror or frightening programmes. There is also sometimes the idea of encouraging the viewing of programmes believed to be educationally desirable—an aspect of television much stressed by parents, possibly in some cases in order to justify their own interest in viewing.

The family's defence of television

Children and parents alike try to present television as a beneficial influence on the family. When children in the main survey were asked: *What are the most important ways in which television has really changed things at home?* 21 per cent of the older and 13 per cent of the younger viewers singled out the fact that the family was at home more or that its members saw more of one another. As many as 18 per cent and 20 per cent respectively of these two age groups made the even more important point that viewing improved the general tone of things at home, that there was more to do and talk about, that the family got on better together, and that there was more 'peace and quiet'.

It is natural that both children and adults should point to television's good effects. The mothers who were interviewed showed a strong tendency to take up a defensive attitude about television, at least as far as their own family was concerned. The majority insisted that television made no difference to their family life and relationships, to conversation within the family, to their children's behaviour, or to their domestic routines. Asked about effects generally, they assumed these must be ill effects, and gave such answers as 'Oh, there are no effects on *our* children'; only sixteen out of the sixty mothers mentioned any bad effects—mainly confined to late nights and bedtime difficulties.[1]

Several factors lie behind this defensiveness. First, much has been said and written about the possible bad effects of television, and it is understandable that parents should interpret 'effects' in an adverse way. It is equally understandable that they should be anxious to exempt their own children from undesirable reactions. It is also possible that parents wish to think of television more as a family bond than as a family menace, and that mothers in particular may see it unconsciously as a means of postponing their children's independence, and of cementing family unity. Parent viewers have a vested interest in presenting television as something of a benefactor, and as a result, especially in working-class families, it tends to be regarded in an uncritical manner.

[1] Maccoby noted the same defensive attitude—the note of 'nothing can change *our* family' (58).

Even fathers can be included in this rosy picture of television as a home-maker:

> Television hasn't changed us. Television holds you together. Before we had television, it was very difficult to keep my husband contented. My children have grown up that bit more, and their interests are inside now; when you have a fire it's very cosy. I only wish we'd had television sooner. They eat up more now because they sit and watch television and don't notice how much they eat . . . before they used to run away. Their interest doesn't end with the programme. I don't have much hope for Mary for the scholarship, but television wouldn't be the cause if she fails. There's more to converse about, with you having television. There's questions, and one thing leads to another. . . . Television doesn't command our life. It gives us a lot of pleasure—for people in our position, by the fire with the children. We haven't always got something to talk about. Television helps to create interest around the family fireside. After being demobbed it was very difficult to keep my husband occupied. Television keeps husbands at home. Young men don't go to the pubs so much.

For the working-class family especially, as in the example just quoted, television may in fact offer a common interest and conversational source such as had hardly existed previously. (Stewart's researches in Atlanta (87) showed much the same result.) Television is also useful as a pacifier—it keeps husband and children quiet; sometimes it is almost thrust at children, especially when very young. One mother, for instance, found she could keep her baby quiet by holding it up to look at television.

Although most mothers denied that they used television as a means of discipline, incidental remarks made elsewhere in the interviews suggested that they sometimes did just this. For instance:

> My children behave rather better now that I have television. You can kind of bribe them with television. If they want to see a programme or a person, they'll behave.

Roughly half the children in both age groups of our main survey sample said that their parents sometimes allowed them to view later as a reward for good behaviour; and 18 per cent of the older children and 32 per cent of the younger said that television was sometimes withheld as punishment.

Maccoby (58) found similar results in the United States: the social life that viewing brought about in the family was parallel rather than interactive, but from the mother's standpoint television appeared to solve rather than to create problems. Partly as a result of this, she found that parents tended to present television in a favourable light. And again, as in our study, she found television often used as a pacifier, as well as a form of discipline.

The sense of increased family unity

There is certainly some evidence that television keeps children indoors more—but only to a very small degree, as Chapter 27 has shown. But even were such a development widespread, it would not necessarily result in improved quality of family contact; in fact, for the adolescent to stay at home more may merely set up a sense of strain.

The mothers' diaries showed little general discussion and sharing of reactions in the normal course of family viewing; but the children made a fair number of comments and sometimes asked questions of the adults present. They did not so much talk about the programmes as react to them. Small children, particularly, tended to express their reactions aloud—partly because they wanted to share them and to receive the reassurance of familiar people around them, and partly because such commentaries represent the normal mode of reaction of young children. But the older children talked far less while viewing—although after the programme they might draw other members of the family into the fantasy it had inspired; here, for instance, is the description of a 10 year old boy, watching *Rin-Tin-Tin*:

> He enjoys this very much—judging by his face—he looks as though he is in the fort. He sits so quiet. Later, he called his dog Rin-Tin-Tin, and he himself was Lt. Rip Masters, and he told Barry (his 7 year old brother) he could be Rusty.

As the child grows older, his viewing experience becomes increasingly personal; he makes fewer attempts either to share it with other members of the family, or to draw them into it afterwards. At this stage, viewing can occur as much in isolation as if the child were physically alone.

Television increased the interests that children shared with their parents to a very limited extent, and on the whole only so far as the younger children were concerned.[1] Among the older children, the outcome was less favourable; while they spent more time viewing with their family, they made up for this by reducing other joint activities (the older girl viewers, for instance, less often than their controls claimed a common interest with their mothers in shopping and housework).

Among 10–11 year old boys, viewers (compared with controls) more often mentioned joint interest with their fathers in building and making things by hand: BBC children's television tries to

---

[1] Children were asked in the main survey: *What are the things which you and your father like to do together?* and *What are the things which you and your mother like to do together?*

encourage such activities. But this increase was apparent only among middle-class boys, and it is likely that middle-class parents pay more attention than working-class parents to these potential uses of television. There was also evidence that more of the younger girl viewers shared their mothers' interest in sewing—but this was mainly because they liked to view and sew at the same time, and not as a result of television programmes on the subject.

Family conflict

Here again, the mothers' diaries were our best source of information. A number of different types of conflict emerged, but easily the most important one concerned bedtimes, followed by difficulties in preventing children from seeing unsuitable programmes. Mealtime conflicts also emerged, with children who ate slowly and distractedly while viewing at the same time, but there were no signs of difficulty in getting children away from television to their meals— possibly because, as has already been seen, mealtimes were sometimes adjusted to coincide with viewing. Other occasional conflicts were over television *versus* homework, or *versus* errands. Surprisingly, there were no instances of conflict about programme choice.[1] Often one family experienced several different types of discord.

Within the limit of the very small sample, girls appeared to be less troublesome than boys, and young children less than older children.[2] There is also evidence to suggest that conflict may occur most often among heavy viewers. When those who showed conflict were matched individually, according to age, sex, and social class, with children who showed no signs of conflict (both very small groups), it was nearly always the 'conflict' child who spent most time watching television. Interviews with mothers suggested the same difference. The emotional unbalance that is elsewhere shown to underlie heavy viewing may itself encourage conflicts with parents or even arise out of them (cf. Chapter 35).

It is also clear from our data that some parents create difficulty through unwise handling of the viewing problems—for instance by assuming, perhaps too readily, that their own needs have priority

[1] It must, however, be remembered that this was only a very small sample, and not all the families involved had sets able to receive both channels. In the United States, where a good deal of choice is available, family conflict over programme choice is frequently reported. One survey (95) found that three families out of five reported conflict of this type.

[2] This age difference may, however, be largely due to the fact that at the time of this study there was a gap in transmission between 6–7 p.m.—and during this time the young children were often put reasonably happily to bed. It is possible that now, with continuous transmission, conflict may arise at any age.

over their child's absorption in his viewing; by switching off the set without warning and before the programme has ended; or by sending the child on an errand in the middle of, or just before, a long-awaited programme. The mother of a girl aged 11 fell into this type of error:

> Television often causes ructions when she wants to see, say, *The Grove Family*, and her homework is still to be finished; or she has to go on an errand for me— then, according to her, everything 'isn't fair'.

Some conflict that occurs is certainly symptomatic of already existing bad relations between parent and child—instances of this emerged both in the mothers' diaries and in personal interviews with children. In such circumstances television may spark off conflicts— and is likely to be cast in the role of scapegoat. No rules for avoiding conflict can be a substitute for unstrained relationships, for perceptive parental handling of the child, and for a home atmosphere which is conducive to the development of many alternative interests to viewing.

The following report from a middle-class mother of four children (aged 6–18 years) shows how conflict can be avoided. This family has rules for viewing, flexibly adhered to, and the children have many other interests:

> Peter (aged 12) likes to see most of the Saturday serials, and those on children's television too, but these are sometimes awkward to fit in as he has a good deal of homework and we like that done first. In fact, until all homework is finished we never have television on, unless there is something exceptional; and occasionally on Wednesdays we let them have a break to watch *Double Your Money*, which is the only ITV item we watch regularly. As my eldest daughter (15) does quite a lot of homework too, the TV is not often on during the evening. We never have any trouble about this, as we made it a condition before we even bought the set. On the whole, I don't think it would worry Peter if the set were disposed of tomorrow, he has so many other things to do. It is just there, with the wireless, gramophone, &c., to use to while away the time when nothing more interesting can be found. Maureen (6) does not seem to be greatly affected by television. The chief reason is, I think, that as a family we are all extremely fond of reading and do not have the TV set on very much, and when we do, it is because we want to see a certain item, and after we have seen it, the set is switched off. For the same reason, we have never had any trouble about watching, as from the beginning we have always watched selectively.

CONCLUSIONS

To sum up: it seems likely that television, although centred on the home, does not greatly strengthen family ties, even though it may offer a spurious sense of unity. As the children grow older, silent viewing increases, and in adolescence the increase in time spent with the family may even cause strain, or a compensatory reduction of other activities shared with parents.

Nevertheless, both parents and children frequently persuade themselves that viewing 'unites' the family; the mother especially finds it useful in keeeping husband and children under her eye, in staving off the children's independence, and in keeping the younger children quiet. Television may be used too easily as a pacifier for young children. Parents, like children, tend to defend television; most of them deny its bad effects and only a minority even admit bedtime difficulties. They lay heavy stress on the educational advantages of viewing and on other incidental uses to which viewing can be put.

Control of children's viewing is widespread with regard to bedtime and homework, but in other respects many parents seem to be unaware of the need for some degree of control.

Parents' best policy probably lies in establishing rules for viewing which, though flexible, are no less binding on themselves than on the child. They can also gain much by encouraging their children to find other interests, by refraining from using television as a bribe and pacifier, and by not viewing indiscriminately and continuously themselves. But when conflict does arise, parents should make sure that television is at the root of the trouble, and that it is not primarily due to strained relationships between themselves and their children, or to emotional strain of other kinds leading to viewing addiction.

35

The Television Addict

A SPECIAL study was made of the television addict (that is, the heavy viewer) to find out what kind of child becomes an addict; also because the intensive viewers are likely to show most clearly any effects that television might have.

WHAT SORT OF CHILD BECOMES A TELEVISION ADDICT?

We designated as addicts the one-third of each age group who spent the longest time viewing.[1] Table 79 gives the distribution of occasional, moderate, and heavy viewers by social class and intelligence. As we wanted to isolate the child who persisted with heavy viewing, once the novelty of having a set had worn off, recent viewers were excluded from this analysis.

On week-days heavy viewers watched television for half the time available between the end of school and going to bed. Since much of this time would be taken up by routine activities, like walking home from school, tidying up, eating, and sometimes homework, the proportion of free time given to viewing was well over half.

We are concerned here not so much with the actual number of hours spent viewing—though this is, of course, important—but rather with the relative amount of viewing done. What type of child, in a given set of circumstances, views the longest?

Intelligence and social background

We have already seen that the more intelligent the child, the less likely is he to be an addict. This is particularly true of the 13–14

---

[1] The point beyond which behaviour is considered excessive is generally fixed arbitrarily (for example, the amount of drink that someone must consume to be described as a heavy drinker) and is selected as a compromise between conflicting considerations: the contrast between this group and the rest must be sharpened, which means fixing the point as far away from the average as possible; yet the group must contain sufficient numbers to permit statistical analysis.

year old; only a fifth of the grammar school children were addicts, compared with half of those of average and below-average intelligence.[1] With the younger children, the difference was less sharp but equally consistent, the figures being a quarter and just over a third, respectively.

TABLE 79. Frequency of different types of viewers by age, intelligence, and social background

13–14 YEAR OLDS

	All %	Grammar school %	Sec. mod. I.Q. 100–114 %	I.Q. below 100 %	Middle class %	Working class %
Occasional viewer	18	26	18	10	20	16
Moderate viewer	48	54	48	40	44	53
Heavy viewer	34	20	34	50	36	31
Total cases (weighted)	490	167	157	176	258	232

10–11 YEAR OLDS

	All %	I.Q. 115+ %	I.Q. 100–114 %	I.Q. below 100 %	Middle class %	Working class %
Occasional viewer	28	32	29	24	33	23
Moderate viewer	41	43	40	40	42	40
Heavy viewer	31	25	31	36	25	37
Total cases (weighted)	464	158	164	141	239	230

NOTE. The occasional viewers would watch on an average less than one hour a day, the heavy viewers three hours or more. These figures are, however, based on the questionnaire and may represent an overestimate. (See Appendix B.)

Dull children may become addicts largely for want of something better to do. One dull boy, when asked what was the most important change that television had brought him, said, 'I can look at television of an evening instead of sitting at home and doing nothing.' For the intelligent child, though, viewing has to compete with other interests once the novelty has worn off.

We further saw that, among the 13–14 year olds, social background was not a factor; there were also no social class differences for bedtimes and cinema attendance. It would appear that the closer control exercised by middle-class parents diminishes when children reach early adolescence. However, we did find the expected class difference

[1] Intelligence, rather than type of school, seems to be the operative factor here: among adolescents the incidence of addicts increased consistently with descending intelligence right down the scale. Had it been a function of type of school as well, we should have expected a sharper division between the grammar school and the two groups of secondary modern school pupils.

among younger children: only a quarter of the middle-class children were heavy viewers compared with a little over a third of the working class. At that age the factors of social class and intelligence seemed to be of equal weight, so that heavy viewing was most frequent among dull working-class children. This also means that there may well be some 10–11 year olds who, given free choice, would have been heavy viewers, while among older children the amount viewed is more clearly a matter of personal preference.

Boys and girls

The proportion of heavy viewers was the same for boys and for girls. This is of interest since we have shown throughout this report that girls, especially adolescent girls, tend to respond more to the medium than boys, to think more about the plays they see, and to be more affected in their outlook by the content of television programmes. This greater impact is not, then, a function of how much they view.

Personality and outlook

As many as a fifth of the grammar school children were heavy viewers, and nearly two-thirds of the duller 10–11 year olds were occasional or moderate viewers; to explain this we had to look for factors other than intelligence and social background. We carried out a comparative analysis of occasional, moderate, and heavy viewers—a kind of comparative case study within the framework of the survey—using teachers' ratings of behaviour and personality, the children's answers to personality inventories, and their diaries. The heavy, moderate, and occasional viewers were individually matched (in trios) for age, sex, social class, and intelligence. Thus, three dull working-class boys would be matched with each other— a heavy viewer, a moderate viewer, and an occasional viewer.

Such stringent matching was necessary to avoid reflecting differences due simply to intelligence and background; this would have vitiated the purpose of the analysis, which was to look beyond these variables for other relevant ones. Inevitably, this procedure reduced the size of the sample very considerably, so that the differences we found were often just below the level of statistical significance. Even so, they were too consistent to have arisen by chance.

A second problem, which matching could not solve, was how to distinguish cause from effect. If addicts were found to have personality features in common or to behave in a way which differentiated them from the other viewers, how could we account for these features, and how could we decide whether they helped to cause excessive viewing or whether they were the result of it? If an addict had few friends, was this the reason he viewed so much, or did the time he spent viewing deprive him of sufficient opportunities for making friends? Might not both the amount and the effect of viewing depend on the type of child?

What is required here is a before-and-after study, observing viewers before they had television and then for some years afterwards. This was not possible. The Norwich study was not suitable either, since viewing for Norwich children was still too much of a novelty to enable us to distinguish between the transient and the confirmed addict. Further, teachers' ratings could not be obtained for the Norwich children, since most of them had moved to new schools; nor was it possible to administer personality tests.

The alternative was to see how far certain personality characteristics and behaviour are common to addicts of different media. We therefore carried out a parallel analysis comparing matched *cinema addicts* with occasional cinema-goers, both drawn from the control group.[1] A 'heavy' cinema-goer was one who went to the cinema two or three times a week. While he saw many more films than the occasional cinema-goer, who went once a fortnight or less, nevertheless the amount of time he spent at the cinema was far less than the time the television addict spent in front of the set.

This parallel analysis will be written up in greater detail as a separate paper, and only the more salient findings are reported here. Once again it must be emphasised that, because of the matching, we are focusing attention on factors other than intelligence or social background.

TYPES OF ADDICT

The confirmed addict

We found, contrary to expectation, that it was not the only child,[2] or the child whose mother goes out to work, who was a heavy viewer, but the insecure child, in particular the child who had difficulties in making friends with other children. The addict, more often than other viewers, was described by his teacher as a follower, not a leader, and as submissive, shy, and retiring (Appendix Table 71). In the addicts' answers to personality inventories and questionnaires,

---

[1] The size of the samples varied a little from one questionnaire to another—there were about 50 cases in each of the three viewing groups and about 130 cases in each of the two groups of cinema-goers.

[2] Seven per cent of the heavy viewers were only children compared with 16 per cent of the occasional viewers.

there were signs of anxiety about getting on with other children. Table 80 lists selected areas from the personality inventories, where we found differences between heavy and occasional viewers and also between heavy and occasional cinema-goers.[1]

TABLE 80. Distribution of moderate to high scores on personality inventories for matched groups of heavy and occasional viewers and matched groups of heavy and occasional cinema-goers

	Viewers		Cinema-goers	
	Heavy %	Occasional %	Heavy %	Occasional %
Moderate-to-high total scores on:				
Worries inventory	50	40	51	47
Ways to be Different inventory . .	32	24	49	47
Fears inventory	34	30	31	22
Moderate-to-high scores about:				
(a) *Feelings of rejection by other children* (including, e.g., not getting on with other children, not being popular, feeling left out of things) . .	58	39	61	48
(b) *General feelings of social insecurity* (including, e.g., my manners, feeling shy, feeling different from other children)	45	35	40	35
(c) *Anxiety about growing up* (including, e.g., the thought of marrying, the thought of having to leave school, finding a job when I am older) .	48	37	45	35
*Total cases**	39	39	103	103

* The numbers varied slightly from inventory to inventory.

The children's personal difficulties were also reflected in their behaviour; for example, when we asked children about visiting and entertaining their friends, more addicts indicated that they 'hardly ever' went to the homes of their friends or invited their friends home. In answer to the question *Are you allowed to bring friends home to watch television if you want to?* more addicts indicated 'I don't want to bring friends home to watch'. Table 81 gives the distribution of the answers for television and cinema addicts.

The heavy viewers consumed more of the mass media generally than the occasional viewers did (Appendix Table 72). They read comics more often, went more often to the cinema (41 per cent went

[1] The frequency of answers of the moderate viewers have not been included in the tables as, with a few minor exceptions, they were intermediate between those of the heavy and occasional viewer.

two or three times a week), and listened more often to the radio serial, *The Archers*, which was on the air during the gap in television transmission between 6 and 7 p.m. Comic-reading and viewing can easily be combined, as this 10 year old boy shows: 'Well, I get a comic and start reading it. My mum, she likes the talking, I think, she tells me when there is something exciting on, and I put the comic down and start looking at it.'

TABLE 81. Frequency of visiting and entertaining as indicated by heavy and occasional viewers and heavy and occasional cinema-goers*

	Viewers		Cinema-goers	
	Heavy %	Occasional %	Heavy %	Occasional %
Hardly ever visits	30	16	21	18
Hardly ever entertains friends . .	23	11	25	16
Does not want to bring friends home to watch television	12	5	—	—
Total cases	52	52	131	133

* The heavy and occasional viewers were matched with one another, so were the heavy and occasional cinema-goers.

Not all viewers have their family so well organised, nor is it only the heavy viewer who watches with a comic in his lap. The pattern for addicts is very consistent. They have a constant desire for ready-made entertainment, demanding little sustained effort.[1] Book-reading does not suit addicts, and fewer of them, compared with occasional viewers, had read a book or even part of a book during the preceding four weeks. Cinema addicts behaved in much the same way; they tended more than others to be great listeners to the radio, to read comics often, and to read relatively few books.

In Chapter 31 we have shown that both viewers and controls prefer to do things for themselves. This is not true of addicts, whether viewers or cinema-goers. Compared with other groups, they preferred to have things done for them rather than to do them themselves or explore things on their own.[2] Also, more of them—but still only a small proportion (16 per cent against 5 per cent)—said they would prefer to see things on television rather than in real life.

We think it would be wrong to attribute these differences to the effects of viewing, since they did not occur between viewers and controls. They do fit in, however, with the general behaviour pattern of the addicts and their need to withdraw from real situations.

[1] Maccoby (59) describes it as 'externally controlled fantasy experience'.
[2] The difference for viewers was significant at the 1-per-cent level; 62 per cent of the heavy viewers, but only 37 per cent of the occasional viewers, had a medium or low initiative score.

In line with this, more addicts than others watched (and would like to watch) in the dark, duplicating at home the setting of the cinema in which familiar surroundings are obscured.[1] These children have to some extent come to rely on television. Asked how much they would miss television, 71 per cent of the addicts said that they would miss it 'very much', compared with 32 per cent of the occasional viewers. When the children were asked: *Why do you feel this way?* occasional viewers as often as addicts said it was because they had 'got used to it'. This explained the reduced interest of the occasional viewer once the novelty had worn off; for the addict it meant 'It has become part of my life'.

Television programmes preferred by heavy viewers

As has been shown in Chapter 8, the addicts' tastes on the whole differed little from those of occasional viewers, except that 52 per cent compared with 36 per cent mentioned plays as their favourite television programme, while the occasional viewer preferred comedy and variety. Among plays, the addict more often chose family serials, adventure, and mystery. Their book choices reflected similar differences (Appendix Table 73).

Adventure and mystery may provide through self-identification the vicarious satisfaction of living an active and dangerous life; the family serial offers the child the means of identifying himself with a happy and united family.

The addict of both cinema and television

Twenty-two adolescents in the survey managed both to view a great deal (about three hours a day) and to go to the cinema two or three times a week. The personality ratings given to them by their teachers differed even more sharply than those of other addicts from the remainder of the viewers. Indeed, the differences were highly significant despite the small numbers involved. Within this group there was an even higher proportion of children who were described as followers, shy, submissive, and retiring. In addition more were said to lack concentration, to be indifferent to school or actively to resent it, and were rated as working below their estimated intellectual ability.

Here are some of the questionnaire responses of one such addict,[2]

---

[1] Thirty-three per cent of the addicts and 14 per cent of the occasional viewers watched in the dark, while 38 per cent and 29 per cent respectively said they would like to do so.

[2] When presented without the purpose for which they were asked, these questions appear a motley collection; it would take too long to give the reasons for them here. Nevertheless, they give an insight into the thinking and feelings of this girl, which fits well with the type of problems we have been discussing.

a grammar school girl from a working-class home, described by her teacher as nervous and highly strung, a follower rather than a leader and immature for her age. Although she had had access to television for some years, she still viewed a great deal, far more than other children of her intellectual calibre. The diary record showed that in addition to her heavy viewing she went to the cinema twice that week. The following are some of her answers given to selected questions in the survey, which bring out clearly the child's picture of her place in the world and her attitudes generally:

> The worst thing about television was that 'there are so many things that come on so late that I can't stay up and see them'. She would like to be a television star or announcer because 'I think it is a nice feeling to think that you are talking to millions of people at a time, yet you can't see them'. She would miss television very much because 'the few times we have had it repaired the house seemed quite empty without it'. She likes all plays, especially love plays, 'it fascinates me to watch them'. Her leisure interests are 'watching television, having tea, playing around in the park'. When in a good mood she draws or knits; when lonely she reads or listens to the radio or watches television; when in a bad mood 'I usually do something wrong and blame it on to someone else, then I read'. She has some friends, but hardly ever visits them or is visited by them. Her insecurity comes out in her answers to projective questions: *What sort of child makes friends easily?* She answered, 'it is best to have just one friend who is not likely to quarrel with you or go off with another girl'. Asked what sort of person she would like to be when 25 years old, she writes, 'I would like to be nice to know'. The age at which one is happiest she puts (a very unusual answer) at 70 because 'they are getting near the end of life and want to make the most of it'.

Heavy viewing for lack of something better to do

Some children (we do not know how many) view a great deal, not because they have emotional problems, but because their environment does not offer enough opportunities for activities or for making friends. In the small sample of children who were intensively interviewed by us, there were one or two who were heavy viewers because they had just moved into a new neighbourhood and had not up till then made many friends. One or two others lived under conditions where there was not enough outlet of the kind needed by energetic children. These heavy viewers, in contrast to those previously described, may well reduce their viewing as soon as their everyday life becomes fuller. Their behaviour and preferences are in fact like those of the moderate and occasional viewers, and their heavy viewing is a temporary reaction to an inadequate environment. One highly intelligent 8 year old boy whom we interviewed on several occasions was a regular and avid viewer of children's television and would gladly have looked at evening television had he been allowed to do so. He was an active, friendly child, and when a year later he moved from a flat to a house with a garden, he viewed relatively little, because, as he said: 'I have no time. I am far too busy helping the workmen and looking after the garden.'

Influence of family background

Does the child addict reflect his family's viewing habits? A number of mothers kept diaries for one week, recording what their children watched. Later they answered questions about each child's reactions to television. One or two of these families seemed to be addicted to television, but the majority were not. Viewing habits varied considerably within one family. One highly intelligent mother of four, an ex-social worker, reported that her 13 year old boy had never viewed indiscriminately, but his 10 year old brother, described as intelligent and easily scared, did view a great deal.

> He has from the start been rather addicted to viewing. . . . We avoid anything at all frightening and even something as remote as a space serial on the radio means that he must hold his father's hand and not go alone to bed.

The third in the family, a girl of 9, described as intelligent and dreamy but a great reader, was least interested in television. The youngest, a girl of 6, however, viewed a good deal, largely because she wanted to be with the rest of the family.

> At the moment she is very independent of television, with a small gang of friends with whom she plays in the garden not wanting even to come in for tea. She is on the whole less addicted to television than the 10 year old boy, but she likes to be with the others.

This mother clearly has more highly trained powers of observation and expression than most others. Even so, the wide variations she depicted were quite usual in other families.

Nevertheless, heavy and indiscriminate viewing by the parents makes it more likely that children will imitate their behaviour; it therefore serves as a predisposing factor.

Results of other research

Our results tie up well with a study by Wilkins (102) of the average adolescent. He brought together various surveys of the leisure and vocational activities of adolescents aged 15–19 and found that those who were heavy cinema-goers had more often changed their jobs since leaving school, were less often members of clubs, and more often described their schooldays as having been unhappy. They gave the impression of being rather disturbed and immature.

Wolfe and Fiske (105) in their study *Why they read comics?* showed that comics were used in qualitatively different ways by the addict and the moderate consumer; they satisfied the needs of normal children for projection and identification with heroes, but

> for the maladjusted child, the comics satisfy just as efficiently an equally intense emotional need; here the need itself is not so readily outgrown . . . the child's problems existed before he became a fan and the comics came along to relieve him.

EFFECTS OF ADDICTION

It is easier to state likely determinants than to feel sure that what are stated as effects are not in fact characteristic reactions of the kind of children who become addicts. One can only make tentative guesses. Such children may not attend youth clubs regularly or may not even belong at all because their time is taken up with viewing. However, the reason may equally well be that they do not feel happy in the company of the children there. An analysis of the diaries shows clearly that, apart from reading comics and going to the cinema, every one of the other activities was curtailed. Heavy viewers spent less time out of doors, played games less often, fewer of them belonged to clubs, especially to Scouts or Guides. The diaries showed that the addicts' leisure life was a much more restricted one, the restriction being probably both a symptom and an effect of such heavy viewing. It is a vicious circle. Emotional insecurity or inadequate facilities at home cause the child to become a heavy viewer. In this way he restricts his outside contacts and so reduces still further his opportunities to mix. With escape through television so readily available, other sources of companionship may demand too much effort and offer too little promise of success.

CONCLUSIONS

How much a child views depends mainly on how intelligent he is: more addicts are to be found among average and duller children than among brighter ones. The younger addicts come more often from working-class than from middle-class homes. But these are not the sole explanations of addiction.[1] It was found that the confirmed addict is not an only child but an insecure one, who finds relationships

---

[1] To find out what type of child tends to become an addict we made a comparative analysis of heavy and occasional viewers, matching pair by pair for the significant background variables such as social class, age, sex, and intelligence, as well as a parallel analysis of controls who were heavy and occasional cinema-goers similarly matched with one another.

with other children difficult and seeks companionship and security in television and other mass media. He also reads comics and goes to the cinema more frequently than others; he even listens more often to the radio when there is no television. He finds it difficult to concentrate and tends to read fewer books. The addict has less desire to do things for himself and is more often prepared to see things on television rather than in real life.

Our findings suggest that these differences were there before television came to the home and explain why the addict views so much more than others of his age, intelligence, and social background. The parallel analysis of cinema addicts showed them to be very similar kinds of children. Television meets a need which the child without television satisfies through the cinema or the radio.

The television addicts' tastes in television programmes were like those of his age group, except that he enjoyed plays rather more, especially family serials, adventure, and mystery—plays which permit identification with the type of active person he would like to be, or with the happy family of which he would like to be a member.

Another type of addict is the transient addict who temporarily finds himself in an environment which provides him with insufficient outlets. His attitude to television and his preferences for different types of programmes resemble those of the occasional viewer rather than those of the confirmed addict.

This means that the child who, for his age, intelligence, and social class, watches television a great deal is either temporarily restricted by his environment or is faced with personal problems which he cannot solve.

The effects of prolonged viewing are difficult to establish. The way addicts spend their free time is much more restricted than that of other children, which is probably both a cause and an effect of heavy viewing.

Wolfe and Fiske (105), in their summing up of why children read comics, state:

> That he becomes a fan can no more be blamed upon the comics than morphine can itself be blamed when a person becomes a drug addict. The drug addict, of course, might have found a better solution for his problems if there were no morphine available.

The same is more or less true of the television addict. He turns to viewing because of the kind of person he is, and viewing in turn reduces his feeling of isolation and insecurity by giving him imaginary companionship and satisfying his need for vicarious excitement.

This analysis has also shown that confirmed addicts of any medium tend to be much the same kind of children. They are often less intelligent than others (in the case of the younger children from working-class homes) and may be withdrawn and insecure, seeking escape from an unsatisfactory reality situation.

Heavy viewing thus expresses a need: it may be temporary and regulate itself, or it may be more lasting. The solution of the problem is not primarily to restrict the children's viewing, but to attack the various underlying causes.

A reduction in the amount a child addict views is likely to be a sign that his personal relations have improved: an increase may well reflect tension and anxiety. Viewing, it would appear, might well serve as a barometer to indicate the extent to which the child's life is satisfactory, provided it is considered in relation to the child's age, intellectual calibre, and background.

PART IX

Future Research

36

Implications for Social and Child Psychology

UNTIL now we have stuck close to our brief, evaluating the findings almost exclusively in terms of the light they throw on the effects of television. In this final chapter, addressed this time to the psychologist rather more than to the general reader, we shall look at the study in a broader context and discuss the implications of the methods used and results obtained for social and child psychology.

This chapter should be read alongside Chapter 3, where, in non-technical language, we have listed the psychological principles and generalisations derived from our findings. It is not our intention to repeat these here, but instead to point to their broader implications and to the questions for future research that they raise. Some of the questions for future research derive from the findings themselves, others concern problems which, for lack of time and resources, we have not studied.

The pattern of children's leisure

From this study, much can be learnt about children's needs and priorities, and about the role of various leisure activities in their lives. The introduction of television into children's homes offers, in a natural field setting, something akin to an experimental conflict or choice situation.

Television takes too much time not to require some adjustment of the child's former leisure-time pattern. Room is made for viewing, not by a proportionate reduction of all activities, but by selective reduction, some being drastically reduced, others hardly at all. In Chapter 3 (pp. 35–36) the manner in which the choice is made has been outlined.[1] It is not a haphazard one, but the result of an inter-play of three factors: the relative significance of the activity to the child; its functional similarity to viewing; and the extent to which it is structured or unstructured.

The more important the activity to the child, the more it relates to needs other than those satisfied by viewing, and the more struc-tured or clearly defined it is, the less likely is the activity to be affected. While the way in which the interplay of these factors expresses itself varies to some extent from child to child, certain common patterns emerge which tell us a good deal about children's priorities.

The central role of active outdoor play and of social activities in the children's lives is high-lighted. In addition (and this was not readily foreseen and is important, from the standpoint of child psychology), children reach satiation-point in their desire for and consumption of ready-made entertainment, almost irrespective of the content of the entertainment. They will sit and watch or listen for a given time and no more.

On the basis of our findings, we predict that if a new form of entertainment were invented, for instance, capable of satisfying three rather than two sensory organs, it would be accommodated by cutting down on viewing, rather than by cutting down on outdoor play or other self-expressive activities. Radio, we have seen, has been virtually ousted from the children's lives because it is per-ceived as functionally equivalent but inferior to television.

Of special importance here is the distinction that needs to be drawn between objective and functional similarity. The 10–11 year olds go to the cinema for entertainment; similar entertainment is provided by television, but at less effort and expense; consequently for them viewing is functionally equivalent to but better than going to the cinema, and such visits are consequently reduced. The older children use the cinema also as a means of meeting friends away from home; this need, which to these children is an important one, tele-vision cannot satisfy. Consequently, adolescents cut down on other activities to make room for viewing, but not on cinema visits.

Comparative study of the choices made by children of different ages, or of the same age but different intelligence, provides useful information about the relative strength of their needs. In the case of adolescents compared with 10–11 year olds, the need for a social life outside the home is very strong; in the case of the dull child compared

---

[1] The child is seldom aware of making such a choice.

with the brighter one, his need for easy, ready-made entertainment was brought out.

A comparative study of children's and adult choices would be of interest; we suspect that adults give greater priority to spectator entertainment and have a correspondingly smaller need for activities which they initiate themselves. For such a comparative study to be of value, two conditions have to be met: first, the examination should be based on changes in actual behaviour and not only on verbal expressions of interest, and secondly, such a study should go beyond the consideration of structured and organised activities.

Analyses of this kind, whether carried out on adults or on children, are of theoretical interest; they are also of practical value in that they show how changes in the consumption of television or of any other mass medium can best be brought about. Our results suggest that changing the content of television entertainment would make little difference; more effective would be changes in the environmental facilities for creative and outdoor activities.

The functional equivalence, or superiority, we have seen, lies in the eye of the beholder. At first, something like a halo effect seems to operate, whereby the new variable (in this case television) is perceived as functionally superior to a number of activities which in fact are capable of satisfying other needs as well. For this, the comparative analysis of recent, experienced, and veteran viewers proved informative. An example of this was the change over time that occurred in the case of book-reading; at first it was much reduced, but after some time viewers stepped up their reading again so that in the long run they read as much as controls (p. 36). How long the halo effect lasts depends on the child's intelligence and on his attachment to television (Chapters 28, 29).

Social background

Contrary to expectation, middle- and working-class children viewed for much the same amount of time. How much a child views, we have seen, is a function of his intelligence, personality, and home life, but not a function of the social level of his parents. This poses an interesting problem, especially since there were also no social class differences for radio listening among the controls.

That matching for intelligence does not iron out social-class differences was shown clearly by the marked variation that we observed with regard to visits to the cinema, the reading of comics, &c.

It is tempting here to speculate about the way social class operates in child-rearing. We suggest that its influence is marked where the activity is not freely available, so that access to it requires specific parental action. This is the case with cinema visits, and to a lesser extent with the purchase of comics, as well as with bedtimes— children rarely go to bed of their own accord, at least until they reach adolescence. Television and radio, on the other hand, are freely available, and as yet no conventions have grown up about the correct amount of viewing. No status question is therefore involved, and any excess can be blamed on the appeal of television rather than on laxity of upbringing. Under these conditions, where in addition the activity is enjoyed by the parents as well as by the children, social-class differences are less likely to develop. If this hypothesis is correct, then further research should show that activities for which some action on the part of the parents is needed will be linked with social class, while those where parents are not called upon to inter- vene will be determined by intelligence, personality, and home background, but will not vary with the social level of the home.

Personality factors

The way an individual's needs and general adjustment affect his perceptions has been the subject of numerous investigations, as has also the way in which different individuals perceive the same com- munication (83). Our study takes the problem one step further by showing that, once intelligence and age are excluded, the personality and needs of the child determine how much he views, what impact programmes make on him, and which programmes he likes or dis- likes.

The study of the television addict is described in the preceding chapter; here reference will be made to the methodological problems that were involved. First, there was the problem of ensuring that any differences found between occasional and heavy viewers were not due to differences in intelligence, age, or social class; this could be overcome through individual matching. The second problem proved more difficult, namely, how to determine which of the differences found were the result and which the cause of viewing so much. An attempt at a differential diagnosis was made by carrying out a parallel analysis of heavy and occasional cinema-goers, similarly matched with one another. Should the addicts of the two media prove to be similar in outlook and personality, even though the two media differed in the time they took up and in the fare they offered, then it would be likely that these similarities pointed to the cause rather than the effect of viewing. This was found to be the case. By means of this comparative analysis, a consistent picture was de- veloped of an insecure type of child who sought refuge in the unde- manding world of make-believe.

While this is a useful beginning, much more needs to be done, this time taking groups clearly differentiated in terms of their personality make-up, in seeing how they react to television, what appeal television has for them, and what is the long-term effect of the vicious circle set up, in which the addicts' initial personality difficulties prompt their heavy viewing, which in turn reduces even further their contact with other people, etc.

Longitudinal studies of children undergoing treatment would show how far changes in programme preferences and reaction to television personalities anticipate or reflect changes (brought about by treatment) in the child's reaction to his immediate environment.

Apart from the study of differences in reactions to television of well- and poorly-adjusted children, there remains the broader question of the link between personality, programme preferences, and programme impact.

Our research has thrown some light on the way in which the emotional needs of children determine their reactions; but here in particular we are much in need of fundamental research into the development of needs in normal children such as, for instance, the desire for reassurance, excitement, mastery of their own impulses, aggression, and dependence. Too little is known about the prevalence and strength of these needs in children of different ages, social and intellectual maturity. Only when such knowledge is available can real strides be made in understanding the extent to which needs determine taste.

In this area there is need for more adequate, properly validated measures of children's adjustment and personality characteristics. The three inventories which we included in the survey proved no more than a useful beginning.

The role of intelligence

While there is much information about the way intelligence relates to school performance and to such pastimes as reading, there has been little research into the manner in which differences in intelligence are reflected in the total picture of children's leisure lives —in their tastes, interests, and attitudes, as well as in their consumption of mass-media. In this study a comparative analysis was made between three groups of children, matched for age, sex, and social class: children with I.Q.s of 115 and above, 100 to 114, and below 100. Except for sport, marked differences were found for almost every activity, interest, and attitude studied. In most cases there was a regular progression through the three intelligence groups; for example, the more intelligent the child was, the more books he would read; the less intelligent, the more often he would go to the cinema or the more time he would spend watching television.[1]

To us the pervasive influence of intelligence was unexpected, the more so since it cannot be explained in terms of different school curricula or school ethos. In educational circles it is often held that differences emerge clearly once children enter the different types of secondary schools. Our research permitted examination of this view (which was not found to be substantiated) by comparing the differences that existed among the bright, average, and dull 10–11 year olds, all of whom attended the same type of primary school, with those found among the three groups of 13–14 year olds. Among the latter, the more highly intelligent children had been at grammar schools for two or three years, where they had been receiving a different type of education from the remainder. In spite of this, the differences in the older group were no more clear cut than those obtained among the younger children, even with regard to such educationally determined attitudes as preferred school leaving age and vocational aspirations (Chapters 19 and 20).

It would appear, therefore, that much of what we attribute to grammar school education is in fact a reflection of the child's intellectual ability rather than of his educational experience.

Differences in ways of behaving and in outlook reflect differences in I.Q. (i.e. in the relation of chronological to mental age). Yet when it comes to assessing children's understanding of the content of television programmes and the impact these make, we have found it more useful to think of these in terms of *mental age* rather than intelligence. We found, for example, that the intelligent 13–14 year olds with a mental age of about 16 were little stimulated by television and hardly at all affected by the views and values it offers. This was also the case with the 10–11 year olds with a mental age of 10 and below. The former were less affected probably because they were the least attached to TV, and also because they had many other sources of information on which to draw; the latter because much of television content was beyond their intellectual grasp. The most responsive groups were those with a mental age of about 12–13, i.e. the bright 10–11 year olds and the 13–14 year olds of average and below average intelligence.

In discussing television's impact on children, it would be misleading to generalise about the bright and the dull children, and better to speak instead of the effects in different spheres. As far as general knowledge was concerned, we found, for instance, that

---

[1] The differences, however, between children of I.Q.s of 115 and over and those of I.Q.s of 100–114 tended to be more marked than those between the latter group and children of below-average intelligence.

only the children with mental ages of 10 and below benefited; the information offered was probably already known to children of greater intellectual maturity, or could more readily be obtained elsewhere. The optimal mental age of responsiveness will, therefore, vary with the topic to be examined. A systematic charting of the effects of a wider range of views and values put over on television would be of great interest here, particularly if extended to other age groups.

Programme comprehension

In this connexion, one aspect in particular needs further inquiry: the manner in which intellectual and social maturity affect the children's ability to comprehend programmes. We know that lack of understanding is not necessarily accompanied by lack of enjoyment, that younger children respond to action rather than to the motives that underly the action, and to isolated incidents rather than to broader themes. More research is needed into the way in which such differences in perception and comprehension affect the meaning of the programmes for the child and his emotional reactions to them.

In considering a dramatic programme we can distinguish between content, and method of presentation. We suggest that reactions to different methods of presentation (especially in the case of programme series) may be linked to the child's intelligence, whereas his reactions to the subject-matter of the play depend more on his social or emotional maturity. We found, for instance, that intelligence as well as age determined children's enjoyment of programmes with such stereotyped predictable pattern as Westerns, but that their reactions (of distaste or of enjoyment) to romantic themes were almost entirely a matter of social maturity. To test this hypothesis further, one would wish to make more detailed studies of children's likes and dislikes and of the reasons underlying them.

Of special interest in this connexion would be a study of children's reactions to programmes which they can understand intellectually, but for which they have as yet little emotional empathy. For example, intellectually the 13–14 year old understands references to divorce and unfaithfulness, and so may correctly recall the story of the plays in which these feature. Yet if he lacks the emotional appreciation of the significance of such events for the characters in the play, he may be unable to identify himself with the characters. Here, as in the field of knowledge and values discussed earlier, there is probably a particular age, this time of maximum *social or emotional* responsiveness, when the child will react strongly to the emotional overtones of a programme which at an earlier age would have escaped him.

Cumulative effects of communication

One of the most difficult methodological problems in this study proved to be the evaluation of the cumulative effect of television on children's outlook and values. Most studies in the field of communication have been concerned with captive audiences (where the subjects were instructed or motivated to be attentive), and with the effects of single or twofold exposure to communications designed to convert. But since television aims to entertain, its effect is likely to be more indirect and less pronounced. We have been able to show the existence of a cumulative impact (Chapters 18–21), and also to delineate the type of conditions under which this is likely to make itself felt (Chapter 3, pp. 37, 38). In general, the factors found to be important in determining how individuals will respond to single propagandistic communications are equally relevant here. For the values we examined, we have been able to indicate the emotional and intellectual age at which children seemed to be most responsive to their influence. We have been particularly struck by the extent to which the children become aware of certain background cues only when their own interest in this type of information has been aroused in their daily lives.

We should like to see this work systematically extended, each time linking objective studies of the content of programmes with investigation of their effects. Both the effects of individual programmes and the cumulative effects of programmes over time need further investigation; in particular, there is need for a systematic evaluation of different methods of presentation and the impact that these make—for example, whether values conveyed in plays which feature children of about the same age as the viewer, make more of an impact than those in plays where there is no such ready object for identification. Such a study might well show that identification depends on perceived similarity of personality or needs, rather than on objective similarity in terms of age and sex. Projective tests like the T.A.T. or the Blacky-test are based on certain assumptions about the conditions which facilitate projection. Studies of the kind just outlined might throw light on their validity, which, so far as we know, has not been investigated.

How far is the model value and impact of characters dependent on the place and setting in which they occur; are these lessened, for example, by occurring in a historical setting or in an unfamiliar country? How far does television build up stereotypes about persons of different walks of life and about different nationalities? (In Chapter 20 we have shown that television can also help to reduce existing stereotypes.)

In studies of this type, special attention has to be paid to Hovland's sleeper effect (46) and also to the role that the child's immediate environment (his friends, family, and teachers) play in reinforcing or decreasing the impact of the views offered by television.

Television personalities

We know as yet too little about the importance and meaning to children of the different personalities who appear on television. What we do know is that no one individual, and no one type of personality, was named as the favourite by more than a small minority of children. The diversity of tastes among children seems, if anything, to be more marked than among adults; what is it, then, that the children look for? Is it that they all tend to value much the same characteristics, but invest different individuals with them? Or is it that different characteristics are valued by different children? We should like to see a study of the types of characteristics and forms of behaviour which children enjoy or admire, and of the link, compensatory or otherwise, which exists between these and their own behaviour and personal needs. For instance, our detailed study of children's identification with the characters in the Grove family suggests that children often enjoy those characters who infringe the social and moral conventions by which the children themselves are bound, provided that the infringement is a mild one and all ends well.

How far do television personalities become invested with a kind of *psychological reality* regardless of their role on television, so that the child considers them on a par with people with whom he mixes every day: his family, teachers, friends, and neighbours; to what extent could this add to, or detract from, their model value for the child? Is Eamonn Andrews, for instance, a fairy-tale figure or a substitute uncle, and in which role would he carry most influence? Equally, how far do the behaviour and attitudes of the characters in the family serials provide standards against which the child evaluates his own family or the family next door?

One other important issue in need of further study is the role of child actors, and the degree to which they, too, serve as models. We have some evidence that children readily identify themselves with actors of approximately their own age, but know little of the factors facilitating such identification, or of the degree to which such identification leads the children to model themselves on these child characters.

Violence and fear

We have been able to develop principles (Chapter 3, pp. 38–39) which throw some light on the fear- or anxiety-potential of different types of programme. For instance, the less stylised, the more personal and realistic the portrayal of violence, and the more play is made of the emotions of aggressors, victims, and spectators, the more disturbing the programme. It is not the amount of injury caused which determines the emotional impact, but rather the manner of its presentation.

Our research has shown the need for grading programmes in terms of the empathy they arouse. Ridicule and anger, for example, with which children can readily identify, disturb more when shown in real-life situations—in quizzes or newsreels—than in fictional programmes; other types of aggressive situations, on the other hand, may prove more disturbing when presented in a fictional or highly dramatic setting than when presented on the newsreel as a real event. We have made a beginning here in the search for criteria or dimensions, but more needs to be done.

We have similarly attempted to see whether the viewers could be graded in terms of their emotional susceptibility to the impact of programmes. As might be expected, we have found the insecure children to be more susceptible, and girls more than boys. What was unexpected, however, was that older and more intelligent children were as often disturbed as younger or less intelligent ones, although by different types of situation.

Learning from television

Our task lay primarily in determining how much children gain or lose in knowledge through spending time viewing. Essentially, this amounted to balancing the information gained through viewing with the loss of information that comes from not using the time in other ways (Chapters 22–26).

We have not, however, examined systematically the way in which the children absorb information from television, and the conditions under which such learning is facilitated. What, for example, is the relation of interest to learning: do children pick up more information from programmes they enjoy or from those about which they feel indifferent? What role does dramatic presentation play? How far is learning made easier if the information is conveyed by a favourite personality? Is incidental learning or motivated learning more effective and more lasting? An almost endless list of useful topics could be compiled.

However, above all we need more fundamental research into the way in which a child's general knowledge is built up; does it depend on a gradual accumulation of facts, or does knowledge advance in dramatic leaps and bounds? Coleridge, for instance, in his *Biographia Literaria*, makes a distinction between those who aim to convey isolated facts and those who seek to discover 'connections or those relative bearings of fact to fact, from which some more or less general law is deducible'. Is this distinction a valid one, or is not a store of facts a prerequisite for the development of general laws and principles? A lot is written about the piecemeal snippet-like way in which knowledge is conveyed on television, rather as if in this it differed substantially from the way in which children pick up information elsewhere. It may well be that, school instruction apart, one's general knowledge is built up in precisely this piecemeal fashion. Many value judgements and opinions are made about desirable and undesirable ways in which general knowledge and understanding should be built up, but there are surprisingly few objective studies of what actually occurs.

OTHER AREAS FOR RESEARCH

Studies of the effects of television on the young child

Even though the two age groups we studied were separated by only two to three years, many differences in their attitudes to viewing and in their reactions to programmes were found. We should like to see more studies of other age groups, especially of young children. The mothers' observations on the under-sevens, which we collected, suggest that young children learn much from television, and are also especially responsive to the leads offered by children's programmes. It would be interesting to see whether with this age group the programmes specifically designed for them make less impact than those aimed at older children; this would be in line with our findings for the two older age groups, with whom adult programmes were more popular than children's programmes.

Here, in particular, one would welcome longitudinal developmental studies.

Trend studies

Our survey was limited to two years of television—itself a new

and rapidly developing medium. A number of trend analyses suggest
themselves:

1. Periodic content analyses of the type described in Chapters 13,
   14 and 17, with special reference to changes in the values and
   views television puts over.
2. Studies of changes in perception and impact that occur when
   the child becomes familiar with the format of a programme.
   We have shown, for instance, that the impact of Westerns
   decreases as the children become familiar with their pattern; it
   would similarly be of interest to see how far this applies to the
   values put over in family serials, or to the extent to which
   children identify themselves with the characters in these. How
   does it affect the model value of television personalities?
3. At the time of our survey, television had been operating for
   less than a decade, and few of the children in our sample had
   been viewing for as long as five years; even so, considerable
   differences were found between the recent and the veteran
   viewers (of three or more years standing). A new generation is
   now growing up who will never have known a home without
   television; it is possible that they will take television more in
   their stride and may be less affected by it than children who
   first met it as something new and coveted. On the other hand,
   such children will grow up in a society in which television and
   the conveying of information through television will have
   become thoroughly accepted and respectable, and to that
   degree possibly more influential. Differences of this kind are
   likely to be largely matters of degree, yet none the less important.
4. An important trend study would be one which charted the
   extent to which television forces other media into more distinctive roles; in the United States, for instance, this has
   occurred with regard to radio listening and book- and magazine-reading (19).

Flicker fusion

We have shown in Chapter 33 that viewers are no more likely to
suffer from eyestrain or visual discomfort than non-viewers. Discomfort of this kind can be produced by many sources: among the
controls, by reading in bed under conditions of poor illumination;
among the viewers, by glare, by viewing from floor level, by prolonged fixation of one small area, &c. While there is no reason to
believe that television causes eyestrain in the average child, the
effects of various viewing conditions on visual discomfort are not as

yet sufficiently well understood. Apart from the effects of glare, posture, and fixation (to which adults are equally susceptible), it would be of considerable interest to investigate children's sensitivity to flicker.

The rate of interruption of the light beam in a modern film projector is too high to be detected by the human eye (usually around 96 times per second), while that of television in this country is very close to the rate at which it can be detected (some 50 cycles per second). We know that sensitivity to flicker decreases with age so that, what appears as a fused image to the adult, may appear as a flickering image to the child. As far as we know there have been no investigations of flicker-fusion frequencies of children below the age of 14. It may well be that individual cases of discomfort which have been reported (once other conditions have been ruled out) are caused by children watching flickering images. Three aspects need study: are children as a group more sensitive to flicker than adults; how great is the variation in sensitivity within a given age group, and how far do some television sets (due to the condition of the phosphorescent screen) produce sensations of flicker more readily than others? The problem is an important one but difficult to investigate since variations in flicker rate in transmitting a moving image would have to be produced while holding other physiological and psychological factors constant. Moreover, one cannot readily draw conclusions from laboratory experiments to the normal home-viewing situation.

Studies of isolated communities

Isolation may well itself result in different reactions, although again it is not easy to foresee the direction such differences would take. Country children, for instance, may be more dependent on television if they are relatively isolated from other sources of ready-made entertainment. Alternatively, they may be more adept at finding their own amusements, and so rely less on mass-entertainment. The teachers from rural districts have commented on the way in which television has helped to break down parochial attitudes and has broadened the children's horizons; it is, however, also possible that children in closely-knit communities may prove resistant to information about people and situations too remote from their way of life.

It would be particularly interesting to undertake a study not only of the children's gain in factual information, but also of the changes in outlook and values that take place when through television they are made familiar with aspects of society of which they have had no previous experience. Do they, for example, reinterpret the 'message' so as to fit in with their existing ideas, or do their basic frames of reference change through contact with television? We have seen that adult drama, a strong source of value information, portrays in the main an urban, middle-class way of life; it is interesting to speculate on the degree to which this will affect the children's ambitions—for instance, will it lead to a greater exodus to the town? Also of interest would be a comparative study of the programme likes and dislikes of urban and rural children. Studies of the manner in which children from isolated communities (for example, from the Highlands of Scotland) react to television, and of the long-term changes which television produces in their individual and community lives, would provide a valuable complement to the present inquiry.

A study of the life-history of programmes

Finally, we would like to support the plea made by Lazarsfeld (53) for research into the life-history of programmes: how they are commissioned, how they are written, and why they are finally put on the air. What, for example, decides programme planners to put on a programme about underwater fauna, how far do chance encounters enter into it, and how far are the interests of the individual producer decisive? In particular, to what extent do programmes reflect problems which are 'in the air'? (The sudden popularity of mental-health programmes is a case in point.) Our study has shown that the notion of producers as slaves of public taste is an imaginary one; producers are in large measure the creators of taste and outlook. It is important, therefore, to study how far programmes are produced which are in advance of the prevalent values of the community, or how far they lag behind.

*   *   *

Communication research of the kind we envisage requires systematic programming, not on a piecemeal, but on a long-term basis, permitting inquiry into some of the fundamental as well as the applied questions we have raised. The research described here should be seen as a first step towards an integrated long-term inquiry into the impact of different mass-media on the community, and into the nature of the communication process itself.

Appendixes

APPENDIX A

Points of Method

Design of Individual Questions

THE children were presented with a number of booklets, each containing a variety of techniques. In the main we made use of two types of questions: 'open-ended' questions, which extracted a free reply from the child, and 'closed' questions, which required the child to select answers from a number of choices prepared by us. We made liberal use of open-ended questions and also of the sentence completion technique (even though the elaborate coding proved costly) whenever we wished the child to draw on his own frame of reference. Here are some examples of the vividness of the children's replies. Question: *Write down the two most important ways in which you think television has really changed things at home*:

> 'Keeps my Mum and Dad in on Saturday night.'
> 'Stops me from quarrelling with my sister.'
> 'You can see things without paying.'

We also used open-ended questions whenever prestige issues were involved; with a ready-made list of alternatives there is always the danger that the child may select what he imagines is the correct answer, rather than give the answer which is true for himself.

Some previous researches failed, in our opinion, because of their conscious emphasis on television. Open-ended questions were therefore often used to see whether the child, without being reminded of television, would spontaneously refer to it; the degree to which he stressed it could then be compared with other activities and interests. For example, we asked three open-ended questions, *What sort of things do you do when you are in a good mood? . . . when you are in a bad mood?* and. . . *when you are feeling lonely?* One boy wrote:

> 'When I am in a good mood I usually help mother get the messages in', when in a bad mood 'kick things around', when lonely, 'read comics or books'. A girl wrote: 'in a good mood I play tennis and help Mummy', in a bad mood 'sulk and go to bed to read a book', when lonely 'turn on the wireless and read'.

Closed questions, offering a choice of alternative answers, were used to obtain measures of frequency (*When did you last go to the pictures? Yesterday; Two days ago; In the last seven days; Two weeks ago; More than two weeks ago;*

I never go), and to ensure that the child had considered all the possibilities in giving his answer. For example, some time after the open-ended question about the changes caused by television, we presented the child with a list headed: *Here are some things that have been said about children and TV. Tick 'true' or 'not true' for each thing.* This list contained a whole range of changes and so forced the child to consider each in turn. The open-ended questions always preceded by a number of pages a closed question dealing with the same issues.

All questions and techniques needed extensive pilot surveys, particularly since the same wording had to be equally appropriate for dull 10 year olds and for relatively sophisticated teen-agers. During this pilot stage of the inquiry some techniques went through as many as eight revisions; in all, 805 children were tested and a considerable number interviewed.

Devices used to facilitate quick answers

Several devices were used to increase the speed of children's answers. Children are often drilled at school to repeat the question in the beginning of their answer. This we did for them in our questionnaires, providing the beginning of the answer—such as:

What sort of things do you do when you are in a good mood?
'When I am in a good mood, I usually . . .'

The general appearance and layout of the questionnaires was important. Everything possible was done to preserve uniformity of layout and instructions. Codes for use in later analysis were kept as unobtrusive as possible. The children were provided with widely spaced lines on which to write, and every effort was made to give an attractive appearance to the questionnaires—by using different colours, and by using a photo-offsetting process rather than stencilling.

Information tests

These are described in Chapter 22.

INVENTORIES

Interest inventories

An inventory of sixty-nine interests was designed in which the child was asked to answer first *How often do you do it?* (Often, sometimes, hardly ever); and second *How much do you like it?* (I like it very much, a little, I do not care for it). This inventory gave a measure of the child's activity in various fields, as well as of his interests. By having both measures, we could see whether television had affected participation and interest in the same way or differently. Since we were ultimately interested in *types* of activity rather than in specific instances, often affected by chance factors, we worked out area scores, grouping individual activities, for interests and for active participation, as well as for the differences between these two measures.

The area scores were computed by adding the scores for the sets of individual inventory items (using a three-point scale for each item), and then computing a mean. It would be well worth while to carry out a factor analysis of these items and to assess whether the factor composition varies with the age, sex, and intelligence of the children.

In addition to the resulting interest and activity area scores, a set of difference scores was computed for each sub-group in the sample, providing by subtraction a measure of the difference between the interest and activity scores. A positive difference score denoted greater interest than activity, a negative score the reverse.

Personality inventories

Three personality inventories were included. One questioned children about their fears, another about their worries, and the third about ways in which they would like to be different. The first of these was specially designed for the inquiry, but the latter two had been used by us in slightly modified form in a previous study.

The inventories served two purposes: first, to provide some information about the emotional stability of each child, which could be drawn on in explaining individual differences in effects; it was important to determine whether perhaps those who said they had been frightened by something seen on television were in fact the more anxious children, in which case fear of certain programmes would be no more than a reflection of general fearfulness. Second, the personality inventories were used to compare viewers and controls for overall adjustment, differences in anxiety or in adjustment to specific life demands, such as school, parents, or growing up.

In constructing these inventories, we tried to cover the main areas in which a child's anxiety might find expression, listing a number of examples for each. For the 'worries' and 'ways to be different' we computed area scores, grouping each of the listed items into broader areas.

The inventory of *worries* included nine areas dealing with various aspects of a child's life. These were:

> Concern about school.
> Concern about school performance.
> Feelings of guilt.
> General feelings of social insecurity.
> Feelings of rejection by other children.
> Anxieties about parent's attitude to the child.
> Anxiety about growing up.
> Anxiety about material aspects of home life.
> Anxiety about material and social factors in the home.

The children were asked to indicate the degree of worry as presented in the following excerpt from the inventory, showing the first seven items:

> Almost everyone at one time or another is worried about some things. Different people are worried about different things. Read through the list and for each thing tick to show whether it worries you a lot, a little, or does not worry you.

Tick what is right for you

	Worries me a lot	Worries me a little	*Hardly ever* worries me
1. Not doing as well at school as I should like			
2. Not having as nice looking a home as I would like			
3. My looks			
4. Not being sure how to behave in company			
5. Starting a thing and then not finishing it			
6. Not getting along well with other children			
7. My father not loving me as much as I would like			

The inventory dealing with *ways to be different* similarly contained nine categories which were:

Desire for improved ability.
Desire for improved parental attitude to child.
Desire to grow up and be independent.
Lack of desire to grow up.
Desire for better social relations with other children.
Desire for improved material conditions.
Desire for improved character.
Desire for better social relations with adults.
Dissatisfactions possibly attributable to television.

The first seven items are given below:

Supposing that your wishes could come true, which of these things do *you secretly wish for yourself*? Tick what is *right for you*.

I wish:	I *often* wish this	I *sometimes* wish this	I *hardly ever* wish this
1. I were younger			
2. I were better at doing things with my hands			
3. Got along better with my mother and father			
4. Other children would like me more .			
5. My family had more money . .			
6. I were not always so tired in the morning			
7. I wish I could choose my own clothes			

The *fears* inventory was developed by asking a large number of children in the pilot inquiry to list three things that had frightened them. To the resulting list we added questions about the four media:

> some plays on television
> some plays on the wireless
> some films
> some stories I have read
> things I have read in the newspaper.

This provided one means of checking whether any one medium was particularly liable to arouse fear. Below are the first seven items:

Grown ups and children all have things which frighten them. Different people are afraid of different things. Read this list and put a tick to the answer which is *right for you*.

Tick what is right for you

	Frightens me *a lot*	Frightens me *a little*	Does *not* frighten me
1. Falling ill			
2. The dark			
3. Going to the dentist . . .			
4. Acting or reciting in front of others .			
5. Some plays on TV			
6. Bees or wasps			
7. People following me . . .			

We have as yet no evidence that these inventories are good measures of adjustment—all we can do at present is to take them at their face value, and to suggest that those who obtain a higher score for anxiety, 'ways to be different' or fears are more likely to be unhappy and tense.[1]

Teachers' assessments of the children's personality and behaviour

The procedure was as follows: each child's code number was placed on top of a page and the teacher supplied with the following schedule:

Rating schedule for teachers.

Here is a list of characteristics. Would you please put a tick against each characteristic which you think applies to the given child.

Wears glasses
Complains of eyestrain

Frequently absent
Rarely absent

[1] We should like to do more research on these inventories, and in particular to determine their significance as neurotic indicators by giving them to children attending child-guidance clinics.

Concentrates adequately
Lacks concentration

Popular, many friends
Some friends
Isolated, few friends

A leader rather than follower
Primarily a follower

Aggressive type of child
Submissive type of child

Unusually imaginative
Moderately imaginative
Unimaginative

Has ability to act/put on plays

Generally likes school
Indifferent to school
Generally resents school

Shows good deal of initiative
Shows some initiative
Lacks initiative

Cheerful and carefree
Moody
Nervous and highly strung

Always seeks the limelight
Shy and retiring

Apes adult ways, e.g. dress and behaviour
Immature for his/her age

Working *above* estimated intellectual ability
Working *up to* estimated intellectual ability
Working *below* estimated intellectual ability

Do you consider that the child's schoolwork or behaviour is affected by some physical disability, illness, or stress? Please state what the nature of the problem is, whether it is physical or emotional disability, illness, or stress, and mention any helpful treatment he or she may be receiving.

Do you consider the child's schoolwork or behaviour is influenced in any way by out-of-school conditions? If so, please give some details below.

THE DIARIES

Introductory letter read to the children before they started the first day's diary

Here at the University of London we are trying to learn as much as we can about what boys and girls think and feel and do. We are especially interested in how young people spend their time when they are not in school. Many people of all ages keep diaries in which they write down the things they do each day. We are now asking boys and girls all over the country to do this for us, and every day to write down at school what they did the day before between coming out of school and bedtime.

We want to know about *all the things* you do, however small they seem to you—we even want to know when you have been doing nothing much at all. Some things (like having tea) you may do every day and at the same time, but you should still write them down each time. Other things will be different on different days. If you have done more than one thing at the same time, write them *both* down. We also want to know who you did things with, or whether you did them by yourself.

You may spend some of your time playing, or going out to clubs. If so, we would like to know *what you played at*, or where you went. In the same way, if you have listened to the wireless, watched TV, gone to the pictures, or read a book, always try to write down each time the *name* of the wireless or TV programme, or what it was about, the *name* of the film you have seen, or the *name* of the book, comic, or paper that you read. All these things are important to us, if we are to find out all we would like to know.

There is no need to worry about your spelling—just write the word as you think it is spelt. If you have written something in the wrong space, just cross it out.

Your teacher will give you a private code number of your own. Put this on your diary sheet every day instead of your name, so that no one will know that it belongs to you. Each day your teacher will put your diary straight into an envelope with all the others, and seal them up for us to collect later.

Thank you very much for filling in the diary as carefully as you can.

THIS IS A VERY LONG LETTER, SO WE WOULD JUST LIKE
TO GO OVER THE MOST IMPORTANT POINTS ONCE MORE

1. Write down all the things you have done, however small they may seem to you.
2. Every time you listened to the wireless, or watched TV, always try to write down the *name* of the programme you heard or saw, or what it was about.
3. Every time you went to the pictures, always try to write down the *names* of the films you saw.
4. If you have been reading, always try to write down the *name* of the book, paper, or comic that you read.
5. If you spent some time playing, or if you have been to a club, write down what you were playing, or where you went.
6. For everything you did, say whether you did it by yourself, or with someone else; if you did it with someone else, say who this was.

The coding of the diaries

A standard format was used for each of the seven diary days, although for Saturday and Sunday allowance had to be made for the morning and afternoon of the day as well.

In order to extract from the diaries just what was wanted, a form of analysis was used which would give:

1. The amount of time spent on each type of activity—reading (separately for comics, books, newspapers), cinema visits, active participation in sports, unorganised outdoor play, 'aimless wandering', spectator sports, walking and cycling and so on, gardening and other outdoor home jobs, visiting relatives, being visited by relatives, visiting peers, being visited by peers, doing indoor jobs, doing indoor hobbies, and of course viewing (separately for evening and children's television) and listening to the radio.
2. The activities carried out immediately before going to bed—on each of the seven days.
3. Mean bedtimes, separately for week-days and for days not followed by school the next morning.
4. Number of times homework was interrupted for viewing.
5. Mealtimes on Saturday, Sunday, and mean mealtimes for week-days.
6. Mentions of museum attendance, extra lessons, club visits, &c., throughout the week.

7. Whether the child's viewing was usually with his family, with friends, or alone. The same for listening to the radio and visiting the cinema.

8. Total amount of time spent out of doors in the course of the week.

9. The number of times television, radio, the cinema, or reading were each mentioned during the week as the child's most enjoyed activity (separately), the second most enjoyed activity, and (separately again) the third most enjoyed activity.

10. The total number of times during the week that television, radio, the cinema, or reading were each mentioned as the child's most enjoyed activity, whether first, second, or third.

THE PROCESS OF INDIVIDUAL MATCHING

This took the form of a number of separate stages which can be compared with using a number of selection sieves of varying sizes.

Briefly, it involved the selection of pairs of children, matched for age, sex, I.Q., and social class, one of whom had had a television set at home for at least three months (the viewer) while the other had no television set at home and viewed television less than once a fortnight (the control case).

We aimed at 40 pairs for each of the 24 cells of the design, i.e. a total of 1,920 cases or of 960 matched pairs. It was thought at the start that such rigorous matching would entail considerable wastage since the majority of children were guest viewers and so did not qualify either as viewers or as control cases. We gave a matching questionnaire to each child at the diary stage of the survey (see p. 421) in which we asked for information about the sex and age of the child, father's occupation, about the ownership of a television set, and the amount of viewing. By getting this information early, we hoped to select the 1,920 cases before the questionnaire stage of the survey, so that special attention could be given to these children during the administration of the questionnaires.

Unfortunately, the matching procedure turned out to be very time-consuming. First, the information on the matching questionnaire had to be scaled or coded. This was done by the Social Survey, who coded the information for some 4,500 questionnaires. Secondly, the I.Q.s had to be obtained for all the children. Most schools had records of the intelligence-test results of the children and made these available to us.

Once the necessary data for each child's social class and intelligence level had been obtained, the matching procedure was started. Initially, a very fine selection sieve was used, but eventually somewhat coarser ones had to be employed to obtain the necessary number of matched pairs for the various cells of our design. In the first and most stringent selection stage, the viewer was matched with his control *within the same class-room*, thus ensuring maximum similarity of school and neighbourhood background.

In order that a viewer and a control child be matched satisfactorily within the same class-room, the following criteria were applied:

1. *Viewer*. These were children whose parents had owned a television set for a minimum of three months at the time the matching questionnaires were filled out, i.e. for four or more months at the time of the survey.

Control case. These were children in whose home there was no television set, and who stated that they viewed *less* than once a fortnight.

THE VIEWING CENSUS

Age Range of Pupils

PART A											
Class . . .											
Stream . . .											
No. present when count was made:											
(a) No. WITH television at home .											
(b) No. WITHOUT television at home . .											
PART B											
Of those WITHOUT television in their home, how many:											
(a) View TWICE a week or more?											
Children's TV only . .											
(b) View ONCE each week? . .											
Children's TV only . .											
(c) View ONCE each fortnight? .											
Children's TV only . .											
(d) View LESS THAN ONCE each fortnight? . .											
Children's TV only . .											
(e) Never view .											

Name of Headmaster/Headmistress: ....

School Address: .... Telephone Number: ....

.... Type of School: ....

.... Boys/Girls/Mixed: ....

Number of Streams: .... Method of Streaming ....

Type of Area: Please indicate something about the homes and the neighbourhood from which the child especially with regard to the work which their fathers do.

....

....

....

....

2. *Age.* Cases were matched within six months either way.

3. *I.Q.* Cases were matched within 5–6 points either way.

4. Cases were only matched if they were of the same *sex*. (This brought about a reduction in numbers of matched pairs in mixed schools.)

5. *Socio-economic class.* All parental occupations were scored on an 8-point occupational prestige scale (the Hall-Jones scale) and matched within one point either way. Children whose fathers did manual work were not, however, matched with those whose fathers were employed on white-collar work, even though these occupations, on the Hall-Jones scale, sometimes differ from one another by only one point (38).

Stages in the matching procedure:

The first stage of the matching operation, which consistently applied the abovementioned criteria yielded approximately 900 cases, or almost half the required number. It then became necessary to relax some of the criteria to permit the inclusion of more cases. This process of adjustment of the matching criteria took place gradually in several stages; at the end of each stage a careful evaluation was made to determine its efficiency in the various cells in the design.

In the second stage the range of permitted I.Q. differences was increased to ten points either way, and for some cases where no I.Q. was available an estimated grading was given according to the stream to which the children belonged. Some children from broken homes were included, provided the data about the mother or the home permitted an approximate assessment of the social level of the child's background. At this stage, within the same city, the viewers from one school were sometimes matched with controls from another school.

In the third stage, without further relaxation of standards, cases from Bristol were matched with those from Portsmouth.

In the fourth stage, again without further relaxation of standards, some cases from Bristol and Portsmouth were matched with London cases.

In the fifth stage, in all cities, the definition of control cases was relaxed to include those who viewed once a fortnight.

In the sixth stage, in all cities, the definition of control cases was relaxed to include those cases who stated on the matching questionnaires that they viewed not more than once a week, and for whom later information showed that such viewing referred *either* to children's television *or* to adult television, but not to both. This final stage brought the yield up to 1,854 cases (see Table 5).

The filling of the required cells in the design proceeded according to expectation. Previous studies led us to expect that there would be few middle-class children in secondary modern schools. Similarly, it was not surprising to find only a small number of dull middle-class children in the primary schools.

Some cells contained more than forty pairs. These were discarded in accordance with the procedure outlined on p. 423.

The Matching Questionnaire

First, please tell us a little about yourself

1. Are you a boy or a girl?

    I am a boy.........
    I am a girl.........

2. How old are you? I am .... years and .... months.

3. How many brothers and sisters have you?...............

4. Describe carefully the sort of job you would like to do when you leave school. ....
....

5. Now, what is the name of your father's job?
....

6. Describe carefully the sort of work he does.
....
....
....

7. Have you a wireless at home?   Yes..........   No..........

8. Have you a TV set at home?   Yes..........   No..........
If yes, how long has there been a TV set in your home? ....

9. Do you listen to the wireless every day?   Yes..........   No..........

10. How often do you go to the pictures?......................................

11. How often do you see TV (it may be at home or it may be in someone else's house)?

    Twice a week or more   ....
    Once a week   ....
    Once a fortnight   ....   (Tick which you do.)
    Less than once a fortnight..........
    Never see television   ....

12. Which sport do you like best? ....

ANALYSIS OF THE DATA

The weighting procedure

When it became clear that the target of forty matched pairs was not going to be achieved in some cells of the research design, consideration had to be given to the effects which this would have upon the analysis and interpretation of the results. So far as the desire for 'orthogonality' was concerned, the effect was that great care would be needed in interpreting the results of the research: it would be necessary to make sure that spurious differences (caused by the differing numbers in the twenty-four basic cells of the design) were recognised as such, and not allowed to mislead the course of the analysis. But there remained the problem of inspecting large numbers of tables with unequal numbers in each cell; in solving it we could choose between two broad courses of action.

On the one hand we could have arranged that all the tabulations to be inspected should be percentaged, so that quick preliminary comparisons would be possible between cells based on different numbers. The sheer magnitude of this operation made it an unsatisfactory solution of our problem, and we therefore turned to the second alternative. This was, to arrange *before* tabulation that the punched cards in each cell (one card corresponding to each matched pair of cases) would be mechanically duplicated in such numbers as could equalise the total number of cards in each cell. This method of card-duplication is quite commonly used for weighting purposes in the processing of market research and other survey data.

The method by which the cell numbers were equalised was a straight-forward one. For each questionnaire, the frequencies achieved in every cell of the design were tabulated; after inspection of these frequencies a revised 'target' figure was arrived at, usually just below the largest of the achieved frequencies. For every cell in the design, the achieved frequency was adjusted to this 'target' figure. Where the achieved frequency was too large, the appropriate number of cases was discarded, the actual cases discarded being selected by a random process. The total number of discarded cases was very small, since only rarely were cell numbers too high. In most cases the cell numbers had to be increased to the 'target' figure, and this was similarly achieved by selecting the appropriate number of cards by a random process, and duplicating them mechanically.

The effects of this procedure of adjustments to equalise cell frequencies are best considered in several stages. In the first place, the fact that the discarded and duplicated cases were selected by a random process meant that *no systematic bias was introduced into the analysis.* Every case in a cell had exactly the same chance of being duplicated (or discarded) as every other case in that cell; which ones were actually selected was simply due to the luck of the draw. It is easy to show that such a procedure has no effect, on the average, on the comparisons between cells; it is in this way that no systematic bias was introduced by the process.

On the other hand, there is no doubt that in every particular case the card-duplication procedure is bound to produce variations in the results obtained for the cell concerned since it superimposes a further source of random variation, due purely to the duplication procedure, upon the genuine variability of the research material. In general, however, such variation was very small (of the order of 3 per cent or less per cell), and in interpreting the research results the effect was additionally guarded against by the constant knowledge of which cells had been most affected by the duplication procedure.

Finally, it will be appreciated that it would be quite improper to allow the augmentation of numbers by card duplication to have the effect of diminishing the apparent sampling errors of the observed differences through the increase in numbers involved. Thus the appropriate tests of significance were based on the true number of cases involved in the comparisons, and not on the inflated numbers resulting from the card duplication procedure.

The machine tabulation

The results of the questionnaires were coded and machine tabulated. Inevitably, the coding process was slow, since so many of the questions were open-ended and in addition often needed coding frames which were interpretative as well as analytical. The coding of the week's diaries for each child proved particularly cumbersome, so that in this case only 84 viewers and 84 controls were analysed for each age group.

Machine tabulation of the results was complex, partly due to the number of Hollerith cards needed for each child (by the time summary and area-score cards had been punched, the total came to over forty 80-column cards per child) and partly as a result of having to deal with matched pairs. In addition, problems were created by the unequal numbers in the cells of the factorial design, with the consequent need for weighting.

From the ultimate machine tabulation, we obtained:

(a) A frequency distribution of all answers to each question for each of the forty-eight cells of the factorial design.

(b) Frequency distributions for each sub-group: intelligence and social class within sex, this within the two age groups, and these of course separately for each of the two parallel samples—viewers and controls.

(c) Frequency distributions of answers correlated with answers to other relevant questions, such as frequency of viewing and length of set ownership. Here further matching was often necessary in order to single out the effect of the particular variable in which we were interested.

(d) Area scores for the inventories, together with other tabulations requiring more complex methods.

EXAMINATION OF RELIABILITY AND VALIDITY

It is sometimes suggested that data obtained from children must be viewed with considerable suspicion, since they might write down anything that comes into their heads or whatever they think the investigator wants to hear. Also, if one were to come back a week later, one would allegedly obtain quite different answers. The following evidence of reliability was obtained:

Reliability. Different questions bearing on the same issue produced very similar patterns of results even though the questions were differently worded, were contained in different booklets, and administered on different days.

For example, we used different techniques to ask for children's favourites on television programmes and for the programmes they disliked. Again and again the same programmes emerged as overall favourites, no matter how the issue was approached, and similar patterns of programme preferences were found with regard to age, sex, and intelligence differences. Children's bedtimes were obtained each day from the diaries and also from two separate questionnaires. The variations were only minimal.

Comparable questions on other subjects produced equally consistent results. As a general rule, there would be some inconsistencies for individual children, but the results for the group as a whole showed a good level of reliability in cases where we could carry out a check.

Validity. We had no means of testing the validity of our answers, but a number of methods were used to encourage full co-operation and frankness. One of the most important of these was the assurance to the children of the anonymity of their answers. This we stressed by giving them code numbers, so that no names appeared on questionnaires; by having the completed questionnaires sealed up in the children's presence to show that the teachers would not read them; and by not having teachers in the class-room when the children were filling in their questionnaires. We also did everything we could to keep the children keen and interested; with some exceptions they took pleasure in the break from normal school routine, in their role as 'advisers', and in the obvious trouble we were taking with them.

We included in the programme-recall lists (the dullest and most mechanical part of the questionnaires) three faked items: two were the names of genuine programmes which in fact had been shown on some other night; the third was the plausible title of a non-existent programme. An average of not more than 8 per cent claimed to have seen these programmes. A similar check was inserted towards the end of the information tests (at a point when children would be getting tired): the question *When is Christmas Day?*, followed by four possible answers—April 1st, July 4th, November 5th, December 25th. If the children had merely been ticking answers at random, the wrong answers would have been frequently given here; in fact fewer than 3 per cent did so.

Lastly, in purely impressionistic terms, the children's answers *sounded* honest. Anyone picking up a handful of completed questionnaires or diaries would be struck by their air of disarming frankness. On most questions only a small proportion of children, bored or anxious to show off, answered frivolously or avoided answering at all.

APPENDIX B

Measurement of Amount of Viewing

IN this appendix we examine some of the methods used to find out how much children view, and present the three approaches employed in our survey, together with some discussion of their strength and weaknesses.

OTHER RELEVANT RESEARCH

American research

In the United States, where most set owners can choose from several channels, a number of research workers have tried to answer this question. The accompanying results show that weekly viewing time ranges from 16 to 30 hours—with a rough average of 21–22 hours. Most investigators agree that children view more at week-ends than on week-days. Otherwise their findings differ widely, partly because they have carried out their studies in different years, selected their samples in different ways, and taken children of different ages. More important, they have also obtained their raw data in different ways. Sometimes the investigator questioned the child's mother, asking her to estimate how many hours the child spent at the television set on a typical week-day and at week-ends. In other studies the children were given questionnaires—either by the research worker or by teachers in class— asking them to estimate their own viewing time. One group of children was asked to keep a diary for a week, after which they were interviewed. Each of these methods has its own inaccuracies and bias, quite apart from genuine variations in children's behaviour. The diary study by Battin (5), for instance, was focused on the child's viewing habits, and the method may have influenced the behaviour it was designed to assess. Free self-estimates are notoriously inaccurate and are readily influenced by the desire to make a particular impression on the interviewer. Parental estimates have the same disadvantages and are also liable to be inaccurate because the parent is not always in the room, or even at home, when the child is viewing. Teacher-administered questionnaires are as inaccurate as self-estimates and may be influenced by the relationship that exists between teacher and child. In short, even when the year, the sample, the days of the week, and the age-range can all be controlled, it is quite difficult to reach an accurate estimate of time.

British research

Investigators in this country have met similar difficulties. One research worker simply asked: 'How many evenings a week do you view?' The

Amount of viewing by child viewers in the United States as measured in sixteen American studies over recent years

Author	Number of cases in sample	Method	Age range School grade	Years	Amount viewed in a week (*hours*)	Remarks
Lewis, P. (57)	1,700	Interview and questionnaire	High School		23·5	—
Sweetser, F. L., Jr. (91)	413	Mother's estimate, weighted		7–20	11·4	For five week-days only
National Council of Churches (72)	650	Doorstep-interview estimates		4–15	13	On regular programmes only
Cunningham and Walsh (25)		Interview			23·3	3·33 hours on a typical evening in 1951
					20·5	2·93 hours on a typical evening in 1952
Fine, B. J. (33)		Interview			23·1	3·3 hours on a typical evening in 1952
Anonymous (3)	223	Questionnaire at school	Junior high school		27·0	3·9 hours daily
Besco, G. S. (13)	223	,,	10th–12th		16·8	—
Clark, W. J. (23)	750	,,	6th–7th		30	3·7 hours on a week-day, 5·5 hours at week-ends
Maccoby, E. (58)	622	Interviews with 332 mothers		4–17	18·5	2·5 hours on a week-day, 3·5 hours on Sunday
Witty, P. A. (103, 104)	2,000 cases each year				19 21 23 27	1950 1951 1952 1954
Battin, T. C. (5)	About 900	7-day diary	1st–6th 7th–12th		18·5 21	1951. Also used interviews in follow-up

BBC, in its studies of adults, has normally relied on interviews based on an aided recall technique concerning the previous day's programmes. In their inquiry on minors in 1954 interviewers asked the children to recall their activities (including listening and viewing) for each quarter hour of the previous day (16). Mitchell (70) used a self-estimate question, together with a prompt list which was read out to the children. He obtained separate data for children's television and evening programmes; the average total for the week was 14·28 hours. A study in a Lincoln grammar school (68) gave an average figure of two hours a night. Other studies simply gave the frequency of viewing—without the duration and so without a weekly total.

TECHNIQUES ADOPTED IN THIS SURVEY

1. *Questionnaire method.* We asked children in the main survey whether they saw evening programmes (and, if so, on which evenings), giving them the option of 'nearly always', 'sometimes', and 'hardly ever' for each evening of the week. This question was repeated for children's television[1] and was set out as follows:

		Nearly always	*Sometimes*	*Hardly ever*
	On Mondays I see evening TV	...	...	...
Tick	On Tuesdays I see evening TV	...	...	...
one	On Wednesdays I see evening TV	...	...	...
for	On Thursdays I see evening TV	...	...	...
each	On Fridays I see evening TV	...	...	...
day	On Saturdays I see evening TV	...	...	...
	On Sundays I see evening TV	...	...	...

We also asked, *How late are you mostly allowed to watch TV in the evenings?* and obtained separate answers for Monday to Thursday inclusive, for Fridays, Saturdays, and Sundays.

(a) *From Mondays to Thursdays*:

> I am not usually allowed to watch evening TV
> I am usually allowed to watch until ... o'clock

(b) *On Fridays*:

> I am not usually allowed to watch evening TV
> I am usually allowed to watch until ... o'clock

(c) *On Saturdays*:

> I am not usually allowed to watch evening TV
> I am usually allowed to watch until ... o'clock

(d) *On Sundays*:

> I am not usually allowed to watch evening TV
> I am usually allowed to watch until ... o'clock

[1] As a check, we asked in another part of the same questionnaire, *Did you watch Children's television yesterday?* The answers for the two questions agreed closely.

The amount of viewing was computed by multiplying each day's permitted viewing hours by 1 (if ticked *Nearly always*), by $\frac{1}{2}$ (*Sometimes*), or by 0 (*Hardly ever*), the separate scores for children's and for evening television then being added to give the total viewing hours for the week. This method of computation results in some degree of overestimation since it assumes that the child views continuously, up to the imposed limits.

2. *Diary method*. We asked the children to keep diaries (see Chapter 6) for one week some time before the main survey—that is, before they knew the purpose of the inquiry. Because the diaries yielded so much information and the scoring was so complex, only 84 viewers and 84 controls were coded in each age group. Where no exact time was recorded for an activity, we adopted the convention of dividing each hour into as many parts as the number of activities the child had mentioned for that hour, and allotting equal parts to each activity. This practice was likely to result in an underestimate of viewing time, because viewing and other activities often took place simultaneously, and because the child did not always recall what he had viewed. While the week we chose, 9–15 May, might not be representative of the year's viewing, it struck a reasonable compromise between summer and winter viewing frequencies. The children were told that we were equally interested in all their leisure activities, and no special reference was made to television.

3. *Programme-recall lists*: Every day during the week following the diaries, each child was presented with a list of all radio and television programmes broadcast the previous afternoon and evening and was asked to tick for each programme whether he had seen (or heard) all or part of it, or not. The duration of each programme was known, and if a child had seen only part of a programme he was credited with half the programme time. In this way we accumulated a time measure for each child and for each day, as well as a total for the whole week. Children were also asked to indicate how much they had liked each of the programmes they had seen (or heard). To some extent, written programme-recall lists run the risk of exaggeration, since some children may watch television or listen to the radio in order to have something to record. To guard against this, we first presented the lists on a Monday morning and inquired about programmes of the preceding Sunday, Saturday, and Friday; on these three days, at least, children did not bias the results with 'duty' viewing.

A second inquiry using programme-recall lists for one week was carried out in London about a year later, to study changes that had taken place since the advent of the second channel.

The programme-recall lists probably gave us our most accurate *time* estimate for a specific week, since the diaries tended to produce an underestimate and in any case were only coded for part of the sample, while the questionnaires gave somewhat of an overestimate, especially for evening television.[1] However, the programme-recall lists referred only to one particular week, which may or may not have been typical. Therefore, when we

---

[1] The overestimate was simply due to our assumption that the child viewed as much as he could on evenings when he 'nearly always' watched evening television.

wanted to relate the amount of viewing to other factors, or to select a sub-sample of addicts, we more often relied on the questionnaire data, because for that purpose accuracy of time measurement was less important than representativeness. The questionnaires gave the child's habitual pattern of behaviour, not merely the results of a particular week, and so were more likely to represent his usual viewing habits, even though the estimate of actual viewing hours may well have been inflated.

APPENDIX TABLE B.1. Average hours of viewing per week (1955) as measured by questionnaires, programme-recall lists, and diaries

13–14 YEAR OLDS

	All	Grammar	Sec. mod.	Boys	Girls
Questionnaires . . . (Total cases: 499)	18·4	16·7	19·3	18·8	18·1
Programme-recall lists . (Total cases: 346)	12·4	11·5	12·8	12·4	12·4
Diaries . . . . (Total cases: 84)	10·4	11·1	10·0	10·0	10·8

10–11 YEAR OLDS

	All	I.Q. over 115	I.Q. 100–115	I.Q. below 100	Boys	Girls
Questionnaires . . (Total cases: 484)	15·4	14·6	15·2	16·6	16·3	14·6
Programme-recall lists (Total cases: 347)	12·5	11·3	12·5	13·7	12·6	12·5
Diaries . . . (Total cases: 84)	9·2	8·7	10·1	8·7	9·4	9·0

In Table B. 1 the results of questionnaires, diaries, and recall lists are placed side by side to illustrate the extent of over- and underestimation. The differences between the questionnaire and the programme-recall lists were smallest among the younger children; this suggests that these children viewed as much as they could of evening television, while the older children were more selective. Table B. 2 illustrates the positive correlation between questionnaire and programme-recall list results for the same children.

APPENDIX TABLE B. 2. Relationship between amount of viewing data obtained by means of questionnaires and by means of programme-recall lists (average hours per week)

	Programme-recall lists			
	13–14 YEAR OLDS		10–11 YEAR OLDS	
Questionnaires:	Boys	Girls	Boys	Girls
Light viewers	9·3	9·5	8·4	9·9
Moderate viewers . . .	14·6	12·3	12·8	12·6
Heavy viewers	13·3	15·4	15·0	14·3
Total cases	168	178	176	171

APPENDIX C

Intercorrelation of Inventory Items

IN Chapter 11 we have frequently made use of a statistical technique known as Kendall's Tau.[1] This is the appropriate device to use as a measure of association in our case, since we were dealing with ordinal data arranged in 3 × 3 contingency tables. The particular coefficient employed here is known as Tau-B.

We have tried to measure associations between programme types by means of this special correlation coefficient. Thus, when comparing preferences for, say, adventure and Westerns, the data were arranged in a small table like the sample shown on this page, and the degree of correlation calculated on the lines described by Kendall.

				Adventure		
Westerns				Would like	Would not mind	Would not like to watch it
Would like				255	12	—
Would not mind				58	42	2
Would not like to watch it				8	6	3

Tau coefficient = 0·48.

Thus 58 of the 321 who said they would 'like' Adventure would 'not mind' Westerns, and 8 of the 17 who would 'not like' Westerns would 'like' Adventure.

Tau coefficients obtained in this way are useful indicators of association, but *they must not be thought of as product-moment correlation coefficients*. Thus, their size gives no indication of the amount of 'variance' which they can account for, nor are they amenable to factor analysis. Also, depending on the marginal frequencies, each 3 × 3 table has a maximum possible coefficient which can be well below unity. In our own case, since marginal frequencies were fixed, the upper limit was frequently found to be lying between 0·70 and 0·80, depending on the degree of skew in the marginal frequencies.

Another problem with Tau coefficients is that the process of estimating their statistical significance is slow and laborious, and has to be done afresh for each 3 × 3 table. Since the computational work involved becomes prohibitive, we may suggest a conservative lower limit of about 0·20, below which the association is mainly determined by chance fluctuations.

[1] Kendall, M. G., *Rank Correlation Methods*, Griffin, London, 1948.

APPENDIX D

Technique of Content Analysis used

Content analysis involves systematic inspection and description of the content of a communication, using specified criteria so that another research worker may repeat the study and arrive at similar results. To take a simple example: in finding out the attitudes of various newspapers to a given minority group, we can both count the different types of epithets used and note the frequency and proportions of favourable to unfavourable comments. Content analyses of fiction are broader and more concerned with evaluation. In radio, there is a further dimension—voice—and in film and television programmes we must take account of gestures, movement, expressions—the whole array of visual information. The analyses of these visual media are therefore especially difficult. How, for example, can we specify a lower middle-class setting? Since we cannot detail how things should look, or what objects should be present, the final evaluation must be qualitative, made more reliable by using trained and experienced investigators, and by having two of them assess each programme.

The content analysis adopted here was intended for the description of adult plays, Westerns, crime and detective programmes, to help answer the following questions:

1. Does television drama teach good or bad morals? For example, how are honesty and dishonesty treated?
2. Is the criminal sometimes a sympathetic character? Is he ever allowed to 'get away with it'? Do people advance themselves by being virtuous or is virtue considered to be its own reward?
3. What values do television plays put over? Do they depict success in terms of money, independence, domination? What does it teach about appearance and manners? Does it invite the questioning of socially desirable values? How far do values cancel each other out within any one programme or as between one programme and another?
4. What are the heroes and heroines like? Since children often identify themselves with the principal characters, what type of models are offered? What characteristics are presented as sympathetic and unsympathetic? How far are they 'black' or 'white' in character, or how far 'grey'—containing elements of both good and bad?
5. Does adults' television drama present themes and relationships involving children? How are children's relationships portrayed—with one another and with adults, especially parents? Are families shown as contented or rebellious?

6. How are violence and aggression depicted? When is violence considered justified? Who is allowed to be aggressive and why, whose aggression is condemned and why? Does the end justify the means?

7. How far are the characters victims of a capricious fate? How far do television plays use *deus ex machina* solutions?

8. How are lighting, music, close-ups, and camera work used to stress situations and produce effects? What situations are given special treatment?

The selection of the plays

Since the BBC and ITV try to present a considerable variety of plays each week, it seemed best to select a random sample from both channels over a period of two months. We chose the calendar months February and March 1956.

Western, crime, and detective programmes. In this comparative analysis, ten Westerns were selected at random from both BBC and ITV, also a number of episodes from each of the following detective series: *Fabian of Scotland Yard* (BBC), *Dragnet*, and *Inner Sanctum* (ITV).[1]

Other adult television plays. We chose six short and two long ITV plays, again at random, taking care to include a play from each of the major production companies. We also selected five BBC plays which together occupied the same amount of time as the (shorter) ITV plays. The analysis had to be restricted to so few plays, as it is very time-consuming.

All three television authorities proved most co-operative. Thanks to them, we were able to view filmed or telerecorded versions and so could compress the viewing of two months' plays into a small number of working days.

The technique of recording used

Two monitors watched each programme, made notes during the showing, and then completed five schedules. They also wrote a short account of the themes and the impressions conveyed by the play.

Two research workers concentrated on the Westerns and the detective series, two on the other plays. The schedules were used to record the following information:

Schedule I asked for a description of the theme, the setting in place and time, and the age, sex, nationality, occupation, social level, and appearance of the main characters and of all child characters.

Schedule II listed a number of values, drawn largely from a manual on value analysis by White (101). Whenever a given value was expressed, the monitor noted whether it was represented in words or in action, which character expressed it and whether the value was given a positive or negative connotation.

Schedule III listed types of relationship between children and adults, especially parents, and also between husbands and wives.

Schedule IV was for the detailed recording of the handling of violence and aggression.

[1] Four episodes of *Dragnet* and three each of the other two series were monitored.

Schedule V gave a 'personality profile'. Following Smythe (85), we expressed each characteristic in terms of opposites—for example, clean–dirty, idealistic–materialistic, and placed every character at some point along a five-point scale linking each pair of opposites. Twenty-eight pairs of characteristics were included.

This type of content analysis gives quantitative data about what must in the last resort be qualitative judgements. We have been able to go beyond the type of content analysis described in the literature because the number of plays we studied was small so that we could employ highly trained monitors who had themselves built up the schedules and had discussed at length the meaning of each term used.

Reliability coefficients were not worked out for every type of assessment, but there was over 90 per cent agreement between two monitors on age and occupations.

APPENDIX E

Programme Reaction Lists

A SPECIAL questionnaire was devised to determine how far children's reactions to potentially disturbing incidents varied with the context, real or fictional, in which the incidents occurred. The questionnaire was headed *How do you feel about seeing these things on television?* It consisted of a number of sheets, each headed with the name of a programme type, such as news, sports programmes, nature programmes, Westerns, variety, detective plays, &c.

The same disturbing incidents, suitably adapted to fit the different types of programmes, were listed on each sheet, and the child asked to indicate whether he liked, disliked, or did not mind them, and whether he was interested in watching them, or bored, or indifferent. The incidents ranged from acts of physical violence or verbal expressions of anger, to loss of face or suffering ridicule. In this way we could see, for instance, whether fighting proved more disturbing when it occurred as a real event in the news, or in sport, than when it formed part of a play. This technique also provided information about the reactions of children to different weapons, and enabled us to test the accuracy of some views of producers on the types of incident children find disturbing.

Samples of the items are given in Table 33 and Appendix Tables 25 and 26.

APPENDIX F

Vocational Values

SELECTED ANSWERS TO QUESTIONS CONCERNING
EXPECTED JOBS AND WISH JOBS

THE following is a selection of answers given by the young adolescents and by the 10–11 year olds. They represent a random selection within given social class and intelligence levels. On the left-hand side the expected and on the right-hand side wish jobs are presented, together with the answers to the subsidiary questions.

In each instance the answers of the viewer and those of his control twin have been presented one *below* the other.

QUESTIONS USED

Expected Job	Wish Job
(a) *Write down the job you expect to do when you leave school.*	(a) *Now supposing you could be anybody, go anywhere, or do anything—what sort of work would you most wish to do when you are grown up?*
(b) *What is it you like about this job?*	(b) *Why would you like this work?*
(c) *How did you come to hear about this job?*	(c) *How did you first come to think about this work?*

GRAMMAR SCHOOL BOYS (MIDDLE CLASS)

V.
(a) Go in a bank as a cashier.	(a) Veterinary surgeon.
(b) There is a lot of hard work and I like counting money.	(b) I like animals.
(c) My father's job is near a bank.	(c) I liked animals so my mother suggested it.

C.
(a) A solicitor.	(a) An airplane designer.
(b) The hours are short.	(b) There is plenty of money in it.
(c) From my father and wireless.	(c) Because a boy's father in our class is one.

GRAMMAR SCHOOL GIRLS (WORKING CLASS)

V.
(a) Domestic Science.	(a) I would like to be a nurse.
(b) I like to do domestic things in my spare time.	(b) It is helping a person to be well again.
(c) Mummy told me about it.	(c) When I went to see a person in hospital.

C.
(a) I would like to be a typist.	(a) I would like to be Doris Day.
(b) I like the noise it makes and the way you have to move your fingers so quickly.	(b) You meet such a lot of people.
(c) Because my sister used to go to do typing with some other girls in her class.	(c) Because when I was at *Tea for Two* Doris Day had to dance, and it was so lovely that I've always wanted to be her.

436

VOCATIONAL VALUES 437

Expected Job

(a) *Write down the job you expect to do when you leave school.*

(b) *What is it you like about this job?*

(c) *How did you come to hear about this job?*

Wish Job

(a) *Now supposing you could be anybody, go anywhere, or do anything—what sort of work would you most wish to do when you are grown up?*

(b) *Why would you like this work?*

(c) *How did you first come to think about this work?*

SECONDARY MODERN SCHOOL BOYS (WORKING CLASS)

V.

(a) Plumbing.
(b) I have seen other men at it and it is a very important job.
(c) Seeing men coming to our house to do this job.

(a) Be a football playing manager.
(b) I like football and hope to play for England.
(c) *Seeing it on television.*

C.

(a) Painter decorator.
(b) My father's very good at it.
(c) When my grandad was alive.

(a) Be a signaller in the Navy.
(b) My father was one.
(c) My father told me.

SECONDARY MODERN SCHOOL GIRLS (WORKING CLASS)

V.

(a) Teacher.
(b) I like looking after children.
(c) From school.

(a) A teacher in Africa.
(b) I like black children.
(c) When I heard about missionary.

C.

(a) Foreign Correspondent.
(b) You can go abroad and learn languages.
(c) One of my relations is training to be one.

(a) Travel.
(b) I want to go abroad.
(c) Because I am interested in other lands.

PRIMARY SCHOOL BOYS
WITH I.Q.S ABOVE 115 (WORKING CLASS)

V.

(a) Electrical engineering.
(b) It is practical but not completely so.
(c) Through newspapers, &c.

(a) I would like to be a driver of a heavy long-distance lorry.
(b) I would like to feel in command of a large vehicle, I also like lorries.
(c) I came to think of it when I was watching these lorries on main roads.

C.

(a) Electrical and radio engineer.
(b) I like most technical things.
(c) From an adult friend.

(a) I would be a freelance air pilot.
(b) I think it would be exciting sometimes.
(c) Reading about them.

QUESTIONS USED

Expected Job

(a) *Write down the job you expect to do when you leave school.*

(b) *What is it you like about this job?*

(c) *How did you come to hear about this job?*

Wish Job

(a) *Now supposing you could be anybody, go anywhere, or do anything—what sort of work would you most wish to do when you are grown up?*

(b) *Why would you like this work?*

(c) *How did you first come to think about this work?*

PRIMARY SCHOOL GIRLS
WITH I.Q.S ABOVE 115 (WORKING CLASS)

V.

(a) I would like to be a secretary.
(b) You get good pay, and it is a clean job.
(c) My friend also would like to be a secretary.

(a) I would like to be a cinema usherette.
(b) You get good pay and most of all you see the films free.
(c) When I went to the cinema.

C.

(a) I would expect to be an infant teacher.
(b) One gets fun teaching and playing with small children.
(c) My older friend is teaching at a school.

(a) Secretary.
(b) I like typing and taking down notes.
(c) One of my cousin's friends is a secretary.

PRIMARY SCHOOL GIRLS
WITH I.Q.S BELOW 100 (MIDDLE CLASS)

V.

(a) I expect to operate a comptometer machine.
(b) I like mathematics.
(c) From Daddy as he used to work at B.A.C.

(a) I would work in Marks & Spencer.
(b) I can fancy myself working or serving behind a counter.
(c) Because my Aunty works there.

C.

(a) Be a shop assistant.
(b) I like serving.
(c) I've always wanted to work in a shop.

(a) I'd like to stay at home and do the housework.
(b) I've had to do it before and I enjoy it.
(c) I've always liked to do it.

PRIMARY SCHOOL GIRLS
WITH I.Q.S BELOW 100 (WORKING CLASS)

V.

(a) A nurse.
(b) It teaches you first aid.
(c) From my friend.

(a) Work in a greengrocer's shop.
(b) You could earn a lot of money.
(c) From my mummy.

C.

(a) Shop assistant.
(b) You sell things.
(c) My friend is one.

(a) I would like to go to India.
(b) I would like to do any work.
(c) . . .

QUESTIONNAIRE TO EXAMINE CHILDREN'S PREFERENCES
FOR DIFFERENT ASPECTS OF WORK

So far, you had many things to choose from. In the next questions, you choose between two things only. Each time, choose the one you like better or would rather do.

1. Which of these would you rather be?

   Very good at school work and not so good at games ...
   Very good at games and not so good at school work ...

2. If you were free to choose, which of these would you rather do when you leave school?

   Go to a university or college ...
   Get a job straight away ...

3. When you grow up, which of these jobs would you rather have?

   A job in which you work mostly with your brains ...
   A job where you work mostly with your hands ...

4. And which of these jobs would you rather have?

   A job where you might get very far, but where you might get the sack ...
   A job where you can't get very far, but are sure you don't get the sack ...

5. And which of these jobs would you rather have?

   A job where it is very necessary for you to be nicely dressed ...
   A job where it doesn't matter how you are dressed ...

6. And which of these jobs would you rather have?

   A job where you have to think things out for yourself ...
   A job where, once you learn it, you always know how to do it ...

APPENDIX G

Measures of Children's Attitudes to School

IN this Appendix we present the techniques used to assess the children's interest in school and their perception of the importance of good school-work for later life.

As before, we have tried to approach the issue in several different ways; sometimes in the form of asking whether children worried about school-work, or wished they could do better, and sometimes in the form of attitude statements with which the child could agree or disagree.

The following is a list of the questions asked in a variety of contexts:

(*a*) People have different ideas about many things. Here are some things that people believe. Read each carefully and tick to show whether you agree, disagree, or are not sure.

Included among forty items dealing with a variety of topics were:

1. *School clubs are a waste of time.*
2. *It is all right to skip school once in a while.*

(*b*) In the worries inventory the following items were included among forty-seven other items dealing with abilities, material circumstances, and personal relations:

3. *My school work.*
4. *Not doing as well at school as I should like.*
5. *Not being able to concentrate on my school work.*
6. *Not getting along with my teacher.*
7. *Not being good at games at school.*

(*c*) In an inventory entitled Ways to be Different the child's concern would express itself as a tick in the columns '*I often wish*', or '*I sometimes wish this*'. The relevant items are: *I wish*—

8. *I was better at lessons.*
9. *I could get along better with my teacher.*

(*d*) In another questionnaire, each child was asked how well he got on with his teacher, and was provided with the answers '*rather less well than other children*', '*about the same as other children*', and '*rather better than other children*'.

(*e*) Finally, the children were asked, *How important do you think it is to get good marks at school, for getting on in the world later?* and asked to tick one of four alternatives: whether they considered good marks to be '*the most important thing of all*', '*very important*', '*fairly*', or '*not very important*'.

APPENDIX H

Guide to Suitable Conditions of Viewing

prepared by the Association of Optical Practitioners

1. Never view television with the room in darkness; the contrast between the bright screen and the dark room is very tiring for the eyes. Have a comfortable amount of light, either overhead or behind you, but not shining directly on the screen.

2. Be sure your set is properly installed, with special attention to the aerial.

3. Tune your set carefully, readjusting after it has warmed up thoroughly. Otherwise the picture may be unsteady and distorted and this strains the eyes.

4. Seat yourself comfortably and do not look up at the screen. It is better to have the picture at eye level, or slightly below, rather than higher.

5. Do not concentrate on the television screen for long periods as this tends to produce eyestrain. Glance round the room occasionally, as a change of focus rests the eyes.

6. It is advisable to sit about 6 to 10 feet away from the television screen.

7. If television makes your eyes ache, have them examined and wear glasses if you need them. If you are over 55 you may need special glasses for television.

APPENDIX I

Appendix Tables 1–73

APPENDIX TABLE 1

Which evening TV programme have you liked most of all?

(Distribution of answers by age and sex)

	13–14 YEAR OLDS			10–11 YEAR OLDS		
	All %	Boys %	Girls %	All %	Boys %	Girls %
Fabian of Scotland Yard .	18	18	17	25	25	25
The Grove Family . .	5	3	7	11	8	13
Plays or serials (excluding *Fabian, Grove Family*) .	14	11	18	9	8	10
Ask Pickles . . .	6	3	9	7	6	8
Variety	19	24	15	15	15	15
Panel games or quiz programes	8	4	11	7	7	6
Documentary programmes, news, interviews, science programmes, the Coronation, newsreels . .	9	14	5	2	4	1
Sport	5	9	—	1	3	—
Nature programmes, animals, birds	1	1	1	1	2	—
Music, singing, ballet, dancing	1	—	2	2	—	3
Miscellaneous . . .	6	5	7	6	4	9
No answer, don't know, or mention of children's or radio programmes . .	8	8	8	14	18	10
Total cases (weighted) . .	521	263	258	501	250	251

Which children's TV programme have you liked most of all?

(Distribution of answers by age and sex)

	13–14 YEAR OLDS			10–11 YEAR OLDS		
	All %	Boys %	Girls %	All %	Boys %	Girls %
Westerns (*Cisco Kid, Range Rider, Hopalong Cassidy*) .	16	22	11	22	30	15
Other plays and serials .	30	21	38	24	16	33
Family Serials (*The Appleyards*)	12	8	15	10	7	13
Hobbies (*All Your Own*) .	12	11	15	6	4	9
Variety (*Jigsaw, Peter Butterworth, Sugar and Spice, Bits and Pieces*) . . .	4	7	1	10	8	11
Animal and nature programmes . . .	1	1	—	4	1	6
Puppets	2	2	2	3	4	2
News, newsreel, sport . .	5	6	3	2	3	1
Panel games and quiz programmes . . .	3	2	4	1	2	—
Miscellaneous . . .	2	3	1	2	3	—
No answer, don't know, or mention of evening or radio programmes . . .	13	17	10	16	22	10
Total cases (weighted) . .	523	257	266	537	267	270

APPENDIX TABLE 3

Distribution of children's first three programme choices obtained in a survey conducted by Research Services Ltd. in 1955 (1)

(Eleven most popular programmes only)

		Sex		Age group		
	All %	Boys %	Girls %	8–10 %	11–13 %	14–15 %
Ask Pickles . . .	31·0	28	34	27	34	33
The Grove Family . .	30·2	21	40	28	39	19
Adult comedies . . .	25·6	30	21	20	25	37
Western films . . .	21·6	30	13	37	15	6
Fabian of Scotland Yard .	20·8	26	15	13	26	26
Children's plays and serials .	18·1	12	24	24	20	4
Sugar and Spice . .	13·2	10	17	14	15	8
Adult panel games . .	12·4	10	15	7	12	22
Watch with Mother . .	12·1	11	14	20	8	5
Adult variety shows . .	11·5	10	13	9	9	19
Sports review . . .	10·6	18	3	4	11	21
Total cases . . .	620	319	301	248	231	141

443

Appendix Table 4

What sort of thing do you like TV plays to be about?

(Distribution of answers by age, sex and intelligence)

13–14 YEAR OLDS

	All %	Boys %	Girls %	Grammar %	Sec. Mod. I.Q. 100– 114 %	Sec. Mod. I.Q. below 100 %
Detective, murder, mystery, thrillers, spies . .	26	31	21	23	31	24
Adventure plays, cowboys, Westerns, exciting plays .	18	19	17	15	21	19
Comedy, funny plays, 'plays that make you happy' .	11	11	11	13	11	9
Love, romantic plays .	14	2	27	13	12	18
War stories . . .	11	19	4	18	6	11
Plays about children or families, detective plays about children, school plays .	8	4	13	10	8	7
Historical, Biblical, classical, plays about old legends .	2	2	3	3	2	2
Plays about nature, animals, life on a farm . . .	1	1	1	2	1	—
Space, science fiction . .	—	—	1	—	1	—
Miscellaneous . . .	8	7	9	12	7	4
Not answered, don't know .	5	6	3	2	8	4
Total cases (weighted) . .	540	270	270	180	180	180

10–11 YEAR OLDS

	All %	Boys %	Girls %	I.Q. 115+ %	I.Q. 100– 114 %	I.Q. below 100 %
Detective, murder, mystery, thriller, spies . . .	28	24	32	25	28	31
Adventure plays, cowboys, Westerns, exciting plays .	18	21	16	22	14	19
Comedy, funny plays, 'plays that make you happy' .	10	9	11	13	9	7
Love, romantic plays . .	3	3	4	2	3	6
War stories . . .	3	6	1	5	3	3
Plays about children or families, detective plays about children, school plays .	10	5	14	9	10	9
Historical, Biblical, classical, plays about old legends .	3	3	4	4	5	2
Plays about nature, animals, life on a farm . . .	1	1	1	2	2	—
Space, science fiction . .	1	2	—	1	2	—
Miscellaneous . . .	10	7	7	9	6	6
Not answered, don't know .	13	16	10	9	14	15
Total cases (weighted) . .	540	270	270	180	180	180

NOTE. The figures may add up to over 100 per cent, since some of the children gave more than one answer.

444

Is there any children's TV programme which you have really disliked? What programme was that? If there has been none you really disliked, which programmes are you not so keen on?

(Distribution of answers by age and intelligence)

| | 13–14 YEAR OLDS | | | | 10–11 YEAR OLDS | | | |
| | | | Sec. Mod. | | | | | |
	All %	Grammar %	I.Q. 100–114 %	I.Q. below 100 %	All %	I.Q. 115+ %	I.Q. 100–114 %	I.Q. below 100 %
Programmes for younger children (puppets, *Watch with Mother*) . . .	12	14	9	11	9	9	8	8
Children's variety programmes (*Jigsaw, Peter Butterworth, Sugar and Spice, Bits and Pieces*) .	9	11	8	9	8	12	7	6
All Your Own . . .	9	8	12	7	6	5	10	3
News, sport . . .	5	3	6	6	8	9	6	8
Music, singing, dancing .	6	8	5	6	5	6	6	3
Plays	6	6	7	4	5	3	2	9
Activity programmes (*Our Port, Our Village*) .	3	5	2	2	7	9	6	6
Nature and animal programmes, birds, botany .	4	4	3	5	4	4	3	6
Westerns	4	3	1	7	3	4	2	2
Panel games, quiz programmes . . .	4	4	2	4	2	2	2	—
Miscellaneous . . .	11	13	7	14	7	6	8	8
No answer . . .	27	21	38	20	36	31	40	41
Total cases (*weighted*) . .	540	180	180	180	540	180	180	180

APPENDIX TABLE 6

Is there any evening TV programme which you have really disliked? What programme is this? If there has been none you really disliked, which have you not been so keen on?

(Distribution of answers by age and intelligence)

	13–14 YEAR OLDS Sec. Mod.				10–11 YEAR OLDS			
	All %	Gram-mar %	I.Q. 100–114 %	I.Q. below 100 %	All %	I.Q. 115+ %	I.Q. 100–114 %	I.Q. below 100 %
Politics, election talks, *In the News, Press Conference* .	18	18	18	19	8	8	8	6
Talks, discussions, *Panorama*, 'serious programmes', 'programmes which are all talking', &c.. . . .	8	8	7	8	10	11	7	13
News, newsreel, weather forecast . . .	3	1	6	4	5	6	4	6
Panel games, quiz programmes	12	16	11	11	9	11	7	7
Music, ballet, singing, opera .	14	17	12	13	5	6	6	4
Plays, stories, serials . .	6	8	6	4	8	10	7	8
Sport	1	1	1	1	5	1	8	7
Documentary programmes .	2	1	3	2	3	2	4	4
Variety	4	4	1	7	1	2	1	1
Miscellaneous . . .	6	8	4	5	4	4	2	4
No answer, don't know .	26	18	31	26	42	39	46	40
Total cases (*weighted*) . .	540	180	180	180	540	180	180	180

APPENDIX TABLE 7

What sort of plays do you not like?

(Distribution of answers of the 34 per cent of the older and the 16 per cent of the younger viewers who gave a positive answer)

	13–14 YEAR OLDS %	10–11 YEAR OLDS %
Detective, murder, mystery, crime, ghosts, gangster, horror plays	16	35
Romantic, love plays	27	19
Shakespeare	20	12
Historical, Biblical, old-fashioned, costume plays	11	16
War plays	1	4
Cowboys, Westerns, plays about Indians .	1	—
Miscellaneous	28	15
Total cases	173	74

NOTE. The figures in this Table add up to more than 100 per cent because some of the children gave more than one answer.

Appendix Table 8

(Young people's discussion groups on television) *What would you like them to talk about?*

(Distribution of first and second choice by age)

	13–14 YEAR OLDS		10–11 YEAR OLDS	
	v %	c %	v %	c %
Political—general, miscellaneous	2·9	2·2	2·4	1·6
Strikes, wage disputes, wages	2·9	4·8	7·1	6·4
Atom, H-bomb, war, peace	3·6	5·0	2·8	2·7
Colour bar, racial prejudice, mixed-colour races living together	2·5	2·8	0·1	0·4
Old Age pensions	0·1	0·7	0·7	0·3
Political discussions *per se*, M.P.s in the news, party broadcasts	0·1	0·5	0·1	0·1
Cost of living, price of food	1·9	1·4	4·6	3·0
Information—general, miscellaneous	5·4	3·0	5·9	5·5
How things are made, how things work (including films and television)	1·8	1·8	2·1	2·6
Government procedures—e.g. how the House of Commons works, how people vote	—	0·2	—	0·6
Art	0·1	0·2	0·1	—
Music	0·4	0·6	1·2	0·6
Books and literature, including plays	1·0	0·6	0·8	1·2
Nature topics, e.g. about bird-watching	0·5	0·7	3·3	3·7
Pets and their care, their ways, &c.	0·4	0·9	2·0	3·0
Other people's lives, life in former times, life in foreign countries	3·3	1·6	0·5	2·1
Television—general, including television stars	2·9	2·7	4·3	3·7
Television programmes—complaints and suggestions	9·9	2·7	8·4	2·6
School—general, miscellaneous	3·0	7·9	6·3	4·4
Leaving age	4·0	6·0	1·0	1·1
Examinations	0·6	1·1	1·1	0·6
Holidays	1·3	1·0	2·7	1·1
Rights of teachers to punish	0·1	0·5	0·3	0·1
Homework	3·5	4·1	1·1	1·1
Social problems applied to young people—general, miscellaneous	4·4	3·4	1·6	2·0
Provision of youth clubs	1·1	1·0	—	0·6
Teddy boys and Teddy girls	3·2	3·6	2·5	1·8
Religion as applied to young people	—	0·6	—	0·1
National Service	1·2	0·1	0·5	—
Personal problems (not including parental control) general, miscellaneous	1·6	0·2	1·5	0·4
Right age to start make-up	0·2	0·6	0·3	—
Right age to go out with members of opposite sex, mixing of sexes, mixed schools, mixing out of school	1·8	1·7	0·1	—

	13–14 YEAR OLDS		10–11 YEAR OLDS	
	V %	C %	V %	C %
Right age for marriage, other marriage problems, divorce	1·4	1·7	1·3	0·6
Shyness, giggling fits, stage fright, blushing	0·1	—	—	0·3
Problems of manners . . .	0·4	0·1	1·2	1·1
Dress and fashion	2·3	1·1	0·8	0·4
Sports (miscellaneous) . . .	5·5	5·7	6·7	8·6
Sports problems, e.g. price of football matches, team selection, fairness of decision	2·2	0·9	1·3	1·0
Job information—how to become a hairdresser, film star, &c. General advice on how to look for a job and what sort of jobs there are . .	5·1	4·0	2·0	3·4
Social—general, miscellaneous, including 'education' in general, national sense	3·6	4·2	4·1	4·8
Relationships with parents, family; *parental control*—general . .	1·6	2·0	2·3	2·2
Time to go to bed . . .	0·6	1·1	1·1	1·5
Time to come in at night . . .	0·6	0·9	—	0·3
Age at which parents should treat you as grown-up	0·1	—	0·1	0·1
Young people today compared with parents' generation. Are young people today as bad as people say? .	0·7	0·9	—	—
Films—general, including discussions on films, film stars . . .	0·8	1·0	2·1	2·5
Miscellaneous—general . . .	3·5	5·2	5·6	12·4
Personality, e.g. singers, explorers .	0·4	0·9	0·7	1·5
Collections of things . . .	—	—	0·5	0·4
Space travel, science fiction . .	0·6	0·1	0·4	0·4
Social concern *re* disasters, aircrashes, racing and road accidents . .	1·0	0·7	0·7	0·6
Cruelty to animals, blood sports, Grand National, &c.	0·7	1·6	1·3	2·3
I am not interested, and 'nothing' .	1·7	2·1	1·7	1·6
Total no. of answers	870	826	747	729

Top favourites for two-channel viewers, 1956

(Children's three favourite programmes distributed by sex, and type of school.)

13–14 YEAR OLDS

	Boys	%	Girls	%
GRAMMAR	Highway Patrol	43	I Love Lucy	73
	Dragnet	35	Robin Hood	27
	I Love Lucy	22	I Married Joan	20
	Rin-Tin-Tin	22	Rin-Tin-Tin	13
			Gun Law	13
Total cases		42		20
SECONDARY MODERN	Highway Patrol	38	Gun Law	50
	Rin-Tin-Tin	38	Rin-Tin-Tin	38
	Gun Law	38	I Love Lucy	25
	Dragnet	29	Dragnet	13
	Robin Hood	24	Highway Patrol	13
Total cases		24		28

10–11 YEAR OLDS

	Boys	%	Girls	%
ALL	Rin-Tin-Tin	42	Rin-Tin-Tin	53
	Robin Hood	37	Robin Hood	43
	Dragnet	32	Roy Rogers	26
	Highway Patrol	24	I Love Lucy	17
Total cases		45		60

APPENDIX TABLE 10

Percentage of children who viewed BBC children's and certain selected evening programmes during the week beginning 13 May 1955

(Distribution of answers by age, sex, and intelligence)

Percentage of viewers who, having seen these programmes, liked them very much

(Distribution of answers by age, sex, and intelligence)

Column groups — **Viewed**: 13–14 year olds [All %, Grammar Boys %, Grammar Girls %, Sec. Mod. Boys %, Sec. Mod. Girls %], 10–11 year olds [All %, I.Q. 115+ Boys %, I.Q. 115+ Girls %, I.Q. below 114 Boys %, I.Q. below 114 Girls %]. **Liked very much**: 13–14 year olds [All %, Grammar Boys %, Grammar Girls %, Sec. Mod. Boys %, Sec. Mod. Girls %], 10–11 year olds [All %, I.Q. 115+ Boys %, I.Q. 115+ Girls %, I.Q. 100–114 Boys %, I.Q. 100–114 Girls %].

Programme	V All	V Gr B	V Gr G	V SM B	V SM G	V All(10–11)	V IQ115 B	V IQ115 G	V <114 B	V <114 G	L All	L Gr B	L Gr G	L SM B	L SM G	L All(10–11)	L IQ115 B	L IQ115 G	L 100–114 B	L 100–114 G
CHILDREN'S TELEVISION																				
Cisco Kid } Friday, 13 May	75	66	70	79	79	81	71	82	81	85	76	63	75	78	82	91	86	82	93	96
Filming in Africa } 13 May	58	46	55	60	63	76	68	78	78	77	76	68	87	80	70	90	86	89	84	97
Sugar and Spice } Saturday	51	46	54	54	55	71	71	75	63	78	41	16	39	44	50	69	52	55	70	81
The Appleyards } Saturday	64	64	60	60	61	74	80	77	69	76	88	81	92	83	96	95	89	95	96	98
Our Port	54	55	62	51	53	68	59	71	67	73	16	25	2	11	25	44	31	27	45	56
Children's Newsreel } Sunday	63	62	71	59	63	70	63	71	69	76	65	45	65	67	73	85	67	86	82	94
Alibi Children	63	63	76	56	63	74	70	85	69	81	83	79	91	72	92	93	95	88	88	94
Cisco Kid	76	68	72	78	82	85	80	71	87	86	77	61	64	82	83	91	86	79	96	94
Devon and Cornwall } Monday	60	55	68	59	58	72	67	67	74	74	57	52	64	53	58	63	56	57	68	65
The Range Rider	75	67	74	76	77	83	75	83	83	87	84	74	79	78	95	93	90	88	96	91
The Explorer (serial) } Tuesday	68	46	74	68	77	82	78	93	82	78	80	76	78	86	78	85	91	88	85	84
Out of Doors	43	28	26	41	46	49	34	55	48	56	42	35	24	20	17	51	50	53	48	51
Comic Turn } Wednesday	45	44	33	72	42	57	37	63	58	63	41	33	55	45	50	70	73	58	76	70
Sport	41	46	38	45	37	53	38	57	59	52	29	42	22	47	37	42	55	55	50	30
Billy Bean	45	26	37	40	56	59	42	66	58	67	24	14	17	22	23	61	63	39	73	63
Ten Minutes' Music } Thursday	40	22	37	30	45	54	34	62	50	64	70	11	47	75	19	31	21	25	29	38
Chessington Zoo } 19 May	35	25	46	35	48	57	40	55	55	68	84	33	66	75	80	84	73	87	79	90
People in Books	35	25	35	35	46	49	39	45	50	56	52	24	72	49	47	53	28	62	54	58
EVENING PROGRAMMES (SELECTED)																				
Science Review	25	32	16	35	15	17	13	6	26	16	52	65	54	68	28	78	73	65	65	81
In Town Tonight	50	42	57	51	52	66	70	73	56	69	92	47	59	53	63	68	86	71	58	72
The Mulberry Accelerator—5	70	66	67	69	74	77	86	83	73	75	92	87	96	91	91	94	98	91	89	97
Secombe Here	71	77	63	81	63	51	57	50	50	51	92	95	88	97	87	92	98	95	89	90
What Every Woman Knows	70	72	64	71	71	44	34	37	51	46	44	44	60	56	62	70	54	77	62	81
Election broadcast—Labour	34	29	37	33	35	47	50	38	51	48	15	8	20	15	14	16	7	16	18	19
Conservative	41	44	47	43	35	47	32	35	51	50	19	28	18	11	12	18	18	17	19	20
Liberal	27	25	24	28	33	34	67	34	34	35	19	10	33	16	19	18	12	4	22	23
Showcase	63	60	60	65	63	72	67	68	36	73	84	94	98	97	97	94	91	91	94	93
Golden Gloves (boxing match)	51	60	23	75	45	22	15	8	29	23	75	91	58	74	74	79	53	50	91	52
Find the Link	52	51	35	53	61	24	18	1	76	35	60	60	79	78	80	82	96	—	91	91
Fabian of Scotland Yard	73	76	79	66	77	73	71	71	76	73	30	92	96	95	99	96	27	25	33	94
Panorama	45	52	28	58	36	25	27	20	24	28	45	32	30	31	25	31	79	62	73	58

Average audience for various types of programme (BBC only, 1955, and BBC and ITV, 1956) and the proportion of the audience retained in the two-channel situation

	Average audiences		
	1955 BBC	1956 BBC or ITV	Proportion of audience kept
	13–14 YEAR OLDS		
	%	%	%
Crime	73	53	73
Film programmes	47	26	55
Westerns	75	38	51
Panel games	54	26	48
Variety	65	28	43
Drama	69	29	42
Children's television excluding Westerns	50	17	34
Information and documentary . .	50	12	24
Total cases (*weighted*) . . .	369	114	
	10–11 YEAR OLDS		
Panel games	45	35	78
Crime	73	46	63
Westerns	83	43	52
Drama	53	27	51
Variety	63	28	44
Children's television excluding Westerns	64	23	36
Film programmes	49	15	31
Information and documentary . .	47	14	29
Total cases (*weighted*) . . .	366	105	

NOTE. The first column lists the average audience size for eight types of BBC programme before the advent of ITV. The second gives figures for directly comparable programmes after the advent of ITV, irrespective of the channel on which they appeared and of what was available on the competing channel. The third column shows the proportion of the original audience retained.

The 1956 sample was much smaller than that of 1955 because it was drawn only from homes with access to both channels.

451

Percentage of children with different favourite programmes who ticked *I would like to watch it* against comparable items in the programme inventory

FAVOURITE PROGRAMMES	INVENTORY ITEMS	13–14 YEAR OLDS %	10–11 YEAR OLDS %
Fabian of Scotland Yard (detectives)	Crime, detectives, and mystery	93	96
Ask Pickles	Variety shows	95	95
The Grove Family (family serial)	About ordinary families	77	72
Cisco Kid and *Range Rider* (Westerns)	Cowboys and the Wild West	79	74
The Benny Hill Show (comedy)	Things that make you laugh	85	100
What's My Line? (panel game)	Quiz games, audience and panel games	91	90
War in the Air (documentary)	{ Things that happened in the war { Flying and aeroplanes	91 83	78 100
Filming in Africa (documentary)	{ Wild animals { Other animals and birds	82 77	94 94
Arthur Askey (comedy)	Things that make you laugh	94	100
The Appleyards (family serial)	{ About ordinary families { Children's plays	60 93	67 96
All Your Own (hobbies)	{ Your hobbies { Children's television	75 87	91 91
Terminus (play cycle)	Serials	100	92

Appendix Table 13

Types of television programme correlated with equivalent items on the inventories for the other three media by means of Tau coefficients.

	Equivalent items on:					
	Radio		Cinema		Reading	
	13–14 YEAR OLDS	10–11 YEAR OLDS	13–14 YEAR OLDS	10–11 YEAR OLDS	13–14 YEAR OLDS	10–11 YEAR OLDS
Type of television programme						
Westerns . .	0·46	0·53	0·55	0·53	0·43	0·51
Crime . . .	0·49	0·45	0·44	0·58	0·33	0·51
Adventure . .	0·32	0·36	0·24	0·38	0·23	0·45
People in other countries	0·34	0·13	0·32	0·30	0·29	0·24
Love and romance .	—	—	0·26	0·29	0·30	0·33
Ordinary families .	0·30	0·30	0·40	0·25	0·25	0·30
Famous people .	0·13	0·32	0·24	0·29	0·24	0·32
Painting . .	0·24	0·30	—	—	0·21	0·28
Ballet . .	0·33	0·37	0·23	0·33	0·26	0·27
News . . .	0·19	0·19	0·20	0·19	0·09	0·10
Total cases (weighted)	416	383	416	383	416	383

Appendix Table 14

Three selected items in the television excitement cluster correlated with items in the excitement clusters of other media

		Correlations with:					
		Radio		Cinema		Reading	
		13–14 YEAR OLDS	10–11 YEAR OLDS	13–14 YEAR OLDS	10–11 YEAR OLDS	13–14 YEAR OLDS	10–11 YEAR OLDS
Television items:	*Excitement items in other media:*						
Crime	Crime .	0·49	0·45	0·44	0·58	0·33	0·51
	Westerns .	0·28	0·13	0·24	0·15	0·19	0·09
	Adventure .	0·32	0·30	0·24	0·23	0·26	0·26
	Ghosts .	0·29	0·34	—	—	0·23	0·34
	Space .	—	—	0·14	0·20	—	—
Adventure	Adventure .	0·32	0·36	0·24	0·38	0·23	0·45
	Westerns .	0·20	0·22	0·17	0·32	0·08	0·20
	Crime .	0·25	0·33	0·21	0·26	0·22	0·31
	Ghosts .	0·20	0·24	—	—	0·16	0·17
	Space .	—	—	0·16	0·18	—	—
Space travel	Space travel	—	—	0·30	0·34	—	—
	Westerns .	0·19	0·20	—	—	0·14	0·19
	Adventure .	0·23	0·20	—	—	0·15	0·17
	Crime .	0·18	0·23	—	—	0·11	0·17
	Ghosts .	0·18	0·25	—	—	0·14	0·20
Total cases (weighted) .		416	383	416	383	416	383

Percentage of children with different favourite pastimes (games, outdoor play, reading) who would like to watch the following types of television programmes

Type of programme	13–14 YEAR OLDS			10–11 YEAR OLDS		
	Games %	Outdoor %	Reading %	Games %	Outdoor %	Reading %
Cowboys and the Wild West .	33	40	60	68	68	70
Other sorts of adventure .	73	58	80	77	79	86
Crime, detectives, and mystery	91	85	89	95	86	78
Space travel and space men .	41	47	40	58	46	39
School life . . .	47	33	58	46	58	50
Love and romance . .	29	35	58	32	37	33
Horror plays or stories .	67	51	58	56	53	42
Things that make you laugh .	91	89	95	86	86	89
Things that make you sad .	32	40	45	23	54	23
Things that happened in the Bible	55	47	55	68	60	64
Things that happened in history	59	56	50	79	56	67
Things that happened in the war	86	64	50	79	60	53
About famous people . .	56	45	45	70	74	53
About ordinary families .	59	44	70	47	65	42
Travel	50	44	45	60	56	44
Science and inventions .	56	55	47	47	37	36
Flying and aeroplanes . .	53	44	35	72	37	39
Your hobbies . . .	73	49	60	67	67	50
Painting and sculpture .	21	22	50	39	46	25
Ballet	9	35	55	11	49	47
Ballroom dancing . .	21	49	70	21	56	58
Wild animals . . .	56	56	60	74	72	78
Other animals and birds .	50	51	50	75	68	69
People in other countries .	59	53	65	67	70	56
People who lived long ago .	62	62	55	75	70	67
About farming and country life	46	45	65	53	70	58
About books . . .	43	42	80	44	56	54
Important news items (current affairs) . . .	26	11	20	19	18	8
Parliament and politics (our Government) . . .	9	11	—	7	32	—
Famous buildings . .	21	16	20	9	37	28
Serious music . . .	12	16	35	19	18	22
Popular light music . .	41	40	70	19	32	39
Singing	55	55	50	32	46	47
Dance music . . .	47	51	60	19	54	48
Opera	11	15	15	16	23	20
Variety shows . . .	97	87	95	93	88	81
Quiz shows, audience and panel games . . .	89	73	90	88	88	89
Serials	94	87	100	93	89	92
Shakespeare's plays . .	32	29	40	46	39	37
Children's plays . . .	68	67	85	93	91	89
Children's television . .	53	56	75	89	86	83
Puppet shows . . .	32	31	65	67	70	80
Fashion parades . . .	16	35	80	19	49	45
Total cases (weighted) . .	66	55	20	57	56	36

454

Classification of answers of 13–14 year old viewers who had chosen different programmes as their favourites, to the following statements and personality measures

	Adult plays %	Variety and comedy %	Docu-mentary %	*Ask Pickles* %
Disliked evening television programme:				
Panels, quizzes	12	8	25	18
Political broadcasts (*In the News, Press Conference*)	18	17	8	26
In TV quiz and panel games, the answers are given on the screen before the guessing starts. You can either look at the answers or shut your eyes. What do you do?				
I try not to look at the answers . .	18	17	23	18
Index of gullibility, as determined by number of agreements with the following statements. High score: . . .	46	35	25	60
Flying saucers are space ships from Mars. There are people living on Mars. We can now visit the moon in a space ship. We are being watched from Mars. The people on TV can see right into your home. Walking under ladders brings bad luck. Seeing a black cat brings good luck. If you cross your fingers when you tell a lie it is all right. Some people can foretell the future.				
Acceptance of clichés (agreement with some of the following statements). High score:	50	65	44	67
My own country is always right. Once people are married, they are sure to be happy. Things always turn out all right in the end. There will always be wars, they are human nature. We are all born to various social positions, and it doesn't do to change them. Girls should only learn things that are useful round the home. Good people always come off best in the end. You can't trust foreigners. Rich people are very seldom happy. Scientists cannot be trusted because they do not believe in God.				
'A good father is a man with a family who . . .' Answers classified in terms of:				
Provider—works hard, earns money, pays bills, is responsible . .	43	46	34	50
Loves his family—is kind, gentle, makes family happy, family love him, helps with troubles . .	39	35	48	41
Anxiety about growing up.[1] High score: .	37	44	44	55
Total cases	146	71	40	34

[1] The items are given on p. 250 in Chapter 20.

Appendix Table 17

Would you say that going to the pictures is better than watching television or not so good?

(Distribution of answers of viewers by age and sex)

Prefer	13–14 YEAR OLDS All %	Boys %	Girls %	10–11 YEAR OLDS All %	Boys %	Girls %
Cinema . . .	38	44	31	25	27	23
Television . . .	34	30	38	41	40	40
Don't know . . .	28	26	31	34	33	37
Total cases (*weighted*) . .	514	256	258	502	253	249

Appendix Table 17a

Imagine that the same story could be seen on television, or at the pictures, or listened to on the wireless, which would you choose?

(Distribution by age and sex)

Would choose	13–14 YEAR OLDS All %	Boys %	Girls %	10–11 YEAR OLDS All %	Boys %	Girls %
Cinema	42	39	44	27	26	27
Television	56	60	52	70	72	68
Radio	2	1	4	3	2	5
Total cases (*weighted*) . . .	480	240	240	480	240	240

Appendix Table 18

Average weekly time devoted to children's programmes of different types (February, July, and November 1956)

	BBC Feb. hrs. min.	July hrs. min.	Nov. hrs. min.	ITV Feb. hrs. min.	July hrs. min.	Nov. hrs. min.
Plays . . .	2 12	2 18	2 31	3 08	3 37	5 29
Light entertainment .	1 34	1 04	1 18	– 53	– 45	– 08
Puppets and cartoons .	– 44	– 23	– 35	– 32	– 59	– 29
Information . .	2 09	1 46	2 06	1 17	1 09	– 56
Sport . . .	– 10	– 32	– 16	– 11	– 02	– 28
Miscellaneous .	– 11	– 15	– 18	– 14	– 04	—

Appendix Table 19

Proportion of time in children's information programmes devoted to different subjects (May–July and September–November 1956)

Subject	BBC May–July %	BBC Sept.–Nov. %	ITV May–July %	ITV Sept.–Nov. %
Animals and nature . . .	25	23	38	41
Doing and making . . .	17	13	5	—
News and newsreels . . .	17	14	4	11
Foreign places and people . .	15	24	—	3
British places and people . .	2	5	6	—
History and archaeology . .	9	5	—	—
Careers	4	—	—	8
Outer space	2	—	21	12'
Sports coaching . . .	2	3	17	24
Books	—	5	3	—
Science	1	5	—	—
Health	—	2	—	—
Miscellaneous	6	1	6	1

Appendix Table 20

Percentage of time allocated to different types of programmes between 5 p.m. and the children's bedtime (February and July 1956)

	13–14 YEAR OLDS BBC Feb. %	BBC July %	ITV Feb. %	ITV July %	10–11 YEAR OLDS BBC Feb. %	BBC July %	ITV Feb. %	ITV July %
Children's television . .	20	17	20	19	22	19	22	21
Adult programmes								
Plays	21	19	32	27	21	18	31	27
Variety Shows . . .	11	10	14	14	11	9	12	11
Information . . .	19	17	6	2	18	18	5	3
Sport	10	20	5	17	10	21	5	19
News	5	6	3	4	5	6	3	4
Light music . . .	4	4	7	2	3	2	8	2
Classical music . . .	5	4	—	—	5	4	—	—
Film news . . .	—	1	3	3	—	—	4	1
Religion . . .	2	1	2	1	2	1	2	2
Panel games . . .	1	1	2	4	2	2	2	3
Give-away programmes .	—	—	5	6	—	—	5	7
Miscellaneous . . .	2	—	1	1	1	—	1	—

Average time devoted each week to adult information programmes
between 7 p.m. and children's bedtime (May to July 1956)

	13–14 YEAR OLDS				10–11 YEAR OLDS			
	BBC		ITV		BBC		ITV	
	hrs.	min.	hrs.	min.	hrs.	min.	hrs.	min.
Subject								
The arts		9		—		2		—
Science		3		—		3		—
History		21		—		12		—
Places abroad	1	10		—		56		—
Places at home		35		—		33		—
Current affairs	1	11		41	1	9		24
News and newsreels	2	6	1	0	2	6	1	0
Industries and economics		16		—		11		—
Nature and animals		19		—		19		—
Doing and making		12		—		12		—
State occasions		2		—		2		—
Miscellaneous		44		—		37		—

Proportion of each type of information programme shown after
the children have gone to bed (May, June, and July 1956)

	BBC		ITV	
	13–14 YEAR OLDS %	10–11 YEAR OLDS %	13–14 YEAR OLDS %	10–11 YEAR OLDS %
The arts	93	56	—	—
Science	63	63	83	83
History and archaeology	31	—	—	—
People and places abroad	19	12	—	—
People and places at home	13	6	28	28
Current affairs	16	13	51	15
Magazines—topical interest	26	12	—	—
News and newsreels	40	40	64	64
Industry and economics	55	39	—	—
Nature and animals	—	—	22	22
Doing and making	—	—	100	100
State occasions	46	46	—	—
Discussions—miscellaneous	—	—	—	—
Outside broadcasts—miscellaneous	13	12	100	100
Other miscellaneous	62	38	—	—

APPENDIX TABLE 23

A typical week's drama on the BBC and ITV during 1956

	BBC			ITV		
Day	Time p.m.	Duration (approx.) min.	Type of play	Time p.m.	Duration (approx.) min.	Type of play
Monday	7.30	30	weekly crime series	varies	30–60 or 90	problem, crime, adventure, or comedy
Tuesday	7.30	30	weekly comedy series	7.0	30	weekly comedy series
	8.0	30–60 or 90	comedy, problem, or crime	10 0	30	weekly crime series
Wednesday	8.0 or 8.30	30	weekly family or comedy series	10.0 or 10.30	30	Western
Thursday	8.30	60–90	problem, crime, or comedy	7.0	60 or 90	problem, crime, adventure, or comedy
Friday	7.30	30	weekly comedy series	7.0 or 10.0	30	swashbuckling adventure series
				9.30		crime series
Saturday	8.30	30	weekly crime series	7.15 or 9.30	30	swashbuckling adventure series
	varies	15	old film excerpt	9.0	30	problem, crime, adventure, comedy
				9.30	30	crime series
Sunday	2.0 or 2.30	30	crime or comedy series	4.0	30	crime series
	8.30	90	problem, comedy or crime	9.0	30	problem, crime, adventure, comedy
				9.30	30	comedy series

Crimes and motives in ten crime and detective programmes shown in February and March 1956

Programme title	Nature of crime	Motive Explicit	Implicit
Dragnet:			
The Big Trunk	Murder.	Curiosity, a desire to see or to steal valuables.	Could not help it. Had not meant to kill. Suddenly went mad when victim made a noise. Obsessively eager to look in trunk. Very neurotic.
The Big Girls	Attack (by shooting) and robbery.	Material gain (unclear what kind).	Transvestist, homosexual.
The Big Rod	Driver runs over pregnant woman who later dies.	No reason given (boy does not speak at all).	No family, no friends, lonely, 18 year old psychopath.
The Big Producer	Selling pornography.	Material gain.	Insane, perverted.
Fabian:			
Sixth Dagger	Attempted murder.	Madman's desire to prove that Shakespeare was Bacon.	Would-be murderer. Admits mental illness and requests treatment.
The Masterpiece	Forgery.	Love for a spiv traps a pitiful young woman into forgery.	
Innocent Victims	Blackmail.	Spite—a sister blackmails her brother even though previously he had gone to prison in her stead.	
Inner Sanctum:			
The Hands	Murder.	A man thinks he has committed murder in a fit of amnesia. In reality, the murder was committed by his wife and her lover who frame the husband for murder to get rid of him.	
Man of Iron	Murder.	An innocent man is due to be executed but, by putting the clock forward by one hour, the wife of the real murderer gets him to confess just in time to save the innocent man.	
The Sisters	Murder.	A spiv makes love in turn to two sisters (wealthy spinsters) and gives each a gun, hoping that they will have a shooting match, and that he will marry the survivor who will then be executed, leaving him free to enjoy the money. His plans fail and both sisters kill him.	

Reactions of seventy-five 11–12 year old viewers to various incidents of physical violence and of disaster shown in different television programmes

		Reactions		
	Liking %	Indiffer- ence %	Dis- like %	Ambiva- lence %
Fighting on ground				
Westerns: When cowboys fight on the ground and roll about in the dust	71	14	8	7
Detectives: When men fight on the ground and roll about on the floor	62	23	7	8
Sport: In rugby matches where men tussle with each other on the ground	45	25	23	7
Newsreels: In rioting when men fight on the ground and roll about the pavement	46	23	20	11
Fighting with fists				
Westerns: When there is a fist fight between cowboys	71	14	9	6
Detectives: When there is a fist fight between two criminals	70	10	6	14
Newsreels: When you see men tussling with fists during rioting	49	18	25	8
Fighting with guns				
Westerns:				
When cowboys shoot at one another	66	17	4	13
When everyone draws their guns to start shooting	80	4	6	10
Detectives: When gangsters shoot at one another	73	10	5	12
Plays: In historical and costume plays when there are battle scenes	42	35	13	10
Newsreels:				
When people run and shoot at each other	53	26	13	8
When people fight with guns	65	19	11	5
When soldiers and tanks fire in war scenes	53	30	14	3
Fighting with other weapons				
Detective: When you see people fighting with pieces of steel or iron	45	14	23	18
Plays:				
In political plays when people are questioned by soldiers or by secret police	48	22	16	14
In space plays when beings or things from other planets fight people from this earth	40	33	13	14
In historical and costume plays when you see two people fighting with swords	51	23	19	7
When you see people using knives or daggers to fight with	49	14	21	16
Disasters				
Plays:				
In science fiction plays when neither audience nor hero knows what awful thing he may have to face or fight with	49	28	18	5
When a building is on fire	36	29	21	14
Newsreels:				
When buildings are on fire	31	27	23	19
When an aeroplane has crashed	33	23	33	11
When people cry after a disaster	20	25	39	16

Reaction of seventy-five 11–12 year olds to potentially disturbing incidents (*not* involving physical violence) in various types of programme

	Liking %	Indiffer-ence %	Dis-like %	Ambi-valence %
Threat to the hero:				
Westerns				
When the good cowboy is getting the worst of it	37	9	25	29
Detective				
When the good man or detective is getting the worst of a fight . . .	45	17	16	22
Panel games				
When someone you like is getting the worst of it	15	15	38	32
Reprimand to the hero:				
Westerns				
When the sheriff tells the good cowboy off because he is not catching the bad man quickly enough . . .	28	22	30	20
Detective				
When the chief tells off the detective for not getting the criminals quickly enough	35	33	14	18
Plays				
When someone is told off when it is not really his fault	31	24	28	17
Panel games				
When a panel member tells somebody off	21	20	40	19
Discussions				
When someone gets told off by others for something he says	24	34	28	14
Sport				
When someone has been told off by a referee or laid off by a sports committee and has a TV interview to say what it's all about	16	45	31	8
Anger				
Plays				
In family plays when grown-ups are angry with one another, but do not raise their voices	53	30	12	5
In family plays when people get angry and leave the room or the house .	41	29	23	7
In family plays when grown-ups are angry with one another and shout .	38	25	23	14
When people slam doors and bang on tables because they are angry . .	33	25	21	11
Panel games				
When someone gets angry . . .	23	18	36	23
Discussions				
When people get angry with each other and raise their voices . . .	45	17	26	12
When people in interviews get very cross and worked up	30	28	30	12
When you know people are really angry but they keep quiet	31	37	23	9
Sports				
In a match when the referee and players disagree and have an argument . .	38	15	31	16
Distress				
Plays				
When young people cry . . .	24	26	31	19
When a man or woman is shown crying .	22	31	29	18

Number of *positive and negative* personality characteristics and behaviour shown by the heroes, heroines, and villains of thirteen adult television plays shown during February and March 1956

Positive Personality Characteristics

	Heroes	Heroines	Villain
Appearance or physical characteristics:			
Good looking	9	12	1
Clean	7	13	7
Tidy	6	11	7
Strong	8	3	6
Healthy	3	—	2
Socially approved characteristics:			
Gentle	7	9	2
Kind	11	11	—
Warm-hearted	11	11	—
Selfless	6	10	—
Loyal	9	11	—
Generous	5	7	—
Idealistic	9	10	1
Just	10	10	—
Honest	10	10	—
Courageous	11	11	3
Strength of character:			
Strong	11	10	6
Sane	10	8	2
Satisfaction and assurance:			
Satisfied	5	1	—
Happy	5	3	2
Assured	11	4	7
Trusting	4	8	—
Social manner:			
Polite	11	11	4
Modest	7	8	1
Humorous	4	1	2
Intelligence and effort:			
Intelligent	11	11	9
Educated	11	10	6
Enterprising	11	8	8
Industrious	6	7	2
Total number of character types	13	14	11

Negative Personality Characteristics

	Heroes	Heroines	Villains
Appearance and physical characteristics:			
Plain, ugly	1	—	4
Dirty	4	—	2
Untidy	5	1	2
Weak	—	—	—
Unhealthy	—	—	1
Socially disapproved characteristics:			
Violent	1	2	8
Unkind	1	—	9
Callous	—	—	10
Selfish	—	2	6
Disloyal	1	—	8
Mean	1	—	5
Materialistic	1	—	5
Unjust	1	1	9
Dishonest	1	—	10
Cowardly	1	—	4
Strength of character:			
Weak	—	—	2
Neurotic/insane	2	1	5
Satisfaction and assurance:			
Dissatisfied	6	8	6
Unhappy	2	8	3
Insecure	2	3	1
Distrusting	4	1	4
Social manner:			
Impolite	1	—	4
Boastful	2	1	5
Dour	—	1	5
Intelligence and effort:			
Unintelligent	—	—	2
Uneducated	—	1	1
Unenterprising	—	1	—
Lazy	1	—	1
Total number of character types	13	14	11

APPENDIX TABLE 28

Vocational expectations and aspirations of adolescent boys and girls aged 13–14 years

(Distribution of answers by sex, type of school, and social class)

	All		Boys		Girls		Grammar		Sec. Mod.		Middle class		Working class	
	v %	c %	v %	c %	v %	c %	v %	c %	v %	c %	v %	c %	v %	c %
Expected job														
Unclassifiable	18	21	24	28	12	14	22	34	15	14	21	22	15	20
Professional, High Administrative (Hall-Jones grades 1, 2, 3)	24	26	22	20	26	31	43	42	12	21	29	27	19	25
Lower-grade inspectional, distributive, clerical	28	27	6	10	50	45	19	18	32	30	27	28	29	26
Manual work (irrespective of degree of skill involved)	30	26	48	42	12	10	16	6	41	35	23	23	37	29
Wish job														
Unclassifiable	23	25	29	30	17	20	21	28	22	26	21	24	25	27
Professional, High Administrative (Hall-Jones grades 1, 2, 3)	45	46	38	46	53	45	52	54	43	38	54	52	37	39
Lower-grade inspectional, distributive, clerical	20	17	15	8	25	27	23	18	17	17	17	13	23	22
Manual work (irrespective of degree of skill involved)	12	12	18	16	5	8	4	—	18	19	8	11	15	12
Total cases (weighted)	504	504	252	252	252	252	168	168	336	336	252	252	252	252

Percentage of children in Norwich with a preference for different aspects of work

	13–14 YEAR OLDS								10–11 YEAR OLDS			
	Grammar				Sec. mod.				All			
	Viewers		Controls		Viewers		Controls		Viewers		Controls	
	1955 %	1956 %	1955 %	1956 %	1955 %	1956 %	1955 %	1956 %	1955 %	1956 %	1955 %	1956 %
A job where:												
You work mostly with your brains	64	64	77	74	29	14	53	31	50	38	55	42
You have to think things out for yourself	78	84	71	77	30	36	29	31	25	25	25	25
You might get very far, but you might get the sack	61	81	72	77	19	36	28	22	23	31	27	29
It is very necessary to be nicely dressed	61	69	73	60	52	50	72	63	66	65	60	60
Which of these would you rather do when you leave school:												
Go to the university or college (*versus* get a job straight away)	61	58	53	61	36	25	38	41	45	35	56	47
Total cases	23	26	30	31	28	28	32	32	124	127	127	125

Appendix Table 30

Vocational expectations and aspirations of 10-11 year olds

(Distribution of answers by sex, intelligence, and social class)

	All		Boys		Girls		I.Q. 115+		I.Q. 114 and below		Middle class		Working class	
	v %	c %	v %	c %	v %	c %	v %	c %	v %	c %	v %	c %	v %	c %
Expected job:														
Unclassifiable	31	30	41	40	20	19	26	34	33	27	36	30	26	27
Professional, High Administrative (Hall-Jones grades 1, 2, 3)	27	32	20	25	34	39	43	39	18	29	30	38	24	27
Lower-grade inspectional, distributive, clerical	25	20	13	8	38	33	18	18	28	21	23	19	27	21
Manual work (irrespective of degree of skill involved)	17	18	26	27	8	9	13	9	21	23	11	13	23	25
Wish job:														
Unclassifiable	28	30	33	37	23	23	28	32	28	29	32	30	24	30
Professional, High Administrative (Hall-Jones grades 1, 2, 3)	40	38	29	28	52	48	45	44	37	34	43	41	37	35
Lower-grade inspectional, distributive, clerical	15	15	13	12	17	19	16	15	15	15	12	19	19	12
Manual work (irrespective of degree of skill involved)	17	17	25	23	8	10	11	9	20	22	13	10	20	23
Total cases (weighted)	504	504	252	252	252	252	168	168	336	336	252	252	252	252

Frequency of response of Norwich children to questions about dress and speech as criteria of social differentiation

	13–14 YEAR OLDS								10–11 YEAR OLDS				
	Grammar				Sec. mod.				All				
	Viewers		Controls		Viewers		Controls		Viewers		Controls	
	1955	1956	1955	1956	1955	1956	1955	1956	1955	1956	1955	1956
	%	%	%	%	%	%	%	%	%	%	%	%
Do you think you can tell how important a man is by the way he is dressed?:												
Usually	25	42	23	39	29	32	47	34	33	36	37	35
Sometimes	67	50	73	48	61	54	47	53	45	51	46	52
Hardly ever	8	8	4	13	10	14	6	13	22	13	17	13
Total cases	24	26	30	31	28	28	32	32	126	125	126	126
Do you think you can tell how important a man is by the way he speaks?:												
Usually	33	35	23	26	29	36	53	44	24	37	38	38
Sometimes	54	54	67	55	61	54	38	50	58	54	45	45
Hardly ever	13	11	10	19	10	10	9	6	18	9	17	17
Total cases	24	26	30	31	28	28	32	32	126	125	126	126

APPENDIX TABLE 32

Here are ten things which may be important in helping a person to get on in the world.
Tick the one which you think is the most important

(Distribution of answers by age, type of school, and intelligence)

| | 13–14 YEAR OLDS | | | | | | 10–11 YEAR OLDS | | | | | |
| | All | | Grammar | | Sec. mod. | | All | | I.Q. 115+ | | I.Q. 114 and below | |
Percentage who ticked the following as being the most important:	v %	c %	v %	c %	v %	c %	v %	c %	v %	c %	v %	c %
Good character	32	40	30	37	34	44	19	24	21	32	18	21
People your family know	11	9	8	8	15	11	1	—	1	—	1	—
Brains	1	1	3	1	1	1	25	22	23	13	26	27
Money	—	—	—	—	—	—	3	3	2	1	3	4
Hard work	22	21	29	25	14	16	13	12	20	12	10	12
Good luck	1	1	1	1	1	—	3	2	2	2	3	2
Dress and speech	2	3	1	2	2	3	2	3	2	4	2	2
Friends	1	1	—	1	—	1	1		1	3	2	3
Education	21	22	19	24	23	21	26	27	20	28	29	26
Not being afraid	9	2	9	1	10	3	7	4	8	5	6	3
Total cases (weighted)	514	520	166	170	348	350	478	494	153	165	325	329

NOTE: This question followed a similar, open-ended question given earlier (see Appendix Table 33).

APPENDIX TABLE 33

What do you think are the three main things that help a man to get on in the world?[1]

(Distribution of answers by age and sex)

| | 13–14 YEAR OLDS | | | | | | 10–11 YEAR OLDS | | | | | |
| | All | | Boys | | Girls | | All | | Boys | | Girls | |
	v %	c %	v %	c %	v %	c %	v %	c %	v %	c %	v %	c %
High principles, being reliable and loyal	45	51	49	50	41	53	47	47	46	38	48	57
Brains, being clever	49	36	53	39	44	33	44	40	46	41	42	39
Being kind, helpful, obedient	32	34	25	30	39	37	36	34	32	28	40	41
Good manners, sportsmanship	23	31	17	30	30	31	21	20	22	15	21	26
Education, schooling, knowledge	23	26	25	29	20	23	22	24	25	27	19	22
Being able to stand up for oneself, confidence, drive	35	25	37	30	33	21	19	14	21	17	18	10
Right appearance, including looks, cleanliness, and dress	17	18	13	15	22	20	15	15	14	13	17	17
Having money	21	16	24	21	18	12	22	25	27	30	16	19
The right type of job	15	15	16	17	15	13	20	19	20	16	21	21
Good health, being strong	9	14	11	12	7	16	15	21	19	24	11	18
Right home background, right home (this includes a happy home as well as a socially suitable home)	14	11	15	9	14	12	19	17	16	11	23	23
Right connexions, pull, and luck	2	5	3	8	1	2	2	1	4	3	1	—
Total cases (weighted)	375	409	186	199	189	210	330	303	160	158	170	145

[1] All three responses were included, therefore the percentages exceed 100.

469

APPENDIX TABLE 34

Percentage of children with preferences for leaving school at different ages

(Distribution of answers by age, sex, social class, and intelligence)

13–14 YEAR OLDS

Sec. mod.

	All		Grammar		I.Q. 100–114		I.Q below 100		Boys		Girls		Middle class		Working class	
	v %	c %	v %	c %	v %	c %	v %	c %	v %	c %	v %	c %	v %	c %	v %	c %
Below 15 years of age	24	28	11	12	26	34	36	35	20	30	29	25	21	26	28	29
15 years	31	28	12	12	42	36	36	35	33	19	29	39	31	23	31	34
16 years	26	22	35	31	21	18	22	18	28	29	23	14	25	29	27	15
Over 16 years of age	19	22	42	45	11	12	6	12	19	22	19	22	23	22	14	22
Total cases (weighted)	440	432	139	129	147	147	154	156	226	220	214	212	215	219	225	213

10–11 YEAR OLDS

	All		I.Q. 115+		I.Q. 100–114		I.Q. below 100		Boys		Girls		Middle class		Working class	
	v %	c %	v %	c %	v %	c %	v %	c %	v %	c %	v %	c %	v %	c %	v %	c %
Below 15 years of age	13	16	12	7	13	15	14	26	13	15	13	17	15	16	15	20
15 years	26	24	10	13	24	28	44	30	25	23	27	24	24	14	27	31
16 years	26	23	24	26	34	22	21	21	27	19	25	26	24	21	27	24
Over 16 years of age	35	37	54	54	29	35	21	23	35	43	35	33	37	49	31	25
Total cases (weighted)	426	425	144	142	141	138	141	145	214	199	212	226	222	211	212	223

A good father is a man who . .

Frequency of mention of (*a*) someone who provides and (*b*) someone who is loving, kind, &c.

| | 13–14 YEAR OLDS | | | | | | | | | | 10–11 YEAR OLDS | | | | | | | | | |
| | All | | Boys | | Girls | | Middle class | | Working class | | All | | Boys | | Girls | | Middle class | | Working class | |
	v %	c %	v %	c %	v %	c %	v %	c %	v %	c %	v %	c %	v %	c %	v %	c %	v %	c %	v %	c %
Someone who:																				
Provides	42	45	49	49	36	42	37	47	46	40	51	51	54	51	49	51	49	54	54	49
Is loving, kind, faithful	46	42	37	36	53	47	50	41	42	43	40	39	38	37	43	41	43	37	38	41
Total cases (weighted)	402	398	187	179	215	219	186	201	216	197	343	342	156	152	187	190	175	171	168	171

APPENDIX TABLE 36

Some common fears selected from the fears inventory

(Percentage distribution of answers by age and sex of 'frightens me a little', 'frightens me a lot')

| | 13–14 YEAR OLDS | | | | 10–11 YEAR OLDS | | | |
| | Boys | | Girls | | Boys | | Girls | |
	v %	c %	v %	c %	v %	c %	v %	c %
The dark	16	17	38	42	31	26	45	48
People following me . .	39	30	81	77	44	37	78	70
Dreams	30	26	40	40	33	32	53	51
Being in a crowd . .	5	6	14	10	8	12	21	20
Being alone at home at night	19	18	50	54	39	31	59	59
Burglars	44	38	81	75	61	56	88	79
Acting or reciting in front of others	74	66	50	44	32	29	47	46
Being made to look silly .	41	45	71	50	34	35	48	54
Total cases (weighted) . .	135	133	154	159	191	183	169	172

APPENDIX TABLE 37

Acceptance as true of four science-fiction statements

	13–14 YEAR OLDS									
					Sec. mod.		Sec. mod.			
	All		Grammar				Boys		Girls	
	v %	c %	v %	c %	v %	c %	v %	c %	v %	c %
Flying saucers are space ships from Mars:										
Agree	8	9	4	2	10	13	8	10	13	21
Disagree . . .	51	50	63	62	45	44	49	45	36	29
Not sure . . .	41	41	33	36	45	43	43	45	51	50
Total cases (weighted) .	300	300	100	100	200	200	100	100	100	100
We can now visit the moon in a space ship:										
Agree	5	10	6	9	5	10	11	11	1	9
Disagree . . .	73	65	78	70	71	62	67	69	74	55
Not sure . . .	22	25	16	21	24	28	22	20	25	36
Total cases (weighted) .	300	300	100	100	200	200	100	100	100	100
There are people living on Mars:										
Agree	10	11	12	11	14	11	19	14	10	8
Disagree . . .	33	38	26	27	32	43	23	30	41	58
Not sure . . .	57	51	62	62	54	46	58	56	49	34
Total cases (weighted) .	300	300	100	100	200	200	100	100	100	100
We are being watched from Mars:										
Agree	6	6	4	7	5	5	9	7	2	3
Disagree . . .	55	50	60	50	53	50	47	47	59	54
Not sure . . .	39	44	36	43	42	45	44	46	39	43
Total cases (weighted) .	300	300	100	100	200	200	100	100	100	100

Attitudes to foreigners

(Distribution of answers given by 13–14 year olds)

| | 13–14 YEAR OLDS | | | | | |
| | All | | Grammar | | Sec. mod. | |
	v %	c %	v %	c %	v %	c %
My own country is always right:						
I agree	11	13	4	10	14	14
I disagree	58	49	76	69	50	40
I am not sure	31	38	20	21	36	46
Total cases (weighted) . . .	300	300	100	100	200	200
You can't trust foreigners:						
I agree	9	11	4	6	11	14
I disagree	73	73	86	81	66	68
I am not sure	18	16	10	13	23	18
Total cases (weighted) . . .	300	300	100	100	200	200
We can learn a lot from foreign people:						
I agree	56	58	66	76	51	50
I disagree	26	22	18	12	31	27
I am not sure	18	20	16	12	18	23
Total cases (weighted) . . .	300	300	100	100	200	200

APPENDIX TABLE 39

Mean test scores of 13–14 year olds on general knowledge test of English literature by sex, intelligence, and social class[1]

| | | 13–14 YEAR OLDS | | | | | |
| | | Boys | | | Girls | | |
Viewers:	All	Middle class	Work-ing class	Total	Middle class	Work-ing class	Total
Grammar . .	3·462	3·375	3·475	3·425	3·600	3·400	3·500
Secondary modern I.Q. 100–114 .	3·468	4·025	3·400	3·712	3·025	3·425	3·225
Secondary modern I.Q. below 100 .	3·074	3·375	3·000	3·187	3·400	2·525	2·962
	3·335	3·592	3·292	3·442	3·342	3·116	3·335

Social class (both sexes) 3·467   3·204

Controls:							
Grammar . .	3·687	3·675	3·775	3·725	3·700	3·600	3·650
Secondary modern I.Q. 100–114 .	3·449	3·600	3·525	3·562	3·125	3·550	3·337
Secondary modern I.Q. below 100 .	2·918	2·925	2·975	2·950	3·400	2·375	2·887
	3·351	3·400	3·425	3·412	3·408	3·175	3·291

Social class (both sexes) 3·404   3·300

[1] See note on following page.

Mean test scores of 10–11 year olds on general knowledge test of English literature by sex, intelligence, and social class

10–11 YEAR OLDS

		BOYS			GIRLS		
Viewers: Primaries	All	Middle class	Working class	Total	Middle class	Working-class	Total
I.Q. 115+	3·618	4·000	3·750	3·875	3·400	3·325	3·362
I.Q. 100–114	3·487	3·875	3·900	3·887	3·050	3·125	3·087
I.Q. below 100	2·887	3·450	3·000	3·225	2·500	2·600	2·550
	3·331	3·775	3·550	3·662	2·983	3·017	3·000

Social class (both sexes) 3·379   3·283

		BOYS			GIRLS		
Controls:	All	Middle class	Working class	Total	Middle class	Working-class	Total
I.Q. 115+	3·606	3·925	3·675	3·800	3·475	3·350	3·412
I.Q. 100–114	3·556	3·800	3·725	3·762	3·500	3·200	3·350
I.Q. below 100	2·762	3·250	3·025	3·137	2·200	2·575	2·387
	3·308	3·658	3·475	3·566	3·058	3·042	3·050

Social class (both sexes) 3·358   3·258

[1] We computed separate scores for each area of knowledge, and subsequently obtained forty-eight cell-means, one for each cell in the factorial design, followed by seventy-two sub-total means for the various cell combinations (viewers and controls) in each area. In computing these additional means, we gave equal weight to all cell-means (instead of the usual weighting procedure). This first set of means, then, represents the distribution of each area score by age, sex, intelligence, and social class, for viewers and controls separately, except that since different tests were given to the three different types of school, age-comparisons are not possible.

In addition, for each area score the control-sample means were subtracted (cell by cell, and sub-total mean by sub-total mean) from the corresponding viewer-sample means. This resulted in a set of difference scores (positive and negative) giving us— besides the normal pattern of scores and differences between viewers and controls—the differential gains and losses between children of different types. We carried out a modified 4-factor analysis of variance for each subject (modified in the sense that it was computed, not on the raw scores, but on the difference scores, and with the aid of sums-of-squares of differences). This analysis, in addition to showing the statistical significance of sex, social class, and intelligence (and their interactions) in determining the results, fully exploits the precision offered by the viewer-cantrol individual matching in the estimation of the significance of gains or losses.

Analysis of variance and mean sub-total scores for each area in the tests of general knowledge

| | | Mean sub-total scores[1] | | | | | | Analysis of variance | |
| | | 13–14 YEAR OLDS | | | 10–11 YEAR OLDS | | | Viewers' overall gains | Effects of main variables |
		Grammar	Sec. mod. I.Q. 100–114	Sec. mod. I.Q. below 100	I.Q. 115+	I.Q. 100–114	I.Q. below 100		
English litera-ture	V	3·462	3·468	3·074	3·618	3·487	2·887		
	C	3·687	3·449	2·918	3·606	3·556	2·762		
	V–C	−0·225	0·019	0·156	−0·012	−0·069	0·125		
History	V	2·950	3·400	3·187	4·368	3·881	3·187		Sex 1% significant. (With dull in both age groups boys gain, girls lose)
	C	3·000	3·274	3·318	4·174	4·006	3·168		
	V–C	−0·050	0·126	−0·131	0·194	−0·125	0·019		
Geography	V	3·224	3·637	2·987	3·824	3·618	2·906	0·1% significant (mainly younger children)	I.Q. 5% significant
	C	3·343	3·347	3·087	3·600	3·343	2·618		
	V–C	−0·119	0·200	−0·100	0·224	0·275	0·288		
Science	V	3·487	3·193	2·562	4·125	3·831	3·324	0·1% significant (mainly dull younger children)	I.Q. 0·1% significant (duller gain more)
	C	3·662	3·056	2·462	4·100	3·825	2·699		
	V–C	−0·175	0·137	0·100	0·025	0·006	0·625		
Religion	V	2·355	3·213	2·647	4·079	3·671	3·263		
	C	2·838	3·088	2·696	4·029	3·818	3·371		
	V–C	−0·183	0·125	−0·049	0·050	−0·147	−0·108		

[1] See note on following page.

475

APPENDIX TABLE 41 (cont.)

| | | Mean sub-total scores[1] | | | | | | Analysis of variance | |
| | | 13–14 YEAR OLDS | | | 10–11 YEAR OLDS | | | Viewers' overall gains | Effects of main variables |
		Grammar	Sec. mod. I.Q. 100–114	Sec. mod. I.Q. below 100	I.Q. 115+	I.Q. 100–114	I.Q. below 100		
Current affairs	V	3·562	4·081	3·412					I.Q. 1% significant (gains for bright secondary modern children only)
	C	3·650	3·693	3·506					
	V–C	−0·088	0·388	−0·094					
Nature and rural studies	V	3·462	3·950	3·231	4·118	3·875	2·893		
	C	3·762	4·012	3·612	3·956	3·693	2·868		
	V–C	−0·300	−0·062	−0·381	0·162	0·182	0·025		
Art Architecture (older children only)	V	2·793	3·350	2·675					
	C	2·900	3·237	2·662					
	V–C	−0·107	0·113	0·013					
Handicrafts and housecrafts	V	3·380	3·330	2·850	3·529	2·997	2·814	5% significant (mainly dull younger children)	
	C	3·354	3·338	2·905	3·446	2·955	2·156		
	V–C	0·026	−0·008	−0·055	0·083	0·042	0·678		
Sport	V	3·437	3·231	2·931	4·556	4·244	3·462	0·001% significant (mainly younger children)	
	C	3·137	3·106	3·067	4·175	3·700	2·975		
	V–C	0·300	0·125	−0·136	0·381	0·544	0·487		
Music	V	3·043	3·937	3·324	4·550	4·493	3·556	1% significant (younger children only)	I.Q. 1% significant (duller gain more)
	C	3·225	3·956	3·306	4·556	4·131	2·993		
	V–C	−0·182	−0·019	0·018	−0·006	0·362	0·563		

[1] Differences between primary, secondary modern, and grammar schools scores arise in part out of the fact that different tests were given to each type of school.

APPENDIX TABLE 42

Proportion of viewers and controls who gave correct answers to eighteen test items which were taken from programmes included in the 1955 programme recall lists

Programme:	Duration (min.)	Proportion of viewers who saw the programme %	Information test item (4 multiple choices) Grammar	Proportion of total in group who ticked the right answer[1]			
				Viewers who saw programme %	Their controls %	Viewers who did not see programme %	Their controls %
The Explorer (serial)	30	50	Which of these explorers is noted for his travels in Africa?	100	96	97	100
The Explorer (serial)	30	50	Stanley was educated at . . .	73	17	48	21
Chessington Zoo	20	29	A golden hampster is a . . .	91	86	96	89
Chessington Zoo	20	29	Which one of these animals is about the same size as a Dexter cow?	56	37	56	60
Panorama[3]	45	33	Doctors and dentists are not the only people who use ether in their jobs. It may also be used by:	88	75	88	76
Cities of Europe—Rome[2]	10	43	On which river is Rome situated?	81	94	86	90
Greta Garbo[2] (film)	30	37	Greta Garbo won fame as . . .	97	94	86	77
Total cases	160						

[1] All the items were shown in the same week; this means that the interval between seeing the information on the screen and being tested as part of our main survey was approximately the same for all of them. The last two columns show in percentages the correct responses for viewers who missed the programmes and their controls. The matching has ensured that these two groups get roughly similar scores: there are only four instances of a difference of more than 10 per cent between them. This suggests that we can obtain a reasonable estimate of previous knowledge of the viewers who *did* see the programmes, by looking at the results of their controls.

[2] Evening programme. All others were taken from children's television.

477

APPENDIX TABLE 42 (cont.)

Programme:	Duration (min.)	Proportion of viewers who saw the programme %	Information test items (4 multiple choices) Secondary modern	Proportion of total in group who ticked the right answer			
				Viewers who saw programme %	Their controls %	Viewers who did not see programme %	Their controls %
Chessington Zoo	20	30	A dromedary is a kind of . . .	62	62	57	47
People in Books	15	33	Who wrote The Three Hostages?	18	15	18	17
The Explorer (serial)	30	60	Members of King Charles I's party in the English Civil War were usually known as . . .	61	61	66	56
Devon and Cornwall	30	44	Which of these towns is in Devon?	61	60	54	65
Panorama	45	39	Doctors and dentists are not the only people who use either in their jobs. It may also be used by:	71	47	67	62
Total cases		330					
			Primary				
Out of Doors	15	47	The leaf of the lime tree has . . .	49	51	42	47
People in Books	15	43	Who wrote The Three Hostages?	29	27	19	32
Chessington Zoo	20	52	A dromedary is a kind of . . .	61	51	60	50
Chessington Zoo	20	52	A baboon is a kind of . . .	91	75	93	90
Devon and Cornwall	30	64	Which of these towns is in Devon?	55	48	53	55
Devon and Cornwall	30	64	Large quantities of china clay are mined in . . .	59	46	43	38
Total cases		486					

If you had been chosen to become one of Jesus' disciples you would probably have found it both easy and difficult. Why do you think it would be easy? And why do you think it would be hard?

(Distribution of answers of 112 pairs of 11–12 year olds in Norwich)[1]

	Viewers %	Controls %
It would be easy because:		
No answer, don't know, illegible	24	32
Reference to a miracle	4	5
Miscellaneous	7	10
Denial—'It would *not* be easy.'	7	12
Reference to television—e.g. 'Because I've seen a play.' .	1	—
Jesus (the practical aspect)		
Jesus helps, defends, provides, calms hostile people, saves you from danger	12	7
Jesus (the human aspect)		
Jesus understands you, makes allowance for weaknesses; people liked Jesus, could trust Jesus. He had such a good nature	6	3
Naïve		
'All you have to do is to follow Him.' 'It would be easy to be with Jesus, and talk to people, preach to people.' 'Just walking around.' 'You need no education, only will-power.' 'You only have to leave your own home and follow Jesus.' 'Because He could do miracles.' . . .	18	15
Jesus (the abstract aspect)		
Jesus gives spiritual support, guidance, inspiration, blessing, courage, inspires you to do good, help from His teaching or His stories	7	12
Doctrinaire		
'You would be forgiven your sins.' 'Because He was the Son of God.' 'You would receive the Holy Ghost.' 'All things are possible with God.'	8	4
Submissive		
Accent on love and faith. 'It would be easy to talk about Jesus.' 'Your faith in Jesus (in God, in the cause) would make it easy.' 'People believed in Jesus.' . . .	6	5
Outside help		
People would help you, would receive you; people would spread the word; no one would stop you. . . .	5	3
Total cases	112	112

[1] The figures exceed 100 per cent because some children gave more than one answer.

APPENDIX TABLE 43 (cont.)

	Viewers %	Controls %
It would be hard because:		
No answer, don't know, illegible	14	18
Miscellaneous	24	14

High moral standard of life required
'It is hard to be good.' 'Jesus was so good.' 'Hard to live with Him.' 'You'd have to pray and set an example so often.' 'You'd have to obey Jesus.' 'Things Jesus asked of you would be difficult.' 'You'd be tempted.' . . . 10 9

Walking involved
'You'd have to do a lot of walking, travelling, wandering.' . 7 6

General hard work implied
'It would be hard work.' 'Followers of Jesus worked hard.' 'You'd do hard tasks.' 'You'd have to do Jesus' work.' 'You'd be very busy.' 4 1

Loss of home, loved ones, and job
'Hard to leave home, friends, work.' 7 3

Loss of physical possessions and comforts
'You'd have to give up everything.' 'You'd have to put up with bad conditions.' 'You'd have no money, no bed.' 'Never know where the next meal would come from.' . 9 6

A feeling for Jesus
Especially His hardships, crucifixion. 'People shouting at Jesus.' 'Need to protect Jesus.' 'Need to be kind to Jesus.' 3 3

Persecution and opposition
'You might be persecuted (condemned, stoned, tortured, killed, crucified, imprisoned).' 'You'd have to face danger, you'd need courage.' 'Many people were against you (Romans, Scribes, Pharisees).' 'Jesus had many enemies, you'd have to watch out for foes.' 13 22

The ridicule of others
'You'd be laughed at, jeered at, mocked, gossiped about.' 'You'd need courage to face up to other people.' . . 2 3

Need for faith
'You'd have to believe firmly or fully in Jesus, in God.' 'Your faith would have to be strong.' 'You may not have enough faith.' 'It was hard to believe in Him.' . . 7 4

Preaching and its difficulties
'People would not listen or believe you or believe Jesus.' 'Hard to make people understand.' 'Preaching or teaching is hard.' 14 17

| *Total cases* | 112 | 112 |

APPENDIX TABLE 44

Some children feel they have learnt something from TV, while others do not. Here is a list of subjects. Tick Yes or No to show whether or not you have learnt something about them that you did not know before

Percentage distribution for each subject, in descending order (positive replies only)

Learnt something about:	13–14 YEAR OLDS %	10–11 YEAR OLDS %
Animals	85	87
Other countries and other people . .	86	85
Cooking, housecraft . . .	86	55
People or happenings in history . .	75	77
Science	75	69
Nature study	66	76
Making small models . . .	59	72
Drawing, painting, and pottery . .	55	68
How to behave in company . .	52	52
How to dress	50	41
Music	48	48
Current affairs	47	33
Dancing, ballet	42	40
Dressmaking or needlework . . .	39	48
English (poetry and literature) . .	34	35
Foreign languages	33	36
Total cases (weighted)	510	510

APPENDIX TABLE 45

Write down the three things you like doing best—that is, in the time after school

Frequency of mention of television by viewers

(Distribution by age and intelligence)

	13–14 YEAR OLDS				10–11 YEAR OLDS			
			Sec. mod.					
	All %	Grammar %	I.Q. 100–114 %	I.Q. below 100 %	All %	I.Q. 115+ %	I.Q. 100–114 %	I.Q. below 100 %
1st choice . .	13	6	16	16	19	16	15	26
2nd or 3rd choice .	27	36	28	19	26	20	32	28
Not mentioned .	60	58	56	65	55	64	53	46
Total cases (weighted)	504	168	168	168	504	168	168	168

Distribution of school performance ratings by intelligence, for both age groups. (The entries in the columns are *raw frequencies*)

Subject:	Controls Better	Same	Viewers Better	Controls Better	Same	Viewers Better	Controls Better	Same	Viewers Better
				13–14 YEAR OLDS					
	Grammar			Sec. mod. I.Q. above 100			Sec. mod. I.Q. below 100		
Reading	13	8	12	12	15	15	7	7	7
Spoken English and drama	12	9	16	10	13	15	5	4	11
Written English	21	10	11	21	5	18	5	4	12
Sports, games	14	11	16	17	13	11	7	5	9
Music, singing	11	21	3	10	12	13	2	6	10
Arithmetic or Mathematics	24	7	14	15	11	17	8	6	7
History	20	7	16	11	12	18	10	5	6
Geography	19	14	13	11	12	20	8	6	7
Current affairs	4	6	3	1	3	3	4	2	3
Art, modelling	15	13	12	14	7	16	6	11	3
Science	13	16	15	14	11	,9	7	5	5
Religious instruction	15	17	7	16	9	13	7	6	6
Domestic subjects	4	3	1	11	3	13	3	4	4
Needlework	1	4	3	12	6	6	7	4	0
Handicrafts	2	3	5	8	5	10	1	7	2
Nature study	5	9	8	5	1	8	2	2	6
Foreign languages	21	3	22	8	2	9	—	—	—
Overall assessment	23	8	15	17	7	20	12	2	7

	Controls Better	Same	Viewers Better	Controls Better	Same	Viewers Better	Controls Better	Same	Viewers Better
				10–11 YEAR OLDS					
	I.Q. 115 and over			I.Q. 100–115			I.Q. below 100		
Reading	9	4	3	14	6	6	7	6	6
Spoken English and drama	10	2	4	10	8	3	3	10	6
Written English	8	5	3	14	3	9	8	6	5
Sports, games	7	3	6	4	10	11	8	4	7
Music, singing	8	5	3	8	12	4	2	12	4
Arithmetic	6	3	7	10	3	13	8	3	8
History	7	5	4	8	9	9	2	10	7
Geography	7	5	4	9	9	8	3	11	5
Art, modelling	8	3	5	7	10	9	5	3	10
Religious instruction	6	7	2	7	13	4	5	13	1
Nature studies	8	4	3	7	12	5	2	10	5
Handicrafts	3	3	3	2	3	5	0	2	2
Overall assessment	8	4	4	12	3	11	9	5	5

Write down the three main things you like doing best—that is, in the time after school

(Distribution of first choices)

13-14 YEAR OLDS

	All		Boys		Girls		Grammar		Sec. mod. I.Q. 100–114		Sec. mod. I.Q. below 100	
	v %	c %	v %	c %	v %	c %	v %	c %	v %	c %	v %	c %
Mass media	26	23	21	16	32	28	18	24	30	24	29	16
Television	13	1	13	—	13	1	6	1	16	—	16	—
Reading	6	7	2	4	11	10	7	12	5	6	7	2
Radio	—	2	—	1	—	3	—	1	—	4	—	1
Cinema, theatre.	7	13	6	11	8	14	5	10	9	14	6	13
Outdoor	53	50	60	62	46	39	60	52	52	47	49	52
Sports, cycling, walking	40	40	49	51	30	28	48	46	39	32	32	39
Playing outside in street, garden, going for walk, window shopping, gardening	13	10	11	11	16	11	12	6	13	15	17	13
Indoor	14	19	12	15	17	24	16	16	12	24	16	22
Hobbies: writing, acting, painting, collecting, indoor games, model-making, musical activities	6	8	8	6	5	9	8	7	7	10	3	9
Helping in the house	4	3	1	1	7	6	3	2	2	6	10	3
Clubs	3	5	3	7	2	4	4	4	2	6	1	6
Dancing	1	3	—	1	3	5	1	3	1	2	2	4
Others												
Playing indoors *or* outdoors (unspecified)	2	3	2	2	1	4	2	4	2	1	—	4
Miscellaneous interests	5	5	5	5	4	5	4	4	4	4	6	6
Total cases (weighted)	502	504	249	251	253	253	168	168	168	168	168	168

10–11 YEAR OLDS

	All		Boys		Girls		I.Q. 115+		I.Q. 100–114		I.Q. below 100	
	v %	c %	v %	c %	v %	c %	v %	c %	v %	c %	v %	c %
Mass media	30	19	25	14	34	24	32	21	25	17	33	19
Television	19	1	18	1	20	1	16	2	15	—	26	1
Reading	10	12	6	8	14	15	14	16	10	11	7	7
Radio	—	3	—	2	—	5	—	2	—	3	—	6
Cinema, theatre	1	3	1	3	—	3	2	1	—	3	—	5
Outdoor	45	52	53	62	35	42	43	48	44	46	46	60
Sports, cycling, walking	36	34	43	46	25	22	34	31	33	31	34	39
Playing outside in street, garden, going for walk, window shopping, gardening	9	18	10	16	10	20	9	17	11	15	12	21
Indoor	19	20	16	17	23	24	19	27	25	27	13	12
Hobbies: writing, acting, painting, collecting, indoor games, model-making, musical activities	13	12	14	13	13	11	15	17	13	17	8	4
Helping in the house	3	4	1	1	6	8	2	4	8	4	2	7
Clubs	2	2	1	3	2	2	2	3	2	4	1	1
Dancing	1	2	—	—	2	3	—	3	2	2	2	—
Others												
Playing indoors *or* outdoors (unspecified)	3	5	3	5	4	4	2	2	4	5	3	7
Miscellaneous interests	3	4	3	2	4	6	4	2	2	5	5	2
Total cases (weighted)	504	504	252	252	252	252	168	168	168	168	168	168

APPENDIX TABLE 48. *Write down the three things you really enjoyed*

Daily diary record. Average number of days in a week on which viewers mentioned various activities

	13–14 YEAR OLDS	10–11 YEAR OLDS
Sport		
Walking, cycling, fishing, football, cricket, tennis, outdoor play	4·1	4·9
Other out-of-home activities		
Outings, shopping, clubs, museums, church and Sunday school, cinema, going out with friends, dating, talking in the street	2·2	1·2
Total out-of-home	6·3	6·1
Home activities		
(except radio and television) meals, preparing for bed, doing domestic jobs, reading, playing, writing, sewing, talking, making things	4·4	4·8
Radio	0·8	0·3
Television	5·5	5·3
Total home	10·7	10·4
Uncertain		
whether activity takes place at home or out-of-home (including hobbies)	1·8	1·8
Total cases (weighted)	132	132
Maximum number of choices possible	21	21

NOTE. The average number of choices adds to less than the total number possible (21) because some children gave no choice, or less than three choices, on one or more days.

APPENDIX TABLE 49. Percentage of children's time between 4 p.m. and bedtime spent on the following activities

	13–14 YEAR OLDS		10–11 YEAR OLDS	
	V %	C %	V %	C %
Total mass media	42	25	35	22
Television	30	1	25	1
Radio	2	8	1	7
Cinema	5	8	3	6
All reading	5	8	6	8
Total outdoor activities	24	33	31	40
Outdoor sports, including swimming, skating	6	8	7	8
Walking, cycling, fishing, birds-nesting, &c.	5	7	5	6
Outdoor play in street, garden or park, including gardening, aimless wandering, chatting	12	16	18	24
Shopping expeditions, watching live sports	1	2	1	2
Total indoor activities	34	42	34	38
Visiting or being visited	10	13	13	11
Clubs	3	4	3	5
Indoors—making things, helping around house, playing, &c.	16	19	16	20
Doing homework	5	6	2	2
Total cases (weighted)	84	84	84	84

NOTE These percentages, derived from the children's diaries, are approximations only. The conventions used in estimating the weekly amount of time spent on each activity have been discussed in Appendix A. Only leisure after 4 p.m. and up to bedtime is covered, which leaves out of account all of Saturday and Sunday before 4 p.m., as well as activities which take place in bed, such as reading, for instance.

APPENDIX TABLE 50

Apart from your school books, how many books have you read during the last four weeks?

(Distribution of answers for viewers and controls by age, sex, and intelligence)

13–14 YEAR OLDS

Number of books read during the last four weeks:	All v %	All c %	Boys v %	Boys c %	Girls v %	Girls c %	Grammar v %	Grammar c %	I.Q. 100–114 v %	I.Q. 100–114 c %	Sec. mod. I.Q. below 100 v %	Sec. mod. I.Q. below 100 c %
None	19	16	30	17	9	13	13	9	26	15	18	21
Part of one	9	5	6	9	12	2	8	6	9	5	11	6
One	16	17	20	14	12	21	17	17	11	11	21	24
Two	22	24	18	22	26	25	22	21	26	31	18	18
Three–five	22	25	16	24	27	26	24	28	20	22	21	25
Six or more	12	13	10	14	14	13	16	19	8	16	11	6
Average number per child	2·2	2·5	1·9	2·5	2·6	2·6	2·8	3·0	1·9	2·7	2·0	1·9
Total cases (weighted)	449	459	222	230	227	229	151	153	148	153	150	153

10–11 YEAR OLDS

Number of books read during the last four weeks:	All v %	All c %	Boys v %	Boys c %	Girls v %	Girls c %	I.Q. 115+ v %	I.Q. 115+ c %	I.Q. 100–114 v %	I.Q. 100–114 c %	I.Q. below 100 v %	I.Q. below 100 c %
None	10	11	13	11	6	10	6	4	7	5	16	22
Part of one	9	8	10	13	7	4	4	6	10	10	12	7
One	21	13	26	15	15	11	15	12	22	14	25	12
Two	21	22	19	19	23	25	21	20	24	18	18	27
Three–five	28	31	21	28	38	34	34	42	30	39	23	19
Six or more	11	15	11	14	11	16	20	16	7	14	6	13
Average number per child	2·5	2·7	2·2	2·5	2·8	2·9	3·3	3·1	2·4	2·9	1·9	2·2
Total cases (weighted)	453	456	225	229	228	227	151	152	152	152	150	152

APPENDIX TABLE 51

Number of comics, children's newspapers or magazines which the children said they read every week

(Distribution of answers by age and social class)

	13–14 YEAR OLDS						10–11 YEAR OLDS					
	All		Middle class		Working class		All		Middle class		Working class	
	v %	c %	v %	c %	v %	c %	v %	c %	v %	c %	v %	c %
Two or less[1] .	39	41	37	49	40	33	39	40	43	46	36	33
Three to six .	46	42	49	35	42	49	36	38	33	35	39	43
Seven or more	15	17	14	16	18	18	25	22	24	19	25	24
Total cases *(weighted)* .	446	452	224	225	222	227	453	451	228	225	225	226

[1] The percentage who did not read comics was 6 per cent or less.

APPENDIX TABLE 52

Comparison of change in comic reading of Norwich viewers and controls, between 1955 and 1956

	13–14 YEAR OLDS		10–11 YEAR OLDS	
	Viewers %	Controls %	Viewers %	Controls %
More in 1956	13	18	16	23
Same in both years	49	53	48	48
Fewer in 1956	38	29	36	29
Total cases (weighted) . . .	37	45	114	115

487

What sort of book do you like best?

	13–14 YEAR OLDS						10–11 YEAR OLDS					
	All		Boys		Girls		All		Boys		Girls	
	v %	c %	v %	c %	v %	c %	v %	c %	v %	c %	v %	c %
Adventure, Westerns, and other stories	45	45	47	45	42	46	50	45	52	49	49	41
Mystery, crime, murder, detective	20	22	21	22	20	21	11	13	10	13	13	14
War, escape	8	10	16	19	—	—	4	2	7	4	—	—
Love, romance	6	5	—	—	11	10	—	—	—	—	—	—
School stories	6	5	1	—	10	10	8	8	3	2	13	13
Comic and funny stories and stories with happy endings	3	2	3	2	3	3	3	4	5	3	1	4
Enid Blyton stories	2	3	1	3	3	3	3	7	—	3	6	10
Stories about families	2	1	—	1	3	2	—	2	1	—	—	4
Stories about animals	3	2	1	—	4	3	4	2	—	—	7	4
Stories about sport, hobbies, travel, exploring	5	5	7	8	4	3	5	6	6	7	4	4
Other types of books	9	10	8	10	10	10	9	12	10	15	7	9
No answer, don't know	2	4	2	1	1	7	7	5	7	6	7	4
Total cases (weighted)	456	456	228	228	228	228	456	456	228	228	228	228

NOTE These figures add to over 100 per cent because some children mentioned more than one type of book.

Appendix Table 54

Viewers' interest in fiction and non-fiction subjects for reading compared with that of controls

13–14 YEAR OLDS

	Significantly more[1]	Insignificantly more	No difference	Insignificantly less	Significantly less[1]
Fiction	school life (0·3%) things that make you sad (5%) the sea (5%) ordinary families (0·3%) poor people (5%) serial stories (0·3%) rich people (0·3%) fairy tales (5%) plays (0·3%)		cowboys other sorts of adventure crime love and romance horror things that make you laugh things that happened in the war	ghosts space travel	
Non-fiction	puppets (5%) science (0·3%) inventions (0·3%) racing (0·3%) flying or aeroplanes (5%) hobbies (0·3%) music (0·3%) wild animals (5%) people in other countries (5%) famous people (0·3%) reference books (0·3%) dictionary (5%)	sport Painting and sculpture	things that happened in the Bible things that happened in history travel and exploring animals and birds people who lived long ago poems	ballet dancing	

10–11 YEAR OLDS

	Significantly more[1]	Insignificantly more	No difference	Insignificantly less	Significantly less[1]
Fiction	cowboys (0·3%) crime (0·3%) ordinary families (0·3%) serial stories (0·3%)	other adventure ghosts school stories things that make you sad the sea rich people	space travel love and romance horror stories things that make you laugh things that happened in the war poor people puppets fairy tales plays		
Non-fiction	travel and exploring (5%) science (0·3%) racing (0·3%) people in other countries (5%) famous people (0·3%) reference books (5%)	sport things that happened in history inventions animals and birds people who lived long ago	things that happened in the Bible flying and aeroplanes hobbies painting and sculpture ballet and dancing wild animals poems	music	dictionaries (5%)

[1] The figures in brackets show the level of significance of the difference.

489

APPENDIX TABLE 55

How many books have you read during the last four weeks?

(Distribution of answers of controls and recent, experienced, and veteran viewers by age and intelligence)

13–14 YEAR OLDS

Number of books read during last four weeks:	Grammar				I.Q. 100–114				Sec. Mod. I.Q. below 100			
	Viewers			Controls	Viewers			Controls	Viewers			Controls
	1 yr.	1–3 yrs.	3–5 yrs.		1 yr.	1–3 yrs.	3–5 yrs.		1 yr.	1–3 yrs.	3–5 yrs.	
	%	%	%	%	%	%	%	%	%	%	%	%
2 or less	64	61	52	53	80	77	59	62	75	64	60	69
3 or more	36	39	48	47	20	23	41	38	25	36	40	31
Total cases	25	63	27	149 (weighted)	24	44	27	153 (weighted)	24	37	20	153 (weighted)

10–11 YEAR OLDS

Number of books read during last four weeks:	I.Q. 115+				I.Q. 100–114				I.Q. below 100			
	Viewers			Controls	Viewers			Controls	Viewers			Controls
	1 yr.	1–3 yrs.	3–5 yrs.		1 yr.	1–3 yrs.	3–5 yrs.		1 yr.	1–3 yrs.	3–5 yrs.	
	%	%	%	%	%	%	%	%	%	%	%	%
2 or less	45	46	48	45	80	72	48	48	75	69	65	68
3 or more	55	54	52	55	20	28	52	52	25	31	35	32
Total cases	35	37	29	152 (weighted)	24	35	29	152 (weighted)	24	26	20	152 (weighted)

APPENDIX TABLE 56

When did you last go to the pictures?

(Distribution of answers by age, social class, and intelligence)

13–14 YEAR OLDS

	All		Middle class		Working class		I.Q. 115+		I.Q. 100–114		I.Q. below 100	
	v %	c %	v %	c %	v %	c %	v %	c %	v %	c %	v %	c %
Within last 2 days	20	23	22	24	19	22	12	13	24	21	26	36
Within last 7 days	54	64	55	62	53	65	42	51	61	59	62	82
Two weeks ago	15	9	15	10	14	9	14	11	14	12	15	4
Over 2 weeks ago	31	27	30	28	33	26	44	38	25	29	23	14
Total cases (weighted)	480	480	240	240	240	240	160	160	160	160	160	160

10–11 YEAR OLDS

	All		Middle Class		Working Class		I.Q. 115+		I.Q. 100–114		I.Q. below 100	
	v %	c %	v %	c %	v %	c %	v %	c %	v %	c %	v %	c %
Within last 2 days	8	16	6	14	9	17	7	6	6	12	10	29
Within last 7 days	32	44	25	39	38	48	24	32	26	45	44	55
Two weeks ago	12	16	12	19	12	14	14	13	14	18	10	18
Over 2 weeks ago	56	40	63	42	50	38	62	55	60	37	46	27
Total cases (weighted)	478	478	240	240	238	238	160	160	158	160	160	158

Appendix Table 57

Would you like to go to the pictures more often?

(Distribution of answers of recent, experienced, and veteran viewers, and of controls)

	13–14 YEAR OLDS			
	Recent viewers %	Experienced viewers %	Veteran viewers %	Controls %
I would like to go more often . .	18	24	26	26
I go as often as I want . . .	82	76	74	74
Total cases	78	150	86	476 (*weighted*)

	10–11 YEAR OLDS			
	Recent viewers %	Experienced viewers %	Veteran viewers %	Controls %
I would like to go more often . .	19	27	33	26
I go as often as I want . . .	81	73	67	74
Total cases	72	99	86	469 (*weighted*)

Appendix Table 58

If you had to be one of these four people, who would you rather be?

	13–14 YEAR OLDS		10–11 YEAR OLDS	
A famous:	v %	c %	v %	c %
Author	28	35	28	39
Wireless star	5	10	5	7
Film star	48	52	43	48
Television star	19	3	24	6
Total cases (*weighted*) . . .	472	473	467	457

What kind of film do you like to see?

Proportion of those who say they would like to see a certain type of film

(Distribution of answers by age and intelligence)

	13–14 YEAR OLDS						10–11 YEAR OLDS					
	All		Grammar		I.Q. below 100		All		I.Q. 115+		I.Q. below 100	
Subjects common to television and the cinema:	V %	C %	V %	C %	V %	C %	V %	C %	V %	C %	V %	C %
Cowboys and Westerns	33	33	29	30	43	55	47	10	53	43	63	47
Other adventure	58	50	61	50	71	69	61	55	76	63	77	63
Thrillers (crime detection, &c)	71	66	72	66	91	86	64	57	80	67	83	71
Horror	50	49	42	47	67	69	38	37	41	39	47	51
Space travel	39	36	38	34	43	52	38	38	45	43	49	45
Musicals (singing and dancing)	42	43	47	56	51	41	35	36	40	43	45	46
Love and romance	40	36	29	33	56	52	33	26	33	28	48	22
Films that make you laugh	77	74	86	87	91	89	74	72	92	90	93	87
Films that make you sad	42	34	38	24	57	54	27	31	28	29	37	42
Subjects more characteristic of television:												
Famous people	50	40	53	45	64	53	55	41	65	61	68	57
Rich people	33	22	30	20	53	30	40	33	40	28	59	50
Poor people	54	33	40	30	59	48	43	41	46	40	59	61
Ordinary families	52	38	54	44	64	46	50	41	56	47	68	53
Serials	59	43	46	41	89	61	63	58	78	65	75	76
Films with children	56	37	46	36	75	50	54	49	66	56	68	62
Information subjects shown on television:												
Sports	47	40	55	59	60	41	42	37	55	45	45	40
Travel	48	43	52	59	61	48	54	51	70	63	66	58
The sea	58	54	64	70	67	62	58	56	74	67	76	71
Flying and aeroplanes	38	38	46	45	45	43	38	41	43	52	52	53
Racing	41	35	51	44	49	40	45	39	55	45	57	45
Ballet	25	30	29	36	27	38	29	33	31	37	37	43
Happenings in the Bible	44	35	40	41	60	44	46	51	41	55	62	72
Happenings in history	43	39	47	49	49	52	49	49	55	56	64	61
Wild animals	47	43	53	46	61	57	58	58	73	69	70	71
Other animals and birds	40	33	42	37	55	48	51	51	67	64	58	65
People who lived long ago	46	38	47	40	60	54	54	53	61	60	70	68
People in other countries	40	37	42	46	51	43	40	19	61	60	56	61
Science	35	26	47	29	39	32	37	34	45	36	45	42
News and newsreels	58	51	52	58	70	55	62	55	55	53	65	50
Total cases (weighted)	416	405	140	135	150	133	383	389	139	129	120	125

APPENDIX TABLE 60

What sort of film do you like best?

(Distribution of answers by age and sex)

	13–14 YEAR OLDS						10–11 YEAR OLDS					
	All		Boys		Girls		All		Boys		Girls	
	v %	c %	v %	c %	v %	c %	v %	c %	v %	c %	v %	c %
Adventure, action	12	10	15	13	9	7	14	12	16	13	11	10
Cowboys, cowboys and Indians, Westerns	4	9	3	8	5	10	21	12	21	15	20	9
Gangster, murder, detective, mystery, crime	27	21	34	22	19	21	11	14	11	18	11	11
War	14	13	24	27	3	—	6	7	12	14	1	—
Space, science fiction	1	—	3	—	1	—	1	—	2	1	1	—
Love, romance	6	7	1	—	11	13	4	3	1	—	8	5
Singing, musical, musical comedy	8	11	2	3	18	18	8	8	2	2	13	14
Comic, funny, make me laugh	7	6	9	5	6	8	8	16	9	12	10	20
Documentaries, true films	1	1	1	2	1	—	—	2	—	2	1	3
Don't know, miscellaneous	18	22	8	20	28	23	26	26	26	23	25	28
Total cases (weighted)	462	477	231	233	231	244	460	454	233	233	227	221

494

Estimated time spent by children on various types of outdoor activity between 4 p.m. and bedtime on seven consecutive days

	13–14 YEAR OLDS		10–11 YEAR OLDS	
	v %	c %	v %	c %
Total time spent outdoors:				
Less than 6 hours . . .	50	40	30	30
6–12 hours	25	28	54	40
Over 12 hours . . .	25	32	16	30
Participating in sport:				
No mention	42	31	38	37
Less than 2 hours . . .	25	33	29	31
Over 2 hours	33	36	33	32
Watching live sports outdoors:				
No mention	82	73	87	81
Less than 2 hours . . .	13	26	11	17
Over 2 hours	5	1	2	2
Walking, cycling, fishing outdoors: including cycling round the block, taking dog for walk, taking baby out, picking flowers, birds-nesting, &c.				
No mention	50	29	48	38
Less than 2 hours . . .	21	34	38	44
Over 2 hours	29	37	14	18
On outdoor play: unorganised play in street, garden, park, kicking a ball around, and so on.				
No mention	49	32	12	17
Less than 2 hours . . .	27	37	26	25
Over 2 hours	24	31	62	58
Gardening, doing outside jobs, repair jobs: including cleaning car, painting fence, mending motor-bike, cleaning shed, &c.				
No mention	72	74	80	69
Less than 2 hours . . .	20	14	18	25
Over 2 hours	8	12	2	6
Aimless outdoor wandering: chatting with friends, loitering, going on long shopping expeditions, &c.				
No mention	24	18	51	40
Less than 4 hours . . .	72	64	46	57
Over 4 hours	4	18	3	3
Total cases	84	84	84	84

We would like to know whether you belong to any of these clubs or groups.
Tick all those you belong to

Do you belong to any other clubs or groups? Write down their names

| | 13–14 YEAR OLDS | | 10–11 YEAR OLDS | |
| | v | c | v | c |
Club:	%	%	%	%
No clubs	32	26	36	34
Scouts, Guides, Cubs, Brownies .	17	18	31	33
Boys'/Girls' Brigades, St. John Ambulance, Girls' Friendly Society, &c.	6	5	5	5
Church	19	18	7	10
Youth, including the YMCA . .	26	27	7	6
Athletics, sports, dancing . . .	14	14	7	5
Hobbies	6	8	3	4
Music, choirs	2	4	3	1
Cinema	15	14	22	27
Television	2	—	3	1
Other	8	14	8	10
Total cases (weighted) . . .	501	504	502	501

NOTE. These figures total more than 100 per cent as some children belonged to more than one type of club.

Which would you rather do?

Percentage of children who would prefer to participate in rather than watch certain activities

13–14 YEAR OLDS

					Sec. mod.			
	All		Grammar		I.Q. 100–114		I.Q. below 100	
	v	c	v	c	v	c	v	c
Activities:	%	%	%	%	%	%	%	%
Swimming	72	77	81	76	71	81	67	77
Skating	70	69	69	79	80	73	64	67
Learn to play musical instrument	47	45	53	47	36	50	57	41
Make something	77	77	82	82	75	81	77	74
Play sport	80	73	82	82	82	74	79	70
Find your way around town . .	89	85	90	93	92	89	86	79
Total cases (weighted) . . .	460	460	153	153	153	153	154	154

10–11 YEAR OLDS

					I.Q. 100–114		I.Q. below 100	
	All		I.Q. 115+					
	v	c	v	c	v	c	v	c
	%	%	%	%	%	%	%	%
Swimming	75	76	72	79	75	81	79	78
Skating	78	77	79	78	84	83	76	77
Learn to play musical instrument	60	62	60	66	62	64	60	58
Make something	82	78	89	87	94	80	63	71
Play sport	82	79	86	86	84	87	83	72
Find your way around town . .	73	74	81	79	78	81	63	70
Total cases (weighted) . .	470	460	156	153	157	153	157	154

Appendix Table 64

Percentage who ticked for more than half the items in a given class '*I am not interested in seeing this at all*'

(Distribution of answers by age and intelligence)

13–14 YEAR OLDS

Class of item:	All v %	All c %	Grammar v %	Grammar c %	Sec. mod. I.Q 100–114 v %	Sec. mod. I.Q 100–114 c %	Sec. mod. I.Q. below 100 v %	Sec. mod. I.Q. below 100 c %
Ceremonial events . .	8	12	15	12	5	9	3	15
Sports events . . .	10	17	12	10	8	16	10	24
Plays and entertainment .	19	29	22	22	19	24	17	41
Famous personalities . .	11	14	12	8	9	13	13	21
Exhibitions and art galleries	26	26	30	20	28	26	20	33
Special places of work .	20	24	26	20	24	23	10	29
Total cases (*weighted*) . .	516	516	172	172	172	172	172	172

10–11 YEAR OLDS

	All v %	All c %	I.Q. 115+ v %	I.Q. 115+ c %	I.Q. 100–114 v %	I.Q. 100–114 c %	I.Q. below 100 v %	I.Q. below 100 c %
Ceremonial events . .	10	14	6	10	9	15	14	16
Sports events . . .	18	25	16	19	16	26	23	31
Plays and entertainment .	15	24	16	20	15	24	15	28
Famous personalities . .	10	19	6	19	12	16	11	21
Exhibitions and art galleries	22	24	15	26	17	20	34	27
Special places of work .	28	35	31	33	23	38	29	34
Total cases (*weighted*) . .	516	516	172	172	172	172	172	172

к k

APPENDIX TABLE 65

Customary ways of watching television

	13–14 YEAR OLDS	10–11 YEAR OLDS
	%	%
Some children, when they are watching television, sit on a chair or settee, others sit on the floor. What do you mostly do? Tick one.		
Sit on the floor	10	21
Sit on a chair or settee	90	79
When you watch TV after dark, what mostly happens?		
All lights on	22	19
Some lights switched off	20	24
Special TV light only	38	33
Watch in the dark	20	24
Total cases (weighted)	526	526

APPENDIX TABLE 66

Mean week-day and week-end bedtimes given in diaries

(The percentages are cumulative)

	Mean week-day bedtime				Mean week-end bedtime			
	13–14 YEARS		10–11 YEARS		13–14 YEARS		10–11 YEARS	
	V %	C %	V %	C %	V %	C %	V %	C %
Went to bed at or before:								
8.30 p.m. . . .	—	—	23	37	—	5	14	34
9.0 ,, . . .	4	2	47	71	11	13	33	51
9.30 ,, . . .	28	20	79	94	22	32	48	69
10.0 ,, . . .	61	57	94	99	53	52	71	83
10.30 ,, . . .	96	87	99	100	86	78	86	84
Went to bed after:								
10.30 p.m. . . .	4	13	1	—	14	22	14	16
Total cases . . .	80	83	82	79	84	84	86	88

Appendix Table 67

Bedtimes on the previous night—questionnaire results

(Distribution of answers by age, sex, social class, and intelligence)

(The percentages are cumulative)

13–14 YEAR OLDS

Went to bed at or before:	All		Boys		Girls		Middle class		Working class		Grammar		Sec. mod. I.Q. 100–114		Sec. mod. I.Q. below 100	
	v %	c %	v %	c %	v %	c %	v %	c %	v %	c %	v %	c %	v %	c %	v %	c %
8.30 p.m.	6	4	5	4	7	5	9	5	2	4	10	4	6	4	3	4
9.0 „	12	21	10	13	13	29	16	23	7	18	14	21	13	18	9	23
9.30 „	29	37	27	29	31	46	32	38	24	37	35	44	26	34	26	34
10.0 „	60	67	56	60	65	74	63	69	57	65	68	76	59	63	56	61
10.30 „	83	83	78	78	89	89	85	84	82	82	90	89	79	78	82	81
Total cases (weighted)	501	486	259	242	242	244	256	241	245	245	164	167	168	162	169	157

10–11 YEAR OLDS

Went to bed at or before:	All		Boys		Girls		Middle class		Working class		I.Q. 115+		I.Q. 100–114		I.Q. below 100	
	v %	c %	v %	c %	v %	c %	v %	c %	v %	c %	v %	c %	v %	c %	v %	c %
8.30 p.m.	37	44	34	34	42	53	41	53	34	35	40	40	44	44	26	49
9.0 „	64	72	62	65	68	77	68	78	60	65	68	69	70	71	54	76
9.30 „	77	81	76	78	79	83	81	85	73	77	82	85	85	81	63	77
10.0 „	92	95	92	91	93	99	94	96	89	93	94	98	95	92	85	95
10.30 „	96	97	97	95	95	99	96	99	96	95	97	98	99	96	91	97
Total cases (weighted)	506	473	257	234	249	239	252	233	254	240	174	161	168	160	164	152

APPENDIX TABLE 68

With whom do you most often view? With whom do you most often listen?

(Distribution of the answers of viewers and controls)

	TELEVISION				RADIO[1]			
	Children's television		Evening programmes		Children's hour		Evening programmes	
	13–14 YEAR OLDS	10–11 YEAR OLDS	13–14 YEAR OLDS	10–11 YEAR OLDS	13–14 YEAR OLDS	10–11 YEAR OLDS	13–14 YEAR OLDS	10–11 YEAR OLDS
	%	%	%	%	%	%	%	%
By myself . .	23	24	9	11	49	51	25	28
With friends of own age .	17	25	20	12	1	4	12	5
With father and mother .	43	47	88	81	27	30	74	70
With brothers and sisters .	58	57	59	52	49	46	52	38
With other relatives and grown-ups . .	12	13	22	22	7	7	10	11
Total cases (weighted) .	504	508	489	481	206	255	368	364

NOTE. Totals exceed 100 per cent because children were allowed to tick more than one response.

[1] Only control cases are included here.

Appendix Table 69

Teachers' ratings of children's concentration, initiative, and school performance

	13–14 YEAR OLDS		10–11 YEAR OLDS	
	V %	C %	V %	C %
Concentration:				
Adequate	67	72	59	62
Lacks concentration	33	28	41	38
Initiative:				
A good deal of initiative	18	16	19	20
Some initiative	64	61	51	45
Lacks initiative	18	23	30	35
School performance relative to estimated intellectual ability:				
Above	3	3	9	7
Equal	72	75	69	74
Below	25	22	22	19
Total cases	262	251	162	205

Appendix Table 70

1. *Are you allowed to bring friends home to watch TV if you want to?* 2. *If you may bring friends home to watch, when are you allowed to bring them?* 3. *May your friends just come, or must you first ask someone at home?* (Viewers only)

	13–14 YEAR OLDS	10–11 YEAR OLDS
1. (a) I don't want to bring friends home to watch . .	6	6
(b) I am not allowed to	5	11
(c) I am sometimes allowed to	23	37
(d) I am usually allowed to	66	46
2. (a) I may bring friends home for children's TV only .	10	52
(b) I may bring friends home for evening TV only .	10	3
(c) I may bring frinds home for children's TV or evening TV	80	45
3. (a) I have to ask first	76	88
(b) I don't have to ask first	24	12
Total cases (*weighted*)	489	453

Percentage of heavy and other seasoned viewers who were rated by their teachers as showing the following personality characteristics and behaviour

	13–14 YEAR OLDS		10–11 YEAR OLDS	
	Heavy viewers %	Other viewers %	Heavy viewers %	Other viewers %
Primarily a follower . . .	65	51	74	49
Submissive	35	20	48	41
Shy and retiring	26	18	35	24
Indifferent to, or generally resentful of school	26	16	13	17
Working below estimated intellectual capacity	30	24	26	13
Total cases	46	119	23	71

APPENDIX TABLE 72

Frequency of book- and comic-reading, cinema attendance, and radio listening of matched groups of heavy and occasional viewers and matched groups of heavy and occasional cinema-goers[1]

	Viewers		Cinema-goers	
	Heavy %	Occasional %	Heavy %	Occasional %
Read no book, or only part of a book, during previous 4 weeks . .	33	23	29	14
Read comics often	75	48	75	60
Went to the pictures 2 or 3 times a week (apart from Saturday mornings) .	41	21	100	—
Listened to the radio for 10 or more hours a week	—	—	21	15
Listened to The Archers often . .	33	14	34	33
Total cases	50	52	131	133

[1] The numbers varied slightly from questionnaire to questionnaire.

APPENDIX TABLE 73

Heavy and occasional viewers' favourite television programme

Favourite type of television programme:	Heavy viewers %	Occasional viewers %
Adult plays	44	25
Children's plays	8	11
Variety shows	14	23
Total cases	45	45

BIBLIOGRAPHY

1. ABRAMS, M., Child audiences for television in Great Britain, *Journalism Quart.*, 1956, **33**, 35–41.
2. ALBERT, R. S., The role of mass media and the effect of aggressive film content upon children's aggressive responses and identification choices, *Genet. Psychol. Monog.*, 1957, **55**, 221–285.
3. ANONYMOUS, One high school surveys television's effect on pupils, *School and College Management*, September 1952, 21–22.
4. BARTLETT, F. C., *Remembering*, Cambridge University Press, Cambridge, 1932.
5. BATTIN, T. C., *The use of diary and survey methods involving the questionnaire-interview technique to determine the impact of television on school children*, Ph.D. thesis, University of Michigan, 1952.
6. BELSON, W. E., Topic for tonight: a study of comprehensibility, *The BBC Quart.*, 1952, **7**, 94–99.
7. —— A technique for studying the effects of a television broadcast, *J. app. Statist.*, 1956, **5**, 195–202.
8. —— Learning and attitude changes resulting from viewing a television series 'Bon Voyage', *Brit. J. educ. Psychol.*, 1956, **26**, 31–38.
9. —— *The effects of television upon the interests and the initiative of adult viewers in Greater London*, Ph.D. thesis, University of London, 1957.
10. —— The ideas of a television public about mental illness, *Mental Health*, 1957, **16**, 95–99.
11. —— Selective perception in viewing a television broadcast, *Audio-visual Commun. Review*, 1958, **6**, 23–32.
12. BERELSON, B., *Content analysis in communication research*, Free Press, Glencoe, Illinois, 1952.
13. BESCO, G. S., Television and its effects on other related interests of high school pupils, *English Journal*, 1952, **45**, 151–152.
14. BRITISH BROADCASTING CORPORATION, *The televison public: its structure and tastes at the end of 1949*, BBC Audience Research Report, 1950.
15. —— *Dick Barton and juvenile delinquency*, BBC Listeners Research Report, 1950.
16. —— *Minors—an enquiry into the interests, listening and viewing, and availability of the 5–20 year old population of the United Kingdom*, BBC Audience Research Report, 1954.
17. —— *The hurt mind*, BBC Audience Research Report, 1957.
18. —— Audience research figures, 1958.
19. BOGART, L., *The age of television*, Frederick Ungar Publishing Co., New York, 1956.
20. BURT, C., *BBC further education experiment, report on the sixth experimental series 'Study of the mind'*, BBC Audience Research Report, 1951.

21. CANTRIL, H., The invasion from Mars in *The process and effects of mass communication*, ed. Schramm, W., University of Illinois Press, Urbana, Illinois, 1954.

22. CHARTERS, W. W., *Motion pictures and youth*, Macmillan, New York, 1933.

23. CLARK, W. J., *Of children and television*, Xavier University, Cincinnati, Ohio, 1951.

24. COFFIN, T. E., Television's effects on leisure-time activities, *J. appl. Psychol.*, 1948, **32,** 550–558.

25. CUNNINGHAM and WALSH, *Videotown, 1948–1955*, Cunningham and Walsh, Inc., New York, 1956.

26. DAISH, A. N., Comics are harming children's eyes, *Vision*, 1952, **6,** 5–8.

27. DUGGAN, E. P., *Times educ. Supplement*, November 11, 1955.

28. DUMAZEDIER, J., *Television and rural adult education*, Unesco, Paris, 1956.

29. DYSINGER, W. S., and RUCKMICK, C. A., *The emotional responses of children to the motion picture situation*, Macmillan, New York, 1933.

30. ECONOMIC RESEARCH COUNCIL, *Regional variations in drunkenness among persons aged under 21 in England and Wales (1953)*, Economic Research Council, London, 1955.

31. EMMETT, B. P., The television audience in the United Kingdom, *J. Roy. statist. Soc.*, 1956, **119,** 284–311.

32. FIELD, M., *Children and films. A study of boys and girls in the cinema*, Carnegie United Kingdom Trust, Edinburgh, 1954.

33. FINE, B. J., *Television and family life, a survey of two New England communities*, Boston University School of Public Relations and Communications, Boston, 1952.

34. FRANCK, I. G., *Über Geschehensgestaltungen in der Auffassung von Filmen durch Kinder*, Johann Ambrosius Barthverlag, Leipzig, 1957.

35. FREIDSON, E., Communication research and the concept of the mass, 1953, *Am. sociol. Rev.* **18,** 313–317.

36. GESSLEMAN, D. B., *Television and reading*, Master's thesis submitted to the University of Utah, 1951.

37. GORER, G., Television in our lives, *The Sunday Times*, April 13–May 4, 1958.

38. HALL, J., and CARADOG JONES, D., The social grading of occupations, *Brit. J. Sociol.*, 1950, **1,** 31–55.

39. HEAD, S. W., Content analysis of television drama programmes, *Quart. Film, Radio and Television*, 1954, **8.**

40. HERZOG, H., *Survey of research on children's radio listening*, Office of Radio Research, Columbia University, New York, 1941.

41. HIMMELWEIT, H. T., HALSEY, A. H., and OPPENHEIM, A. N., The views of adolescents on some aspects of the social class structure, *Brit. J. Sociol.*, 1952, **2,** 148–172.

42. —— Social status and secondary education since the 1944 act: some data for London, in *Social Mobility in Britain*, ed. Glass, D. V., Routledge & Kegan Paul, London, 1953.

43. HOLADAY, P. W., and STODDARD, G. D., *Getting ideas from the movies*, Macmillan, New York, 1933.

44. Home Office, *Report of the departmental committee on children and the cinema*, H.M.S.O., London, 1950.
45. Horowitz, E. L., The development of attitudes toward the Negro, *Arch. Psychol.*, 1936, **194,** 34–35.
46. Hovland, C. I., Effects of the mass media of communication in *Handbook of Social Psychology*, ed. G. Lindzey, Addison Wesley Publishing Co., Inc., Cambridge, Mass., 1954.
47. ——Janis, I. L., and Kelley, H. H., *Communication and persuasion*, Yale University Press, New Haven, 1953.
48. Hulton Readership Surveys, published annually by the Hulton Press, London.
49. Instructional television research report, No. P-1544, U.S. Naval Training Devices Center, Port Washington, L.I.N.Y.
50. Jones, D. B., Quantitative analysis of motion picture content, *Pub. Opin. Quart.*, 1942, **6,** 411–428.
51. Johns-Heine, P., and Gerth, H. H., Values in mass periodical fiction, 1921–40, *Pub. Opin. Quart.*, 1949, **13,** 105–113.
52. Kay, H., and Nias, A. H. W., Immediate memory of a broadcast feature programme, *Brit. J. educ. Psychol.*, 1954, **24,** 154–160.
53. Kefauver, E., *Television and juvenile delinquency—a part of the investigation of juvenile delinquency in the United States*, United States Senate Subcommittee Report No. 1466, Government Printing Office, Washington, 1956.
54. Keilhacker, M., *Jugend und Spielfilm: Erlebnisweisen*, Ernst Klett Verlag, Stuttgart, 1953.
55. Klapper, J. T., *Children and television*, Bureau of Applied Social Research, Columbia University, New York, 1953.
56. Lazarsfeld, P. F., and Stanton, R. N., *Communications research, 1948–1949*, Harper & Brothers, New York, 1949.
57. Lewis, P., TV and teen-agers, *Educational Screen*, 1949, **28,** 159–161.
58. Maccoby, E. E., Television, its impact on school children, *Pub. Opin. Quart.*, 1951, **15,** 421–444.
59. —— Why do children watch television?, *Pub. Opin. Quart.* 1954, **18,** 239–244.
60. Martin, F. M., Some subjective aspects of social stratification, in *Social mobility in Britain*, ed. Glass, D. V., Routledge & Kegan Paul, London, 1953.
61. Mayer, J. P., *Sociology of film*, Faber & Faber, London, 1946.
62. —— *British cinemas and their audiences*, Dennis Dobson Ltd., London, 1948.
63. McGeehan, J. R., and Maranville, R. L., *Television: Impact and reaction in Lexington, Kentucky*, University of Kentucky, Lexington, 1953.
64. McPhee, W. N., *New strategies for research in the mass media*, Bureau of Applied Social Research, Columbia University, New York, 1953.
65. Merton, R. K., *Mass persuasion*, Harper, New York, 1946.
66. —— *Social theory and social structure*, Free Press, Glencoe, Illinois, 1957.

67. MEYERSOHN, R., *Television research: an annotated bibliography*, Bureau of Applied Social Research, Columbia University, New York, 1953. (Mimeographed.)

68. MIDDLETON, L. R., Television and the grammar school pupil, *University of Nottingham Inst. of Ed. Bulletin*, 1956, **22**, 1–4.

69. MINISTRY OF EDUCATION, *Standards of reading, 1948–56*, Pamphlet No. 32, H.M. Stationery Office, London, 1957.

70. MITCHELL, W. W., *Television watching in a secondary modern school*, thesis submitted to the Department of Education, University of Manchester, in part fulfilment of requirements of Diploma of Education, 1956.

71. OPPENHEIM, A. N., *A study of social attitudes of adolescents*, Ph.D. thesis, University of London, 1956.

72. PARKER, E., Parents, children and television, Information Service, Central Department of Research and Survey, National Council of the Churches of Christ in the U.S.A., 1954, **33**.

73. PETERSON, R. C., and THURSTONE, L. L., *Motion pictures and the social attitudes of children*, Macmillan, New York, 1933.

74. PIAGET, J., *The moral judgement of the child*, Harcourt, Brace & Co., New York, 1932.

75. PURDUE OPINION PANEL, *Four years of New York television 1951–1954*, Monitoring Study No. 7, National Association of Educational Broadcasters, Urbana, Illinois, 1954.

76. REMMERS, H. H., HORTON, R. E., and MAINER, R. E., *Attitudes of high school students towards certain aspects of television*, Purdue Opinion Panel, Report No. 36, 1953.

77. RIESMAN, D., *The lonely crowd*, Yale University Press, New Haven, 1956.

78. RILEY, M. W., CANTWELL, F. V., and RUTTIGER, K .F., Some observations on the social effects of television, *Pub. Opin. Quart.*, 1949, **13**, 223–234.

79. —— and RILEY, J. W., Jr., A sociological approach to communications research, *Pub. Opin. Quart.*, 1951, **15**, 445–460.

80. ST. PANCRAS PUBLIC LIBRARY SERVICE, *The arts in St. Pancras, 1955–56*, presented to the Public Libraries Committee, November 1956.

81. —— *The arts in St. Pancras, 1956–57*, presented to the Public Libraries Committee, November 1957.

82. SCHRAMM, W. (Ed.), *The process and effects of mass communications*, University of Illinois Press, Urbana, 1954.

83. —— How communication works, in *The process and effects of mass communications*, ed. Schramm, W., University of Illinois Press, Urbana, Illinois, 1954.

84. SMYTHE, D. W., *New Haven television, May 15–21, 1952*, Monitoring Study No. 5, National Association of Educational Broadcasters, Urbana, Illinois, 1953.

85. —— *Three years of New York television 1951–1953*, Monitoring Study No. 6, National Association of Educational Broadcasters, Urbana, Illinois, 1953.

86. —— and CAMPBELL, A., *Los Angeles television, May 23–29, 1951*, Monitor-

ing Study No. 2, National Association of Educational Broadcasters, Urbana, Illinois, 1953.

87. STEWART, F., *The social impact of television on Atlanta households*, Division of Journalism, Emory University, Atlanta, 1952.

88. STOUFFER, S., A sociologist looks at communications research, in *Print, radio and film in a democracy*, ed. Waples, D., University of Chicago Press, Chicago, 1942.

89. SUCHY, J., *British television, August 12–25, 1953. A content analysis of programmes*, M.A. thesis, University of Iowa, 1954.

90. SWANSON, C. E., and JONES, R. L., Television ownership and its correlates, *J. appl. Psychol.*, 1951, **35**, 352–357.

91. SWEETSER, F. L., *Grade school families meet television*, Research report No. 1, Department of Sociol. and Anthropol., Boston, Mass., 1953.

92. Television and the eyes, *Vision*, 1952, **6**, 9–11.

93. *The Financial Times*, 2 March 1958.

94. TRENAMAN, J., Understanding of broadcasts on science, *Proceedings* of the British Association for the Advancement of Science, 1950.

95. USHER, A., Is TV good or bad for your children?, *Better Homes and Gardens*, 1955, **33**.

96. VERNON, M. D., Perception and understanding of instructional television programmes, *Brit. J. Psychol.*, 1953, **44**, 116–126.

97. VERNON, P. E., Investigations of the intelligibility of educational broadcasts, *Proceedings* of the British Association for the Advancement of Science, 1950.

98. WALL, W., and SMITH, E. M., Film choices of adolescents, *Brit. J. educ. Psychol.*, 1949, **19**, 121–136.

99. WARD, J. C., *Children out of school*, Social Survey Report No. S.S. 110, Central Office of Information, London, 1948.

100. —— *Children and the cinema*, Social Survey Report No. S.S. 131, Central Office of Information, London, 1949.

101. WHITE, R. K., *Value-analysis: the nature and use of the method*, Society for the Psychological Study of Social Issues, 1951.

102. WILKINS, L. T., *The adolescent in Britain*, Social Survey Report No. S.S. 148 P, Central Office of Information, London, 1955.

103. WITTY, P., Children's reaction to TV—third report, *Elementary English*, 1952, **29**, 469–473.

104. —— Children and TV—a fifth report, *Elementary English*, 1954, **31**, 310–357.

105. WOLFE, M. K., and FISKE, M., Why they read comics, in *The process and effects of mass communications*, ed. Schramm, W., University of Illinois Press, Urbana, 1954.

106. ZAZZO, B., Analyse des difficultés d'une sequence cinematographique par la conduite du récit chez l'enfant, *Revue internationale de filmologie*, 1952, **3**, 25–36.

GLOSSARY

THE words in this glossary have been included either because they are technical terms which may be unfamiliar to the general reader, or because for the purposes of this study an ordinary word has been given a special meaning and usage. The definitions are intended to be of help to the reader, and are not meant to be authoritative.

Addict. The terms 'television addict' and 'cinema addict' are defined in Chapter 35.

Area. The word as used in this report denotes an aspect of behaviour or a complex of attitudes.

Area score. The inventories were designed to give a measure of overall adjustment, but also to provide information about different areas in the child's life, his relationship to his family, his attitude to school, &c. For each inventory a *total score* was computed consisting of answers to all the items, as well as a number of *area scores*. Each area score consists of the answers to all the items pertaining to that area.

Boomerang effect. A term used in communication research to describe an effect which is the opposite of the one intended by the author of the communication.

Channel. In Britain this term is used to denote a television wavelength allocated to a particular programme authority. Until 1955 there was only one channel, on which BBC television was broadcast. A second channel was subsequently allocated to the newly founded Independent Television Authority. Several programme companies broadcast on this channel on different days of the week, and in different parts of the country.

Content analysis. A systematic analysis of the content of a communication. There are many different types of content analysis, ranging from a simple frequency count of acts of violence per programme, for instance, to more qualitative assessments of the underlying theme and values of a programme (Appendix D).

Controls. In this report we use the terms *controls* or *control sample* to indicate those children who have no television at home and who also view in other people's homes less often than once a fortnight. The purpose of a control sample is to indicate what the experimental sample would have been like if it had not been exposed to the experimental variable, in this case, television. In this study, each control was matched with a viewer of the same age, sex, social class, and intelligence, and, wherever possible, both viewer and control were drawn from the same class-room.

Correlation. The tendency for two or more measures to vary concomitantly, so that knowledge of the one gives us a basis for making predictions regarding the other, depending on the degree of the correlation. The degree of correlation is measured by a variety of statistical procedures; the two referred to in this report are the *product moment correlation coefficient* and the *tau coefficient* (Appendix C).

Displacement effects. Effects of television which are due not so much to programme content as to the time taken up by viewing, which necessarily displaces other activities.

Eleven-plus examination. In Britain almost all children in state schools sit for an examination at the end of their primary school career, at the age of about 11. On the basis of this examination, and teachers' reports, the child is allocated to one or another type of secondary school.

Experienced viewers. See *Recent viewers*.

Extrapolation. Extension of the findings of a particular survey or experiment to a different sample or a different set of conditions.

Factorial design. An experimental design in which the cases are selected in such a way that the effects of one variable can be studied while holding the other variables constant. This requires equal or proportional numbers of cases in all the cells of the design (p. 75).

Format. Here used to indicate the ingredients that make up a given programme series; those aspects which characterise it.

Functional equivalence or similarity. Different activities or situations may be used to satisfy the same psychological needs. Where this is the case, these activities become functionally equivalent.

Future viewers. In the Norwich study (q.v.) we tested the children in 1955, before television was generally available, and again in 1956. Those children who in the intervening period acquired a television set are referred to as viewers when we discuss their 1956 answers and as future viewers when we refer to the answers they gave in 1955.

Grammar school. See *Secondary modern school*.

Guest viewer. Someone who does not have a television set, but sees television in other people's homes.

Halo effect. A source of bias in making assessments which occurs when *one* aspect of a person or a situation is allowed to colour the entire picture.

Heavy cinema-goers. See *Occasional cinema-goers*.

Heavy viewers. See *Occasional viewers*.

I.Q. (Intelligence Quotient). A measure of the child's tested intelligence in relation to other children of the same age. The intelligence test gives the child's *mental age*; by dividing this by his chronological age, and multiplying the answer by 100, we obtain an index figure, or I.Q., which indicates whether the child is advanced or retarded for his age; the average I.Q. of the population being 100. Most children who are selected for a grammar school (q.v.) have I.Q.s of at least 115.

I.T.V. Independent television is the term used to denote collectively the various programme companies broadcasting under the auspices of the Independent Television Authority. In this study the term refers to the two companies broadcasting in the London area (Associated-Television and Associated-Rediffusion), and not to all programme companies that broadcast under the auspices of the I.T.A.

Main survey. Here used to indicate the survey carried out in London, Bristol, Portsmouth, and Sunderland, and to distinguish it from the Norwich study. (See Chapters 1 and 6.)

Matching. See *Controls*, also Chapter 6 and Appendix A.

Mental age. See *I.Q.*.

Moderate cinema-goers. See *Occasional cinema-goers.*

Moderate viewers. See *Occasional viewers.*

Mothers' diaries. For one week a sample of mothers kept diaries about their families' viewing. They noted in particular the amount younger children viewed, and their reactions to the different programmes.

Multiple-choice questions or items. These terms refer to questions in a questionnaire, or to items in an inventory, where the child is provided with ready-made answers from which to select the one(s) appropriate for him. Multiple-choice questions should be distinguished from *open-ended* questions, to which the child formulates his own answers.

Norwich study. The two surveys carried out in Norwich in 1955 and 1956 (see Chapters 1 and 6).

Occasional, moderate, heavy cinema-goers. Here defined as children who went to the cinema once a fortnight or less (occasional), between once a fortnight or once or twice a week (moderate), and twice a week or more (heavy).

Occasional, moderate, heavy viewers. Here defined (on the basis of their questionnaire responses) as children who were allowed to view up to a maximum of 12, 22, or more than 22 hours per week, for the 13–14 year olds; for the 10–11 year olds the equivalent divisions were up to 12, up to 18, and more than 18 hours per week. The average hours of viewing were well below these upper limits (see Appendix B).

Passivity. For several definitions and forms of measurement used in this study see Chapter 31.

Personality inventories. The inventories included in this study concerned children's wishes, anxieties, and fears (see Chapter 6 and Appendix A).

Programme reaction list. A questionnaire in which the child is presented with brief descriptions of different situations found in television programmes, and is asked to describe his feelings about them by selecting one of a number of prepared answers (Appendix E).

Programme recall lists. A list of radio or television programmes of the previous day and evening, on which the subject was asked to record whether he saw or heard each of the programmes listed. In addition, the subject was asked whether he had liked the programme 'a little', 'a lot', or had not liked it at all. The percentage of respondents liking a programme (either a little or a lot) out of those who saw or heard it is referred to as a *Reaction index* (see Appendix B and Chapters 6, 8, 10).

Projective questions. The answers to this type of question reveal something about the individual's personality and needs.

Rating. A mark or numerical value assigned to some characteristic or behaviour of an individual, according to an objectively defined scale or series of grades.

Reaction index. See *Programme recall lists.*

Recent, experienced, and veteran viewers. The viewers were divided into three groups depending on the length of time they had had television in their homes. A recent viewer was one who had had television for more than three months and for less than a year; an experienced viewer one who had had television for between one and two years, and a veteran viewer one who had had television for three or more years. We excluded all children from the analysis who had had television for under three months, as we did not want to obscure the picture by studying children for whom television had maximum novelty value.

Reliability—or consistency—is the degree to which an instrument will yield the same results if repeatedly applied to the same subjects under the same conditions (see Appendix A).

Sampling. Selection of cases for a survey or an experiment. There are many different types of sample, depending on the purpose of the investigation. A *representative* sample is a miniature replica of the population of origin. In a *factorial design* (q.v.) a special kind of stratified sample and not a representative one is used.

Secondary modern school. For their secondary schooling most children in British state schools go to one of three types of school: grammar, secondary modern, or technical schools. Their allocation depends on the results of the 11 plus examination (q.v.). Broadly speaking, grammar schools take the top 20 per cent (generally with I.Q.s of 115 and above), and provide a more academic education leading to university, while technical colleges offer more vocational courses. The majority of children go to secondary modern schools and leave at the age of 15. There are numerous exceptions and local variants to this tripartite system of secondary education.

Significance. Depending on the number of cases involved, and on a number of other conditions, any research finding should be regarded with greater or lesser confidence, according to the likelihood of its having arisen by chance. Statisticians have worked out various methods for assessing the degree of confidence or statistical significance. It is often expressed in percentage terms, indicating the frequency with which the observed difference would have arisen by chance. If a difference is 'significant at the 1 per cent level of confidence', this means that it would have arisen by chance in less than one out of a hundred comparisons. The higher the percentage, the less significant the difference observed. In our inquiry, we speak of '*trends*' to denote differences above the 5 per cent level of confidence.

Sleeper-effect. A term coined by Hovland to denote the effect of a communication which does not become apparent until some time after the communication has been received. Sleeper-, or long-term, effects may be different from the immediate, short-term ones.

Stimulation effect. Here used to indicate any activity, attitude, or interest which has been strengthened or initiated through watching television.

Trend. See *Significance.*

Trend analyses are analyses repeated over a period of time so as to obtain an indication of change.

Veteran viewer. See *Recent viewer.*

Viewer. Here used to describe a child who has had a television set at home for a period of not less than three months.

Weighting. A statistical procedure whereby a sample can be adjusted for certain shortcomings without biasing the results (see Appendix A).

INDEX

[To avoid needless repetition, the word 'and' has only been inserted before and after subheadings where its absence would alter the sense; otherwise, where necessary, it should be implied. References to the Bibliography are made in brackets after a page reference, when the author's name is not mentioned on the page referred to.]